Also in the Variorum Collected Studies Series

MICHAEL LECKER
Jews and Arabs in Pre- and Early Islamic Arabia

Y. TZVI LANGERMANN
The Jews and the Sciences in the Middle Ages

AMNON SHILOAH
The Dimension of Music in Islamic and Jewish Culture

T.D. BARNES
Early Christianity and the Roman Empire

ELENA LOURIE
Crusade and Colonisation: Muslims, Christians and Jews under the Crown of Aragon

ANNA SAPIR ABULAFIA
Christians and Jews in Dispute: Disputational Literature and the Rise of Anti-Judaism in the West (1100–1150)

J.H.G.W. LIEBESCHUETZ
From Diocletian to the Arab Conquest: Change in the Late Roman Empire

BRENT D. SHAW
Rulers, Nomads, and Christians in Roman North Africa

HAN J.W. DRIJVERS
History and Religion in Late Antique Syria

DAVID F. GRAF
Rome and the Arabian Frontier from Nabataeans to Saracens

C.R. WHITTAKER
Land, City and Trade in the Roman Empire

JOSEPH MÉLÈZE-MODRZEJEWSKI
Statute personnel et liens de famille dans les droits de l'Antiqué

DAVID T. RUNIA
Exegesis and Philosophy: Studies on Philo of Alexandria

JOSEPH GUTMANN
Sacred Images: Studies in Jewish Art from Antiquity to the Middle Ages

VARIORUM COLLECTED STUDIES SERIES

The Jews in the Roman Empire: Legal Problems, from Herod to Justinian

Professor Alfredo Mordechai Rabello

Alfredo Mordechai Rabello

The Jews in the Roman Empire: Legal Problems, from Herod to Justinian

Routledge
Taylor & Francis Group
LONDON AND NEW YORK

First published 2000 by Ashgate Publishing

Published 2016 by Routledge
2 Park Square, Milton Park, Abingdon, Oxon OX14 4RN
711 Third Avenue, New York, NY 10017, USA

Routledge is an imprint of the Taylor & Francis Group, an informa business

A CIP catalogue record for this book is available from the British Library.

Transferred to Digital Printing in 2011

ISBN 9780860786627 (hbk)

VARIORUM COLLECTED STUDIES SERIES CS645

CONTENTS

This volume contains x + 364 pages

PREFACE

This collection embraces a number of articles, all of which are linked by their topic, namely, the legal status of the Jews in the Roman Empire. Foremost among the scholars in this field is Jean Juster, who in 1914, published his work: 'Les Juifs dans l'Empire Romain'. My article on this work 'The Legal Condition of the Jews in the Roman Empire' (published in *Aufstieg und Niedergang der Römischen Welt* II, 13 [Berlin–New York, 1980], pp. 662–762) does not appear in this collection.

Among the topics discussed here are: the capacity in which Herod judged his wife and sons; prohibition on Gentiles entering the Temple; early stages of Jewish settlement in Roman Spain; the legal basis for Emperor Hadrian's decree banning Jewish circumcision; the attitude of the Emperor Diocletian – infamous for his persecution of the Christians – towards the Jews. Two articles focus on the opportunities offered by the Roman Empire to Jews for observing the Sabbath and festivals. One deals especially with the various problems caused by the observance of the Purim Festival. Two other articles deal with problems relating to marriage and divorce. Another deals with the Roman attitude towards conversion to Judaism. Three of the articles discuss Jewish jurisdiction in the Roman Empire. Finally, one article examines the legal status of the Samaritans, derived from special legislation in Justinian's *Corpus Iuris Civilis.* Closing the collection is 'A Tribute to Jean Juster'.

Those interested in my point of view on a number of other issues related to these topics are referred to my work: *Giustiniano, Ebrei e Samaritani alla luce delle fonti storico-letterarie, ecclesiastiche e giuridiche*, 2 vols (Milano, 1987–88).

Alfredo Mordechai Rabello

Hebrew University of Jerusalem, Mount Scopus

July 1999

PUBLISHER'S NOTE

The articles in this volume, as in all others in the Collected Studies Series, have not been given a new, continuous pagination. In order to avoid confusion, and to facilitate their use where these studies have been referred to elsewhere, the original pagination has been maintained wherever possible.

Each article has been given a Roman numeral in order of appearance, as listed in the Contents. This number is repeated on each page and quoted in the index entries.

ACKNOWLEDGEMENTS

It is my pleasant obligation to express gratitude to my research mentors: the late Professor Giuseppe Ignazio Luzzatto, who guided me in my first steps in the academic world at Bologna University; Professor Vittore Colorni, a leading authority in this field and Professor Reuven Yaron of the Hebrew University of Jerusalem, under whose direction I have worked for many years.

In the course of the years I have benefited from the advice and lessons of the late Professors Elias Bickerman, Arnaldo Momigliano, Menachem Stern and Ephraim Elimelech Urbach. I am greatly indebted to them for these and for discussions I had with them.

I am very grateful to Professor Joseph Mélèze Modrzejewski of the University of Paris, and to Dr John Smedley of Variorum, Ashgate Publishing Ltd, for their helpful advice regarding this collection.

Dulcis in fundo: I would like to thank the following editors and publishers of the books and journals in which the articles first appeared for generously giving their permission to reproduce them in this volume: Bar-Ilan University Press, Ramat Gan (I); Institute of Jewish Law, University of Boston and Brill, Leiden (II and IX); Israel Ministry of Religions, Jerusalem (III); University of Tel Aviv (IV); Israel Law Review Association, Faculty of Law, Hebrew University of Jerusalem (V, XI, XIII and XV); Oxford Centre for Postgraduate Hebrew Studies (VI); *Revue historique de droit français et étranger*, Paris (VII); Walter de Gruyter GmbH, Berlin (VIII); Accademia Romanistica Costantiniana, Naples (X); Clarendon Press, Oxford (XII); Harry and Michael Sacher Institute for Legislative Research and Comparative Law, Hebrew University of Jerusalem (XIV).

To the blessed memory of my father and teacher
Dr Emilio Marco Rabello ז"ל
(Milano 1908–1999)

'... when a perfect man is stricken with years and approaches death, this apprehension increases very powerfully, joy over this apprehension and a great love for the object of apprehension become stronger, until the soul is separated from the body at that moment in this state of pleasure ..."

(Moses Maimonides, *The Guide of the Perplexed*, III, 51)

I

Civil Justice in Palestine from 63 BCE to 70 CE

The purpose of this study is to determine how the problem of justice (*iurisdictio*) was solved in Palestine between Pompey's conquest and the Great Revolt (70 CE). In particular we shall examine what system of civil justice was available to litigants seeking legal recourse: Jewish justice or Roman justice? We will not analyze here the internal organization of the systems of justice, but will refer occasionally to the essential works on the subject.

I am particularly happy to dedicate this article in honor of Prof. David Sohlberg—on the occasion of his retirement from his activities at Bar Ilan University—as a mark of appreciation for his great contribution to Classical Studies in Israel, and to Bar Ilan in particular, in the special period of building a new University with the attempt to harmonize the classical and the Jewish traditions.

1. Pompey's Conquest (63 BCE) and the Example of Macedonia

In 63 BCE Pompey sacked the Hasmonean kingdom and established a new order in Palestine. From a legal perspective this new order could not be termed a province, as Ammianus Marcellinus calls it.[1] Rather, it constituted an intermediate situation, differing both from a province and an allied state. In particular, institutions of rule and national laws were preserved.[2]

1 *Res gestae* 14.8.11-12; on this subject see the interpretation of M. Stern, *Greek and Latin Authors on Jews and Judaism*, II (Jerusalem 1980), No. 505. See also D. Piattelli, "Ricerche intorno alle relazioni politiche tra Roma e l'ἔθνος τῶν Ἰουδαίων dal 161 a.C. al 4 a.C.," *Bullettino dell'Istituto di Diritto Romano* (= *BIDR*) 74 (1971) 219-349 at 281-323.

2 A. Momigliano, *Ricerche sull' organizzazione della Giudea sotto il dominio romano (63 a.C.-70 d.C.)* (Bologna 1934; repr. Amsterdam 1967) 19.

Scholars have emphasized the similarity between the order which was established in Palestine and the policy followed by the Romans in Macedonia. After the battle of Pydna in 168 BCE, in which the consul Aemilius Paullus defeated Perseus, the last Macedonian king, Rome sent a special committee to establish a new order in Macedonia. Macedonia was divided into four completely independent regions. The residents of these regions did not even retain the rights of commerce (*commercium*) or marriage (*conubium)* among themselves, despite the fact that only recently they had been subjects of the same kingdom. Rome's aim was to create divisions among these four regions in order to prevent their reunion: (*divide et impera*).

Thus, each region had its own *synedrion*, an organization that served as a political and judicial authority, and which could mint its own coins. Rome intended not to create the *feeling* of subjugation, but to convince the residents that their freedom was greater than it had been. Tax collection was assigned to local governments, and taxes were reduced by half; local laws and institutions of the government continued to operate. These actions did not in themselves establish a province, but they did constitute the laying of the groundwork for the province that was established in 146 BCE.

Here, too, the question arises of what system of justice was in effect between the conquest of 168 and the annexation of 146. No specific name was given to the kind of rule that existed at that time. In fact, Rome avoided defining it in order to reinforce the *impression* of continued freedom. In practice, this was an intermediate form differing both from a province and from an allied state.[3] However, this intermediate situation should not mislead us. We know the ultimate result: as Arangio Ruiz writes, "there was no end to expansionism until the entire world which was geographically and militarily attainable was under Roman rule."[4]

3 F. De Martino, *Storia della Costituzione Romana*, II^2 (Napoli 1973) 315-17. See also J. A. O. Larsen, "Representation and Democracy in Hellenistic Federalism," *CP* 40 (1945) 65-97; *idem*, "Consilium in Livy XLV,18,6-7 and the Macedonian Synedria," *CP* 44 (1949) 73 ff.; M. Feyel, "Paul Émile et le synedrion macédonien," *BCH* 70 (1946) 187-98 at 195-98; W. Dahlheim, *Gewalt und Herrschaft. Das Provinziale Herrschaftssystem der römischen Republik* (Berlin-New York 1977); A. M. Rabello, *Giustiniano, Ebrei e Samaritani alla luce delle fonti storico-letterarie, ecclesiastiche e giuridiche* (Milan, vol. I 1987; vol. II 1988), in the index s.v. "sinedrio," vol. II, 948.

4 V. Arangio Ruiz, *Storia del Diritto Romano* (Napoli 1964) 183.

To turn to the situation in Palestine, Rome was well aware of the degree to which the Jews valued the *πάτριοι νόμοι*, the "customs of the fathers," which were above all of religious importance. Rome had no motivation to involve itself in internal institutions, apart from the desire to determine who would be responsible to Rome for providing internal order. More extreme intervention would have brought negative reactions and could have led to a revolt, which Rome wished to prevent.

Thus Pompey left Judaea under the rule of Hyrcanus II, as Ethnarch and High Priest. His duties were primarily religious, and related to the Temple in Jerusalem. Hyrcanus was subordinate to the supervision of the ruler of Syria. What is worthy of note is that Hyrcanus retained the right to administer justice to the nation on an internal basis according to the *πάτριοι νόμοι*, "customs of the fathers"[5] and, therefore, the principle of judicial autonomy was preserved.

2. Gabinius' Division (57 BCE)

A short time later, in 57 BCE, Gabinius divided the area into five regions (*συνέδρια*, *σύνοδοι*), each ruled by the local elite.[6] These *συνέδρια* undoubtedly judged on the basis of traditional Jewish law. As Jean Juster realized, Gabinius diminished the Jews' unity, but he did not attack their judicial autonomy.[7] The local courts, which were established in each city, undoubtedly judged according to Jewish law.[8]

According to Momigliano:

> the legal form addressed by Josephus is the rule of the elite of the

5 A. Schalit, *King Herod—Portrait of a Ruler* (Jerusalem 1964) 17 ff. (Hebrew; German trans. by J. Amir, *König Herodes. Der Mann and sein Werk* [Studia Judaica, 4] [Berlin 1969]); E. M. Smallwood, *The Jews under Roman Rule from Pompey to Diocletian* (Leiden 1981) 32 ff.; M. Stern, *The Kingdom of Herod* (Tel Aviv 1992).

6 Josephus, *Ant.* 14.91; *BJ* 1.167-70. See E. Bammel, "The Organisation of Palestine by Gabinius," *Journal of Jewish Studies* 12 (1961) 159-62; E. Schürer, *The History of the Jewish People in the Age of Jesus Christ (175 B.C. – A.D. 135)*, a new English version revised and edited by G. Vermes & F. Millar, I (Edinburgh 1973) 268-69; M. Stern, *Hasmonaean Judaea in the Hellenistic World* (Jerusalem 1995) 216 ff. (Hebrew).

7 J. Juster, *Les Juifs dans l'Empire Romain* II (Paris 1914) 94, n. 3.

8 See in general, G. I. Luzzatto, "Sulla condizione delle città suddite nelle cosidette ἀρχαί durante il principato," *Symposion 1971* (Köln 1975) 105-23, now in G. I. Luzzatto, *Scritti minori epigrafici e papirologici* (Bologna 1984) 571-91.

Sanhedrin, cut off from its traditional ties with the High Priest and duplicated in all five regions.... It is clear that after Rome based its division of the Jewish state on the upper classes, it granted them full rulership. This explains why these classes were pleased with the situation. This matter strengthens the comparison with Macedonia, which provides the best example for the use of the word *συνέδριον*, *synedrion*, in the meaning used by Josephus in our case.[9]

3. Hyrcanus II, Ethnarch and High Priest (47 BCE)

However,the order established by Gabinius did not last long. In 47 BCE Julius Caesar returned full political and judicial power as Ethnarch and High Priest to Hyrcanus II. He recognized that the position was hereditary, in accordance with tradition: "And if, during this period, any question shall arise concerning the Jews' manner of life, it is my pleasure that the decision shall rest with them."[10]

Taubler was correct in seeing this statement as relating to internal justice in Judaea[11]; the picture seems complete. Julius Caesar explicitly mentions the administering of justice as one of the obligations of the Ethnarch: the renewed agreement permitted living and behavior according to "the laws of the fathers." Hyrcanus acted by means of the "council of elders," "the council of the Sanhedrin," and thus strove to respect the traditional structure. Apparently, this power did not arouse the opposition of Antipater, Herod's father, who had obtained the title "Epitropos of Judaea" and Roman citizenship from Julius Caesar.[12] By contrast, Herod himself acted differently when, as ruler of the Galilee, he executed

9 Momigliano (supra n. 2) 7. Many researchers tried to study the meaning of the word *συνέδριον* in the literature regarding the land of Israel at the period under discussion. *Inter alia*, there has been debate on whether there was more than one Sanhedrin (one—of politics, law, and religion; the second—of politics and religion; the third—of the Priests, the Pharisees and the Elite, each one having a different role). See the discussion on this question and literature in H. Mantel, *Studies in the History of the Sanhedrin* (Cambridge, Mass. 1961).

10 *Ant.* 14.194-97; *BJ* 1.199.

11 E. Taubler, *Imperium Romanum* (Leipzig 1913; repr. 1964) 161, n. 3. See also H. A. Wolfson, *Philo* (Cambridge, Mass. 1947) II 346, n. 168.

12 A. Gilboa, "L'octroi de la citoyenneté romaine et de l'immunité à Antipater, père d'Hérode," in *Revue historique de droit français et étranger* 50 (1972) 609-14.

"bandits" without trial,[13] an action for which he was called to account before the Sanhedrin.[14] We will forgo explication of this instance here, as it pertains to criminal and not civil law; we wish only to emphasize the fact that Herod did not demonstrate respect for the Sanhedrin or the traditional Jewish legal norms.

4. Herod (37 BCE), Hellenistic King

It may be correct to suggest, as Schalit does, that the judicial autonomy granted to Hyrcanus by Caesar ended with the Hasmonean dynasty when Herod, with Roman support, took Jerusalem from Antigonus in 37 BCE. Herod enjoyed the support of Antonius and later of Augustus. This was his central power base, as his rule never achieved legitimacy in the eyes of the Jews, by whom he was always regarded as a foreign king and as a slave.[15] Herod was well aware of this situation and, despite his title of "Allied king and friend of the Roman people" (*Rex socius et amicus populi romani*), he was above all else subservient to Rome (*in dicione populi romani*).[16]

Nevertheless, it seems likely, considering Rome's traditionally liberal attitude towards the internal institutions of the provinces,[17] that Augustus allowed Herod to choose whether to preserve the traditional system of

13 *Ant.* 14.159-67; *BJ* 1.204-209; Schalit (supra n. 5) 31.

14 H. Mantel, "The Trial of Herod," *Annual of Bar-Ilan University* 1 (1963) 165-71 (Hebrew); A. Gilboa, "On the Trial of Herod," *Jerusalem in the Second Temple Period, A. Schalit Memorial Volume* (Jerusalem 1980) 98 ff. (Hebrew), emphasizes the interference of Sextus Iulius Caesar, governor of Syria, since Herod was a Roman citizen. On this problem, see also A. Kirschenbaum, "Jewish Law of Agency for Illegal Acts, Part II," *Shenaton hamishpat ha-ivri. Annual of the Institute for Research in Jewish Law* (1974) 219-30 (Hebrew). The author tries to examine Herod's trial within the limits of the Pharisaic halacha.

15 Talmud Bavli, *Bava Batra* 3b, 4a; *BJ* 2.87; Mantel (supra n. 14) 165 ff.

16 A. H. M. Jones, *The Herods of Judaea* (Oxford 1938); A. Momigliano, "Herod of Judaea," in *CAH* X (1934) 316-39 at 329-30; Schalit (supra n. 5); M. Stern, "The Politics of Herod and the Jewish Society toward the End of the Second Commonwealth," *Tarbiz* 35 (1965) 235-53 (Hebrew); A. M. Rabello, *Effetti personali della Patria Potestas, I, Dalle Origini al periodo degli Antonini* (Milan 1979) 363 ff.; *idem*, "Herod's Domestic Court? The Judgment of Death for Herod's Sons," *The Jewish Law Annual* 10 (1992) 39-56; M. Stern, *The Kingdom of Herod* (Tel Aviv 1992) (Hebrew).

17 O. Karlowa, *Römische Rechtsgeschichte* I (Leipzig 1885) 329 ff.

I

justice or to replace it with Roman justice on the pretext that Rome was interested in the wide use of Roman law in Judaea as well.[18] What happened practically? We know that the vassal king saw himself primarily as a Hellenistic king, and that he did all he could to give his kingdom a Hellenistic coloring. At the same time it is clear that the highest political and judicial authority was the Sanhedrin. Herod executed most of the members of the Sanhedrin who had judged him, and stripped the Sanhedrin of most of its political authority.[19] However, it seems that Herod did not want to take steps more far-reaching than these, and that he did not dare to abolish the Sanhedrin's judicial authority. Clearly, the vassal king, who saw himself as a Hellenistic king, did not feel subservient to the traditional Sanhedrin.[20] We should not be surprised that obviously Hellenistic institutions appear in that period, such as "Synhedrion of relatives and friends."[21]

It is also understandable that Herod occasionally promulgated laws which contradicted the traditional order when he felt it was justified by reason of state, as in the case of the "bandits."[22] However, Schalit is mistaken when he assumes that Herod changed the laws of debts. This assumption is based on the unproven premise that Jewish law in that period did not recognize self-help, and that such an action was necessarily a Hellenistic practice.[23]

We will see, in contrast to this, that the scholars who felt that self-help was accepted in Jewish law in Herod's time were correct. Particularly in contracts of debts, a clause had been introduced which allowed the lender to take the borrower's property directly, without a court order, at the end of a predetermined period.[24] Such a practice existed both in Jewish and

18 Schalit (supra n. 5) 121-34; see also infra n. 56.

19 Schalit (supra n. 5) 60-61.

20 Mantel (supra n. 14).

21 On this point, see Rabello, "Herod's Domestic Court?" (supra n. 16).

22 Josephus, *Ant.* 16.1.1. On this law see A. Gulak, "The Law of King Herod on the Punishment for Thieves," *Festschr. Klausner* (Tel Aviv 1937) 132-35 (Hebrew), and Schalit's criticism (supra n. 5) 126, 421 ff.

23 Schalit (supra n. 5) 133-34.

24 L. Beauchet, *Histoire du Droit privé de la République athénienne* III (Paris 1897; repr. Amsterdam 1969) 232: "s'il ne remplit point exactement l'obligation que lui impose le contrat, pourra être soumis à exécution 'comme s'il eut été condamné' envers le créancier par jugement passé en force de chose jugée '*καθάπερ ἐκ δίκης*' suivant la formule généralement employée;" L. Mitteis, *Reichsrecht und Volksrecht in den Östlichen Provinzen des Römischen Kaiserreichs* (Leipzig 1891) 411 (with

Hellenistic law. Similarly, I believe that Herod showed no lack of respect for the Sanhedrin when he made an independent law regarding the Arabian king Syllaeus.[25] Josephus emphasized that the matter related to international problems, and that it was not by chance that Herod had informed the Roman government before he acted.[26]

In general, therefore, we can conclude that as far as civil law goes, Herod did not interfere overtly by changing the "laws of the fathers." Local courts continued to function in accordance with traditional norms.[27] Clearly the internal conflicts between classes and sects, particularly between the Sadducees and the Pharisees, bore no connection at all to the question of whether Rome allowed autonomy of civil justice to remain—as apparently it did.

It seems likely that in this period the opportunity for choice between the courts existed. Jews who wanted to remain faithful to the "laws of the fathers" were not compelled to turn to Roman courts. This state of affairs became more pronounced later on.[28]

5. Judaea as a Roman Province (6 BCE)

In the year 6 BCE Judaea became a Roman province,[29] and its ruler became the highest authority in both criminal and civil law. Josephus explains: "The territory of Archelaus was now reduced to a province, and

reference to a passage from Josephus); A. Gulak, *History of Jewish Law. Talmudic Period I, Law of Obligations and Guaranties* (Jerusalem 1939) (Hebrew) 125-30. In my opinion, Gulak is correct in that the development was the opposite to what Schalit has described. Therefore, civil justice was afterwards limited; M. Elon, *Freedom of the Debtor's Person in Jewish Law* (Jerusalem 1964) 31-37 (Hebrew).

25 *AJ* 16.343-45.

26 Z. W. Falk, *Introduction to Jewish Law of the Second Commonwealth* I (Leiden 1972) 97.

27 Falk (supra n. 26) 88-92 ("The Town Court").

28 B. Cohen, "Arbitration in Jewish and Roman Law," in *Jewish and Roman Law* (New York 1966) 651-709, and the bibliography mentioned there.

29 M. Stern, "The Status of Provincia Judaea and Its Governors in the Roman Empire under the Julio-Claudian Dynasty," *Eretz Israel* 10 (Shazar Volume) (1971) 274-82 (Hebrew); Momigliano (supra n. 16) 337-39; M. Stern, "The Province of Judaea," in S. Safrai & M. Stern eds., *The Jewish People in the First Century* (Compendia Rerum Judaicarum ad Novum Testamentum 1,1) (Assen 1974) 308-76.

Coponius,[30] a Roman of the equestrian order, was sent out as procurator, entrusted by Augustus with full powers, including the infliction of capital punishment."[31] Yet, even after Judaea became a Roman province, he maintained the principle of leaving civil justice to the local Jewish institutions.[32]

In this region in particular, where Rome was well aware of the value placed on the "laws of the fathers," it decided to preserve local institutions of government, judges, and national law. Rome defined autonomy as the right to live according to independent laws (*suae leges*)—"autonomy in the broad sense of independent civil justice."[33]

Like Judaea, other nations sought autonomy. Cicero tells us of the decree he made as ruler of Cilicia, in which he permitted local judges to continue to perform their functions. Cicero describes the Greeks' reactions

30 He was under the control of the Syrian legatus, P. Sulpicius Quirinius. There is a discussion on the question of whether his title was Praefectus (*cum iure gladii*) or Procurator; See A. Schalit, *Roman Administration in Palestine* (Jerusalem 1937) (Hebrew); H. G. Pflaum, *Les carrières procuratoriennes équestres sous le haut Empire Romain*[3] (Paris 1961) 1082; *idem*, *Les Procurateurs équestres sous le haut Empire Romain* (Paris 1950) 110 ff. ("Le pouvoir judiciare des procurateurs--goverveurs"); A. H. M. Jones, "Procurators and Prefects in the Early Principate," in *Studies in Roman Government and Law* (Oxford 1960) 115-25. For references and summary of discussion since the discovery of an inscription identifying Pontius Pilate as *praefectus*, see L. H. Feldman, *Josephus and Modern Scholarship (1937-1980)* (Berlin-New York 1986) 317-20.

31 *BJ* 2.117; see Pflaum, *Les Procurateurs équestres* (supra n. 30) 119; Stern, "The Status of Provincia Judaea" (supra n. 29) 275.

32 H. Volkmann, *Zur Rechtsprechung im Prinzipat des Augustus* (Münchener Beiträge zur Papyrusforschung 21) (Munich 1935) 128 ff.; F. Millar, "Some Evidence on the Meaning of Tacitus Annals XII, 60," *Historia* 13 (1964) 180-87; *idem*, "The Development of Jurisdiction by Imperial Procurators: Further Evidence," *Historia* 14 (1965) 362-67; Stern, "The Province of Judaea" (supra n. 29) 336 ff.; see the criticism of the essay of W. Dahlheim (supra n. 3) by G. I. Luzzatto, *SDHI* 43 (1977) 654-66. Luzzatto emphasizes that the jurisdictional autonomy of the citizens had limited the interference of the authorities; the principle of personal law, which was dominant in the ancient period, has to be mentioned as well; thus, a large part of the subjects had preserved their private law (p. 657).

33 De Martino (supra n. 3) 366-70; compare Polybius 4.27; Th. Mommsen emphasizes that with regard to Greece the situation is ἐλευθερία, and with regard to Syria and its surrounding areas the situation is αὐτονομία. See also R. Martini, *Ricerche in tema di editto provinciale* (Milan 1969) 48: "This recognition of the autonomy of the citizens was in the eyes of the provincial citizens primarily the possibility, derived therefrom, of recourse to local judges."

in his letter to Atticus, written in 50 BCE,[34] "The Greeks are most pleased,[35] because they have foreign judges.[36] You may say the judges are base fellows; but the Greeks believe they have received autonomy."

"There can be no doubt," writes De Martino, "that having local judges constituted the most important aspect of autonomy." However,

> there was no firm standard principle requiring preservation of national norms.... We must remember that Roman policy adapted itself to different situations. In a few cases local law and national institutions indeed were preserved with unsure status, always subject to suspension by the ruler. In other cases even these were changed or else national institutions were changed fundamentally, Roman judges and courts were imposed, and the traditional norms of the subjugated people were not honored.[37]

Judaea was among those states that had their own law restored to them —*leges suas reddere*. The residents had the status of foreigners using their own law (*peregrini qui suis legibus utuntur*), and thus lived "in accordance to local law" (*secundum propriae civitatis iura*).[38]

Nevertheless, even in cases where there was no official provision for it, in practice, the local law continued to hold force in relations between the inhabitants "except," writes De Martino, "for instances in which the

34 Cicero, *ad Att.* 6.2.4; A. H. I. Greenidge, *The Legal Procedure of Cicero's Time* (London 1901; repr. New York 1971) 117-18; G. Pugliese, "Riflessioni sul- l'Editto di Cicerone in Cilicia," *Synteleia Arangio-Ruiz* II (Napoli 1964) 972-86.

35 This pleasure shows that the situation could have been different. See D. Stockton, *Cicero, A Political Biography* (Oxford 1971) 227-53.

36 Martini (supra n. 33) 24 ff., 33 ff.; A. Biscardi, "Nuove testimoniaze di un papiro arabo-giudaico per la storia del processo provinciale romano," *Studi Scherillo* I (Milan 1972) 111 ff., 131 ff.; *idem*, *Aspetti del fenomeno processuale nell'esperienza giuridica romana* (Milan 1973) 181 ff.; *idem*, "xenokritai," *Novissimo Digesto Italiano* XX (1975) 1087-90; *idem*, "Sulla identificazione degli 'Xenokritai' e sulla loro attivita in *P.Oxy.* 3016," *Fest. Seidl* (Cologne n.d. [1975]) 15-24. See the extensive bibliography mentioned in these studies.

37 De Martino (supra n. 3) 371.

38 See the list of texts in De Martino (supra n. 3) 377, n. 60: Cic., *Verr.* 2.2.13.23; 2.2.22.53; 2.2.37.90; Livy 25.23.4; 38.39.12; Gellius, *NA* 16.13.4; Livy 33.32.5; Polybius 18.46.5; Livy 37.54.26; 38.44.4; Cic., *de leg. agr.* 2.31.86; *Att.* 6.1.15; 6.2.4; *FIRA* I 35.19 (*Sc. de Asclep.*); *OGIS* 449; Dio Cass. 37.20.2; see also A. H. M. Jones, "Another Interpretation of the Constitutio Antoniana," *JRS* 26 (1936) 222 ff., 223-35 esp. 229.

ruler made specific decrees of his own, and except for the various principles which he was able to establish in the process of the carrying out of justice."[39] This last point should be limited, in my opinion, to cases which were brought before Roman judges; the local judges continued to judge according to the traditional law.

Thus, it is possible to establish that Jewish courts in Palestine were able to judge conflicts between Jews, just as in other places conflicts between local residents were decided by local courts or by a *iudex peregrinus*.[40]

We may assume that this authority was also recognized in cases involving Jews and non-Jews. Despite some skepticism engendered in a number of apologetic speeches by Josephus, there does not appear to be any serious reason to doubt the factual picture he presents, as it does not contradict other sources available to us.[41] In a speech which Josephus puts in Titus' mouth, the Roman emperor seeks to know what the causes were of the Jewish revolt: "... ever since Pompey reduced you by force."[42] He concludes: "No, assuredly you were incited against the Romans by Roman humanity.[43] To begin with, we allowed you to occupy this land and set over you kings of your own blood; then we maintained the laws of your forefathers and permitted you, not only among yourselves but also in your dealings with others, to live as you willed."[44]

In addition, Rome preferred this approach of autonomy because it avoided the huge expenditure involved in establishing Roman courts everywhere for the local populations.

In a case of judgment between a local resident and a Roman citizen

39 De Martino (supra n. 3) II, 377 ff.

40 Cic. *Verr.* II.2.13.32. *Siculi hoc iure sunt, quod civis cum cive agat, domi certet suis legibus...* See Greenidge (supra n. 34) 118; De Martino (supra n. 3) 380; Pugliese (supra n. 34) 975: The *lex Rupilia*, of the year 111 BCE, permitted litigants from the same town to be judged before their own judges, in their own courts, according to their own laws. Martini (supra n. 33) 21, nn. 16, 27 f., 46.

41 On this last problem, see M. Stern, "Josephus and the Roman Empire," in *Josephus Flavius Historian of Eretz Israel in the Hellenistic-Roman Period* (Jerusalem 1982) 237-45 (Hebrew with English summary).

42 *BJ* 6.329.

43 ἡ 'Ρωμαίων φιλανθρωπία.

44 *BJ* 6.333-334; see also S. Safrai, "Jewish Self-government," in Safrai & Stern (supra n. 29) 377-419 at 379 ff.; B. S. Jackson, "On the problem of Roman Influence on the Halakah and Normative Self-Definition in Judaism," in E. P. Sanders ed., *Jewish and Christian Self-Definition* II (Philadelphia 1981) 157-203 at 159-60.

it would seem that the *lex Rupilia* applied. This law of 111 BCE required that the judge and defendant be of the same nationality, and that the law in effect be that of the lender.[45] In other cases, the case could be tried before a Roman court (*ex conventu civium romanorum*) or a local court. Apparently referring to this principle is a letter from Octavius to Rhosos, where it states that citizenship is granted to Seleucus and his relatives along with the right to choose the manner of justice if he should be a defendant; however, as plaintiff he would be required to follow the local law.[46]

At the same time, there were many exceptions, such as the one granted to the city of Chios by a *senatusconsultum* of the year 80 BCE, according to which even Romans living in the city were subject to local law.[47] Another exception was that established by the *senatusconsultum de Asclepiade* (78 BCE),[48] in which three navigators and their children, friends of the Roman people, were permitted to choose between Roman and local justice, or that of the free cities. In cases tried in their absence they were entitled to the right of *restitutio in integrum*. We have no sources that would indicate the legal situation of Roman-born citizens, but it certainly was no worse than that of newly created Roman citizens.[49]

6. The Archives

As in Greek cities, alongside the courthouse were located archives in which various legal documents could be checked and approved. Josephus speaks of archives that were burned by the Sicarii:[50]

> They next carried their combustibles to the public archives (ἀρχεῖα), eager to destroy the money-lenders' bonds and to prevent the recovery of debts, in order to win over a host of

45 H. Lewald, "Conflits de lois dans le monde grec et romain," *Labeo* 5 (1959) 338 ff.; G. Broggini, "'Fictio civitatis' strumento dell'arbitrio giurisdizionale di Verre?" *Synteleia Arangio-Ruiz* II (Napoli 1964) 934-43 at 942; Martini (supra n. 33) 44, 46 and n. 75.

46 *CIL* XVI 11 = *FIRA* I 55, lines 53-55; G. I. Luzzatto, *Epigrafia giuridica greca e romana* (Rome 1942) 300; Martini (supra n. 33) 35, n. 46.

47 *SIG*³ II, No. 785, lines 14-19.

48 *FIRA* I 35. See A. Berger, *Encyclopedic Dictionary of Roman Law* (Philadelphia 1953) 697.

49 De Martino (supra n. 3) 21, 29, 384-87; Martini (supra n. 33) 46 ff.

50 *BJ* 2.427.

grateful debtors and to cause an uprising of the poor against the rich, sure of impunity. The keepers of the Record Office having fled, they set light to the building.

It would appear from Josephus' account that the archives were burnt a second time by Roman soldiers: Titus "then gave his troops permission to burn and sack the city. For that day they refrained; but on the next they set fire to the Archives, the Acra, the Council Chamber, and the region called Ophlas"[51]

7. Roman Justice

It is clear that in Palestine, as in other provinces, the Roman ruler had judicial authority along with the local governments. The authority of justice (*iurisdictio*),[52] both civil[53] and criminal, was among his most important responsibilities.[54] He exercised this authority in the courts that were established in various areas (*διοικήσεις*), *conventus*.[55] The ruler judged civil cases primarily between Roman citizens, with an authority similar to that of the *praetor urbanus*. He upheld the norms of provincial decrees (*edicta*) and the norms established by the law of the province (*lex provinciae*).[56] We should not forget that at this time there were many

51 *BJ* 6.353-54.

52 G. I. Luzzatto, "Giurisdizione (Storia, diritto romano)," in *Enc. dir.* XIX (1970) 190 ff.; Stern, "The Province of Judaea" (supra n. 29) 336-40; Safrai (supra n. 44) 397-400.

53 *D.* 1.16.7.2; 1.18.10-12.

54 P. De Francisci, *Storia del diritto romano*, II,1 (Milan 1944) 356 ff.

55 On the judges in the provinces, see G. Pugliese, *Il processo civile romano* II, 1 (Milan 1963) 110-13, 118 ff., 183. On the *conventus*, see F. Grelle, "Conventus," *Novissimo Digesto Italiano* IV (Turin 1959) 801-802; G. Foti Talamanca, *Ricerche sul processo nell' Egitto Greco-romano* I: *L'organizzazione del 'Conventus' del 'Praefectus Aegypti'* (Milan 1974) on page 2, n. 6 a comprehensive bibliography; on pp. 1 and 23 the examination of the relation between the Conventus and permanent jurisdiction.

56 On the Lex Gabinia for Syria and Palestine, see Cic., *Prov. Cons.* 5.10-21; On that, see G. I. Luzzatto, "Provincia," *Novissimo Digesto Italiano* XIV (Turin 1967) 377-82; Stern (supra n. 1) 202 ff. Scholars of Roman law have emphasized, generally, the influence of the local laws, which, as a result of the local autonomy, continued to exist side by side with the Roman law. However, Luzzatto emphasizes the fact that there was imperial interference, the aim of which was to limit the local autonomy and to influence the development of the law in the province, according

Roman citizens in Palestine. They were members of the provincial government, soldiers, newly created Roman citizens (such as Herod's family), slaves freed by Roman masters,[57] or non-Jewish citizens living in Palestine. The Roman judge had to decide cases involving Roman citizens, at least when the citizens were the defendants.[58] Clearly, we cannot exclude the possibility of tyranny along the lines of that perpetrated by Verres during his rule of Sicilia.

8. Conclusion

In light of this inquiry we can conclude that the civil jurisdiction in Palestine, which was a Roman province between 6 BCE and 70 CE, was as follows:

— Civil cases among Jews: Jewish justice

— Civil cases between Jews and non-Jews: Jewish justice

— Civil cases in which the plaintiff was Roman: apparently the law of the defendant was followed, unless there existed a special privilege which required Roman law to be followed or which allowed the Roman defendant to choose between Roman justice (before the *conventus* of the magistrate) and Jewish justice (before a Jewish judge).

— Civil cases in which the defendant was Roman: the defendant could choose between Roman and Jewish justice.

It is reasonable to assume that, as in the period of the Principate,

to the *princeps*' will and instructions. See G. I. Luzzatto, "Processo provinciale e autonomie cittadine," *JJP* 15 (1965) 49-64 (at 49 ff. and 58 ff. there are interesting notes on the question of the foreign judges, "aloteria" and "autonomy," and on the possibility of choosing between the local law and the Roman law).

On the *edictum provinciale*, see particularly A. Guarino, "Gaio e l'edictum provinciale," *IVRA* 20 (1969) 154-71; R. Katzoff, "The Provincial Edict in Egypt," *Tijdschrift voor Rechtsgeschiedenis* 37 (1969) 414-37; H. Ankum, "La législation des préfets d'Égypte et l'edictum provinciale," in *Annales de la Faculté de Droit et des Sciences Economiques de Toulouse* 18 (1970) 357 ff.; J. Modrzejewski, "La Règle de droit dans l'Égypte Romaine," in *Proceedings of the Twelfth International Congress of Papyrology* (Toronto 1970) 317-77 at 341-44; *idem*, *Droit impérial et traditions locales dans l'Egypte romaine* (Hampshire 1990); *idem*, "Diritto e diritti locali," in *Storia di Roma* III,2 (Turin 1993) 985-1009.

57 A. M. Rabello, "The Legal Condition of the Jews in the Roman Empire," *ANRW* II, 13 (1980) 662-762 at 724-26.

58 Martini (supra n. 33) 9 ff., 35, n. 46.

there was some supervision of local justice by the Roman governments.[59, 60]

59 On this problem, see J. Juster, *Les Juifs dans l'Empire Romain. Leur condition juridique, économique et sociale* II (Paris 1914) 94; V. Colorni, *Legge ebraica e leggi locali* (Milan 1945) 103 ff.; Rabello, *Giustiniano, Ebrei e Samaritani* (supra n. 3) II 658-96.

60 It should be noted that the following passage in the Palestinian Talmud, Sanhedrin 1,1, has not been relied upon in the present study: "It was taught: Forty years before the destruction of the Temple the right to judge capital cases was withdrawn, and it was in the days of Simeon b. Shatah that the right to judge property cases was withdrawn. Said R. Simeon b. Yohai, 'Blessed be the All merciful that I am not a sage required to make court decisions.'" Tr. J. Neusner, *The Talmud of the Land of Israel*, vol. 31, Sanhedrin 1.1 p.12 III [A], [B].

Simeon b. Shatah was a scholar at the turn of the first century BCE, while Rabbi Simeon b. Yohai was a scholar of the second century CE. Although the period of the former, in the days of King Yannai, was complicated, I do not believe the civil Jewish traditional law was cancelled. We should note that the reading is far from certain; in the parallel text in Sanhedrin 7.2, instead of Simeon b. Shatah, Simeon b. Yohai appears. Neusner ignores this difference: "In the time of R. Simeon b. Shatah, the right to judge property cases was taken away from Israelite courts," ibid. 7.2, p. 201 III [B]. On Neusner's translation of the Palestinian Talmud, see the critical remarks of Saul Lieberman, "A Tragedy or a Comedy?" *Journal of the American Oriental Society* 104.2 (1984) 315-19. This reading (i.e., Bar Yohai) corresponds with the continuation of the Talmudic text and it seems to correspond with the historical period (in the days of the Emperor Hadrian and the Bar-Kochba revolt). This reading is accepted by A. Buechler and G. Alon; see also Jackson (supra n. 44) 159 ff.

For an examination of the subsequent period, see A. M. Rabello, "Jewish and Roman Jurisdiction," in N. S. Hecht, B. S. Jackson, S. M. Passamaneck, D. Piatelli, & A. M. Rabello eds., *An Introduction to the History and Sources of Jewish Law* (Oxford 1996) 139-65.

II

HEROD'S DOMESTIC COURT?
THE JUDGMENT OF DEATH FOR HEROD'S SONS

This study is dedicated to *Professor Reuven Yaron*, teacher and friend, with acknowledgement on the occasion of his retirement from the Hebrew University of Jerusalem.

A. *Introduction*

The life of Herod the King[1] seems at times a true tragedy even in the intimate domestic sphere. However, before embarking upon a discussion of the question of whether Herod judges his wife Mariamne and his sons, Alexander and Aristobulus, as a Roman *pater familias* — as many scholars contend — we shall consider a number of basic points.

Herod's father, Antipater, received Roman citizenship from Julius Caesar (πολιτεία τε αὐτὸν τῇ 'Ρωμαίων ἐδωρήσατο καὶ ἀτελείᾳ[2]), as a result of which, the sons of Antipater and their wives also received Roman citizenship, including *patria potestas* over their son.[3] It is therefore clear that Herod had Roman citizenship,

1 A. Schalit, *Koenig Herodes, der Mann und sein Werk* (Berlin: 1969); see also W.E. Filmer, "The Chronology of the Reign of Herod Great", *Journal of Theological Studies* 16 (1966), 2683; M. Pani, *Roma e i re d'Oriente da Augusto a Tiberio*, 114.

2 Josephus, *Wars of the Jews* [hereinafter: Wars], I:194. The passages from Josephus are from the translations by H. St.J. Thackeray (Wars) and R. Marcus (Antiquities) in the Loeb Classical Library.

3 On this point see E. Schürer, *Geschichte des* Jüdischen *Volkes I*, (Leipzig: J.C. Hinrichs, 1898), 402 n.108; A. Gilboa, "L'octroi de la citoyenneté romaine et de l'immunité à Antipater, père d'Hérode, *Revue Historique de Droit Français et Etranger* 50 (1972), 609. Gilboa points out, *inter alia*, the connection with the granting of citizenship to Seleucus of Rhosos. See E. Volterra, "Sulla condizione dei figli dei peregrini cui veniva concessa la cittadinanza romana", *Studi Cicu*, 645ff.

as well as φίλος καὶ σύμμαχος, *socius et amicus* of the Romans.[4] What emerges is that Herod was permitted to have legal marital relations, to the extent that there was *connubium* (ἐπιγαμία) between himself and the woman.[5] Hence, the issue of these relations were subject to the *patria potestas* of their father.[6]

After referring to "Herod's court" — בית דין של הורדוס (like the Hasmonean Court referred to in the Talmud), Schalit writes:

> Roman law in another format in the Herodean kingdom emerges when we look at the juridical essence of the trials of Mariamne and her sons, the trial of Antipater the son of Herod and possibly also the complaint of Herod against Aristobulus prior to the appointment of the young Aristobulus to the position of High Priest. There is no doubt that Mariamne, her sons and Antipater were brought before a court constituted as a domestic court which was the practice in Rome and which was assembled in the family circle by the Roman *pater familias*, in order to judge a family member who committed or plotted a crime against the *pater familias* himself, or against an outsider or against Roman society in general. The decision lay in the hands of the *pater familias* on the basis of his *patria potestas*.[7]

4 Josephus, *Antiquities of the Jews* [hereinafter: Antiquities] XVII:246; see A. Momigliano, *Ricerche sull'organizzazione della Giudea sotto il dominio romano* (63 a.C.-70 d.C.) (Bologna: Annali della R. Scuola Normale di Pisa, Serie 2, Vol. 3, 1934; Amsterdam: A.M. Hakkert, 1967), 54.

5 See also the Edict of Rhosos (line 40): F. de Visscher, "Le statut juridique des citoyens romains et l'inscription de Rhosos", *L'Antiquité Classique* XIV (1946), 25, 39; E. Volterra, *Il matrimonio romano* (Rome: Ed. Ricerche, 1961), 157; E. Volterra, "Matrimonio in Diritto Romano", *Enciclopedia del Diritto* (1975), XXV 726, 775; M.A. Levi, "La grande iscrizione di Ottaviano trovata a Roso", in *Il tribunato della plebe* (Milano, 1978), 143.

On the problem of Herod's polygamy, which was contrary to Roman law, see: J. Juster, *Les Juifs dans l'Empire Romain* (Paris: Gabalda, 1914), II.53. On the custom of polygamy amongst Jews in the Roman Empire, see A.M. Rabello, "Sui rapporti fra Diocleziano e gli Ebrei", *Atti della Accademia Romanistica Constantiniana* (Perugia: Libreria Universitaria, 1976), 157, 171. However, with respect to Herod it must be recalled that he divorced his first wife, Doris, prior to his marriage to Mariamne. See Josephus, *Antiquities* XIV:300; *Wars* I:241, 432. And see also E.M. Smallwood, *The Jews under Roman Rule* (Leiden: E.J. Brill, 1976), 102, n.148.

6 Gaius, *Institutiones* I.55; A.M. Rabello, *Effetti personali della patria potestas in diritto romano* (Milano: Giuffrè, 1979), 174 .

7 Schalit, *supra* n.1, at 132-133; see also at n.345, in which he quotes

It is true that many scholars held, and some still hold, that there was such a thing as a domestic court with juridical jurisdiction,[8] but following the studies of Volterra,[9] the number of doubters grew as to the legal obligation (as opposed to social custom) applying to the holder of the *patria potestas* to expand the *consilium necessariorum* (in which, often, influential *amici* participated, alongside the relatives),[10] and to obtain the consent of the majority in order that he be able to exercise his *vitae necisque potestas*[11] (power over life and death).

In one note in his book on Roman criminal law, Mommsen refers to the trial of Herod's two sons, saying that "the most vivid picture of the domestic court is provided by Josephus ..."[12]

It is interesting, however, that Jean Juster, who also held that *les juifs citoyens romains eurent surement le droit de constituer un tribunal domestique* (Jews who were Roman citizens surely had the right to constitute a domestic court)[13] does not interpret in this manner the case of the court that judged the two sons of Herod. Juster writes as against Mommsen: "*C'est un cas exceptionnel, qu'on peut ex-*

Mommsen and Volkman, and comments: "The customary term for these tribunals is "domestic court" (*Hausgericht*). I have sometimes preferred the expression "family" for the sake of linguistic convenience."

8 See recently W. Kunkel, "Das Konsilium im Hausgericht", *Zeitschrift der Savigny Stiftung für Rechtsgeschichte, Romanistische Abteilung* [hereinafter: ZSS] LXXXIII (1966), 219. At 225ff., there is a discussion of the trial of the sons of Mariamne and Herod, which we shall discuss below. See also A. Balducci, "Intorno al iudicium domesticum", *Archivio Giuridico* 191 (1976), 69ff.

9 E. Volterra, "Il preteso tribunale domestico in diritto romano", *Rivista Italiana per le Scienze Giuridiche* I (1948), 102n.; *idem*, "Il matrimonio romano", *supra* n.5, at 43ff.

10 Cf. A. Guarino, "Il preteso tribunale domestico", *Labeo* XIII (1967), 124.

11 See R. Yaron, "Vitae necisque potestas", *Tijschift voor Rechtsgeschiedenis* 30 (1972), 243; Rabello, *supra* n.6, at 30, 144 .

12 Th. Mommsen, *Roemisches Strafrecht* (Leipzig: C.H. Beck, 1899), 25 n.4.

13 J. Juster, *Les Juifs*, *supra* n.5, at II.55 n.1. See also my critique on the occasion of the reprinting of the work: *Jura* XVIII (1967), 312 n.26 and see, in general, A.M. Rabello, "The Legal Condition of the Jews in the Roman Empire", *Aufstieg und Niedergang der Römischen Welt*, II, 13 (Berlin — New York: W. de Gruyter, 1980), 662-762.

pliquer autrement"[14] (this is an exceptional case, which could be interpreted otherwise). Juster's comment appears to us to be correct. If we reexamine the sources, we shall see how it is possible to explain in another way the trials conducted by Herod for some of the members of his family, and that they can be viewed other than as actions done by virtue of his power as *pater familias*.

B. *The Trial of Mariamne*

The marriage of Herod to Mariamne the Hasmonean was solemnized in the year 37 B.C.E. in the city of Samaria, at the time that Herod was besieging Jerusalem. To him, this marriage was πάρεργον ... τῆς πολιορκίας (a matter that was secondary to the siege).[15] Mariamne, the daughter of Alexandra (the daughter of Hyrcanus II) and Alexander (the son of Aristobulus II),[16] may have brought a measure of legitimacy to the reign of Herod before the Hasmonean kings. Herod's great love for Mariamne was spoiled due to his jealous rivalry with the Hasmonean dynasty,[17] and due to the hatred of Herod's sister and mother for the proud queen. To all these must be added the decree issued secretly by Herod to his followers, first Antonius and later Octavius, to put Mariamne to death if he should die. The conduct of Mariamne towards Herod, when he returned home jubilant and triumphant, aroused his jealousy and ire, and Mariamne was brought before the Court. Josephus relates the incident thus:

> He did say, however, that the hatred which his wife felt for the king had arisen from the things which Soemus had told her. And while he was still speaking, the king cried aloud, saying that Soemus, who had all along, been most faithful to him and his realm, would never have betrayed his instructions if he had not gone too far in his intimacy with Mariamme. And so he gave orders that Soemus should be arrested

14 Juster, *supra* n.5; see also Z. W. Falk, *Introduction to Jewish Law of the Second Commonwealth I* (Leiden: E.J. Brill, 1972), and see my critique: *Jura* XX (1969), 681 n. 11.

15 *Wars* I:344. On this point, See J. Klausner, *History of the Second Temple* (Heb., Jerusalem: Ahiasaf, 1959), III. 268-269.

16 *Antiquities* XV:23-25.

17 As it manifests itself in the murder of Aristobulus III (the brother of Mariamne) on Herod's orders, and the execution of Hyrcanus II.

and put to death at once, while to his wife he conceded the right to a trial. Calling, together those who were closest to him, he brought an elaborately framed accusation against her concerning the love-potions and drugs which she was alleged to have prepared. Since he was intemperate in speech and too angry to judge (calmly), those who were present realized in what a state he was, and finally condemned her to death. But after sentence had been passed, it occurred both to him and to some of those present that she ought not to be done away with so hastily but be put away in one of the fortresses of the kingdom. But Salome and her friends made every effort to get rid of the poor woman, and they prevailed upon the king to do so by advising him to take precautions against the popular disturbances which would break out if she should be allowed to live. That is how Mariamme came to be led to execution.[18]

In Greek, the principal sentence in the above section is as follows: τῇ δὲ γυναικὶ κρίσιν ἀπεδίδου συναγαγὼν τοὺς οἰκειοτάτους αὐτῷ (and he brought his wife to trial, assembling his closest friends).[19]

We do not know if the marriage of Mariamne was accompanied by *conventio in manum*, as a result of which the wife is considered as *filiae loco* in the house of her husband.[20] A negative answer seems more reasonable to us, and therefore it cannot be said with certainty that Herod was acting by virtue of his *patria potestas*. Prior to the enactment of the *lex Julia de adulteriis* in the year 13 B.C.E. (Mariamne was executed in the year 29 B.C.E.), the Roman husband was, apparently, permitted to execute his adulterous wife only if he caught her *in flagrante*, as an instance of self defence."[21] Here, how-

18 *Antiquities* XV:228-231. See H.H. Mantel, *Studies in the History of the Sanhedrin* (Cambridge Mass.: Harvard University Press, 1961).

19 On the marriage of Herod and Mariamne, see also S. Zeitlin, *The Rise and Fall of the Judean State* (Philadelphia: The Jewish Publication Society of America, 1968), I.383. On the problem of the political judicature see Zeitlin at 202ff., and also A.M. Rabello, "A Tribute to Jean Juster", *Israel Law Review* XI (1976), 216, 227; M. Lepri, *Sui rapporti di parentela in diritto attico, Saggi terminologici*, (Milano, 1959), 37, 73f., 89ff.

20 See Gaius, *Institutiones* I.108ff.; on recent studies, see Volterra, *supra* n.5, at 1961:89ff.; Volterra, *supra* n.5, at 1975, citing literature on the subject.

21 See L. Chiazzese, "Adulterio", *Novissimo Digesto Italiano* (1957), I.322; G. Branca, "Adulterio", *Enciclopedia del Diritto* (1958), I.620; A.M. Rabello, "Il ius occidendi iure patris della lex Julia de adulteriis coercendis e la vitae necisque potestas del paterfamilias", *Atti del Seminario*

ever, there were only mere suspicions![22]

Obviously, Herod is not acting here in accordance with the Scriptural law of the adulterous woman[23]. Therefore, the question arises: by virtue of what is Herod acting when he orders the execution of Sohemus? Had Herod been an ordinary citizen, it is reasonable to assume that in such a case he would have been tried as a murderer; Herod, however, was acting *as a king*. The trial of Mariamne can be explained, in our opinion, on the same basis. It is almost certain that Herod also had political reasons which led him to the conclusion that he must execute his wife, Mariamne the Hasmonean.[24] We shall discuss the nature of this court below, in our discussion of the trial of the sons of Herod and Mariamne. Josephus himself, in his description, does not conceal his great admiration for Mariamne.[25]

C. *Herod's Relations with his Sons from his Wife, Mariamne*

In the year 23 B.C.E., six years after the execution of Mariamne, Herod sent his sons, Alexander and Aristobulus, and another, to Rome. (The third son died there.) In Rome, the boys grew up in the house of Pollio,[26] and Augustus himself was fond of them. In the year 18 B.C.E., Herod brought his sons back to his kingdom. Alexander married Glaphyra, the daughter of Archelaus, king of Cap-

---

Romanistico Internazionale, Perugia (Roma: Arti Grafiche E. Cossidente, 1972), 228; Rabello, *supra* n.6, at 210ff.

22 For an explanation of other cases in which it appears that the wife is judged in a domestic tribunal, See *Dionysius* II, 25; Gellius, *N.A.* 10,23,3-4; Tacitus, *Ann.* XIII, 32; and see the explanation of Volterra, *Il matrimonio romano, supra* n.5, at 49.

23 *Numbers* 5:2-31.

24 Cf. Smallwood, *supra* n.5, at 71.

25 *Antiquities* XI:235-239. See the story as it is related in the Babylonian Talmud, *Bava Batra* 3b. And see the explanation of J. Derenbourg, *Essai sur l'Histoire et la geographie de la Palestine d'apres les Thalmuds et les autres sources rabbiniques* (Paris: Imprimerie Imperiale, 1867), 150.

26 On the death of Herod's third son, See *Wars* I:435. On Asinius Pollio, or possibly Vedius Pollio, See E. Schürer, *The History of the Jewish People in the Age of Jesus Christ (175 B.C. — A.D. 135)*, edited by G. Vermes & F. Millar (Edinburgh: T & T Clark, 1973), 321 n.132.

padocia, and Aristobulus married Berenice, the daughter of Salome, Herod's very influential sister.[27]

The sons of Mariamne, who inherited their Hasmonean mother's proud nature,[28] did not hide their longing for their mother and their desire to avenge her death. This aroused the suspicions of those close to Herod, and of Herod himself. As a first step, Herod brought back to his household his first-born son, Antipater, the son of his first wife Doris, whom he had divorced preceding his marriage to Mariamne the Hasmonean.[29] Antipater did not sit idly by, and through his actions he succeeded in further deepening the suspicions of Herod towards his sons. He did the same in the year that he spent in Rome for the purpose of studies. Finally, Herod decided to bring the two sons to trial before Augustus. Since Augustus was not in Rome at the time, Herod took his sons with him to Aquila, where Augustus was staying.

Josephus describes the trial before Augustus in the following terms:

> One of them, at any rate, namely Alexander, was dragged by his father to Rome and there accused at Caesar's tribunal of attempting to poison him. The young man, finding himself at last at liberty to vent his grievances and in the presence of a judge with far more experience than Antipater, more sagacity than Herod, modestly threw a veil over his father's faults, but forcibly exposed the calumnies directed against himself. He next proved that his brother, his partner in peril, was equally innocent, and then proceeded bitterly to complain of Antipater's villainy and of the ignominy to which he and his brother were exposed. He was assisted not only by a clear conscience but by his powerful oratory, for he was an extremely able speaker. Concluding with the remark that it was open to their father to put them to death, if he really believed the charge to be true, he reduced all his hearers to tears, and so deeply affected Caesar that he acquitted the accused and brought Herod to a reconciliation on the spot. The conditions of the agreement were that the sons.should render implicit obedience to their father, and that he should be at liberty to bequeath the kingdom to

27 On Alexander, See A. Schalit, *Encyclopedia Judaica* II.567. On Aristobulus, see J. Gafni, *Encyclopedia Judaica* III.442.

28 *Wars* I:445.

29 *Wars* I:448. See M. Stern, "Herod and the Herodian Dynasty", in S. Safrai and M. Stern, eds., *The Jewish People in the First Century* (Assen: Van Gorcum 1974), 264 (*Compendia Rerum Judaicarum ad Novum Testamentum* I, 1).

whom he would.[30]

Clearly, Augustus deigned to preside over this trial concerning Herod only because the latter was a king, and from what Herod himself says, it emerges clearly that he acted as he did because of his role as a king, even though he did not disregard the natural ties:

> ὦ παῖδες ἀγάθοι, πρῶτον μὲν ἐνθυμούμενοι τὴν ἱερὰν φύσιν, ἧς καὶ παρὰ θηρίοις αἱ στοργαὶ μένουσιν.
>
> As for you, my good children, think first of the sacred ties of nature and the constancy of affection which she instils even into the beasts;[31]

Josephus describes the return of Herod to Jerusalem thus:

> On reaching Jerusalem, Herod assembled the people, presented to them his three sons, made his excuses for his absence, and rendered profuse thanks to God, and no less to Caesar, who had re-established his disordered household and had given his sons a greater boon than a kingdom, namely concord. "The ties of that concord," he continued, "I shall bind more closely myself; for Caesar has appointed me lord of the realm and arbiter of the succession, and I, in consulting my own advantage, also repay my debt to him. I now declare these my three sons kings, and I beseech first (God, and then you, to ratify my decision."[32]

Of particular interest is the following passage, which Josephus attributes to Herod:

> I myself shall select the advisers and attendants who are to consort with each of my sons, and shall hold them responsible for keeping the peace, being well aware that factions and rivalries among princes are produced by the malign influence of associates, while virtuous companion.s promote natural affection. I must require these persons however, and not them only but also the officers of my army, for the present to rest their hopes on me alone; for it is not the kingdom, but the mere honours of royalty, which I am now delivering over to my sons. They will enjoy the pleasures of power, as if actual rulers, but upon me, however unwilling, will fall the burden of office.[33]

In another passage, too, while continuing his description of the bad relations between Herod and his sons, Josephus stresses the conduct of Herod as a king and as a father: βραχέα μὲν ἠπείλησεν ὡς

30 *Wars* I:452, 456; cf. *Antiquities* XV:105ff, 129ff.

31 *Wars* I:465.

32 *Wars* I:457-458.

33 *Wars* I:460-461.

βασιλευς τὰ πολλὰ δ 'ἐνουθέτησεν ὡς πατήρ[34] (He threatened them curtly, as a king, and censured them with many words, as a father).

Affairs of the realm remain the primary interest, precious above all, in the eyes of Herod.

D. Συγγενεῖς καὶ φίλοι (*Relatives and Friends*)

Note ought also to be taken of the expression, συγγενεῖς καὶ φιλους, which Josephus attributes to Herod regarding his sons advisers.[35] The συγγενεῖς were already well-known in the court of the Persian kingdom, from whence they passed over to the Hellenist kingdoms. The φίλοι and συγγενεῖς are those people who are close to the king, whether family relatives or fictitious "relatives". The term "relative" appears in the singular — συγγενής — and does not indicate affiliation to a body of "relatives".[36] The φίλοι, apparently, were originally comrades-in-arms of the King. Later, they became the King's advisers and his senior clerks. They owe their status to the friendship of the king. There were various degrees of φίλοι, in accordance with the degree of kinship with the King.[37] We have emphasised this matter only in order to indicate again the fact that Herod's court was organized as a Hellenistic court: "All that we know leads us to the proof that the state of Herod was organized, in general terms, according to the model of the Hellenist states."[38]

34 *Wars* I:481.

35 *Wars* I:460; M. Rostovtzeff, "Syria and the East", *Cambridge Ancient History* VII.164; Ch. Habicht, "Die herrschende Gesellschaft in den hellenistichen Monarchien", *Vierteljahresschrift fur Sozial und Wirtschaftsgeschichte* XLV (1958), 1.

36 Cf. *I Maccabees* 10:65, 89; 4:32; 11:27, 57, 58; *II Maccabees* 11:1, 35; see G. Corradi, "Συγγενεῖς", *Studi Ellenistici* (1929), 281; E. Bickerman, *Institutions des Seleucides* (Paris: P. Geuthner, 1938), 42.

37 G. Corradi, "φίλοι", *Studi Ellenistici* (1929), 318; Momigliano, *supra* n.4, at 68; Bickerman, *supra* n.36, at 40; J. Gaudemet, *Institutions de l'Antiquite'* (Paris: Sirey, 1967), I.227; J. Crook, *Consilium Principis. Imperial Councils and Counsellors from Augustus to Diocletian* (Cambridge: The University Press, 1955).

38 Momigliano, *supra* n.4, at 67.

E. *The Trial of Herod's Sons*

Let us return to Herod's domestic affairs. Even the intervention of Augustus did not succeed in restoring the father's true love for his sons. Herod's ear was always attuned to whatever was told to him about the plotting of his two sons. The attempt of Archelaus, king of Cappadocia, to save his son-in-law Alexander, succeeded only for a time. Herod decided to get rid of Mariamne's two sons, who were also his sons. However, he did not dare to do this without the consent of Augustus — the political significance of which was clear to all, including himself.[39]

Josephus quotes the reply of Augustus:

> And so, being reconciled with Herod, Caesar Augustus wrote to him, saying that he was distressed because of his sons, and that if they had been so reckless as to attempt an unnatural crime, he ought to punish them as parricides — for this power was granted him —,but if they had planned to flee, he should merely admonish them and not inflict irreparable punishment upon them. He also advised him to appoint and convene a council at Berytus, where Romans were settled as colonists, and to take along the governors (of Syria), Archelaus, the king of Cappadocia, and as many others as he thought conspicuously friendly or important, and with their advice to determine what should be done. These were the instructions that Caesar gave.[40]

The central section states as follows in Greek:

> συμβουλεύειν δὲ ἔχειν αὐτῷ συνέδριον ἀποδείξαντα περί Βηπυτον.

In the Wars of the Jews, we find:

> εἰ μετὰ κοινοῦ συέδριον τῶν τε ἰδιων συγγενῶν καὶ τῶν κατὰ τῆν ἐπαρχίαν ἡγεμόνων.

Augustus tries to steer Herod towards leniency by means of his "suggestion" to get together an assembly of συνέδριον in Berytus,

39 This did not go unnoticed by Kunkel either, who is of the opinion that this is a case of domestic judgment: "Und wenn dies der Fall ist darf man in diesem hochpolitischen Fall noch von einem Hausgericht sprechen": Kunkel, *supra* n.8, at 225. Kunkel correctly stresses, at 226: "Herods war besides, Vater und Konig, sein Verfahren gegen die Sohne also sowohl Hausgericht als auch Staatsgericht".

40 *Antiquities* XVI:356-357; see S. Zeitlin, "The Political Synedrion and the Religious Sanhedrin", *Jewish Quarterly Review* XXXVI (1945-46), 109; Schalit, *supra* n.1, at 303.

which was the location of the Roman delegation of Syria.[41] This detail, too, attests to the political importance of the matter. Furthermore, Augustus suggests involving Archelaus, king of Cappadocia, father-in-law of Alexander, in the trial, for Archelaus was experienced in matters of conciliation and his presence would certainly have an effect in swinging the balance in favour of the sons.

Herod was not unaware of this, and he "therefore sent messengers to those people that he decided to assemble as a judicature other than Archelaus. He did not want to meet Archelaus either because of hatred or also because he was of the opinion that Archelaus would constitute an obstacle (in the execution) of his plan."

In the Wars of the Jews, Josephus describes the assembling of the δικαστήριον,[42] stressing that Augustus himself wrote about the matter to the most venerable Romans:

> Saturninus and his legates, Pedanius and others; with them was associated Volumnius[43] the procurator. Next came the king's relatives and friends,[44] including Salome and Pheroras, and after these all the aristocracy of Syria, with the exception of King Archalaus; for, as Alexander's father-in law, he was regarded by Herod with distrust. His sons were not produced by Herod in court — a very wise precaution, for he knew that their mere appearance would be sure to arouse compassion, while, if they were further permitted to speak, Alexander would have no difficulty in rebutting the charges. So they were detained in custody at Platana, a village in the territory of Sidon.[45]

Contrary to every proper procedure in pursuit of justice, the accused were not heard. Herod's suspicion was clear; and concerned that there might be someone in the judicature who would require the presence of the accused, Herod brought them to a nearby place. But these judges did not feel such a need, and the "trial" was conducted as

41 Berytus (Beirut) was elevated to the status of colony by Augustus: Colonia Julia Augusta Felix Berytus. See A. Schalit, "Beirut", *Enc. Ivrit* 8 (1956), 535. On Herod in Beirut, See *Academie des Inscriptions et Belles Lettres, Comptes Rendus* 243f.; Schürer, *supra* n.26, at 323 n.150.

42 *Wars* I:538. On the term "dikasterion", see A. M. Rabello, "On the Relations between Diocletian and the Jews", *Journal of Jewish Studies* XXXV (1984), 165 n. 96.

43 Volumnius was called στρατοπεδάρχος (Wars I:535), ἐπίτροπος (Wars I:538).

44 οἱ τοῦ βασιλέως συγγενεῖς καὶ φίλοι.

45 *Wars* I:538-539.

Herod wished:

> All alone, therefore, and by himself he went before the hundred and fifty men seated there, and made the accusation, which was not painful as would benefit an unfortunate necessity but very unlike what a father should say about his sons. For he was violent and emotional in demonstrating their guilt, and he gave the strongest signs of fury and savagery. He did not permit the members of the council to examine the proofs but offered arguments in advocacy of these that were a disgrace for a father to use against his sons. When he read aloud the letters written by them, there was no plot or any notion of filial disloyalty mentioned in them, only that they were planning to flee, and some offensive remarks about Herod that included reproaches for his ill-will toward them. When he came to these passages, he cried out even more loudly and exaggerated their excessive language into a confession of a plot formed against him by his sons, swearing that he would much rather lose his life than hear such words as these. Finally, he said that both by nature and by Caesar's grant he himself had authority to act, but he added that there was also a law in his country that provided that if a man's parents, after accusing him, placed their hands on his head, the bystanders were bound to stone him and to kill him in this way. This, he said, he was prepared to do in his own country and realm but he still awaited their judgment.[46]

What did Herod (or Josephus) mean in referring to πάτριος νόμος? Schalit writes on this matter as follows: "Even though Herod stresses the *patria potestas*, he does not judge the sons in accordance therewith, that is, according to the law of the rebellious son, for had he done so, he would have had to act in accordance with the dictates of Scripture on this matter (*Deuteronomy* 18:21)."[47]

It is very clear that Herod is not acting in accordance with patriarchal law. The law of the rebellious son is designed to ensure to the maximum extent that the father shall not be cruel to his son, and one of the means is to accord absolute equality to the status of the father and the mother.[48]

46 *Antiquities* XVI:362-366.

47 Schalit, *supra* n.1, at 132.

48 On the law of the rebellious son, See A. M. Rabello, "Patria Potestas in Roman and Jewish Law" (Heb.), *Diné Israel* 5 (1974), 130, and references there; A.M. Rabello, "Les effets personnels de la puissance paternelle en Droit Hébraïque, à travers la Bible et le Talmud", Mélanges à la mémoire de Marcel-Henri Prévost (Paris: Presses Universitaires de France (1980), 94; Zeitlin correctly observes: "It is strange that Herod, who had transgressed every law of the Pentateuch, should invoke this

Attention should also be paid to the form in which, according to Josephus, the stoning of the rebellious son was carried out.[49]

Nevertheless, one cannot ignore the fact that Herod was speaking to people who, for the most part, were not aware of the substance of the Jewish law of the rebellious son. The reference to πάτριος νόμος is made, therefore, in order to make it easy for the people sitting in the "court" to to decide to agree to the execution of the sons. Herod does not mention his *patria potestas* nor his *vitae necisque potestas* over his sons, for good reason. The Romans sitting on the "court" were surely more expert on this subject than he, and they could explain to Herod the actual nature of this *potestas*, which was *ius proprium civium Romanorum*.[50] Herod was apparently afraid to get into this subject.

All this leads us to the view that in the trial of his sons, as in

---

law which had been rendered inoperative ...": S. Zeitlin, *The Rise and Fall of the Judean State* (Philadelphia: JPSA, 1969), II.77.

49 Cf. also *Antiquities* IV:260, 264. Note should be taken of the differences between the formulation appearing in Josephus and that of Scripture. In particular, the Bible does not mention the requirement that the hands of the parents be placed on the head of the accused. There is no mention of this in the Septuagint either: and see P. Walters & D. W. Gooding, *The Text of the Septuagint* (London: Cambridge University Press, 1973), 150; A. Freyman, "Ben Sorer Umoreh" (Heb.), *Enc. Mikrait* II.160-162. It would seem, however, that the custom in the case of stoning was in accordance with the law of the blasphemer: "And let all that heard him lay their hands upon his head ..." (*Lev.* 24:14). Cf. the Apocryphal *Additions to the Book of Daniel, Susanna* 34, and see A. Kahane, *Haṣefarim haḥitsyonim* (Tel-Aviv: Masada, 1959), Vol.I, ad loc.: "The one who lays on hands accepts responsibility for the trouble and attests that the one upon whom hands were laid had done to him that which he deserves." And cf. Philo, *De mutatione nominum* 206; *De Ebrietate* 13-94; *De Specialibus Legibus* II, 232. And see also the comment of Colson (Colson, *Philo*, Loeb Classical Library, VII.629). This is not the place to discuss this matter, which has been treated extensively: see in particular B. Ritter, *Philo und die Halacha* (Leipzig: J.C. Hinrichs, 1879), 42; E. Goodenough, *The Jurisprudence of the Jewish Courts in Egypt* (New Haven: Yale University Press, 1929), 69; I. Heinemann, *Philons griechische und judische Bildung* (Breslau: M & H Marcus, 1932), 250; D. Goldenberg, *Halakah in Josephus and Tannaitic Literature: a Comparative Study* (Ph.D. dissertation, Dropsie University, Philadelphia, 1978), 36-56.

50 Gaius, *Institutiones* I:55.

the trial of Mariamne his wife, Herod did not act by virtue of his *patria potestas*, nor according to the accepted procedures of the Romans, but as a Hellenistic king.

This "court" should be seen as the same as that of the Hellenistic kings, which dealt with the most difficult political or military matters, and which also had jurisdiction in capital matters.[51] In general, in such a "court", the opinion of the king carried decisive weight. He was the one to decide in the final analysis. In fact, the opinion of the "court" carried weight only in an advisory capacity. Corradi correctly writes:

> And also in cases in which the "court" exercised its jurisdiction, so that it appeared that the absolute rule of the king was affected, in truth they were only thereby respecting an ancient Macedonian custom, and the king always found a way to carry out his will. Indeed, later we find in Herod's court a similar arrangement to that found in the Hellenistic courts. And here, too, we find the assembly of the φίλοι συγγενεῖς or συνέδριον or σύλλογος, which Herod consults, in cases of difficult decisions, and which we see as a High Court of Justice for the most serious political trials. For example, in the case of the trial of Mariamne and Antipater, the first-born son of Herod. In Herod's court, too, the judicature was not a decision-making assemblage, since the decision in fact lay in the hands of the king; rather, as we saw in the other Hellenistic states, its role was purely advisory.[52]

There is a certain proximity between the judicature and the *consilium* of the Roman magistrates, and this possibly explains why so many scholars wanted to regard this judicature as a "domestic tribunal", which even in Rome itself had no juridical power in the precise sense of the term. Bickerman writes as follows:

> It would be mistaken to regard these assemblies as meetings of a permanent body, similar to the "King's Council" in the *Ancien Régime* ... this judicature, which was selected from amongst the "friends" of the king, was more similar to the *consilium* of the Roman magistrates. The friends expressed an opinion and the king decides alone ...[53]

51 See Corradi, *supra* n.36, at 248.

52 Corradi, supra n.36, at 251. At n.2, Corradi also mentions the *consilium* which convened in Beirut. Corradi's view was accepted by Momigliano, *supra* n.4, at 69.

53 Bickerman, *supra* n.36, at 189. And see also E. Bickerman, "The Sanhedrin", *Zion* 3 (1938), 356, in which there is reference to the conclusions of Corradi (at 358 n.14).

The "trial" proceeded according to Herod's wishes: the people voted, for various reasons, according to his will. Of Saturninus, who tried to inject a spirit of *pietas* into the hearts of the members of the judicature, Josephus writes:

> Moreover, they had come not so much to be judges of the clear crimes of his sons, from which he had almost fatally suffered, as because they had an opportunity to share his anger, since it was not right for anyone, even those far removed, to be unconcerned about so serious a plot. After the king had spoken in this manner, without letting the youths be produced even long enough to defend themselves, the members of the council, being agreed that they were in no position to soften him or effect a reconciliation, confirmed his authority. The first to speak was Saturninus, a man of consular rank and of great influence, who expressed a most moderate opinion, taking the circumstances into account. For he said that while he condemned Herod's sons, he did not think it right to put them to death, since he himself had sons, and such a penalty was too great, even granted that all his misfortunes were due only to them. After Saturninus had spoken, his sons — there were three of them, accompanying him as legates — expressed the same opinion, that Volumnius on the contrary said that they should put to death sons who had been so unfilial to their father. The same sentiment was expressed by the majority of the following speakers, so that it seemed no other verdict had been given than that the youths should be sentenced to death. From there Herod at once went to Tyre, taking them along, and when Nicolas sailed from Rome to meet him there, Herod, after first telling him what had happened in Berytus, asked him just what his friends in Rome thought about his sons. Nicolas said that while they thought that his sons' intentions toward him were unfilial, nevertheless he ought merely to imprison them and keep them in chains. "And if, indeed, you are resolved to punish them in some other way, do not appear to be giving way to anger rather than using your judgment. If, on the contrary, you choose to absolve them, do not let your unfortunate position remain unremedied. This same opinion is held by most of your friends in Rome." Thereupon Herod, after remaining silent in deep thought, ordered Nicolas to sail with him.[54]

The sentence was carried out on the order of Herod at Sebastia in the year 7 B.C.E. Their death by strangulation took place exactly thirty years after Herod took for a wife, at the same place, Mariamne the Hasmonean. Augustus did not succeed in preventing the murder of the sons at the hands of their father. In the *consilium* on which Augustus himself sat, in Rome, he was witness to a successful

54 *Antiquities* XVI:366-372.

attempt of a father to save his son accused of *parricidium* by "judgment" in front of friends and relatives, where the punishment imposed was only exile.[55] Augustus apparently did not know that Herod's sons would not appear before the judicature. He also did not know that Archelaus would not be invited to sit amongst the friends, and did not know the great hatred felt for Herod.[56]

The people did not forget the two sons. At least once, Herod was beset by doubts, that the execution may have been unjust.

F. *The Trial of Antipater*

After Herod had tried the wife of his brother Pheroras before the συγγενεῖς καὶ φίλοι[57] (in this case, it is certainly not possible to contend that Herod was acting as a Roman *pater familias*), it was the turn of Antipater, who was the first person responsible for the domestic troubles of Herod.[58] Antipater, who together with Pheroras drove Herod to murder his sons, now became frightened by his deeds.[59] Antipater's plots were coming to light, and Herod now knew that his first-born son had plotted to kill him. This time, too, Herod assembled the judicature:

> Armed, then, with these weapons he entered the palace, without his friends, for they had been insolently stopped at the outer gate. At the time there was a visitor within — Varus, the governor of Syria. Antipater proceeded to his father's presence and, seeking courage in audacity, approached as though to kiss him. Herod, with arms extended and head averted, cried out: "That too betrays the parricide: he would embrace me, with such accusations against him! Perdition take thee,

55 Cf. Seneca, *De Clementia* I:15; and see the interpretation of Volterra, *Il matrimonio romano, supra* n.5, at 61ff. Volterra stresses the tendency of Augustus to intervene between fathers and sons in order to prevent the former from exercising their *potestas* with cruelty.

56 *Wars* I:564: "When the king perceived what disposition he was in towards the orphans, he was angry at it, and a suspicion came into his mind as to those sons whom he had put to death, whether that had not been brought about by the false tales of Antipater; so at that time he made Antipater a long and peevish answer, and bade him begone." And cf. *Wars* I:662; *Antiquities* XVII:94.

57 Cf. *Wars* I:571.

58 Cf. *Wars* I:595.

59 Cf. *Wars* I:586, 589.

most impious wretch and touch me not until you have cleared yourself of the charges. I offer you a tribunal and for judge this timely visitor, Varus. Go and prepare your defence for to-morrow; I leave you that interval for your artifices." Unable through consternation to utter a word in reply, Antipater withdrew, and his mother and his wife came to him and told him in detail of all thee vidence against; him. Then he collected himself and applied himself to preparing his defence.

On the following day the king assembled a council of his relatives and friends, inviting Antipater's friends to attend as well. He himself presided, with Varus, and ordered all the informers to be produced. Among these were some domestics of Antipaters mother, recently arrested in the act of carrying a letter from her to her son in these terms: "As your father has discovered all, do not come near him, unless you have obtained support from Caesar." When these witnesses had been brought in with the rest, Antipater entered and, falling prostrate at his fathers' feet, said: "I beseech you, father, do not condem me in advance, but lend an unprejudicd ear to my defence; for I shall, if you permit, establish my innocence."

Herod burst out upon him to be silent and then addressed Varus: "That you, Varus, and every honest judge will condemn Antipater as an abandoned criminal, I am fully persuaded. What I fear is that my fate may also appear hateful to you and that you may judge me deserving of every calamity for having begotten such sons. And yet you ought rather to pity me for having been the most devoted of fathers to such abominable wretches. My late sons, who when they were quite young I thought fit to destine for the throne, whom I not only expensively educated in Rome, but introduced to Caesar's friendship and made all object of envy to other sovereigns, these I found to be conspirators. They have died, mainly to further Antipater's interests: he was young, he was the heir, and to secure him was the object which I had most at heart."[60]

A report was again sent to Augustus, to inform him of the political importance of the matter:

60 *Wars* I:617-623; cf. the passage in *Antiquities* XVII:89ff. Regarding the use of the term "ἀσεφάλεια" (Wars I:623), see S. Lieberman, *Greek and Hellenism in Jewish Palestine* (Jerusalem: Bialik Institute, 1962), 6 (Heb.); R. Taubenschlag, *The Law of Greco-Roman Egypt in the Light of the Papyri* (Warsaw: Panstowowe Wydawnictwo Naukowe, 1955), 54 n.13, 275 n.18, 296 n.21, 413 n.5; Tcherikover, Fuks, Stern & Lewis, *Corpus Papyrorum Iudaicarum III* (Jerusalem: Magnes Press and Cambridge, Mass.: Harvard University Press, 1964), pap. 508 (13), pap. 513; Z. Gothold, "On the Types of Benedictions", *D. Kotlar Jubilee Volume* (Tel Aviv: Am Hasepher, 1975), 142.

> The governor, thereupon, called for the poison and had it applied to a prisoner under sentence of death, who drank it and instantly expired. Then, after a private interview with Herod, Varus drafted his report of the meeting for Caesar, and a day later took his departure. The king had Antipater put in irons and dispatched messengers to the emperor to inform him of the catastrophe.[61]

Augustus himself answered Herod, and confirmed Antipater's punishment:

> At the moment when he was giving these instructions, he received letters from his ambassadors at Rome, informing him that Acme had been executed by Caesar's orders and Antipater condemned to death; but, the letter continued, if his father were content with banishing him, he had Caesar's permission to do so.[62]

Therefore, this case, too, refers to a judicature with a primarily political function, and not to a domestic court. The last attempts of Antipater to save his life were not successful, and Herod commanded that he be executed. Five days later, Herod himself died.[63] It is said that Augustus, hearing of the fate of Herod's sons, mumbled: *Mallem Herodis porcus esse, quam filius* (I would rather have been Herod's swine than his son).[64]

Conclusion

It seems to me that we can conclude that in none of the abovementioned cases did Herod act as a Roman *pater familias*, on the basis of his *patria potestas*; it is clear, moreover, that Herod did not act as the patriarch of a Jewish family in the days of the second Temple.

The assembling of the "relatives and friends" should not be viewed as an assembly for the purpose of judging the members of his household — the convening of a domestic tribunal. In all these cases, Herod acted as a Hellenistic king, and adapted himself to Hellenistic customs, even in assembling the "court". The attempt of Herod to base himself on ancient custom might have convinced only those to whom such customs were totally foreign.

61 *Wars* I:640.

62 *Wars* I:661; cf. *Antiquities* XVII:182.

63 *Wars* I:663-665.

64 Macrobius, *Saturnalia* II:41.

IIIa

THE 'LEX DE TEMPLO HIEROSOLYMITANO', PROHIBITING GENTILES FROM ENTERING JERUSALEM'S SANCTUARY

'Who shall ascend the hill of the Lord?'
(Psalm 24:3)

In 1871, the French archaeologist C. Clermont-Ganneau discovered an inscription in Jerusalem north of the Temple area and not far from it.[1] The inscription is of great interest as allowing us to view at first hand one of those injunctions, which Josephus Flavius mentions, against the entry of Gentiles into the Sanctuary of Jerusalem. The inscription reads as follows: 'No foreigner to enter within the balustrade and embankment around the sanctuary. Whoever is caught will have himself to blame for his death which follows."

We must first examine the origin of this ban, then determine who set up the inscription, and, finally, discover who had the authority to inflict the death penalty upon foreign violators.

A. THE PROBLEM IN THE BIBLE

Even before the Sanctuary was built, when there was only the Tabernacle (*Mishkan*), the Torah had made special arrangements and regulations for the priests on the one hand, and for lay members of the nation on the other, and also with regard to strangers. In Leviticus 22:10, for example, it is forbidden for an outsider (*zhar*, that is, one who is not a priest) to eat anything sacred (*qodesh*). In the preceding verse, after a pressing invitation to priests to observe certain precepts, there is added: 'they shall not incur sin because of sacred things nor shall they die because of them'[2], a penalty which, according to Jewish tradition, was threatened directly *bide Shamaim*, that is, by direct Divine intervention, and for which there is no earthly tribunal (see Rashi *in loco*). More directly pertinent to the subject-matter of our investigation is Leviticus 16:2: 'The Lord said to Moses, "Speak unto Aaron thy brother that he come not at all times into the holy place within the veil...'" In this case, too, death was threatened directly by God. Thus, Rashi, with his usual exactness and loyalty to Jewish tradition, can write in his commentary on this passage: 'that he (Aaron) die not as his sons have died.' Is it well known that the sons of Aaron died 'by the hand of Heaven' itself (Leviticus 10:2ff.). In Numbers 1:51, too, with its reference to the Tabernacle (*Mishkan*), death is decreed as the fate of the *outsider* (non-Levite) who approaches (Rashi: "to take on this service'). The doom envisaged is again that which comes 'by the hand of Heaven' (Rashi, *in loco*).[3]

In nearly all the instances where the death penalty is enjoined for sacrilege to sacred objects of the Sanctuary itself, the punishment is threatened immediately from Heaven and not by any human court.[4] As we have seen (and as we shall find stressed in subsequent documents), it was forbidden for anyone not a Priest or a Levite — and all the more so for a non-Jew — to perform certain actions or to enter specified places.

When King Solomon built the *Beth Hamiqdash*, he spoke this prayer to the Lord: וגם אל־הנכרי אשר לא מעמך ישראל... ובא והתפלל אל־הבית הזה... ('Moreover concerning the stranger that is not of Thy people Israel... when he shall come and pray toward this house...') (I Kings 8:41-43).

Some have tended to see[5] a contradiction between Solomon's words and the ban pronounced by the prophet Ezekiel against Gentiles entering the

Sanctuary (to serve God) כה אמר ד׳ יי כל־בן־נכר ערל לב וערל בשר לא יבוא אל־מקדשי... ('Thus saith the Lord God: No alien, uncircumcised in heart and uncircumcised in flesh, shall enter into My sanctuary...') (Ezekiel 44:9-10) [6] A discrepancy, to say the least, is commonly seen in respect of this ban as we find it in subsequent periods. To my mind, no contradiction exists.

From the outset, account is to be taken of the fact that the verse, I kings 8:43, is usually translated as reading, 'in the Temple.' [7] In my opinion, the correct rendering is, 'towards the House;' the main argument on which the discrepancy theory is based would thus be weakened.

In the second place, we should not lose sight of the special character of the *Beth Hamiqdash*, which was not a 'house of assembly' (*Beth Hakenesset*) for the people. It was out of bounds for Jews themselves and only the priests could enter, but they, too, had to observe special precautions, and the Holy of Holies was accessible to the High Priest alone and on the Day of Atonement alone.
Ceremonies connected with Jewish worship and assembly took place in the *courts* which surrounded the Sanctuary properly — so-called on three sides: north, west and south. Of these, the first was reserved for the priests and Levites: 'Another court, called the outside enclosure, on a lower level than the preceding (called the inner enclosure), was reserved for Israelites who were present round about at the celebration of sacrifices — to the exclusion of Gentiles. Solomon did not have time to complete this. It was finished by his successors.' [8]

This seems to be substantiated by a paragraph in Josephus (*Ant. Jud.*, VIII, 3, 9): 'He also surrounded the temple with a parapet called *geision* in the native tongue and *thrinkos* by the Greeks, which he raised to a height of three cubits; it was to keep the multitude from entering the sacred precinct and to signify that entry was permitted only to the priests. Outside of this he built another sacred precinct in the form of a quadrangle and erected great and wide porticoes which were entered by high gates, each of which faced one of the four quarters and was closed by golden doors. Into this precinct all the people who were distinguished by purity and their observance of the laws might enter...'

B. THE SANCTUARY BUILT BY ZERUBBABEL

Of the Second Temple, built by Zerubbabel, Josephus (*Ant.* XII, 3, 4) tells us that it was forbidden 'for any foreigner to enter the enclosure of the temple which is forbidden to the Jews, except to those of them who are accustomed to enter after purifying themselves in accordance with the law of the country.'

There is the matter of a *prostagma* [9] of Antiochus III of Syria (223-187 BCE). The attention of scholars has been called to it by E. Bikerman, who has devoted a profound commentary to the whole passage,[10] stressing the consideration which it merits. The Books of the Maccabees confirm that in this sanctuary, too, there were outside premises for the Levites and the public: 'and they built the shrine and the inner quarters and they consecrated both temple and temple courts,' (1 Maccabees, 4:48) 'for the temple had been full of Gentile licence and revelry and dallying with harlots, and women making their way into the sacred precincts, and bringing in of things abominable.' (3 Macc. 6:4). There must have been a third court, also, to which even the Gentiles had access. (Actually, the Letter of Aristeas has *hoi periboloi treis;* 84.)

The barring of the stranger from the inmost part of the Sanctuary was nothing new in antiquity.[11] Nevertheless, it is made expressly clear that there was no issue of a *racial* motive but only of a *religious* one. If the stranger became a convert and had observed the prescription of purification like any other Jew, he could certainly enter just as far as was lawful for a Jew. Thus, the passage under consideration allows of a negative solution to the doubt raised by Clermont-Ganneau as to whether 'stranger' included the converted stranger, the proselyte.[12] Punishment consisted of a money-fine of three thousand silver drachmas.[13]

Further confirmation of the ban is found, indirectly, in the account by Josephus (*Bellum Judaicum* I, 7, 6): 'Of all the calamities of that time none so deeply affected the nation as the exposure to alien eyes of the Holy Place, hitherto screened from view. Pompey indeed, along with his staff, penetrated to the sanctuary, entry to which was permitted to none but the high priest, and beheld what it contained...'

C. THE SANCTUARY BUILT BY HEROD

When Herod rebuilt the Temple, the whole appeared outwardly to be a copy of Solomon's.[14] This has to be borne in mind, for we have to explain the steles which give clear directions as to how far a non-Jew could proceed on the Temple Mount.[15]

The Sanctuary as seen in Professor M. Avi-Yonah's model of Jerusalem at the time of the Second Temple

The stele discovered by Clermont-Ganneau (now in the Museum of Istanbul) runs: 'Mēthena allogenē eisporeuesthai entos ton peri to hieron truaktou kai peribolou. Os d'an lēfthē eautōi aitios estai dia to exacolou thein thanaton.

('No foreigner is to enter within the balustrade and embankment around the sanctuary. Whoever is caught will have himself to blame for his death which follows.,) [16]

In his *Römische Geschichte,*[17] Mommsen refers to the 'Warning Tablets' in Latin and Greek. He contends: 'These tablets were hardly set up by the Jewish kings, who would scarcely have added a Latin text, and had no cause to threaten the penalty of death with this singular anonymity. If they were set up by the Roman government, both are explained; Titus also says (in Josephus, *Bell Jud.* VI. 2, 4), in an appeal to the Jews: "Did we not give you leave to put to death those who trespass, even though there be question of a Roman?" if the tablet really bears traces of axe-cuts, these came from the soldiers of Titus.'

The opinion of the great historian has had a powerful influence on scholars. The number still prepared to subscribe to it today is considerable. Thus, for example, Dittenberger [18] faithfully follows Mommsen when he writes: 'That the Romans, who in the year 6 CE reduced Judaea to a province, carved these inscriptions is evident both from the words of Titus in Josephus and a comparison of Latin and Greek practice. If this decree were the work of native kings, you could not think of any plausible reason for its origin.'

Gabba [19] likewise welcomes the opinion of Mommsen and observes: 'In fact, we cannot see why King Herod would have had to post Latin transcriptions of the prohibition also....' Then, referring to *Bellum* VI, 125-126, he notes that this excerpt 'testifies to full Roman recognition of the decree and explains very well the presence of the Latin text side by side with the Greek.'

I am unable to go along with such theories. It seems to me that Josephus, when treating of the steles barring Gentiles from entering the Sanctuary, speaks of them in reference to the *construction* done by Herod. This provided an excellent reason for putting them up.

Stele bearing the prohibition against Gentiles entering the Sanctuary (Vincent, 'Revue Biblique' 30,1921)

Bellum V, 5, 2: 'Proceeding across this towards the second court of the temple, one found it surrounded by a stone balustrade, three cubits high and of exquisite workmanship; in this at regular intervals stood slabs giving warning, some in Greek, others in Latin characters, of the law of purification, to wit that no foreigner was permitted to enter the holy place, for so the second enclosure of the temple was called. It was approached from the first by fourteen steps; the area above was quadrangular, and screened by a wall of its own.' [20]

In *Antiquitates* XV, 11, 5: 'Such, then, was the first court. Within it and not far distant was a second one, accessible by a few steps and surrounded by a stone balustrade with an inscription prohibiting the entrance of a foreigner under threat of the penalty of death.'

The use of Greek and Latin can easily be explained. The inscriptions were meant to be read and understood by strangers. Therefore they had to be written in languages known to the majority. Greek was very widespread in Palestine and Syria. Bikerman has fully demonstrated the existence of similar inscriptions in the Greek world.[21] Then, in view of contacts with Rome, Latin was already beginning to be a widely known medium. In the light of its conquests, Rome was now recognized as the main power in the Mediterranean (*mare nostrum*). Further, it is known that Herod was practically a subject of Augustus.[22]

We should not be surprised, therefore, if he wanted the inscriptions posted in Latin, too. On the one hand, he could thereby show the people that he desired the rules to be kept by Roman citizens also, thus achieving something which would please the folk. On the other hand, since it was done on the most sacred site, the gesture was an implicit recognition of the importance which Rome was assuming in the public life of Judaea. Finally, we must not overlook a third reason: it is likely that Herod wished to avoid the possibility of incidents with Rome arising from religious causes. Having made it clear enough to the Roman citizen that he was barred from the Sanctuary, Herod could eventually justify himself with the Romans if such a person met his death after setting foot in it.

So it seems to me that the date for the setting up of the inscriptions must be fixed during the building of Herod's Temple. They were the work of Herod himself and not of the Roman authority some time after, viz., when Judaea had become a Roman province.

1 For detailed information, see the description by Clermont-Ganneau, 'Une stèle du Temple de Jérusalem,' in *Revue Archéologique* 23 (1872) 214-234; 290-296 (with reproductions), hereinafter: Clermont-Ganneau, 'Stèle.'

2 S. D. Luzzatto, I. Reggio, Luzzi, M. E. Artom and Diodati translate thus: 'and may not die for it, if they profane this *my ordinance.*' Ricciotti (in a version which seems unacceptable) has: 'They should observe my commandments, so as not to incur guilt of sin in the sanctuary after having profaned it.'

3 See, also, Numbers 3:38 and Babylonian Talmud, *Menachot* 27 b.

4 The following may also be consulted: Derenbourg, M. J., 'Une Stèle du Temple d'Hérode,' in Journal Asiatique, 6 Ser. 20 (1872) 178-195 (hereinafter Derenbourg, 'Stèle'). Daube, in Symbolae Friburgenses in honorem O. Lenel (Leipzig, 1931). On the penalty of *karet, cfr.* B. Cohen, 'Testimonial Compulsion in Jewish, Roman and Moslem Law,' in *Jewish and Roman Law* (New York, 1966), Vol. II, pp. 741-744. Loewenstamm, *sub voce KARET* in *Enziclopedia Mikrait* (in Hebrew), Vol. IV, cols. 330-332.

5 See, also, Derenbourg, 'Stèle', p. 180. He translates, 'The stranger also... that he may enter and pray in this house.' He comments, 'As is apparent, it is an invitation rather than a prohibition.' Spadafora, *Ezechiele* in *La Sacra Bibbia,* under the supervision of Msgr. Garofalo (Turin, 1951), p. 39, note on 44:9, says, 'There then follows the more absolute prohibition: no pagan shall enter the Temple.... Even Solomon prayer God to show himself favourable to the pagans who will come to pray in His Temple. Ezechiel admits of no exeptions.'

6 The note by Fisch recalling the stèle found by Clermont-Ganneau is exact: 'Non-Israelites were forbidden to come into certain parts of the Temple area.' *Cfr. Ezechiel* in *Soncino Books of the Bible* (London. 1950) p. 304. *Cfr.* also the comment by Radak (Rabbi David Kimchi) *in loco.*

7 See, for example, the translations by Diodati, Luzzi, S. D., Luzzato, Ricciotti, Sierra (in *Bibbia Disegni*). The influence of the Vulgate seems evident: 'et horaverit in hoc loco.' The Septuagint does not have vv. 41-42 and translates: *eis ton topon touton*. On the contrary Slotki has the accurate translation: 'When he shall come and pray toward this house' — 'toward' and not 'inside'; *cfr. Kings* in *Soncino Books of the Bible*. See also, the translation, likewise by Slotki, in 2 *Chronicles* in *Soncino Books of the Bible*. *Cfr.* J. M. Myers, 2 *Chronicles* (New York, 1965), p. 33.

8 Thus, Vigoroux in *La Sainte Bible Polyglotte*, Tome II (Paris, 1901), p. 908. Regarding archaeological problems, *cfr.* Y. Yadin, 'The First Temple', in *Sefer Jerushalaim* (in Hebrew; Jerusalem, 1956), pp. 176-191 — complete with sketches and tentative reconstructions.

9 In the past, it was customary to use the word *programma*. On this, see E. Bickerman, 'Une proclamation séleucide relative au Temple de Jérusalem,' in *Syria* 25 (1946-1948) 67-85 — hereinafter: Bickerman, 'Séleucide'. See, also, the highly regarded studies by G. I. Luzzatto, 'Epigrafia giuridica greca e romana, III', in *Studia et Documenta Historiae et Juris* 17 (1951) 156. I. Modrzejewski, 'The *prostagma* in the papyri', in J.J.P. V (1951) 187-206.

10 Bickerman, 'Séleucide', pp. 67ff. (especially pp. 69-73). See the remark by G. I. Luzzatto in *Epigrafia giuridica*, p. 166.

11 In this connection, see, also, 'Le citoyen et l'étranger', in *La cité antique* by Fustel de Coulanges (Paris: Hachette). *Cfr.* also Bikerman, 'The Warning Inscriptions of Herod's Temple', in *The Jewish Quarterly Review* 37 (1947 387-405 — hereinafter: Bikerman, 'Warning') p. 389: 'A pagan visitor had no reason to be offended in finding himself excluded from the holy ground. In all ancient religions there were sancta inaccessible to the profane crowd and separated by a rail of wood or stone.'

13 On this see Bickerman, 'Séleucide', pp. 79, 81, 84.

13 On this see Bikerman, 'Séleucide', pp. 79, 81, 84. Bikerman's whole study deserves special attention. *Cfr.* also Abel, F.-M., *Histoire de la Palestine depuis la conquête d'Alexandre jurqu'à l'invasion arabe*, Tome I (Paris, 1952), pp. 88ff.

14 For a description of Herod's Temple: Hollis, F. J., *The Archaeology of Herod's Temple* (London, 1934) with numerous reproductions and sketches. Abel, F.-M, *Histoire de la Palestine*, Tome I, pp. 372ff., especially the chapter on 'La reconstruction du Temple de Jérusalem'. Parrot, A., *Le Temple de Jérusalem* (Paris, 1954). M. Avi-Yonah, 'The Second Temple', in *Sefer Jerushalaim* (in Hebrew; Jerusalem, 1956), pp. 392ff. In the appendix there is a bibliography.

15 Cfr., also, the remarks of A. Büchler, 'The Levitical Impurity of the Gentile', in *The Jewish Quarterly Review* 17 (1926-1927) 1-8. See also S. Lieberman, *Hellenism in Jewish Palestine* (New York, 5711:1950, especially p. 164, notes 1-8), and *Greek and Hellenism in Jewish Palestine* (in Hebrew; Jerusalem, 5723: 1962), pp. 272ff. G. Alon, *Studies in Jewish History in the times of the Second Temple, the Mishna and Talmud*, Vol. I (in Hebrew; Tel Aviv, 1957), art. 'Thumat nochrim' (pp. 121ff.). Contesting some of Büchler's statements, see now H. Mantel, *Studies in the History of the Sanhedrin* (in Hebrew; Tel Aviv, 1969), p. 328 n. 347.

16 Another stéle was found in 1936 in the course of studies by the Department of Antiquities of Palestine. The stele (incomplete) is now in the Rockefeller Museum in Jerusalem. *Cfr.* Iliffe, J. H., 'The THANATOU Inscription from Herod's Temple', in *QDAP* VI (1936) 1-3. The followin is the text of the stele: [Mē]thena all[ogenē eisporeuesthai en] tos tou p[eri to hieron truphak] tou kai [peribolou. Os d'an l]ēphthē au[tō aitios estai d] ia to ex [akolouthein] thanat [on].

On the subject, *cfr.* also V. Arangio-Ruiz, *Epigrafia giuridica greca e romana* (II), in Studia et Documenta Historiae et Iuris, 1939; p. 21 of offprint.

17 Vol. V (6 ed.), p. 513, note 1. *Die Römischen Provinzen von Caesar bis Diokletian.*

18 In *Orientis graeci inscriptiones selectas* II (section VIII, Imperii Romani provinciae orientales, n. 598: Templus Hierosolymitanum), p. 294-295.

19 *Iscrizioni greche e latine per lo studio della Bibbia* (Turin, 1958), pp. 83-86.

20 See, also, *Bellum Judaicum* V, 5, 6: 'To strangers arriving in *the city* it (the Sanctuary) looked from afar like a mountain covered with snow, for where it was not gilded it was glistening white. Like a garland around the Sanctuary and the altar he fashioned a graceful, low parapet of fine stone about one cubit high. This kept the people outside, separate from the priests. The whole city was out of bounds to those suffering from gonorrhoea or leprosy. The Temple was inaccessible to women during their monthly period. Even when they were legally clean they could not lawfully go beyond the above-mentioned limits. Men who were not wholly clean were excluded from the inner court. Priests who were not in a state of purity were also excluded from it. To the altar and the sanctuary those alone amongst the priests who were spotless went up...'

See also Philo, *The Virtutibus et legatione ad Caium*, par. 31 and 39 and *De ebrietate* par. 34.

Finally, we have the evidence of the following passage from Josephus (*Contra Apionem* II, 8): 'All who saw the building of our Temple knew what it consisted of. They are aware of the insuperable barriers which defended its purity. It was comprised of four concentric porticoes and each one, according to the law, had its guardian. It was so arranged that all had access to the outer portico, even foreigners. Only women, during their monthly, impure period, were denied entry. Into the second, all Jews with their wives could go, provided they were quite clean. Into the third went male Jews who were spotless and purified. Into the fourth entered the priests, clothed in their priestly vestments. As to the Holy of Holies the High Priest alone had entry, clothed in his special vestments.'

21 Bikerman, 'Warning', p. 388-389. See, also, M. Schwabe, 'Josephus u-bitui bemichtavo shel melech elenisti,' in *Tarbiz* 17 (5706) 197. In John's Gospel (19:20) it is recorded that Pilate had the inscription posted on the cross: 'and the inscription was in Hebrew, Greek and Latin.'

22 F.-M. Abel, *Histoire de la Palestine*. I, pp. 355ff.: 'Herode dans la vassalité d'Auguste'; pp. 359ff. According to Abel, work on building the Temple was begun after Augustus' journey to Syria (20 BCE); p. 375, n.l. *Cfr.* also the recent work (in Hebrew) by A. Schalit, *King Herod: Portrait of a Ruler* (Jerusalem, 1964). On pp. 240-273 there is an inquiry regarding the relationships between Herod and the Jewish people, on the one hand, and Herod and the Roman government, on the other.

IIIb

THE 'LEX DE TEMPLO HIEROSOLYMITANO' PROHIBITING GENTILES FROM ENTERING JERUSALEM'S SANCTUARY

In Part One of our article, we saw how the prohibition against Gentiles entering the Temple in Jerusalem was already in existence in the period of the First Temple (Solomon) and was repeated at the time of the Second Temple (Zerubbabel). We also determined that the inscriptions in Greek and Latin in which the prohibition appears, were set up by King Herod.

D. BELLUM JUDAICUM VI, 2, 4

In this connection, we have still to examine the worth of this passage in Josephus: 'Titus, yet more deeply distressed, again upbraided John and his friends. "Was it not you," he said, "most abominable wretches, who placed this balustrade before your sanctuary? Was it not you that ranged along it those slabs, engraved in Greek characters and in our own, proclaiming that none may pass the barrier? And did we not permit you to put to death any who passed it, even were he a Roman?"

The first two sentences would seem to confirm our theory that the steles were put up by Jews on the order of King Herod. The last sentence, however, seems to speak of an express authorization granted by the Romans. Here, two hypotheses can be advanced: either there was tacit recognition of the *status quo ante* by reason of the fact that the Romans did not want to change a religious rule in the province of Palestine, or the report in Josephus is devoid of foundation.

We should not forget the special nature of Josephus' works.[23] Accordingly, we can imagine that, by putting such words in Titus' mouth, he might, on the one hand, have sought to exalt the Jews by showing how highly the Romans esteemed them.[24] On the other hand, he might have wished to enhance the prestige of the Flavian family in the eyes of the Jews (let us remember that Titus himself belonged to it). The aim would have been to better relationships between the Jews and the reigning house and thus, perhaps, to minimize the gravity of Josephus' own treason, while, at the same time, attracting the sympathy of his overlords.[25]

We may adduce additional proof thereof, albeit incidentally, from the accounts of the burning of the Temple. According to Josephus (*Bellum*, 6, 4), it was Titus' desire that the Temple be allowed to stand. Other sources, however, indicate that it was Titus himself who gave the command to burn the Temple, which, by virtue of the central role that it played in the hearts of Jews already in a Diaspora, was an institution of great political and moral significance. This information comes from the writings of Sulpicius Severus. So it is clear that one must be cautious about accepting the testimonies of Josephus.[26]

E. THE PROBLEM OF THE DEATH PENALTY

At this stage, we must look into a question which has been widely argued: *What kind of death was in view* and *who had the duty to inflict it?* From the outset, I must affirm that I, too, in line with what is usually taught, cannot accept that the death which was threatened should come exclusively 'by the hand of Heaven.'[27] This is the theory of Derenbourg,[28] which Graetz has made his own.[29] Such an interpretation runs counter to the text of the inscriptions studied: *Lēphthē* ('whoever is caught')[30] is certainly not meant to have the Divinity make the execution of the penalty dependent on the 'catching' of the criminal by some human agency.[31] Besides, the interpretation, to my mind, clashes with certain rabbinic sources which, while adduced by Derenbourg, have not been interpreted in the right sense. I think it fitting to make a brief survey of those rabbinic sources.

In Tractate *Kelim* (I, 8), the Mishna defines the various degrees of holiness (*qedusha*): from the Land of Israel to the Holy of Holies. It lays down that 'the Temple Mount is still more holy, for no man or woman that has a flux, no menstruant, and no woman after childbirth may enter therein. The Rampart is still more holy, for no gentiles and none that have contracted uncleanness from a corpse may enter therein. The Court of the Women is still more holy,. . ." From this it is evident that, in complete harmony with what Josephus has to say, strangers could go as far as the Temple Mount, commonly called 'the Court of the Gentiles' (though this expression is not found in Jewish sources).

We must, however, note that the ancient commentators had already observed that we are face to face with a rabbinic ordinance. According to the prescriptions of the Torah itself, strangers could have gone into 'the Women's Court,' that is, up to Nicanor's Gate, seeing that the Sanctuary properly so-called (the *Mahane Shehina*) began there.[32]

Regarding the penalty which a violator of the prohibition would incur, the text under consideration is silent. On the other hand, there is mention of various punishments in the Mishna itself,[33] in the Tosephta[34] and in the Talmud,[35] but always with reference to violations on the part of a Jew. Thus, to my mind, it is impossible to extend such ordinances analogically to a Gentile who had violated the prohibition. However, it seems useful to draw attention to the fact that, in the Mishna, *Keritoth* I, 1 makes mention of, amongst others, the penalty of *karet*[36] for 'him that eats what is consecrated while unclean, or enters the Temple while unclean.'[37] It seems to me that the similarity of penalty for the unclean Jew who eats something sacred or who enters the Sanctuary could be extended also to the non-Jew who partakes of something sacred or goes into the Sanctuary.

Now, while the traditional Jewish sources are silent regarding the pagan who enters the Sanctuary, they do report an episode relative to a pagan who ate sacred foods. The Babylonian Talmud (Pesachim 3b) tells us that 'A certain Syrian (i.e., non-Jew) used to go up and partake of the Passover sacrifices in Jerusalem, boasting: It is written, *there shall no alien eat thereof . . . no uncircumcised person shall eat thereof,*[38] Yet I eat of the very best. Said R. Judah b. Bathyra[39] to him: Did they supply you with the fat-tail?[40] No, he replied. (Then) when you journey up thither say to them. Supply me with the fat-tail. When he went up he said to them, Supply me with the fat-tail. But the fat-tail belongs to the Most High! they replied. Who told you (to do) this? they enquired. R. Judah b. Bathyra, answered he. What is this (matter) before us? they wondered. They investigated his pedigree, and discovered that he was a Syrian, and killed him.[41] Then they sent (a message) to R. Judah b. Bathyra: "Peace be with thee, R. Judah b. Bathyra, for thou art in Nisibis yet thy net is spread in Jerusalem." '

Derenbourg feels disquiet at this passage and tries to explain it by way of the idea that the killing was the work of zealots and not accurately observed by Rabbi Jehuda ben Batira. It remains a fact, however, that in the Talmud there is not the slightest reference to zealots, and there is no note of disapproval whatsoever, so much so that, in his mediaeval commentary *in loco*, Rashi explains that Rabbi Jehuda ben Batira had to have recourse to this stratagem because, as he was resident in a foreign land, he could not kill the offender himself. Thus, from the text, it is clear enough that there might be the contingency of the death penalty for a pagan who had eaten something sacred. Therefore, analogically, we can conceive the same thing in relation to a pagan who might have set foot in the Sanctuary. It should also be noted that, in the traditional Jewish sources, we find other cases of killings effected immediately after the violation of the statute, namely, after a premeditated trespass which was witnessed by many. In the Mishna (*Sanhedrin* IX, 6), the case is envisaged of the profanation of the Sanctuary on the part of a priest: 'If a priest served (at the Altar) in a state of uncleanness his brethren the priests did not bring him to the court,[42] but the young men among the priests took him outside the Temple Court and split open his brain with clubs.[43]

Thus, on the evidence of the Mishna itself, the death penalty could be exacted for such violation. There is no weight in Derenbourg's objection that this

IIIb

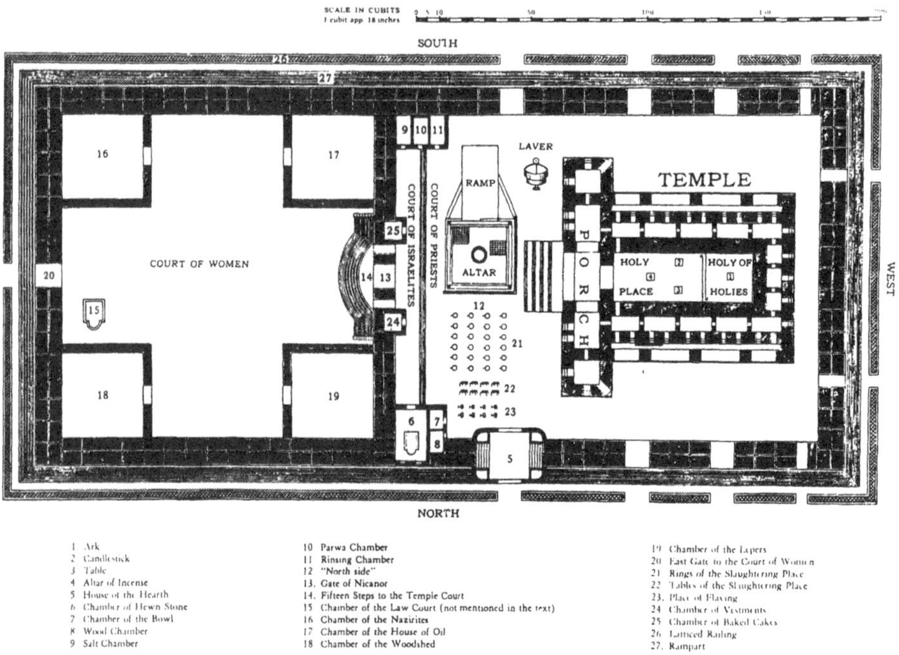

Plan of the Sanctuary, according to Maimonides (after *The Codex of Maimonides VIII*, London 1957). No. 26 indicates the balustrade.

must be an isolated case, to be viewed against the background of differences between Pharisees and Sadducees. True, such violations may not have been frequent, but it is also true that it is precisely from the occurrence of such transgressions that we can learn what laws were provided for them.

It seems to me that this passage warrants us in concluding with certitude that to comminate the death by the hands of the members of the public who had witnessed a transgression for which such a penalty was provided was not unknown to the Jewish juridical system. Bikerman has rightly observed that there is no question of lynching as such, seeing that the offender had previously been warned.

Examination of the pertinent texts leads us to reject Juster's theory that 'in countries and towns Roman public law made reservation (of the power to execute) only with regard to their own nationals. The Sanhedrin could exercise capital jurisdiction even over a non-Jew, even a Roman citizen, in the case, and only in the case, where he had presumed to pass beyond the Temple enclosure.'

All this formulation is based on the words put by Josephus into Titus' mouth; we have already shown how suspect they are in our eyes.[44] Juster himself stresses how unusual the whole thing is in relation to Roman law — a feature apparent even from the language attributed to Titus. It remains a fact that no source, either Roman or Jewish (except for the excerpt from Josephus under review — let us not beg the question!), gives any ground for holding that the Sanhedrin could condemn a Roman citizen to death. The silence of the sources on a matter of this kind (whose exceptional gravity needs no emphasis) seems to me a further proof that Josephus' statement cannot be given credence — nor, consequently, can the theory of Juster.[45]

Juster's hypothesis gains no support, either, from the account in the *Acts of the Apostles* (chaps. 21-23). There is uncertainty in the text. Specifically, the report of the trial before the Sanhedrin and of the tribune's intervention are amongst the sections most suspect by the critics.[46]

In view of this uncertainty, the fact that there were various accusations against Paul[47] does not allow us to conclude from *Acts* that we have 'an additional proof of the competence of the Sanhedrin.' Furthermore, if we give credence to the whole report, account must be taken of the fact that Paul was a Roman citizen, and that it is likewise true that he was a Palestinian Jew. Therefore, we must enquire whether or not we are confronted with a case of dual citizenship and, if so, with the question of what law was brought to bear. (Numerous studies have been devoted to the admissibility or otherwise of dual citizenship.)

Regarding the detail of the episode of the pagan Trophimus entering the Temple (*Acts* 21:27-30), we must take note of the whole context[48] for a better understanding of the passage. There is the matter of Paul's return to Jerusalem after his third journey. In Asia Minor, the Jews had shown dislike for his activity: 'And this is what has come to their ears about you: that you teach all Jews to break away from the Law of Moses, telling them not to circumcize their children, and not to follow the tradition' (*Acts* 31:21-22).

In an attempt to avoid such hostile demonstrations, Paul betook himself to the Temple. 'And when the seven days were all but at an end, the Jews from Asia saw him in the Temple. Whereupon they threw the whole multitude into an uproar, and laid hands upon him, crying out: Men of Israel, come to the rescue! Here is the man who goes about everywhere, teaching everybody to despise our people, and our law, and this place. He has brought Gentiles into the Temple, too, profaning these sacred precincts. They had seen Trophimus, who was from Ephesus, in the city with him, and it was he whom they suspected Paul of introducing into the Temple' (*Acts* 21:27-29).

Usually, stress is laid on Trophimus' entry into the Temple.[49] Yet he seems to have had but a minor place in the accusations laid by the Jews who challenged Paul. In any case, Paul will deny the fact itself, (Acts 21:29; 25:8). At all events, the Temple seems to have been the only place where the uproar, which Paul had expected, actually began — and this independently of the episode of Trophimus. Consequently, the whole narrative has only relative importance for the solution of our problem.

We have said that, to our way of thinking, the account of the transfer of the case to the Sanhedrin does not warrant the exploiting of any element in favour of Juster's theory. We must, nevertheless, add that, even if Paul had met with death in the uproar, we should not have been able to formulate decisive solutions from the narrative. Paul was a Jew. So far as I know, we do not have any source which speaks of a Jew suffering such a penalty for introducing a pagan into the Sanctuary. The text of *Acts* does not speak in absolute fashion of Trophimus, therefore we can retain the conclusions reached in our examination of Jewish and epigraphic sources.

In summary, the death penalty was not carried out by direct Divine intervention, as Derenbourg and Graetz thought, but by human hands. The executioners were not the Roman authorities, as Mommsen and many others thought, or the Sanhedrin, as Juster believed. It is maintained that, from the examination of the sources presented herein, the conclusion to be drawn is that the killing of a Gentile who violated the ban was carried out by the people present who with their own eyes saw that deliberate breach.

NOTES

23 With regard to *Contra Apionem*, one might consult the interesting article by A. Momigliano, 'Un'apologia del Giudaismo: il 'Contra Apione' di Flavio Giuseppe', in *Rassegna Mensile di Israele* 5691:1931, Vol. VI, pp. 33-41. Momigliano also examines about the character and personality of Josephus. *Cfr.*, now, the study by V. Tcherikover, 'Jewish Apologetic Literature Reconsidered.' *EOS* XLVIII:3 (Varsavia, 1957), Symbolae Taubenschlag, III, pp. 169ff. *CPJ*, pp. 12 and 40.

24 This is the theory put forward by Clermont-Ganneau, 'Stèle', p. 293. Personally, I would not be inclined to stress this factor.

25 Others, on the contrary, find worth in the passage, for example, Bikerman, 'Warning', p. 394-395, who thus rejects the hypothesis of Clermont-Ganneau ('Stèle', p. 290, m. 3) in which a lynching is suggested. Previously, Juster had already written (in *Les Juifs dans l'Empire Romain*, Vol. II, chap. XIV, p. 143, note 5): it cannot be admitted that 'the execution was to be carried out by lynching and this by legal prescription!' Nevertheless, it seems to me that there can be cases in which the law forewarns against the possibility of reactions, yet of a kind which the law itself does not consider as meriting punishment. We ourselves will examine one of these cases of Rabbinic Law (Mishna. *Sanhedrin*, IX, 6). See, on the point, Bikerman, who makes

a distinction between what the stele could have meant for the pagan and for the Jew. He avers that, for the pagan reader, the significance was quite clear: 'The trespasser will be executed by the outraged community which he had polluted by his act' ('Warning', p. 398). As we shall see, for us the meaning is the same in the case of the Jewish reader equally.
Again, in opposition to Juster's judgment, we may recall the case of the *homo sacer* in Roman law. According to the definition preserved for us by Festus, '*homo sacer* is he on whom the people has passed judgment because of a crime. While it is not lawful to slay him, neither would one who kills him be condemned for parricide.'

26 Sulpicius Severus, *Historia Sacra* 11, 30, 5-7 (Migne, Patrologia Latina, 20 p. 146); Sulpicius used more ancient sources and perhaps also Tacitus' Histories. See also Orosius: Historiae adverous paganos, 7, 9, 5-6; he also blames Titus. A detailed discussion concerning this problem appears in G. Alon's article 'The Burning of the Temple' in *Studies in Jewish History*, I, pp. 206 *et seqq.*

27 It is even extremely likely that it was so according to *strictum ius*. I say 'likely', seeing that the Mishna (*Sanhedrin*, IX, 6) reports a divergence of opinions on a similar case: 'If a layman (one not a priest) has performed service in the Sanctuary, Rabbi Akiva holds that he should be strangled. The other Sages teach: (he is struck) by the hand of Heaven.'

28 Derenbourg, 'Stèle', *passim*.

29 *Histoire des Juifs* (French translation by M. Bloch, Paris, 1884), p. 235.

30 It seems difficult to grant that *Lēphthē* (3rd person, aorist passive of *lambanō*) can in this instance mean, 'anyone who would risk it' (as Graetz holds). In this regard, it is helpful to note the various uses of the verb. *Cfr.* Rocci, *Vocabolario greco-italiano* (Città di Castello, 1955), p. 1120ff., where it is stated that the verb means, amongst other things, 'take', 'catch', 'arrest', 'and that it was also used (as customarily in Persian) 'to indicate the death sentence.'

31 It is this argument which is quoted by all opponents of the abovementioned theory, mostly with apologetic ideas in mind. Amongst such opponents, see, for example, E. Schürer, *Geschichte des Jüdischen Volkes im Zeitalter Jesu Christi*, Vol. II (Leipzig, 1907), p. 329, n. 57. But his theory that the death penalty was threatened by the Roman authority is just as inconsistent.

32 *Cfr.*, also, *Siphre Zuta* on Numbers 5:2 and the *Tosephta Kelim* I, 6; I, 8; 1, 10. On the Rabbinic restrictions, see all the commentaries by Rabbenu Asher (Rosh and Rabbi Ovadia of Bertinoro on the Talmud and Mishna respectively (*in loc.*). Amongst modern commentators, see the explanation by Albek on the Mishna.

33 Keritot I, 1 (about which see *infra*) and Makkot 3, 2.

34 Tosephta Kelim I, 6; I, 8; I, 10.

35 Babylonian Talmud, Menachot 23, b.

36 On the penalty of *karet*, see note 4.

37 *Ofr.*, also, the English translation of I. Porush (Epstein), Keritot, p. 1: 'when an unclean person eats of sacrificial food, or when one enters the precincts on the Temple in an unclean state....'

38 Exodus 12:43; 12:48.

39 A famous master from Nisibis in Babylonia. For a bibliographical note, *cfr. Encyclopedia of Talmudic and Geonic Literature. A Bibliographical Dictionary of the Tannaim, Amoraim and Geonim*, (in Hebrew; Jerusalem, 1964), Vol. I, p. 412.

40 The prohibition on eating fat foods is contained in the Torah: Exodus 29:22; Leviticus 7:3; 8:25; 9:9.

41 In his translation of the Talmud into English, Epstein notes accurately: 'for a non-Jew might not even penetrate beyond a certain point within the Temple precincts on pain of death, and a public notice gave due warning of this. Josephus ant. XV, 11, 5.' *The Babylonian Talmud. Seder Mo'ed, Pesahim* (London, 1938), p. 10, note 7.
On the point that 'they wrote to Rabbi Jehuda ben Batira', the *Margalioth* (*cfr. Encyclopedia of Talmudic and Geonic Literature*) has it that the allusion is to the *chachamim*, that is to say, the wise men, the Masters. This interpretation seems to be fully logical and concincing, seeing that we must suppose that it would have been the Master's task to institue the inquiry and then write to their colleague in Babylonia. This is another element to be taken into account against Derenbourg's interpretation (*cfr. infra.*).
With reference to Derenbourg's observations that it was above all the *zealots* who applied the penalty, see the whole passage devoted to the subject by Foakes-Jockson in *The Beginnings of Christianity* (London, 1920), p. 424. Also against Derenbourg, *cfr.* G. Alon, *Studies in Jewish History*, p. 103, n. 61 and p. 134, no. 35.

42 In Court, the sentence would be to scourging (*malkut*) only, since it was considered as otherwise punishable directly by God. All this is to be understood, naturally, if the priest acted with premeditation and therefore with the obvious purpose of committing an offence. To my mind, the posting of the inscriptions would show clearly that premeditation was required in the case of pagans also.

43 On this sentence, see Z. Falk, *Introduction to Israel Law in the Time of the Second Temple*, (in Hebrew; Tel Aviv, 1969), pp. 33ff.

44 We can add the observation of Clermont-Ganneau that these arraignments are often a work of the imagination. On the trial of Paul, see too Mantel, *Studies, etc.*, pp. 328ff. Mantel also holds that Roman citizens could have been punished by the Jewish authorities. (He relies on *Bellum Judaicum* VI, 2, 4, p. 336, n. 410).

45 Juster's theory is fully accepted by Gabba in *Iscrizioni Greche e Latine etc.* p. 25.

46 *Cfr.*, among others, A. Loisy, *Les Livres du Nouveau Testament* (Paris, 1922), p. 498-499; also E. de Faye, *Les Actes des Apôtres* in *Le Nouveau Testament* supervised by 'Société Biblique', 1928, p. 218-219 (notes).

47 *Acts of the Apostles* 23:29; 24:5, 12, 13ff.; 25:7, 8, 27; 26:6. On these passages, *cfr.*, also, G. Alon, *Studies in Jewish History*, I, pp. 99ff.

48 *Cfr.*, also, Juster, *Les Juifs, etc.*, I, p. 143, note 1.

49 C. S. C. Williams, for example, comments: 'The implication was that Paul had taken Gentiles beyond the Court of the Gentiles and within the Court of Israel ignoring the barrier on which Greek and Latin notices warned Gentiles against going within on pain of death. *Cfr.* Josephus, *Bellum Judaicum* V, 5, 2 (in *A Commentary on the Acts of the Apostles* (London, 1957), p. 241). See also the comment of Foakes-Jackson (*The Beginnings of Christianity*. Part I: *The Acts of the Apostles* (London, 1920), p. 6): 'The Gentile, who might wander at liberty among the porticoes of the outer court was confronted with rows of pillars on which were inscribed warnings in Greek and Latin that he might go no farther.'

IV

THE SITUATION OF THE JEWS IN ROMAN SPAIN

1) The Beginning

Many legends are told about the beginning of Jewish settlement in Spain. Some of these attribute the beginning of this diaspora to the days of Nebuchadnezzar. There were families who claimed that they could trace their genealogy to the families Titus brought from *Iudaea capta*[1]

1. E.g. the *Aibalia* family has a tradition that one of their ancestors, Baruch - who had a post in the Temple of Jerusalem - accepted an invitation to visit Spain at the time of Titus; see especially A. De Castro, *The History of the Jews in Spain*, London, 1857 (repr. 1972); S. Applebaum, "The Diaspora of the Mediterranean coast in the Hellenistic - Roman age" (in Hebrew), in *The Mediterranean: its place in the History and Culture of the Jews and other nations*, Jerusalem, 1970, p. 54.

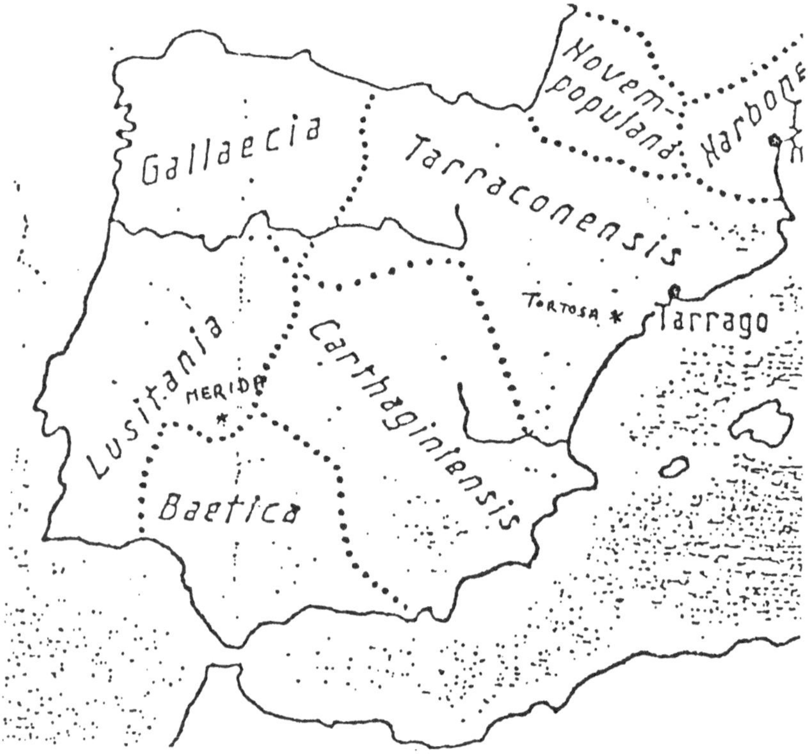

Fig. 1: Spain at the end of the IVth century

after the conquest. It is obvious that we cannot verify these legends which were partly spread in order to "purify" families of Jews and Marranos from the suspicion that their ancestors were associated with the killing of Jesus. There were some who tried to explain the great wisdom of the Sefardic Jews by the tradition according to which the tribe of Judah was exiled to Spain after the destruction of the First Temple.[2] It is probable that a Jewish settlement already existed there at the end of the Second Temple period or immediately after the destruction of the Temple in 70 C.E. Paul in his *Epistle to the Romans* says:

" I shall come to you on my way to Spain...." (15.24), and

" I shall cross your land to get to Spain" (15.28).

Even if scholars today believe that Paul never reached Spain, it may be deduced from his intention to visit there that Jewish communities existed in Spain, and that it was in those communities that Paul wished to preach Christianity.[3]

In the Talmudic sources we find several references to Spain *(Aspamia)*, and even if these sometimes point to a distant place and no more, it would seem that the Sages referred to Ispamia as a land in

In general on the Jews in Roman Spain see: L. Garcia Iglesias, "Los Judíos en la España Romana" , *Hispania Antiqua*, 3, 1973, pp. 331 ff: J. Juster, *The Legal Condition of the Jews under the Visigothic Kings* (brought up-to-date with a Tribute by A.M. Rabello) Jerusalem, 1976.

2. J.F. Baer, *A History of the Jews in Christian Spain*, vol. 1, Philadelphia, 1961, p.3 ff. ; see also: H. Beinart, "Two *Shalom al Israel* inscriptions from Spain", *Eretz Israel*, 8, 1967, pp. 298 ff. (In Hebrew; English summary p. 78).
3. S. Baron, *A Social and Religious History of the Jews*, vol. 1. New York, 1952, p. 170, vol. III,p. 33 f. ; H. Beinart, "Cuándo llegaron los Judíos a España", *Estudios del Instituto Central de Relaciones culturales Israel-Iberoamerica, España Y Portugal*, III, 1961, 1, ff.; M. Smallwood, *The Jews under Roman Rule*, Leiden, 1976, p.122.

which Jews lived. In the *Mishnah (Bava Batra*, 3,2,) we read:

"R. Judah said: They have prescribed a limit of three years only that if the owner was in Spain (Ispamia) ..." and in the *Babylonian Talmud*, (*Yevamot* 63a):

"Even vessels which come from *Gallia* to *Ispamia* are not blessed but for the sake of Israel..."; and again, *Bab. Talmud Nidda*, 30, b):

"A man sleeps here and sees a dream in *Aspamia.* "

Finally, in *Midrash Vayikra Rabbah* (3, 6) we read:

"He brought his offering from *Gallia* and from *Ispamia...*"[4]. And again: "God said to him : "Do not fear my servant Jacob, and do not let Israel fear becouse I am going to save you from far away (Jeremiah, 30, 10): *from Gallia and from Ispamia and from her friends.*"

In the book of Ovadiah it is written:

"....and the diaspora of Jerusalem which is in *Sefarad*[5] will inherit the towns of the Negev" (1, 20);

in the *Targum Yonatan* they interpret *Sefarad* as Spain.

4. It is clear that we cannot determine from these quotations whether in the name *Aspamia* the sages referred to *Spain* or perhaps to other nearer places, such as *Apamia* in Syria. On this issue see especially: A. Neubauer, *La Géographie du Talmud*. Paris, 1868, p. 304, 417; P. Neeman, *Encyclopedia of the Geography of the Talmud*. Tel-Aviv, 1972 (1), p. 118 ff. (in Hebrew), and also notes of the editor in *ʾAruch Hashalem*, entry *Aspamia*, on what the Midrash says in Vayikra Rabbah.
   Nevertheless, it seems quite clear that sometimes the name *Aspamia* refers to Spain itself. See M. Margaliot's note concerning *Vayikra Rabbah*, 70, 68-69, in which he emphasizes that the names Aspamia and Gallia actually refer to present day Spain and France, and not to other places nearer to Israel, "for the main aim of the Midrash is to stress the great trouble and pain endured in travelling a long distance in order to bring a sacrifice".
5. Sefarad is the name generally used in Hebrew for Spain, see S. Krauss, "The names Ashkenaz and Sefarad", *Tarbitz* 3, 1932, pp. 423 ff. (in Hebrew), and also I.N. Epstein's important note in "On the name Spain", *ibid*, p. 435.

We may note here that the status of the Spanish Jews was generally no different from the status of Jews elsewhere in the Roman Empire, especially in the western part of the Empire.

Judaism was considered *religio licita*, a *nation* with its own privileges permitting the free exercise of the Jewish cult and exemption from public duties in conflict with the monotheistic faith of the Jews. It is especially important to point out that after the grant of Roman citizenship to all the inhabitants of the Empire by Antoninus Caracalla *(Constitutio Antoniniana de Civitate)* in 212, all the Jews of Spain became Roman citizens. Thus on the one hand we see that the Jews enjoyed Roman citizenship and everything that it involved, and on the other hand it enables us to understand the continuity of the Roman laws which relate to the Jews.[6]

2) The council of Elvira and the Jews

The first reference of the Catholic Church to the Jews of Spain is found at the Council of Elvira. It was the first Church Council in the world to regulate the relationship between Christians and Jews.

Elvira is the name of a place, or more precisely, the name of two towns in Spain: One in the province of Narbona and the other in the Baetic province, today Andalusia, not far from the present site of Gerona. It is most probable that it was in this latter town that the Bishops' council took place. In the opinion of some scholars, the council was held between the years 300-303; others say it took place between 306-312.[7]

6. This is not the place to give a full bibliographic list. It is sufficient to refer the reader to: J. Juster, *Les Juifs dans l'Empire Romain*, Paris, 1914; L. Garcia Iglesias, "Los Judíos en la España Romana", *Hispania Antiqua*, 3, 1973, pp. 331 ff.; A.M. Rabello, The Legal Condition of the Jews in the Roman Empire, *ANRW*,II, 15, 1980, pp. 662-762; A.M. Rabello, *The Jews in Visigothic Spain in the Light of the Legislation* (in Hebrew), Jerusalem, 1983.
7. On the Elvira Council see: C.I. Hefele - H.Leclerq, *Histoire des Conciles d'après les documents originaux*, II, Paris, 1908; G. Bareille, "Elvire",

From the decisions taken at the council which concerned Jews, at a time of syncretism for the Spaniards, we may learrn about the influence the Jews had on the Christians (there was probably influence in the other direction too !). The Spanish Church, like other churches, was afraid of too much contact between Jews and Christians. It decided not to permit mixed marriages *(Can. 16)*,[8] and to forbid adultery with a Jewish woman *(Can. 78)*,[9] which presumably meant a prohibition on taking a Jewish concubine. It also prohibited dining with Jews *(Can.*

Dictionnaire de théologie catholique, 4,2, 2378-2392; A.M. Rabello, *Giustiniano, Ebrei e Samaritani alle luce delle fonti storico-letterarie, ecclesiastiche e giuridiche*, vol. II, Milano, 1988, pp. 497 ff. In general, see: A. Momigliano, *The Conflict between Paganism and Christianity in the Fourth Century*, Oxford, 1962.

8. Can. 16: "*Women believers are forbidden to marry non-believers.*
If heretics refuse to join the Catholic Church, it shall be prohibited to give them Catholic girls. The reason for prohibiting an attachment with Jews or heretics is that there cannot be any kind of a partnership between a believer and a non-believer. If parents will not follow this prohibition they will be excluded for five years from the *communio*". Cf. P. Lombardia, "Los matrimonios mixtos en el Concilio de Elvira (a. 303 ?)", *A.H.D.E.*, 24, 1954, pp. 543 ff.; A.M. Rabello, "Il problema dei matrimoni fra Ebrei e Cristiani nella legislazione imperiale e in quella della Chiesa (IV-VI secolo), in *Atti della Accademia Romanistica Costantiniana*, VII, Napoli, 1988, pp. 213 ff.

9. *Can. 78: "About the loyal married men who commit adultery with a Jewish or a Pagan woman.* If any believer who has a wife commits adultery with a Jewish or a Pagan woman, he shall be expelled from the *communio*; if someone else catches him in the act (and accuses him), he shall be allowed to return to the holy *communio* after five years of penitence" (*poenitentia*).
The aim of the Canon forbidding the possession of Jewish or Pagan mistresses is to prevent the believer from being influenced by foreign customs. The Canon does not relate to non-married men, but the issue will be dealt with by the non-religious legislation.

50).[10]

Canon 49, which states that a Christian must not ask a Jew to bless his crop, shows that the Jews were landowners at the time and that they enjoyed good relations with their neighbours.[11]

Canon 26, prevents the Christians from keeping Saturday as a holy day (Exodus, 20, 8; Deut. 5, 12)[12]. At that period and also for some

10. Can. 50: "*About the Christians who dine with the Jews.*
If anyone from the clergy or a believer eats his food in the company of a Jew, a decision will be taken to suspend him from the *communio* so that he can repent". see B. Blumenkranz, "Judaeorum convivia: à propos du Concile de Vannes (465), c. 12, in *Études du droit canonique dediées à Gabriel Le Bras*, II, Paris, 1965, pp. 1055 ff. *(=Juifs et Chrétiens. Patristique et Moyen Age*, London, 1977, n. XX)
11. Can. 49: "*That the Jews shall not bless the fruit of the believers.* We think landowners ought to be warned not to let Jews bless their fruit, fruit which is a gift from God, so that our blessing will not seem a false and unimportant blessing. If anyone continues in this way after the prohibition, he shall be expelled from the Church".
12. Can. 26: "*That they shall fast every Saturday.* Whoever wishes to make amends for a sin, must keep all the fasts which were established every Saturday".
It seems that the aim is to prevent the Christians from keeping Saturday as a day of joy. It should not be forgotten that for a long period of time there were Christians who continued keeping Saturday as a holiday and a rest day, while there were other Christians who used to keep two days as a holiday, both Saturday and Sunday. On the concurrence between Saturday and Sunday in the Church, see: J. Juster, *Les Juifs dans l'Empire Romain*, I, p.280; P. Cotton, *From Sabbath to Sunday*, Bethlehem, 1993; M. Simon, *Verus Israel: Étude sur les rélations entre chrétiens et Juifs dans L'Empire Romain (135–425)*, Paris, 1948 pp. 374 ff., 383, 422., S. Bacchiocchi, *A Historical investigation of the Rise of Sunday observance in Early Christianity*, Roma, 1977,; A. Weiss, "The Sabbath-observance of Gentiles", *Bar-Ilan Anuual* 1963, pp. 143 ff. (Hebrew); Y.D. Gilat, "On Fasting on the Sabbath",

time afterwards, there were many Christians influenced by the Bible and by the Jews who wanted to keep Saturday as a day of solemn rest, or both days (Saturday and Sunday) combined.

Canon 36[13], at a later period of time, was the cause of very strong controversy, and until this very day Christian theologians differ in their opinions about its precise meaning. This Canon forbade pictures in Church. Some assume that by taking this action, the council wanted to prevent the contempt and mockery of the Jews, but it would logical to think that the conference was aiming at a ritual of a more spiritual nature.

Tarbiz, 52,1,1982. pp. 1 ff. (Hebrew); R. Bonfil, "Tra due mondi: prospettive di ricerca sulla storia culturale degli Ebrei nell'alto medioevo", *Italia Judaica*, Roma, 1983, pp. 135 ff.; A.M. Rabello, "L'observance des fêtes juives dans l'Empire Romain", *ANRW* II, 21, 2, Berlin-New York, 1983, pp. 1288 ff.

13. Can. 36: "*That there will be no pictures in church.* The decision to forbid any kind of picture in church was taken in order that what is to be worshipped and honoured should not be painted on the walls." On the prohibition of pictures in church see also E.E. Urbach, "The Rabbinical Laws of Idolatry in the Second and Third Centuries in the Light of Archaeological and Historical Facts", *Israel Exploration Journal*, 9, 1959, pp. 149 ff. More generally see: E.J.Martin, *A History of the Iconoclastic Controversy*, London, 1930.

14. Can. 61: "*That a man shall not marry two sisters.* If a man, after the death of his wife, marries her sister, and even if she is a believer, it has been decided that they shall be excluded from the *communio* for five years unless, in case of a disease, it will be necessary to ease their conscience at an earlier stage and enable them to return to the *communio* before the five years are over". See *Babylonian Talmud, Mo'ed Qatan* (tractate on intermediate days of a festival), *23a: Jerusalem Talmud. Yevamot*, 84, 11, and *Masekhet Semahot* (tractate on mourning laws and manners), 87. See also discussion on this issue: R. Yaron, "Duabus sororibus coniunctio". *Revue Internationale des Droits de l'Antiquité*, 10, 1963, pp. 115 ff.

Finally, another item, *Canon 61*, is aimed at preventing Christians from adhering to the Jewish custom by which the unmarried sister of a deceased woman was expected to marry her brother-in-law and take care of the sister's little orphans. In any case, Judaism did not consider this kind of marriage as defective.[14]

From these Canons we can learn that Spanish Jews were considered by the local Church to be of great importance in the area, thus the Church passed laws against them in order to limit their influence on Christians.

3) The Incident of Minorca

In this discussion of the relations between Jews and Christians in Spain it is important to mention an incident which occured in Minorca, one of the Balearic islands. In an epistle from the year 418, *Epistula de Judaeis*, Severus, the bishop of Majorca and Minorca, gives us a report on Christianity's victory over the Jews on the island, and tells us about their conversion.[15]

15. Severus Majoricensis, *Epistula de Judaeis* (=Migne, P.L.,20, 731 ff.) 41, 822, ff.; G.G. Segni Vidal, *La carta encíclica del Obispo Severo. Estudio critico de su autenticidad e integridad con un bosquejo histórico del cristianismo balear anterior al siglo VIII*, Palma de Mallorca, 1936. In this study the author sets out to prove the authenticity of the document. He argues with scholars who do not accept his theory.
Blumenkranz has since claimed that the *epistula* attributed to Severus reflects the reality of the seventh century and not the fifth. This claim is based on literary grounds: B.Blumenkranz, *Les auteurs Chrétiens latins de Moyen age sur les Juifs et le Judaïsme*, Paris, 1963, p. 106, ff.: Blumenkranz, *Juifs et Chrétiens dans le monde occidental* (430-1096) , Paris, 1963. p. 76 n. 34, pp. 263-284, but his claim does not seem fully proven.
Among the many scholars who accept Severus' letter as an historic document are: Juster, *Juifs*, 1, 464, nt. 3, 500; 2, 200-201, 253, 261-262; Baer, *A History of the Jews in Christian Spain*, 1, 17, 382, n. 2; Garcia, *Judíos*, 17 ff., 20 ff., 32 ff.; Baron, *Social and Religious History*, I, 370 and III, 33 ff.

At first, the relationship between Jews and Christians was good, but then in 415 Orosius brought over the bones of Stephan, a saint of Church. He had been put to death by the Jews in the Land of Israel. The act of bringing over his bones inflamed the Christians who wanted to take vengeance on the Jews of the island.[16] Riots erupted. The Jews, headed by their leader Theodorus, gathered at the synagogue. The Christians were convinced that the Jews were armed and ready for battle. Therefore, they asked for a debate to take place.

Here we findoneof the first examples of a theological debate in Spain, one of those debates in which our forefathers proved the might of their wisdom in spite of the obstacles facing them. And so also here, Theodorus "spoke with great wisdom about the Torah until he made a total mockery of all the objections he confronted." When the Christians realised they could not win this debate, they asked for a miracle from heaven. But Severus could not hide his treacherous activities: even while saying how ugly it is to have a war between brothers, he was trying to find out how much truth there was in the rumours that the Jews were carrying weapons. Once he became aware that there was no reason to doubt that the Jews were in fact unarmed, he himself organized the treacherous attack: "Even the Jews, taking their example from the period of the Maccabees, wished for the deaths of their relatives." The women, in particular, were willing to sacrifice their lives for the sake of martyrdom; the synagogue was burnt, but in the end, five hundred and forty Jews converted to Christianity in four days.[17]

This story mentions several Jewish characters who held public positions, such as Lectorius for example, who was the governor of the

16. G. Rinaldi, "Stefano", *Enciclopedia Cattolica*, vol. XI, col. 1928 f.; G. Madoz, "Severo di Minorca", *Enc. Cattolica*, XI, col 465f.; "Saint Stephan'", *Hebrew Encyclopedia*, (in Hebrew) vol. 25, p. 722 ff.

17. See E. Gibbon, *The History of the Decline and Fall of the Roman Empire*, (ed. by J.B. Bury), London, 1909, vol. 3, p. 224 n. 91.

Balearic islands,[18] and Caecilianus, considered "an honest man, not only in the eyes of the Jews, but also in the city where until now he occupied a leading position, so that he had just been elected defender of the town (the civilians).... *(defensor civitatis)*".[19] Theodorus is also described as knowledgable in the Torah, and a landowner who was greatly respected by both Jews and Christians, and who officiated as mayor of the town Mahon in Minorca.

18. *Arthemisia siquidem, Lectorii, qui nuper hanc provinciam rexit et nunc comes esse, dicitur, filia...* (cap. 17), Migne, *Patrologia Latina*, 20, 744; cf. Juster, *Juifs* 2, pp. 250, 261 ff. The position of *comes* occupied by a Jew is also mentioned in an inscription from Sepphoris dated to the first half of the fourth century. See the context of the inscription and discussion about it in: Frey, *Corpus Inscriptionum Judaicarum*, 2, 1991; B. Lifshitz, *Donateurs et fondateurs dans les Synagogues Juives*, Paris, 1967, n. 74.
19. Ibid, chapter 14; Attention should be paid to the fact that in the year 409 anyone who was not a Christian was forbidden to hold the position of defender of the town *(defensor civitatis)*. This position was considered very important, especially in the Land of Israel (*Codex Justinianus* 1.55.8). Parkes considers that an explanation can be found in the fact that the command did not reach the island for nine years, or that the facts are not true, and this is simply an example of the literary tradition of telling about the wonders of heroes of a particular story (J. Parkes, *The Conflict of the Church and the Synagogue*, Cleveland, 1961, p. 204). In my opinion, it is possible that in places where good relations were achieved between Jews and Christians, the law was ignored. It is also important to note that Caecilianus probably held the position after his conversion to Christianity, and that Theodorus also held other positions, so that it is not clear whether he was the defensor after 409. That the Jews were prohibited from holding this position may be understood from the third Novella of Theodosius II (436) and from the constitution of Justinian *C.J.*1.9.18.

We do not intend to go into further details on this epistle.[20]

The main facts to be deduced from this document are as follows: in the island of Minorca, at the beginning of the fifth century there were many Jews who maintained good relations with the Christians of the island. Among the Jews there were some who managed to reach high public positions. The Jews had a synagogue and among them there were learned people, but it seems that the women had stronger faith. The relations between Jews and Christians started to crumble following the hostile activities of the Catholic Church on the island.

4) The Epigraphic evidence: The Jewish inscriptions from Spain.

Attention must be paid to the Jewish inscriptions which come from Spain.[21] These inscriptions tell us about the community life of the Jews in Spain, and this is very important since most of the information

20. For more particulars see: A.M.Rabello, "Gli Ebrei nella Spagna romana e ariana-visigotica", *Atti dell'Accademia Romanistica Costantiniana*, 4°, Perugia, 1981, pp. 807 ff. ; idem, *The Jews in Visigothic Spain in the light of the Legislation.* (in Hebrew), Jerusalem, 1983.
21. Bibliography and main abbreviations: Cantera-Millas, *Inscripciones* = F. Cantera-Burgos-Millas, *Les Inscripciones hebraicas de España*, Madrid, 1956;
Ferrua, *Inscripciones* = A. Ferrua, "*Inscripciones griecas y judias*", in J. Vives, *Inscripciones cristianas de la España Romana y visigoda*, Barcelona, 1942, 2e ed., 1969;
Frey, *C.I.J.* = J.B. Frey, *Corpus Inscriptionum Judaicarum. Recueil des inscriptions juives qui vont du IIIe siècle avant J.C. au VII siècle*, vol. I, Europe, Città del Vaticano, 1936 (reproduction with Prolegomenon by B. Lifshitz, New York, 1975);
Garcia, *Judíos* = L. Garcia Iglesias, "*Los judíos en la España romana,*" *Hispania Antiqua*, 3, 1972, pp. 331 ff.;

we have about the Jews in that time comes from laws passed against them.[22]

From these inscriptions we learn that the Jews settled mainly in coastal towns, such as Tarragona, Tortosa, Elche and Adra. Nevertheless, there is also evidence that Jews lived inland, for instance, in the town of Merida "a town which resembled Rome more than any of the big cities of Spain".[23]

The inscriptions are written in the following languages: Hebrew, Latin, Greek,[24] and sometimes there are even expressions taken from the Jewish liturgy: among the typical Jewish symbols we find the *Menorah*, the Star of David *(Magen David)* and the palm-branch *(lulav)*. Among the community roles which appear in the inscriptions we find the *Archisynagogus*.[25] The use of Latin and Greek in Spain shows that the Jews who spoke those languages came from distinguished and highly cultured families.

We shall discuss the inscriptions in geographical order: Hispania Tarraconesis; Hispania Carthaginesis; Hispania Baetica; Hispania Lusitanesis. (Fig. 1).

Goodenough, *Jewish Symbols* = E Goodenough, *Jewish Symbols in the Greco-Roman Period*, New York, 1953–1968;

Hubner - Mommsen, *CIL* = Th. Mommsen, *Corpus Inscriptionum Latinarum*, vol. 2, *Inscriptiones Hispaniae Latinae*, ed, A. Hubner, 1869;

B. Lifshitz, *Prolegomenon* = B. Lifshitz, "Prolegomenon" to Frey, *CIJ*.

22. J. Juster, *The legal Condition of the Jews under the Visigothic Kings*, (brought up to date by A.M. Rabello), Jerusalem, *Israel Law Review*, 1976.
23. E. Albertini, "Les étrangers residents en Espagne à l'époque romaine", *Mélanges Cagnat*, Paris, 1912, p. 313.
24. See: V. Colorni, "L'uso del greco nella liturgia del Giudaismo ellenistico e la Novella 146 di Giustiniano", *Annali di Storia del Diritto*, 8, 1964. pp. 15 ff. with special attention to Jewish inscriptions from Spain.
25. See below, inscription N.1, nt.3.

HISPANIA TARRACONENSIS

This is the name of the region in the north-east of the Spanish peninsula: to its east lies the Mediterranean sea and to the north - the Pyrenees. The capital was Tarragona (Tarraco), a port about one hundred kilometers south of Barcelona. The town was also important economically on account of the linen and wine trades. It would seem that there was a Jewish settlement in Tarragona already in the Roman era.

In 1955 an inscription was found in Tarragona (Fig. 2), which was later published by Cantera Burgos.[26]. The inscription is written in three languages: Hebrew, Latin, and Greek. The dating of this inscription is very similar to the dating of the three-language inscriptions from Tortosa: either the sixth century or, at least, the seventh.[27] It is possible that this could be a dedicatory inscription in a synagogue. In Hebrew we read:

שלום על ישראל
ועלינו ועל בנינו אמן

"Shalom al Israel ve-aleinu ve-al baneinu amen."

["May there be peace on Israel and on us and on our sons, amen"]

There are pictures of a *Menorah* and of the tree (the tree of life ?) , and of a *shofar* and two peacocks. These may present the idea of resurrection. In Latin we read: *Pax Fides.*

The expression pax is an attempt at translating the expression *shalom* into Latin. The second expression, *fides* - "faith" is not common in either Jewish or Christian inscriptions, and may be used here to emphasize that the place is dedicated to the faith of Israel.

In Greek there are a number of signs which are not comprehensible:

26. F. Cantera-Burgos, "Nueva inscripcion trilingue tarraconense?, *Sefarad*, XV, 1955, pp. 151-156.
27. This is the opinion of Cantera-Millas; *but Beinart and others think it might belong to the IInd Century*: "Two *Shalom al Israel* Inscriptions from Spain", *Eretz Israel*, 8, 1967, p. 298 f.

"TAH" or "πAHE" (according to the reading suggested by Cantera): some other letters in Latin and Greek can not be read. The expression *ve-aleinu ve-al baneinu amen* - "and on us and on our sons, amen"[28] reminds us of similar expressions we find in the book of Psalms, 115, 14: "G-d will add to you, to you and to your sons" as in prayers like the "Kaddish": "On Israel and on its teachers and on their pupils and on all the pupils of the pupils..."[29]

H. Beinart thought that it was likely that this inscription was engraved on a sarcophagus: "the only Jewish sarcophagus ever found in Spain and outside the Land of Israel up till now";[30] however, in my humble opinion, it is more probable that the inscription was engraved on a laver-basin which was placed at the entrance to the synagogue in Tarragona, as Cantera-Burgos suggested.[31]

28. "Which seems uncommon in Jewish inscriptions" says Cantera-Burgos ("que nos parece exceptional en lapidas hebraicas"). On the expression שלום על ישראל - "shalom al Israel" - "peace on Israel " see discussion below on the trilingual inscription from Tortosa.
29. On this see now M. Weinfeld, "The Inscriptions of the Synagogues and the Jewish Liturgy", *An Annual for Biblical and Ancient Near Eastern Studies*, IV, 1980, pp. 288 ff. (in Hebrew); J. Yahalom , "Synagogue Inscriptions in Palestine - A Stylistic Classification" *Immanuel*, 10, 1980, pp. 47 ff.
30. H. Beinart, op. cit
31. Cantera-Millas, *Inscripciones*, n. 243, pp. 350-354 with a drawing and three photographs. This opinion is shared by B. Lifshitz, *Prolegomenon*, n. 650 c., p. 55 f.; J. Naveh, *On Stone and Mosaic. The Aramaic and Hebrew Inscriptions from Ancient Synagogues*, Jerusalem, 1978, n. 111. p. 148 (in Hebrew).
For other dedicatory inscriptions engraved on laver-basins see :
Frey, *CIJ*, 2, 754; B. Lifshitz, *Donateurs et fondateurs dans les Synagogues Juives*, Paris, 1967, p. 31, n. 28; M. Ben Dov, "Fragmentary Synagogue Inscriptions from Tiberias", *Qadmoniot*, 9, 1967, p. 79 f. (in Hebrew); L.

Fig. 2: Tri-lingual inscription on a laver – basin from Tarragona

An inscription from Tarragona in Latin and Greek probably dating back to the fourth century[32]

IN NOMINE [DOMI
NI REQVIESCI[T IN IS
TA INQVISIO[NE RAB
LASIES .S. NE[POS ? ?)
DIDASCALI R[EQVIES (?)
CIT CVM PAC[E
ΕΝΘΑ ΚΑΤΑΚ[ΕΙΤΑΙ
ΡΑΒ ΑΑΤΟΥΕ[Σ ΠΑ
ΡΑ ΤΟΥ ΜΑΚΑ[ΡΙΣ
ΤΟΥ ΚΥ ? ? [??
ΑΡΞΗΣΥΝ [ΑΓΩ̂ΓΟΥ
ΚΥΖΗΚΕ [ΝΟΣ
ΔΗΚΕΩ [Σ
ΓΗΑΝΗ [Α
ΚΕΥ ΛΩ [ΒΗS
ΚΕΥΡΗΕ
ΤΕΘΝΕ

Roth-Gerson, "On the Donation of a Laver-Basin to a Synagogue", *Qadmoniot*, 10, 1977, p, 79 (in Hebrew).

32. J.M. Millas Vallicrosa, "Una nueva inscripcion judaica bilingue en

[In the name of G-d - in this grave rests Rab Lasies, the grandson of the teacher (?) rests in peace [Greek text] here rests Rab Latoyes, by the pious Archisynagogus. He was from Cysicus, a righteous....from Hell (will keep him ?) will rest in peace (in ?) G-d].

The inscription is written in Latin and Greek. Its style resembles the inscription in three languages from Tortosa which is nearby. It ought to be mentioned that the Latin always appears first. Many Jews from that area came from the east and spoke more than one language, and this is also the reason for their lack of fluency in all the languages and especially Latin; for instance, they use the term *inquisio* (= *incisio*) instead of *tumba*.

The above is an inscription concerning a Rabbi or a sage by the name of Lasies (or Latoyes) who came from Cysicus which is in Asia Minor.[33] It seems that this is the correct interpretation of the inscription since it is not logical that the head of the congregation, who laid the stone, would mention his own place of origin. The position of *Archisynagogus* was well known in the Jewish congregations of the Roman empire.[34] Thus we have evidence that the Jewish congregations in Spain were organized similarly to other Jewish congregations

Tarragona", *Sefarad*, 17, 1957, p. 3 f. (from which the text of the inscription is taken); Garcia, Judíos, p. 13 f., 35.

33. J. Juster, *Les Juifs dans l'Empire Romain*, Paris, 1914, I. p.190; M. Stern, "The Jewish Diaspora", *Compendia Rerum Judaicarum ad Novum Testamentum*, Sect. I: *The Jewish People in the First Century*, vol. I (ed. S. Safrai and M. Stern), Assen, 1974, p. 120 f., 143 ff.

34. This title usually indicated the head of the Jewish congregation . See: J. Juster, *Les Juifs dans l'Empire Romain*, Paris, 1914, I, 450 ff.; H.J. Leon, *The Jews of Ancient Rome*, Philadelphia, 1960, p. 171 ff. : M. Floriani Squarciapino, "Plotius Fortunatus Archisynagogus", *Scritti Milano, La Rassegna Mensile di Israel,* 1970, p. 184 ff.; S. Applebaum, "The Organisation of the Jewish Communities in the Diaspora", *Compendia Rerum Judaicarum ad Novum Testamentum*, ed. Stern-Safrai, I, 1, pp. 429 ff.

elsewhere in the empire. As mentioned above, the writer knew Greek better than Latin. Here we have remnants of evidence about the life of the large Jewish congregation at Tarragona.

This congregation was probably founded by immigrants from east of the Mediterranean sea. Arab historians called Tarragona *Madinat-il-Yahud* which means the town of the Jews.[35],[36]

Another inscription, which is currently to be found in the Archeological Museum of Tarragona, was found in Pallaresos (Fig. 3), not far from Tortosa.[37] In the opinion of several scholars, it belongs to the first century, but others think that the Latin which is used in the inscription suits the style of the third century. Nevertheless, it seems that it is apparently from the sixth century, a time in which the important families in the area spoke both Latin and Greek.[38] The father holds a Jewish name, the mother a Greek name and the daughter's name is in Latin:

35. Cfr. J.M.Milla Vallicrosa, "Els textes d'historiadorors musulmans referents a la Catalunyas carolingia". *Quaderns d'Estudi*, 14, 1922, pp. 125 ff.
36. On the short form "Ku" instead of "Kuriou" see below, inscription N. 4, nt. 9; alas, we cannot be sure that this is also a shortened form.
37. See: Ferrua, *Inscripciones*, n. 430; A. Ferrua, "Addenda et corrigenda al *Corpus Inscriptionum Iudaicarum", Epigraphica*, 3, 1941. pp. 30 ff.; Goodenough, Jewish Symbols: Cantera-Millas, *Inscripciones*, n. 290; B. Lifshitz, *Prolegomenon*, n. 660 d (from which the text of the inscription is taken).
38. Goodenough thinks the lettering is excellent and appropriate to the first century; but the use of *bone* instead of *bonae* seems to Hendrikson (quoted by Goodenough) a sign that we are in the third century, so Goodenough himself is prepared to compromise: "Though it might have been written in the second century".

HI C EST
MEMORIA BONE RE
CORDATIONIS ISID
ORA FILIA BENE ME
MORII IONATI ET AX
IAES PAVSET ANI
MA EIVS IN PACE CV
M OMNE ISRAEL
[AM] EN AMEN AMEN

[This is the grave of Isidora, of blessed memory, the daughter of Jonathan, of blessed memory, and Axia: rest her soul in peace with all Israel amen, amen, amen.]

At the top of the inscription there are two lamps and three palm-tree branches, which could either be Lulavim or a reference to the Psalms: צדיק כתמר יפרח[39]. The name Isidora[40] was given to both Jews and Christians, and it probably tells of some Byzantine influence. The name Jonati is the genitive of Jonatus (Jonathan) according to the paradigma *Juda - Judanti*, Cantera reads: *Jonati et Axiaes*; Ferrua does not agree and suggests: *Jonatie Taxiaea*. In Cantera's opinio, it is the mother of Isidora who carries a Greek name. Ferrua claims that the expression *cum omne Israel* (with all Israel) is "new", but it is a well known expression in the Jewish liturgy .[41]

39. Psalms, 92, 13: "The Righteous will blossom like a palm-tree".
40. On this name see M. Cassuto Saltzman, "Greek Names among the Jews " *Eretz Israel*, 3, 1954, pp. 1 f.; on Jewish names in general, see N.G. Cohen's Ph.D. thesis, *Jewish Names and their significance in the Hellenistic and Roman Periods in Asia Minor*, Jerusalem, 1969.
41. See e.g. the text of the *Kaddish*. Cf. L. Zunz, *Zur Geschichte und Literatur*, Cap. 4: "Das Gedächtnis des Gerechten" pp. 304 ff.; M. Weinfeld, "The inscriptions of the Synagogues and the Jewish Liturgy", *An Annual for Biblical and Ancient Near Eastern Studies* (in Hebrew) IV, 1980, pp. 280 ff.

Fig. 3: A burial inscription from Pallaresos

From Tortosa (Dertosa) , another town in the north-east, south of Tarragona, a very interesting inscription has come down to us, written in three languages: Hebrew, Latin and Greek. At the beginning of the Hebrew there is a five-pointed star or what may be "Solomon's seal" : at the end there is a *Menorah* and the same star appears.[42]

42. See Fig. 4. On this inscription see: Frey, *CIJ*, n.661; Goodenough, *Jewish Symbols*, 2, p. 58 f. ; Ferrua, *Inscripciones*, n. 428; H. Beinart, "Cuando llegaron los judíos a Espana ?", *Estudios del Instituto Central de Relaciones culturales Israel - Iberoamerica, España y Portugal*, III, n. 3, 1962, p. 19 ff.; Cantera-Millas, Inscripciones, p. 198; Garcia, Judíos, p. 13. ; V. Colorni, "L'uso del greco nella Liturgia del Giudaismo Ellenistico e la Novella 146 di Giustiniano" *Annali di Storia del Diritto*, 8, 1964, p. 19 f. We have quoted the inscription following Ferrua's reading which is similar to Frey's. The reading is identical.

✡ שלום על ישראל
הקבר הזה של מללי ושא[43] בת[44]
יהודה ולקירא מרים[45] זכרונה תהי[46]
לברכה נשמתה לחיי העולם הבא[47]
נפשה בצרור החיים אמן[48]
שלום
✡

IN NOMINI ΔOMINI
HIC EST MEM[O]RIA VBI RE
QVIESCIT BENEMEMORIA
MELIOSA FILIA IVΔANTI [9] ET
CYR[I]A [10] MARIES VIXIT AN [NOS]
[VIGI}NTI ET QUATTOUR
OUM PACE AMEN

[ἐν] ὠνώ[μα]τη Κ(υρ[ο)υ. | ὧδε ἔστην με|[3]μν[εῖο]ν ὅπου ἀνά|π[αυ]σαν πάμμνη|[στος Μελιώσ]α Ἰούδαντ|[6][ος καὶ κυρίας Μά]ρες, ζήσ[ασα |ἔτη εἰκοσι] τέσ(σ)ερα(ς). ἠν | [εἰρήνη. ἀμήν].

43. Cantera-Millas read מיללאשא
44. Cantera-Millas read ר ברת instead of בת. The use of Aramaic is odd in a inscription which is written wholly in Hebrew.
45. Cantera-Millas read מארים or מארים. This reading is interesting since it suits the Latin writing of the name (*scriptio plena*).
46. Cantera-Millas read צדקת [זכר]
47. Cantera-Millas read תנוח
48. On the expression בצרור החיים, see the book of *Samuel* I, 25, 29. See also this expression in an inscription from Merida, of the Visigothic period, in A.M. Rabello, *The Jews in Visigothic Spain in the Light of the Legislation*, Jerusalem, 1983 (in Hebrew), p.120. no. 30, nt. 3.

Fig 4. A three language inscription (Hebrew, Latin, Greek) from Tortosa

[In the name of G-d. Here lies the memory in which Meliosa rests, may her memory be blessed, the daughter of Juda[49] and Lady[50] Maria. She lived twenty-four years in peace, amen]

(The Greek translation is identical to the Latin)

The inscription is clearly a Jewish one. The Hebrew text is typical of Jewish grave inscriptions. The star is "Solomon's seal" which was common among the Jews of Persia in the fifth and fourth centuries B.C.E..[51] Can we detect a reference to the days of Solomon, with which the Jews of Spain were trying to find a connection? Finally, beside another star appears the *menorah* with five branches.[52]

The expression שלום על ישראל "Peace on Israel" appears very often

49. On the name Judas in the Jewish and Christian world see: A.M.Rabello, "Sui rapporti fra Diocleziano e gli Ebrei", *Atti della Accademia Romanistica Costantiniana*, Perugia, 1976, pp. 186 ff. See also the remarks of Cantera-Millas, above.
50. Ferrua reads *Quira*. Cantera-Millas read *cura* or *cuira*. This name which means "lady" appears in several other Jewish inscriptions: see B. Lifshitz, *Donateurs*, 70. On the shortened form *Ku* instead of *Kuria* see Beinart, "Two inscriptions", pp. 302 ff.
51. On "Solomon's seal" see: N. Avigad, "Seal", *Biblical Encyclopedia*, 3, 81, ff.; "Star of David", *Hebrew Encyclopedia*, 22, pp. 149 ff (in Hebrew).
52. Probably according to the Talmudic tradition which forbids the making of a *Menorah* with seven branches, like the one which was placed in the Temple: "Said Abaye: The Torah forbade the making of ritual articles that can be made identical .... a *Menorah* opposed to a *Menorah*: the making of a *Menorah* with five, six or eight branches is permitted, but not seven..." (*Babylonian Talmud, Rosh Hashana*, 24a-b; see also *Menahot*, 28b, and *Avoda Zara*, 43a). The prohibition was interpreted with reference to a three dimensional *Menorah*, so that we usually find a seven-branched *Menorah* in inscriptions. Nevertheless, there are other examples of *Menorot* with five branches, e.g. in

in Jewish inscriptions.[53] Here it is used to show the loyalty of the family to the tradition of their forefathers. The blessing "Peace on Israel" can be interpreted as an expression of prayer and a wish concerning the fate of the nation following the death of the deceased, rather than a hint about the afterworld or the words of the deceased! The feeling of leavetaking from the deceased is combined with a prayer for the welfare of the small community of which the deceased was a member, and for all Israel.

The inscription was found in the town of Tortosa, in 1771. As to date of inscription, some scholars consider it goes back to the second or third century; most scholars think it belongs to the sixth century, and maybe Beinart was right in fixing the date at the end of the fourth century or beginning of the fifth. It should be noted that the family compiled the inscription in the vernacular, so as to be understood by the Christian families in the neighbourhood, while using the Hebrew language to give expression to its faith.

HISPANIA CARTHAGINENSIS

In the south-east region of Spain, an area which includes Toledo, three inscriptions belonging to the same building were found in the

inscriptions from Narbona, or the house of Kyrios Leontis in Scythopolis (VI century) ; See: Goodenough, *Jewish Symbols*, IV, pp. 71 ff. ; N. Zori, "The House of Kyrios Leonthis, *Israel Exploration Journal*, 19, 1966, p. 130 and nt. 15. Alas, it is possible that sometimes it occurs not from loyalty to the Talmud, but as the result of ignorance on the part of the artist. This assumption is brought forward by A. Negev, "The Chronology of the Seven-Branched Menorah". *Eretz Israel*, 8, 1967, p. 196 nt. 55.

53. On the expression שלום על ישראל see Psalms, 125, 5, and 128, 6; the expression often appears in inscriptions found in Israel and in the diaspora, as can be seen in Frey's *Corpus*. In the Monteverde catacomb in Rome, the expression appears with *alef mater lectionis* after the *shin* in שאלום .See A.M.Rabello, "Catacombs", *Enc. Judaica*, 5, 1971, pp. 294 ff.

town of Elche (Alicante), not far from the sea. At first, scholars assumed that they relate to a Christian basilica, but later most of them were conviced that they are Jewish inscriptions. Albertini even published a second article in which he withdrew from his first assumption, and explained that the text of these inscriptions does relate to a synagogue (Fig. 5). In any case, even if we accept the assumption that the inscriptions do belong to a synagogue and to the Jews, this does not rule out the possibility that the synagogue was later turned into a church. This was Schlunk's assumption. The inscriptions date to the fourth and fifth centuries, the time of Byzantine rule in the area, and the sixth century when the Visigoths ruled. But in Melida's opinion, the art seems to be Decadent-Roman.

The three inscriptions are written in Greek:[54]

The first is written in black letters on a white background:

πρ[οσ] ευχή λαο[ῦ]

(Frey) which means "the Synagogue of the people of...." or "the Synagogue of L........" The name προσευχή together with συναγογή is the most common expression for a synagogue or a Community.

The leaf design, in the eyes of Frey, seems to be a citron (*ethrog*), a motif which was popular on inscriptions from the ancient period.

54. On these inscriptions see: Juster, *Juifs*, 1, p. 183; 446 nt. 1; Hubner, *CIL*, 2, 515; Frey, CIJ, nn. 662-664; Goodenough, *Jewish Symbols*, 7, p. 177; Ferrua, *Inscripciones*, nn. 431-433; Cantera-Millas, *Inscripciones*, nn. 284-286; Garcia Iglesias, *Judíos*, pp. 11, 16 f.,pp 34, VI, 36; B. Lifshitz, *Donateurs et fondateurs dans les synagogues juives*, Paris, 1967, n. 101.
On the synagogue of Elche see: F. Cantera Burgos, *Sinagogas Españolas*, Madrid, 1955, pp. 212 ff.; Don E. Halperin, *The Ancient Synagogues of the Iberian Peninsula*, U. of Florida 1969. p. 27; Garcia Iglesias, *Judíos*, pp. 11, 34.

Fig. 5: The Synagogue of Elche: Sketch by Ibarra

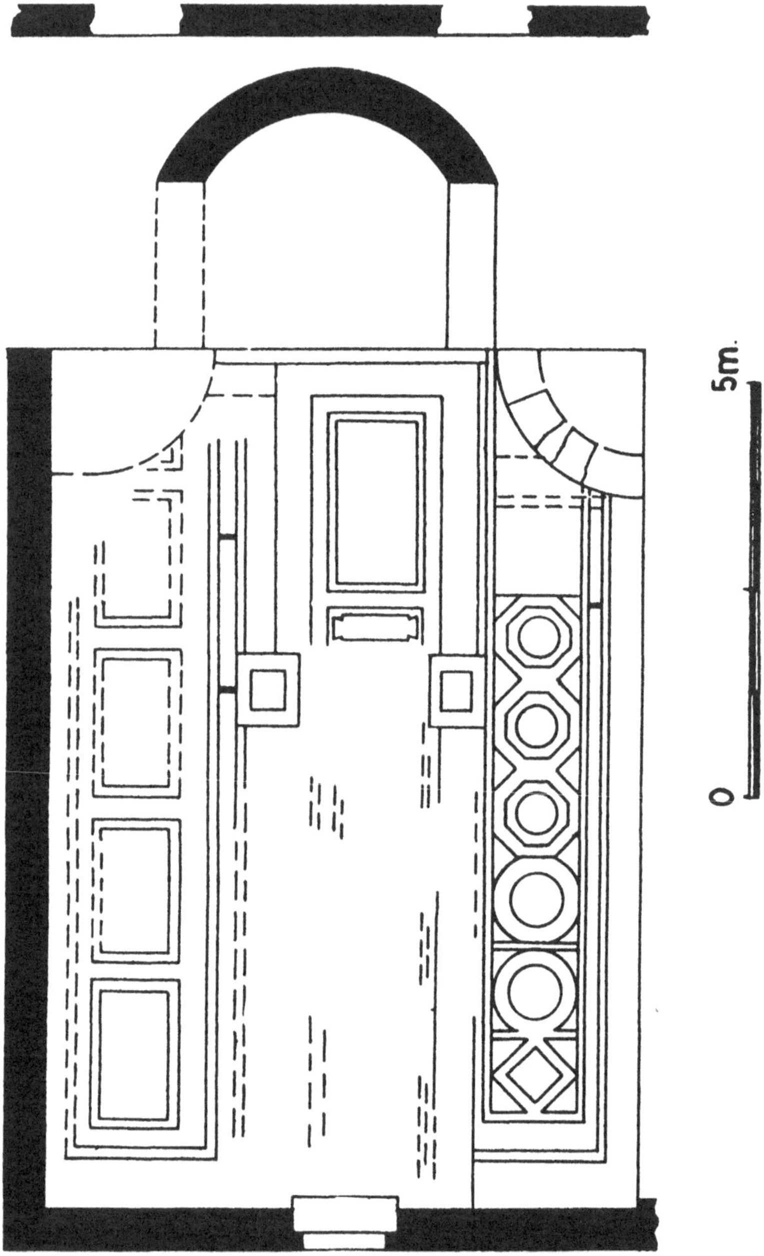

The second inscription is placed at the north of the Synagogue and it reads:

χροχοντον (χησχοντων)κε πρεβυτερων (Ibarra)

ʾαρ]χόντων (?) κε πρε[σ]βυτέρων (Albertini, Ferrua)

It tells of the members of the committee, some who were *Presbyteri* and other special members who were *Archontes.*

The third inscription may be read like this:

εὔπγοια(ν) θ συγχ[ώρησον ʾεμῆ] εὐχὴ

(Ferrua) (.........a pleasant voyage.....)[55],[56],[57],[58],[59],[60],[61]

55. The word προσευχή to indicate a synagogue appears early on and is used continuously. See, for example, inscriptions from the middle of the third century B.C.E. in *Orientis Graeci Inscriptiones Selectae*, ed. W. Dittenberger, Leipzig, 1903, v. i, p. 96, v. 2, p. 726; Frey, *CIJ*, No. 683) from the first century B.C. (and No. 684; Lifshitz, *Prolegomenon* No. 683b from the second century. On this matter see S. Krauss, *Synagogale Altertumer*, Berlin-Vienna, 1922, pp. 11 ff. ; Lifshitz, *Donateurs*, index, p. 91.
56. H. Schlunk, "El arte de la época paleocristiana en el sudeste español. La Sinagoga de Elche y el 'martyrium' de la Alberca", *Cronica del III Congreso Arquelogico del Sudeste Español*, Murcia, 1947, pp. 335 ff.
57. J. Ramon Melida, "El arte romano cristiano", in R. Menendez Pidal, *Historia de España*, vol. II, *España Romana, Madrid*, 1935, p. 721 f.
58. On this term see: J Juster, *Les Juifs dans l'Empire Romain*, I, pp. 413 ff.; A.M. Rabello, *The Legal Condition of the Jews in the Roman Empire*, op. cit., p. 720, nt. 214.
59. H.J. Leon, *The Jews of Ancient Rome* , Philadelphia, 1960, p. 196.
60. J. Juster, *Les Juifs dans l'Empire Romain*, I, pp. 440 ff.
61. See Schlunk, *op. cit.*; see also Cantera-Millas, *Inscripciones*, p. 409.

Albertini[62] is almost certain that it tells of a metaphorical voyage, which means that it is either a voyage in our present world (on earth) or a voyage of the soul to the afterworld. In my opinion, Frey is right in suggesting that the subject in question is expressing gratitude (maybe in the dedication of the synagogue itself ?) following a successful voyage, or even perhaps expressing a wish for a successful voyage. In this matter many speculations can be made, and maybe we can detect a hint that some of the Jews of the congregation earned their living though trade, and therefore used to travel to countries across the sea.

We must not forget that the town was close to the sea, and that it was not very far from Africa.[63] Schlunk reckons that underneath the inscription there must have been a drawing with marine elements but that the drawing was damaged when the inscription was revealed.

HISPANIA BAETICA

Another inscription which was found in Adra (or Abdera) in Baetic Spain brings us back to the beginning of the third century (Fig. 6). This inscription is one of the most ancient pieces of evidence about the Jews of Spain. Baetic Spain is the name of the most southerly province of the peninsula. The name was derived from the name of the river Baetis which crosses the land. The use of Latin was widespread all over Baetic Spain as were many Roman customs. The area was known as very rich, and this was one of the reasons many merchants settled there. The inscription which was found in the area reads

[AN]NIA SALO
[MO]NVLA AN I
MENS IIII DIE I
IVDAEA

62. E. Albertini, "Rapport sommaire sur les fouilles d'Elche (Espagne), *Comptes rendus de l'Académie des Inscriptions et Belles Lettres*, 1905, pp. 619 ff.

63. See, in general, H.Z. Hirschberg, *A History of the Jews in North Africa*, vol. I, *From Antiquity to the Sixteenth Century*, London, 1974.

[Annia (or Yunia or Licinia) Salo(mo)nola one year, four months, one day (old). Jewish].[64]

It is possible that the girl's name was Hanna, and it is interesting to see that in such a small inscription (which suits a little girl) her religious identity is mentioned in the bottom line: *Iudaea* (Jewish). Adding *Iudaeus* to the name was very common, especially in a period in which Christians also used Jewish names.[65] According to García Bellido, the name *Salomonula* indicated a maidservant.[66]

Fita reckons that at the beginning of the inscription there was a drawing of a *menorah*. This view is shared by Cantera-Millas.

In the first, second and third lines of the inscription there are three leaves (perhaps a sign that the little girl passed away like a leaf?) or, according to another interpretation, three citrons.[67]

64. T. Mommsen, *CIL*, 2, n. 1932; J.B. Frey, *CIJ*, n. 665; Ferrua, *Inscripciones*, n. 429; Cantera-Millas, *Inscripciones*, n. 283, (pp. 405-406); F. Fita, "Epigraphos romanos de la cividad de Adra" , *BRAH*, LXXX, 1917, pp. 142-144.
65. On the custom of writing IUDAEUS in inscriptions next to the name, see J. Juster, *Les Juifs dans l'Empire Romain*, I, p. 172 ff.; II, p. 233 f. To Ferrua the matter seems "very rare" in Hebrew inscriptions.
66 A. Garcia, Y. Bellido, "El elemento forestero en Hispania Romana" *BRAH*, 144, 1959, p. 142; Garcia-Iglesias, Judíos p. 35.
67. The citron was a Jewish symbol, used together with the *lulav* at the festival of Succot.

Fig. 6: An inscription from Adra with the reconstruction by Cantera

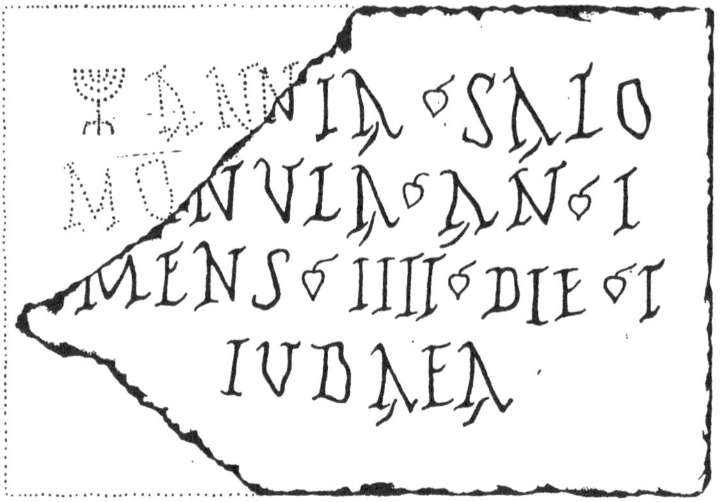

HISPANIA LUSITANENSIS

Lusitania is in the south-west region of the Iberian peninsula. Its capital, founded by Augustus in the year 25 B.C.E. was called *Emerita Augusta*. The area was not directly influenced by Roman culture. The river which crosses the town and reaches the sea had a significant importance for trade, since the town was already known as an important agricultural centre. This is the reason many foreigners settled there, and among them there were also many Jews.[68] From Emerita Augusta we have a number of inscriptions. The most ancient one is probably the inscription of Justinus which is from the second century.[69]

IVSTINUS. MENANDRI. FILIUS
FLAVIVS. NEAPOLITANVS. ANNO

68. E. De Ruggiero, "Hispania", *Dizionario Epigrafico*; E. Albertini, *Les divisions administratives de l'Espagne Romaine*, Paris, 1923.

69. Hubner, *CIL*, 2, 525; Garcia, Judíos, p. 11, 34 (from which the text of the inscription is taken).

XLVI. H.S.E.S.T.T.L.[70] SABINA. MARITO
OPTIMO. ET.MERENTISSIMO.ET
MENANDER FILIVS CVM.SERORIBVS
SVIS.RECEPTA.ET. SALVINA
PATRI PIISIMO [
P[[71]

[Justinus, son of Menander, Flavius Neapolitanus in his forty sixth year. This is where he was buried. May the earth be light for you. Sabina (a tombstone) was placed for the fine and highly privileged husband, and Menander, the son, with his sisters Recepta and Salvina for the very pius father].

In order to identify this inscription as a Jewish one, it ought to be mentioned that the name Justinus which comes from Iustus (Zaddok) is a name which often appears in Jewish inscriptions from the Roman era. Stating the place of origin is also typical of Jews. Flavius Neapolitanus means from the town of Nablus (Flavia Neapolis, the Jewish Shkhem):[72] in this place there was also a strong Samaritan group....

5. Conclusions

In this article we have discussed the special conditions of the Jews in Roman Spain as reflected in general historical sources, Church sources and Jewish inscriptions.[73]

The picture we get is of a society which leads a good way of life.

70. *H*ic *S*epultus *E*st (=is buried here) ; *S*it *T*erra *T*ibi *L*evis (=may the earth be light for you).
This version, like שלום עפרך "peace on your ashes" appears sometimes on tombstones. Compare, for example, with the tombstone of Clandia, *CIL*, 12 1211.

71. *P*osuerunt (= [they] placed).

72. A. Garcia, Y. Bellido, "El elemento forestero en Hispania Romana", *BRAH*, 144, 1959, p. 142

73. The numismatic sources will be checked by Dr. Kindler in the appendix.

This society is loyal to the forefathers' traditions, but also has good relations with its Spanish neighbours, also Christians. Because of this good relationship between the Jews and the Christians the Church became worried and held its first conference relating to the Jews in Spain, in order to separate Jews and Christians.

Realisation of these intentions took place in Spain when Christianity ruled in the Roman Empire As a result, the Jews' legal status worsened, even though at the beginning Imperial legislation passed against the Jews was not applied with full rigor in distant provinces.

However, the basic tenets of the Theodosian Code (438) towards the Jews were applied in Spain.[74]

Two chapters of the *Codex Theodosianus* deal particularly with the Jews: Book XVI. chapter 8: "On Jews, Caelicolae and Samaritans" , and chapter 9: "A Jew may not own a Christian slave". Chapter 8 contains twenty-nine statutes: chapter 9 - four. Laws relating to Jews, sixteen in number, are, however, found also in other chapters, while in other places mention is made of statutes which have not come down to us. Alas, it is important to note that the Code was applied not only in Spain but also in other parts of the Roman Empire, and from a legal point of view, the status of the Jews in Spain was no different from their status elsewhere in the Empire.

The Theodosian Code was cancelled in the year 506 in favour of the *Breviarium Alaricianum* or *Lex Romana Visigothorum*,[75] but this takes us away from Roman Spain to Visigothic Spain.[76]

74. Cf. L. De Giovanni, *Chiesa e Stato nel Codice Teodosiano, Saggio sul libro XVI*, Napoli, 1980; A. Linder, *Roman Imperial Legislation on the Jews*, Jerusalem, 1983.

75. J. Juster, *The Legal Condition of the Jews under the Visigothic kings* (brought up-to-date with a Tribute by A.M. Rabello) Jerusalem 1976.

76 For more on this subject, see A.M. Rabello, *The Jews in Visigothic Spain in the light of the Legislation* (in Hebrew), The Zalman Shazar Centre for the Furtherance of the Study of Jewish History, Jerusalem, 1983.

V

THE BAN ON CIRCUMCISION
AS A CAUSE OF BAR KOKHBA'S REBELLION*

To Reuven and Shoshanna Yaron
with love and gratitude

A) *Circumcision in Roman Sources Before Hadrian*

As far as we can determine from papyri and from Greek and Roman historians, circumcision was practiced among various nations in the

* This is a revised and expanded version of my Hebrew paper, under the same title, in: A. Oppenheimer and U. Rappaport (eds.), *The Bar-Kokhba Revolt — A New Approach*, (Jerusalem, 1984) 27-46.
I would like to thank Mr. Amitai Spitzer for his help with the new version of this article. Additionally, I would like to thank Mr. Noah R. Feldman, Mr. Michael Bar-Yaakov and Mr. David Eisen for their assistance in translating the text.

Roman Empire, particularly in Egypt and Arabia.[1] A few of the most important examples will suffice.

Herodotus addresses circumcision in Egypt and elsewhere:

> ... but my better proof was that the Colchians and Egyptians and Ethiopians are the only nations that have from the first practised circumcision. The Phoenicians and the Syrians of Palestine acknowledge of themselves that they learned the custom from the Egyptians, and the Syrians of the valleys of the Thermodon and the Parthenius, as well as their neighbours the Macrones, say that they learnt it lately from the Colchians.[2]

Diodorus Siculus believes the Egyptians taught this practice to other nations:

1 On this issue and with regard to the sources see in particular: J. Juster, *Les Juifs dans l'Empire Romain. Leur condition juridique, economique et sociale*, I, (New York, 1967; Paris, 1914) 263 ff.; Zmigryder-Konopka, "Les Romains et la circoncision des Juifs", (1931) 33 *Eos* 334 ff.; E.M. Smallwood, "The Legislation of Hadrian and Antoninus Pius against Circumcision", (1959) 18 *Latomus* 342 ff.; Addendum, (1960-1961) 20 *ibid.* 93 ff.; E. Schürer, *The History of the Jewish People in the Age of Jesus Christ, 175 B.C.-135 A.D.*, revised and edited by G. Vermes and F. Millar, I, (Edinburgh, 1973) 537 ff.; A.M. Rabello, "The Legal Condition of the Jews in the Roman Empire", (1980) 13 *Aufstieg und Niedergang der Römischen Welt*, vol. II,, pp. 662 ff. (see in particular pp. 699 ff).
The texts of the Classic authors are discussed by M. Stern in: M. Stern, *Greek and Latin Authors on Jews and Judaism*, (= Stern, GLA), I-II, (Jerusalem, 1974-1980). See also: T. Reinach, *Textes d'auteurs grecs et romains relatifs au Judaïsme*, (Paris, 1895); L.H.Feldman, *Jew and Gentile in the Ancient World*, (Princeton, 1993) 153 ff. For a recent bibliography see: P. Schäfer, "Hadrian's Policy in Judaea and the Bar Kokhba Revolt: a Reassessment", Ph.R. Davies and R.I. White (eds.), *A Tribute to Geza Vermes*, (Sheffield, 1990) 281-303 (= *Journal for the Study of the Old Testament. Supplement Series 100*); A. Kloner, "Underground Hiding Complexes from the Bar Kokhba War in the Judaean Shephelah", (1983) 46 Biblical Archaeologist 210-221; A. Opppenheimer and B. Isaac, "The Bar Kokhba Revolt — Modern Scholarship", in: A. Kloner and Y. Tepper (eds.), *Underground Hiding Complexes in the Judaean Shephelah*, (Tel-Aviv, 1987, in Hebrew); B. Isaac, *The Limits of Empire — the Roman Army in the East*, (Oxford, 1990); I. Shatzman, "The Limits of Empire: Review Article", (1994) 44 IEJ 129-135.

2 Herodotus, *Historiae*, II, 104, 2-3. The English translation by A.D. Godley, *Loeb Classical Library*. On the text of Herodotus see: Stern, *GLA*, no. 1. Note especially his extensive remarks, as we shall concentrate our discussion mainly on the legal aspects grounded in the sources.

> They say also that those who set forth with Danaus, likewise from Egypt, settled what is practically the oldest city of Greece, Argos, and that the nation of the Colchi in Pontus and that of the Jews, which lies between Arabia and Syria, were founded as colonies by certain emigrants from their country; and this is the reason why it is a long-established institution among these two peoples to circumcise their male children, the custom having being brought over from Egypt.[3] And the proof which they offer of the Egyptian origin of this nation is the fact that the Colchi practise circumcision even as the Egyptians do, the custom continuing among the colonists sent out from Egypt as it also did in the case of the Jews.[4]

The idea that the origins of circumcision lay in Egypt also appears in Strabo of Ameseia (one should point out that Judaism never practiced female circumcision, *ektome*).

> One of the customs most zealously observed among the Egyptians is this, that they rear every child that is born, and circumcise the males, and excise the females, as is also customary among the Jews, who are also Egyptians in origin, as I have already stated in my account of them.[5]

It is thus clear that circumcision existed among various peoples and that this was known to classical writers. At the same time some writers, such as Petronius, saw circumcision as an indicator of Judaism: '*Circumcise us, so that we will appear to be Jews*'.[6] Others saw circumcision as a sign that served to make Jews distinct, as Tacitus states: '*They established circumcision so that it would be a sign for them to distinguish them from others*'.[7] Such a view also existed in the fourth century:

3 Diodorus Siculus, *Bibliotheca Historica*, I,8:2-3 (= Stern, *GLA*, no. 55; trans. A.D. Godley, *Loeb Classical Library*).

4 *Ibidem*, I,55:5 (= Stern, *GLA*, no. 57; trans. C.H. Oldfather, *Loeb Classical Library*).

5 Strabo, *Geographica*, XVII,2:5 (= Stern, *GLA*, no. 124; trans. H.L. Jones, *Loeb Classical Library*).

6 Petronius, *Satyricon*, 102:14 (= Stern, *GLA*, no. 194; trans. M. Heseltine, *Loeb Classical Library*): '*circumcide nos, ut Iudaei videamur*'; see also: Satyricon, 68:4-8 (= Stern, *GLA*, no. 193) and Stern's remark on p. 443 concerning 'recutitus'; see also Poem no. 24 (*Fragmenta*, no. 37 = Stern, *GLA*, no. 195), and the discussion further down.

7 Tacitus, *Historiae*, V,5:2 (= Stern, *GLA*, no. 281 and note on p. 41); see *infra* n. 35.

Sallustius Neoplatonicus writes of the Hebrews who circumcise themselves.[8] Finally, this attitude appears in a later legal text which speaks of circumcision as the '*Jewish sign*'.[9]

There can be no doubt that historically Jews attached great importance to circumcision as a tangible sign of God's covenant with the people of Israel:

> God further said to Abraham, 'As for you, you shall keep My covenant, you and your offspring to come, throughout the ages. Such shall be the covenant, which you shall keep, between Me and you and your offspring to follow: every male among you shall be circumcised. You shall circumcise the flesh of your foreskin, and that shall be the sign of the covenant between Me and you. At the age of eight days, every male among you throughout the generations shall be circumcised, even the homeborn slave and the one bought from an outsider who is not of your seed. The slave that is born in your household or bought with your money shall be circumcised! Thus shall my covenant be marked in your flesh as an everlasting pact. An uncircumcised male who does not circumcise the flesh of his foreskin — such a person shall be cut off from his kin; he has broken My covenant'.[10]

In the Hasmonean period another religious aspect became involved with the Jewish practice of circumcision — that of sanctifying God's name through martyrdom. After Antiochus IV Epiphanes banned circumcision, many chose to ignore the command of the mortal king rather than that of the divine King, and suffered for it a terrible death:

> The women who had their sons circumcised they put to death according to the decree, hanging their babes from their mothers' necks and executing also their husbands [or: families] and the men who had performed the circumcision.[11]
> Two women were brought to trial for having circumcised their children. Their babes were hanged from their breasts, and the women

8 Sallustius Neoplatonicus, *De Deis et Mundo*, IX,5 (= Stern, *GLA*, no. 448).

9 *Codex Theodosianus*, XVI:8:22: '*nota Iudaica*'.

10 *Genesis*, 17:9-14.

11 I *Maccabees*, 1:60-61 (trans. J.A. Goldstein, *Anchor Bible*).

were paraded publicly through the city and hurled down from the walls.[12]

In the Roman Empire circumcision was not banned before the reign of Hadrian. Thus we can understand Herod's insistence that Syllaeus the Arabian become circumcised before marrying Herod's sister Salome: the marriage never took place because of Syllaeus' refusal.[13] A similar incident occured in the case of the proposed marriage between Agrippa I's daughter and Epiphanes, the son of the king of Commagene.[14] Aziz, king of Emasa, was circumcised in 52 C.E.,[15] and Polemus, king of Pontus and Cilicia, was circumcised in 63 C.E.[16]

Domitian established a penalty for castration,[17] but not for circumcision. At the same time he took the opportunity to enact reforms in the eunuch trade. "This contradiction, intended or not, constituted the source for repeated and long lasting failures in the enforcement of the laws".[18] Thus Suetonius explains: "He prohibited the castration of males, and he lowered the price of the eunuchs who remained in the hands of the slave dealers".[19] Cassius Dio also mentions Domitian's ban on castration, and he attempts to provide the reason for the ban.[20] It seems likely that Domitian's ban stemmed simply from moral motives, from the struggle for modesty and against lack of decency. However, Prof. Dalla suggests another cause. Despite the ban on castration, commerce

12 II *Maccabees*, 6:10 (trans. J.A. Goldstein, *Anchor Bible*): On this problem see: Y. Efron, *Studies of the Hasmonean Period*, (Tel-Aviv, 1980, in Hebrew) 50 ff.

13 Josephus Flavius, *Antiquitates Judaeorum*, 16:7:6 (225); see also: J. Juster, *supra* n. 1, at 264; B.J. Bamberger, *Proselytism in the Talmudic Period*, (Cincinnati, 1939) 21 ff.; A. Shalit, *King Herod — Portrait of a Ruler*, (Jerusalem, 1964, in Hebrew) 227.

14 Josephus Flavius, *ibid.*, 19:9:1 (355), 20:7:1 (139).

15 *Ibid.*

16 *Ibid.*, 20:7:3 (145).

17 On the relations between this controversial Emperor and the Jews see: E.M. Smallwood, "Domitian's Attitude toward Jews and Judaism", (1956) 51 Classical Philology 1 ff.; A.M. Rabello, "Domitian", *Enc. Judaica*, VI, 1971, col. 164; S. Applebaum, "Domitian's Assassination: The Jewish Aspect", (1974) 1 *Scripta Classica Israelica* 116 ff.

18 D. Dalla, *L'incapacità sessuale in Diritto Romano* [= Dalla] (Milano, 1978) 78 (our translation).

19 Suetonius, *Domitianus*, 7: '*castrari mares vetuit; spadonum, qui residui apud mangones erant, pretia moderatus est*'.

20 According to Cassius Dio (67:2:3), the motive was Domitian's contempt of the memory of his brother, Titus. On this subject see: Dalla, *supra* n. 18, at 82, n. 28.

in eunuchs continued through imports. Dalla reminds us of a passage from Marcianus (*Dig.* 39:4:16:7) which indicates that Indian eunuchs were a commodity on which tax had to be paid:

> We cannot absolutely eliminate the possibility that in addition to trying to rule in a society which more and more devoted itself to corruption and pleasures of the flesh, there was also the desire to impose a tax on the eunuch trade in order to obtain not insignificant revenues for the treasury. The ban required purchasers to turn to the import market and strove to prevent circumvention of the law.[21]

Dalla's point is logical, and seems particularly reasonable in the context of the terrifying and cruel investigation of the *fiscus Iudaicus*. Suetonius recounts:

> Besides other taxes, that on the Jews was levied with the utmost rigour, and those were prosecuted who without publicly acknowledging that faith yet lived as Jews, as well as those who concealed their origin and did not pay the tribute levied upon their people. I recall being present in my youth when the person of a man ninety years old was examined before the procurator and a very crowded court, to see whether he was circumcised.[22]

It is obvious that ban on circumcision was not the issue in this case, and that Domitian clearly did not ban circumcision. "Domitian's ac-

21 Dalla, *supra* n. 18, at 83.

22 Suetonius, *Domitianus*, 12:2 (= Stern, *GLA*, no. 320; see his notes on pp. 129-131; trans. J.C. Rolfe, *Loeb Classical Library*): *Praeter ceteros Iudaicus fiscus acerbissime actus est; ad quem deferebantur qui vel ut inprofessi Iudaicam viverent vitam vel dissimulata origine imposita genti tributa non pependissent. Interfuisse me adulescentulum memini, cum a procuratore frequentissimoque consilio inspiceretur nonagenarius senex, an circumsectus esset.*
See also: M. Hengel, *Judaism and Hellenism. Studies in their Encounter in Palestine during the Early Hellenistic Period*, II, (London, 1974) 204, n. 303: 'After A.D. 70 the *fiscus Judaicus* was levied from every circumcised Jew, even the proselytes. Intrinsically a punitive tax for the rebellious "ethnos" of the Jews (see Suetonius, *Domitian*, 12:2: *imposita genti tributa*), it also affected the Jews as a "religious association"'. And see also *ibid.*, at 306.

tions", argues Juster, "resulted from his greediness".[23] The Emperor's intervention against castration was achieved by extending the application of the already existing ban on murder included in the *Lex Cornelia de Sicariis*, although we do not know to what extent.[24]

In the year 96 C.E., Domitian's successor, the moderate Nerva, abolished the investigation of the *fiscus Iudaicus* (although not the tax itself) by means of a *senatus consultum*. To commemorate the occasion a coin was struck: '*Fisci Judaici calumnia sublata*'.[25] Nerva also dealt with the ban on castration, according to Cassius Dio (68:2:4). The decree mentioned in *Dig*. 48:8:6 (of Venulius Saturninus, *De officio proconsulis*, Book 1) can be attributed to Nerva:

> It is provided by a *senatus consultum* given in the consulship of Neratius Priscus and Annius Verus that whoever hands his slave over for castration is fined half his property.[26]

This decree, which apparently originated in the year 97 C.E., establishes that one who castrates a slave will forfeit half of his property. In contrast to Mommsen's opinion, nothing whatsoever is said about the fate of the slave himself, particularly not that he would be granted freedom on

23 With regard to the fiscal reasons for Domitian's decree, Juster assumes *(supra* n. 1, vol. 2, at 284, n. 3) that there was a discrimination between the rich and the poor with regards to the Jewish proselytes (vol. 1, p. 257 f., n. 1): "It is also possible that Domitian used double standards: he imposed taxes on the poor who practiced Judaism without asking more, but in accordance with custom he preferred to prosecute the rich and to put them in a situation where they would refuse to worship the 'official gods', this in order to take control of their possessions". (our translation).

24 For an essential bibliography on '*Lex Cornelia de Sicariis*' see: A.M. Rabello, *Effetti personali della 'patria potestas'*, I: *Dalle Origini al periodo degli Antonini*, (Milano, 1979) 144; on the background story concerning Domitian's edict see: F. Grella, "La 'correctio morum' nella legislazione flavia", (1980) 13 *Aufstieg und Niedergang der Römischen Welt*, Vol. II, 340 ff., esp. n. 18 and 19.

25 On '*fisci iudaici calumnia sublata*' see: F. Bruce, "Nerva and the Fiscus Judaicus", (1964) 96 Palestine Exploration Quarterly 34 ff.

26 *Dig*. 48:8:6: '*Is, qui servum castrandum tradiderit, pro parte dimidia bonorum multatur, ex senatus consulto, quod Neratio Prisco et Annio Vero consulibus factum est*'. Some scholars attribute the edict to Domitian (Mommsen, Rohden, Pernice, Hitzing, Buckland, Stein, Orestano and others); Karlowa, however, leaves this question open. For bibliography and discussion see: Dalla, *supra* n. 18, at 85 and n. 37.

the basis of this alone.[27] In addition, *Dig.* 48:8:3:4 (Marcianus, *Institutiones*, Book 14) mentions a *senatus consultum* regarding castration:

> Again, anyone who castrates a man for lust or for gain is by *senatus consultum* subject to the penalty of the *lex Cornelia.*[28]

In the same book of the *Institutiones*, Marcianus indicates (*Dig.* 48:8:3:5):

> The penalty of the *lex Cornelia* on murderers and poisoners is deportation to an island and forfeiture of all property. However, nowadays capital punishment is customary, except for those persons of a status too high to be subject to the modern [statutory] punishment; those of lower rank are usually either crucified or thrown to the beasts while their betters are deported to an island.[29]

Our purpose is to give just a few basic facts to investigate the background for the ban on castration. Thus it is sufficient to emphasize

27 Th. Mommsen, *Römisches Strafrecht*, (Leipzig, 1955; 1899) 637, n. 6: "Following the castration of the slave, he becomes free, and half of his master's property is confiscated". Following Mommsen, Juster wrote, *supra* n. 1, vol. I, p. 269): ". . . en recompense de la mutilation qu'ils ont subie, le legislateur — à l'époque païenne comme à l'époque chrétienne leur rend la liberté"; and also (*ibid.*, n. 2): "La chose est certaine pour l'esclave chatré, *Dig.* 48:8:6". The lack of precision in this interpretation has already been noticed by E. Volterra, 'Intorno ad alcune costituzioni di Costantino', *Rendiconti Accademia Nazionale dei Lincei*, rend. morali, ser. VIII, vol. 13, fasc. 3-4 (1958), p. 87 ff., although he refers only to Juster (p. 87, n. 62). About the text under discussion Volterra has to say: "*Come si può constatare dalla semplice lettura del testo, il senatusconsulto puniva la castrazione dello schiavo, comminando la multa della metà dei beni all'autore del fatto, ma non concedeva affatto la libertà allo schiavo. Una norma siffatta non avrebbe mai potuto essere dichiarata nel diritto classico, in quanto contrastante con i piu elementari principi giuridici in tema di schiavitú*".

E.E. Urbach too follows Juster: "The Laws regarding Slavery as a Source for Social History of the Second Temple, the Mishnah and Talmud", *Papers of the Institute of Jewish Studies*, (London, 1964) 52, n. 131; see in contrast, without giving reference to Mommsen or Volterra: A. Linder, "The Roman Imperial Government and the Jews under Constantine", (1974-1975) 44 *Tarbiz* 134, n. 210. Dalla does not discuss this issue.

28 *Dig.* 48:8:3:4: '*et qui hominem libidinis vel promercii causa castraverit, ex senatus consulto poena legis Corneliae punitur*'. See: Dalla, *supra* n. 18 at 86 ff.

29 *Dig.* 48:8:3:5: '*Legis Corneliae de sicariis et veneficis poena insulae deportatio est et omnium bonorum ademptio. Sed solent hodie...*'. See: Dalla, *supra* n. 18, at 87 ff.

that Domitian undertook a legislative action with the purpose of banning castration, and that he named as punishment that which is fixed by the *lex Cornelia de sicariis*. Nerva continued this action, broadening it and changing a number of details. However, the ban remained based on the *lex Cornelia de sicariis*.

Thus, along the whole period before Hadrian's reign, circumcision remained permitted. Since the Empire had not passed laws against circumcision, a few Christians escaped persecution by pretending to be circumcised Jews, and therefore entitled to the privileges enjoyed by the Jews. First among these was the right not to participate in the cult of the Emperor. Even if it was worthless from a legal perspective, practically it was difficult to distinguish between circumcised Jews and circumcised Christians. This is particularly noticable in Jerome's commentary on the Epistle to the Galatians:

> Gaius Caesar, Octavianus Augustus, and Tiberius, Augustus' successor, promulgated laws which established that the Jews, spread throughout the Roman Empire, could live according to their religion and follow their fathers' practices. Therefore, anyone circumcised, even if he were a Christian, was thought by the gentiles to be a Jew, but someone [i.e., a Christian] not circumcised, whose foreskin revealed that he was not a Jew, was subject to persecution by both Jews and gentiles. These persecutions destroyed the Galatians, and in their desire to escape them they convinced their students to circumcise themselves for their own protection ... For neither Jews nor gentiles could persecute them, when they saw them both circumcising their proselytes and fulfilling the commandments of the Law.[30]

30 *Ad Gal.*, 6:12 (Migne, *Patrologia Latina*, 26, col. 435): "*Gaius Caesar, et Octavianus Augustus, et Tiberius successor Augusti, leges promulgaverant, ut Judaei qui erant in toto Romani imperii orbe dispersi, proprio ritu viverent, et patriis caeremoniis deservirent. Quicumque igitur circumcisus erat, licet in Christum crederet, quasi Judaeus habebatur a Gentibus. Qui vero absque circumcisione se non esse Judaeum praeputio praeferebat, persecutionibus tam Gentilium, quam Judaeorum fiebat cbnoxius. Has igitur persecutiones hiqui Galatas depravaverant declinare cupientes, circumcisionem pro defensione discipulis persuadebant etc... Nam nec Judaei persequi eos poterant nec Gentiles, quos videbant et proselytos circumcidere, et ipsos Legis praecepta servare*".
However, it must be remembered that the opposite phenomenon existed: Christian-Jews or assimilated Jews, in most cases preferred to have an operation — the *epispasmos* — that will conceal the signs of circumcision, to be exempted from paying the '*fiscus Judaicus*'.

V

B) *The Period of Hadrian*

1) *The New Ban on Castration and Bar Kokhba's Revolt*

Hadrian[31] reiterated the ban on castration. Apparently, as we may infer from Juvenal's *Sixth Satire* (lines 368-376), the earlier bans were not enforced. It was for this reason that Hadrian intervened, as Ulpian reports in the seventh book of *De officio proconsulis*:

> Likewise deified Hadrian wrote in a rescript: It is laid down, that none shall become eunuch. Yet those who shall be found guilty of this crime are to be liable to the penalty of the *lex Cornelia*, and their goods must deservedly be forfeit to my imperial treasury. Slaves, however, who become eunuchs are to be punished with the extreme penalty. And if those who are liable on this charge fail to appear in court, sentence is to be pronounced in their absence as if they were liable under the *lex Cornelia*. It is certain that if those who have suffered this injury announce that they have lost their manhood, the provincial governor must give them a hearing; for no one should castrate another, freeman or slave, willing or unwilling, nor should anyone voluntarily offer himself for castration. Should anyone act in defiance of my edict, the doctor performing the *excision* shall suffer a capital penalty, as shall anyone who voluntarily offered himself for excision.[32]

31 About Hadrian see: T. Henderson, *The Life and Principate of the Emperor Hadrian*, (London, 1923); F. Pringsheim, "The Legal Policy and Reforms of Hadrian", (1934) 24 Journal of Roman Studies 141 ff. (now in: *Gesammelte Abhandlungen*, I, Heidelberg 1961, pp. 91 ff.); A. D'Orgeval, *L'Empereur Hadrien. Oeuvre legislative et administrative*, (Paris, 1950); A. Thornton, "Hadrian and his Reign", (1975) 2 *Aufstieg und Niedergang der Römischen Welt*, II, 432 ff. With regard to certain legal aspects see: Rabello, *supra* n. 24, at 239 ff.

32 *Dig.* 48:8:4:2: *Idem divus Hadrianus rescripsit: Constitutum quidem est, ne spadones fierent, eos autem, qui hoc crimine arguerentur, Corneliae legis poena teneri eorumque bona merito fisco meo vindicari debere, sed et in seruos, qui spadones fecerint, ultimo supplicio animadvertendum esse, et qui hoc crimine tenetur, si non adfuerint, de absentibus quoque, tamquam lege Corneliae teneantur, pronuntiandum esse. Plane si ipsi, qui hanc iniuriam passi sunt, proclamaverint, audire eos praeses provinciae debet, qui virilitatem amiserunt: nemo enim liberum seruumue inuitum sinentemue castrare debet, neque quis se sponte castrandum praebere debet. At si quis adversus edictum meum fecerit, medico quidem, qui* exciderit, *capitale erit, item ipsi qui se sponte* excidendum *praebuit.*
On other compilations similar to Ulpian, see: A. Dell'Oro, *I libri de officio della Giurisprudenza Romana*, (Milano, 1960). On Ulpian's style see R. Yaron, "Semitisms in Ulpian?" (1987) 55 *Tijdschrift voor Rechtgeschiedenis* 3 ff.

Clearly, there now existed a need to seek means of circumventing the ban.[33] This led to the legal equation of castration by crushing (*thlibias facere*) with castration by normal means (*Dig.* 48:8:5, Paulus, Book 2: *De officio proconsulis*):

> Under the constitution of the deified Hadrian to Ninnius Hasta, those who crush the testicles are under the same legal case as those who castrate [with a knife].[34]

A short time before Hadrian, Tacitus spoke of the circumcision of converts to Judaism without reference to prohibition of the practice. Had the practice been prohibited, it seems unlikely that such a scrupulous historian would have failed to mention it:

> They adopted circumcision to distinguish themselves from other people by this difference. Those who are converted to their ways follow the same practice, and the earliest lesson they receive is to despise the gods.[35]

33 See: Dalla, *supra* n. 18, at 90 f.; A. Linder, *supra* n. 27, at 126 f. and n. 103.

34 *Dig.* 48:8:5 (Paulus, 1:2, *De officio proconsulis*): '*Hi quoque, qui thlibias faciunt, ex constitutione divi Hadriani ad Ninnium Hastam in eadem causa sunt, qua hi qui castrant*'. See Dalla, *supra* n. 18, at 91 f. According to J. Geiger ("The Ban on Circumcision and the Bar-Kokhba Revolt", [1976] 41 *Zion* 141, n. 8), this is the clearest proof that Hadrian's edict (in *Dig.* 48:8:4:2) did not include circumcision; otherwise, how could it be assumed that Ninnius Hasta approached Hadrian and asked him whether *thlibias facere* was included in the ban? In my opinion, the problem is solved by taking a close look at the edict's last sentence. We shall discuss this further later on.

35 *Historiae*, V,5:2 (English translation by C.H. Moore, *Loeb Classical Library*): '*Circumcidere genitalia instituerunt, ut diversitate noscantur. Transgressi in morem eorum idem usurpant...*'. On this paragraph, which was only partly quoted (see also *supra* n. 10) see especially: Juster, *supra* n. 1, at 264-265, n. 2: '*s'il y avait eu peine, Tacite aurait, avec son admirable concision, ajoute un mot, ou deux, pour dire qu'ils le firent contrairement à des lois précises*'. See also: Stern, *GLA*, II, p. 41. On the diffusion of Judaism even amongst the Senatorial class see especially: J. Derenbourg, *Essai sur l'histoire et la geographie de la Palestine*, (Paris, 1867) 334 ff.; Bamberger, *supra* n. 13, especially 255 ff.; M. Stern, "Sympathy for Jews among Roman Senatorial Circles in the Ancient Empire Period", (1964) 29 *Zion* 155 ff.; A.M. Rabello, *supra* n. 1, at 696 ff.

Did Hadrian forbid *circumcision* as well as *castration*? If so, did the ban *precede* Bar Kokhba's revolt? Although many scholars feel otherwise, we maintain that Hadrian did ban circumcision, and that this was one of the factors leading to the outbreak of the revolt. There are a number of relevant Latin and Hebrew passages which indicate this.

The first evidence is that of Pseudo-Spartianus: "At that time the Jews too began war because they were forbidden to mutilate (*mutilare*) the sexual organs" (*Scriptores Historiae Augustae*,[36] *Vita Hadriani*, 14:2).[37]

36 As is well known, scholars have argued for a long time about the historic value of the '*Historia Augusta*'. Amongst recent studies see especially: A. Momigliano, "An Unsolved Problem of Historical Forgery: The Scriptores Historiae Augustae", in *Secondo contributo alla Storia degli Studi Classici*, (Rome, 1960) 105 ff. with two appendices; *Atti del Colloquio Patavino sulla Historia Augusta*, (Rome, 1963); *Historia Augusta. Colloquium*, (Bonn, 1964-1975/6); R. Syme, *Ammianus and the Historia Augusta*, (Oxford, 1968); and its criticism by Momigliano, included in: *Quinto contributo alla storia degli studi classici e del mondo antico*, I, (Rome, 1975) 93 ff., 104 ff.; Barnes, *The Sources of the Historia Augusta*, (Bruxelles, 1978); Stern, *GLA*, II, pp. 612 ff.

37 *Scriptores Historiae Augustae, Vita Hadriani*, 14:2: '*Moverunt ea tempestate et Iudaei bellum quia vetabantur mutilare genitalia*'. The issue is widely discussed by scholars without reaching an agreement. The following scholars accept the historic value of this statement and argue that the ban on circumcision should be attributed to Hadrian, that it occurred prior to the Bar Kochba revolt, and that it was one of its causes (some even claim that it was its only cause): E. Schürer, *Geschichte des Jüdischen Volkes*, I, (Leipzig, 1901) 675 ff.; *Idem*, in the new, English edition, *supra* n. 1, at 536 ff.; J. Juster, *supra* n. 1, II, at 190 ff. and especially note 1 on 191; Th. Mommsen, *supra* n. 27, at 567 ff., G. Alon, *The Jews in their Land in the Talmudic Age*, II, (Jerusalem, 1984) 520 ff.; S. Safrai, "Sicaricon", (1962) 17 *Zion* 56 ff.; Smallwood, *supra* n. 1, 1959, pp. 344 ff.; 1961, pp. 93 ff.; S. Liebermann, "The Martyrs of Caesarea", *Annuaire de l'Institut de Philologie et d'Histoire Orientales et Slaves*, VII (1939-1944) 423-424: "From both Jewish and non-Jewish sources it appears that Hadrian's prohibition preceded the Jewish rebellion . . . There can be no doubt that the prohibition was one of the causes which stimulated the Jewish rebellion"; M.D. Herr, "Persecutions and Martyrdom in Hadrian's Days", *Scripta Hierosolymitana*, XXII (1972) 86, n. 1; S. Follet, "Hadrian en Egypte et en Judée", (1968) 42 *Revue de Philologie de Litérature et d'Histoire Anciennes* 54 ff.; S. Applebaum, "Some New Aspects of the Second Revolt", in *Studies in the History of the Jewish People and the Land of Israel*, II, (Haifa, 1972, in Hebrew) 39 ff.; E.E. Urbach, *The Sages — Their Concepts and Beliefs*, (Jerusalem, 1979, index); A. Linder, *supra* n. 27, at 132 ff,;

Spartianus relates to events preceeding the Bar Kokhba revolt, and considers in explicit terms the ban on circumcision as the cause of the revolt. Scholars have correctly seen the phrase *'mutilare genitalia'* as a reference to the ban on castration renewed by Hadrian (*Dig.* 48:8:4:2). However, it is our position that in this renewal not only castration, but circumcision as well, could be banned and punished by means of the *Lex Cornelia de sicariis*. It is reasonable to assume that like the ban on castration, the ban on circumcision held force over Jews and non-Jews throughout the Empire. We have no information on any attempt to enforce the ban in Rome, and no reason to believe the Jews in Rome gave

M.D. Herr, "The Causes of the Bar-Kokhba War", (1978) 43 *Zion* 1 ff.; Dalla, *supra* n. 18, at 91 ff.; A.M. Rabello, "A Tribute to Jean Juster", (1976) 11 Is. L. R. 223 ff.; S. Applebaum, "Prolegomena to the Study of the Second Jewish Revolt (132-135 A.D.)", *BAR*, Supplementary Series 7 (1976), pp. 6 ff.: "It is therefore to be assumed that the decisions to prohibit circumcision and to found Aelia were taken in the same period if not at the same time, and that they involved a major change of policy on the part of the Emperor". (p. 9); E.M. Smallwood, *The Jews under Roman Rule from Pompey to Diocletian*, (Leiden, 1976) 428 ff.; Stern, *GLA*, no. 511; A.M. Rabello, *supra* n. 1, at 739-741; L.H.Feldman, *supra* n. 1, at 100.

Yet, as we have stated, not all scholars agree with this interpretation. Some accept only Cassius Dio's' version (see *infra*): D. Rokeah ("Kosbaean Remarks", [1966] 35 *Tarbiz* 127 ff.) claims that the ban on circumcision was an outcome of the revolt, not one of its causes. C.D. Mantel too ("The Causes of the Bar-Kochba Revolt", [1968] 58 Jewish Quarterly Review 224 ff.) is of the opinion that not only Spartianus but also Cassius Dio confused cause and result, and that the revolt was actually caused by the Jewish people's desire for freedom. He claims that various decrees were inflicted on the Jews and their religion after the revolt. J. Geiger, *supra* n. 34, at 129 ff., arrives at the conclusion that Hadrian did not announce a general edict prohibiting circumcision; the decree was inflicted only locally as a punishing act following the revolt. In his opinion, the first to announce a general edict against circumcision was Antoninus Pius. This theory however was not accepted. We refer the reader to Herr's criticism in the second study mentioned here (1978), p. 9, n. 41. Schäfer has a similar theory (P. Schäfer, "The Causes of the Bar-Kochba Revolt", in *Studies in Aggadah, Targum and Jewish Liturgy in Memory of Joseph Heinemann* (Jerusalem, 1981) 11 ff.; *Idem*, 1990, *supra* n. 1, at 293ff.) which we cannot accept: The Bar Kokhba Revolt was a result, not only of the Jewish-Roman conflict, but also a result of the internal conflict between the Jews, in which Hadrian's role was much less prominent than has hitherto been thought (1981, p. 94). According to him, it is not possible to rely on Spartianus. See our remarks on Schäfer's opinion *infra*.

up one of Judaism's most basic practices.[38] Yet, the ban was probably enforced, in particular in the Eastern regions of the Empire (Syria, Palestine, Arabia, Egypt): i.e., the regions where circumcision was most heavily practiced.

Thus if we accept Spartianus as a reliable source (as we choose to do), Hadrian initiated the ban on circumcision *before* Bar Kokhba's revolt.[39] But why does no other Roman source mention explicitly that Hadrian banned circumcision? It seems very unlikely that such an apparently important decree would reach us only on the authority of Spartianus and in the echo of a statement by Modestinus (*Dig.* 48:8:11). The answer to this question lies in the passage quoted above in which Ulpian speaks of Hadrian's ban (*Dig.* 48:8:4:2).

As we saw, Hadrian renewed the ban on castration. But was the ban simply renewed, or was something added to it? In the text, the phrases *castrare* and *spadones facere* are followed *for the first time* by the more general term *excidere* — to cut out: *medico quidem* (relating to the doctor) *qui exciderit* (who has cut); *item ipsi* (or to him) *qui se sponte excidendum praebuit* (who voluntarily agreed to cut). Might there have been a significant difference between *excidere* and *circumcidere*?

2) *Succidere — Excidere — Circumcidere;* מול (mwl) — גזר (gzr)

In order to answer this question we will first investigate the meaning of *excidere* and other similar concepts; then the sense of the biblical Hebrew root מול (*mwl*), generally translated as *circumcidere*.

38 See, *inter alia*, M. Stern, *GLA*, II, p. 621: "It may only be suggested that the general ban on circumcision, as ordained by Hadrian, left some room for special permission to be granted to Jews to circumcise their children, similar to the permission given to them later by Antoninus Pius and that given to the Egyptian priests. Thus, we may assume that the later Roman legislation relating to Jews was foreshadowed under Hadrian. Such an innovation, implying a limitation on proselytism, could well constitute one of the causes of the revolt". Already in a review published in 1968, I wrote that: "The Jews of Rome were not those who revolted; on the other hand, we do not have any information about restrictions against the Jews of Rome, except for the ban on circumcision". I have also stated, although with some reservation, that "it was precisely in Rome where they avoided the ban, taking into consideration that we do not have any evidence regarding punishments which were supposedly inflicted as a result, and the Jews most probably did continue to circumcise their sons" (1969) 15 *Labeo* 110).

39 On the passage by Spartianus, *cf.*: Derenbourg, *supra* n. 35, at 419, n. 5.

Forcellini's Latin dictionary[40] gives many examples of the use of the term *excidere*, beginning with the general meaning of 'to cut' and continuing to 'mining precious stones'[41] and 'cutting out of a person's tongue'.[42] One phrase mentioned is *partum mulieri excidere*, meaning 'to perform a Caesarean delivery'. A number of examples resemble, though are not identical with, the meaning 'to castrate'.

Ovid (*Fasti* 4:361) asks: '*Cur igitur Gallos, qui se excidere, vocamus*'? which J.G. Frazer translates as '*Why then do we give the name Galli to the men who unman themselves?*'[43]

In his *Epigrams*, (3:91:9) Martialis speaks of: '*continuo ferrum noxia turba rapit excidunt senem spondae*', which W. Ker translates '*and mutilate the old sire who lay in his part of the bed*'.[44] That *excidere* is translated as '*to mutilate*' is important for understanding Spartianus' use of *mutilare genitalia* (mutilation of the genitals).[45]

According to E. Forcellini's *Lexicon totius latinitatis*, *circumcidere* means 'cutting all around'. This term also carries a wide range of meanings, including 'to cut off the foreskin', by extension 'to cut', and 'to remove that which is extra'. *Circumcisus* is defined as 'one who has been circumcised', or 'one whose foreskin has been removed by a knife which was drawn around the organ'. For *circumcido* the *Oxford Latin Dictionary* yields, among other things, 'to cut or make an incision round', and 'to remove by cutting round a thing', referring to Cornelius Celsus (6:18:2:1), *cutis ipsa circumcidenda est*, relating to cicumcision.[46]

40 Vol. II, p. 218, there is a list of sources; see also: *Oxford Latin Dictionary*, 1968, s.v. *excido*².

41 Cicero, *De officiis*, III,2.

42 Cicero, *De oratore*, III,1.

43 *Loeb Classical Library*. The French translation of Nisard (Paris, 1943, p. 607) is also interesting: '*Mais pourquoi le nom de Galles donné à ces pretres qui se sont mutilés...*'. This resembles Spartianus' '*mutilare genitalia*'.

44 *Loeb Classical Library*. Izaac too (ed. *Les Belles Lettres*, Paris, 1961) translates: '*Mutile le vieux qui couchait au bord du lit*'.

45 *Vita Hadriani*, 14:2. See also Seneca, *Con. exc.*, 10:4: '*excisorum greges*'. In the *Historia Augusta* '*mutilare*' does not appear anymore, but '*excidere*' appears twice: *Avidius Cassius*, 4:5: '*Multis desertoribus manus excidit*'; *Clodius Albinus*, 9:6: '*Caput eius excisum pilo circumtilet*'.

46 See also: *Thesaurus Linguae Latinae*, for a long list of citations from Classical sources, from Latin translations of the Bible and from Patristic sources. Since our issue here is not philological but rather legal-historical, we refer the reader to the *Thesaurus* for a more profound study.

Clearly *circumcidere* can be understood as belonging to the broader category of *excidere*. It is not impossible that *circumcidere* was just the technical term, translated from Greek, *peritome*, but that there existed other words in common speech which also denoted circumcision. Petronius, for example, uses *succidere* in place of *circumcidere* or *excidere*: '*ni tamen et ferro succiderit inguinis oram*' ('But unless he also cuts back (*succiderit*) with a knife the region of his groin').[47] Thus it appears possible that a broader definition of *excidere* as containing also *circumcidere* could have been perfectly legitimate.[48]

It is noteworthy that the Greek equivalent of *excidere*, *ektome* is also used both in the narrow sense of castration and in a wider sense of excision of women's organs. In the latter sense it appears as the female counterpart of *peritome*, the male's circumcision, and is related explicitly to Jewish customs:

> ... *kreophagoi, koloboi tas balanous kai ai gunaikes ioudaikws ektetmhmenai*' ('to the Creophagi, of whom the males have their sexual glands mutilated and the women are excised in the Jewish fashion'.[48a]

Interestingly, Hebrew sources also support this hypothesis. Gesenius translates the verb מול (*mwl*) as *praecidere*, and in other forms as *succidit—excidit*, with the interesting comment: 'There is no reason to doubt this usage of the word, as the meaning *circumcidere* is by no means primary, but comes from *abscindere*, see גזר (*gzr*), *secuit*, Syriac

47 Poem 24, *Fragmenta*, no. 97 (trans. M. Heseltine, *LCL*); but Reinach translates more freely: '*s'il ne se decide à pratiquer sur lui même la circoncision*'. For '*recutitus*', see Petronius, *Satiricon*, 68:8, and Martialis, *Epigrammata*, 7:30:5 (Stern, *GLA*, nos. 193, 240).

48 A similar use in Greek is found in: Strabo of Amaseia, *Geographica*, XVI 2:37 and is translated by Rocci in his dictionary: '*taglio, intaglio, recisione, amputazione, segmento, spaccatura, apertura, mutilazione, castratura, incisione*'.

48a Strabo of Amaseia, *Geographica*, 16:4:9, translated by H.L. Jones, *LCL*. See also: *ibid.*, 16:2:37 (M. Stern, *GLA*, I, no. 115, p. 295, 306; no. 118, p. 312; III, Index, s.v. *ektome*. Notice that the same Greek expression used by Strabo to describe circumcision, *kolobos tas balanous*, is used by Ps. Spartianus, *mutilare genitalia*.

circumcidit'.[49] The new English Gesenius[50] translates 'circumcise: to cut off'.[51] The Aramaic targumim of the Old Testament translate the root מול (*mwl*) as גזרתא (*gezarta*), from the verb, גזר (*gzr*), to cut; occasionally they translate חתך (*hthkh*), to cut off.[52] Neither the Biblical verb nor the Aramaic translations bear any relation to the concept of *circum*. Deissmann writes: "In comparison to the verbs הסיר (*hesir*) כרת (*karath*), and מול (*mwl*), translated into Greek as *peritemno,* the Greek word has an additional sense. None of the Hebrew verbs carry the sense of the Greek *peri*. The choice of this verb can be ascribed to the fact that the translators of the Septuagint were familiar with it as a technical term used to describe an Egyptian practice similar to biblical circumcision".[53]

We conclude this short discussion with a definition for circumcision given in a modern medical dictionary: "A simple operation whose purpose is complete or partial excision of the foreskin".[54] Here too the word *excidere* recurs.

Thus we may determine that Hadrian's use of *excidere* in the *Dig*. 48:8:4:2 could include both castration (*excidere testiculos*) and circumcision (*excidere praeputium*). Such an interpretation seems more than likely. If it is indeed accurate, a number of the phenomena we will discuss later become significantly clearer.

49 Gesenius, *Thesaurus Philologicus Criticus Linguae Hebraeae et Chaldaicae Veteris Testamenti*, (Lipsiae, 1829) 776. Here too we refer the reader to the *Thesaurus Linguae Latinae* for details.

50 *Hebrew and English Lexicon of the Old Testament* (Gesenius, Robinson, Brown etc.), (Oxford, 1972) s.v מול.

51 See also: F. Zorell, *Lexicon Hebraicum et Aramaicum Veteris Testamenti*, (Rome, 1962) 417: '*abscidit praeputium, excidam*'.

52 E. Krupnik-Silbermann, *A Dictionary of the Talmud, the Midrash and the Targum*, I, (Tel-Aviv, 1970; London, 1927) 156. On this issue see lately: J. Bleich, "Survey of Recent Halakhic Periodical Literature: Hypospadias and Circumcision", (1980) 18 Tradition 295 ff.: "The question hinges primarily upon the meaning of the Hebrew word "yimol — he shall circumcise" (Leviticus 12:3), i.e., whether the word means "he shall cut" or whether its connotation is "he shall remove" as is the apparent meaning of the term in Deuteronomy 10:16 and Deuteronomy 30:6" (p. 299).

53 G.A. Deissmann, *Bibelstudien*, (Marburg, 1895) 149 ff.; *Idem*, *Bible Studies*, (Edinburgh, 1909) 151 ff. The quotation is from p. 152.

54 G. Bolognesi, s.v. *Circoncisione*, in: *Enciclopedia Italiana*, X, (Rome, 1929-1939) 412. See also historical introduction by Levi Della Vida (p. 410).

3) *Legal Results of the Ban on Circumcision* (excidere)

Our interpretation justifies our explaining the absence of general legislation against circumcision. Such legislation did not exist on its own, but was included in the general ban on castration (*Dig*. 48:8:4:2). Like castration, circumcision was punishable under the *Lex Cornelia de Sicariis*. Both *castrare* and *circumcidere* were forms of *excidere*, enforced by means of Hadrian's edict.

This explains Spartianus' use of *mutilare genitalia*. His terminology can be understood in light of Hadrian's general terminology. Had Spartianus used *excidere* in place of *mutilare*, all the scholars would have understood immediately that he was referring to Hadrian's order.

A broad interpretation such as this one was not necessarily applied everywhere in the empire on an immediate basis, even if, as we assume, the source for such an interpretation was Hadrian himself. Thus, for example, we can explain the apparent lack of enforcement of the ban on circumcision in Rome.[55]

We can also understand the precise meaning of *Dig*. 48:8:11, in which Antoninus Pius permits the Jews alone to circumcise their children. Antoninus created this privilege for the Jews, overriding the Hadrianic ban. He did not institute the law banning circumcision itself.

We may attribute the ban to the years 129-130, a short time before Hadrian's journey to Syria.[56] We do not know for certain the causes for the decree.[56a] However, although it was a general decree, it seems unlikely that Hadrian did not consider the particular effects of such a decree on Jews. Indeed it seems impossible to many scholars who have been impressed by the emperor's cultured and intellectually curious character.[57]

55 See A.M. Rabello, *supra* n. 38, at 110; and *Babylonian Talmud, Shabbath*, p. 130a. J. Geiger, *supra* n. 34, n. 40, suggests a different approach: in his opinion, the Rabbinical sources prove that the ban on circumcision was local and that it was related to the governor, Tineius Rufus. In our opinion, however, Rufus' role was limited only to applying a severe interpretation to the ban on '*excisio*' in the province under his rule.

56 J. Geiger, *ibid*., at 141, n. 8, rightly argues that there is a connection between the ban on circumcision and the passage in the *Digesta* (48:8:5), but he does not draw the conclusions mentioned *supra*. On this text see Dalla, *supra* n. 18, at 91. Dalla says, *inter alia*, that Ninius Hasta was proconsul of Asia not before 130, and that the order attributed to him must have been later than stated in the *Digesta*, 48:8:4:2.

56a Yet see below the discussion on the Roman policy in the Near-East.

57 C.D. Mantel, *supra* n. 37, and others.

The Rabbinic texts themselves depict him as holding discussions with Jewish sages on philosophical and theological questions such as the nature of Creation.[58] Yet, the phenomenon of the friendly ruler who acts against a befriended people is hardly historically original. Circumcision may have seemed a barbaric custom to an adherent of Greek aesthetics, a custom to be combatted in order to prevent pollution of the Roman world.[59] Judaism could easily have seemed diametrically opposed to the popular ideals of the classical Hellenistic world, even to a person (and perhaps particularly to him) who was interested in Eastern paganism.[60]

As for the punishments for this crime, the death penalty applied to:

1. Anyone who consents to be circumcised (*Dig.* 48:8:4:2)
2. A doctor who performs the circumcision (*ibid.*)
3. A slave who goes through circumcision (*ibid.*)
4. It seems likely that one who performs circumcision against the will of the circumcised/cut/castrated person is also punished by death (*Dig.* 48:8:4:2; *Pauli Sententiae* 5:23:13). Yet a free man who circumcises/cuts/

58 See, *inter alia*, the dialogue between Hadrian and Rabbi Yehoshua ben Rabbi Hanina in *Midrash Bereshit Rabba*, 10, 3 (Theodor and Albeck, eds., pp. 75-76). For analysis of the Talmudic sources see: M.D. Herr, "The Historical Significance of the Dialogues between Jewish Sages and Roman Dignitaries", *Scripta Hierosolymitana*, XXIII (1971) 123 ff., esp. 142 ff.

59 See F. Grelle, *L'autonomia cittadina fra Traiano e Adriano. Teoria e prassi dell'organizzazione municipale*, (Napoli, 1972) 226 ff. (in our translation):
"The *Vita Hadriani* states explicitly that the order came prior to the revolt and was one of its causes; it is hard to envisage any motive the editor might have had to change the original text. Equally, it is hard to assume that the writer himself had distorted the original text, no matter what his attitude toward Hadrian was. The ban on circumcision should be understood as an expression of intolerance toward the custom, which the emperor thought was so repulsive, that he stated that whoever conducted circumcision did not belong to a civilized people".

60 See Zmigryder-Konopka, *supra* n. 1, at 345, and the scholars quoted there. See also Fanizza's correct words in: 'Il parricidio nel sistema della Lex Pompeia', (1979) 25 *Labeo* 27 ff.) (in our translation):
"Hadrian's ban on murder comes in the frame of normative interventions, their purpose being the assurance of compliance between the relations between man and man and the natural order; there is a parallel version to this in the law against castration. Also in this case Hadrian intervened with a drastic step implementing the death penalty giving no other alternative. He did not even act according to the principle which he himself set more than once, punishing according to the offender's status. The idea is to establish relations between human beings in a manner that will suit the nature, but these relations must also be *based on ethnic-religious concepts*". (the emphasis is mine, A.M.R.)

castrates, was punished by exile to an island (*Dig.* 48:8:5:3) and the confiscation of his property (*Dig.* 48:8:4:2). Those not present would be judged *in absentia*.[61]

4) *Jewish Sources on Circumcision*

We will now consider Jewish sources dealing with circumcision. These sources will enable us to complete the picture obtained from the classical Greek and Roman sources. We assume that most of these sources deal with the period before and shortly after the Bar Kokhba revolt, although some scholars have expressed doubt about some of them.

Mekhiltha de-Rabbi Yishma'el, explains the words '*To those who love me and those who keep my commandments*' (Exodus 20:5), as follows:[62]

> Rabbi Nathan[63] says: 'Of them that love me and keep my commandments', refers to Israel who live in the land of Israel, and risk their lives for the commandments. 'Why are you being led out to be decapitated'? 'Because I circumcised my son'.[64]

The rest of the passage indicates that the quotation deals with the period of the persecutions under Hadrian. It reflects the harshness of

61 On these texts see especially: Th. Mommsen, *supra* n. 27, at 637 ff.; J. Juster, *supra* n. 1, vol. I, pp. 263 ff.; vol. II, pp. 190 ff.; Dalla, *supra* n. 18, at 89 ff. On the physicians in this period see: C. Maschi, 'Operae liberales', *Bull. Scuola di perfezionamento in Diritto del lavoro, Trieste*, 2 (1955) 9.

62 See: M.D. Herr, s.v. *Mekhilta of R. Ismael*, in: *Enc. Judaica*, 11 (1971), col. 1267 f. The quotation is from 'Ba-Chodesh' portion, *Exodus*, 19:1-20, 26 (eds. Horowitz-Rabin, 1931, p. 227).

63 A Tannah (Sage of the Mishnah) from the fourth generation, the son of the Head of the Golah in Babylon, who emigrated to Judaea before the Bar-Kokhba revolt and held important positions.

64 Lauterbach's translation. See: S. Lieberman, *supra* n. 37, at 423 ff.; G. Alon, *supra* n. 37; Lieberman returns to this issue in "Religious Persecution in Israel", in *Jubilee Volume in honour of Shalom Baron*, III, (Jerusalem, 1975, in Hebrew) 213-245, in particular pp. 216 ff. In this important research Lieberman goes back to the issue of persecution in the time of Hadrian, and examines carefully the Rabbinical sources on this matter. There he explains the difference between בשעת הסכנה (at a time of danger) and שמד (religious persecutions), with which he dealt also in *op. cit.*, p. 427.

the Jews' situation in Palestine during that time.[65] The harsh punishment inflicted on the father who circumcised his son corresponds with that of the *Lex Cornelia de sicariis*.

We began with Rabbi Nathan, because this text enables us to respond to P. Schäfer, who argues strongly (a) that the ban was not introduced before the revolt but rather during the revolt or immediately after, (b) and that the danger was pending over the circumcised person, being either a new-born or a convert. The above quotation shows clearly that the danger was to the father who performed or authorised the circumcision.

Schäfer disputes Mary Smallwood's deduction from Antoninus Pius' privilege of 138 C.E. that it must have been preceded by a general prohibition on circumcision, which was applied not just on Jews and would-be converts to Judaism, but on all people. Her main evidence that the ban preceded the revolt and was its immediate cause is the Tosefta *Shabbath* (15[16]:9). She argues that the passage refers to circumcised Jews who later concealed it by an operation, known as *epispasmos*, out of fear of being caught transgressing Hadrian's prohibition, and later, in the days of Ben Kozba, restored their circumcision. The Tosefta *Shabbath* 15[16]:9) says:

> A משוך (*mashukh*) [A circumcised person who has his prepuce drawn forward] requires to be [re]circumcised. R. Yehudah said: he should not be [re]circumcised because such an operation is dangerous. They said to him: Surely many were [re]circumcised in the days of Ben Kozba and yet had children and did not die ... And 'he has broken My covenant' (Gen. 17:14), to include the משוך.[66]

A parallel passage in the Palestinian Talmud, *Yevamoth* 8:1, adds:

65 It is true that such words coming from a Rabbi who came from Babylon might indicate that there the situation was different from that in Judaea. However, as we saw above (nn. 38, 55), it seems that the situation in Judaea was extremely severe even in comparison to the other parts of the Empire. We also learn from *Midrash Bereshit Rabba* (ed. Albeck, p. 73) that Tineius Rufus ordered that no one be circumcised. Here the prohibition is attributed to the local governor; thus there were some who wished to see this order as a local one, applied only in Judaea, based on the 'coercitio'. In our opinion, this was not a local enactment, but a local interpretation given to the word *excidere*, included in Hadrian's general order.

66 See S. Lieberman, *The Tosefta, Mo'ed, Sabbath*, (New York, 1962) 71; *Idem, Tosefta ki-fshuṭah, A Comprehensive Commentary III*, (New York, 1962) 251.

> The משוך and one born circumcised and the one who was already circumcised when converted [but has not as yet dripped blood] may not eat *terumah*. R. Zerekan, R. Yannai of the house of R. Yishma'el in the name of R. Yohanan [says it is] because of punishment. R. Yirmiyahu R. Shmuel son of R. Yitzhak in the name of Rab [says it is because] they made a decree. What is the practical difference? If another [person] extended his foreskin or if it became extended by itself, if you say [he may not eat *terumah*] because of punishment, there is no punishment here. If you say [he may not eat] because they made a decree, even so they made a decree [based on the verse] 'He shall surely be circumcised 'circumcision' [And therefore he shall repeat the circumcision and until then he may not eat *terumah*.][67]

Schäfer, on the other hand, claims that the ban was introduced at a later date, and that the משוכים those who performed the *epispasmos* on themselves — mentioned by the Tosefta and *Yevamoth* are adult hellenized Jews who did it voluntarily as an act of assimilation, not because of fear of the ban. He argues against Smallwood's interpretation:

> Smallwood's argument is both illogical and historically unlikely. If Hadrian had issued a decree prohibiting circumcision before the war (for whatever reason), this can only have meant that it was forbidden to circumcise all new-born children. Persecution of Jews who were already circumcised would have been nonsensical, since logically only those Jews who had themselves circumcised after the decree were affected, and these were either new-born children or proselytes. Besides, the procedure of drawing forward the prepuce artifically (by surgical operation) and then shortly afterwards carrying out a second circumcision (and the time between operations must have been very short) was hardly advisable on medical grounds.[68]

Schäfer points to two different dangers faced by the circumcised babies and new converts. The first is from the Romans, who might punish them for breaking the ban on circumcision, the other is the

67 *Cf.* also the Baraitha in Babylonian Talmud, *Baba Batra*, 60b [trans. in G. Alon, *supra* n. 37, at 584].

68 P. Schäfer, *supra* n. 37, at 90.

health risk to the recircumcised person. Obviously, the danger facing the משוך discussed in the Tosefta is of the second kind — the health risks to his life and the danger of his becoming sterile.

Concerning the passages from the Tosefta and *Yevamoth*, there can be no doubt that the משוך refers to a person who has undergone the operation of the *epispasmos* to hide the signs of circumcision. Schäfer assumes that it refers only to persons who themselves arranged the operation, as an act of assimilation, and that during the revolt they were forced to recircumcise. Yet it does not seem as clear as he suggests. As R. Nathan's saying in the *Mekhiltha* makes clear, the danger threatened the person who performed the act, e.g. the fathers, etc., and not only the circumcised new-born son. Likewise it is abundantly clear in the passage from *Yevamoth* — '*if another extended his foreskin or if it became extended by itself*' — that the person may have undergone the operation without his consent (while a child, on the authority of his father or someone else interested in hiding the signs of his circumcision). It is also possible that he himself authorized the operation, as Schäfer understands it, not because of any fear but in order to assimilate and to become 'hellenized', a phenomenon encountered elsewhere in Jewish history.[69]

The motives for such an operation were either fear of Hadrian's ban or the wish to assimilate, and there may have been some who did it because of both reasons — their wish to assimilate was augmented by a healthy dose of fear. No doubt there were many who did it or caused it to be done to their sons because of their fear. There was good reason for such a fear in the period before the revolt, for it is difficult to imagine that the Romans who enforced the ban went from village to village with precise lists of who was circumcised before the ban and who after. Given the tense political situation, there was probably a tendency towards

69 The event occurred in the days of Antiochus IV Epiphanes. According to I *Maccabees*, 5:15, and Josephus (*Jew. Antiq.*, 14:5:1 [241]), the hellenized Priest Jason founded a gymnasium in Jerusalem, located north-west of the Temple, where Jews also used to frequent. These Jews did not wish to be distinguished from the non-Jews during their training naked in the stadium, and had removed the signs of circumcision by restoring their foreskins in the operation known as *epispasmos*. See also: Epiphanius, *De mens.* 16 (*P.G.* 43, col. 264):
Imo vero, quod molestius est, post circumcisionem rursus ad praeputium redeunt. Etenim, medica quadam arte, eoque quem spathistherem vocant, glandis cuticulum attrahentes consuunt, ac glutino cicumstringunt, atque ita praeputium recuperant. See also F.M. Abel, *Les livres des Maccabées*, (Paris, 1949) 8.

stringency.[70] There might have been fear that the Romans would punish not just innocent people, parents who performed it on their children, but also older boys, who might be suspected of consenting to be circumcised, although they were circumcised a long time before the ban. Such persons prefered to secure themselves by this means.

Contrary to Schäfer's logic, it is sensible to assume that this very fear may have changed a parent's mind, after he had performed the circumcision, to wish to conceal his deed and to hide its signs by the *epispasmos*. During the Bar Kokhba revolt the fear of the Romans was temporarily removed, and the משוך could — or perhaps was forced to — be recircumcised, as is stated in the Tosefta *Shabbath*.[71]

An example of such a complicated situation may be reflected in the tractate *Avoth* (3:12):

> R. Eleazar of Modiim said: If a man profanes the hallowed things and despises the set feasts and puts his fellow to shame publicly and makes void of the covenant of Abraham our father, and discloses meanings in the Law which are not according to the *Halakhah*, even though a knowledge of the Law and good works are his, he has no share in the world to come.[72]

This person, who makes void the covenant, was not necessarily an assimilated Jew, for he is described as knowledgeable in the Torah and a pious man. R. Eleazar of Modiim lived in the era of Bar Kokhba and died tragically on the eve of the fall of Bethar. Thus, the problem discussed here arose before the revolt or during it, not after its suppression.

Among the sins mentioned in the statement is making "void the covenant of our father Abraham", that is, not being circumcised. This[73] could mean more than one thing. It can be understood in one of three,

70 Compare with the situation described in I *Maccabees*, 8:60-61 (see *supra* n. 11).

71 See S. Lieberman, *supra* n. 66, and P. Schäfer, "Hadrian's Policy in Judaea and the Bar Kokhba Revolt: A Reassessment", in Ph.R. Davies and R.I. White (eds.), *A Tribute to Geza Vermes* (Sheffield, 1990) 281-303, at 294-298. (Journal of the Study of the Old Testament, Supplement Series 100).

72 H. Danby, *The Mishnah* (Oxford, 1950) 451. For biographic particulars on Rabbi Eleazar see: Mendelsohn, s.v., *Jewish Encyclopedia*, V, 1903, p. 102 ff.; S. Safrai, s.v., *Enc. Judaica*, VI, 1971, p. 603; G. Alon, *Toledoth Hayehudim*, (Tel-Aviv, 1955, in Hebrew) II, p. 41. On the interpretation of this passage as a polemic with Christian-Jews see: E.E. Urbach, *supra* n. 37, at 263.

73 *Cf.* also the texts in S. Lieberman, *supra* n. 66.

non-exclusive, ways: (a) either as abstention from circumcision altogether — a solution allowed by some Sages[74] — out of fear of Hadrian's ban; or as one of two types of משוכים as the Tosefta *Shabbath* defines clearly that 'he who makes void the covenant — to include the משוך': (b) either those who did it out of fear, (c) or as an act of assimilation.

Despite the three possible interpretations, Schäfer maintains that the passages in the Tosefta and *Yevamoth* refer only to men who performed the *epispasmos* because they wished to assimilate, and later were compelled by Bar Kokhba to be circumcised once again. The two passages thus relate to the situation during the revolt and after it, not to the years before the revolt. He believes it was the Jewish internal struggle between Bar Kokhba's supporters and the assimilated Jews of Jerusalem that led to Roman intervention, and thus to the outbreak of the Bar Kokhba revolt against Rome. I quote Schäfer *verbatim*, to avoid any distortion of his position:

> If we start from the assumption that, in Jerusalem, there was a fairly large group of assimilated Jews, who were friendly to Rome, and who had gone so far as to perform the *epispasmos*, then it is only logical to assume that this particular political group in Jerusalem supported Hadrian's policy of 'Hellenisation'. According to Garzetti, Hadrian had created a kind of 'uniform Hadrianic art . . . extending . . . over an area of unparalleled extent and overflowing with its influence even the boundaries of the empire — something that had never happened before . . . One of the results was a widespread enthusiasm for restoration and renewal.[75]

The evidence we have indicates that after the Great Revolt, Jerusalem was utterly destroyed. The city remained in ruins for some time, serving as a base camp for the Tenth Roman Legion, Fretensis.[76] Slowly,

74 *Cf.* n. 67.

75 A. Schäfer, *supra* n. 37, at 92; see also the conclusions on p. 94.

76 B. Lifshitz, "Roman Legions in Palestine", *Bulletin of the Israel Exploration Society*, XXIII (1959) 53 ff. In the article appears, *inter alia*, the claim that the Sixth Legion, Ferrata, was transferred to Palestine before the Bar Kokhba revolt and not as a result of it. See also the French version in: *Homm. à Renard*, II, Coll. *Latomus*, CII, (Bruxelles, 1969) 458 ff. Its headquarters were in Kefar Otnay, near Meggido, on the Caesaria-Beth Sh'ean road. There is a suggestion that an army was brought there even earlier, at the time of Trajan. See: B. Isaac, *Limits of Empire*, (Oxford, 1990) 432 and n. 53. On the Tenth Legion, Fretensis, and its base in Jerusalem before the

small groups of Jews and Jewish-Christians began to dwell in the city, apparently remaining after performing the pilgrimage to Jerusalem.[77] It seems extremely unlikely that any serious conflict arose between these two small groups. The Jews, Christians, and Jewish-Christians must have understood the tenuousness of their situation, and at all costs tried to avoid public conflict. They knew the Roman Legion could expel them from the ruins of the city at any time if they became disruptive. Even if we were to assume that on the site of the ruined Jerusalem the Jews did struggle amongst themselves, how likely does it seem that an entire Roman Legion not only failed to root out those who disturbed the peace, but allowed the situation to deteriorate to the point of a conflict as serious as Bar Kokhba's rebellion?[78]

revolt see: B. Isaac, *ibid.*, at 323-325, 427-429, 434. An inscription in memory of Tiberius Claudius Fatalis Ropanus shows that a Roman soldier from the Tenth Legion, Fretensis, was posted in Jerusalem with his family: M. Avi-Yonah, "Greek and Latin Inscriptions from Jerusalem and Beisan. Tombstone of Tiberius Claudius Fatalis", (1938) 8 QDAP 54 ff.; B. Lifshitz, "Jérusalem sous la domination romaine. Histoire de la ville depuis la conquête de Pompée jusqu'à Constantin (63 a.C.-325 p.C.)", (1977) 8 *Aufstieg und Niedergang der Römischen Welt*, II, 444 ff.

77 B. Lifshitz, *ibid.*, at 471 f.: "*En résumé, les indices que nous venons d'énumérer attestent l'existence à Jerusalem d'une population juive peu nombreuse, dont les habitations se trouvaient probablement dans un faubourg ou dans un village près de la ville* . . ." (p. 473). On the pilgrimages to Jerusalem see: S. Safrai, "Pilgrimage to Jerusalem after the Destruction of the Second Temple", in *Jerusalem in the Second Temple Period, Schalit Memorial Volume*, 3, (Jerusalem 1980, in Hebrew) 376 ff.; reprinted: *In Times of Temple and Mishnah*, (Jerusalem, 1994) vol. I, pp. 85-102. See also B. Mazar, "The Archaeological Excavations Near the Temple Mount", in *Jerusalem Revealed. Archaeology in the Holy City 1968-1974*, (Jerusalem, 1975) 25 ff.: "Following the destruction of Jerusalem by Titus's legions, in 70 C.E., which entirely depopulated the city . . . With the stationing of the Tenth Legion as occupation force in the desolate city . . ." (p. 32); see also 'Aelia Capitolina', pp. 33-35; Avigad, "Excavations in the Jewish Quarter of the Old City, 1969-1971", *ibid.*, at 51; J.W.. Hirschberg, "The Remains of an Ancient Synagogue on Mount Zion", *ibidem*, at 116.

78 It should be noted that Schäfer's interpretation runs counter to Eusebius's *Chronicles*, which states that in the 17th year of Hadrian (133 C.E.) Bar Kokhba executed the Christians who refused to collaborate with him against the Roman troops; from here it is clear, not only that there was not a conflict between Jews and Christians *before* the revolt, but also that Bar Kokhba had thought of getting assistance from the Christians against the Romans! It should also be remembered, that there was always hope for the participation of Gentiles in the revolt for the sake of human freedom and for the sake of fighting Roman absolutism. See S. Applebaum, *supra* n. 37, at 56 f.

5) *Bar Kokhba Revolt and the Ban on Circumcision Revisited*

P. Schäfer discusses the question of the causes leading to the Bar Kokhba revolt in his book on that subject, in 1981, and in a recent article in 1990.[79] In the first work, he surveyed all the literary evidence concerning the causes, and reaches the conclusion that the revolt was an outcome of the internal Jewish conflict in Judaea rather than of any Jewish-Roman conflict or strained relationship in the province, or of any provocative Roman policy towards the Jews during the Hadrianic reign, in the years 117-130 C.E. What concerns us here is his claim that the Romans did not ban circumcision before the outbreak of the revolt, contrary to the explicit statement by Ps. Spartianus in the *Scriptores Historiae Augustae*, but rather as one of the Roman retributions following its suppression.

In his reassessment of the question of the revolt's causes, Schäfer defends his thesis, yet admits that any further discussion is unproductive and is furthermore methodologically questionable.[80] The scholarly dispute over the concrete causes has been exhausted, so it seems, without either side being able to convince the other. He therefore turns to studying the question indirectly, by examining the Roman policy toward the Jews in Judaea, on the one hand, and the Jewish reaction to that policy on the other hand. By doing so, he tries to define the "political and intellectual climate which existed before the revolt", and the "mentality among the Jews".[81] This might prove whether there was any political unrest or strained relationship between the Jews and the Roman rule in Judaea, which might have led to the outbreak of the Jewish revolt against Rome, without the need to discuss the futile subject of its direct causes.

Yet, in his reassessment, Schäfer does not produce any arguments which alter the present state of research, and in some respects, he even weakens his own thesis. In his survey of the various views, he refers to my Hebrew article of 1984, but ignores my interpretation of the legal evidence. There I show that the prohibition of circumcision was enacted

79 P. Schäfer, *Der Bar Kokhba-Aufstand. Studien zum zweiten jüdischen Krieg gegen Rom*, (Tübigen, 1981): *Idem*, "Hadrian's Policy", *supra* n. 71, at 281-303.

80 P. Schäfer, *Der Bar Kokhba-Aufstand*, *supra* n. 79, at 281. And see his conclusion on p. 303.

81 P. Schäfer, "Hadrian's Policy", *supra* n. 71, at 281, 292.

prior to the revolt, in the edict reported in *Dig.* 48:8:4:2, which was implemented in the province of Judaea with a severe interpretation. This evidence thus gives a clear answer to the dispute over the causes leading to the revolt and over the reliability of Ps. Spartianus' account. It supplies additional evidence to the view that the revolt broke out, *inter alia*, because of the strained relationships between the Jewish population and Rome, and because of a Roman policy which was considered offensive by the Jews. It supplements our own sources concerning the causes leading to the revolt, Cassius Dio and the *Vita Hadriani*, with a third one, the actual legislation which authorized the ban.

Schäfer has put great emphasis on Hadrian's policy of hellenizing the East. In his view, this policy was welcomed by the urban Jewish population and rejected by the rural sector.[82] The Roman policy itself was not anti-Jewish as such, nor was it seen as provocative and offensive by the Jews themselves. It was even supported by the assimilated circles within Judaism. It cannot therefore be regarded, in his opinion, as one of the causes leading to the revolt. Yet, it can be argued against Schäfer's opinion, that this very policy can no less support the argument that the ban on circumcision was part of this policy of hellenization, and that it was not inflicted upon the Jews as a punishment for their uprising. Indeed, the edict *Dig.* 48:8:4:2 prohibiting castration (*excidere*) was not an expression of any specifically anti-Jewish policy, and was implemented throughout the Empire.[83] The severity of its implementation in Judaea, as including also circumcision, was a local interpretation by the local governor. When seen in the wider context of the Roman policy in the Near East, it is apparent that this local interpretation of the edict conformed with the imperial policy to enforce the Roman norms and values on all oriental nations, rather than being a provincial or local policy. Between the years 106 and 155 C.E., the Roman government imposed a prohibition on all nations south of Syria, i.e., on the provinces of Judaea (including Samaria), Arabia, and Egypt to perform circumcisions and ordered them to abolish their ancient custom of circumcision. They had started with this policy already at the time of Trajan, when shortly after the annexation of the Nabatean kingdom into the empire in 106 C.E., the Romans abrogated ancient laws, and in particular that

82 *Ibid.*, at 295.

83 See also M.D. Herr, "The Causes of Bar Kokhba Revolt", (1978) 43 *Zion* 8.

of circumcision.[84] The punishment of transgressors was the same as in the *Lex Cornelia de sicariis*. Hadrian's ban on circumcision, in approx. 129-130 C.E., was applied not just to the Jews, but also to the Samaritans, Samaria being part of the province of Judaea. The ban on the Jews was lifted later, by Antoninus' rescript *Dig.* 48:8:11, but not from the Samaritans, who are recorded in about 180 C.E. as not being allowed to perform circumcision, while the Jews were allowed.[85] A similar ban on circumcision appears to have been in force also in Egypt. The date of its introduction is not known, yet here too, as in Judaea, the ban was eased on certain conditions, and some Egyptian priests were exempted. This priviledge was renewed in 155 C.E., and the date of its original grant must have been earlier, perhaps about the time of Antoninus' rescript.[86] It was thus during less than fifty years, and probably in less than thirty, that circumcision was banned in all the Roman provinces in the south-east region of the empire, and the exemptions were made to reach a *modus vivendi* with that rule.[87] Seen in this wider context of the Roman policy in the Near East, Ps. Spartianus' statement concerning Judaea gains credibility, and the assumption that the ban was implemented as a punishment ought to be discarded. The theory that the Jewish-Roman relationship in Judaea during Hadrian's early years were amicable and the period was a peaceful one, has to take into account the vast military presence in the area, and moreover, its increase immediately after Hadrian's nomination by at least 20,000 sol-

84 According to Bardesanes, written in approx. 180 C.E., in *The Book of Laws of Countries*, trans. by H.J.W. Drijvers, (Assen, 1965) 56. See M. Stern *GLA* II, p. 620.

85 Origenes, *Contra Celsum*, 2:13.

86 Regarding the prohibition of circumcision in Egypt, see the summary of M. Stern, *GLA II*, p. 620.

87 The *Epistle of Barnabas*, a Christian work from Egypt, written probably during Hadrian's rule, discusses circumcision from a Christian point of view (ch. 9). It speaks of circumcision of the heart against that of the flesh, which is still practiced by the Jews (9:4). He states that 'every Syrian and Arab and all the priests of the idols have been circumcised (. . .) even the Egyptians' (9:6). The writer was unaware of the prohibition laid on circumcision in these nations, and lists the nations which keep this custom, beside the Jews, i.e. the Syrians, Nabataeans, Arabs, as well as the priests of other nations, and the Egyptians. The *Epistle of Barnabas* (16:3) is aware of Hadrian's plans to rebuild the Temple in Jerusalem as a Jewish temple, on which see below.

88 B. Isaac, "The Limits of Empire", *supra* n. 76, at 106, 118. For the cost of maintaining 'one legion and some cavalry' in Britain, which would equal the whole income from the custom duties collected there, see *ibid.*, at 388. the position of the two legions in Judaea, in addition to another legion in Arabia (since 106 C.E.), must have been a very heavy financial burden on the empire and the provinces.

diers.[88] Schäfer claims, contrary to the accepted view, that it was not done as a precaution against possible political unrest in Judaea, or because of fear that the Jewish revolts in other areas of the empire during Trajan's rule might spread into that province; nor was it a reaction to any unrest already existing there. The introduction of a second legion to Judaea was done for peaceful purposes: to defend the peace in the area, to defend the eastern borders of the empire, and to take an active part in Hadrian's development programmes of urbanization and road construction, to allow prosperity to the province and to improve civil and military communications between Syria and Egypt.[89]

This claim, however, is very weak and unconvincing. Much more evidence is needed to claim that such amassing of military forces and the vast resources needed to maintain them in the province of Judaea was done only for the purpose of policing the province, defending the borders and constructing roads.

Contrary to Schäfer's argument, the province of Judaea at the time of Hadrian's accession did not suffer from special security problems on its eastern frontiers. The Partian border was far away and the nomad tribes in the east did not present a serious problem to the Romans.[90] On the contrary, just a few years earlier, in 106 C.E., the Nabataen kingdom was annexed to the empire and a Roman legion, the III Cyrenaica, was stationed in Bostra, thus transferring the 'eastern frontier' far away from Judaea, to the eastern 'borders' of Arabia. Recently, B. Isaac summed up the whole issue of the Roman army's role in the imperial policy in the Near East, and in Judaea in particular, and of the function as well as the concept of the *Limes*, and the defensive function of the army along the eastern frontiers.[91] He showed quite convincingly that the purpose of the military installations in Judaea and her frontiers were not for defensive purposes, and neither was the army's role there of that nature. Only a small fraction of the Roman army was stationed on the eastern frontier, while the main army was positioned in Caesaria,

89 P. Schäfer, "Hadrian's Policy", *supra* n. 71, at 285-287, 289, 295.

90 B. Isaac, *supra* n. 76, at 119.

91 B. Isaac, *ibid.*; Idem, "The Meaning of 'Limes' and 'Limitanei' in Ancient Sources", (1988) 78 Journal of Roman Studies 125-147; I. Shatzman, "The Limits of Empire: Review Article", (1994) 44 IEJ 129-135, esp. 131 f.

around Jerusalem and in several other cities, as well as along the network of roads.[92]

The conclusion must be reached that one of the army's main duties, aside from constructing new roads and maintaining existing ones or defending the passage, was undoubtedly to prevent local unrest in the province. The scale of the military presence is clear evidence as to how serious the problem of internal security was during Hadrian's early years. The same would apply to Schäfer's other argument that there was no unusual political and military unrest which required the large military presence. Though Schäfer underestimates the serious problem which the brigands (*lestés*) posed to the public safety along the inter-city roads,[93] this alone is not enough to explain the permanent position of a second legion in the province. The military presence must have reflected therefore the political tension in the area during Hadrian's early reign. This tension does not necessarily contradict the existence of amicable relationships with the Romans on other levels, nor the existence of assimilated circles in Judaea. Yet, besides the military evidence, there are two more pieces of evidence which indicate that there was a very strong anti-Roman under-current, which was known to the Roman governor, but did not come out into the open before the outbreak of the Bar Kokhba revolt. This would account for the reason why there are no records of any Roman-Jewish military collusions during these years. The first evidence is Cassius Dio, who states clearly that as long as Hadrian was present in the Near East, both the Jews and the Romans were careful to avoid confrontation. Yet, the Jews used this time to prepare themselves for a future confrontation, building up an arsenal and subterranean passages and preparing for long sieges.[94] This statement by Cassius Dio has recently been corroborated by the second piece of evidence, the several hiding places which were discovered mainly in Southern Judaea, the region which was the center of the Bar-Kokhba revolt, but also in the Galilee and the Coastal Plain.[95] There is evidence that

92 For the list of military sites, around the cities and along the road system rather than on the eastern and southern frontiers, see B. Isaac, "The Limits of Empire", *supra* n. 76, at 707 and App. I pp. 427-435. For the Roman military presence along the eastern frontiers of Arabia during the second and third centuries, before Septimius Severus, see *ibid.*, at 123, 131.

93 See the evidence collected by B. Isaac, *ibid.*, at 83-85, 289.

94 Cassius Dio, *Romana*, 69:12:1.

95 A. Kloner & J. Tepper (eds.), *The Hiding Places in the Judaean Shephelah*, (Tel-Aviv, 1987, in Hebrew).

some of these subterranean hiding places were prepared and stocked with products needed for time of siege and war about the time before the Bar Kokhba revolt. It is therefore clear that during Hadrian's early years there was a buildup of military preparations, which eventually broke out in the Bar Kokhba revolt, and that it was not a development which caught the Romans surprised and unprepared.[96]

One of Schäfer's main proofs for his thesis, that the hellenized and assimilated Jews in Judaea supported Hadrian's hellenizing policy, and that there was no exceptional political unrest in Judaea before the revolt, is the fifth Sibylline oracle.[97] The first fifty verses are a list of Roman emperors with corresponding appreciations, up to the reign of Hadrian, who is described as follows:

> And after him [i.e. Trajan] another shall reign, a silver-helmeted man. He shall have the name of a sea. He shall be a most excellent man and shall understand everything. *And in thy time, most excellent, most noble*, dark-haired prince, and in the time of thy scions, all these days shall come.[98]

Schäfer puts much weight on the phrasing of the praise of Hadrian, 'the most excellent, most noble' (5:49), as evidence that these assimilated Jews saw in Hadrian a sort of *restitutor* or *soter*,[99] greeting him enthusiastically in almost messianic tones.[100] He argues that this praise by an Egyptian Jew reflects 'a broader mentality among the Jews' and expresses also the climate among the Jews in Judaea during Hadrian's early years, between 117 and 130, and of their high expectations from his rule and their support for his peace policy during this period.

Yet, the fifth Sibylline oracle cannot be used, in this context at least, as evidence for the situation in Judaea during Hadrian's reign, for it does not reflect any Jewish attitude towards his rule there. The oracle,

96 See now, B. Isaac & A. Oppenheimer, "The Revolt of Bar-Kokhba: Ideology and Modern Scholarship", (1985) 38 JJS 36-60; a Hebrew version in A. Oppenheimer & B. Isaac, "The Bar-Kokhba Revolt: the Modern Scholarship", in A. Kloner-J. Tepper (see the previous note) at 405-428; reprinted in I.M. Gafney (ed.), *Studies in Jewish History in the Mishnah and Talmud Period*, (Jerusalem, 1994) 110-133, esp. 122.

97 P. Schäfer, "Hadrian's Policy", *supra* n. 71, at 291-293.

98 Translation by Lanchester, in Charles' *Apocrypha*.

99 P. Schäfer, *Der Bar Kokhba-Aufstand*, *supra* n. 79, at 93.

100 P. Schäfer, "Hadrian's Policy", *supra* n. 71, at 293 f.

as a whole, the first fifty verses included, does not show any kind of knowledge or familiarity with events in Judaea after the suppression of the great revolt in 70 C.E. Furthermore, it shows no interest at all in the events there or in the 'earthly' Jerusalem. In the verses which were composed during Hadrian's reign, 5:1-50, there is only one single reference to any event in Judaea during the Roman imperial rule, the description of Vespasian's exploits in Judaea: 'Then there shall come a great destroyer of godly-men' (5:36). It is remarkable how he ignores the destruction of the Temple itself, and it is more so when compared with the fourth Sibylline oracle, which mentions twice the destruction and burning of the Temple, as well as the ruin which Titus brought upon the great land of the Jews (4:115-127). Not less puzzling is that an Egyptian Jew, writing sometime between 117-30 C.E., would describe Trajan's exploits in the East (5:43-44), yet fail to mention the fatal blow which he brought upon the writer's own community just a few years earlier, in 116-117 C.E. Surely, the writer does not reflect any Jewish sentiment towards the Roman rule in Egypt, let alone in Judaea. His greeting of Hadrian ought to be understood simply as a salutation to the reigning monarch. In fact, it cannot be described as reflecting any 'Jewish mentality' at all.[101]

101 The later verses, 5:246;286, and in particular 5:250, 262-264, dealing with the future of Judaea, have no relationship to our subject. They belong to the earlier stratum of the oracle. They present an anti-Roman and anti-hellenic vision, unlike the pro-Roman feelings which Schäfer ascribes to the later additions, of verses 7-50. It expects the renewal of Jewish settlements in Judaea around Jerusalem, surrounded by a huge wall, reaching up to Jaffa, and not destroyed by the raging invaders. It does not speak of any political restoration. Yet, even here the oracle is systematic in its disregard towards the Temple in Jerusalem, whether that which was destroyed or that to be built in the future. The Judaean Jews' expectations that Hadrian will build the Temple in Jerusalem were not shared by those Egyptian Jews from whom the fifth oracle emerged. Their expectations are in fact directed to the restoration of the Jewish temple in Alexandria, closed down by Titus in 70 C.E. (5:501-503).
The fifth Sybilline oracle, as an expression of Egyptian Jewish feeling concerning Jerusalem and the Temple, ought to be compared with the Christian *Epistle of Barnabas* ch. 16. The Epistle, like the oracle, is an Egyptian work from Hadrian's early reign. It states that the Temple in Jerusalem is now going to be built by those who destroy it (16:3-4), referring most probably to Hadrian's plans to build a pagan temple, dedicated to Jupiter, on the site of the old Jewish Temple. This difference might be explained either by wrong information reaching the *Epistle*'s author, or by its being written during Hadrian's very first years of reign, before it became clear that the temple is going to be dedicated to Jupiter, not to the "Jewish" God. He certainly

C) *Conclusion and Some Notes on the Ban on Circumcision*

The rebellion clearly had a number of causes, and I have no intention to seek for new ones. The list of causes described in the various sources are an adequate explanation. The uprising was not an isolated event, but followed in the footsteps of the rebellions of 70 C.E. and of 115-117 C.E. Both Cassius Dio and the Midrash emphasize the plans to rebuild Jerusalem as a pagan city, Aelia Capitolina, with a pagan temple in place of rebuilding a Jewish temple to God.[102] Archaeological investigations reveal a period of renewed building, not necessarily Jewish, in the period preceding the rebellion.[103] Spartianus and several Hebrew sources emphasize the ban on circumcision: 'At that time the Jews too began a war because they forbade them to injure (*mutilare*) their sexual organs'. *Midrashim* which recount debates between Romans and Jewish sages

was not well informed about the situation in the late 20's, when the ban on circumcision was laid. The *Epistle*'s author, unlike the sybilline's, does not ignore Jerusalem and the Temple. Yet, he does not praise Hadrian, but criticizes the Jews who wish to consecrate God in it, and he rejects the need for such a temple altogether. If we shall treat both sources as that of assimilated Jews, we cannot see in them any expression of support for Hadrian's policies in Judaea, and in particular not for his plans to rebuild the Jewish ruined temple.

102 Cassius Dio, *Histories*, 69:12:1: "At Jerusalem he [Hadrian] founded a city in place of the one which had been razed to the ground, naming it "Aelia Capitolina", and on the site of the temple of the God he raised a new temple to Jupiter". (trans. by E. Cari, *Loeb Classical Library*) On this see especially: F. Millar, *A Study of Cassius Dio*, (Oxford, 1964) 68; A.M. Rabello, *supra* n. 1, at 740 and n. 308; M. Stern, *GLA*, no. 440 (with an extensive commentary); and more recently, see the very cautious survey by B. Isaac, *Limits of Empire*, *supra* n. 76, at 323-325, 352-354, 427, based on the archaeological survey by H. Geva, "The Camp of the Tenth Legion in Jerusalem: an Archaeological Reconsideration", (1984) 34 IEJ 239-254. With regard to *Midrash Bereshit Rabbah*, chap. 64:9 (T. Albeck, ed., p. 710), see G. Allon's interpretation in *Toledot Hayehudim*, (Tel-Aviv, 1954), I, p. 272; C.D. Mantel, *supra* n. 37, at 36 ff.; M.D. Herr, *Persecutions and Martyrdom*, *supra* n. 37, at 79; S. Applebaum, *Prolegomena*, p. 4 f.; M.D. Herr, *The Causes*, *supra* n. 37, at 5, n. 17.

103 B. Lifshitz, *supra* n. 72; *Idem*, "Sur la date de la transfert de la legio VI Ferrata en Palestine", (1960) 19 *Latomus* 109 ff.; M. Hecker, "The Roman Road from Legio to Sephoris", (1961) 25 Bulletin of the Israel Exploration Society 3. According to the author, the road was constructed in the 14th year of Hadrian (130 C.E.), probably in connection with the Emperor's visit to Judaea, its purpose being the strengthening of the Roman authority. Therefore the author is of the opinion, that the building of the road was one of the causes of the revolt and not a result of it. See S. Follet, *supra* n. 37.

or laymen indicate that a question of importance was whether man's works or God's works were preferable: why should any one change God-given nature and undergo circumcision? The Jewish sages answered to that question that God wished man to particiapte in the creative process of his own body.[104] These *Midrashim* indicate the gravity of the situation. The Jewish sages had the almost impossible task of convincing the pagan Hellenistic world, represented by 'the Divine Hadrian', that God's commandments are superior to nature, which itself is subject to His laws. But even more serious from their perspective, the Sages had to convince the Jewish people of the indispensability of circumcision as a sign of God's covenant, a task particularly difficult in the wake of the appearance of Christianity.[105]

D) *Circumcision in Roman Sources after Hadrian*

As we have seen, the Romans had been familiar with circumcision for a long time and knew it to be practiced among various nations, although they viewed it as a sign of Judaism in particular. Literary sources indicate that many were repelled by this practice. A legal campaign against castration began under Domitian and Nerva, enforced by means of the *Lex Cornelia de sicariis et veneficis*. Hadrian reiterated the ban on castration by means of a decree using broader language, *excidere*, which can be understood as including *circumcidere*. Hebrew sources

104 *Midrash Tanhuma*, 'Tazria', 5; *Bereshit Rabbati*, at 72 ff. (ed. Albeck); on this see: M.D. Herr, *supra* n. 58, at 131 ff. and 146, n. 127.

105 We would like to emphasize clearly that we have not dealt here with all the relevant Hebrew sources; this is due to our opinion, based on several inquiries, that these sources do not include important information that we do not already have from other sources, and also because we have reached the same conclusions as earlier scholars, especially M.D. Herr, *supra* n. 36, at 93 f., ns. 27, 28; p. 98, n. 51, as well as Applebaum, *supra* n. 37, at 7 f. We also have not dealt with the problem of the *Sikarikon*: on this see the bibliography mentioned in my article, *supra* n. 37, at 702, n. 165. The Christian approach was not mentioned in this study either, since it does not relate directly to the legal solution of the problem at that period. We have also not discussed the similarities and differences between Hadrian's attitude towards the Jews and his attitude towards the Christians. On this see: E. Bickerman, "Trajan, Hadrian and the Christians", (1968) 96 *Rivista di Filologia e di Istruzione Classica* 290 ff.; K. Waters, "The Reign of Trajan and its place in Contemporary Scholarship (1960-1972)", (1975) 2 *Aufstieg und Niedergang der Römischen Welt*, II, 406 ff.

support this construction. The Hadrianic edict forbidding circumcision (before 130) held general force, yet it seems likely that interpretation was left to those responsible in a given location. Although doubtless there were many other causes, this would support Spartianus' suggestion (doubted by many scholars) that Bar Kokhba's rebellion stemmed from a ban on circumcision. Rabbinic texts indicate the severity of the ban. We may conclude from these texts that the ban preceded Bar Kokhba's rebellion and held force during and after the rebellion. A *modus vivendi* was reached under Antoninus Pius, whose decree appears in *Dig.* 48:8:11, in the *principium*:

> *Modestinus libro sexto regularum. Circumcidere Iudaeis filios suos tantum rescripto diui Pii permittitur: in non eiusdem religionis qui hoc fecerit, castrantis poena irrogatur.* By a rescript of the deified Pius it is allowed to Jews to circumcise only their own sons; he who does so to a person not of that religion suffers the penalty of one carrying out castration.[106]

Scholars have tried to understand the exact significance of Modestinus' passage dealing with the privilege granted by Antoninus Pius. Did the Emperor give permission *only* to the Jews to circumcise their sons, or did he permit the Jews to circumcise *only* their sons? We shall enlarge a little on this topic in order to bring to the attention of historians some sources and methods of research commonly employed by the legal historians.

The basic passage is that of Modestinus, *Dig.*48.8.11:

The corresponding passage in Greek is to be found in *Basilica*[107] 60:39:7, which we present here in the Latin translation:

106 See the discussion above on the chapter dealing with the causes of the Bar-Kokhba revolt. Scholars who feel that the prohibition against circumcision preceded the revolt, are, among others, E. Schürer, Th. Mommsen, G. Allon, S. Lieberman, S. Mazzarino, E.M. Smallwood, S. Safrai, M.D. Herr, S. Appelbaum, and A. Linder. Opposed to this view is Mantel who feels that the revolt preceded the prohibition. In a study published recently, Geiger, reaches the conclusion that Hadrian did not legislate a general law and the first general law concerning circumcision stems from Anotonius Pius: J. Geiger, "The Ban of Circumcision and the Bar-Kokhba Revolt", (1976) 41 *Zion* 139ff.; but see now the answer of M.D. Herr, "The Causes of the Bar-Kokhba War", (1978) 43 *Zion* 1 ff.

107 The '*Basilica*' is a Byzantine codification of Roman law. Historians generally neglect it because of its late date. However, legal historians have proven that "the *Basilica* constitute a legal monument of the highest importance for our knowledge of Justinian

Modest: Iudaeis filios suos circumcidere permittitur. Sed si alium circumciderint, capite puniuntur, et bona eorum publicantur.

1. Qui servum vendit sine iudice, et cum bestiis depugnet, tenetur lege de sicariis, et etiam, qui emit.
2. Ex iusta tamen causa per iudicem servus datur, ut cum bestiis depugnet.[108]

Two scholia in *Basilica* also refer to the passage of Modestinus:

Iudaeis] Solis Iudaeis constitutione Pii filios suos circumcidere permittitur: qui vero non Iudaeus hoc fecerit, castrantium poenae subiicitur.
sed si alium circumciderint] Iudex habet; Quodsi quis non Iudaeus hoc fecerit, castrantium poenae subiacet.[109]

From the passages in the *Basilica* it is quite clearly evident that *only Jews* were allowed to circumcise, and furthermore that they were allowed to circumcise *only their own sons.*[110]

and post-Justinian law in the Byzantine Empire, and for our criticsm of some texts of Justinians' *Digesta* and *Code* in instances in which the Greek text of the *Basilica* and their *scholia* is better preserved than in the Latin manuscripts of Justinian's legislation." (Berger, *E.D.*, 372).

108 Here too we bring the Latin translation of the *Basilica* by Heimbach. On the basis of these sections it is possible to understand better the section of Modestinus in the *Digesta* and it becomes clear that based on this, there was no reason for most of the discussion between Smallwood and Rokeach. See D. Rokeach, *supra* n. 37, at 127-129.

109 See P. Lenel, *Palingenesia Juris Romani*, I (Leipzig, 1889), 136 n. 230. Compare this also with a section of 'Pauli Sententiae' (generally considered post-classical) *P.S.*, 5,22,3: *Cives Romani, qui se iudaico ritu vel servos suos circumcidi patiuntur, bonis ademptis in insulam perpetuo relegantur; medici capite puniuntur. P.S.*, 5,22,4: *Iudaei si alienae nationis comparatos servos circumciderint, aut deportantur aut capite puniuntur.* On these paragraphs see also J. Juster, "The Legal Condition of the Jews under the Visigothic Kings", brought up to date by A.M. Rabello (Jerusalem, 1976 = (1976) 11 Is. L. R. 405-406 n. 134) with a recent bibliography on the topic.

110 S. Solazzi, "Fra norme romane antisemite", (1937) 44 *Bulletino dell'Istituto di Diritto Romano* 369ff. Solazzi compares a section of the *Digesta* with the *Basilica* and *Nomocanon* 1:14. The deletion of the word "slaves" in the *Digesta* is a result of the attempt of Christianity to widen the prohibition against circumcision.

V

We must take into account also the context of this passage in Modestinus' work. It is clear from the *Palingensia* of Lenel[111] that the place in which this fragement occurs is in the chapter which deals with the power of the owner over his slaves (*de potestate dominorum*): indeed Siro Solazzi has claimed that the original passage of Modestinus was concerned expressly with the prohibition to circumcise non-Jewish slaves.[112] It must also be borne in mind that there have been scholars who wished to draw conclusions about the meaning of the word *siqariqin* from the fact that the statute which dealt with circumcision was the *lex Cornelia de sicariis*.[113]

Anyone (whether Jew or gentile) who circumcised a non-Jew, no matter whether the person circumcised was punished according to his status in society, could face the death-penalty or banishment with consfication of his property. If he was a physician, he was always liable to the death-penalty. Furthermore, whoever was an accessory to the circumcision, such as a master who allowed his slaves to be circumcised, was liable to penalties.[114]

The person undergoing circumcision could also expect to be punished: if a freeman, he faced confiscation of his property and, at a later period, the death-penalty. If he was a slave, he did not face any penalty, since

111 On this topic there is much literature. See especially H. Graetz, "Das Sikarikon Gesetz", in *Jahresbericht des jüdisch-theologischen Seminars* (Berlin, 1892); F. Rosenthal, "Das Sikarikongesetz", (1893) 37 *MGWJ* 1ff.; I. Elbogen, (1925) 69 *ibid.*, 249ff.; A. Gulak, "Siqariqin", (1934-1935) 5 *Tarbiz* 23ff.; E.E. Urbach, "The Laws Regarding Slavery as a Source for Social History of the Period of the Second Temple, The Mishnah and Talmud", *Papers of the Institute of Jewish Studies*, (London, I, 1964) 1; D. Rokeah, *supra* n. 37, (1966) 35 *Tarbiz* 228ff.; M. Gil, "Land Ownership in Palestine under Roman Rule", (1970) 17 *Revue Internationale des Droits de l'Antiquité* 11ff., 45ff.; S. Shiloh, *The Law of the State is Law* (Jerusalem 1974, in Hebrew) 41ff.; A. Linder, *supra* n. 27, at 127, *cf.* 183; see also Applebaum's *Jewish Revolt (A.D. 132-135)* (Oxford, 1976), 74 n. 96, and Applebaum's observations on Rokeach's article in S. Applebaum, "Judaea as a Roman Province: the Countryside as a Political and Economic Factor", in *ANRW* II, 8 (Berlin - New York, 1977), 355ff. and 388 n. 183.

112 Juster is of the opinion that the situation already existed in an earlier period and he refers the reader to a paragraph of Venuleius dealing with castration, *Digesta*, 48:8:6. However, this does not prove that the slave won his freedom.

113 Compare the situation with the Samaritans and see Novella 6 of Justinian and Canon 18 of Epiphanios, Patriarch of Constantinople (520-530).

114 See my book *Giustiniano, Ebrei e Samaritani*, (Milano, 1987-1988).

he was considered to have no free will. From the Christian period on, a Jew's Christian slave who was circumcised could go free.[115] Therefore, as we have attempted to prove, Justinian adopted the passage of Modestinus in his *Digesta* (48:8:11) and expanded its force by granting wide interpretation to the passage. Moreover, his Codex devoted great emphasis to the subject of circumcision, which was depicted in a most harsh manner. However, it must be observed that in practice the law was very often not carried out;[116] a fact which explains how it came to be that many succeeded in undergoing circumcision right down to medieval times.[117]

115 On this entire issue, including relevant texts of 'Codex Theodosianus' and bibliography see Juster - Rabello, *supra* n. 109, at 406 n. 137.

116 See my book, *supra* n. 114, at 944, s.v. "Circoncisione".

117 The problem of the Hadrianic ban on circumcision and its consequences concerning Jewish family law has been dealt with by Joseph Mélèze Modrzejewski in a paper entitled "*Filios suos tantum*: Roman Law and the Personal Status of the Jews", delivered at the International Conference on Jewish-Gentile Relations, Haifa, 13-16 November 1995 (to be published in the Proceedings of the Conference); *cf.* also G. De Bonfils, *Gli schiavi degli Ebrei nella legislazione del IV secolo. Storia di un divieto* (Bari, 1992) 134 ff.

VI

On the Relations between Diocletian and the Jews

The Emperor Diocletian (284-305 C.E.) is mentioned several times in rabbinic sources (*Talmud* and *Midrashim*) which do not make a clear differentiation between history and legend.[1] The student of legal history will find his task easier, therefore, if certain historical situations are clarified.

The Palestinian Talmud (*Terumot* 8,12) refers to the humble origins of the Dalmatian Emperor: "When Diocletian was only a swine-herd he was ill-treated by some young pupils of Rabbi Judah the Patriarch". Other sources also bear witness to his background; for instance, he is mentioned as *virum obscurissime natum* (*Eut.* 9. 19, 2), and the Coptic Hagiographa mentions the time when he was a goat-herd in Egypt. The continuation of the talmudic passage relates that when Diocletian was proclaimed Emperor he wanted to know whether the Jews would continue to despise him. He therefore sent a message to the Rabbis of Tiberias[2] ordering them to appear before him at Paneas[3] at the end of the Sabbath, but told the messenger to deliver the message only on the Friday evening, that is to say, at the

[1] On Diocletian see in particular: O. Seeck, *Geschichte des Untergangs der antiken Welt,* 4 Stuttgart, 1921: W. Ensslin, "Zur Ostpolitik der Kaisers Diocletians", *Sitzungsberichte Bayer. Akad. Wissensch,* 1942, 1; K. Stade, *Der Politiker Diokletian und die lezte grosse Christenverfolgung,* Baden, 1926; W. Seston, *Dioclétien et la Tétrarchie, I, Guerres et Réformes (284-300),* Paris, 1946; W. Ensslin "Valerius Diocletianus", *PW, RE,* 2, Reiche 14, 1948, col. 2419ff. (especially 2479ff.); E. Stein-Palanque, *Histoire du Bas Empire, I (284-476),* Paris, 1959; A. H. M. Jones, *The Later Roman Empire, 284-602,* Oxford, 1964, II, pp. 944ff.; III pp. 321ff. (footnotes); A. H. M. Jones, *The Decline of the Ancient World,* London, 1974, pp. 278ff. For juridical aspects see in particular: R. Taubenschalg, *Das Römische Privatrecht zur Zeit Diokletians* (1920), *Opera minora,* Warsaw, 1959 3 ff.; M. Amelotti, *Per l'interpretazione della legislazione privatistica di Diocleziano,* Milan, 1960; G. I. Luzzatto, "Sul regime del suolo nelle provincie romane. Spunti critici e problematica", *Atti del Convegno Internazionale sul tema: 'I diritti locali nelle provincie romane con particolare riguardo alle condizioni guiridiche del suolo'* (Rome, 26-28 Oct. 1971), Rome, 1974, 9ff. Finally, for an analysis of Diocletian's image, especially with regard to public law, see F. De Martino, *Storia della Costituzione Romana,* V, Naples, 1967, *passim* and VI (General Indexes), 1972, under term "Diocletian" (imp.). For a study of the Jewish sources, see the essay by A. Marmorstein, "Dioclétian à la lumière de la littérature rabbinique", *REJ* 98 (1934), 19ff.

[2] On Diocletian's stay in Tiberias see: T. Mommsen, *Ueber die Zeitfolge der Verordnungen Diocletians und seiner Mitregenten,* 1860 (*Gesammelte Schriften,* 2, 202ff. and especially 216, pp. 217, 269, referring to Justinian's Codex 1, 51, 1; 4, 10, 3; 5, 17, 3): H. Kottek, "Der Kaiser Diokletian in Palästina", *Jahrbuch der Jüdisch-Literaturischen Gesellschaft,* Frankfurt, 1, 1903, 213ff.; W. Seston, *Dioclétien op cit.,* 374ff.

[3] On Diocletian's stay in Paneas (i.e. Banyas): A. Neubauer, *La géographie du Talmud,* Paris, 1968 (reprint 1967), 236ff.; H. Kottek, "Paneas", *Jahrbuch, op. cit.,* 220ff.; L. Szczepánski, *Geographia historica Palestinae Antiquae,* Rome, 1926, 255ff.; A. H. M. Jones, *The Cities of the Eastern Roman Provinces,* Oxford, 1937, 281ff.

beginning of the Sabbath. By a miracle, the rabbis arrived at Paneas without desecrating the Sabbath and successfully withstood severe ordeals reminiscent of those endured by Daniel.

On the basis of this passage, Baer[4] claimed that the Jews as well as the Christians suffered religious persecution at the time of Diocletian.[5] But the talmudic passage is unclear in this respect; it speaks only of forced desecration of the Sabbath or of being subject to the death penalty unless a miracle occurs. "Diocletian's name is alluded to in various talmudic sources. It may be said that an equal share of attention was obtained only by those emperors who afflicted Israel such as Vespasian, Titus, Trajan and Hadrian, or by rulers whose personalities were bound up with eschatological hopes, an exception being the name of Constantine, which was not uttered by the rabbis of the Talmud".[6]

Baer's arguments are not convincing. It is true that in general the Talmud refers to those emperors who were extremely antagonistic to Judaism, but if one examines the names mentioned – Vespasian, Titus, Trajan and Hadrian – it will be realized that they were the rulers in power at the time of the Jewish revolts in Palestine and the Diaspora which led to the destruction of the Temple and the final loss of political independence.[7] Other emperors

[4] Y. F. Baer, "Israel, the Christian Church and the Roman Empire from the time of Septimius Severus to the Edict of Toleration of A.D. 313", *Scripta Hierosolymitana,* VII, 1961, 117 ff., especially p. 127f.

[5] On the persecution of Christians during Diocletian's reign see in particular: Lactantius, *De Mortibus Persecutorum;* Eusebius, *Historia Ecclesiastica* (especially books VIII and IX); *idem, De Martyribus Palestinae.* Among modern authors: K. Stade, *Der Politiker . . . op cit.*; H. Grégoire, *Les persécutions dans l'empire romain,* Paris, 1950, 78ff.; W. Seston, "A propos de la Passio Macelli centurionis. Remarques sur les origines de la persécution de Dioclétien", *Mélanges M. Goguel,* 1950, 239ff.; G. Lanata, *Gli atti dei martiri come documenti processuali,* Milan, 1973.

[6] Y. F. Baer, "Israel, the Christian Church . . ." *op cit.,* p. 123; on the relations between Constantine and the Jews see A. Linder, "The Roman Imperial Government and the Jews under Constantine", *Tarbiz,* 44, 1975, pp. 95ff. (in Hebrew, with English summary, p. V) and the literature cited therein.

[7] On the war of 70 C.E. and its repercussions in the Diaspora see in particular: J. Juster, *Les Juifs dans l'Empire romain. Leur condition juridique, économique et sociale,* II, Paris, 1914, 183ff.; A. Momigliano, "The Jewish Rebellion, the Campaigns of Vespasian, the Siege and Fall of Jerusalem", CAH, vol. 10, 1934; M. Aberbach, *The Roman-Jewish War (66-70 A.D.): Its Origin and Consequences,* London, 1966; E. Schürer, G. Vermes, F. Millar, *The History of the Jewish people in the Age of Jesus Christ,* vol. 1, Edinburgh, 1973, pp. 484ff. On the Jewish revolt during Trajan's reign in Egypt, Cyprus, Cyrene and Mesopotamia see in particular V. Tcherikover, *Corpus Papyrorum Judaicorum (CPJ),* I, Prolegomena, Jerusalem, 1957, 85ff.; A. Fuks, "Aspects of the Jewish Revolt in A.D. 115-117", *JRS* 51 (1961), 98ff.; S. Appelbaum, "The Jewish Revolt in Cyrene in 115-7", *JJS,* 2 (1951), 177ff. On the revolt in Palestine under Trajan, see D. Rokeah, "The War of Kitos: towards a clarification of a philological-historical problem", *Scripta Hierosolymitana,* vol. 23, 1972, 79ff. On the Bar-Kokhba revolt under Hadrian: H. Mantel, "The Causes of the Bar-Kokhba Revolt", *JQR,* 58 (1968), 224ff. 274ff.; M. D. Herr, "Persecutions and Martyrdom in Hadrian's Days", *Scripta Hierosolymitana,* 23, 1972, 85ff.; A. M. Rabello, "A Tribute to Jean Juster", *Israel Law Review,* II (1976), 242f.; J. Geiger, "The Ban on Circumcision and the Bar-Kokhba Revolt", *Zion,* 41 (1976), 139ff.; M. D. Herr, "The Causes of the Bar-Kokhba Revolt", *Zion,* 43 (1973), 1ff.; A. M. Rabello, "Il problema della 'circumcisio' in Diritto Romano fino ad Antonino Pio", *Studi in onore di A. Biscardi,* Milano, vol. II, 1982, pp. 187ff.

known for their hostility towards Judaism,[8] such as Domitian, are barely mentioned; but the Talmud does allude to several Roman emperors who did not persecute the Jews.[9]

Baer emphasizes Diocletian's adherence to polytheistic beliefs, but on this issue Juster correctly observed that the privileges granted to the Jews were reconfirmed, "probably because the anti-Christian policy of the pagan emperors obliged them to act favourably towards the Jews".[10] Also worthy of note is Stade's remark: "It was even possible to bear the intolerant monotheism of the Jews, as their proselytisation was not very dangerous since they were a nation".[11] It seems that Baer did not keep in mind the fact that Judaism was considered, even after the defeats of 70 and 135, a *natio* and not only a *religio,* as Mommsen maintains.[12]

The spirit of Diocletian's policies is only too well expressed in the famous Constitution against the Manichaeans, reported in the *Collatio legum*

[8] E. M. Smallwood, "Domitian's Attitude towards the Jews and Judaism", *Classical Philology,* 51 (1956), 1ff.; A. M. Rabello, "Domitian", *Enc. Judaica,* 1971, vol. 6, col. 164.

[9] See, e.g., the dialogues between "Antoninus and Rabbi", and in particular the following studies: S. Krauss, *Antoninus und Rabbi,* 1910; M. Stern, "Caracalla, Marcus Aurelius Antoninus", *Enc. Jud.,* 5, 1971, 156ff.; M. D. Herr, "The Historical Significance of the Dialogues between Jewish Sages and Roman Dignitaries", *Scripta Hierosolymitana* 22, 1971, 123ff.

[10] J. Juster, *Les Juifs, op. cit.* 1, p. 226.

[11] K. Stade, *Der Politiker Diokletian,* p. 136.

[12] Th. Mommsen, "Der Religionsfrevel nach römischen Recht" (1890), *Gesammelte Schriften,* III, 389ff. According to Mommsen all Jews in the Empire became *dediticii* after 70 C.E.; Judaism therefore lost its national character, becoming simply a *religion.* This theory was opposed by Juster, *Juifs, op. cit.* 2, 19ff., who demonstrated that the war of 70 C.E. had no effect upon the *status civitatis* of the Jews of the Roman Empire: the Jewish people continued to be considered a *natio* and to enjoy certain *privilegia.* Later research, however, has shown that, at least with regard to the Palestinian Jews, it is impossible to generalize in view of the different attitudes adopted by various Jewish communities towards Rome. It is, therefore, legitimate to speak only of *dediticiae* communities. See in particular: A. Momigliano, "Ricerche sull'organizzazione della Giudea sotto il dominio romano", *Annali della R. Scuola Normale Superiore di Pisa* II series, 1934 (reproduced in Amsterdam, 1967) and related commentary by G. I. Luzzatto, *SDHI,* 2, 1936, 218ff.,; V. Colorni, *Legge ebraica e leggi locali,* Milan, 1945, 16ff.; G. I. Luzzatto, "Peregrini", *NNDI,* 12, 1965, 931ff.; E. Volterra, "Nuovi documenti per la conoscenza del diritto vigente nelle provincie romane", IURA, 14, 1969, 29ff.; E. Volterra, "I diritti locali" in *I diritti locali nelle provincie romane con particolare riguardo alle condizioni giuridiche del suolo* (A Paper of the *Accademia Nazionale dei Lincei*), Rome, 1974, 55ff.; G. I. Luzzatto, "Sul regime del suolo nelle provincie romane", *ibid.* 43ff.; S. Applebaum, "The Legal Status of the Jewish Communities in the Diaspora", in Safrai-M. Stern in co-operation with D. Flusser and W.C. van Unnik, *The Jewish People in the First Century (Compendia Rerum Judaicarum ad Novum Testamentum*), Assen, 1974, 420ff.; A. M. Rabello, *A Tribute to Jean Juster, op. cit.,* 231ff. and notes 58-63.

Mosaicarum et Romanarum (XV, 3,1).[13] It is clear that this Constitution did not concern the Jews, whose doctrines were ancient (*scitote, iurisconsulti, quia Moyses prius hoc statuit*)[14] and fully recognized under Roman law, but it was clearly offensive to the Christians. Volterra has even claimed that the original text openly referred to the Christians; this may provide an explanation for the fact that no mention is made of this Constitution by Christians in their polemics and in their legislation against the Manichaeans.[15] For several centuries, pagan Rome had allowed the Jewish people to enjoy certain privileges enabling them to observe the norms of their ancestral religion-nation, privileges which were continued even under emperors notorious for their persecution of the Christians.[16] This also explains how Origen "in the *Passio Pionii,* which contains an account of events that occurred under Decius, related that before dying the martyr exhorted his brethren to resist the advances of the Jews when, he said, they invite some of you to the synagogue, and not to avoid suffering at that price".[17] Further confirmation of this situation may be found in another passage of the Palestinian Talmud: "When Diocletian arrived in Palestine he commanded all the nations, except the Jews, to offer libations to the idols; after the Samaritans offered libations, their wine was declared forbidden". (*'Avodà Zarà* 5,4).

Scholars have discussed this passage at length. Graetz claims that the talmudic text refers to the period of persecutions and draws the conclusion that the Samaritans were excluded from the community because they refused to sanctify God's name, although they were put to death for not having offered wine to the idols.[18] Halevy firmly rejects this viewpoint, noting that the Samaritans were guilty of having offered libations to the idols of their *own free will,* not availing themselves of the exemption permitted *to Jews;* they thus excluded themselves from the community and

[13] On the edict against the Manichaeans see in particular E. Volterra, *Collatio legum Mosaicarum et Romanarum,* Rome 1930, 107ff.; W. Seston, "De l'authenticité et de la date de l'édit de Dioclétien contre les Manichéens", *Mélanges Ernout,* 345ff.; E. H. Kaden, "Die Edikte gegen die Manichäer von Diokletian bis Justinian", *Festschrift Lewald,* 1953, 55ff.; L. Gil Fernandez, "Observaciones sobre el edictum de Manichaeis de Diocletiano", *Actas II Congro. esp. est. class.,* 1865, 214ff.; E. Volterra, "La costituzione di Diocleziano e Massimo contro i Manichei", *Problemi attuali di scienza e cultura,* 76 (1966), 27ff.; A. M. Rabello, "On the Collatio legum Mosaicarum et Romanarum", *Annual of Institute for Research in Jewish Law,* Jerusalem, 1974, vol. 1, 246ff. (in Hebrew); P. Brown, "The Diffusion of Manichaesim in the Roman Empire", *JRS* 59 (1969), 92ff.

[14] Coll. VII, 1; an argument well-known to Jewish apologetics.

[15] E. Volterra, *Collatio legum . . . op cit.,* 103ff., 107ff.

[16] See J. Juster, *Juifs,* I, 114ff.; A. M. Rabello, *A Tribute to Jean Juster, op. cit.,* notes No. 21ff.

[17] M. Simon, *Verus Israel. Étude sur les relations entre Chrétiens et Juifs dans l'Empire Romain* (135-425), Paris, 2nd ed., 1964, p. 135; on *"Passio Pionit"* see also J. Juster, *Juifs, op. cit.,* p. 270, footnote.

[18] Graetz, *Geschichte* IV, 277 s.

their wine was subsequently declared forbidden as pagan wine.[19] This does not constitute the end of the discussion,[20] but all scholars, including Baer, agree that the Jews enjoyed the privilege of exemption from idol-worship. There remains the problem of dating. Juster, Volterra and other scholars[21] hold the view that the edict was proclaimed at the time of the religious persecutions of 303; Halevy and Baer[22] think that, in keeping with the *principium* of the passage, the date is earlier – 286. I personally agree with those scholars who see a connection between the edict and the persecutions of 303. It is true that Diocletian was not in Palestine in that year, but it may well be that the people remembered his last journey to Palestine, in 297.[23] The rabbis may then have reminded the Emperor of the privileges enjoyed by the Jews, in accordance with Roman law. However, even if the edict is associated with Diocletian's *first* visit to Palestine in 286, I think there can be no doubt that the Jews were effectively exempted from pagan rites, while the Christians were persecuted. The edict shows that the Emperor was well aware of this privilege and was thereby giving renewed force to accepted practice. The fact that in imperial circles a distinction was made between Jews and Samaritans would suggest that one was also made between Jews and Christians. If we agree that the date of the edict is 286, we have further proof that the episode in *Terumot* should be understood in this light. We are then faced with the problem of seeking a reason – without having definite sources as proof for the Romans' subsequent change in attitude.

I do not agree with Baer's view on the following passage of the *Midrash*

[19] I. Halevy, *Dorot Harishonim* II, 337ff.

[20] In a comprehensive study of this subject Lieberman rejects Halevy's interpretation in part. Although he agrees with Halevy that if the Samaritans had really been *coerced,* their wine would not have been banned by the Rabbis as the wine of idolaters he maintains that the Samaritans had no alternative, as it is well-known that they opposed idolatry and followed the precepts of the Bible. It seems that the local administration adopted a restrictive interpretation of the privilege granted to the Jews. Moreover, the conflict between Samaritans and Jews was already taking shape, and the Rabbis may therefore have used the case as a pretext. S. Lieberman, "The Martyrs of Caesarea", *Annuaire de l'Institut de Philologie et d'Histoire orientales et slaves* VII (1939-44), 395ff. and especially p. 403f. But see also the remarks made by L. I. Levine in his recent volume *Caesarea under Roman Rule,* Leyden, 1975, 111ff. and 229 n. 53.

[21] For Graetz see above, note 18; J. Juster, *Juifs,* I, 247, n. 1; E. Volterra, *Collatio,* 120, n. 1; J. Gutmann, "Diocletianus", *Enc. Judaica,* 5, 1971, col. 1123; M. Simon, *Verus Israel,* 135, n. 3.

[22] Halevy, *op. cit.,* above note 19; Y. F. Baer, "Israel, the Christian Church", op. cit., 124ff.

[23] In this sense see also the recent study by L. I. Levine, *Caesarea under Roman Rule,* 111 and 229, n. 51; with reference to the duty of sacrifice, from which even the closer relatives of the Emperor were not exempt, in a Hebrew text (Midrash Shemot Rabba, XV, 12), see S. Lieberman, *Hellenism in Jewish Palestine,* New York, 1950, p. 4f.; also Lactantius *De mor. Pers. XV: "et primam omnium filiam Valeriam coniugemque Priscam sacrificio pollui coegit".*

to the Song of Songs[24]: "R. Hiyya bar Abba said:[25] If a man says to me, give thy life for the sanctification of the Name, I give it, if only they slay me at once. But I cannot bear what they are doing in the age of persecution. For what do they do in such an age? They bring iron balls and make them white-hot and place them beneath the arm-pits and so take their souls . . . It was concerning this that David said: 'Unto Thee, O Lord, do I lift up my soul' (Ps. XXV, 1), the meaning of 'lift' being that they give up their souls for the sanctification of the Name of God".[26]

In this connection Baer writes: "Anyone comparing the words of the Christian teacher must confess that R. Hiyya bar Abba's references to 'the generation of persecution' do not allude to an old tradition only, but he is speaking in defence of those of his generation who had failed in the ordeal; unlike the Christian theologians, the rabbi makes himself a partner to the plight of his tormented and persecuted Jewish contemporaries".[27]

It should be noted that Rabbi Hiyya bar Abba refers to the "generation of persecution", that is to say, the persecution under Hadrian during the Bar-Kokhba revolt,[28] a period in Jewish history memorable for its many martyrs.[29] It is therefore not surprising that Rabbi Hiyya explains in this connection that there are also degrees in martyrdom, for a person who is willing to lay down his life may not be able to bear all the tortures. Moreover, even without taking into account actual religious persecution, the Jews could not be considered a flourishing community under the Roman Empire at this time, and there was a lingering fear that their situation would deteriorate. The rabbis' task was therefore to prepare the people for all eventualities, and to show understanding of, and identification with, the persecuted.

[24] On this issue see E. E. Urbach, "The Homiletical Interpretations of the Sages and the Expositions of Origen on Canticles, and the Jewish-Christian Disputation", *Scripta Hierosolymitana* xxii, 1971, 247ff.; see also M. D. Herr, "Song of Songs Rabba", *Enc. Judaica,* 15, 1971, 152ff.

[25] On this Rabbi also see Z. Kaplan, "Hiyya bar Abba", *Enc. Judaica,* 8, 1971, 796; W. Bacher, *Tradition und Tradenten in den Schulen Palästinas und Babyloniens,* Leipzig, 1914, index p. 686.

[26] Song of Songs Rabba, 2, 7; Y. F. Baer, "Israel, the Christian Church . . ." *op. cit.,* p. 126f.

[27] Y. F. Baer, *op. cit.*, p. 121, with reference to Cyprian's passage *De lapsis,* 13, 11.

[28] See S. Lieberman, "Roman Legal Institutions in Early Rabbinics and in the Acta Martyrum", JQR 35 (1944-5), 1ff. On p. 17, referring to our passage, Lieberman writes: "A Rabbi, who flourished under Diocletian, thus described the methods of torture during the Hadrianic persecutions . . ." Cf. Lieberman, "On Persecution of the Jewish Religion" (in Hebrew), *S. W. Baron Jubilee Volume,* Jerusalem, 1975, vol. III, pp. 213ff. and especially 234ff.

[29] M. D. Herr, "Persecutions and Martyrdom in Hadrian's Day", *Scripta Hierosolymitana,* vol. 23, 1972, 85ff.; on the concept of sanctification of God's name (*Kiddush HaShem*) in this period see also D. Daube, *Collaboration with Tyranny in Rabbinic Law,* London, 1965; "Limitation on Self-Sacrifice in Jewish Law and Tradition", *Theology* (1969), 291ff.; E. E. Urbach, *The Sages, Their Concepts and Beliefs,* Jerusalem, 1975, 352ff. and index.

Indeed, Baer might find support for his interpretation in the following passage from the Babylonian Talmud (which is, however, a secondary source in our case, the primary being the Palestinian Talmud): "At the time of Rabbi Zeira there were persecutions (*sh^{e}mada*) and it was forbidden even to pray for the revocation of the decree".[30] Lieberman has, however, provided an interesting comment on this passage: the meaning of *sh^{e}mada* is not certain since the word *shmad* has various connotations, for example, forced labour involving desecration of the Sabbath, or payment of taxes. If the latter interpretation is correct, we have here an allusion to the Emperor's oppressive monetary policy which is mentioned in other talmudic passages.[31] Less acceptable, it seems to me, is the *argumentum e silentio* that Baer finds in Eusebius: "But nowhere did Eusebius dare to say or to hint to the Jews: you have not stood firm in the present battle for the sanctification of the heavenly name against the pagan idolaters, for by virtue of your national privileges you have exempted yourselves from all duties and rights . . ."[32] Would the non-existence of such a reproach prove that the Jews at that time were also subjected to persecution? I do not think that is likely. The Church itself was seeking a *modus vivendi* within the Empire; martyrdom and suffering cannot be viewed as Jewish or Christian ideals.[33] Christian writers well know that the Jews were ready to lay down their lives for the unity of God, and it was, perhaps, in order to teach the Jewish concept of martyrdom and remember the past that the rabbis of that era drew attention to the persecutions under Hadrian.[34]

It would therefore seem clear that Diocletian's reign saw neither religious persecution of the Jews nor a drastic change from the tolerant policies adopted by the later Antonine emperors and the Severi. Judaism and Christianity may be said to have been fighting on two different fronts at this time:[35] against each other, and against paganism. This is the period when

30 B. Ta'an, 8b; R. Zeira lived at the time of Diocletian; see W. Bacher, *Tradition* . . ., index p. 703.

31 S. Lieberman, "Palestine in the Third and Fourth Centuries", *JQR* 36 (1946), 329ff. and especially 335. See also his criticism of A. Marmorstein, "The Age of R. Yohanan", *Tarbiz* 3 (1932), 161ff.

32 Y. F. Baer, "Israel, the Christian Church . . .", 133f. For some accurate observations on the silence of Christian sources (*Acta Martyrum*) with regard to the rôle of the Jews, see M. Simon, *Verus Israel* . . .,152ff.

33 See Costa, "Diocletianus", *DE,* 2, 3, 1852ff; Lanata,*Gli atti dei martiri come documenti processuali,* 53f. For Jewish precedents on martyrdom, see *ibid.,* 14ff.

34 See also Lieberman, "Palestine in the Third and Fourth Centuries", p. 370: There is no evidence either for the persecution of the Jewish religion during the third and fourth centuries, or for Jewish rebellions during that time . . . There is no proof that the burden of taxes levied on the Jews was heavier than that on the other provincials. The Rabbis very often complain against the Romans, not as Jews but as oppressed citizens denouncing the lawlessness and the wickedness of the rulers".

35 In this sense see E. E. Urbach, *The Sages* . . ., *op. cit.,* 545ff. See also at p. 933 criticism of Baer's interpretation of the relations between Jews and Christians at this period.

the distinction between Christianity and Judaism became more marked, and which ended with a major offensive of the Church against the "Church of Circumcision".[36]

Mention should be made, too, of certain matrimonial constitutions of Diocletian which were in keeping with the tradition of Roman jurists but which could have encountered opposition among certain Jewish groups. Thus, in a constitution of 285 Diocletian and Maximian declare: *Nemine, qui sub dicione sit Romani nominis, binas uxores habere posse vulgo patet* (c.5.5.2).[37] Some scholars, including Mommsen,[38] consider the passage to be the source of the autonomous crime of bigamy, although it is likely that this new offence was not created by Diocletian but by later emperors acting under the changing influence of Christian concepts of marriage and divorce.[39] In any case, although Juster thinks this constitution also applied to the Jews, he suggests that they continued to practise polygamy until expressly forbidden to do so in 393 (c.I.9.7).[40] The other constitution concerns the prohibition of certain marriages, such as between maternal uncle and niece (Coll. 6.4.5; c.5.4.I7),[41] but here again Juster is not sure that the Jews observed the prohibition until 393, when Jewish matrimonial customs were forbidden (c.1.9.7.).[42] In addition, it should be borne in mind that the oppressive economy and fiscal policy of the Emperor must have had a profound effect on the community in Palestine and it is possible that

[36] P. B. Bagatti, *L'Eglise de la circoncision,* Jerusalem, 1965; L. I. Levine, *Caesarea under Roman Rule, op. cit.,* 130ff.; see also the *Travaux du Centre d'Etudes Supérieures Spécialisé d'Histoire des Religions de Strasbourg: Aspects du Judéo-Christianisme,* Colloques de Strasbourg 23-25 avril 1964, Paris, 1965; S. Pines, *The Jewish Christians of the Early Centuries of Christianity according to a New Source,* Jerusalem, 1966.

[37] See E. Volterra, *"Lezioni di Diritto Romano. Il Matrimonio Romano",* Rome, 1961, 315 ss.

[38] Th. Mommsen, *Römisches Strafrecht,* 701.

[39] E. Volterra, *Il Matrimonio Romano, op. cit.,* 317, see also M. Amelotti, *Per l'interpretazione della legislazione privatistica di Diocleziano,* Milano, 1960, 78, 153.

[40] J. Juster, *Les Juifs dans l'Empire romain* II, 52ff. and n. 4; for the following period see V. Colorni, *Legge Ebraica e Leggi Locali,* 193ff. Talmudic legislation did not actually approve of polygamy; L. G. Lévy, *La famille dans l'antiquité israélite,* Paris, 1905, 148ff. Significant in this context is the text of the Aramaic Targum of the Book of Ruth (4,6) in which Ruth's relative apologizes for being unable to marry the young widow: "I cannot marry her since I am already married and I am not allowed to take a second wife together with the first. This would ruin my domestic peace. But you, who are not married, wed her yourself". See Z. W. Falk, *Jewish Matrimonial Law in the Middle Ages,* Oxford, 1966, 1ff., "Monogamy", with bibliography.

[41] See E. Volterra, *Il Matrimonio Romano,* 244; also V. Colorni, *Legge Ebraica e Leggi Locali,* 185; A. M. Rabello, "Divorce of Jews in the Roman Empire", *The Jewish Law Annual,* IV, 1981, pp. 79 ss.

[42] J. Juster, *op. cit.,* II, 49ff.

there was even forced labour on the Sabbath.[43] In general, it may be said that the talmudic sources provide us with a realistic portrait of the Emperor, but persecution of the Jews in the strict sense of the word may be discounted.[44]

* * *

In the light of these remarks, let us now examine some legal texts.

First, it should be borne in mind that the *Collatio legum Mosaicarum et Romanarum* was compiled, in my opinion, by a Roman Jew. It is to Volterra's great merit that he upheld the Jewish authorship of the *Collatio,* claiming 324 as the *dies post quem.*[45] However, this dating has been rejected by Levy and Scherillo[46] with perfectly valid arguments and today Volterra considers that the *Collatio* was probably completed "in a Jewish milieu at the beginning of the 4th century C.E."[47] In this connection I shall refer to two studies rejecting Volterra's thesis by Oestersetzer and Bossowski.

Oestersetzer[48] agrees that the author of the *Collatio* was Jewish but believes that he wished to prove that Jewish laws were similar to those of Rome in a desperate attempt to safeguard Jewish jurisdiction. The compilation should therefore be connected to the constitution of 398, as reported in CTh.2,1,10.[49] "We believe that we can solve the problem by admitting that the author was a Jew who wanted to show the authorities the

[43] S. Lieberman, "Palestine in the Third and Fourth Centuries", II, "Taxation and Imaginary Religious Persecutions", On the economic situation see in particular: A. Büchler, *The Economic Condition of Judaea after the Destruction of the Second Temple,* London, 1912; M. Rostovtzeff, *The Social and Economic History of the Roman Empire,* Oxford, 1957; D. Sperber, *Roman Palestine (200-400): Money and Prices,* Tel-Aviv, 1974; L. I. Levine, *Caesarea under Roman Rule;* D. Sperber, *Roman Palestine (200-400): The Land,* Ramat Gan, 1978; see also new edition of M. Giacchero, *Edictum Diocletiani et Collegarum de pretiis rerum venalium,* Genoa, 1974.

[44] See also *ySheb* 9,2. This passage has also been interpreted as an indication of persecutions against the Jews at the time of Diocletian, e.g., by Frankel; but according to Lieberman ("Palestine in the Third . . .", *op. cit.*, 350), "we have here a typical petition to the emperor, asking for the reduction of taxes". On the various forms of taxation (*tributum soli, tributum capitis, annona, angaria*), see M. Avi Yonah, *The Jews of Palestine,* New York, 1976, 94ff.

[45] E. Volterra, *Collatio legum mosaicarum et romanarum, Memorie della Reale Accademia Nazionale dei Lincei,* Rome 1930.

[46] E. Levy, *Zeitschrift der Savigny-Stiftung für Rechtsgeschichte, Romanistische Abteilung* (=ZSS), 50, 1930, 698ffr.; G. Scherillo, *Archivio Giuridico* (=AG), 104, 1930, 225ff.; and now also *Idem,* "Collatio legum mosaicarum et romanarum", *Novissimo Digesto Italiano* (=NNDI), 3, 446ff.

[47] *Istituzioni di Diritto Privato Romano,* Rome, 1961, p. 15.

[48] J. Oestersetzer, "La Collatio Legum Mosaicarum et Romanarum, ses origines, son but", *REJ* 97 (1934), 54ff.

[49] On this constitution see A. M. Rabello, "The Legal Condition of the Jews in the Roman Empire, Aufstieg und Niedergang der römischen Welt, Berlin – New York II, 19, 1980, pp. 728ff. and the bibliography quoted therein.

importance of Mosaic law in force amongst the Jews and its affinity with Roman law . . . show the perfect harmony of Biblical law and Roman law and prove that their application by Jewish or by Roman courts led to exactly the same results. This was the author's true aim. The author's point of view is not theologico-dogmatic but wholly politico-legal''.[50]

Oestersetzer's opinion in unacceptable. Apart from the question of dating (which has recently interested scholars again),[51] I fail to see why a Jew should wish to prove that Jewish law is exactly the same as Roman-pagan law just at the very height of the Roman-Christian period when the victorious Church was about to change that law.[52] It is obvious that, to be effective, the Collatio had to agree with the views of its intended readers, who were, according to Oestersetzer, Christian; otherwise a grave political error would have been committed, likely to increase Christian dislike of the Jews. There would have been no point in referring to the norms permitting marriage between a man and his brother's daughter (Coll. VI, 2; VI, 3, 1; VI, 4,5) when such a practice had already been declared a capital offence (CTh. 9,12,1 of 342); or, in the mistreatment of slaves, to the difference between murder and assault followed by death (Coll. III, 1), when the *dierum distinctio* had already been abolished (CTh. 9, 12, 1 of 319); or in referring to crucifixion (Coll. 1,2,2; VIII, 4, 2; XIV, 2,2,) as a form of death penalty still in use, when it had been forbidden by Constantine in *circa* 320.[53] These points corroborate my view that the *Collatio* was compiled in the pagan era.

Bossowski, however, does not accept that the author was Jewish. Disagreeing with Volterra, he considers him to be a Christian who wished to show that the Mosaic laws were superior to Roman laws in upholding what was right and just. Bossowski claims that since Roman laws were mainly hostile to Christianity, it would not be unreasonable to suppose that the author was a Christian seeking to urge fellow-Christians to keep the Mosaic rather than the Roman laws. He notes that Christians used the *Collatio* in the Middle Ages, which fact would support Christian authorship of the

[50] Oestersetzer, *op. cit.*, pp. 84-5.

[51] A. Masi, "Contributi ad una datazione della Collatio Legum Mosaicarum et Romanarum", *Bollettino Istituto Diritto Romano (BIDR)*, 64 (1961), 285ff.: G. Cervenca, "Ancora sul problema della datazione della Collatio Legum Mosaicarum et Romanarum" *Studia et Documenta Historiae et Juris, SDHI* 29 (1963) 253ff., a study praised by P. De Francisci, "Ancora intorno alla 'Collatio legum Mosaicarum et Romanarum', *BIDR* 66 (1963), 97ff.; A. Masi, "Ancora sulla datazione della Collatio Legum Mosaicarum et Romanarum", *Studi di Senesi*, 14, 1965, 415ff., and M. A. de Dominicis' answer, "Ancora sulla Collatio Legum Mosaicarum et Romanarum (a proposito di una recente critica)", *BIDR* 69 (1969), 337ff.

[52] See B. Biondi, *Il Diritto Romano Cristiano*, 1, Milan, 1952, p. 57.

[53] See again the arguments raised by E. Levy in his analysis of Volterra's work *ZSS* 50 (1930), 698ff.

Collatio, otherwise it would be difficult to understand why they should adopt the work of a Jew, an *infidelis,* when they were overtly opposed to the Jews.[54]

This theory does not in my view withstand critical analysis. Except for a short period when the Church, for political reasons, recognized the value of Roman law, it considered Christian law superior to that of Rome and determined to adapt Roman law to it.[55] If the author of the *Collatio* were a Christian, he would not have carried weight by praising both Judaism and the Roman-pagan world, for these were the two main institutions to which Christianity was opposed. In addition, there is no known Christian document which does not mention the Gospels, so that it would be difficult to designate as Christian one that refers only to the Torah. Even Bossowski's claim that the *Collatio* was intended to discourage the practice of Roman law seems inexact; while the antiquity of biblical law was noted (*scitote iurisconsulti quia Moyses prius hoc statuit . . .)* the author also wished to demonstrate the similarity between the two legal codes.[56] It is true that Christians made use of Scripture, but they did so in order to support Christian doctrine, which regarded the Church as the offspring of the Bible. They often used it in their polemics against the Jews since it formed the common basis of both their religions. But they thought that the Jews had made a grave mistake in not believing that the messianic prophesies referred to Jesus. In their view, the events in the Old Testament were but a preparation for the advent of Christ,[57] and with his coming the divine covenant with Israel had been abrogated, with the result that the Jews were no longer the chosen people.[58] Why then should a Christian encourage the observance of the Mosaic law which, according to his belief, had been repealed?

Regarding the medieval period, Savigny, in his history of Roman Law in the Middle Ages,[59] is of the opinion that the *Collatio* was known and used

[54] F. Bossowski, "Suntne in jure romano, suadente usu forensi audientiae episcopalis, quaedam praecepta ad instar juris privati hebraici introducta?" *Rocznik Prawniczego Wileńskiego,* X, 1939, 1ff, and in particular p. 26, n. 32.

[55] See above, n. 52. Also Bossowski's thesis that the *episcopalis audientia* may have been instrumental in permitting the penetration of Greek and Jewish laws into the Roman code does not seem convincing Biondi. (*Diritto Romano Cristiano,* p. 456) rightly observed that the *episcopalis audientia* made possible the introduction of the Christian spirit into Roman law.

[56] An argument similar to Bossowski's figures in Rudorff, *Ueber den Ursprung und die Bestimmung der Lex Dei oder Mosaicarum et Romanarum legum Collatio,* Berlin, 1868, and in Hohenlohe, *Ursprung und Zweck der Collatio,* Vienna, 1935, according to which the *Collatio's* author is St. Ambrose. See criticism by S. Solazzi, "Per la data della Collatio Mosaicarum et Romanarum Legum", *Atti dell'Accademia di Scienze Morali et Politiche di Napoli,* 1935, 262ff. (*Scritti di Diritto Romano,* Napoli, 1960, vol. 3, 481ff., p. 484f.).

[57] On this point see M. Simon, *Verus Israel . . ., op. cit.,* 92, 177ff.

[58] M. Simon, *Verus Israel . . ., op. cit.,* 203.

[59] C. F. Savigny, *Geschichte des römischen Rechts im Mittelalter,* Ed. II, ch. 15, 28ff.

by the Church at that time; Volterra, however, has provided many valid objections to this point of view.[60] It may be stated that there is no clear proof that ecclesiastical circles knew and made use of the *Collatio* in the Middle Ages, for the phrases quoted by some scholars may also be attributed to other sources. Moreover, no other text exists of a Latin translation of biblical passages similar to the translation in the *Collatio,* and the Roman legal sources used only in the *Collatio* and not in other compilations are not mentioned. While it cannot be denied that the *Collatio* may have been known to medieval Christian circles, that is surely a long way from declaring, as does Bossowski, that it was known for certain, and therefore that the author must have been Christian. I think that we may assume that the *Collatio* was compiled by a Roman Jew between 294 and 313, with the purpose of broadening the Jews' knowledge of Roman law during Diocletian's reign.[61]

* * *

Another issue to be considered is that of the relationship between Diocletian and the Patriarch. I agree with the view of various scholars that, even after the Antonian Constitution, local laws and customs survived in Palestine.[62] In particular, it is certain that jurisdictional autonomy and Jewish courts of law existed in Palestine side by side with Roman courts of law. Unlike the more complicated situation in the Diaspora, it may be stated that in Palestine the Jews, "although enjoying the rights of local and Roman citizenship, maintained until 398 their own personal ethnic-religious statute and their own courts of law which applied this statute in competition with the law of the state. Hence the existence until 398 of Jewish jurisdiction is limited to the eastern provinces, although Juster claimed that it extended to the whole of the Diaspora; it may be noted with regard to these same states that the Roman administration, even after 212, recognized *de iure* the Jewish personal statute necessarily connected with jurisdiction . . . This recognition is in keeping with the Romans' general system of preserving

[60] E. Volterra, "La collatio . . .", *op. cit.,* 23ff., ch. "La conoscenza della Collatio nel Medio Evo".

[61] A. M. Rabello, "Alcune note sulla Collatio Legum Mosaicarum et Romanarum e sul suo luogo d'origine" *Scritti G. Bedarida,* Firenze, 1966, 177ff.; *idem,* "Sull ebraicità della Collatio legum Mosaicarum et Romanarum", *Rassegna Mensile di Israel* 33 (1967), 339ff.; *idem,* "Collatio legum Mosaicarum et Romanarum", *Enc. Judaica,* 5, 1971, 734ff.; *idem,* "On the Collatio legum Mosaicarum et Romanarum", *Annual of the Institute for Research in Jewish Law* (in Hebrew), Jerusalem, 1, 1974, 231ff.; D. Sperber, "Laesio Enormis and the Talmudic Law of Ona'ah", *Israel Law Review* 8 (1973), p. 272, n. 35.

[62] V. Colorni, *Legge Ebraica e leggi locali,* 106ff.; E. Volterra, "I diritti locali" in *Atti del Convegno internazionale sul tema: I diritti locali nelle provincie romane con particolare riguardo alle condizioni giuridiche del suolo,* Rome, 1974, 63f.

local laws even after citizenship had been granted to all the *peregrini*''.[63]

''After the fall of Jerusalem, as before it'', notes Juster in his basic study, ''the Jews brought their lawsuits not only before Jewish judges – who might possibly be considered arbiters – but before true Jewish courts empowered to dispense justice in accordance with Jewish law, and authorized by the Romans to do so. That is to say, a Jewish court of law was constituted [as a recognized tribunal]; this court then had authority over the defendant; could summon and compel him to appear before it or convict him by default, subsequently carrying out sentence by whatever means were at its disposal. The Roman government recognized that the verdict was founded in lawful judicial authority. Nevertheless, as in other parts of the Empire, it seems that Roman rule provided some kind of supervision over the moral standards and professional competence of the Jewish judges''.[64]

How was this Jewish court of law constituted so that it was considered competent in accordance with both Jewish and Roman law?

It should be noted, in this respect, that there was heated controversy between the rabbis and the Patriarch. The rabbis claimed the exclusive right to ordain, whereas the Patriarch claimed unto himself a similar privilege; the dissension between some of the rabbis and the patriarchs was particularly violent and the situation in the legal field was far from satisfactory.[65] It is perhaps in this context that a rescript by Diocletian, reported in Justinian's Code, should be understood.

The problem of the *inscriptiones* of Diocletian's constitutions is well known. Volterra has recently published two articles on this subject ''seeking to show that the original inscriptions were very different from those found in the Gregorian, Hermogenian, Theodosian and Justinian codes, in the pre-Justinian collections of *iura* and *leges* and from those appearing in jurists' collections . . . Even the name of the addressee was followed, if he was a civil servant, by details of his duties and title, or, if he was a private citizen, by his name, first name, patronymic and sometimes by his profession''.[66]

[63] V. Colorni, *op. cit.*, 115ff. See also H. P. Chajes, ''Les juges juifs en Palestine de l'an 70 á l'an 500'', *REJ* 39 (1899), 39ff.; J. Juster, *op. cit.*, 296 n. 2, 106 n. 2; A. Büchler, *The Political and the Social Leaders of the Jewish Community of Sepphoris in the Second and Third Centuries,* London, 1909; A Gulak, *Yesodei Hamishpat Ha'Ivri,* Jerusalem, 1922, vol. 4, 23ff.; G. Alon, *Toledot Hayehudim Be-Eretz Israel,* Tel Aviv, 1, 1952, 136ff.; H. Mantel, *Studies in the History of the Sanhedrin,* Harvard University Press, 1961, 223; see also Sh. Albeck, *Law Courts in Talmudic Times,* Jerusalem, 1980 (in Hebrew).

[64] J. Juster, *op. cit.*, II, 96-97.

[65] A. Marmorstein, ''L'Opposition contre le Patriarche R. Juda II'', *REJ* 64 (1912), 59ff.; H. Albeck, ''Semikha and Minnui and Beth Din'', *Zion* 8 (1943), 85ff. (in Hebrew) and *idem,* ''The Sanhedrin and its President'', *Zion* 8 (1943), 165ff.; I. F. Baer, ''The Origins of the Organization of the Jewish Community of the Middle Ages'', *Zion* 15 (1950), 1ff.

[66] E. Volterra, ''Sulle *inscriptiones* di alcune costituzioni di Diocleziano'', *BIDR* 76 (1973), 245ff. and *idem, Il problema del testo delle costituzioni imperiali,* Florence, 1971.

Had the *inscriptio* of the rescript we shall examine here been more complete, there doubtless would have been fewer questions to ask. The text has reached us through the Justinian Code. Book three, chapter thirteen, *De iurisdictione omnium iudicum et de foro competenti,* paragraph 3, reads as follows:

> "*Idem* (Diocletianus et Maximianus) *AA. et CC. Iudae.* Privatorum consensus iudicem non facit eum, qui nulli praest iudicio, nec quod is statuit rei iudicatae continet auctoritatem. *S. vi K. Ian. AA. conss.* (a.293)".[67]

Selden,[68] Gothofredus,[69] Mitteis,[70] and more recently Taubenschlag,[71] interpret this passage as being addressed to a Jew named *Juda* and as referring to Jews. Mitteis, in particular, sought support for the view, mentioned above,[72] that after the loss of national independence the Jews, from the legal point of view, became *peregrini dediticii* who might have constituted a *collegium* of worship but not a nation and hence could not have enjoyed national jurisdiction.[73] Mitteis saw in Diocletian's rescript and in the constitution reported in CTh. 2,1,10 of 398 proof that nothing had changed with regard to our problem from 70 onwards.

We have already mentioned that scholars today do not agree with this theory, mainly as a result of Juster's research. He dealt briefly with our text; however, since Diocletian's rescript seems, *prima facie,* to conflict with the assertion that there was permanent jurisdictional autonomy in Palestine up to 398 (when the CTh. 2,1,10 was promulgated), Juster considered that Diocletian's rescript was not addressed to a Jew and did not refer to Judaism.[74]

About thirty years ago historians were divided on the interpretation of this rescript. Dinaburg, in an original explanation, claimed that it was

[67] Cf. text in the *Basilica,* 7, 3, 39.

[68] J. Selden, *De synedriis et Praefecturis Juridicis Veterum Ebraeorum libri tres,* Frankfurt, 1691, 118.

[69] Gothofredus *in loco* remarks: *Fallit hac regula, quoties fori privilegio renunciat.*

[70] L. Mitteis, *Reichsrecht und Volksrecht,* Leipzig, 1891, p. 34 and n.5.

[71] R. Taubenschlag, *Das Römischen Privatrecht zur zeit Diokletianus, Opera Minora,* Warsaw, 1959, p. 149, n. 1044.

[72] See above, note 12.

[73] It was for this reason that Mitteis excluded the Talmud from his analysis of the relations between *'Reichsrecht* and *Volksrecht',* while recently R. Yaron showed that the Talmud too can offer some valuable clues for the study of the problem: R. Yaron, "Reichsrecht, Volksrecht and Talmud", *Revue Internationale des Droits de l'Antiquité* II (1964), 281ff.

[74] J. Juster, *op. cit.,* II, 104, n. 4.

addressed to the Patriarch;[75] Albeck[76] and Baer[77] generally concurred with this opinion. By contrast, G. Alon agreed with Juster and sought to combat Dinaburg's arguments.[78] Since then no scholars have dealt with it.[79]

I think that Dinaburg is right, that the text refers to Jewish jurisdiction and that it was addressed to the Patriarch. To begin with, the name of the person to whom the rescript was addressed: *Iudae. Iuda* does not appear in Jones' Prosopography.[80] Without delving deeply into the problem, it should be pointed out that in the East some Christians bore this name *Iuda,* evidently following the example of Judas Taddeus whose epistle is included in the New Testament. Eusebius, in his *Historia Ecclesiastica* (VI, 7), mentions a Christian chronicler by the name of *Iudas,* living at the time of the Severi.[81]

In other cases, it is not clear to which religious faith those bearing the name *Iuda* belonged. For instance, CIJ. 2 mentions the inscription found in the Basilica of San Valentina, on the Flaminian Way: *qui nomen habuit*

[75] B. Z. Dinaburg (Dinur), "Diocletian's Rescript to Jehuda", *Memorial Volume in Honor of A. Gulak and S. Klein,* Jerusalem, 1942, 76ff. (in Hebrew); see also M. Schwabe, "Libanius' Letters to the Patriarch in Eretz Israel", *Tarbiz* 1 (1929-30), Part 2, 85ff. (in Hebrew); *idem,* "A New Document concerning the History of the Jews in the Fourth Century", *ibid.,* part 3, 107ff.

[76] H. Albeck, "Semikha and Minnui and Beth Din", *Zion* 8 (1943), 85ff. and especially p. 90; we quote the English summary, published in the same journal: "The term 'Semikha' was at first used for the granting of an appointment as teacher to the recipient, Nismakh; but there was no laying on of hands. For this reason 'Semikha' is referred to in Palestine as 'Minnui' or appointment. At a later stage the term 'Semikha' evolved into an honourable epithet indicating that the 'nismakh' was worthy of appointment. After the death of Rabbi Judah the Patriarch, Rabbi Hanina was appointed the 'Rosh Yeshiva', and at a later date appears to have become the Head of the Great Yeshiva. At first, a single authority made the appointment. At a later time it was decided that a Beth Din of three was required and that the *Nassi* or President must approve of the appointment even if he himself did not appoint. This led to disputes as those who had received 'Semikha' from a Beth Din considered that their status did not require the approval of the President. The latter appealed to the Roman authorities and received a favourable 'rescript'. Finally the Beth Din and the President reached a compromise and ordered that the approval of both was necessary for Minnui".

[77] I. F. Baer, "The Origins of the Organization . . .", *op. cit.,* 16.

[78] G. Alon, *Studies in Jewish History,* Tel-Aviv, 1957 (in Hebrew), vol. 2, 15ff. and especially 55ff.

[79] On this issue see the recent essays by H. Mantel, *Studies in the History of the Sanhedrin,* Harvard University Press, 1961, 206ff. "Ordination and the Appointment of Judges"; A. Linder, "The Roman Imperial Government and the Jews under Constantine", *Tarbiz* 44 (1974-75), 118 n. 137, in which the author abstains from expressing a personal opinion in the above-mentioned polemics.

[80] A. H. M. Jones – J. R. Martindale – P. Morris, *The Prosopography of the Later Roman Empire,* Cambridge, I, 1971; see also A. H. M. Jones, *The Later Roman Empire (284-602),* Oxford, 1964, II, 944ff.; III, 321ff.

[81] F. Jacobi, "Judas", *PW,RE,* 9^2, 2641.

Iuda;[82] in CIJ. 206 there is an inscription from the Appian Way: *Cocotina qui et Juda . . .* followed by the brother's name *Abundantius,* a typically Christian name like *Hilarius, Anastasius, Clemens.* If *Abundantius* was in fact a Christian, it may be assumed that his brother *Juda* was too, although this must evidently remain a hypothesis.[83] It is, nevertheless, true that its association with Judas Iscariot discouraged more and more Christians from adopting this name at a time when the separation between Judaism and Christianity was becoming more distinct. However, I prefer to consider the *Iuda* of the rescript we are studying to have been a Jew.[84] It will be remembered that *Iuda* not only dates back to the patriarchal era (Jacob's son Judah), the name of one of the tribes and later of one of the Jewish kingdoms; it was also the name of the Patriarchs in the Mishnaic and talmudic periods. After Rabbi *Judah HaNassi* who compiled the Mishna,[85] it was borne by his grandson Rabbi *Judah II* (= Rabbi Judah Nesia I)[86] and the latter's grandson Rabbi *Judah III* (= Rabbi Judah Nesai II) who was Patriarch from 290 to 320.[87] Hence it follows that Rabbi *Judah III* was Patriarch at the time of Diocletian. He lived in Tiberias and, although the patriarchate had lost much of its popular prestige, was respected and must have been on good terms with the Roman administration.[88] It may well be that Rabbi *Judah III* is the *Iuda* of Diocletian's rescript, so we may assume

[82] *Corpus Inscriptionum Judaicarum,* by J.-B. Frey, Vatican City, I, 1936 (new Photostat edition, with Prolegomenon by B. Lifshitz, 1975), p. 7. Frey writes: "According to Marucchi and Le Blant we are concerned with a Jew converted to Christianity who, at the time of his baptism, rejected the name Judas. However, it is pure conjecture to assume that the deceased was a Christian. What is certain is that the name Judah is definitely Jewish . . ."

[83] J.-B. Frey, *CIJ* 657, on the use of the name Judah in Egypt, see Tcherikover, *CPJ* 1, 180 (index).

[84] On the use of the name Judah in the Roman Empire, see in particular: H. Leon, *The Jews of Ancient Rome,* Philadelphia, 1960, p. 105 and inscriptions 12, 33, 121, 122, 345, 346, 347, 348, 349, 350, 351; Naomi G. Cohen, *Jewish Names and their Significance in the Hellenistic and Roman Period in Asia Minor* (thesis, Jerusalem, 1969, in Hebrew), 37ff. I wish to thank Dr. Naomi Cohen for the information provided on the name Judah.

[85] On Rabbi Judah the Patriarch, or Rabbi, see H. Albeck, *Introduction to the Mishna,* Tel-Aviv, 1959, 231ff.; E. E. Urbach, "Rabbi Yehuda Hanasi", *Enziklopedia Ivrit,* 19, 1968, 207ff., with bibliography; *idem,* "Judah HaNasi", *Enc. Judaica,* 10, 366ff. The genealogical tree of the Patriarchs up to Rabbi Judah III is as follows: Rabbi Judah HaNasi – Rabban Gamaliel III – Rabbi Judah II – Rabban Gamaliel IV – Rabbi Judah III.

[86] On Rabbi Judah II, see A. Marmorstein, "L'opposition contre le Patriarche R. Juda II", *REJ* 64 (1912), 59ff.; W. Bacher, "Juda II", *JE,* 1916, 7, 337ff.; G. Blidstein, "A Roman Gift of Strenae to the Patriarch Judah II", *IEJ* 22 (1972), 150ff.

[87] On Rabbi Judah III see I. Halevy, *Dorot Harishonim: Die Geschichte und Literatur Israels,* IIa, Frankfurt, 1901, 344ff. (in Hebrew); W. Bacher, "Juda III", *JE,* 1916, 338ff.; I. Ta-Shma, "Juda III", *Enc. Judaica,* 10, 333.

[88] In Talmudic sources we find mention, for instance, of his slave Germanius, the Gothic guard received as a gift from the government (*yShab,* 6,9; *yYom* 5,5).

that he himself petitioned the Emperor.[89] What prompted the Patriarch to take this step at the beginning of his term of office? The reason must be sought in the dispute, mentioned above, between the Patriarch and the rabbis over the question of who should appoint the judges.[90] The Patriarch claimed the prerogative of appointing the judges directly; it happened that those appointed were often wealthy but incompetent in legal matters and ignorant in religious matters (two aspects of the same phenomenon because "legal" and "religious" norms are inseparable in Judaism). The Patriarch preferred rich judges for two main reasons: (1) so that they might be above suspicion of corruption and could serve without requiring remuneration; (2) so that, in times of economic difficulties, their financial aid, given in gratitude for their appointment, could be relied upon; their money was used for the living expenses of several rabbis and, in particular, for the maintenance of schools, even in small population centres.[91] The rabbis did not find such reasons acceptable; they considered them compromising. In their view it was essential that the judges be wise, knowledgeable and God-fearing. The rabbis also claimed that it was their prerogative to appoint these judges. An echo of these disputes, *inter alia,* can be found in a passage of the Palestinian Talmud:[92]

> Pt Sanhedrin 1, 4(5); 19a: Rabbi Abba said: At first everyone used to ordain his own students like Rabban Johanan ben Zakkai (who) ordained R. Eliezer and R. Joshua, and R. Joshua (who ordained) Rabbi Akiva, and Rabbi Akiva (who ordained) Rabbi Meir and R. Simeon.
>
> He (R. Akiva) said: Let R. Meir sit first. R. Simeon became distraught. Said R. Akiva to him: Enough – I and your creator recognize your worth.
>
> They returned to their original practice of honouring the Patriarchate (granting honour to this house, i.e. Patriarchate). They said: A court which ordains against the will of the Patriarch – its ordination is invalid. A Patriarch who ordains against the will of the court – his ordination is valid.

[89] As is known, the *rescripta* are written opinions by the emperors handed down on controversial juridical issues submitted by magistrates or by private individuals; on the *rescripta* see F. Schulz, *History of Roman Legal Science,* Oxford, 1953², 152ff.; V. Arangio-Ruiz, *Storia del Diritto Romano,* Naples, 1964, 245ff,; A. Nicoletti, "Constitutiones Principum", *NNDI,* 4, 295ff.

[90] See above n. 65; regarding the continued existence of jurisdictional autonomy, a problem often mentioned in this article, see also the remarks by Th. Reinach, "Judaei", *Daremberg-Saglio,* 3,2,626: "The juridical autonomy of the Rabbis was in force even after the Jews became Roman citizens; it was then that the supreme jurisdiction of the Patriarch at Tiberias became all important". On the question of the appointment of judges, see also H. Mantel, *Studies in the History of the Sanhedrin, op. cit.,* 206ff.: "Ordination and the Appointment of Judges".

[91] It was also for these reasons that the Patriarch used to send emissaries (*apostoli*) to the various Jewish centres; on the functions of the Patriarch see J. Juster, *Juifs, op. cit.,* I, 391ff.; H. Mantel, *Studies in the History of the Sanhedrin, op. cit.,* 175ff.: "The Offices of the Nasi".

[92] *ySanh* I, 4(5), see L. I. Rabinowitz, "Talmud, Jerusalem", *Enc. Judaica,* 15, 772ff.

"Once again they changed their position and laid down that a court should not ordain against the will of the Patriarch and that the Patriarch should only ordain in accordance with the will of the court".

Now that we have established that the rescript was addressed to the Patriarch, Rabbi Judah III, we come to the interpretation of its contents. Regarding *Privatorum consensus,* it should be noted (as Dinaburg has done, although he did not examine this point very thoroughly) that the rescript does not speak of *partium consensus* but *privatorum.* We learn from Cicero that *privatus homo dicitur qui in magistratu non est;*[93] upon examining certain passages in the Justinian Code (selected from Mayr's *Vocabularium Codicis Iustiniani*) *privatus* appears as the antithesis of *publicus* (see e.g. C. 3,12,7), whereas no similar comparison may be made between *privati* and *partes.* The word *partes* appears several times in the Justinian Code and it is interesting to note the use of *partium consensus* (instead of *privatorum consensus* in C. 3,13,3) in C. 3,1,14,1: . . . "*per* quam sancimus omnes iudices sive maiores sive minores, sive qui in administrationibus positi sunt vel in hoc regia civitate vel in orbe terrarum, qui nostris gubernaculis regitur, sive eos, quibus nos audientiam committimus vel qui a maioribus iudicibus dantur vel qui ex iurisdictione sua iudicandi habent facultatem vel qui ex recepto (id est compromisso, quod iudicium imitatur) causas dirimendas suscipiunt vel qui arbitrium peragunt vel ex auctoritate sententiarum et partium consensu electi, et generaliter omnes iudices Romani iuris disceptatores non aliter litium primordium accipere, nisi prius ante iudicialem sedem sacrosanctae deponantur scripturae . . ."[94]

Having excluded the possibility that the original text of the rescript may have referred to the consent of the parties, we must explain the meaning of *privatorum consensus.* The *privati* in this case would be the rabbis who played an important rôle in the lives of the Jewish people but, in contrast to the Patriarch, had no public standing in Roman law.[95] Diocletian's rescript lays down that the consent of these private persons (that is, the agreement of the rabbis) is insufficient for the appointment of a judge; a judge must

[93] Cicero, *Catil.* 1.1.3; Forcellini, *Lexicon totius latinitatis,* under title "*privatus*".

[94] On C. 3.1.14.1 see in particular M. Kaser, *Das römische Zivilprozessrecht,* Munich, 1966 (= RZPR), 421ff.

[95] Also of interest is the use of the word in the corresponding passage of the *Basilica,* 7,3,9; "individual, private, simple citizen" (Rocci); in the second meaning of the word, "ignorant, lay", the word is used in the Talmudic expression *"Bet Din shel Hediotot"* (court of the laymen); on the use of this expression see J. Buxtorfius, *Lexicon Chaldaicum, Talmudicum et Rabbinicum,* Basle, 1539, 595ff.; A. Gulak, *Yesodei Hamishpat Ha'ivri,* Berlin, 5682 (Tel-Aviv, 5727, 1967), III, 119; IV, 32, 166; G. Alon, *Studies . . ., op. cit.,* II, 15ff.; M. Elon, *"Jewish Law. History, Sources, Principles",* Jerusalem, 1973, 1, 18ff. ("Lay Jewish Tribunals").

head a court of law or legal authority (*iudicium,* dikastērion in the Basilica). There are in fact some texts where *iudicium* indicates a court.[96]

The meaning of the rescript, therefore, from the historical point of view, would be as follows. Roman law does not recognize as judge a person appointed by private individuals. To be a judge, that person must stand at the head of a court of law or legal authority.[97] For that purpose a judge must be appointed by the competent authority – in our case, the Patriarch, who, after the destruction of the Temple and loss of political independence, assumed ever-increasing importance as a political leader, and eventually was recognized as such by the Roman administration.[98] Moreover, whenever the parties turned to judges appointed only by the rabbis, the decisions of these judges would not have been recognized in Roman law as *res indicata;* this is confirmed in the *Pauli Sententiae* 5.5a,1: "Res iudicatae videntur ab his, qui imperium potestatemque habent vel qui ex auctoritate eorum inter partes dantur, itemque a magistratibus municipalibus usque ad summam, qua ius dicere possunt, itemque ab his, qui ab imperatore extra ordinem petuntur. Ex compromisso autem index sumptus rem iudicatam non facit: sed poena inter eas promissum sit, poena re in iudicium deducta ex stipulatu poeti potest".[99] The fact that the *sententia* of the *arbiter* did not constitute *res iudicata* clearly gave the losing party the opportunity to take his case *ex novo* to a *iudex qui praest iudicio.*[100]

[96] On the use of the word *'iudicium'* in post-classic courtroom terminology, see in particular G. Pugliese, "Iudicium", *NNDI,* 9, 1963, 355ff. and especially 338ff. On the use of the corresponding term in the *Basilica,* 7,3,9 ("Judgment, Tribunal" – Rocci), see F. De Martino, *Storia della Costituzione Romana,* Naples, 1965, IV, 2, 771; see also the remarks of S. Mendelsohn, *The Criminal Jurisprudence of the Ancient Hebrews,* New York, 1890 (reproduced 1968), p. 87, n. 190: "The individual members of the several courts are frequently styled Dayanim (Judges), and in the aggregate Beth Din (house, court of justice), similar to the Attic appellation *Dicasterion,* which indicated the judicial body (*Dicastes*) that sat in court, as well as the place at which they held their sessions (Smith 356b). In Rome the reverse was the case. There the term *jus* was transferred from the *law* to the *place* where the law was dispensed: an application of the name of what is done to the place where it is done (*ibid.* 562a)".

[97] See G. I. Luzzatto, "Giurisdizione . . ." *Enc. del Diritto* (= EdD) in particular 196 ff.

[98] On the functions of the Patriarch and his status in the Roman Empire, see in particular: J. Juster, *Juifs . . ., op. cit.,* I, 391 ff.; I. S. Zuri (Rzezak), *History of Hebrew Public Law. The Reign of the Patriarchate and the Sanhedrin,* London, 1933 (in Hebrew); M. Simon, *Verus Israel . . ., op. cit.,* 82 ff.; H. Mantel, *The Sanhedrin . . ., op. cit.,* 175 ff.; A. Linder, *The* Roman Imperial Government, *op. cit.,* 117, notes 136-166; A. M. Rabello, "A Tribute to Jean Juster", *op. cit.,* 227 ff. L. Levine, "The Jewish Patriarch (Nasi) in Third Century Palestine", *ANRW,* II, 19, 2 (1979), 649ff.

[99] On P.S. 5.5a1 see in particular E. Betti, "Regiudicata", *NNDI* 15 (1968), 216 ff.; G. Crifò, "Arbitrato", *EdD* 2 (1958), 893 ff.

[100] On the validity of the decisions of the arbiters see: M. Wlassak, "Arbiter", *PW.RE,* 2, 408 ff. and *idem,* "Arbitrium", *ibidem,* 412 ff.; F. Bonifacio, "Arbitro e Arbitratore", *NNDI* 1[2] (1958), 925 ff.; G. Crifò, "Arbitrato", *EdD* 2 (1958), 893 ff.; see also G. Salvioli, *Storia della Procedura Civile e Criminale* (in P. del Giudice, *Storia del Diritto Italiano,* vol. III, part II, Milan, 1927), 114 ff. "Il tribunale degli Ebrei."

This interpretation of C. 3,13,3 is consistent with the Roman administration's reinforcement of the Patriarchate at that time. The title *Patriarch* given to the *Nasi* by the Romans (CTh. 16,8 passim) is the Latin form of *Ethnarch* conferred by Julius Caesar on Hyrcanus II and his descendants.[101] In the Theodosian Code the Patriarch is defined as *spectabilis* (CTh. 16,8,15),[102] *clarissimus* (CTh. 16,8,8),[103] *illustris* (CTh. 16,8.8; 16,8,13),[104] *honoraria praefectura* (CTh. 16,8,22).[105] During the period when they were centralizing their administration, it seem that the Romans were interested in encouraging a recognized central authority among the Jews in Palestine.[106] It is therefore clear that, even if Diocletian's rescript refers to the Jews, as we claim, it did not change the jurisdictional situation: Jewish jurisdictional autonomy continued to be recognized.[107] Nor is there reason to suppose that the Emperor wished to intervene in a dispute between the rabbis and the Patriarch which did not concern him; in reply to the Patriarch's petition the Emperor states that only judges recognized by the governing authorities may hand down decisions admissible as *res iudicata.* Hence the decisions of the judges appointed by the Patriarch continued to be recognized by the Roman administration as *res indicata.* The Emperor's intervention may well have persuaded the rabbis to come to an understanding with the Patriarch whereby judges were to be appointed by mutual agreement between the two parties.[108] The real change in the juridical field – the abolition of Jewish jurisdictional autonomy and the withdrawal of recognition from its courts – was to occur in the Christian period, with the promulgation of the famous Constitution

[101] Josephus, *Ant. Jud.*, 14, 10.2, on which see in particular: A. Momigliano, *Ricerche sull'organizzazione della Guidea*, 12 ff.; F. Fabbrini, *L'impero di Augusto come ordinamento sovrannazionale*, Milan, 1974, 378; D. Piattelli, Ricerche intorno alle relazioni politiche tra Roma e l'*ethnos tōn Ioudaiōn* dal 161 a.C. al 4. a.C.", *BIDR* 74, 19 p. 303; H. Mantel, *Studies in the History of the Sanhedrin*, 236.

[102] On the use of the title *spectabilis* see J. Gaudemet, *Institutions de l'antiquité*, Paris, 1967, 706; F. De Martino, *Storia della Costituzione Romana*, Naples V, 1967, 245.

[103] On the use of the title *clarissimus* see J. Gaudemet, *Institutions . . ., op. cit.*, 706; De Martino, *Storia . . ., op. cit.*, V. 314; 366 ff.

[104] On the use of the title *illustris* see U. Brasiello, "Illustres", *NNDI*, 7, 1962, 181; J. Gaudemet, *Institutions . . ., op. cit.*, 706; De Martino, *Storia . . ., op. cit.*, V. 314, 331, 335.

[105] H. Mantel, *Studies in the History . . ., op. cit.*, 239.

[106] Juster explains the legalization of the patriarchate by the Roman administration as an attempt to supervise the activities of that institution and thus prevent eventual rebellion (*Juifs . . .*, 1, 393). Schlatter, on the other hand, maintains that the Romans acted thus because the Jews of Babylon enjoyed a similar privilege, in the institution of the Exilarch (*Geschichte Israels*, Stuttgart, 1925, 351). On the history of the Jews in Babylon and the authority of the Exilarch, see in particular: J. Neusner, *A History of the Jews in Babylon*, Leiden, 1965-68; M. Beer, *The Babylonian Exilarchate in the Arsacid and Sassanian Periods*, Tel-Aviv, 1970 (in Hebrew).

[107] J. Juster, *Juifs . . .*, II, 93 ff.; V. Colorni, *Legge ebraica e leggi locali, 103 ff., 311; idem, Gli Ebrei nel sistema del diritto comune fino alla prima emancipazione*, Milan, 1956, 1 ff.; A. M. Rabello, "A Tribute to Jean Juster", *op. cit.*, 236 ff.; see also above, note 90.

[108] See above, notes 75-78 and 92.

of 398 reported in CTh. 2,1,10.[109]

As for the position of the rescript in the Justinian Code, it should be noted that CTh. 2,1,10 is not located together with the other constitutions concerning the Jews, in book 16, chapters 8 and 9 of the Code. In the second book of the Theodosian Code, the first subject concerns *de iurisdictione et ubi quis conveniri debeat.* C. 3,13 also deals with *de iurisdictione.* Nevertheless, in the course of time, when the Patriarchate no longer existed,[110] the rescript certainly lost its original meaning and became of more general import.[111] Thus Lemosse explains: "The fact that the *iudices dati* were not appointed by the parties was announced by Hadrian. Diocletian only repeated in practice what was an undoubted principle (CTh. 3,13,3)".[112]

We may therefore conclude that, despite everything, Diocletian's reign was not a time of great oppression for the Jews. It is in this light that the following episode reported in the Palestinian Talmud (yBer. 3:1) should be understood: "when Diocletian came to Tyre, Rabbi Hiyya son of Abba (who was a *Cohen*) was seen crossing a cemetery in order to meet the Emperor".[113]

[109] On this constitution, see in particular J. Juster, *Juifs. . .*, II, 101 ff.; V. Colornin, *Legge ebraica . . ., op. cit . . .*, 115 ff.; J. Gaudemet, *L'Eglise dans l'Empire Romain (IV-V siècles)*, Paris, 1958, 628; A. Berger, "C.Th. 2.1.10 and CJ. 1.9.8. pr. A Perfect Example of an Interpolation through Cancellation of a 'non' ", *IURA* 10 (1959), 14 ff. and n. 49 above.

[110] In 415 the Patriarch Gamliel was deposed (C.Th. 16.8.22) and in the following years the office of the Patriarch disappeared. In 429 Theodosius II took advantage of the situation to impose a new tax, the *aurum coronarium* (C.Th. 16.8.29). On this subject see S. Solazzi, "Fra norme romane antisemite", *BIDR*, 44, 1937 396 ff. (*Scritti*, 3, 1960, 579 ff.); J. Parkes, *The Conflict of the Church and the Synagogue, op. cit.*, 235; J. Gaudemet, *L'Eglise dans l'Empire . . ., op. cit.*, 623 ff.; A. Swinderek, *"Ioudaikos Logos", The Journal of Juristic Papyrology. JJP.* 16-17, 1971, 45 ff.; I. Gafni, "Aurum Coronarium", *Enc. Judaica*, 3, 854; A. M. Rabello, "Honorius Flavius", *ibid.*, 8, 968: *idem.* "Theodosius II et la fête de Pourim", *Revue Historique de Droit Français et Etranger* 55, 1977, pp. 545 ff.

[111] It may be of interest to note that in a medieval commentary on the Justinian Code, compiled by various authors, we find side by side the two interpretations of *Privatorum consensus* given here: "Codicis D. N. Iustiniani . . . libri novem priores; ad vetustissimorum exemplarium, et ad ipsius etiam Noricae editionis (quam Haloandro debemus) fidem recogniti et emendate". Lugduni, 1558, 350; "Priuatorum casvs. Ego & tu in causa quam habebamus, in iudice, qui nullam alias habuit iurisdictionem, consensimus, vt inter nos iudecaret an sit iudex, quaeritur respon. quod non, nec si iudicaverit, autoritatem rei iudicatae obtinet iudicatum. Priuatorum, puta duorum vel trium, vel etiam decem, nam secus in consensu alicuius collegii, puta cerdonum, pellipariorum & similium: vt infra eodem. l. fina. Item secus in consensu uniuersitatis: vt in uthenti, de defen, ciui, crica pin. & j. in fi. col. iij. Sed obstat quod ibi dicit, quod est confirmandus a praefecto, praetoria. Sed dico, quod statim facta electione habet iurisdictionem, sed non effectum iurisdictionis".

It may be useful, for the exact interpretation of the Constitution in the Justinian text, to examine also D. 5.1.1. and D. 5.1.2.

[112] M. Lemosse, *Cognitio. Etude sur le rôle du Juge dans l'Instruction du procès civil antique,* Paris, 1944, 228; on C. 3, 13, see in particular: Liebs, *Hermogenianus iuris epitomae. Zum Stand der römische Jurisprudenz im Zeitalter Diokletians,* Göttingen, 1964, 30; A. Cenderelli, *Ricerche sul 'Codex Hermogenianus'*, Milan, 1965, 35, 143; R. Bonini, *Ricerche di Diritto Giustiniano,* Milan, 1968, 108, 118, n. 79.

[113] I wish to express my gratitude to my teacher, Professor Reuven Yaron, and to Professor Daniel Sperber for their interesting remarks and observations.

La première loi de Théodose II, C. Th. XVI, 8, 18 et la fête de Pourim

Résumé. — L'a. examine la loi du *C.Th.* XVI, 8, 18 sur la crucifixion d'Haman et l'observance de Pourim. Pour la datation, on confirme que cette loi doit être du 29 mai 408. On examine aussi l'aggravation de la situation religieuse des Juifs sous Théodose II et l'incident de Inmestar. On conclut par les considérations concernant la signification politico-religieuse de la loi concernant Pourim et l'influence de la tradition de la crucifixion d'Haman sur Dante et Michel-Ange.

La fête de Pourim a toujours été chère aux Juifs — surtout à ceux de la Diaspora — qui y voient le symbole de l'intérêt persistant et providentiel que Dieu porte à Son peuple partout où il se trouve. Célébrée d'abord par le peuple, ce n'est que plus tard que la fête prit un caractère officiel. Dès l'origine, il s'agissait d'une fête populaire : « Et les Juifs s'engagèrent à faire ce qu'ils avaient déjà commencé et ce que Mardochée leur écrivit » (*Esther,* 9, 23) [1].

Le *Talmud* précise de façon explicite que l'homme a le devoir de boire (du vin) à Pourim jusqu'à ce qu'il soit incapable de distinguer « Maudit

1. Sur la fête de Pourim et son histoire, voir surtout N. S. Doniach, *Purim or the Feast of Esther,* Philadelphie 1933. Voir aussi P. Goodman, *The Purim Anthology,* Philadelphie 1949; J. T. Levinsky, *Sefer ha-Mo'adim,* vol. VI : Yemei Mo'ed Vezikaron, *Purim, Lag ba-Omer, Tu be-Av,* Tel-Aviv 1966; J. C. H. Lebram, *Purimfest und Estherbuch, Vetus Testamentum* 22, 1972, p. 208 ss.; R. E. Herst, *The Purim Connection,* dans *Union Seminary Quarterly Review* 28, 1972-73, p. 139 s.; M. Smith, *Pseudepigraphy in the Israelite Literary Tradition,* dans *Pseudepigraphica,* I (*Entretiens sur l'Antiquité classique,* 18), 1972, p. 191-223; C. Roth, *The Feast of Purim and the Origins of the Blood Accusation,* dans *Speculum* 8, 1933, p. 520-526.

soit Haman » de « Bénit soit Mardochée » (*Megillah,* 7b). La *Guémara* elle-même rapporte l'anecdote suivante : Rabbah et R. Zera fêtaient ensemble la fête de Pourim. Ils s'enivrèrent, Rabbah se leva et coupa la gorge de R. Zera. Le lendemain il pria pour lui et R. Zera ne survécut que par miracle. L'année suivante, il invita de nouveau R. Zera à venir fêter avec lui la fête de Pourim, mais R. Zera refusa en alléguant qu'un miracle ne se reproduit pas tous les ans.

Les autorités rabbiniques se fondèrent sur cette anecdote pour essayer d'en déduire la nature exacte de l'obligation de boire du vin et de s'enivrer à Pourim [2]. Il semble bien, en fait, que les Juifs se soient parfois réjouis de façon quelque peu excessive de la mort d'Haman et de ses fils; au cours des siècles, Haman devint le symbole de l'antisémite, en tout temps et en tout lieu [3]. Le livre d'Esther mentionne expressément « La pendaison d'Haman » (*Esther,* 9, 10) mais d'autres sources mentionnent apparemment « la crucifixion d'Haman ». Est-ce que cette « crucifixion » d'Haman n'était pas de nature à rappeler la crucifixion de Jésus ? C'est sans doute pour cette raison — il me semble — que la fête de Pourim méritait une mention spéciale dans la législation romaine chrétienne, et il n'est pas impossible que cette législation ait eu à son tour une influence sur l'idée que les peuples occidentaux se firent de cette fête à travers les âges [4].

Avec l'élévation de Théodose II (Flavius Theodosius junior) au trône de l'Empire Romain d'Orient le 1er mai de l'an 408, les conditions de vie des Juifs de l'Empire empirèrent notablement [5]. Né en avril 401, il succéda à son père Arcadius, à l'âge de sept ans, laissant le pouvoir réel entre les mains d'Anthemius. La politique de Théodose II était en fait dictée par ses conseillers, mais les choses ne changèrent guère lors-

2. Sur cette question, voir l'étude halachique du rabbin Sh. J. ZEVIN, *Ad de-Lo Yada,* dans : *Ha-Mo'adim ba-Halakha,* 4e éd.; Jérusalem 1954, p. 203 et s.

3. Mais on ne doit pas penser que l'aversion pour Haman ait un caractère racial. Les Sages du *Talmud* soutiennent le principe de la responsabilité individuelle et dans le *Talmud,* Sanhedrin, on trouve que « ... les fils des fils d'Haman ont enseigné la Parole de Dieu à Bnei Berak... » Pour une vision d'Haman chez les Juifs hellénistiques, voir E. J. BICKERMAN, *Notes on the Greek Book of Esther,* dans *Proceedings of the American Academy for Jewish Research* 20, 1951, 101 ss. (= E. J. BICKERMAN, *Studies in Jewish and Christian History,* 1, 1976, p. 246 ss. et part. p. 263, n. 54 : Haman « Macedonian »); M. HENGEL, *Judaism and Hellenism. Studies in their Encounter in Palestine during the Early Hellenistic Encounter in Palestine during the Early Hellenistic Period,* London 1976, 1, p. 101 *Period,* London 1976, 1, p. 101 et 2, p. 70.

4. Sur l'influence de la loi romaine sur les Juifs du Moyen Age, voir S. GRAYZEL, *The Jews and Roman Law,* dans *JQR* 59, 1968, p. 93 et s.

5. Aujourd'hui encore, près de soixante ans après sa publication, l'étude de Juster reste fondamentale : Jean JUSTER, *Les Juifs dans l'empire romain,* Paris 1914. Sur Jean Juster et son ouvrage voir maintenant A. M. RABELLO, *A Tribute to Jean Juster,* dans *Israel Law Review* 11, 1976, p. 216 ss.

qu'il prit lui-même en main la gestion des affaires publiques. C'est lui qui collationna l'ensemble des lois impériales (*constitutiones*), depuis le règne de l'empereur Auguste jusqu'au sien [6].

La loi concernant la fête de Pourim se trouve dans *C. Th.* XVI, 8, 18 :

IMP. HONOR(IUS) ET THEOD(OSIUS) AA. ANTHEMIO P(RAETORI)O. *Iudaeos quodam festivitatis suae solemni Aman ad poenae quondam recordationem incendere et sanctae crucis adsimulatam speciem in contemptum Christianae fidei sacrilega mente exurere provinciarum rectores prohibeant, ne iocis suis fidei nostrae signum inmisceant, sed ritus suos citra contemptum Christianae legis retineant, amnisuri sine dubio permissa hactenus, nisi ab inlicitis temperaverunt.* DAT. IIII KAL. IVN. CONSTANT(INO)P(OLI) BASSO ET PHILIPPO CONSS. [7].

Cette loi est la première loi de Théodose II [8], et ce n'est pas par hasard qu'elle concerne les Juifs; comme nous l'avons dit, elle ne fait que marquer le début d'une législation hostile au judaïsme et aux Juifs. En l'an 408, l'année même où elle fut promulguée, Honorius, empereur d'Occident, connu pour sa sympathie pour les évêques, promulgua lui-aussi des lois contre les mécréants [9].

Cette constitution pose un certain nombre de questions qu'il nous faut aborder maintenant. En premier lieu, quand, exactement, fut-elle promulguée ? Deuxièmement, et surtout, la promulgation d'une telle constitution était-elle vraiment juste ? Les Juifs « crucifiaient-ils » vraiment Haman ? Quelle était la nature exacte de ces réjouissances de Pourim ? Troisièmement, nous analyserons un événement survenu près de la ville d'Antioche en Syrie. Enfin, nous devrons nous poser la question de savoir si la promulgation de cette loi ne constituait pas une intervention dans

6. Comme cela est reconnu, le *Codex Theodosianus* (438) fut accepté et promulgué par l'empereur Valentinien III dans l'empire d'Occident, où il fut longtemps et largement appliqué, même après la publication du *Corpus Iuris Civilis* qui est supérieur au *Codex Theodosianus* à bien des égards. Pour une explication de ce phénomène et l'importance du *C. Th.*, voir surtout P. VINOGRADOFF, *Roman Law in Medieval Europe,* Oxford 1929, p. 17-21; F. CALASSO, *Medio Evo del Diritto,* I, Milan 1954, p. 47 et suiv.

7. Th. MOMMSEN et P. KRUEGER, *Theodosiani libri XVI cum Constitutionibus Sirmondianis,* Berolini 1926, p. 891; P. R. COLEMAN-NORTON, *Roman State and Christian Church. A Collection of Legal Documents to A.D. 535,* II, London 1966, p. 510-511.

8. Sur l'attitude de Théodose à l'égard des Juifs, voir B. BLUMENKRANZ, *Juifs et chrétiens dans le monde occidental* (430-1096), Paris 1960, p. 295 ss.; A. M. RABELLO, *Theodosius II,* dans *Encyclopaedia Judaica,* XV, 1971, Col. 1101-2 (avec bibliographie).

9. Sur l'attitude d'Honorius à l'égard des Juifs, voir RABELLO, *Honorius,* dans *Encyclopaedia Judaica,* VII, col. 968 (avec bibliographie). De façon générale, sur l'attitude des empereurs romains à l'égard des Juifs, voir RABELLO, *Roman Emperors,* dans *Encyclopaedia Judaica,* XIV, col. 229-30.

les affaires intérieures des Juifs et une atteinte portée à leur liberté religieuse.

I. — Date de C. Th. xvi, 8, 18.

Dans les manuscrits et dans les éditions de *C. Th.* la date figure de la façon suivante : DAT. IIII KAL IUN. CONSTANT(INO)P(OLI) BASSO ET PHILIPPO CONSS. « Rendu le quatrième jour avant les calendes de juin à Constantinople, l'année du consulat de Bassus et de Philippus. » En d'autres termes, la loi fut publiée le 29 mai 408. Cette date ne soulève aucune question particulière. Mais nous ne devons pas oublier la remarque d'un des principaux interprètes du *C. Th.*, Jacques Godefroy [10] : ce dernier suggère dans son commentaire de lire plutôt *ian.* que *iun.*, c'est-à-dire janvier et non juin. Si l'on tient compte de cette correction, la loi aurait donc été publiée le 29 décembre. Mais de quelle année ? Janvier 408, et donc décembre 407, ou janvier 409, et donc décembre 408 ?

Anthemius était préfet du Prétoire de 405 à 414 si bien qu'en ce qui le concerne, les deux dates sont possibles [11]. Mais, il n'est pas de même de Théodose II et de ses deux consuls : Théodose II n'ayant accédé à l'empire que le 1er mai 408 et ses deux consuls, Bassus et Philippus, n'ayant occupé leurs fonctions que pendant l'année 408 [12], il est clair que, si l'on retient la suggestion de Godefroy, la seule date possible est celle du 29 décembre 408. Toutefois, la note de Godefroy ne me semble pas devoir être retenue. L'examen de la procédure législative de Théodose pendant les premières années de son règne montre clairement qu'en 408, des lois impériales ne furent successivement publiées qu'entre la fin du mois de mai et le mois de juillet [13]. Mais il y a une autre objection, moins formelle, mais plus fondamentale.

La fête de Pourim est traditionnellement célébrée le 14 et le 15 du mois d'Adar, qui correspond aux mois de février-mars. Mais il y a dans le calendrier hébreu d'autres dates que celles du 14-15 Adar qui sont liées, d'une façon ou d'une autre, à la fête de Pourim : « pour prescrire ces jours de Pourim aux temps fixés, comme le Juif Mardochée et la reine Esther les avaient établis pour eux-mêmes et leur postérité »

10. Jacques Godefroy (1587-1653), comme son père Denis, était un calviniste, célèbre professeur de droit. La plus importante de ses œuvres est l'édition du *Codex Theodosianus* (Lyon, 1665), avec un commentaire qui est considéré, jusqu'à ce jour, comme un des meilleurs.

11. Sur Anthemius, voir l'article de O. SEECK dans PAULY-WISSOWA, *Realencyklopädie der classischen Altertumswissenschaft*, I (1894), p. 2365 et suiv.; IDEM, *Regesten der Kaiser und Päpste für die Jahre* 311 *bis* 476 *n. Chr.*, Stuttgart 1919, p. 475.

12. *Ibid.*, p. 313-317.

13. *Ibid.*, p. 313-317.

(*Esther* 9, 31). Il semble qu'il existe un lien entre Pourim et la Pâque. Dans le cantique liturgique qui est lu traditionnellement la première nuit de la Pâque après la section *nirtza* de la Haggadah, se trouve la liste des miracles qui eurent lieu pendant cette nuit. Nous y lisons, *inter alia :* « *l'Agaguite se livra à la haine et écrivit des lettres pendant la nuit* », phrase qui fait allusion aux mauvaises pensées d'Haman et aux ordres qu'il rédigea pour faire périr les Juifs, ainsi qu'il est rapporté dans le Livre d'Esther : « Au premier mois, qui est le mois de Nissan, la deuxième année du roi Assuérus, on jeta le « pour », c'est-à-dire le sort devant Haman » (*Esther* 3, 7); « Les secrétaires du roi furent appelés le treizième jour du premier mois, et l'on écrivit aux satrapes suivant ce qui fut ordonné par Haman... » (*Esther*, 3, 12.). Le cantique liturgique ajoute : « et Vous réveillèrent votre puissance conquérante en dérangeant le sommeil du roi pendant la nuit », faisant allusion au roi Assuérus qui « cette nuit-là, ne put pas dormir » (*Esther* 6, 1), et au début de l'ascension de Mardochée et de la chute d'Haman. Selon le *Midrach* (*Pesikta de R. Kahana, sur le verset 6, 1*), cet événement eut lieu la première nuit de Pâque. La deuxième nuit de la Pâque toujours selon le *Midrach* (*Esther Rabbah*), Haman fut pendu à l'arbre [14].

Une autre date encore, celle du 23 Sivan, est liée à la fête de Pourim : « Les secrétaires du roi furent appelés en ce temps, le vingt-troisième jour du troisième mois, qui est le mois de Sivan, et l'on écrivit... » (*Esther* 8, 9.) Godefroy, dans son commentaire, estime que la loi se rapporte au 23 Sivan (qui tombe au mois de mai) : « *quod in mensem maium sivan incidit* ». Il est vrai qu'une étude approfondie des sources juives révèle d'autres allusions au fait que les Juifs célébraient également le 23 Sivan [15]. Je ne pense pas néanmoins que nous puissions retenir la suggestion de Godefroy, et ceci pour une raison bien simple : en 408, qui correspond à l'année 4168 du calendrier hébreu, le 23 Sivan tombait un mercredi, le 3 juin [16]. Il est donc clair que la loi fut promulguée avant le 23 Sivan,

14. Voir, aussi, H. MALTER, *Purim,* dans *Jewish Encyclopaedia,* X, p. 274 et suiv.; M. SEL, *Haman the Agagite,* dans *Jewish Encyclopaedia,* VI, p. 189 et suiv.; E. WIND, *The Crucifixion of Haman,* dans *Journal of the Warburg Institute* I, 1937, p. 245 et suiv.

15. Sur ce point, voir tout particulièrement JELLINECK, *Beit ha-Midrash,* V, Jérusalem 1938, p. 46-49. Par exemple, « le rêve de Mardochée et les Additions au Livre d'Esther » : « Ecrit et signé le treizième jour de Sivan, dans la douzième année du règne d'Assuérus dans la capitale de Chochane. Moi, l'auteur, Jacob, au nom de R. Makkir. » Il est également intéressant de noter que dans Esther 8.9, les LXX parlent du 23 Nisan au lieu du 23 Sivan. Il semble que les traducteurs aient voulu souligner le fait que les événements se sont déroulés si vite que, dans la semaine même qui vit la disgrâce et la pendaison d'Haman, les secondes lettres furent envoyées dans toutes les provinces.

16. Voir A. A. AKAVIA, *Calendar for 6000 — Comparative Calendar from the Creation until then End of the Sixth Millenium,* Jérusalem 1976, p. 580. Je remercie ici le dr. A. Kimmelmann, de l'Institut de Recherche en Droit Hébraïque de l'Université Hébraïque de Jérusalem, pour son aide sur ce problème.

et nous devons en conclure qu'elle concerne la fête de Pourim au mois d'Adar. Il ne faut pas oublier qu'il fallait un certain temps pour qu'une nouvelle loi parvint à toutes les provinces : trois mois environ après Pourim est une date raisonnable pour promulguer une telle loi. Par ailleurs, il n'y a aucune raison de penser que la promulgation de cette loi ait nécessité des mesures plus expéditives : à peine quelques jours si nous en croyons Godefroy. Il n'y a donc aucun doute dans mon esprit : la loi concernait la fête de Pourim que le peuple juif célébrait traditionnellement au mois d'Adar [17].

II. — La crucifixion d'Haman et Haman brulé en effigie.

Comme nous l'avons dit, le *Livre d'Esther* ne parle que de la *pendaison* d'Haman à l'arbre : « Le roi dit : Qu'on y pende Haman ! Et l'on pendit Haman au bois qu'il avait préparé pour Mardochée » (*Esther* 7, 9-10). Et pourtant, le texte de la loi d'Honorius et Théodose II (*C. Th.* XVI. 8. 18) laisse entendre que les Juifs célébraient la *crucifixion* d'Haman. Comment concilier la *pendaison* d'Haman et sa crucifixion ? En examinant les sources juives, nous constaterons qu'elles mentionnent bien la tradition de la crucifixion d'Haman. Certaines d'entre elles sont peut-être postérieures à la loi du C. Th., mais seules les *sources* sont postérieures, et non pas les anciennes pratiques qu'elles décrivent.

Le *Targoum* du Livre d'Esther traduit le passage « et l'on pendit Haman » de la façon suivante : « et l'on crucifia Haman sur un arbre ». Le *second Targoum* [18] contient ce commentaire détaillé du passage « et le roi dit : Qu'on y pende Haman : « Haman répondit à Mardochée, avant que l'on vienne me prendre pour me pendre, je te supplie, Mardochée le juste, ne me *crucifie* pas comme on crucifie un homme ordinaire... On ne pend pas un homme de mon âge vénérable à un arbre; tue-moi comme tu voudras, décapite-moi avec l'épée du roi, avec laquelle sont exécutés les ministres de l'Etat... Ben-Hamdata (Haman) va être pendu à l'arbre... Ecoute-moi, dit le cèdre, pends Haman à une de mes branches, à l'arbre qu'il s'est préparé pour lui-même. »

La traduction de la Bible en latin due à s. Jérôme (*Vulgate*) parle aussi de la crucifixion de Haman et de ses fils : *denique et ipsum et filios eius affixerunt cruci* [19].

17. Voir, aussi, II. Macch. 15, 36 : « ... un jour avant le jour de Mardochée » : voir H. Bardtke, *Der Mardochäustag,* dans *Tradition und Glaube,* p. 97-116.

18. Sur le second *Targoum,* voir Y. Komlosh, *Targum Sheni,* dans *Encyclopaedia Judaica,* XV, col. 811 et suiv. Les différentes opinions concernant la date de cette œuvre sont présentées à la col. 813 : certains la font remonter au quatrième siècle, d'autres au sixième et d'autres au onzième.

19. Il convient à cet égard de consulter l'article « Hanging » dans Cheyne-Sutherland Black, *Encyclopaedia Biblica,* II (1901), col. 1958-9.

La coutume de prendre sa revanche sur Haman connue sous le nom de *machvarta depuraya* est déjà notée dans le *Talmud :*

Rabi Judah dit : « Celui (qui donne de sa semence à Moloch) ne doit être puni que s'il fait en sorte que sa semence traverse (le feu) d'une manière normale : Pourquoi cela ? Abaye dit : il y avait un tas de briques branlantes au milieu du feu et des deux côtés. Rava dit : C'était comme la *machvarta de puraya* (Sanhedrin 64 *b*). »

Selon le commentaire de Rachi « comme la *machvarta de puraya* signifie qu'il ne fait pas passer (sa semence) en étant debout, mais plutôt, en sautant au-dessus (du feu) comme font les enfants à Pourim, il en résulte qu'un trou était creusé, que l'on y allumait un feu, et qu'il sautait au-dessus, de part en part » [20].

La crucifixion d'Haman est également mentionnée dans des textes postérieurs qui semblent faire état de l'existence de deux traditions différentes : l'une parle de pendaison, qui était alors couramment effectuée par crucifixion, et la seconde de pendaison proprement dite (forme à laquelle le *second Targoum* fait également allusion). Nous ne nous arrêterons ici que sur les textes traitant de la crucifixion d'Haman.

L'écrivain Moché Chaltiel nous donne un témoignage vivant des coutumes des Juifs yéménites : « Quand les préparatifs de Pourim ont lieu au mois d'Adar, les enfants, dans certaines parties du Yemen, prennent deux bâtons, les lient en forme de croix, et les affublent de chiffons. Ils appellent cela Haman, et le crucifient, d'où le dicton « Adar crucifie Haman » [21]. A Tunis, les enfants célébraient ordinairement Pourim en fabriquant une sorte d'épouvantail (généralement en forme de croix) qu'ils jetaient ensuite dans un feu de joie [22].

20. A Babylone, les *Gheonim* interprétèrent *mashvarta depuraya* de la façon suivante : « Les jeunes gens font un simulacre d'Haman et le pendent sur leurs toits pendant quatre ou cinq jours. Le jour de Pourim ils faisaient un feu de joie dans lequel ils jetaient le simulacre, et se tenaient autour du feu, chantant et dansant. Et ils suspendent un anneau au-dessus du feu, s'y accrochent et sautent ainsi d'un côté du feu à l'autre. » (L. GINZBERG, éd. *The Responsa of the Geonim,* p. 90). Voir aussi GINZBERG, *Geonica,* II, New York 1909, p. 1-2; « *meshavra* » dans *Aruch Completum,* V, p. 268; LEVINSKY, *Keitzad Hikku et Haman be-Tfutzot Yisrael,* dans *Yalkut Folklori le-Purim,* Tel-Aviv 1947.

21. Cité dans *ibid.,* p. 82.

22. S. MAMO, *Hag Teliyat Haman U-Sreifato, ibid.,* p. 70 et suiv. Selon M. Gil (dans *ibid.,* p. 73), les Juifs d'Afghanistan célébraient la fête de la manière suivante : « A Pourim, à midi les enfants de tous les quartiers se rassemblent. Ils plantent en terre une sorte de mât, et y pendent des simulacres d'Haman, faits de papier, de bois, de chiffons et de paille. Après cela, ils allument un feu au pied du mât, et tous les « Hamans » qui y pendent son brûlés. » Sur les coutumes de Damas, voir LEVINSKY, *Sefer ha-Moadim,* p. 119 : « Pendant la nuit de la fête d'Haman, c'est-à-dire Pourim, les Juifs lisent le Livre d'Esther et prient dans la synagogue jusqu'à minuit, implorant Dieu de prendre Haman et de lui donner une telle leçon qu'il ne puisse plus jamais se relever. Le jour suivant, ils érigent une effigie d'Haman, un simulacre fait de chiffons et d'autres matériaux combustibles, près de la synagogue. Après la fête, ils se rassemblent, font feu sur « Haman » avec de vrais fusils, et lui enfoncent leurs épées dans le « corps ».

La coutume qui consistait à brûler une effigie d'Haman était donc très répandue dans les communautés juives [23]. Il y avait aussi d'autres coutumes observées dans les synagogues lorsque le nom d'Haman était mentionné au cours de la lecture du Livre d'Esther; Godefroy lui-même y fait allusion dans son commentaire du Code Théodosien [24].

III. — La loi d'Honorius et de Théodose II et l'incident d'Inmestar.

Toutes ces coutumes sont très vraisemblablement antérieures à l'arrivée du christianisme au pouvoir politique, c'est-à-dire qu'elles remontent à l'époque du paganisme [25]. Comme nous l'avons vue, la plus répandue était la coutume de brûler Haman en effigie; quelquefois, l'effigie était crucifiée et pendue sur une croix.

Il est certain que ces pratiques n'étaient pas vues d'un bon œil par les chrétiens; bien au contraire : ils y voyaient une attaque portée contre la religion chrétienne. L'Eglise fit évidemment tout ce qui était en son

23. Voir Doniach, *Purim*, p. 72 et suiv. : « La coutume de brûler un simulacre d'Haman, coutume qui prévalait anciennement en Israël, tomba rapidement en désuétude, excepté en Orient. A l'époque talmudique et gaonique, Haman était brûlé en effigie et les jeunes dansaient joyeusement autour du feu. Le texte qui mentionne cette coutume en offre deux versions : ou bien les hommes dansaient autour du feu, ou bien ils sautaient par-dessus... »; voir aussi p. 115, 171 et suiv., 194; Goodman, *Purim*, p. 322.

24. « *et quoties Amanis sit mentio, pugnis et malleis scanna Iudaei pulsare solent, Amanemque maximo strepitu explodunt, cui similem consuetudinem retinet hodie ecclesia romana ipsa passionis dominicae nocte in Iudae detestationem...* » Voir aussi Gregorovius, *Wanderjahre in Italien*, 1925, p. 269 et suiv.; J. G. Frazer, *The Scapegoat*, Londres 1913.

25. Il était en fait plus facile pour les Juifs, à cette époque ancienne, de se livrer à ces activités. Plus tard, à l'époque chrétienne, ils continuèrent à pratiquer les coutumes qui s'étaient déjà enracinées d'elles-mêmes. A cet égard, voir Juster, *Les Juifs*, II, p. 207, note 2 : « ... mais l'habitude de représenter Haman en image (ce qui est contraire à la loi juive, cf. *supra*, ch. 2, section III, § I, t. 1, p. 348 ss.) ne s'implanta chez les Juifs de la Diaspora qu'assez tard. Ils faisaient peut-être alors avec Haman ce que les païens faisaient avec leur *Mimus* (cf. H. Reich, *Der Mimus*, 2 vol., 1902 B.). Je trouve après coup un rapprochement semblable dans H. Wollmer, *Der König mit der Dornenkrone*, dans *ZNTW*, 1905, p. 196, note 3. Il se peut aussi que de même que pendant les 2ᵉ et 3ᵉ siècles les païens firent du *Mimus* une caricature du Christ (cf. H. Reich, *op. cit.* I., 80-109; cf. Idem, *Der König mit der Dornenkrone*, 1895 L. (extrait de *Neue Jahrbücher für das klass. Altert.*) et P. Wendland, *Iesus als Saturnalien-König*, dans *Hermes* 33, 1898, p. 175-179 : « Les Juifs en firent aussi une de l'image d'Haman vers la même époque. En effet, l'habitude de fixer l'image d'Haman sur la croix doit dater de l'époque où la religion païenne étant dominante, les Juifs pouvaient, comme leurs concitoyens, se permettre des moqueries contre le Christ. » Je ne peux pas accepter la thèse de Juster selon laquelle cette coutume était en contradiction avec la loi juive, et il n'en donne aucune preuve dans la première partie de son livre (p. 348 et s.); s'il en avait été ainsi, les *Gheonim* se seraient certainement opposés à cette pratique. Ginzberg prouve que, bien au contraire, les *Gheonim* l'approuvaient. Voir Ginzberg, *Geonica*, II, p. 1 ss.

pouvoir pour y mettre un terme : d'où l'intervention d'Honorius et de Théodose II (*C. Th.* XVI, 8, 18) qui demandèrent aux gouverneurs de leurs provinces de veiller à ce que les Juifs ne célèbrent pas la fête de Pourim de cette manière, sous peine de se voir retirer les privilèges leur permettant de célébrer cette fête.

Cette loi du *C. Th.* XVI, 8, 18 est liée à l'incident rapporté par l'historien de l'Eglise grecque Socratès [26], dans son *Historia Ecclesiastica* (Livre VII, Chap. XVI). Cet incident, d'après lui, aurait eu lieu dans la ville d'Inmestar, entre Antioche et Chalcis. Célébrant leur fête de Pourim avec une joie excessive, les Juifs de cette ville commencèrent par se moquer des chrétiens, et certains affirment qu'ils allèrent jusqu'à se moquer de Jésus lui-même. Ils firent des plaisanteries au sujet de la croix et sur le compte de ceux qui y croient. Au milieu de ces réjouissances, la foule des Juifs se saisit d'un enfant chrétien, le plaça sur une croix et le porta en procession à travers les rues de la ville. Pour finir, ils assassinèrent sauvagement l'enfant. Un grave conflit éclata entre Juifs et chrétiens. Lorsque les empereurs eurent vent de l'incident, ils donnèrent l'ordre aux gouverneurs de la province de torturer et de mettre à mort les responsables de cet acte criminel.

Godefroy rapporte lui aussi cet incident dans ses commentaires et y voit le motif de la promulgation de la loi [27]. Mais Juster fait remarquer à juste raison que l'incident relaté dans l'*Historia Ecclesiastica* s'est produit *après* la loi du *C. Th.* [28]. Godefroy n'a peut-être pas remarqué que l'année 408, citée par exemple par Theophanes, est l'année alexandrienne « qui commence le 1er septembre de l'année 415 de notre calendrier » comme Migne nous l'indique [29]. Plus récemment, Parkes a affirmé que « c'est une erreur que de voir dans cet incident un " meurtre rituel ", bien qu'il n'y ait aucune raison de mettre en doute l'authenticité du récit,

26. Sur le *Scholasticus* de Socratès et sa composition, voir l'article d'ELTESTER dans PAULY-WISSOWA, *Realencyklopädie,* III A, 1 (1901), p. 893-901.

27. « ... *quod huic legi occasionem dedit quod memorat Socrates* », 7, *cap.* 16 ».

28. On trouvera d'autres arguments contre cette explication de Godefroy dans JUSTER, *Les Juifs,* II, p. 207, n. 1.

29. MIGNE, *Patrologia Graeca,* LXVII, col. 770 n.h. : « *Idem Theophanes, anno* 408 *secundum Alexandrinos, qui kalend. septemb. Nostri* 415 *inchoatur...* » En ce qui concerne la date, voir aussi JUSTER, *Les Juifs,* II, p. 204, n. 2. Plus récemment, cf. aussi SEAVER, *Persecution of the Jews in the Roman Empire* (300-438), Lawrence 1952, p. 17 : « The chronographer Theophanes, writing much later, asserts this this even took place in 408. He says : *In the year 408 which was the first year of the Bishop Cyril of Alexandria.* In this year the Jews abducted a Christian boy during the festival of Haman; in the midst of their games they hung this same boy from a beam in mockery of the cross and killed him under torture; because of this the emperor found out and executed those Jews who were liable for punishment. » Il semble que cette histoire, de même que celle de Cassiodore, n'est qu'une copie du récit de Socrates; Theophanes ajoute malheureusement à la confusion par son manque de précision en ce qui concerne la date. Aussi p. 69 Seaver, lui non plus, n'a pas tenu compte de la remarque de Migne !

ainsi que l'a fait Juster »[30]. Juster lui-même écrivait : « Mais c'est à tort qu'on y a vu un exemple de meurtre rituel juif. »[31] Nous n'aborderons donc pas la question de savoir s'il s'agit-là d'un meurtre rituel ou non : nous nous bornerons à analyser l'incident en lui-même.

Il est utile de résumer tout d'abord la situation des Juifs dans la région d'Antioche, où résidait une importante communauté juive dès la fondation de cette ville, ainsi qu'en témoigne Flavius Josèphe (*Guerres,* VII, 4, 4)[32]. Il semble que les Juifs aient eu dans cette région une influence considérable sur les chrétiens. Nous savons, par exemple, qu'en 341, le Synode d'Antioche interdit aux chrétiens de célébrer Pâques en même temps que les Juifs fêtaient la Pâque[33]. Plusieurs années plus tard, entre

30. J. PARKES, *The Conflict of the Church and the Synagogue,* Londres 1934, p. 234, n. 2. Après Parkes, voir aussi SEAVER, *Persecution,* p. 61 : « It is certainly a black mark on the Jewish record. » Parkes avance, et Seaver après lui, que si l'histoire n'avait pas été vraie, elle aurait fait état d'un miracle qui sauva l'enfant au dernier moment. Mais, à son avis, cet argument n'est pas convaincant : car si les chrétiens avaient rapporté que l'enfant avait été sauvé par un miracle, ils auraient privé l'histoire de son caractère tragique et cette histoire n'aurait pas eu un tel impact sur la chrétienté.

31. JUSTER, *Les Juifs,* II, p. 204. Voir, aussi, C. H. KRAELING, *The Jewish Community at Antioch* dans *JBL,* 51, 1932, p. 130 ss. Kraeling écrit p. 159 : « a ritual murder is said to have been perpetrated », mais il me semble qu'il n'ait pas suffisamment pesé la valeur des mots qu'il utilisait. Voir aussi la note de Manzini, selon laquelle il n'y avait rien dans ces événements qui rappelât l'*omicidio rituale :* « Neppure queste uccisioni, quand'anche fossero accertate, si potrebbero classificare fra gli omicidi rituali, dovendo esse considerarsi come fatti di vendetta contro le violenze esercitate dai Cristiani. Così invero mostrano di giudicarle gli scrittori dell'epoca. » V. MANZINI, *L'Omicidio rituale e i sacrifici umani, con particolare riguardo alle accuse contro gli Ebrei, Ricerche storico-sociologiche,* Torino 1925. Nous ne pouvons pourtant pas ignorer les graves erreurs historiques commises par ce célèbre spécialiste du droit criminel. C'est ainsi qu'il affirme (p. 85) que « la révolte de Bar Kochba eut lieu au temps d'Adrien (395-408) » ! Il ajoute (p. 85) que l'incident d'Inmestar eut lieu au temps de l'empereur Hadrien (« an 44 de notre ère » !).

32. Sur la communauté juive d'Antioche, voir surtout S. KRAUSS, *Antioche,* dans *REJ* 45, 1902, p. 27 et suiv.; A. NEUBAUER, *La Géographie du Talmud,* Paris 1868 (réédition, Hildesheim 1967), p. 311 et suiv., 431; KRAELING, *Antioch;* V. TCHERIKOVER, *Hellenistic Civilization and the Jews,* Philadelphie 1959, p. 30, 289, 328-9; M. SIMON, *Verus Israel : Etude sur les relations entre Chrétiens et Juifs dans l'empire romain* (*135-425*), Paris 1965; G. DOWNEY, *A History of Antioch in Syria from Seleucus to the Arab Conquest,* New Jersey 1961, p. 447 et suiv. Downey ne mentionne pas l'incident d'Inmestar, bien qu'il se soit produit non loin d'Antioche.

33. Cette décision n'était pas la première de cette nature. Le Concile de Nicée avait précédemment menacé de châtiment les chrétiens célébrant la Pâque en même temps que Pâques. Selon Eusèbe et d'autres Pères de l'Eglise, Constantin transforma les décisions de l'Eglise en lois civiles. Mais il semble que ces mesures furent inefficaces, si le problème se posait encore au temps de Justinien. D'après Procope (*Historia Arcana,* 128, 16-18), Justinien décréta que les Juifs ne pourraient célébrer la Pâque qu'après Pâques. Mais trois ans plus tard, Justinien lui-même repoussa la date de Pâques, agissant ainsi en contradiction avec sa propre loi. Sur ce point, voir JUSTER, *Les Juifs,* I, p. 282 ss., 356 ss.; S. BARON, *A Social and Religious History of the Jews, III,* New York 1957, p. 4 ss.; SIMON, *Verus Israel,* p. 361 et suiv.; RABELLO, *A Tribute to Jean Juster, op. cit.,* p. 225, n. 19.

366 et 387, Jean Chrysostome reprochait aux chrétiens de fréquenter les synagogues et de s'adresser aux tribunaux juifs. Il protestait aussi contre le fait que l'empereur Valens ait lui-même donné aux Juifs « des jardins... pour s'y livrer au culte de leur Dieu » [34].

Il est certain que lorsque le christianisme devint religion d'Etat, la situation des Juifs empira : les chrétiens allèrent jusqu'à détruire la synagogue d'Antioche (423). L'essai, fait par Théodose II de la rendre aux Juifs fit enrager Siméon Stylite [35], dans cette affaire, comme dans bien d'autres, l'empereur, tout en reconnaissant le bien-fondé de la cause juive, capitula devant la pression des autorités ecclésiastiques [36].

Tout ceci montre que les dirigeants de l'Eglise d'Antioche souhaitaient manifestement porter préjudice, de toutes les manières possibles, aux bonnes relations qui prévalaient encore entre Juifs et chrétiens, et écarter les chrétiens des pratiques religieuses juives qu'ils continuaient à observer. Il est logique que les Juifs aient essayé de se défendre contre ces tentatives, mais leurs ressources étaient faibles, le christianisme ayant l'appui de l'autorité gouvernementale. Il me semble qu'il suffit de connaître cette atmosphère pour bien comprendre l'incident d'Inmestar, et que Parkes et tous les chercheurs qui admettent la vérité du récit de Socratès, ne tiennent pas compte de cette réalité historique. Je suis d'accord avec Juster lorsqu'il affirme qu'il faut voir dans cet incident un affront fait par les Juifs aux rites des chrétiens, affront qui entraîna un grave conflit entre chrétiens et Juifs [37]. Compte tenu des circonstances précitées, je pense que nous pouvons reconstruire l'incident de la façon suivante : malgré l'interdiction d'Honorius et de Théodose II, des Juifs excités brûlèrent un simulacre de poupée crucifiée le jour de Pourim, ou bien le second jour de la Pâque (le jour de la mort d'Haman, qui fut aussi le jour de la mort de Jésus) : le résultat fut un violent conflit.

Pour jeter de l'huile sur le feu et séparer davantage encore les chrétiens des Juifs, les chrétiens racontèrent que les Juifs avaient non pas brûlé un *simulacre* de poupée, mais assassiné un *enfant*, dans lequel chacun pouvait voir une sorte de caricature de l'enfant Jésus. Cette rumeur fut

34. Sur ce point, voir M. Simon, *La polémique anti-juive de st. Jean-Chrysostome et le mouvement judaïsant d'Antioche*, dans *Mélanges Cumont, Annuaire de l'Institut de Philologie et d'Histoire orientales*, IV, Bruxelles 1936, p. 403-429. Voir aussi Downey, *Antioch*, p. 448 et suiv. ,

35. *PG*, 114, 381 : voir aussi *PG*, 86, 2456; Evagrius, *His. Eccl.*, I, 13.

36. L'ascète Siméon Stylite fut le premier des stylites. Pour s'infliger une pénitence physique prolongée, il vécut plus de trente ans sans descendre, sur une petite plate-forme en haut d'une colonne. Du haut de cette colonne, il prêchait des sermons anti-Juifs, et avait une grande influence sur son auditoire. Voir G. Ricciotti, dans *Encic. Italiana*, XXXI, p. 796 et XXXII, p. 735; Downey, *Antioch*, p. 459 ss.; Simon, *Verus Israel*, p. 266; Seaver, *Persecution*, p. 76.

37. Juster, *Les Juifs*, II, p. 297 et suiv. Voir aussi H. Graetz, *History of the Jews*, II, Philadelphia 1949, p. 231, 613; Krauss, *Antioche*, p. 46; J. Gaudemet, *L'Eglise dans l'Empire Romain* (*IVe-Ve siècles*), Paris 1958, p. 632.

admise comme vérité d'évangile par Socratès qui la reprend à son compte comme un fait historique. En fait, son récit montre quelles tensions entre Juifs et chrétiens provoquait la célébration de la fête de Pourim, tensions qui entraînaient périodiquement de sérieux incidents et des accusations de meurtre réel au lieu du simple meurtre symbolique qui, nous en sommes persuadés, avait été commis.

IV. — La signification politico-religieuse de la loi concernant Pourim.

La loi d'Honorius et de Théodose II constitue une intervention manifeste de la part des autorités séculières et ecclésiastiques dans la vie religieuse de la communauté juive vivant dans l'Empire romain. A partir de cette date (408), l'observance de la fête de Pourim est toujours permise, mais *sub conditione :* les Juifs peuvent observer leurs coutumes, mais *à la condition* de ne pas offenser les sensibilités chrétiennes. Dans ce cas, comme dans bien d'autres — et surtout les lois concernant les synagogues [38] — les meneurs exploitent la calomnie classique selon laquelle les Juifs insultent la religion chrétienne. Les lois de Théodose, quand bien même, en surface, elles réprouvent les actions de masses, accordent en fait une grande liberté d'action aux éléments hostiles aux Juifs. Nous nous trouvons dans une période de pression ecclésiastique croissante, pas seulement sur les Juifs, mais aussi sur les hommes au pouvoir [39]; les autorités séculières capitulent et la situation des Juifs s'aggrave.

La Novelle 146 *De Hebraeis* (année 553) de l'empereur Justinien mit le comble à cette intervention impériale [40]. Justinien incorpora la loi concernant Pourim à son propre *Codex* (*C. J.*, I, 9, 11), avec de très légères modifications par rapport au texte du *C. Th.* [41]. Mais les lois

38. Sur la législation concernant les synagogues et les nombreux incidents entre Juifs et chrétiens sur cette question, voir particulièrement Seaver, *Persecution*, p. 65 ss.; M. Avi-Yonah, *Bi-Ymei Roma u-Bizantyon*, Jérusalem 1970, p. 188 ss. Il est intéressant de noter que dans de nombreux cas les gouverneurs de provinces rapportèrent à l'empereur que les chrétiens étaient à blâmer, mais en raison de l'intervention des dirigeants de l'Eglise, les empereurs se voyaient obligés d'agir à l'encontre de la vérité et de la justice. Cette regrettable situation n'est pas inconnue des hommes d'Etat de notre époque.

39. Sur la nature absolue et intolérante de l'Eglise, voir B. Biondi, *Il Diritto Romano Cristiano*, I, Milano, 1951-54, p. 256-306; V. Colorni, *Israeliti*, dans *Novissimo Digesto Italiano*, IX, Torino, 1963, p. 203 ss.

40. Sur la Novelle 146, voir Colorni, *L'uso del Greco nella Liturgia del Giudaismo Ellenistico et la Novella 146 di Giustiniano*, dans *Annali di Storia del diritto*, VIII (1964), p. 19 ss. Voir la critique de Rabello dans *Labeo*, 12 (1966), p. 140 ss.

41. Le texte, tel qu'il apparaît dans le *C.J.*, est le suivant : « Impp. Honorius et Theodosius A.A. Anthemio PP. *Iudaeos quodam festivitatis suae sollemni Aman ad pœnae quondam recordationem incendere et sanctae crucis adsimulatam speciem*

concernant les Juifs qui se trouvent dans le *Codex Theodosianus* ne furent pas toutes reprises dans le *Codex Justinianus* [42] : il n'est donc pas possible de prétendre que l'inclusion de la loi concernant Pourim dans le *C. J.* est sans importance. Je pense pour ma part que les passions n'étaient pas encore apaisées, et que l'empereur voulait se protéger contre toute recrudescence éventuelle d'actes pouvant être interprétés comme affronts à la religion chrétienne. Mais il me semble plus raisonnable encore de supposer que Justinien qui, nous l'avons vu, était partisan d'une intervention maximum de l'Etat dans la vie communautaire, n'était pas prêt à renoncer à une loi qui limite la liberté religieuse des Juifs et facilite l'intervention ecclésiastique et séculière dans la vie religieuse de la communauté juive. Comme nous l'avons dit, cette loi de Théodose n'est que le début d'une législation plus vaste qui viole les principes essentiels de la liberté religieuse, principes qui, dans une certaine mesure, avaient été respectées jusqu'au règne de l'empereur Arcadius (395-409) [43].

Immédiatement après la proclamation de cette loi, d'autres lois furent promulguées interdisant la construction de nouvelles synagogues : bien pis, l'autonomie du patriarcat juif d'Eretz-Israël fut circonscrite de façon très étroite, jusqu'au jour où il fut entièrement aboli (*C. Th.* XVI, 8, 29) [44]. Quelques années plus tard, en 438, Theodose II appelait les Juifs « ennemis de la loi romaine et de l'autorité suprême » (Novelle 3) [45].

Il me semble donc que nous ne devons pas être surpris si les Juifs, en

in contemptu Christianae fidei sacrilega mente exurere provinciarium rectores prohibeant, ne locis suis fidei nostrae signum immisceant, sed ritus suos citra contemptum Christianae legis retineant, amissuri sine dubio permissa hactenus, nisi ab illicitis temperaverint. D. IIII K. IUN. CONSTANTINOPOLI BASSO ET PHILIPPO CONSS (*anno* 408). »

42. Les lois qui furent abolies sont : *C. Th.* XVI, 8, 2-6; 13, etc.

43. Seaver, *Persecution*, p. 56 ss.; Rabello, *A Tribute to J. Juster, op. cit.*, p. 247.

44. Sur le statut légal du patriarcat dans l'Empire romain, voir Juster, *Les Juifs*, I, p. 385-408; S. Dubnov, *History of the Jews*, II, New York 1968, p. 96 ss.; G. Alon, *Toledot ha-Yehudim be-Eretz Yisrael bi-Tekufat ha-Mishna ve-ha-Talmud*, II, p. 125; Seaver, *Persecution*, p. 65 ss., 71 ss.; E. E. Urbach, *The Sages. Their Concepts and Beliefs*, Jérusalem 1975, p. 599 ss.; A. M. Rabello, *A Tribute to Jean Juster, op. cit.*, p. 226 s. et 261, n. 5.

45. Seaver (p. 84-5) fait le commentaire suivant sur la Novelle 3 de Théodose : « Finally Theodosius II summed up all this anti-Jewish legislation in his Novella III, crystallizing in bombast and elaborate verbiage all the orthodox sentiments of the pious Roman emperors of the late fourth and early fifth centuries. Many of these laws were embodied in canons by the ecclesiastical contemporaries of the imperial legislators and later passed into the tradition of western Europe by way of the church in the great collections of canons which were made during the Carolingian Age. The canons of the church councils of the fourth century helped make anti-Jewish sentiments traditional in the Christian church... The effect of this body of religious legislation coupled with the Theodosian laws was disastrous to Jewry. The church canons and the Theodosian laws together officialy stamped the mark of Cain on the Jews, and permanently separated them socially and economically from their fellow Roman citizens. »

célébrant la fête de Pourim, priaient et demandaient à Dieu qu'il leur épargnât de nouvelles souffrances. Haman symbolisait la descendance d'Amalek, les nouveaux et dangereux adversaires des Juifs.

Il est peut-être intéressant de rappeler que la crucifixion d'Haman est un thème qui a été repris par deux grands artistes. Dante Alighieri décrit l'apparition d'Haman crucifié au chant XVII du Purgatoire :

Poi piovve dentro all'alta fantasia
un crucifisso[46] dispettoso e fero
nella sua vista, e cotal si moria :
intorno ad esso era il grande Assüero,
Ester sua sposa e il giusto Mardocheo
che fu al dire ed al far così intero.

Il est probable que Michel-Ange se souvint de ces vers lorsqu'il peignit Haman dans la chapelle Sixtine[47].

46. Il est intéressant de noter que la plupart des interprètes ne voient aucun problème dans le mot *crucifisso,* « crucifié ». C'est ainsi que N. Sapegno, dans son commentaire de la *Divine Comédie,* écrit : « questi ordinò che fosse crocifisso » (Ester, 3-7); voir aussi le commentaire de A. Momigliano : « Fece appendere Aman alla croce, che il feroce ministro aveva destinato a Mardocheo. »

47. Le premier à avoir soupçonné la source d'inspiration de cette peinture de Michel-Ange fut R. DUPPA, *Michelangelo,* Londres 1846, p. 120. Après lui : WIND, *The Crucifixion of Haman,* p. 245 et suiv.; Ch. de TOLNAY, *Michelangelo,* vol. II; *The Sistine Ceiling,* Princeton 1949, p. 1881 et suiv. et Tableau 131.

VIII

L'observance des fêtes juives dans l'Empire romain*

Table des matières

I. Introduction. Le problème de l'historicité des Actes 'Pro Iudaeis' dans Josèphe

L'objet de cet article est d'étudier le problème de l'observance des fêtes juives dans l'Empire romain, surtout à la lumière des textes historiques et juridiques, romains ou non; autrement dit, nous n'étudierons ici ni la valeur théologique et sociale de chaque fête, ni les réactions des Romains à l'observance de ces fêtes, comme nous pouvons l'apprendre par les sources littéraires[1].

* A mon Maître SERGIO JOSEPH SIERRA qui m'a appris la valeur éthique des fêtes bibliques, en témoignage de gratitude et d'estime.

[1] J. JUSTER, Les Juifs dans l'Empire romain, I, Paris, 1914, pp. 354 ss.; pour le problème de la valeur du Sabbat et des fêtes du point de vue juif, on peut étudier la Bible, l'ordre de la Mishna Mo'ed et les traités du même ordre du Talmud Palestinien ou de Jérusalem, et du Talmud Babylonien; pour le Talmud de Jérusalem, on peut consulter aussi la traduction française de M. SCHWAB, vol. 2, Paris, 1960.
Pour les textes d'auteurs grecs et romains relatifs au Sabbat et aux fêtes, v. TH. REINACH, Textes d'auteurs grecs et romains relatifs au Judaïsme, Paris, 1895, et maintenant M. STERN, Greek and Latin Authors on Jews and Judaism. Edited with Introductions, Translations

Les premiers contacts entre Juifs et Romains eurent lieu au temps de la révolte des Maccabées et aboutirent à la formation d'une première alliance entre la Judée et Rome au deuxième siècle avant l'ère chrétienne. En cette occasion Rome eut certainement l'opportunité d'apprendre combien les Juifs tenaient à l'observance de leur Torah, Loi du Seigneur.

Plus tard, lorsque Rome conquit la Judée, il se posa pour elle le problème des contacts avec le Judaïsme. Comme chaque nouveau conquérant, elle eut le choix entre la tolérance et les persécutions. Rome, on le sait, était généralement tolérante envers les religions de ses provinciaux. Pour les païens, ce n'était pas un problème très grave que d'adorer dix dieux de plus ou de moins; pour les Juifs, au contraire, le problème était capital: l'absolu monothéisme juif ne permettait pas au Juif d'adorer un seul dieu à côté de l'Unique Dieu, Créateur du ciel et de la terre. Mais tolérer le Judaïsme, lui permettre de vivre *suis legibus* signifiait pour les Romains décréter une série de privilèges permettant de mettre en pratique le principe général que Rome appliquait aux autres peuples.

Ainsi se pose le problème de la survivance des privilèges juifs après la chute de Jérusalem et la perte de l'indépendance nationale. On connaît bien la théorie de THÉODORE MOMMSEN, selon laquelle après 70 le Judaïsme perdit son caractère national et devint pour l'Empire une religion comme les autres; mais il est aussi bien connu qu'aujourd'hui – surtout grâce à JEAN JUSTER (et après lui, grâce à MOMIGLIANO, à COLORNI et à LUZZATTO) –, la plupart des savants sont convaincus que le Judaïsme continua à être considéré par le gouvernement romain comme une nation et non comme une simple religion. Les privilèges juifs furent maintenus, mais Rome ajouta une nouvelle condition pour pouvoir en jouir, à savoir le payement d'une nouvelle taxe au profit du *fiscus judaicus* qui venait souligner symboliquement la victoire romaine sur le «Dieu des Juifs»[2].

Parmi ces privilèges, nous nous occuperons ici de ceux qui concernent l'observance des fêtes.

Dans ses 'Antiquités Juives', Flavius Josèphe nous a conservé le texte des privilèges concernant le Sabbat et les fêtes, et les savants sont généralement d'accord pour en admettre l'historicité[3].

and Commentary, I: From Herodotus to Plutarch, Jerusalem, 1974; II: From Tacitus to Simplicius, Jerusalem, 1980. Sur l'observance du Sabbat et des fêtes juives, voir: J. MANN, The Observance of the Sabbath and the Festivals in the First Two Centuries of the Current Era according to Philo, Josephus, the New Testament and the Rabbinic Sources, Jewish Review, 4, 1914, pp. 433ss., 498ss. (maintenant reproduit dans: J. MANN, Collected articles, I, Gedera, 1971, pp. 1ss.); S. SAFRAI, Religion in Everyday Life, Compendia Rerum Iudaicarum ad Novum Testamentum, II, Assen, 1976, pp. 793ss. (en particulier pp. 804ss.); voir maintenant aussi R. GOLDENBERG, The Jewish Sabbath in the Roman World up to the Time of Constantine the Great, dans: ANRW II 19,1, Berlin–New York, 1979, pp. 414ss.

[2] J'ai résumé ici mes conclusions sur la situation juridique des Juifs dans l'Empire romain; pour les détails de la question et pour la bibliographie, je renvoie à A. M. RABELLO, The Legal Condition of the Jews in the Roman Empire, dans: ANRW II 13, Berlin–New York, 1980, pp. 662ss.

[3] Voir pour tous E. BIKERMAN, Une question d'authenticité: Les privilèges juifs, dans: Mélanges I. Lévy, Bruxelles, 1953, pp. 11ss., p. 33.

Il est vrai que dernièrement H. R. MOEHRING a voulu nier la valeur des documents 'Pro Judaeis' contenus dans les 'Antiquités' et il est arrivé à la conclusion que: *"Their direct use as historical evidence is impossible. They can be used for that purpose only after full allowances have been made for their apologetic character and after their original* Sitz im Leben *has been clearly established"*[4].

A mon avis cependant, en règle générale, on peut faire confiance à ces privilèges sur les fêtes: non seulement nous savons qu'ils ont précédé – en leur contenu – la conquête romaine, mais nous voyons aussi qu'ils furent généralement respectés après elle.

MOEHRING rappelle le caractère apologétique de l'ouvrage de Josèphe, et cela est hors de discussion; mais on peut observer aussi que son ouvrage était destiné à un public cultivé, connaissant le grec et que, s'il pouvait peut-être inventer le nom d'un personnage, il pouvait plus difficilement inventer le contenu même du privilège: il y aurait certainement eu des personnes qui auraient pu faire voir à Josèphe qu'il avait écrit un faux historique! Or, dans la plupart des cas, le fond de l'intervention romaine était la situation précaire des Juifs dans les villes hellénistiques: donc nous voyons ici reflétée une situation que nous savons être véritable, comme on peut le vérifier par les écrits de Philon sur la situation des Juifs à Alexandrie, et en deuxième lieu, nous voyons que Josèphe décrit cette situation qui n'était pas favorable aux Juifs, c'est-à-dire une situation d'inégalité pour des motifs religieux et dont seulement l'intervention romaine a pu corriger les effets, et nous savons bien que des interventions des Romains en faveur des Juifs étaient connues déjà du temps des premiers contacts entre Rome et la Judée.

Pour le problème de la tradition des textes et surtout sur l'incertitude des noms des fonctionnaires romains on doit rappeler qu'on avait beaucoup de difficultés à trouver les textes dans les archives, comme nous l'atteste quelques années après la correspondance entre Pline le Jeune et Trajan, à propos, par exemple, du problème des θρεπτοί ou enfants exposés: *Recitabatur autem apud me edictum, quod dicebatur divi Augusti . . .*[5].

Ainsi il me semble qu'on peut reconnaître l'historicité de ces privilèges et qu'on peut passer à leur examen direct.

II. Les privilèges concernant le Sabbat et les fêtes

Le premier document est celui de Julius Caesar à la ville de Parium, à l'est de l'Hellespont: «Les Juifs de Délos et d'autres Juifs voisins . . . se sont plaint

[4] H. R. MOEHRING, The Acta pro Judaeis in the Antiquities of Flavius Josephus, dans: Christianity, Judaism and other Greco-Roman Cults. Studies for Morton Smith at Sixty, ed. by J. NEUSNER, III: Judaism before 70 (Studies in Judaism in Late Antiquity, 12), Leiden, 1975, pp. 124ss. et p. 157 (pour les conclusions). Cf. aussi ID., Joseph Ben Matthia and Flavius Josephus. The Jewish Prophet and Roman Historian, ci-dessus dans ce même volume (ANRW II 21.2), pp. 864ss.

[5] Plinius, Epistulae, 10. 65; pour la problématique et la bibliographie, v. A. M. RABELLO, Effetti personali della Patria Potestas, Milano, 1979, pp. 230ss.

devant moi de ce que vous ne leur permettez pas légalement d'observer leurs coutumes nationales et leurs rites sacrés»[6].

Et voilà la lettre de Dolabella à la ville d'Ephèse: «. . . les Juifs . . . ne pourront pas prendre part au service militaire parce qu'ils ne peuvent pas porter des armes ou marcher le jour du Sabbat . . . Pourtant, comme les gouverneurs qui m'ont précédé, je les assure de l'exemption du service militaire . . .»[7].

Ou encore la lettre des magistrats de Laodicée à Gaius Rabirius: «. . . ce sera une loi pour eux que d'observer leur Sabbat et d'accomplir leurs rites, selon leurs coutumes . . .»[8], ou encore la lettre de Publius Servilius Galba à la ville de Milet: «. . . et m'a informé qu'à l'encontre de notre clair désir vous attaquez les Juifs et leur défendez d'observer leur Sabbat . . . J'ai décidé que les Juifs ne doivent pas être empêchés d'observer leurs coutumes . . .»[9].

Et voici deux décrets. Le premier est du peuple d'Halicarnasse: «. . . pour l'amitié et l'alliance avec les Juifs . . . d'observer leurs fêtes nationales et religieuses . . . nous avons aussi décrété que ces Juifs, hommes ou femmes, qui le désirent, peuvent observer le Sabbat . . .»[10].

Le second décret est du peuple d'Ephèse: «Les Juifs . . . peuvent observer leurs Sabbats et faire toutes les choses en accord avec la loi de leurs pères . . . en outre il est établi par le conseil que personne ne doit leur causer de troubles le jour

[6] Ant. J. 14.213: Ἰούλιος Γάιος στρατηγὸς ὕπατος Ῥωμαίων Παριανῶν ἄρχουσι βουλῇ δήμῳ χαίρειν. ἐνέτυχόν μοι οἱ Ἰουδαῖοι ἐν Δήλῳ καί τινες τῶν παροίκων Ἰουδαίων, παρόντων καὶ τῶν ὑμετέρων πρέσβεων, καὶ ἐνεφάνισαν ὡς ὑμεῖς ψηφίσματι κωλύετε αὐτοὺς τοῖς πατρίοις ἔθεσι καὶ ἱεροῖς χρῆσθαι. Pour le texte grec de Josèphe je me suis servi de l'édition de R. Marcus dans la Loeb Classical Library. Selon quelques auteurs (Ritschl, Mendelssohn, Viereck) ce document est de 46 a. E. C.; selon Juster il est de 44 a. E. C. (?); v. aussi A. C. Johnson, P. R. Coleman–Norton, F. C. Bourne, Ancient Roman Statutes (=ARSt.), Austin, 1961, doc. no. 109.

[7] Ant. J. 14.225–227: ἐνεφάνισέ μοι περὶ τοῦ μὴ δύνασθαι στρατεύεσθαι τοὺς πολίτας αὐτοῦ διὰ τὸ μήτε ὅπλα βαστάζειν δύνασθαι μήτε ὁδοιπορεῖν αὐτοὺς ἐν ταῖς ἡμέραις τῶν σαββάτων . . . ἐγώ τε οὖν αὐτοῖς, καθὼς καὶ οἱ πρὸ ἐμοῦ ἡγεμόνες, δίδωμι τὴν ἀστρατείαν καὶ συγχωρῶ χρῆσθαι τοῖς πατρίοις ἐθισμοῖς . . . ἁνίων συναγομένοις. Selon Juster le document est de 43 a. E. C.; Dolabella a été gouverneur de la Syrie; v. ARSt. doc. no. 118.

[8] Ant. J. 14.242: . . . ἵνα τά τε σάββατα αὐτοῖς ἐξῇ ἄγειν καὶ τὰ λοιπὰ ἱερὰ ἐπιτελεῖν κατὰ τοὺς πατρίους νόμους . . . Selon Juster le document est de 45 a. E. C. et le grand prêtre doit être Hyrcane II; Reinach, au contraire, suppose qu'il s'agit d'Hyrcane I.

[9] Ant. J. 14.245–246: . . . προσφέρεσθαι καὶ κωλύειν αὐτοὺς τά τε σάββατα ἄγειν καὶ τὰ ἱερὰ τὰ πάτρια τελεῖν καὶ τοὺς καρποὺς μεταχειρίζεσθαι, καθὼς ἔθος ἐστὶν αὐτοῖς, αὐτόν τε κατὰ τοὺς νόμους τεθεικέναι τὸ ψήφισμα. βούλομαι οὖν ὑμᾶς εἰδέναι ὅτι διακούσας ἐγὼ λόγων ἐξ ἀντικαταστάσεως γενομένων ἐπέκρινα μὴ κωλύεσθαι Ἰουδαίους τοῖς αὐτῶν ἔθεσι χρῆσθαι. Juster est d'avis que le document doit être postérieur à 46 a. E. C. puisque avant cette époque Milet n'a pas eu des assemblées ni d'autonomie civique.

[10] Ant. J. 14.257–258: . . . καὶ οἷς περὶ τῆς Ἰουδαίων φιλίας καὶ συμμαχίας πρὸς τὴν πόλιν ἔγραψεν, ὅπως συντελῶνται αὐτοῖς αἱ εἰς τὸν θεὸν ἱεροποιίαι καὶ ἑορταὶ αἱ εἰθισμέναι καὶ σύνοδοι, δεδόχθαι καὶ ἡμῖν Ἰουδαίων τοὺς βουλομένους ἄνδρας τε καὶ γυναῖκας τά τε σάββατα ἄγειν καὶ τὰ ἱερὰ συντελεῖν κατὰ τοὺς Ἰουδαϊκοὺς νόμους . . .

du Sabbat . . .»[11]. Comme nous pourrons le voir, c'est un principe qui sera confirmé jusqu'au temps de Justinien.

Comme nous pouvons le constater, dans cette période Rome envoyait aux villes grecques des *senatusconsulta* qui leur imposaient d'annuler toute disposition contraire à l'observance du Sabbat et leur demandaient d'éviter, pendant les Sabbats, toute corvée, l'encaissement des impôts et les citations en justice. La ville d'Halicarnasse fit même voter un décret punissant d'amende quiconque «magistrat ou particulier empêcherait les Juifs de célébrer les Sabbats».

Auguste garantit aux Juifs aussi la célébration de la veille des fêtes, ἡ παρασκευή, c'est-à-dire surtout le vendredi après-midi[12].

On constate, d'une manière générale, qu'à cette époque le problème qui se pose au gouvernement romain est de faire respecter le Sabbat par les villes grecques, qui empêchaient cette célébration; un tel problème ne se posa pas, en principe, à l'égard des Romains eux-mêmes. Mais il y eut des exceptions. Philon nous raconte à propos de la conduite du préfet d'Egypte Avilius Flaccus: «. . . Un puissant personnage qui, ayant reçu le gouvernement de l'Egypte, résolut de troubler nos usages nationaux et particulièrement de détruire la loi très sainte et très vénérable concernant le septième jour; il nous forçait à le servir et à faire d'autres choses contre nos coutumes ancestrales; il pensait que ce serait le commencement d'un changement complet d'habitudes et d'une transgression de l'ensemble de la loi, s'il pouvait détruire la loi concernant le septième jour. Et voyant que ceux qu'il violentait ne cédaient pas à ses ordres, et que par ailleurs la foule se soulevait . . . dans le deuil et l'accablement . . . il jugea bon de leur apprendre par un discours à transgresser la loi: si une invasion soudaine de l'ennemi, un débordement du Nil, un incendie, la foudre, la famine, la peste, un tremblement de terre ou tout autre malheur se produisait le samedi, resteriez-vous

[11] Ant. J. 14.263–264: . . . ὅπως ἄγωσι τὰ σάββατα καὶ πάντα ποιῶσι κατὰ τὰ πάτρια αὐτῶν ἔθη μηδενὸς αὐτοῖς ἐμποδὼν γινομένου . . . μηδένα κωλύεσθαι παρατηρεῖν τὴν τῶν σαββάτων ἡμέραν μηδὲ πράσσεσθαι ἐπιτίμιον, ἐπιτετράφθαι δ' αὐτοῖς πάντα ποιεῖν κατὰ τοὺς ἰδίους αὐτῶν νόμους.

[12] Comme on le sait, le Sabbat juif commence le vendredi soir. Sur le problème des noms des jours de la semaine, du Sabbat et de la veille du Sabbat ou des fêtes (παρασκευή, προσαββάτων, ערב שבת, ערובתא), v. E. Schürer, Die siebentägige Woche im Gebrauche der Christlichen Kirche der ersten Jahrhunderte, Zeitschrift für die neutestamentliche Wissenschaft und die Kunde des Urchristentums, 6, 1905, pp. 1ss.; S. Zeitlin, The last supper as an ordinary meal in the fourth Gospel, Jewish Quarterly Review (= JQR), 42, 1951–52, p. 252, n. 3: "*The Hellenized Jews did not use the word παρασκευή but πρὸ σαββάτων, comp. Ant. 3.10.7 [= iii. 255]; Judith 8.6; II Macc. 8.26*"; A. Pelletier, Pour une histoire des noms grecs du Sabbat et de la Pâque, Comptes rendus de l'Académie des Inscriptions et Belles-Lettres, 1971, pp. 71ss., et l'intervention de A. Dupont-Sommer, ibidem, pp. 77ss.; A. Pelletier, Σαββατα. Transcription grecque de l'araméen, Vetus Testamentum, 1972, pp. 436ss. Sur le calendrier juif en général, v. M. D. Herr, The Calendar, Compendia Rerum Iudaicarum ad Novum Testamentum, II, Assen, 1976, pp. 834ss.; M. Sibony, Le calendrier juif et ses problèmes, Revue des Etudes Juives (= REJ), 136, 1977, pp. 139ss.; S. Sandmel, Judaism and Christian Beginnings, Oxford, 1978, pp. 209ss., chap. 8: 'The Calendar. The Festival Days and the Sabbath', et aussi pp. 224ss.: 'Penitence and fast-days'.

encore tranquillement chez vous? Ou selon votre habitude, vous promèneriez-vous dans les rues les mains cachées dans vos habits pour ne pas être tentés d'aider ceux qui organiseraient le sauvetage? Ou resteriez-vous dans vos Synagogues en réunion solennelle à lire vos livres sacrés, à en expliquer les passages obscurs et à faire des sermons prolixes sur votre philosophie? Certes non: sans perdre un moment, vous chercheriez à mettre à l'abri vos parents, vos enfants, et tout ce qui vous est cher. Or voilà, moi je suis tout cela réuni: tempête, guerre, inondation, foudre, famine, tremblement et fatalité, et cela non en abstrait, mais comme une force présente et agissante»[13].

III. La période des persécutions

La situation se fit plus grave dans la période connue dans la littérature talmudique comme celle du פולמוס של קיטוס (*polemos shel Quietus*).

[13] Philon, De somniis, 2. 123–129: Χθὲς δ' οὐ πρῴην ἄνδρα τινὰ οἶδα τῶν ἡγεμονικῶν, ὅς, ἐπειδὴ τὴν προστασίαν καὶ ἐπιμέλειαν εἶχεν Αἰγύπτου, τὰ πάτρια κινεῖν ἡμῶν διενοήθη καὶ διαφερόντως τὸν ἁγιώτατον καὶ φρικωδέστατον περὶ τῆς ἑβδόμης ὑπάρχοντα νόμον καταλύειν καὶ ὑπηρετεῖν ἠνάγκαζεν ⟨ἐν αὐτῇ⟩ αὐτῷ καὶ τὰ ἄλλα ποιεῖν παρὰ τὸ καθεστὼς ἔθος, νομίζων ἀρχὴν ἔσεσθαι καὶ τῆς περὶ τὰ ἄλλα ἐκδιαιτήσεως καὶ τῆς τῶν ὅλων παραβάσεως, εἰ τὸ ἐπὶ τῇ ἑβδόμῃ πάτριον ἀνελεῖν δυνηθείη. καὶ μήθ' οὓς ἐβιάζετο ὁρῶν εἴκοντας τοῖς ἐπιτάγμασι μήτε τὴν ἄλλην πληθὺν ἠρεμοῦσαν, ἀλλὰ βαρέως καὶ τραχέως φέρουσαν τὸ πρᾶγμα καὶ ὡς ἐπ' ἀνδραποδισμῷ καὶ πορθήσει καὶ κατασκαφῇ πατρίδος πενθοῦντάς τε καὶ κατηφοῦντας, ἠξίου λόγῳ διδάσκειν παρανομεῖν, φάσκων· εἰ πολεμίων ἔφοδος αἰφνίδιον γένοιτο ἢ κατακλυσμοῦ φορὰ τοῦ ποταμοῦ ταῖς πλημμύραις παραρρήξαντος τὸ χῶμα ἢ ῥιπὴ πυρὸς ἢ κεραυνία φλὸξ ἢ λιμὸς ἢ λοιμὸς ἢ σεισμὸς ἢ ὅσα ἄλλα κακὰ χειροποίητα καὶ θεήλατα, μεθ' ἡσυχίας πάσης οἴκοι διατρίψετε; ἢ μετὰ τοῦ συνήθους σχήματος προελεύσεσθε, τὴν μὲν δεξιὰν εἴσω χεῖρα συναγαγόντες, τὴν δὲ ἑτέραν ὑπὸ τῆς ἀμπεχόνης παρὰ ταῖς λαγόσι πήξαντες, ἵνα μηδ' ἄκοντές τι τῶν εἰς τὸ σωθῆναι παράσχησθε; καὶ καθεδεῖσθε ἐν τοῖς συναγωγίοις ὑμῶν, τὸν εἰωθότα θίασον ἀγείροντες καὶ ἀσφαλῶς τὰς ἱερὰς βίβλους ἀναγινώσκοντες κἂν εἴ τι μὴ τρανὲς εἴη διαπτύσσοντες καὶ τῇ πατρίῳ φιλοσοφίᾳ διὰ μακρηγορίας ἐνευκαιροῦντές τε καὶ ἐνσχολάζοντες; ἀλλὰ γὰρ ἀποσεισάμενοι πάντα ταῦτα πρὸς τὴν ἑαυτῶν καὶ γονέων καὶ τέκνων καὶ τῶν ἄλλων οἰκειοτάτων καὶ φιλτάτων σωμάτων, εἰ δὲ δεῖ τἀληθὲς εἰπεῖν, καὶ κτημάτων καὶ χρημάτων, ὡς μηδὲ ταῦτα ἀφανισθείη, βοήθειαν ἀποδύσεσθε. καὶ μὴν οὗτος αὐτὸς ἐγὼ τὰ λεχθέντα, ἔφη, πάντα εἰμί, τυφώς, πόλεμος, κατακλυσμός, κεραυνός, λιμηρὰ καὶ λοιμώδης νόσος, ὁ τινάττων καὶ κυκῶν τὰ παγίως ἑστῶτα σεισμός, εἱμαρμένης ἀνάγκης οὐκ ὄνομα, ἀλλ' ἐμφανὴς ἐγγὺς ἑστῶσα δύναμις. τί οὖν τὸν ταῦτα λέγοντα ἢ διανοούμενον αὐτὸ μόνον εἶναι φῶμεν; ἆρ' οὐκ ἐκτόπιον; ὑπερωκεάνιον μὲν οὖν ἢ μετακόσμιόν τι καινὸν κακόν, εἴ γε τῷ πάντα μακαρίῳ ὁ πάντα βαρυδαίμων ἑαυτὸν ἐξομοιοῦν ἐτόλμησεν. Le gouverneur est souvent identifié avec A. Flaccus, persécuteur des Juifs, et cela même si dans le 'In Flaccum' Philon ne fait pas allusion à un épisode de ce genre; mais on sait bien que le 'In Flaccum' ne nous est pas arrivé complet; d'autres pensent au contraire qu'il s'agirait de l'un des deux prédécesseurs immédiats de Flaccus, Iberus ou Vitrasius Pollio. Voir aussi l'édition, avec traduction française et notes, du 'De Somniis' par P. SAVINELLE, Paris, 1962, pp. 178ss.

Nous avons à ce propos un intéressant passage du Talmud Palestinien qui se rapporte à la fête de Hanoucca qui venait célébrer la victoire des Maccabées sur les «Grecs» d'Antioche Epiphane. Or pendant la domination romaine et le règne d'Hérode il devint de plus en plus difficile de pouvoir célébrer une victoire «politique» qui rappelait la purification du Sanctuaire, et ce serait pour ce motif là, justement pour éviter que la fête ne fût plus célébrée et la mémoire des Maccabées oubliée, que les Maîtres du Peuple auraient donné plus d'importance aux lumières. De toute façon on comprend bien que les Romains ne voyaient pas d'un bon œil une fête qui pouvait provoquer le désir d'indépendance des Juifs.

Le Talmud Palestinien nous rapporte un épisode que nous retrouvons aussi dans d'autres sources: «Trajan le tyran eut un fils le 9 du mois d'Av (anniversaire de la destruction du Temple) et les Juifs observèrent leur jeûne; puis il perdit une fille pendant les journées de Hanoucca (où le souvenir des victoires des Maccabées est fêté) et les Juifs illuminèrent. La femme de Trajan fit alors dire à son mari: Au lieu de faire des conquêtes parmi les Barbares, viens achever la soumission des Juifs qui se sont révoltés contre toi . . .»[14]. Selon quelques interprétations il s'agirait ici du rapport voilé de faits historiques liés au nom de Marcius Turbo qui aurait vu l'ἡγεμών romain offensé dans son honneur et qui voulait se venger pour des affronts personnels en violant les femmes juives[15]. De toute façon peut-être le Talmud veut nous indiquer aussi que le motif de la révolte contre Trajan était le désir d'indépendance, symbolisé dans le rappel du Temple détruit (9 av) et l'exemple des Maccabées (Hanoucca)[16].

Des épisodes plus graves eurent lieu au temps d'Hadrien, dans la période qui est connue dans la littérature talmudique comme דור השמד ou génération de la destruction. Dans son article «Quelques notes sur la guerre de Bar-Kôsêbâ et ses suites», J. Derenbourg écrivait il y a cent ans: «Trois siècles auparavant, lorsque le temple était debout et que tout le culte se concentrait dans la capitale, il suffisait à Antiochus de souiller l'autel de Jéhova et d'arrêter à la source même les eaux vivifiantes de la Loi, pour concevoir l'espérance d'en finir avec le judaïsme. Sous Hadrien, il n'y avait plus de point central. Le Sanhédrin et le Nâsî siégeaient bien à Iabneh, mais il y avait des écoles partout . . . La célébration des fêtes ne

[14] Talm. Palest., Soucca, 5, 1:
בימי טרוגיונוס הרשע נולד לו בן בתשעה באב והיו מתענין. מתה בתו בחנוכ׳ והדליקו נירות
ושלחה אשתו ואמרה לו עד שאת מכב׳ את הברבריי׳ בוא וכבוש את היהודים שמרדו בך.

[15] S. Krauss, La fête de Hanoucca, REJ, 30, 1895, pp. 24ss., 204ss., et aussi la critique de I. Levi, Hanoucca et le Jus primae noctis, ibidem, pp. 220ss., et la réponse de S. Krauss, REJ, 32, 1896, pp. 39ss.; E. Bickerman, The Maccabees, New York, 1947, pp. 42ss.; J. Morgenstern, The Chanukah Festival and the Calendar of Ancient Israel, Hebrew Union College Annual (= HUCA), 20, 1947, pp. 90ss.; voir aussi la critique de L. H. Feldman, Scholarship on Philo and Josephus (1937–1962), New York, s.d., p. 49; M. D. Herr, s.v. Ḥanukkah, Enc. Judaica, VII, 1971, col. 1280ss.

[16] Il peut être intéressant de constater les changements qu'a subis l'observance de la fête de Hanoucca à cause des persécutions d'Hadrien et d'autres persécutions; le Talmud même nous enseigne qu'en principe on doit exposer les bougies de Hanoucca, mais que dans une période de péril, il suffit d'allumer les bougies sur une table chez soi (T. Bab., Shabbat, 21b; Scolion à Meghillat Ta'anit, Kislev, 25 [éd. Lichtenstein, p. 342]).

provoquait plus de pèlerinage à Jérusalem, où jadis la nation se réunissait trois fois par an; elle était devenue une affaire de chaque famille; et la Pâque, comme le Sabbat, était sanctifiée par le chef de la maison au milieu des siens. Comment empêcher ces agapes, comment saisir les contrevenants? . . . Pour assurer l'exécution d'une telle série de lois vexatoires, il fallait l'organisation d'une police active, taquine et inquisitoire . . . Le Talmud de Jérusalem (Ḥaguîgâh 2.1.77) rapporte à propos de Rabbi Elisée ben Abouyyâ, un des hommes les plus instruits de la Palestine, qui aurait fourni aux Romains les indications les plus minutieuses, pour qu'ils pussent distinguer un acte religieux, qui était interdit, d'une action indifférente et permise: ʿAinsi les Romains ayant obligé les Juifs à porter des charges le jour du Sabbat, ceux-ci cherchaient à les porter à deux, parce que le péché devenait moindre, en n'exécutant pas le travail seul. Elisée conseillait alors aux Romains de faire toujours faire l'ouvrage par un seul individu' »[17].

Peut-être les décrets impériaux ne regardaient que la Palestine; en tout cas les textes rabbiniques rappellent expressément – entre autres vexations, et en particulier celle qui empêchait la circoncision[18] – la prohibition – mentionnée aussi dans des sources romaines – d'observer le Sabbat et les Fêtes sous peine de mort.

Ainsi nous lisons dans la ʿMehilta de Rabbi Ishmaël'[19]: « Rabbi Nathan dit: ʿPour ceux qui aiment mes Commandements . . . il se réfère aux Juifs qui vivent en Terre d'Israel et risquent leur vie pour les Commandements. Pourquoi sortez-

[17] Bibliothèque de l'Ecole des Hautes Etudes, Paris, 1878, pp. 167ss.; sur l'épisode rapporté dans le Talmud Palestinien, Haguigah, 2,1, et dans Avot de Rabbi Natan, B. XXI, A. XI (éd. SCHECHTER, p. 44), v. M. D. HERR, Persecutions and Martyrdom in Hadrian's Days, Scripta Hierosolymitana, 23, 1972, pp. 85ss., p. 101: "*Yet although no positive decree had been promulgated to compel the active desecration of the Sabbath, it is clear that Jews were not granted exemption from forced labour etc., when this was to be performed on the Sabbath. Such were the cases alluded to in the story about Elisha b. Avuia: ʿDuring the period of persecution, too, they were forced to carry loads on the Sabbath'. The overall conclusion follows, then, that the Romans, for various psychological and tactical reasons, only enacted prohibitions against the observance of positive precepts*".

[18] V. A. M. RABELLO, ANRW II 13, pp. 699ss., avec la bibliographie. [Voir Addendum ci-dessous p. 1312.]

[19] Itrò, Bahodesh, 6, éd. HOROWITZ-RABIN, p. 227:

רבי נתן אומר, לאוהבי ולשומרי מצותי, אלו ישראל שהם יושבין בארץ ישראל ונותנין נפשם על המצות. מה לך יוצא ליהרג, על שמלתי את בני, מה לך יוצא לישרף, על שקראתי בתורה, מה לך יוצא ליצלב, על שאכלתי המצה, מה לך לוקה מאפרגל, על שנטלתי את הלולב; ואומר אשר הוכיתי בית מאהבי, מכות אלו גרמו לי ליאהב לאבי שבשמים.

Dans le Leviticus Rabba, 32,1, on trouve la version: « Pourquoi sortez-vous pour être brûlé? Parce que j'ai observé le Sabbat »: מה לך יוצא לשרף? על ששמרתי את השבת. Sur le problème des contraintes de violer le Sabbat, voir M. D. HERR, Concerning the Problem of War on the Sabbath during the Second Temple Period, Tarbiz, 30, 1961, pp. 242ss., 336ss. (en particulier voir pp. 344ss.) (en hébreu); M. D. HERR, Persecutions and Martyrdom in Hadrian's Days, Scripta Hierosolymitana, 23, 1972, pp. 85ss. Sur les moyens de persécution, voir S. LIEBERMAN, Roman Legal Institutions in Early Rabbinics and in the Acta Martyrum, JQR, 35, 1944, pp. 1ss. Sur le Sabbat, voir aussi les Papyrus no. 457a–c du C. P. J. de TCHERIKOVER, vol. III (1964), pp. 14ss.

vous pour être tué? – Parce que j'ai circoncis mon fils. Pourquoi sortez-vous pour être brûlé? – Parce que j'ai lu la Torà. Pourquoi sortez-vous pour être crucifié? – Parce que j'ai mangé le pain azyme[20]. Pourquoi sortez vous pour être flagellé? – Parce que j'ai accompli la cérémonie de la palme (Loulav)'»[21].

D'autres sources nous apprennent la prohibition de la lecture publique du livre biblique d'Esther[22], de la sonnerie du Shofar[23] ou de la construction des Cabanes de Souccot[24].

D'un autre côté, nous possédons aujourd'hui, pour cette même période, des lettres de Bar-Kochbà où le Nesi Israel (Président d'Israel) ordonne au destinataire de donner l'hospitalité le jour du Sabbat aux soldats juifs:

«De la part de Simon (Bar Kosba) à Yeshua fils de Galgula, salut!

Tu dois te mettre à faire l'envoi de 5 kor de blé par les gens de ma maison, que cela soit connu de toi. Prépare-leur donc à chacun sa place d'Hôte. Qu'ils restent chez toi pendant le Sabbat. Pourvoyez à ce que le cœur de chacun soit satisfait. Sois courageux et soutiens le courage de l'endroit. Sois en paix. Et j'ai ordonné à quiconque te donnera son blé: qu'ils le ramènent le jour après le Sabbat»[25].

[20] Voir aussi Lev. Rabba, 32,1, et Midrash Tehillim, 12,5; sur la Pâque dans la période romaine, voir aussi: J. B. Segal, The Hebrew Passover. From the Earliest Time to A.D. 70, London, 1963.

[21] Voir aussi Lev. Rabba, 32,1.

[22] Tosefta Meghillah, 1,3 (éd. Lieberman, p. 344), et 2,4 (p. 349); sur la fête de Pourim: E. J. Bickerman, Notes on the Greek Book of Esther, dans: Idem, Studies in Jewish and Christian History (Arbeiten zur Geschichte des antiken Judentums und des Urchristentums, 9), Leiden, 1976, I, pp. 246ss.; M. Hengel, Judaism and Hellenism. Studies in their encounter in Palestine during the early Hellenistic Period, I, London, 1974, pp. 70, 101; A. M. Rabello, La première loi de Théodose II, C. Th. XVI, 8,18 et la fête de Pourim, Revue historique de droit français et étranger (RH), 55, 1977, pp. 545ss.

[23] Pour le son de Shofar, précepte caractéristique de la fête du Nouvel An, voir Talm. Bab., Rosh Hashanah, 32b. Voir aussi J. Mann, Changes in the divine service of the Synagogue due to Religious Persecutions, Hebrew Union College Annual, 4, 1927, pp. 241ss.; p. 299ss.: "*The time of Blowing the Shofar on New Year*": "*. . . the sounding of the Shofar caused excitement among the Roman Garnison as a revolutionary signal*".

[24] Tosefta Soucca, 1,7 (éd. Lieberman, p. 257); Lev. Rabba, 32,1; sur la fête des Cabanes, voir: A. Büchler, La fête des Cabanes chez Plutarque et Tacite, REJ, 37, 1898, pp. 181ss.; G. Alon, La fête des Cabanes à Jérusalem dans la période du Second Temple, dans: Idem, Studies in Jewish history in the times of the Second Temple, the Mishna and the Talmud, Jérusalem, I, 1967, pp. 77ss. (en hébreu).

[25] Murabba'ât 44, lettre:

משמעון לישוע בן גלגולה שלום שתשלח תבו חמשת כורין ח[טי]ן [ ]ש לביתי אצלך בדעת ותתקן להן מקום פניו יהו בו אצלך תשבת חזו אם יחפצו לבו והתחזק וחזק ת מקום הוא שלום ופקדתי ת מי שיתן לך תחטין שלה אחר השבת יטלון.

Voir P. Benoit, J. T. Milik, R. de Vaux, Discoveries in the Judaean Desert, II: Les grottes de Murabba'ât, Oxford, 1961, pp. 161ss., qui notent: «En dépit de son caractère anecdotique, la lettre atteste un fonctionnement énergique de l'intendance pendant la Seconde Révolte. A un autre point de vue, noter la stricte observance du repos sabbatique, qui rappelle l'attitude des Asidéens, maquisards religieux de l'insurrection maccabéenne». Voir aussi la lettre n. 8:

Dans une autre lettre, en araméen, Bar-Kochbà se soucie de procurer à ses soldats les palmiers et les autres plantes nécessaires pour célébrer régulièrement la fête des Cabanes: «Simon à Yehūda bar Menašeh, à Qiryat ʿArabaya. Je t'ai envoyé deux ânes afin que tu envoies avec eux deux hommes à Yehōnatan bar Baʿayan et à Massabala pour qu'ils les chargent et les envoient à ton camp avec des palmes et des citrons. Et toi, de ton côté, envoie d'autres hommes qui t'apporteront des myrtes et des saules. Veille à ce qu'ils soient soumis à la dîme et envoie-les au camp»[26]. Peut-être la lettre est-elle de l'an 134, c'est-à-dire qu'elle a été écrite peu de mois avant la chute de Bethar, signe que malgré les dangers, malgré la lutte difficile, les Juifs continuaient à observer les Sabbats et leurs fêtes avec foi et abnégation. Il est aussi bien connu que dans les inscriptions sur les pièces de monnaie et sur les tombes juives de cette époque on trouve des palmiers, des cèdres et des *shofarot*, comme pour symboliser la foi dans le Messie, dans la vie du monde futur et l'attachement aux préceptes du Seigneur[27].

«Shim'on Bar Kosiba	שמעון בר כשבה
à Yehonatan Bar Ba'ayan	ליהונתן בר בעין
et à Masabala Bar Shim'on,	ולמשבלה בר שמעון
envoyez-moi immédiatement Eléazar	די תשלחון לי ית אלעזר
Bar Hittah, avant le Sabbat.»	בר חטה שוה קדם שבה

L. HUTEAU-DUBOIS, Les sursauts du nationalisme juif contre l'occupation romaine de Massada à Bar Kokhba, REJ, 127, 1968, p. 191, écrit: «Malgré les conditions précaires dans lesquelles il mène son combat, Simon n'oublie pas qu'il l'a entrepris pour satisfaire les aspirations religieuses de son peuple». Pour le texte du Papyrus, voir l'édition de Y. YADIN, Expedition D, Israel Exploration Journal, 11, 1961, pp. 36ss.

26 Voir Y. YADIN, ibidem, p. 48:

שמעון ליהודה בר מנשה לקרית ערביה. שלחת לך תרי חמרין די תשלח עמהן (תר)! גברין לות יהונתן בר בעין ולות מטבלה די יעמרן וישלחן למחויה לותך ללבין ואתרגין ואת שלח אחרון מלותך וימטון לך הדסין וערבין ותקן יתהן ושלח יתהן למחניה . . . הוא שלם.

Voir aussi S. LIEBERMAN, 'The Importance of the Bar-Kokhba letters for Jewish History and Literature', maintenant reproduit dans S. LIEBERMAN, Texts and Studies, New York, 1974, p. 208s.: "*The testimony of contemporary Rabbis regarding the attitude of the People towards the minute observance of Jewish ritual law is fully substantiated by the letters of Bar-Kokhba*". Voir aussi le Papyrus no. 452 a du C. P. J. de TCHERIKOVER, vol. III (1964), pp. 5ss. Le papyrus du IIe siècle fait mention de la fête des Cabanes: διὰ Ἀμαράντου τῇ παννυ[χί]δ(ι) τῆς σκηνοπηγίας (δρ.) ρ ("*By Amarantos, on the pannychis of the Feast of Tabernacles, 100 dr. etc.*"); voir aussi la note de M. STERN, ibidem, p. 6. La fête des Tabernacles est mentionnée aussi dans une inscription de Bérénice: [Ἔ]τους ν̅ε̅, Φαῶφ κ̅ε̅, ἐπὶ συλλόγου τῆς σκηνοπηγίας («L'an 55, le 25 du mois de Phaôph, lors de la fête des Tabernacles, . . .»); sur ce décret du *politeuma* des Juifs de Bérénice, honorant Marcus Titius, fils de Sextus, du 22 octobre 25, voir J. JUSTER, Juifs, I, p. 438 n. 4; J. G. ROUX, Un décret du Politeuma des Juifs de Bérénikè en Cyrénaïque au Musée Lapidaire de Carpentras (Planches III et IV), Revue des Etudes Grecques, 62, 1949, pp. 280ss.; SH. APPLEBAUM, Greeks and Jews in Ancient Cyrene, Jérusalem, 1969, pp. 137ss. (en hébreu).

27 E. R. GOODENOUGH, Jewish Symbols in the Greco-Roman Period, vols. I–XIII, Princeton, 1953–1968, passim, et en particulier vol. IV, pp. 145ss.: "*The Lulab and Ethrog*", pp. 167ss.: "*The Shofar*"; selon GOODENOUGH "*the lulab and ethrog* (sc. dans les monnaies du période de Bar-Kochba) *are indications of the hope of triumph in general . . .*"; mais voir aussi le compte-rendu de E. BICKERMAN, Syria, 44, 1967, pp. 131ss., et les

IV. Dioclétien

Un autre problème se pose pour l'époque de Dioclétien. Le Talmud de Jérusalem nous rappelle l'humble origine de cet Empereur: «Dioclétien, lorsqu'il n'était encore que porcher, a été maltraité par les jeunes gens de Rabbi Yehuda hanasì. Lorsqu'il fut nommé empereur romain, il voulut savoir si on continuerait à le mépriser: il se rendit à Pameas (ville sise loin du séjour des Juifs) et envoya un écrit aux rabbins leur enjoignant de se rendre auprès de lui dès l'issue de samedi; et il recommanda au messager de ne remettre l'ordre que le vendredi soir, à la tombée de la nuit, de façon à ce que ne pouvant voyager pendant le sabbat, ils soient en retard, ce que le messager exécuta. Or, R. Yejuda hanasì et R. Samuel bar Nachman étaient allés au bain de Tibériade. Le démon Antigoras se rendit auprès d'eux. R. Yehuda voulut le chasser. 'Laisse-le', dit Rabbi Samuel bar Nachman, 'c'est probablement dans un but miraculeux qu'il est apparu'. – 'Comment vont mes Maîtres?', dit-il. Et ils racontèrent ce qui se passait. 'Baignez-vous sans crainte', dit-il, 'votre Créateur saura opérer un miracle'. En effet, le samedi soir il les emporta sur ses épaules; et peu après, ils étaient arrivés à destination. On dit à l'empereur qu'ils étaient dehors, attendant la réception. 'Qu'ils n'apparaissent pas devant moi', dit celui ci, 'avant de s'être baignés dans le bain chauffé depuis sept jours et sept nuits'. L'esprit alla aussitôt se placer devant eux, afin de les protéger dans leur séjour et qu'ils ne soient pas brûlés. 'Est-ce parce que votre Créateur accomplit des miracles en votre faveur', dit le Romain, 'que vous venez mépriser le souverain?' 'Du tout', s'écrièrent-ils 'et si l'on a pu avoir peu d'égards pour le porcher, nous savons combien l'on en doit au roi!' Et de plus, il est bon de ne mépriser ni le dernier des Romains, ni le plus infime des adeptes de Zoroastre (ou Perses, par lesquels on sera toujours vaincu s'ils arrivent un jour, comme Dioclétien, au pouvoir)»[28].

observations de A. MOMIGLIANO, Problemi di metodo nella interpretazione dei simboli giudeo-ellenistici, dans: IDEM, Secondo contributo alla storia degli studi classici (Storia e letteratura, 77), Roma, 1960, pp. 355ss.; voir aussi H. J. LEON, The Jews of Ancient Rome, Philadelphia, 1961, passim.

[28] Talm. Palest., Teroumoth, 8,12:

דיקלוט חזירא מחוניה טליי דרבי יודה נשייא. איתעביד מלך נחת לפמיים. שלח כתבין בתר רבנין תיהוון גביי במפקי שובתא מיד. אמר ליה לשלוחיא לא תתן להון כתבין אלא בערובתא עם מטמעי שמש׳. ואתא שליחא גבהון בערובתא עם מטמעי שמשא. והוה ר׳ יודן נשייא ורבי שמואל בר נחמן וחתין למיסחי בדימוסין דטיבריא. אתא אנגיטרים גבהון ובעא ר׳ יודן נשייא למינזף ביה. א״ל רבי שמואל בר נחמן ארפי ליה לניסיון הוא מיתחמי. אמר לון מה רבנין עבדין תנון ליה עובדא. אמר לון סחון. דברייכון עביד ניסון במפקי שובתא. טען יתהון ואעיל יתהון. א״ל הא רבנין לבר. אמר לא ייחמון אפיי עד דאינון סחיין. הוה ההיא ביבני אזייה שבעה יומין ושבעה לילוין. נפק ואנצח קדמיהון ועללון וקמון ליה קדמיהון. אמר לון בגין דברייכון עביד לכון ניסין אתון מבזין מלכותא. אמרין ליה דיקלוט חזירא בזינן. ריקליטיאנוס מלכא לא בזינן. ואפי׳ כן לא מכסי לא ברומי זעיר ולא בחבר זעיר:

Se fondant également sur ce passage, BAER[29] a cru pouvoir penser que les Juifs aussi, comme les Chrétiens, avaient dû subir des persécutions religieuses au temps de Dioclétien. Le passage talmudique les aurait voilées dans le récit: obligation de profaner le Sabbat, condamnation à mort dont on ne peut se sauver que miraculeusement.

Mais à notre avis, les Juifs n'ont pas eu à supporter de vraies persécutions au temps de Diocletien et le Judaïsme continua, à la différence du Christianisme, à faire valoir son caractère de religion nationale antique: *scitote, iurisconsulti, quia Moyses prius hoc statuit*[30]. Sans doute on ne peut pas exclure catégoriquement qu'il n'y a pas eu des cas de travaux forcés qui ont impliqué la profanation du Sabbat; mais je ne pense pas qu'il puisse s'agir là de brimades à caractère religieux[31].

V. Privilèges particuliers: la dispense de comparaître en justice le jour du Sabbat

Un privilège d'une importance particulière pour les Juifs les dispensait de comparaître en justice le jour du Sabbat et les jours de fêtes juives; nous le trouvons déjà dans le premier livre des Maccabées: « Que toutes les solennités, les sabbats, les néoménies, les jours fixés et les trois jours qui précèdent et qui suivent une fête solennelle soient des jours d'immunité et de franchise pour tous les Juifs qui sont dans mon royaume, et personne n'aura la faculté de poursuivre et d'inquiéter quelqu'un d'entre eux pour n'importe quelle affaire »[32].

29 Y. F. BAER, Israel, the Christian Church and the Roman Empire from the time of Septimius Severus to the Edict of toleration of A. D. 313, Scripta Hierosolymitana, 7, 1961, pp. 117ss.

30 Collatio legum Mosaicarum et Romanarum, VII, 1.

31 S. LIEBERMAN, The Martyrs of Caesarea, Annuaire de l'Institut de philologie et d'histoire orientales et slaves, 7, 1939–1944, pp. 395ss.; S. LIEBERMAN, Palestine in the third and fourth centuries, JQR, 36, 1946, pp. 329ss.; S. LIEBERMAN, On Persecution of the Jewish Religion (en hébreu), dans: S. W. Baron Jubilee Volume, III, Jérusalem, 1975, pp. 213ss.; A. M. RABELLO, Sui rapporti fra Diocleziano e gli Ebrei, dans: Atti dell'Accademia Romanistica Costantiniana, Perugia, 1976, pp. 155ss. E. E. URBACH, The Times of the Second Temple and the Mishna According to Y. Baer, Acta of the Israel Academy of Sciences and Humanities, 6,4, Jérusalem, 1980, pp. 59ss. (en hébreu).

32 1. Macc. 10. 34ss.: καὶ πᾶσαι αἱ ἑορταὶ καὶ τὰ σάββατα καὶ νουμηνίαι καὶ ἡμέραι ἀποδεδειγμέναι καὶ τρεῖς ἡμέραι πρὸ ἑορτῆς καὶ τρεῖς ἡμέραι μετὰ ἑορτὴν ἔστωσαν πᾶσαι αἱ ἡμέραι ἀτελείας καὶ ἀφέσεως πᾶσι τοῖς Ἰουδαίοις τοῖς οὖσιν ἐν τῇ βασιλείᾳ μου, καὶ οὐχ ἕξει ἐξουσίαν οὐδεὶς πράσσειν καὶ παρενοχλεῖν τινα αὐτῶν περὶ παντὸς πράγματος. καὶ προγραφήτωσαν τῶν Ἰουδαίων εἰς τὰς δυνάμεις τοῦ βασιλέως εἰς τριάκοντα χιλιάδας ἀνδρῶν, καὶ δωθήσεται αὐτοῖς ξένια, ὡς καθήκει πάσαις ταῖς δυνάμεσι τοῦ βασιλέως. Observer F. M. ABEL, Les livres des Maccabées, Paris, 1949, p. 188: « 34. Les jours convenus, déterminés, *dies decreti*, ימי המועדים, KAHANA; chez les LXX *mô'ed* devient ἑορτή ou καιρός s'appliquant aux grandes fêtes prescrites par la Torah. C'est non seulement aux jours fixés pour chacune de ces solennités (y compris peut-être l'octave) mais encore aux trois jours qui précèdent et aux trois jours qui suivent, assignés sans doute au voyage d'aller à Jérusalem et de retour, que s'étendront l'exemption

Le Juif n'était pas obligé de comparaître devant les tribunaux païens, romains ou grecs, le samedi, les jours de fêtes juives et la veille de ces jours. Josèphe nous rapporte les plaintes des Juifs des villes ioniennes à Agrippa parce que les Grecs les citaient en justice justement le jour du Sabbat pour les tracasser; Marcus Agrippa, gendre d'Auguste et son vice-roi, ami d'Hérode, reconnut les raisons des Juifs[33] et il dut confirmer ce privilège[34]. Auguste reconnut aussi ce privilège par un édit général, et défendit à tous les tribunaux de l'Empire de citer les Juifs en justice le samedi ou bien le vendredi après la neuvième heure, c'est-à-dire le milieu de l'après-midi, pour permettre la préparation du Sabbat, qui pour les Juifs commence justement le vendredi soir[35].

L'observance du Sabbat concernait aussi le cas des distributions gratuites de grains, auxquelles les juifs participaient dès l'époque d'Auguste, selon le témoignage de Philon: « Mieux encore, jusque dans les distributions mensuelles (à la *plebs urbana*) dans sa propre cité (c'est-à-dire Rome) où tout le peuple reçoit argent ou blé selon le cas, jamais il n'admit une réduction de cet avantage pour les Juifs, mais s'il arrive que la distribution eut lieu pendant le sacro-saint septième jour, où il ne leur est permis ni de recevoir ni de donner, bref de faire quoi que ce soit qui se rapporte à la vie courante et spécialement au commerce, il avait prescrit aux distributeurs de mettre en réserve pour les Juifs jusqu'au lendemain la libéralité accordée à tout le monde »[36].

des droits d'octroi (ἀτέλεια) et la remise temporaire des dettes (ἄφεσις)». Voir aussi M. Stern, The Documents on the History of the Hasmonaean Revolt, Tel-Aviv, 1972, p. 103 s. (en hébreu).

[33] Ant. J. 16.27: Τότε δὲ περὶ τὴν Ἰωνίαν αὐτῶν γενομένων πολὺ πλῆθος Ἰουδαίων, ὃ τὰς πόλεις ᾤκει, προσῄει καιροῦ καὶ παρρησίας ἐπειλημμένοι, καὶ τὰς ἐπηρείας ἔλεγον ἃς ἐπηρεάζοντο, μήτε νόμοις οἰκείοις ἐώμενοι χρῆσθαι, δίκας τε ἀναγκαζόμενοι διδόναι κατ' ἐπήρειαν τῶν εὐθυνόντων ἐν ἱεραῖς ἡμέραις ...

[34] Ant. J. 16.168: ἔγραψα δὲ καὶ Σιλανῷ τῷ στρατηγῷ ἵνα σάββασιν μηδεὶς ἀναγκάζῃ Ἰουδαῖον ἐγγύας ὁμολογεῖν.

[35] Ant. J. 16.163: ἔδοξέ μοι καὶ τῷ ἐμῷ συμβουλίῳ μετὰ ὁρκωμοσίας, γνώμῃ δήμου Ῥωμαίων τοὺς Ἰουδαίους χρῆσθαι τοῖς ἰδίοις ἐθισμοῖς κατὰ τὸν πάτριον αὐτῶν νόμον, καθὼς ἐχρῶντο ἐπὶ Ὑρκανοῦ ἀρχιερέως θεοῦ ὑψίστου, τά τε ἱερὰ [χρήματα] εἶναι ἐν ἀσυλίᾳ καὶ ἀναπέμπεσθαι εἰς Ἱεροσόλυμα καὶ ἀποδίδοσθαι τοῖς ἀποδοχεῦσιν Ἱεροσολύμων, ἐγγύας τε μὴ ὁμολογεῖν αὐτοὺς ἐν σάββασιν ἢ τῇ πρὸ αὐτῆς παρασκευῇ ἀπὸ ὥρας ἐνάτης. Voir S. Zeitlin (supra, n. 12) et aussi S. Zeitlin, The Edict of Augustus Caesar in Relation to the Judaeans of Asia, JQR, 55 (1964–1965), pp. 160ss., qui veut expliquer l'usage du terme παρασκευή chez les Juifs hellénistiques et veut corriger la lecture du mot ἀαρῶνος: "*The word* ἀνδρῶνος *is the correct reading . . . Augustus Caesar in this edict exempted Judaeans from appearance in court on the Sabbath day*" (p. 162); voir aussi ARSt., doc. n. 150.

[36] Philo, Legatio ad Gaium, 23,158: οὐ μὴν ἀλλὰ κἀν ταῖς μηνιαίοις τῆς πατρίδος διανομαῖς, ἀργύριον ἢ σῖτον ἐν μέρει παντὸς τοῦ δήμου λαμβάνοντος, οὐδέποτε τοὺς Ἰουδαίους ἠλάττωσε τῆς χάριτος, ἀλλ' εἰ καὶ συνέβη τῆς ἱερᾶς ἑβδόμης ἐνεστώσης γενέσθαι τὴν διανομήν, ὅτε οὔτε λαμβάνειν οὔτε διδόναι ἢ συνόλως τι πράττειν τῶν κατὰ βίον καὶ μάλιστα τὸν πορισὴν ἐφεῖται, προσετέτακτο τοῖς διανέμουσι ταμιεύειν τοῖς Ἰουδαίοις εἰς τὴν ὑστεραίαν τὴν κοινὴν φιλανθρωπίαν. Et voir la note de F. H. Colson: « "*πατρίδος suspectum," says Reiter, and a correction to σπυρίδος = sportulae has been suggested. But cf. the application of πατρίς to Jerusalem in § 278. It is an essential*

Pour compléter ce tableau il faut ajouter qu'on permettait aux juifs de faire des pèlerinages à Jérusalem; Philon nous donne une touchante évocation des fêtes de pèlerinage: «A chaque fête des milliers de Juifs accourent au Temple, de milliers de villes, par l'eau et par terre, de l'Est et de l'Ouest, du Nord et du Midi»[37/38].

Permettre aux Juifs d'observer leurs fêtes signifiait aussi reconnaître le calendrier juif et en permettre son usage aux Juifs, mais seulement dans le domaine religieux; c'est pourquoi on pouvait écrire la date juive sur des épitaphes juifs, parce que tout le monde reconnaît le caractère religieux des tombeaux[39]. Mais ce privilège ne devait pas s'étendre au-delà de la vie religieuse; au contraire, les Romains insistaient sur l'usage de leur calendrier, et c'est probablement pour cela que les Maîtres du Talmud ont ordonné que la date romaine devait figurer dans les contrats civils et dans les libelles de divorce. Citons ici la Mishna de Ghittin: «Si un mari date l'acte de divorce d'après un comput de gouvernement non convenable (ou bien: d'un autre royaume), par exemple selon le règne des Mèdes ou celui des Grecs, ou en comptant les années depuis la construction du Temple ou depuis sa destruction . . . l'acte n'est pas valable . . .»[40]. Dans le Talmud de

part of the argument that Augustus's favour was shown to the Jews in his own city». Cf. aussi le commentaire de M. Smallwood, Philo Alexandrinus: Legatio ad Gaium, Leiden, 1961, p. 242, et sur les distributions de blé à la *plebs urbana*, voir: D. van Berchem, Les distributions de blé et d'argent à la plèbe romaine sous l'empire, Genève, 1939.

37 Philo, De Specialibus Legibus, 1, 69–70: καὶ τοῦδε σαφεστάτη πίστις τὰ γινόμενα· μυρίοι γὰρ ἀπὸ μυρίων ὅσων πόλεων, οἱ μὲν διὰ γῆς, οἱ δὲ διὰ θαλάττης, ἐξ ἀνατολῆς καὶ δύσεως καὶ ἄρκτου καὶ μεσημβρίας καθ' ἑκάστην ἑορτὴν εἰς τὸ ἱερὸν καταίρουσιν οἷά τινα κοινὸν ὑπόδρομον καὶ καταγωγὴν ἀσφαλῆ πολυπράγμονος καὶ ταραχωδεστάτου βίου, ζητοῦντες εὐδίαν εὑρεῖν καὶ φροντίδων ἀνεθέντες, αἷς ἐκ πρώτης ἡλικίας καταζεύγνυνται καὶ πιέζονται, βραχύν τινα διαπνεύσαντες χρόνον ἐν ἱλαραῖς διάγειν εὐθυμίαις· ἐλπίδων τε χρηστῶν γεμισθέντες σχολάζουσι τὴν ἀναγκαιοτάτην σχολὴν ὁσιότητι καὶ τιμῇ θεοῦ, φιλίαν καὶ πρὸς τοὺς τέως ἀγνοουμένους συντιθέμενοι καὶ κρᾶσιν ἠθῶν ἐπὶ θυσιῶν καὶ σπονδῶν εἰς βεβαιοτάτην πίστιν ὁμονοίας ποιούμενοι. Cf. aussi Josephus, Bellum J. 6.421; sur le pèlerinage à Jérusalem, voir S. Safrai, Pilgrimage at the Time of the Second Temple, Tel Aviv, 1965 (en hébreu).

38 On peut rappeler que la dispense du service militaire (temporaire ou complète) était aussi justifiée par le devoir de l'observance du Sabbat.

39 F. de Visscher, Le droit des tombeaux romains, Milano, 1963 (en particulier pp. 43ss., pp. 65ss., pp. 93ss.).

40 Mishna, Ghittin, 8,5:

כתב לשם מלכות שאינה הוגנת לשם מלכות מדי ולשם מלכות יון לבניין הבית ולחורבן הבית היה במזרח וכתב במערב במערב וכתב במזרח תצא מזה ומזה וצריכה גט מזה ומזה אין לה לא כתובה.

V. aussi Tosefta Baba Bathra, 11,2, et Tosefta, Ghittin, 7,6, et voir le commentaire de S. Lieberman, Tosefta Ki-fshuta, VIII, order Nashim, New York, 1973, pp. 904s.; cf. aussi Mishna, Yadaim, 4,8, et le commentaire de H. Albeck, ad locum. Cf. aussi, par exemple, Murabba'ât, Papyrus n. 18, reconnaissance de dette de l'an 55/56 de l'E.C., avec le commentaire de Milik, Les grottes de Murabba'ât, cit., pp. 100ss.; papyrus no. 19, acte de répudiation, en araméen de l'an 111, ou bien du IIIe siècle (?), selon Milik, Les grottes, cit., pp. 104ss., mais plus probablement de l'an 71, comme l'ont démontré Yadin et Yaron: Y. Yadin, The Excavation of Masada 1963/64, Jerusalem, 1965, p. 119 n. 112; R. Yaron, The Meṣada Bill of Divorce, dans: Studi in onore di Edoardo Volterra, VI,

Jérusalem on explique: «R. Yochanan dit au nom de R. Janai: 'la raison essentielle pour laquelle on a adopté l'usage d'insérer le nom du règne dans les actes était d'éviter tout danger de persécution, au point qu'à défaut de cette formalité les sages ont déclaré illégitime l'enfant né d'une telle union' . . .»[41].

VI. La période chrétienne: Sabbat et Dimanche

Le problème de l'observance des fêtes devient plus grave dans l'Empire romain chrétien, et cela surtout pour des raisons théologiques. Des discussions surgirent d'abord dans les milieux chrétiens mêmes[42], ensuite entre Juifs et Chrétiens. Le problème faisait partie d'une question plus vaste, celle de la valeur des préceptes bibliques avant et après Jésus. La circoncision et l'observance du Sabbat soulevaient des difficultés particulières.

Alors que les Juifs ne pouvaient transgresser la règle générale du caractère sacré de la Loi que dans des circonstances exceptionnelles et définies (ainsi en cas de guerre pouvait-on se défendre les jours de Sabbat et les Maccabées ont en fait combattu le jour du Sabbat[43]), cette transgression devenait pour les Chrétiens une

1971, 441 ss.; A. M. Rabello, The Divorce of the Jews in the Roman Empire, The Jewish Law Annual, 4, 1981, pp. 79 ss., et le papyrus 115, contrat de mariage: [1]Ἔτ̣ους ἑβδόμου Αὐτοκρά[τ]ορος Τραϊανοῦ Ἁδριανοῦ Καίσαρος Σ̣εβαστοῦ ὑ̣[π]α[τευόντω]ν Μανίου Ἀκ[ιλίου Γλ]αβρίωνος καὶ Βελλικίου Τορκουάτου πρὸ ιδ κ(αλανδῶν) Νοενβρίων [2]Δύστρου ιε ἐν Βαιτοβαι̣σσαιας . ι̣ω̣ . . κ . τ̣ο̣παρχείας Ἡρω̣δεί̣ο̣[υ] Ἐ̣ξομο̣λ̣[ογ]ήσα̣[το καὶ σ]υνεγράψατο Ἐ̣λ̣ε̣α̣ῖ̣ος Σίμωνος τῶν ἀπὸ κ(ώμης) Γαλωδῶν τῆς περὶ Ἀκραβα̣τ̣-τῶν: «[1]L'an sept de l'empereur Trajan Hadrien César Auguste, sous les consuls Manius Acilius Glabrio et Bellicius Torquatus, le 14 avant les calendes de novembre, (qui est) le 15 de Dystros, à Bethbassi . . . de la toparchie de l'Hérodion. A été convenu et conclu par Éléaios (fils) de Simon, du village de Galôda qui relève d'Aqraba» (traduction Milik).

41 Talm. Pal., Ghittin, 8,5:

רבי יוחנן בשם רבי ינאי עשו את הוולד ממזר מפני הסכנה.

Voir H. I. Boornstein, The Dates of Israel, Hatequfa, 8, 1930, pp. 285 ss.; G. Allon, A History of the Jews in Eretz Israel in the Mishna and Talmud Period, I, Tel Aviv, 1952, p. 336 (en hébreu); M. D. Herr, The Roman Rule in Eretz Israel, Jerusalem 1969 (Ph. D. thesis, polyc., pp. 77 ss.); E. E. Urbach, Halakha and History, dans: Jews, Greeks and Christians. Religious Cultures in Late Antiquity. Essays in Honor of W. D. Davies, ed. by R. Hamerton-Kelly and R. Scroggs (Studies in Judaism in Late Antiquity, 21), Leiden, 1976, pp. 112 ss., p. 121.

42 M. Simon, Verus Israel. Etude sur les relations entre Chrétiens et Juifs dans l'Empire Romain (135–425) (Bibliothèque des écoles françaises d'Athènes et de Rome, 166), Paris, 1948; Idem, Réflexions sur le Judéo-Christianisme, dans: Christianity, Judaism and other Greco-Roman Cults. Studies for Morton Smith at Sixty, ed. by J. Neusner, II: Early Christianity (Studies in Judaism in Late Antiquity, 12), Leiden, 1975, pp. 53 ss.

43 Sur le problème de la guerre pendant le Sabbat, voir M. D. Herr, Concerning the Problem of War on the Sabbath during the Second Temple Period, Tarbiz, 30, 1961, pp. 242 ss., 336 (en hébreu); S. Safrai, Religion in Everyday Life, Compendia Rerum Iudaicarum ad Novum Testamentum, II, Assen, 1976, pp. 804 ss.

règle générale[44]. Les pères de l'Eglise affirment que les prescriptions formulées dans la Bible n'ont qu'un caractère transitoire, qu'elles doivent être interprétées dans un sens allégorique seulement et les Chrétiens peuvent se dispenser des observances. On sait que Sabbat et dimanche ont coexisté dans l'Eglise pendant une certain période; mais assez vite le dimanche a supplanté le Sabbat[45]. En plus, observer le Sabbat, σαββατίζειν est devenu synonyme de ἰουδαΐζειν; on devait éviter à tout prix le synchronisme entre fête chrétienne et fête juive. On devait, en plus, éviter l'influence que le Judaïsme continuait à exercer sur les esprits chrétiens et pour cela on transformait le Sabbat en un jour de pénitence[46]. Mais même longtemps après que le dimanche fut devenu un jour saint, le samedi continua dans certains milieux à être considéré comme un jour saint aussi; et nous pouvons lire dans les Constitutions Apostoliques par exemple: «les esclaves travaillent cinq jours et le samedi et le dimanche ils se reposent»[47]. Cela n'a pu durer longtemps. Le Concile de Laodicée fait «défense aux Chrétiens de judaïser et d'observer le repos du Sabbat; qu'ils travaillent ce jour-là, qu'ils sanctifient spécialement le dimanche autant que possible en se reposant; s'il s'en trouve pour judaïser, qu'ils soient anathèmes au nom du Christ»[48].

Quoique mon propos ne soit pas théologique, on ne peut pas comprendre le sens de certaines lois, leur esprit, sans comprendre la situation interne de l'Eglise et ses rapports avec le Judaïsme; le Christianisme, après être devenu la religion de l'Empire, lutte non seulement contre le Judaïsme et le paganisme, mais aussi contre l'Eglise de la Circoncision, contre les nombreux «Judaïsants dans l'Eglise», comme les appelle Marcel Simon dans son 'Verus Israel'.

Nous devons aussi faire allusion aux épisodes du temps de la révolte contre Gallus (351), qui échoua et à laquelle ni le Patriarche ni les Sages n'avaient participé. Après la révolte il y eut une occupation militaire très lourde pour les

[44] M. Simon, Verus Israel, op. cit., pp. 374ss.; voir aussi A. L. Williams, Adversus Iudaeos. A Bird's Eye View of Christian Apologiae until the Renaissance, Cambridge, 1935, pp. 104, 167. N. R. M. de Lange, Origen and the Jews. Studies in Jewish-Christian Relations in third-century Palestine, Cambridge, s.d., pp. 92ss.; C. Aziza, Tertullien et le Judaïsme, Nice, 1977, pp. 172ss.

[45] P. Cotton, From Sabbath to Sunday. A Study in Early Christianity, Bethlehem, Pa., 1933; M. Simon, Verus Israel, op.cit., pp. 374ss., 383, 422; C. K. Barrett, Jews and Judaizers in the Epistles of Ignatius, dans: Jews, Greeks and Christians. Religious Cultures in Late Antiquity. Essays W. D. Davies, Leiden, 1976, pp. 220ss.; E. Schweizer, Christianity of the Circumcised and Judaism of the Uncircumcised – The Background of Matthew and Colossians, ibidem, pp. 245ss.

[46] Didaché, 5,20, et autres textes ap. J. Juster, Les Juifs dans l'Empire Romain, cit., I, p. 280 n. 2; M. Simon, Verus Israel, cit. p. 363; J. P. Audet, La Didachè, Paris, 1958.

[47] Const. Apostol. 8.33. 1–2; M. Simon, Verus Israel, p. 374; voir aussi B. Bagatti, L'Eglise de la circoncision, Jérusalem, 1965, et les observations de M. Simon, Réflexions sur le Judéo-Christianisme (cit. supra, n. 42), p. 72. Voir aussi le Papyrus No. 457d du C.P.J., du IVe siècle: . . . καὶ ἀπελθοῦσα [εἰ]ς τὸ κυριακὸν ἐν Σαμβάθῳ . . . (. . . "*and having gone away to the church on the Sabbath . . .*").

[48] Concile de Laodicée, Canon 16 et Can. 29; voir J. Parkes, The Conflict of the Church and the Synagogue. A Study in the Origins of Antisemitism, Philadelphia, 1961, pp. 174ss.

habitants de la Palestine; le nom du *magister militum* était Ursicinus[49]. A ce propos là nous avons un récit dans le Talmud palestinien: «Rabbi Yona et Rabbi Yossa décidèrent qu'il est permis de cuire du pain le samedi pour Ursicinus. Rabbi Mena dit: ‛j'ai présenté devant R. Yona mon père cette question: l'on sait par Rabbi Zeira et Rabbi Yohanan, au nom de Rabbi Yanaï, que Rabbi Jérémie et Rabbi Yohanan avec Rabbi Simon ben Yoçadak se sont réunis dans la salle d'étude de Lobza à Lydda pour commenter la Loi. Là, ils ont résolu que lorsque un païen commandera à un Israélite de transgresser l'un des préceptes mosaïques, celui-ci ne devra résister à un tel ordre, au péril de sa vie, que s'il s'agissait de ces trois crimes capitaux: idolâtrie, inceste ou meurtre'. Toutefois, cette condescendance n'est vraie que dans l'intimité; mais, si en public on demandait de transgresser le moindre commandement, il ne serait pas permis d'écouter le païen, dût-on perdre la vie. Ainsi agirent les frères Lolenos et Pappos; lorsqu'on les engagea à imiter les païens en buvant de l'eau dans un verre coloré, ils refusèrent et périrent (comment donc se fait-il que la cuisson du pain a été permise publiquement le samedi)? C'est que, par cette dernière contrainte, le gouvernement n'avait pas pour but de faire renoncer Israel à sa loi, seulement le gouverneur voulait manger du pain frais»[50]. Et encore: «Un jour, Rabbi Eliézer, Rabbi Aba Maré et Rabbi Matnia professèrent aussi qu'il est permis le samedi d'apporter des mets au gouverneur Ursicinus, car peut-être l'ensemble des habitants aura besoin de recourir à lui»[51].

Comme nous pouvons le voir, il y a ici sans doute des transgressions au précepte sabbatique, mais les Sages d'Israel ont cru devoir les autoriser en premier lieu parce qu'il ne s'agit pas de persécutions religieuses: Ursicinus ne s'intéressait pas à l'observance du Sabbat, il voulait simplement manger du pain frais tous les jours . . .; en deuxième lieu, en période politique difficile, l'intérêt public était de ne pas irriter le gouverneur et d'éviter ainsi un péril possible, après la cruelle réaction de Constance. De toute façon on peut voir qu'il n'y avait ici aucune

[49] Sur Ursicinus et sur la révolte des Juifs sous Gallus, voir: S. Lieberman, Palestine in the third and fourth centuries, JQR, 36, 1946, pp. 336ss.; S. Lieberman, Jewish Life in Eretz Yisrael as Reflected in the Palestinian Talmud, dans: Israel: Its role in Civilization, ed. by M. Davis, New York, 1956, pp. 82s.; M. D. Herr, Concerning the Problem of War on the Sabbath . . ., Tarbiz, 30, 1961, pp. 341ss.; A. Lippold, s.v. Ursicinus, RE IX A 1, 1961, col. 1058ss.; M. Avi-Yonah, The Jews of Palestine. A Political History from the Bar-Kokhba War to the Arab Conquest, New York, 1976, pp. 176ss.

[50] Talmud Pal., Šebi'it 4,2:

רבי אבונה זעירא חמנונוה פרי חורי חמרא בשכתא רבי יונה ורבי יוסי הורין מפי לארסקינם בשובתא אמר רבי מנא קשיתי קומי רבי יונה אבא לא כן אמר רבי זעירא רבי יוחנן בשם רבי ינאי רבי ירמיה רבי יוחנן בשם ר׳ש בן יוצדק נמנו בעליית בית נתזה בלוד על כל התורה כולה מניין אם יאמר עכו׳ם לישראל לעבור על אחת מכל מצות האמורות בתורה חוץ מן העבודה זרה וגילוי עריות ושפיכת דמים יעבור ולא יהרג הרא דתימא כינולבין עצמו אבל ברבים אפילו מצוה קלה לא ישמע לו כגון לוליינוס ופפוס אחיו שנתנו להם מים בכלי זכוכית צבועה ולא קיבלו מהן אמר לא אתכווין משמדתון ולא אתכווין אלא מיכל פיתא חמימה.

[51] Talmud Pal., Beza, 1,7:

לא סוף דבר שצורך לרבים בו אלא שמא יצרכו לו הרבים דלמא רבי ליעזר ור׳ אבא מרי ורבי מתניה הורי פיתא לארסקינם בשובתא שמא יצרכו לו הרבים.

intention de la part du gouverneur de provoquer la profanation du Sabbat en soi-même[52].

Du point de vue légal on continua à reconnaître le privilège qui dispensait les Juifs de comparaître en justice le jour du Sabbat. Des constitutions impériales de 412 nous l'apprennent: C. Th. 2.8.26 et C. Th. 16.8.20.

C. Th. 2.8.26 = C. Th. 8.8.8:

> *Idem AA. (Impp. Honorius et Theodosius) Johanni P(raefecto) P(raetori)o. Post alia: „Die sabbata ac reliquis sub tempore, quo Judaei cultus sui reverentiam servant, neminem aut facere a(li)quid aut ulla ex parte conveniri debere praecipimus, cum fiscalibus conmodis et litigiis privatorum constat reliquos dies posse sufficere. Et cetera. Dat. VII K. Aug. Rav(enna) DD. NN. Hon(orio) VIII et Theod(osio) III AA. conss.* (409[412] Jul. 26)[53].

C. Th. 16.8.20:

> *At cum vero Iudaeorum memorato populo sacratum diem sabbati vetus mos et consuetudo servaverit, id quoque inhibendum esse censemus, ne sub obtentu negotii publici vel privati*[54] *memoratae observationis hominem adstringat ulla conventio*[55], *cum reliquum omne tempus satis publicis legibus sufficere videatur sitque saeculi moderatione dignissimum, ne delata privilegia violentur: quamvis retro principum generalibus constitutis satis de hac parte statutum esse videatur. Dat. VII Kal. Aug. Rav(ennae) Honor(io) VIII et Theod(osio) V AA. conss.* (412 Jul. 26)[56].

FERRARI DALLE SPADE voit dans cette loi l'expression de la liberté religieuse[57], mais BIONDI écrit dans son 'Diritto Romano Cristiano'[58]: „*Mentre il calendario pagano è caduto in pieno (CT 2,8,22; Arc. Hon. 395), almeno nel suo significato religioso, la legislazione è più tollerante per le festività ebraiche. Nel giorno di sabato e negli altri giorni* quo Iudaei cultus sui reverentiam servant, neminem aut facere aliquid aut ulla ex parte conveniri debere praecipimus; *però è tolta alla festività ogni contenuto religioso, poichè quella disposizione si giustifica con la considerazione che per far valere i diritti del fisco e dei privati bastano gli altri giorni (CT 2,8,26 = CT 8,8; Hon. Theod. 409?); lo stesso concetto tro-*

52 Voir J. JUSTER, Les Juifs dans l'Empire Romain, cit., II, p. 197.

53 Pour la datation 412, voir O. SEECK, Regesten der Kaiser und Päpste für die Jahre 311 bis 476 n. Chr., Stuttgart, 1919; voir aussi J. GAUDEMET, L'Eglise dans l'Empire Romain (IV–V siècles) (Histoire du droit et des institutions de l'Eglise en Occident, 3), Paris, 1958, p. 627 et p. 663.

54 „*Id est conventionibus et actionibus*" (GODEFROY).

55 « Citation en justice » (JUSTER).

56 Sur le texte, voir J. E. SEAVER, Persecution of the Jews in the Roman Empire (300–438), Lawrence, 1952, pp. 62ss.

57 G. FERRARI DALLE SPADE, Privilegi degli ebrei nell'impero romano-cristiano, dans: Festschrift für L. Wenger, II (Münchener Beiträge zur Papyrusforschung und antiken Rechtsgeschichte, 35), München, 1944, pp. 102ss. = IDEM, Scritti Giuridici, III, Milano, 1956, pp. 267ss., à p. 270s.

58 B. BIONDI, Il Diritto Romano Cristiano, I, Milano, 1952, p. 167.

Certainement la prohibition faite aux Juifs de citer les Chrétiens orthodoxes en justice ne pouvait pas être considérée comme gênante pour un Juif observant; on peut au contraire expliquer cette défense de Justinien en ce sens que si le dernier jour pour citer un Chrétien au tribunal tombait un samedi, le Juif pouvait correctement le citer le lundi suivant. De même on peut interpréter la défense de Justinien comme expression de sa volonté de faire respecter la règle de réciprocité (cfr. D. 2.2.1 pr.).

Enfin il faut tenir compte du fait que l'Empereur se sentit autorisé à intervenir même dans la vie religieuse des Juifs, comme nous pouvons le constater fort bien dans la Novelle 146 'De Hebraeis'[60].

On peut conclure que, pour ce qui regarde l'observance du Sabbat par les Juifs, il ne devait pas subsister de problème particulier; le problème de la valeur du Sabbat restait un problème interne dans l'Eglise, problème qui a donné lieu à des conflits entre l'Eglise d'Occident, qui avait bientôt abandonné l'observance du Sabbat, et celle d'Orient, qui continua de l'observer pendant longtemps. Il pourrait être intéressant de lire le jugement de Jean Chrysostome sur l'observance juive du Sabbat: « N'avez-vous pas honte en considérant les Juifs? Leur exemple ne vous fait-il pas rougir? Avec quelle exactitude ils observent le sabbat, et, dès la veille au soir, ils s'abstiennent de tout travail! S'ils voient le soleil prêt à se coucher le jour de la préparation, ils interrompent leurs transactions et suspendent leurs affaires; si quelqu'un, leur ayant acheté quelque chose avant le soir, arrive le soir pour leur en apporter le prix, ils ne le souffrent pas, ils refusent de recevoir cet argent. Que dis-je? il ne s'agit là que d'un prix de vente ou d'un contrat, mais fût-il question de recevoir un trésor, ils aimeraient mieux perdre ce gain, que de fouler la loi aux pieds »[61].

VII. La fête de Pourim

Une texte d'une importance particulière pour notre sujet est finalement la Constitution de Théodose II, C. Th. 16.8.18, qui concerne la fête de Pourim, qui commémore les épisodes rapportés par le livre biblique d'Esther. On sait par le Talmud que les Sages d'Israel ont hésité avant de fixer la fête de Pourim, probablement pour éviter des incidents entre Juifs et non-Juifs; mais finalement le désir populaire vainquit et Pourim fut fixée comme fête.

60 Voir V. Colorni, L'uso del greco nella liturgia del Giudaismo ellenistico e la Novella 146 di Giustiniano, Annali di Storia del Diritto, 8, 1964, pp. 19 ss., avec les observations de G. I. Luzzatto, SDHI, 31, 1935, pp. 443 ss., et de A. M. Rabello, Labeo, 12, 1966, pp. 140 ss.

61 Homélie, In illud si esurierit inimicus, 3 (Migne, P. G., 51, 176) (trad. franç. de M. Jeanin 4, p. 118); voir aussi J. Juster, Les Juifs dans l'Empire romain, cit., I, p. 355 n. 1; M. Simon, La polémique anti-juive de St. Jean Chrysostome et le mouvement judaïsant d'Antioche, dans: Mélanges Cumont, Annuaire de l'Institut de Philologie et d'Histoire orientales, IV, Bruxelles, 1936, pp. 403 ss.

tienne. Les lois de Théodose, quoiqu'elles réprouvent en apparence les actions des masses, accordent en fait une grande liberté d'action aux éléments hostiles aux Juifs. Nous nous trouvons à une période de pression ecclésiastique croissante, pas seulement sur les Juifs, mais aussi sur les hommes au pouvoir; les autorités séculières cèdent et la situation des Juifs s'aggrave. La Novelle 3 de Théodose et la Novelle 146 de Justinien marquent le point culminant de cette intervention impériale.

Justinien incorpora la loi concernant Pourim à son propre Code (C.J. 1.9.11), avec de très légères modifications par rapport au texte du Code Théodosien; nous savons que les lois concernant les Juifs qui se trouvent dans le Code Théodosien ne furent pas toutes reprises par Justinien; il n'est donc pas possible de prétendre que l'inclusion de la loi concernant Pourim dans le Codex Justinianus est sans importance. On peut penser que les passions n'étaient pas encore apaisées et que l'Empereur voulait se protéger contre toute recrudescence éventuelle d'actes pouvant être interprétés comme des affronts à la religion chrétienne. Mais il me semble plus raisonnable de supposer que Justinien, qui était partisan d'une intervention maximale de l'Etat dans la vie communautaire, n'était pas prêt à renoncer à une loi qui limitait la liberté religieuse des Juifs.

VIII. La fête de Pâque

Un problème plus compliqué encore était celui de la fête de Pâque. Pour les Juifs, on le sait bien, la fête de Pâque tombe chaque année le 14 du mois de Nisan pour célébrer la sortie d'Egypte: il s'agit d'une fête joyeuse célébrée dans chaque famille juive par une cérémonie domestique appelée *seder*. Les Pâques chrétiennes commémorent la passion et la résurrection de Jésus, qui selon la tradition chrétienne eurent lieu justement pendant la Pâque juive; c'est pour cela que l'Eglise des origines trouva naturel de fixer la date de Pâques selon la date de la Pâque juive; or, on sait qu'à cette époque les Juifs n'avaient pas encore un calendrier lunaire fixe, comme aujourd'hui, mais on fixait chaque fois le début du mois selon l'apparition de la nouvelle lune; quelques pères de l'Eglise commencèrent bientôt à trouver insupportable une situation dans laquelle on devait attendre que les Rabbins eurent fixé la date du nouveau mois pour pouvoir eux-mêmes fixer la date de leur fête; lorsque la fête fut introduite à Rome, ils la célébraient d'abord (160) le dimanche après la Pâque juive, comme à Alexandrie; après de nombreuses discussions entre l'Eglise d'Occident et celle d'Orient, la question fut portée au concile de Nicée[66], qui menaça de châtiment les chrétiens célébrant Pâques en même

[66] L. Duchesne, La question de la Pâque au concile de Nicée, Revue des Questions historiques, 1880, pp. 1ss.; M. Simon, Verus Israel, cit., pp. 373ss. Voir aussi E. Werner, Melito of Sardes, the first Poet of Deicide, Hebrew Union College Annual, 37, 1966, pp. 191ss.; S. Hall, Melito in light of the Passover Haggadah, Journal of Theological Studies, 22, 1971, pp. 29ss.; R. C. White, Melito of Sardis. Sermon "on the Passover". A

temps que la Pâque; selon Eusèbe, Constantin transforma les décisions de l'Eglise en loi d'Etat; en 341 le Synode d'Antioche revient sur la prohibition faite aux chrétiens de célébrer Pâques en même temps que les Juifs fêtaient la Pâque; le problème était évidemment difficile à résoudre et on peut imaginer que beaucoup de Chrétiens continuaient à ignorer les décisions de l'Eglise[67].

Peut-être est-ce justement à ce propos-là que les Sages d'Israel sont arrivés à la décision de fixer un calendrier lunaire. SAUL LIEBERMAN écrit: "*It was*

new English translation with Introduction and Commentary, Lexington, 1976; M. PAVAN, I Cristiani e il mondo ebraico nell'età di Teodosio 'il Grande' (Annali della Facoltà di lettere e filosofia, 3 [1965–66], Perugia, 1966, pp. 438ss.); J. PARKES, The conflict of the Church and the Synagogue, cit., pp. 165, 175s.; E. CHADWICK, The Early Church, Middlesex, 1967, pp. 84ss., 258s.

[67] Conc. Laodicée, can. 38, et d'autres textes chez J. JUSTER, Les Juifs, I, p. 283 n. 4; voir aussi le Nomocanon, titulus VII, cap. IV, in: PITRA, Juris ecclesiastici graecorum historia et monumenta, II, Roma, 1868, p. 519s.: Περὶ τοῦ μὴ χρῆναι ἐν κυριακῇ θεώρια γίνεσθαι, ἢ γόνυ κλίνειν ἐν κυριακῇ, ἢ ἐν ταῖς ἡμέραις τῆς πεντηκοστῆς, καὶ ὅτι κατὰ τὸ ἐγχωροῦν δεῖ σχολάζειν τὴν κυριακὴν, οὐ μὲν τὸ σάββατον, καὶ ὅτι δεῖ γραφὰς ἀναγινώσκειν τὸ σάββατον. Συνόδου Νικαίας κανὼν κ'. Συνόδου Λαοδικείας κανὼν κθ'. Συνόδου Καρθαγένης κανὼν ξα'. [Συνόδου ς' κανὼν ιθ'. ξς'] Πέτρου κανὼν ιε'. Θεοφίλου ἐκ τῆς περὶ τῶν θεοφανείων προσφωνήσεως. Ὁ νόμος. Ἡ ς' διάτ. τοῦ ιβ' τίτ. τοῦ γ' βιβλίου τοῦ κώδικος λέγει τὴν κυριακὴν ἄπρακτον εἶναι· ἡ δὲ θ' διάτ. τοῦ αὐτοῦ τίτ. ὅτι ἐν αὐτῇ οὐχ ὑπομιμνήσκεταί τις, ἢ ἐγγύας ἀπαιτεῖται, ἢ δημόσιον ἢ ἰδιωτικὸν χρέος, οὔτε δικάζεται, οὔτε σκηνικὴ θέα ἢ κυνήγια ἢ ἱπποδρόμιον τελεῖται, ἀλλ' εἰ καὶ φθάση βασιλέως νατάλιον ἐν κυριακῇ, ὑπερτίθεται τὸ θεώριον· ὁ δὲ θεωρῶν ἐν κυριακῇ ἀποστρατεύεται καὶ δημεύεται, καὶ ὁ ἐμβιβαστὴς παραβὰς τὸν νόμον· ἔξεστι δὲ πακτεύειν καὶ διαλύεσθαι ἐν κυριακῇ. Εἴρηται δὲ βιβλίῳ α' τίτ. θ' διάτ. β' καὶ ιγ', ὅτι οἱ Ἰουδαῖοι ἐν τῷ σαββάτῳ καὶ ταῖς ἄλλαις αὐτῶν ἑορταῖς, οὔτε σωματικῶς λειτουργοῦσιν, οὔτε τι ποιοῦσιν, οὔτε διὰ δημοσίαν ἢ ἰδιωτικὴν αἰτίαν ἐνάγονται, ἢ Χριστιανοῖς ἐνάγουσιν. Cap. IV. *Non oportere die dominica fieri spectacula, vel genuflectere in dominica, vel diebus pentecostes; et quod oportet, quoad eius fieri potest, die dominica feriari, non tamen sabbato; et quod oportet legere scripturas sabbato.* Syn. nic. canon XX. Syn. laodic. can. XXIX. Syn. carthag. can. LXI. [Syn. VI canon XIX, LXVI.] Petri canon XV. Theophili ex compellatione de Theophaniis. *Lex.* Sexta constitutio XII tit. III lib. Cod. dicit, diem dominicum esse feriatum. IX autem eiusdem tit. constitutio, quod in eo non interpellatur quispiam aut sponsio petitur, aut publicum aut privatum debitum, nec iudicatur; nec scenicum spectaculum, vel venatio, equorumve cursus peragitur. Sin autem contigerit imperatoris natalem esse dominico, differuntur spectacula. Qui autem spectat die dominico, militia privatur, et bonis mulctatur, et apparitor, qui legem transgressus est. Licet autem pacisci et transigere in die dominico. Dictum est autem in libro primo, tit. IX constitut. II et XIII, quod Judaei sabbato, et aliis suis festis, nec corporale ministerium exercent, nec aliquid faciunt, nec propter publicam vel privatam causam in eos actio intenditur, vel ipsi in christianos intendunt. M. SIMON, Verus Israel, p. 374, écrit: « Le synchronisme entre fêtes chrétiennes et fêtes juives était, pour les milieux exposés à la contagion, comme une invitation au syncrétisme ». « Du moment où l'on célébrait la fête le 14 », note DUCHESNE à propos de la Pâque, « on était assez porté à la célébrer à la juive et à observer le rite comme on observait la date ». La remarque vaut pour les autres fêtes d'origine juive. Mais il n'a pas suffi, pour écarter le danger, de modifier les dates. Car les Judaïsants ont alors célébré deux fêtes au lieu d'une ». Sur cette problématique, voir aussi M. PAVAN, I cristiani e il mondo ebraico nell' età di Teodosio 'il Grande' (Annali della Facoltà di lettere e filosofia, 3 [1965–66]), Perugia, 1966, pp. 74ss.

therefore natural for the Christian emperors to render a service to the church which they earnestly strove to unify by forbidding the Patriarch to compute and proclaim in advance the date of Passover; and especially to despatch messengers, who had to take roads to the Jewish diaspora in the East, which ran through Syria and Mesopotamia. The sectarian churches of these countries would thus be deprived of information about the date of the Passover . . . Realizing that this prohibition, unlike any other, was conceived not to annoy the Jews but to achieve that unity, of such vital importance to the Christian government, the Patriarch concluded that the measure was not a temporary one and consequently created a permanent calendar"[68]. De toute façon le problème est encore actuel au temps de Justinien et l'empereur tout-puissant pensa alors le trancher une fois pour toutes! Dans l'année 543, il décréta, d'après Procope, que les Juifs ne pourraient célébrer leur Pâque qu'après les Pâques chrétiennes: «Mais – ce sont les paroles de Procope – l'Empereur prit la peine aussi d'abolir les lois que les Juifs respectaient. Si par chance la fête de Pâque (juive) tombait avant les Pâques des Chrétiens, il ne permettait pas aux Juifs de célébrer leur fête à la date fixée, et ne leur permettait pas non plus de faire leur offrande à Dieu, ni d'accomplir chaque cérémonie selon leurs propres coutumes. Et beaucoup parmi eux ont été poursuivis par les autorités pour avoir mangé la viande d'agneau de lourdes amendes, sous prétexte de violation de lois d'Etat»[69]. Nous avons ici, sans doute, une grave atteinte à la liberté des fêtes juives, comme écrit JUSTER; mais il semble que trois ans plus tard, en 546, lorsque les Pâques chrétiennes devaient coïncider avec la Pâque juive, Justinien préféra repousser la date de la fête chrétienne.

[68] S. LIEBERMAN, Palestine in the Third and Fourth Centuries, JQR, 36, 1946, p. 334. Voir aussi: A. RENOUX, Le Codex arménien Jérusalem 121. I. Introduction. Aux origines de la liturgie hiérosolymitaine, in: F. GRAFFIN (éd.), Patrologia Orientalis, tome XXXV, fasc. 1, no. 163, Turnhout, 1969, pp. 68s.: «C'est à la Pâque juive que fait allusion la rubrique du samedi de Lazare du Jérusalem 121, conservant vraisemblablement la rédaction la plus ancienne de l'ordo hagiopolite, toujours soucieux de correspondances évangéliques. L'*Itinerarium Egeriae* fait également allusion à la Pâque juive . . .» (p. 69, avec n. 7); le Codex arménien Jérusalem 121 est du Ve siècle; voir IDEM, Edition du texte, ibidem, tome XXXVI, fasc. 2, no. 168, Turnhout, 1971, p. 255 et p. 265.

[69] Procope de Cesarée, Anecdota, 28,16–19: Ταῦτα δὲ οὐ μόνον ἐς τοὺς νόμους ἀεὶ καὶ καθ' ἑκάστην εἰργάζετο τοὺς Ῥωμαίων, ἀλλὰ καὶ οὓς Ἑβραῖοι τιμῶσι καταλύειν ὅδε βασιλεὺς ἐν σπουδῇ εἶχεν. ἢν γάρ ποτε αὐτοῖς ἐπανιὼν ὁ χρόνος τὴν Πασχαλίαν ἑορτὴν πρὸ τῆς τῶν Χριστιανῶν ἀγαγὼν τύχοι, οὐκ εἴα ταύτην τοὺς Ἰουδαίους καιροῖς τοῖς καθήκουσιν ἄγειν οὐδέ τι ἐν ταύτῃ ἐξοσιοῦσθαι τῷ θεῷ ἢ ἐπιτελεῖν τῶν ἐν σφίσιν αὐτοῖς νομίμων. πολλούς τε αὐτῶν οἱ ἐπὶ τῶν ἀρχῶν τεταγμένοι ἅτε προβατείων κρεῶν ἐν τούτῳ γευσαμένους τῷ χρόνῳ, τῆς ἐς τὴν πολιτείαν παρανομίας ὑπάγοντες χρήμασιν ἐζημίουν πολλοῖς. ἔργα μὲν οὖν καὶ ἄλλα τοιαῦτα Ἰουστινιανοῦ ἀνάριθμα ἐξεπιστάμενος οὐκ ἄν τι ἐνθείην, ἐπεὶ πέρας δοτέον τῷ λόγῳ· ἀποχρήσει γὰρ καὶ δι' αὐτῶν τὸ τοῦ ἀνθρώπου ἦθος σημῆναι.

IX. Conclusions

Jean Chrysostome nous apprend que les fêtes solennelles du mois de Tishri aussi, c'est-à-dire le Nouvel An, le grand Pardon et les Tabernacles, ont exercé une grande influence dans l'Eglise d'Antioche et que beaucoup de Chrétiens jeûnaient le jour de Kippour, par exemple: «Beaucoup de ceux qui se comptent des nôtres – proclame Chrysostome dans sa première homélie contre les Juifs – et qui prétendent partager nos idées, s'en vont, les uns assister comme spectateurs aux fêtes juives, les autres participer à leur célébration et s'associer au jeûne. C'est de cette détestable pratique que je veux maintenant débarrasser l'Eglise»[70].

Nous n'avons pas de lois à ce propos, dans la période romaine, mais nous savons bien que dans la législation postérieure, par exemple dans l'Espagne visigothique[71], il y a eu des limitations pour la célébration de ces fêtes-là.

C'est là aussi une des fatalités du Peuple du livre: après avoir donné au mode le concept du repos hebdomadaire, après avoir donné le concept de Dieu Un et Unique, le Judaïsme a dû lutter pour conserver son droit à servir Dieu selon Son enseignement; les fêtes, qui auraient dû être des moments de délassement et de joies de l'esprit, sont souvent devenues une cause de souffrance et de Martyre[72].

[70] M. SIMON, Verus Israel, cit., pp. 379ss. V. aussi J. DANIÉLOU, La fête des Tabernacles dans l'exégèse patristique, Studia Patristica, 1 (Texte und Untersuchungen zur Geschichte der altchristlichen Literatur, 63), Berlin, 1957, pp. 262ss.; M. PAVAN, I cristiani e il mondo ebraico, cit., pp. 74ss., 78ss.; L. CRACCO RUGGINI, Pagani, Ebrei e Cristiani: odio sociologico e odio teologico nel mondo antico, in: Gli Ebrei nell'alto Medioevo, Settimane di Studio del Centro Italiano di Studi sull'alto Medioevo, 26, Spoleto, 1980, I, p. 34, n. 32, et p. 64, n. 85.

[71] J. JUSTER, The Legal Condition of the Jews under the Visigothic Kings, Brought up-to-date by A. M. RABELLO, The Israel Law Review Association, 1976, pp. 394ss.

[72] La base de cette étude a été une communication faite à Paris, au Centre G. GLOTZ (Université de Paris I Sorbonne), le 2 avril 1979 et je désire remercier le Directeur de l'Institut, M. le Prof. J. MÉLÈZE-MODRZEJEWSKI, pour sa collaboration. Je désire remercier aussi mon collègue, M. le Prof. M. D. HERR, de la faculté des sciences humaines de l'Université Hébraïque de Jérusalem, pour avoir lu le manuscrit et pour les observations qu'il a bien voulu me faire, et le Dr. H. NERSON qui a bien voulu faire la révision du texte français. Mes vifs remerciements aussi à la 'Memorial Foundation for Jewish Culture' pour sa contribution appréciée.

Addendum: A la fin de note 18 adde: A. M. RABELLO, Il problema della 'circumcisio' in Diritto Romano fino ad Antonino Pio, Studi A. Biscardi, II, Milano, 1982, pp. 187ss.

IX

DIVORCE OF JEWS IN THE ROMAN EMPIRE

1. *Introduction*

In this study, we wish to examine the problem of the divorce of Jews in the Roman Empire. Clearly, we are confronted here with the two different legal systems, the Roman and the Jewish; it may be useful, therefore, to make a brief historical examination of the Roman conception of divorce, and then to give an exposition of the Jewish conception of divorce also in the light of recently discovered documents. After this brief comparative examination, we may be able to draw certain conclusions as to divorce among Jews, both Roman citizens and foreigners (*peregrini*), in the Roman Empire.[1]

Part I. Divorce in Roman Law

2. *Divorce in classical Roman law*

The judicial conception of divorce is intimately connected with that of marriage, divorce being *one* of the causes of the untying of the marriage bond. Therefore, given that the Roman marriage of classical times depended on the continuing wish of the parties—of both the parties—to remain husband and wife, it follows that the discontinuance of that wish, at one moment or another in married life, leads to the dissolution of the marriage (*divortium*).[2]

It is clear, therefore, that if both spouses agreed on a divorce, there was no problem; Gaius, a jurist of the 2nd century, C.E., defined divorce in the eleventh book *ad edictum provinciale* thus: "The term *divortium* is derived either from the *difference* of minds (of the parties),

---

[1] For bibliography, see E. Volterra, "Divorzio", *Novissimo Digesto Italiano* (Turin: U.T.E.T., 1960), VI. 62ff.; A. Morongiu, "Divorzio", *Enciclopedia del Diritto* (Milan: Giuffrè, 1964), XIII. 432ff.; M. Sargenti, *Index* (Ticini: Alma Ticinensis Universitas, 1978), 474ff.

[2] E. Volterra, *Lezioni di diritto romano, Il matrimonio romano* (Rome: Edizioni Ricerche, 1961), 123ff.

or from the fact that the parties who are tearing the marriage asunder are going their *different* ways."[3] It was also sufficient that one of the spouses—whether it was the husband or the wife was immaterial—no longer wanted to continue in that capacity: the later sources speak in such cases of a *repudium*.[4]

The divorce, like the marriage, had to be completely free. It was considered wrong to bind oneself not to divorce or to pay a penalty in the event of divorce: "It is dishonourable to bind together a marriage, whether existing or anticipated, by means of a penal bond."[5]

Further, as regards form, divorce was completely free of formality:[6] what was required was that a real will to divorce should be manifested, so that it was not a case of simple abandonment in a moment of anger.[7]

Certainly, problems of definition created by such absolute freedom were not lacking: the question was, when was the divorce established in fact? The problem emerges, for example, in a passage from Cicero, where he recounts the case of a Roman citizen who, leaving his pregnant wife in Spain, arrived in Rome and set up house with another woman *more uxorio*, without having given notice of his intentions to the first wife. His sudden death, and the birth of a son to each of the women after his death, posed the question of whether the son of the second woman was illegitimate, because of the persistence of the first marriage—the second woman then being considered merely as a concubine; or whether he was indeed legitimate, the second "wedding" being seen as an indication of an effective divorce of the first marriage. On the one hand, it seems clear that it was not legally necessary to make a declaration that one did not wish to be considered any more as husband or wife; instead, that fact could be deduced from the conduct of the

---

[3] *Dig.* 24.2.2.pr.: *Divortium autem vel a diversitate mentium dictum est, vel quia in diversas partes eunt, qui distrahunt matrimonium.*

[4] See A. Berger, *Encyclopedic Dictionary of Roman Law* (Philadelphia: American Philosophical Association, 1953), 626 s.v. *repudium mittere.*

[5] *Dig.* 45.1.134: *inhonestum visum est vinculum poenae matrimonia obstringi, sive futura, sive iam contracta.* See also *C.J.* 8.38(39).2 and *Schol. Sin.* 6; *Dig.* 45.1.19; *C.J.* 6.46.2; 8.38.2; 5.4.14.

[6] A. Watson, *The Law of Persons in the Later Roman Republic* (Oxford: The Clarendon Press, 1967), 53f.

[7] As for the most ancient period, E. Levy, *Der Hergang der römischen Ehescheidung* (Weimar: H. Böhlaus Nachfolger, 1925), 15ff., has maintained that there were certain formalities; *contra*, R. Yaron, "Minutiae on Roman Divorce", *Tijdschrift voor Rechtsgeschiedenis* 28 (1960), 1ff., who holds that even in that period divorce must have been completely free.

spouses. On the other hand, such a system created difficulties. As Cicero explains:

> Then as to freedom, the most serious issue there can be, may not controversy arise out of the common law, on the question whether a slave, enrolled with his master's consent on the censor's list, is to date his enfranchisement from that moment, or from completion of the lustrum? And what of a case that really happened, within our fathers' recollection, of the head of a family coming from Spain to Rome, and leaving in the province his wife with child: at Rome he married another wife, without having sent notice of divorce to the first, and afterwards died intestate, when each woman had borne a son; was it but an ordinary dispute that thereupon arose, involving as it did the civil rights of two citizens, the boy born of the second consort, and his mother? She, if it were held that the first wife could be divorced only by using some specific formula, and not by marrying again, would be regarded as being in the position of a concubine.[8]

Later on, Cicero underlines the differences of opinion among legal experts:

> Indeed in all those suits, as in that very one of Manius Curius, recently conducted by yourself, and in the dispute over Gaius Hostilius Mancinus, and again in the matter of the boy born of the second wife, before her predecessor had received notice of divorce, dissent as to the law was complete in the most learned circles.[9]

The principle of liberty of form was also fully confirmed by Diocletian:

> Diocletian and Maximilian to Phoebus. Even though a bill of repudiation was not delivered or known to the husband, the marriage is dissolved. A.D. 294.[10]

The problem of whether the divorce was effective (*verum divortium*) was in issue when the "divorced" couple lived together afterwards: was this to be considered as merely a continuation of their existing marriage, or was it an entirely new marriage? If there was, between one marriage and the other, a marriage by one spouse to a third party, or if a period of time had elapsed sufficient to evidence the dissolution of the preceding marriage, one could speak of a *verum divortium*.[11]

---

[8] *De Oratore* I, XL, 183, translation of E. W. Sutton in the Loeb Classical Library.

[9] *De Oratore* I, LVI, 238. On such passages see esp. Levy, *supra* n. 7, at 15f.; E. Costa, *Cicerone Giureconsulto* I (Bologna: Zanichelli, 1927), 55f.; E. Volterra, "Per la storia del reato di bigamia in diritto romano", *Studi in onore di Umberto Ratti* (Milan: Giuffrè, 1934), 387ff., 392f.; Watson, *supra* n. 6, at 53f.

[10] *C.J.* 5.17.6: *Idem AA. et CC. (Diocletianus et Maximianus) Phoebo. Licet repudii libellus non fuerit traditus vel cognitus marito, dissolvitur matrimonium. D. XVIII K. Ian. Nicomediae CC. consules* (A.D. 294). See R. Yaron, "Divortium inter absentes", *Tijdschrift voor Rechtsgeschiedenis* 31 (1963), 54ff.; R. Yaron, "Ad secundas nuptias convolare", *Symbolae iuridicae et historicae Martino David dedicatae*, ed. A. Ankum, R. Feenstra, W. F. Leemans (Leiden: E. J. Brill, 1968), I.263ff.; M. Humbert, *Le Remariage à Rome. Étude d'Histoire juridique et sociale* (Milan: Giuffrè, 1972), 135.

[11] R. Yaron, "De divortio varia", *Tijdschrift voor Rechtsgeschiedenis* 32 (1964), 533ff., arguing against Levy, *supra* n. 7, at 91: "The essence of the concept of *idem*

In the earliest period, divorce must have been a rarity, but, towards the end of the Republic, the mores of Roman society were very decadent, and divorce was abused: Plautus put into the mouth of a wife a lamentation on the sad condition of woman—she had to endure all the freedoms permitted to her husband, while she could not even go out without his knowledge.[12]

The law did not require any special grounds for divorce; as has been noted, it was sufficient that the *affectio maritalis* no longer existed.

It is also necessary to take account of a distinction which we have not made but which still forms part of 'Romanist' doctrine, that between marriage *cum manu* and marriage *sine manu*. There is, in fact, only *one* marriage; *manus* does not pertain to the elements of the marriage—it is formed and broken independently of the marriage.[13]

The fact that it was also easy for Roman women to obtain divorces aroused the interest of satirists and the disapproval of some writers: thus, Seneca complains that there are women who do not number the years by consuls but by husbands—they divorce to marry, and they marry to divorce.[14] Likewise, Martial remarks, concerning a woman who in thirty days had married and divorced ten husbands: "Women who marry so often do not contract marriages; in law it is adultery."[15]

It is, however, unnecessary to assume that this situation was general. As always, dissolute morality was typical of the nobles and the rich; among the middle and lower classes and in the provinces the situation must have been different and the family unit more settled.[16]

It was not easy to restrain this situation by legislation. Legislative intervention here would have contradicted the Roman conception of mar-

---

matrimonium then is, that if the marriage is renewed within a short time, the interlude is to be disregarded. What occurred is dismissed as a mere *iurgium* "altercatio, dispute" (see D.23.2.31, 23.4.27), and ex post facto the spouses are deemed to have stayed married all along. The divorce proves not to have been *verum*, which here means something like "real, final, definite"." (at 542).

[12] Plautus, *Merc.* 817ff.; see other cases recounted in Valerius Maximus 6.3.10-12, especially for the case of Servius Sulpicius Gallus, who divorced his wife for having walked bareheaded in the street, with which compare *M. Ket.* 7:6.

[13] P. Bonfante, *Corso di diritto romano I. Diritto di famiglia* (Rome: Samparolesi, 1925, repr. Milan: Giuffrè, 1963), I². 346; Volterra, *supra* n. 2, at 89ff.

[14] Seneca, *De beneficiis* 3.16.2.

[15] *Epigrammata* 6.7. *Quae nubunt totiens, non nubunt: adultera lege est.*

[16] V. Arangio-Ruiz, *Istituzioni di diritto romano* XIV (Naples: Jovene, 1960), 451; J. Carcopino, *La vie quotidienne à Rome à l'apogée de l'Empire* (Paris: Hachette, 1939); Bonfante, *supra* n. 13, at 347, who observes, besides: "Nel dipingere a fosche tinte il quadro agisce in tutti, più o meno, il preconcetto della grande regenerazione morale portata dal cristianesimo."

riage and divorce as well as the liberty of citizens. It is therefore understandable that Augustus needed to overcome severe obstacles to secure approval for his two laws—*de adulteriis* and *de maritandis ordinibus*—which favoured marriage, and the birth rate, and opposed adultery.[17]

The *lex Iulia de adulteriis* also laid down that a divorce must be witnessed in the presence of seven Roman citizens over the age of puberty.[18]

The probable significance of this was that a solemn form was to be required in the case of unilateral divorce, in order to release a husband from a public accusation of *crimen lenocinii* and to establish exactly when an accusation of adultery against the woman might become appropriate.[19]

3. *Divorce in Hellenistic law*

In Hellenistic Egypt too, we may note that both spouses could dissolve a marriage of their own volition; as in Rome, the marriage could be dissolved without any formalities by the simple wish of one party (expulsion or abandonment of the other) or by mutual consent. Any document had merely evidential, not constitutive effect.[20]

4. *Divorce in Roman-Christian law*

Clearly, this situation of complete freedom changed with the coming to power of Christianity. The influence of Christian doctrine,[21] opposed

---

[17] For bibliography on the legislation of Augustus and in particular on the two laws here mentioned, reference may be made to my book, *Effetti personali della patria potestas* (Milan: Giuffrè, 1979), I.210ff.

[18] *Dig.* 38.11.1.1; 24.2.9; 24.1.35.

[19] An interesting case of divergence as between the civil law and the criminal law. P. E. Corbett, *The Roman Law of Marriage* (Oxford: The Clarendon Press, 1930), 234; Volterra, *supra* n. 9, at 413ff.

[20] See H. J. Wolff, *Written and Unwritten Marriages in Hellenistic and Postclassical Roman Law* (Hanerford Penn.: American Philological Association, 1939); R. Taubenschlag, *The Law of Greco-Roman Egypt in the Light of the Papyri* (2nd ed., Warsaw: Pańistwowe Wydawnictwo Naukove, 1955), 121ff.; C. Préaux, "Le Statut de la femme à l'époque hellénistique, principalement en Égypte", *Recueils de la Société Jean Bodin* 11 (1959), 127ff.; C. Vatin, *Recherches sur le mariage et la condition de la femme mariée à l'époque hellénistique* (Paris: De Boccard, 1970); H. J. Wolff, "Hellenistic Private Law", *Compendia Rerum Iudaicarum ad Novum Testamentum* (Assen: van Gorcum, 1974), I.1, 534ff.

[21] *Cf. Mt.* 19:3-9; *Lk.* 16:18; *Mt.* 5:27-32; Paul, *1 Cor.* 7:10-11; J. Bonsirven, *Le Divorce dans le Nouveau Testament* (Paris: Desclée, 1948); D. Daube, "The New Testament Terms for Divorce", *Theology* 47 (1944), 65ff.; J. M. Myaud, *L'indissolubilité du*

to divorce,[22] must have been felt quickly in the legislative field, even if a clear prohibition, which would have conflicted with the principles then permeating Roman society, was not issued. It is perhaps on account of this conflict that we cannot establish a "continuity" in the Imperial interventions on the divorce issue.

The first constitution is that of Constantine in 331, drawn up, it seems, in an ecclesiastical setting (*C. Th.* 3.16.1):

> Emperor Constantine Augustus to Ablavius, Praetorian Prefect.
>
> It is Our pleasure that no woman, on account of her own depraved desires, shall be permitted to send a notice of divorce to her husband on trumped up grounds, as, for instance, that he is a drunkard or a gambler or a philanderer, nor indeed shall a husband be permitted to divorce his wife on every sort of pretext. But when a woman sends a notice of divorce, the following criminal charges only shall be investigated, that is, if she should prove that her husband is a homicide, a sorcerer, or a destroyer of tombs, so that the wife may thus earn commendation and at length recover her entire dowry. For if she should send a notice of divorce to her husband on grounds other than these three criminal charges, she must leave everything, even to her last hairpin, in her husband's home, and as punishment for her supreme self confidence, she shall be deported to an island. In the case of a man also, if he should send a notice of divorce, inquiry shall be made as to the following three criminal charges, namely, if he wishes to divorce her as an adulteress, a sorceress, or a procuress. For if he should cast off a wife who is innocent of these crimes, he must restore her entire dowry, and he shall not marry another woman. But if he should do this, his former wife shall be given the right to enter and seize his home by force and to transfer to herself the entire dowry of his later wife in recompense for the outrage inflicted upon her.
>
> *Given ... in the year of the consulship of Bassus and Ablavius.—331.*
>
> INTERPRETATION: The right to send notice of divorce is extended to a wife or husband for certain approved reasons and causes; for they are forbidden to dissolve a marriage for a trivial charge. If perchance a woman should say that her husband is

---

mariage. Étude historico-canonique (Strasbourg: 1952); J. Dom Dupont, *Mariage et divorce dans l'Évangile* (Bruges: Abbaye de Saint-André, 1959); M. Zerwick, "De matrimonio et divortio in Evangelio", *Verbum Domini* 38 (1960), 193ff.

[22] It should be noted, however, that within the church itself opposition to divorce in any situation was not uncontested: on the basis of the two Matthaean passages in which mention is made of divorce *excepta fornicationis causa* (Vulgate), various church fathers allowed divorce in cases of rape or adultery or in other cases of serious offences, such as idolatry; besides the study of Bonsirven (*supra* n. 21, at 38ff.), see P. Rasi, *Consensus facit nuptias* (Milan: Giuffrè, 1946), where the author maintains that one must distinguish between the Italian tradition, opposed to divorce, and that of the East, more disposed to allow it. According to B. Biondi, *Il Diritto Romano-Cristiano* (Milan: Giuffrè, 1954), III. 164ff., the differences of opinion were serious and persisted throughout the first centuries in the teaching of the church; this explains too the about-turns in the legislative positions of the Christian Roman emperors. See also G. D'Ercole, "Il consenso degli sposi e la perpetuità del matrimonio nel diritto romano e nei padri della Chiesa", *Studia et Documenta Historiae et Iuris* 5 (1939), 18ff.; F. Delpini, *Divorzio e separazione dei coniugi nel diritto romano e nella dottrina della Chiesa fino al V secolo* (Turin: Marietti, 1956).

> either a drunkard or given to licentiousness, she shall not send him notice of divorce on that account. But if perchance she should prove that he is either a homicide, a sorcerer, or a violator of tombs, the husband who is convicted of these crimes appears to be justly divorced, without any fault of the woman; and she may recover her dowry and depart. If the woman should not be able to prove such crimes, she shall be subjected to the following punishment: namely, that she shall forfeit both the dowry which she had given or which had been given on her behalf and the gift which she received, and she shall also be liable to exile by relegation. But if a man should cast off his wife, he also is not permitted to divorce her for a trivial quarrel, as often happens, unless perhaps he should be able to prove that she is guilty of certain crimes, that is, if he is able to prove that she is an adulteress, a sorceress, or a procuress. But if he cannot prove this, he shall restore her dowry to the woman, and he shall not presume to take another wife. But if perchance he should attempt to do so, the woman who was cast off, though innocent, shall have the right to vindicate for herself her husband's home and all his substance. It is recognized that this is ordained in order that if a woman should be unjustly divorced, she is ordered to acquire the dowry of the second wife also.[23]

Unilateral divorce is admitted, according to the law, only for a *iusta causa*: for example, wives would not be able to divorce their husbands by accusations of drunkenness, gambling or womanising; in order to obtain a divorce the wife would need to prove that the husband was guilty of homicide, sorcery or violation of graves; the husband, on the other hand, could divorce when the wife was guilty of adultery or was a procuress or poisoner. According to another interpretation, however, instead of "poisoner" the law referred to those who were dedicated to the black arts.

Bilateral consensual divorce continued to be free; unilateral divorce still resulted in the dissolution of the marriage bond with civil effect, but, excepting the above-mentioned cases of *iustae causae*, there were accompanying sanctions such as loss of dowry or the obligation to restore it, deportation of the woman, who thus became unable to contract another marriage, or, in the case of fault on the man's part, the possibility of the first wife invading his home and appropriating the dowry of the "new" woman. Discrimination between the sexes is evident here.

This system was abolished by the Emperor Julian in 363 C.E. in his attempt to reinstate the pagan conception of divorce and with it complete freedom to divorce.[24] However, this was but a brief interlude and his successors had to return to the system of Constantine: Honorius and

---

[23] Pharr's translation. On this constitution, see Bonfante, *supra* n. 13, at 350ff.

[24] Augustine, *Quaestiones de utroque testamento* 9, 115 (144); Ambrosiaster, *Quaestiones Veteris et Novi Testamenti*, 115.12; see also *C.Th.* 3.13.2 and Bonfante, *supra* n. 13, at I.351.

Constantinus promulgated a new constitution (*C.Th.* 3.16.2),[25] which propounded in more legal language the system of the constitution of *C.Th.* 3.16.1: the woman could only obtain a divorce if the husband had been guilty of *magna crimina*, and she could marry again only if 5 years had passed since the day of the divorce. If one takes account of the fact that for a woman in particular it was very important to be able to marry

---

[25] In Pharr's translation:

Emperors Honorius, Theodosius, and Constantius Augustuses to Palladius, Praetorian Prefect.

If a woman should serve notice of divorce upon her husband and separate from him and if she should prove no grounds for divorce, the gifts shall be annulled which she had received when betrothed. She shall also be deprived of her dowry, and she shall be sentenced to the punishment of deportation. We deny her not only the right to a union with a subsequent husband, but even the right of postliminium. But if a woman who has revolted against her marriage should prove merely flaws of character and ordinary faults, she shall lose her dowry and restore to her husband all gifts, and never at all shall she be associated in marriage with any man. In order that she may not defile her widowhood with wanton debauchery, We grant to the repudiated husband the right to bring an accusation.

1. It remains to say that if a woman who withdraws should prove serious grounds and a conscience involved in great crimes, she shall obtain possession of her dowry and shall also retain the betrothal bounty, and she shall regain the right to marry after a period of five years from the day of the divorce. For then it will appear that she has done this from loathing of her own husband rather than from a desire for another husband.

2(1). Certainly if the husband should be the first to give notice of divorce and if he should charge his wife with a grave crime, he shall prosecute the accused woman in accordance with the law, and when he has obtained his revenge, he shall both get possession of her dowry and recover his bounty to her, and he shall acquire the unrestricted right to marry another woman immediately. 3. If it is a fault of character and not of criminality, the husband shall recover his gifts but relinquish the dowry, and he shall have the right to marry another woman after a period of two years. 4. But if the husband should wish to dissolve the marriage because of a mere disagreement and should charge the repudiated woman with no vices or sins, he shall lose both his gifts and the dowry and be compelled to live in perpetual celibacy; he shall suffer punishment for his insolent divorce in the sadness of solitude; and the woman shall be granted the right to marry after the termination of a year. Moreover, We order to be preserved the guarantees of the ancient law in regard to the retentions from dowries, on account of children.

Given on the sixth day before the ides of March at Ravenna in the year of the consulship of Eustathius and Agricola.—March 10, 421.

INTERPRETATION: If a woman should be the first to serve a notice of divorce upon her husband and should not prove the statutory grounds for divorce, she shall forfeit the betrothal bounty, and she shall not recover that which she gave her husband as dowry. In addition, she shall also be sent into exile by relegation, and she shall not have the right to marry or to return to her own. Indeed, if she should prove slight faults in her husband, for which she appears to seek a divorce, she shall forfeit her dowry and shall restore the betrothal gifts, and she shall not have the right to marry another man. If, however, after divorcing her husband, she should become involved in adultery, her husband shall have the right to prosecute her even after the divorce. But if a woman who has separated from her husband should prove that he is guilty of grave and definite crimes, she shall both recover her dowry and vindicate that which her husband bestowed upon her as a betrothal bounty, and she shall have the unrestricted right of marriage after five years.

young—also in order to have children—one understands that the rule made the woman's second marriage very difficult; in a case then of *morum vitia ac mediocres culpae* of the husband, the woman could obtain a divorce but could not remarry. If she divorced without satisfying any of the grounds laid down by law she suffered a proprietary sanction (loss of dowry and of the husband's *donatio*) and was liable to deportation. More favourably to the husband, the law established that he could divorce and remarry in the event of a serious *crimen* by the wife; in the case of *morum culpa* he could divorce and then remarry after two years; in the case of divorce for *dissensus*—incompatibility of character—he would have had to live in perpetual celibacy. This system appeared too rigid to Theodosius II who in C.E. 436 abolished it by the *Novella Theodosiana* No. 12: it is not known, however, to what extent this was applied in practice and, in any case, the same Emperor, together with Valentinian III, had to revive the earlier system, prohibiting *repudium* without *iusta causa* and bringing to 14 the number of *iustae causae* for which husband or wife could obtain a divorce. In a case where the spouses had children, the divorce had to be made more difficult.[26]

In 497 C.E. Anastasius established (*C.* 5.17.9) that in the case of divorce by consent (*communi consensu*), with the reciprocal exchange of the *libellus repudii*, the wife could contract a second marriage after one year had passed. According to *communis opinio*, the *divortium communi consensu* had continued to be legal from Constantine to Anastasius: differences of opinion in the Church would have favoured

---

Indeed, if the husband should be the first to serve notice of divorce, he shall secure his revenge on grounds approved by law, he shall vindicate the dowry of his repudiated wife, shall recover his betrothal gifts, and shall have the right to marry another woman immediately if he wishes. If indeed there were no definite crimes, but, as often happens, the husband is displeased with the frivolity of his wife's character, he shall recover his gifts and shall restore to her immediately anything which he has received from her, and after a period of two years he shall have the right to marry another wife. But if no defect of character should be proved but merely mental discord, the innocent woman who is rejected by her husband shall both vindicate the gifts made to her by the man and shall recover her dowry. But he shall remain alone forever and shall not presume to associate himself in marriage with another woman. The woman, however, is permitted to proceed to another marriage after a year if she should so wish. But for the sake of their common children, if there should be any, the Emperor orders those rules to be observed which have been established in the law concerning retentions according to the number of children, which law Paulus sets forth in his *Book of Responses* under the title, *A Wife's Property*.

[26] On the problems of entrusting the children of divorced persons, see especially D. Daube, "Dividing a Child in Antiquity", *California Law Review* 54 (1966), 1630ff.; R. Bonini, "Criteri per l'affidamento della prole dei divorziati in diritto romano", *Archivio Giuridico* 181 (1971), 24ff. (= *Problemi di Storia delle Codificazioni e della politica legislativa* (Bologna: Patron, 1973), I.3ff.); Rabello, *supra* n. 17, at 250ff.

the persistence of this type of divorce.[27] Other scholars maintain, on the contrary, that with the advent of Christianity this type of divorce was prohibited, and that Anastasius would have had to permit it *de novo*.[28]

Justinian showed interest in the problem of divorce on a number of occasions:[29] his earliest interventions were indirect, made by interpolating earlier texts: thus, he laid down that it was necessary to renounce formally the wish to divorce; then he added new *iustae causae*, such as dangerous incurable madness on the part of one of the spouses, or that a spouse was taken as a prisoner of war for at least 5 years (*divortium bona gratia*: the term had already appeared in the classical texts, though in a different sense—then it indicated a divorce arrived at amicably; now it indicated a unilateral divorce for cause which did not involve a penalty for any party).

The direct interventions of the Emperor were by means of the *Novellae*: the first, *Novella* 22 of 535 C.E., regulated the question more or less *ex novo*; divorce could be *cum poena* or *sine poena*, four forms being distinguished:

> by mutual consent, leaving it to the judgement of the spouses;
>
> by an innocent event, which included a vow of chastity as well as being taken prisoner of war and *servitus superveniens*;
>
> without just cause;
>
> for just cause.

It was, in a certain sense, to define the terms of the situation, as appears from the constitution of the code. Seven years later, in 542, Justinian again turned to the question of regulating divorce, with *Novella* 117, cap. 10, restricting whatever remained of the freedom to divorce. The *divortium communi consensu* was limited to cases of impotence, vows of chastity, entering monastic life, and presumption of husband's death after an absence of more than five years. Unilateral divorce was also restricted: it was permitted to a man or woman whose spouse had plotted against the Emperor's life or failed to reveal a plot or where one spouse had attempted to kill the other or had not exposed the intrigues

---

[27] Thus, *inter alia*, Bonfante, Biondi, Volterra, Bonini.

[28] Thus V. Basahoff, "Les sources chrétiennes de la loi de Constantin sur le repudium", *Studi in onore di Salvatore Riccobono* (Palermo: G. Catiglia, 1936), III.175ff.; Rasi, *supra* n. 22; Yaron, *supra* n. 7/11.

[29] On Justinian's divorce legislation see especially Bonfante, *supra* n. 13, at 353ff.; Biondi, *supra* n. 22, at III.164ff.; R. Bonini, "Il divorzio consensuale dalla *Novella Iustiniani* 117.10 alla *Novella Iustini* 140", *Bullettino dell'Istituto di Diritto Romano* 75 (1972), 41ff. (= *Problemi, supra* n. 26, at I.27ff.), with the most recent bibliography; Humbert, *supra* n. 10, at 449ff.

of third parties against the other spouse. The other instances related to the moral conduct of the spouses in relation to one another: thus, the husband could divorce if his wife was found guilty of adultery or of having taken part in banquets or assisting in public performances, attending the baths with other men, or taking lodgings with another without her husband's consent and authority. The wife, on the other hand, had recourse to proceedings if her husband unjustly accused her of adultery or had attempted to dishonour, defame, disgrace or prostitute her, or if he took another woman into his house or habitually cohabited with another woman. In all other cases divorce was regarded as unjust and punishable: if it occurred because of the woman, she was incarcerated in a convent and deprived of her possessions; a guilty husband, on the other hand, suffered only patrimonial damages. Penalties were also laid down for magistrates who did not immediately hand the woman over to the custody of the bishop or administer the husband's punishment. The Church's influence in this *Novella* was evident—probably inspired by Bishop Pelagius who had a convent specially constructed for guilty women. The Bishop's intervention is recalled on a number of occasions in this *Novella*.

The disparity of treatment between spouses was eliminated with *Novella* 127 of 548 C.E., in which the penalties against wives were extended to husbands divorcing without cause.

In 556 C.E., Justinian returned to the question with *Novella* 134, laying down new penalties of a patrimonial and personal nature (perpetual enclosure in a convent). Spouses could escape the penalties by declaring, before being sent to their respective institutions, that they were prepared to live together. Thus, it became permissible to a husband to take back an adulterous wife within two years of "permanent" reclusion in a convent.

It is clear that with Justinian the Church made the greatest anti-divorce effort which was possible in the Romano-Byzantine era. The most drastic curb, it seems, was that which limited the divorce *communi consensu*.

In 566, Justin II, successor to Justinian, pressured by numerous demands, revived—with *Novella* 140—the divorce *communi consensu*, defined as *therapeia*, especially in cases of incurable mutual hatred between spouses: this consent was defined as *iusta causa*. Numerous requests for consensual divorces were made after the promulgation of this *Novella*, but later it fell into disuse and the prohibition on consensual divorce was revived.

In the waverings of Roman-Christian law on the divorce theme we can discern two conceptions: the Roman state conception according to which "mutual consent creates marriage ... for amongst men whatever is bound together may be loosed" (*nuptias consensus facit mutuus nam inter homines quidquid ligatur omne dissolubile*) and that of the Church, which after numerous divergences, tended ever more drastically to affirm, in an absolute manner, that what God has joined together man may not break asunder (*Quod Deus coniunxit, homo non separet*). The complete victory of Church doctrine was achieved in later times when marriage became an indissoluble *sacramentum*; though, as Bonfante outlines in his conclusions, forced marriage continuing under duress is always "a moral fiction".[30]

Part II. Divorce of Jews in the Roman Empire

5. *Introduction: Jewish divorce from biblical times to the end of the period of the Second Temple*

We come now to examine certain problems relating to divorce among Jews in the Roman Empire; for this purpose it will be useful to examine briefly the Jewish conception of divorce. Jewish law recognised on principle divorce as a unilateral act of the husband—as may be seen from *Deut.* 24:1-4:

> When a man has married a wife, but she does not win his favour because he finds something shameful in her, and he writes her a note of divorce, gives it to her and dismisses her; and suppose after leaving his house she goes off to become the wife of another man, and this next husband turns against her and writes her a note of divorce which he gives her and dismisses her, or dies after making her his wife—then in that case her first husband who dismissed her is not free to take her back to be his wife again after she has become for him unclean. This is abominable to the Lord; you must not bring sin upon the land which the Lord your God is giving you as your patrimony.[31]

---

[30] Bonfante, *supra* n. 13, at 366.

[31] On the passage in Deuteronomy, and further generally on Jewish divorce in the biblical period, see L. G. Levy, *La Famille dans l'Antiquité Israélite* (Paris: F. Alcan, 1905), 211ff.; L. M. Epstein, *Marriage Laws in Bible and Talmud* (Cambridge Mass.: Harvard U.P., 1942); E. Neufeld, *Ancient Hebrew Marriage Laws* (London: Longmans, 1944); Y. Y. Rabinowitz, "Gerushin", *Entsiḳlopediyah miḳra'it*; R. Yaron, "On Divorce in Old Testament Times", *Revue Internationale des Droits de l'Antiquité*, 3 Ser., 4 (1957), 117ff.; R. de Vaux, *Ancient Israel. Its Life and Institutions* (London: Darton, Longman & Todd, 1961), 60ff.; Z. W. Falk, *Marriage and Divorce. Reforms in the Family Law of German-French Jewry* (Jerusalem: Mif'al hashichpul, 1961, Hebrew); *idem, Hebrew Law in Biblical Times* (Jerusalem: Wahrmann Books, 1964), 154ff.; A. Toeg, "Does Deuteronomy XXIV: 1-4 incorporate a General Law on Divorce?", *Diné Israel* 2 (1970), vff.; Z. W. Falk, *The Divorce Action by the Wife in Jewish Law* (Jerusalem: Institute for Legislative Research and Comparative Law, 1973, Hebrew).

Divorce continued to remain legal afterwards; it was considered as a necessary remedy for an evil.

At the beginning of the Second Temple period, in the 5th century B.C., the Prophet Malachi delivered a rebuke to husbands who repudiated the wives of their youth in order to take up with young pagan girls:

> Yet ye say: 'Wherefore?' Because the Lord has been witness between thee and the wife of thy youth, against whom thou hast dealt treacherously, though she is thy companion and the wife of thy covenant. Therefore take heed to your spirit, and let none deal treacherously against the wife of his youth. For I hate putting away, saith the Lord, the God of Israel.[32]

However, the Prophet did not doubt the legal validity of divorce. We can also discern from his words how great an influence was exerted on the Jewish family by foreign customs.

Some scholars have seen a limitation on divorce in the stipulation of *ervat davar*, but this thesis is far from certain and it seems preferable to maintain that the Bible did not wish to limit the husband's power.[33] Rather, from the practical point of view, it seems that the writing of the *libellus repudii* was of greater importance. It required knowledge on the part of the writer and thus very often implied using the services of a competent person for drafting purposes. It may therefore be supposed that such action was not taken in a transient moment of anger; the man contemplating divorce had to take account of the eventual censure of society and particularly that of the woman's family, but no more.

The influence of foreign conceptions (Egyptian according to Yaron, or perhaps Babylonian, as Volterra maintains) is strongly in evidence from the documents of the Jewish colony of Elephantine in the 5th century B.C.E.,[34] from which it is clear that the wife as well as the husband could obtain a divorce (*sin'ah*), contrary to Jewish practice: "The most interesting feature of divorce at Elephantine is the equal capacity of the spouses, as far as the power of dissolution of the marriage is concerned.

---

[32] *Malachi* 2:14-16: On this passage see Z. W. Falk, *Introduction to Jewish Law of the Second Commonwealth* II (Leiden: E. J. Brill, 1978), 307ff. It should be noted that this prophetic passage is referred to at the end of the (Babylonian Talmud) tractate Gittin as an expression of sorrow caused by divorce.

[33] Yaron, *supra* n. 31, at 127ff.; Toeg, *supra* n. 31, at viiff. In *Marriage and Divorce, supra* n. 31, at 96f., Falk holds that originally divorce was restricted to cases of *ervat davar*, and that only gradually did a more liberal attitude develop, which found expression in the interpretation of Bet Hillel. But in a later study, he has reversed his opinion, without offering reasons for the change: *Introduction, supra* n. 32, at 308.

[34] Cowley, AP 15; Kraeling, AP 2 and 7.

This is in striking contrast to the situation which on the whole obtains in the ancient East, and also in Talmudic Law, where the husband alone is entitled to dissolve the marriage (the only mitigation being the court's power to bring pressure upon him to divorce). The equality at Elephantine is probably due to the Egyptian environment."[35]

6. *From the Second Temple period to the end of the Roman period*

Coming to the end of the Second Temple period—a period in which contacts already existed between the Roman and Jewish worlds—we can ascertain that there existed diverse views among the Pharisees on the problem of divorce: the school of Hillel interpreted the biblical texts to mean that divorce was permitted to men without limitation as to grounds; the school of Shammai adopted a sterner line, requiring the existence of grave moral reasons:

> The School of Shammai say: A Man may not divorce his wife unless he has found unchastity in her, for it is written, *Because he hath found in her* indecency *in anything*. And the school of Hillel say: [He may divorce her] even if she spoiled a dish for him, for it is written, *Because he hath found in her indecency in* anything. R. Akiba says: Even if he found another fairer than she, for it is written, *And it shall be if she find no favour in his eyes.*[36]

In Flavius Josephus' story about the *repudium* sent by Salome to her husband, it is noteworthy that the writer expressly underlines the fact that this *repudium* was contrary to Jewish law, according to which it should have emanated from the husband. Evidently Salome conducted herself according to Hellenistic and Roman usages:

---

[35] R. Yaron, *Introduction to the Law of the Aramaic Papyri* (Oxford: The Clarendon Press, 1961), 53ff., and see the review by G. I. Luzzatto, *Studia et Documenta Historiae et Iuris* 28 (1962), 376. On this subject see also E. Volterra, "Osservazioni sul divorzio nei documenti aramaici", *Studi Orientalistici in onore di G. Levi Della Vida* (Rome: Istituto per l'Oriente, 1956), II.586ff.; R. Yaron, "Aramaic Marriage Contracts from Elephantine", *Journal of Semitic Studies* 3 (1958), 1ff.; *idem*, "Aramaic Marriage Contracts: Corrigenda and Addenda", *Journal of Semitic Studies* 5 (1960), 66ff.; E. J. Bickerman, "The Historical Foundations of Postbiblical Judaism", in *The Jews. Their History, Culture, Religion*, ed. L. Finkelstein (3 ed., New York: Harper, 1960), 83ff.; J. Modrzejewski, "Les Juifs et le droit hellénistique: Divorce et égalité des époux (CPJud. 144)", *IURA* 12 (1961), 184; Falk, *Hebrew Law in Biblical Times, supra* n. 31, at 157; A. Verger, *Ricerche giuridiche sui papiri aramaici di Elefantina* (Rome: Centro di Studi Semitici, 1965), 116ff., and the review by Yaron, *Journal of Semitic Studies* 12 (1967), 308; B. Porten, *Archives from Elephantine. The Life of an Ancient Jewish Military Colony* (Berkeley and Los Angeles: University of California Press, 1968), 261ff., and Yaron's review, *Journal of Semitic Studies* 16 (1971), 243.

[36] *M. Gitt.* 9:10, Danby's translation. See the commentary of H. Albeck, *The Mishnah, Seder Nashim* (Tel-Aviv: Dvir, 1958), 407f.; Toeg, *supra* n. 31, at xxlff. ("Additional Note on Mishnah *Gittin* IX, 10"). The passage has often been studied also by authors concerned with the problem of divorce in the New Testament; see *supra* n. 21.

> Some time afterwards Salome had occasion to quarrel with Costobarus and soon sent him a document dissolving their marriage, which was not in accordance with Jewish law. For it is (only) the man who is permitted by us to do this, and not even a divorced woman may marry again on her own initiative unless her former husband consents. Salome, however, did not choose to follow her country's law but acted on her own authority and repudiated her marriage, telling her brother Herod that she had separated from her husband out of loyalty to Herod himself.[37]

We cannot draw any legal conclusions about Jewish divorce from the conduct of Herodias, daughter of Aristobulus (son of Herod the Great and Miriam the Hasmonean). According to Josephus, in 41 C.E. she divorced her husband Herod Philip to marry his brother;[38] this affair, considered incestuous by the *Torah*, provoked a negative reaction among the people, including John the Baptist.[39] Josephus stresses that her attitude was contrary to Jewish law: here, as in other cases connected with Herod and his family, one is not dealing with Jewish, but rather with Hellenistic and Roman customs, given the marked assimilation of this family.[40]

From the above two passages of Josephus we cannot discern anything denoting a change in the Jewish norms; though we can deduce that if a Jewish woman who was also a Roman citizen wished to divorce her husband, she could do so in virtue of her Roman citizenship and the divorce was valid according to Roman law.

There are those who wish to discover an exception to the general rule, noted by Josephus, in the life of Josephus himself. Thus in the *Vita*, 75, 415[41] they see a case of divorce by a woman. Certainly, however, it ap-

---

[37] *Ant.* XV.7.10 (259-60), translation of R. Marcus in the Loeb Classical Library. According to Boaz Cohen, Jewish law would have recognised divorces of gentiles which conformed to their own laws: see "Concerning Divorce in Jewish and Roman Law", in *Jewish and Roman Law* (New York: Jewish Theological Seminary of America, 1966), I.377ff.

[38] *Ant.* 18.5.4 (136): "Their sister Herodias was married to Herod, the son of Herod the Great by Mariamme, daughter of Simon the high priest. They had a daughter Salome, after whose birth Herodias, taking it into her head to flout the way of our fathers, married Herod, her husband's brother by the same father, who was tetrarch of Galilee; to do this she parted from a living husband."

[39] *Mt.* 14:3-10; the end of the passage is considered without "historical foundation" by A. Schalit, "Herodias", *Encyclopedia Judaica* (Jerusalem: Keter, 1971), VIII. 388; *cf.* also *Mk.* 6:17ff.; *Lk.* 3:19ff.

[40] Rabello, "Tribunale domestico in casa di Erode il grande?", in *Effetti personali, supra* n. 17, at 363ff.

[41] *Vita* 75, 414-415: "... and it was by his [of Vespasian] command that I married one of the women taken captive at Caesarea, a virgin and a native of that place. She did not, however, remain long with me, for she left me on my obtaining my release and accompanying Vespasian to Alexandria." On this passage see B. Motzo, *Saggi di Storia e di Letteratura Giudeo-ellenistica* (Firenze: Le Monnier, 1924), 214ff.

pears from the text that such a marriage—between him, a priest, and her, a prisoner—so badly regarded by Jewish law,[42] was imposed by the Emperor himself. We do not know, therefore, if it was celebrated according to law, though if it was it is not stated if the woman left without asking for a divorce, in order not to be bound to live with Josephus who, being viewed as a traitor, was hateful to her,[43] or if Josephus assented to the woman's wish and divorced her in regular fashion.

The particulars did not interest Josephus, who underlined two aspects, relating to the beginning and the end of the union: the union was created by the will of the Roman Emperor; it was terminated on the woman's initiative. Josephus does not enter into the details of the legal problem; if the woman had acted contrary to the Jewish norm Josephus would not have omitted to underline the fact, which would have contributed to placing the woman in a bad light.

Others have wished to see a concession to the school of Shammai in the fact that in a subsequent divorce Josephus makes us aware of his disapproval of his wife's conduct;[44] it is notable, however, that those who regard a divorce for whatever reason as acceptable from the strictly legal point of view, cannot ignore the social reactions provoked by unjustified divorces—above all in Rome after the Augustan reforms described above.

---

[42] *Cf. M. Ket.* 2:5 and also *Ant.* 3.12.2; 13.10.5 and *c.Ap.* 1:7, and refer to J. Juster, *Les Juifs dans l'Empire Romain* (Paris: Geuthner, 1914), II. 44 n. 2 (2 ed., New York: Franklin, 19).

[43] Thus M. Stein in a note in his Hebrew translation of the *Vita* of Josephus (Ramat-Gan: Masada, 1968), 167 n. 5. It must be noted that recently D. Daube has suggested that Vespasian did not *impose* the marriage with the captive, but *permitted* it. For this reason Josephus tells us that the wife was a virgin: D. Daube, "Three Legal Notes on Josephus after his Surrender", *Law Quarterly Review* 93 (1977), 191ff.

[44] Modrzejewski, *supra* n. 35, at 179. The author writes about "l'inconduite de sa première femme"; in fact the text deals with ... the third wife! On the wives of Josephus, see Juster, *supra* n. 42, at II. 44 n. 2, but Juster too is somewhat inaccurate: he writes that Josephus had only one son from this third wife, but according to *Vita* (76, 426) he had three sons from her, although only one survived; moreover Juster states that the fourth wife, who came from Crete, bore him three sons, whereas in fact there were only two sons, the second having two names. As Josephus himself says, *Vita* 76, 426-428:

> At this period I divorced my wife, being displeased at her behaviour. She had borne me three children, of whom two died; one, whom I named Hyrcanus, is still alive. Afterwards I married a woman of Jewish extraction who had settled in Crete. She came of very distinguished parents, indeed the most notable people in that country. In character she surpassed many of her sex, as her subsequent life showed. By her I had two sons, Justus the elder, and then Simonides, surnamed Agrippa. Such is my domestic history.

Josephus always took care to present himself well, and it is clear therefore that in a work which was defined as an *apologia pro vita sua*, he wanted his conduct in private life to be fully justifiable in the eyes of every reader. We can, therefore, conclude from the above that Josephus' conception of divorce was in conformity with that of traditional Judaism.

A *geṭ* discovered at Murabbaᶜât and known as P. Murabbaᶜât 19[45] probably dates from this period. The document reads as follows:[46]

I

באחד למרחשון שנת שת במצדא
שבק ומתרך מן רעתי יומא דנה אנה {יהוסף
בר נ} יהוסף בר נקסן מן [ ]ה יתב במצדא לכי אנתי
מרים ברת יהונתן [מ]ן הנבלטא יתבא
במצדא די הוית אנתי מן קדם דה די את
רשיא בנפשכי למהך ולמהוי אנת לכול גבר
יהודי די תצבין ובדי]ן להוי לכי מני ספר תרכין
וגט שבקין בדין [ ]קא יהבנא וכול חריבין
ונזקן ו...ן ◦[ ]◦ע לכי כדן יהי קים
ומשלם לרבעין ובז[מן]די תמרין לי אחלף לכי
שטרה כדי חיא

---

[45] P. Benoit, J. T. Milik, R. de Vaux, *Discoveries in the Judaean Desert* II, *Les Grottes de Murabbaᶜât* (Oxford: The Clarendon Press, 1961), 104-109; see also E. Volterra, "Nuovi documenti per la conoscenza del diritto vigente nelle provincie romane", *IURA* 14 (1963), 43ff. Against D. Piatelli, see also M. Modrzejewski, "Chronique", *Revue Historiqye de Droit Français et Etranger* 47 (1969), 157; but about his remarks on the name "Sambathion" as a Jewish name, see N. Cohen, *Jewish Names and their Significance in the Hellenistic and Roman Periods in Asia Minor* (unpublished thesis, Jerusalem, 1969, p. 6 of the English summary and pp. 99-162 of the Hebrew text).

[46] In Milik's French translation:

> [1] Le premier de Marḥešvan, an six, à Maṣada. [2] 'Je divorce et (te) répudie, de mon propre gré, aujourd'hui, moi, [3] Yoseph, fils de Naqsan, de [...]ah, résidant à Maṣada, toi, [4] Mariam, fille de Yonatan de Hanablaṭa, résidant [5] à Maṣada, (toi) qui étais ma femme antérieurement, de telle sorte que tu es [6] libre pour ta part de t'en aller et de devenir femme de tout homme [7] juif que tu voudras. Et puis, voici de ma part l'acte de répudiation [8] et la lettre de divorce. Puis, [*la do*]*t, je* (*te la*) *rends.* Et tous les (biens) détruits, [9] endommagés et ... s te seront [*rembour*]*sés, comme* (*je m'*)*y oblige par ceci,* [10] et je (les) paierai au quadruple. Et à quelque moment que tu me le demandes, je te remplacerai [11] le document si je suis (encore) en vie.'
>
> [26] Yoseph, fils de Naqsan, pour lui-même
> [27] Eliᶜazar [fils de] Malka, témoin
> [28] Yoseph fils de Malka, témoin
> [29] Eleazar fils de Ḥanana, témoin.

II

בא[ח]ד למרחש[ון]שנת שת במצדא
שבק֯ ומתרך֯ א֯[נ]ה֯ מן רעתי יומא דנה
יהוסף בר נ֯[קסן]לכי אנתי מרים ‹ברת›
יהונתן [מ]ן [ה]נבלטא יתבא
במצדא די ה֯[וי]ת אנתתי
מן קדמת דנא די אתי רשיא
בנ֯פשכי למ[ה]ך למהי אנתא
לכול גבר יהודי די תצבין
בדין להי לכי מני ס[פ]ר תרכין
וג֯ט֯ שבק[ין ב]דין כו[ל]ק יהב֯נה
וכל חר[יבי]ן֯ [ונזקן ו. . .]ן]◦ כ֯דן
[יהי קים] ו֯[מש]ל֯ם לרבעין ובזמן
[די ת]מרין לי֯[א]חלף לכי שטרה כדי
[חי]א֯

יהוסף בר נק[סן] על נפש[ה]
אליעזר [בר] מ֯לכה שהד
יהוסף בר מלכה שהד
אלעזר בר חננה שהד

Before us is the form of a *geṭ*, which corresponds in essentials to the traditional *geṭ*, including the formula of a *repudium*, which authorises the woman to remarry whomsoever she wishes, and a formula of delivery of the document.[47]

If scholars are generally agreed in identifying *Metsada* with the famous Massada, bastion of Jewish-Zealot Resistance to the Romans, grave problems arise as to dates: Milik thinks that it is the sixth year of the Eparchate of the province of Arabia, which began on the 22nd of March, 106, and that the document therefore dates back to October-November 111 C.E.;[48] Yaron and Yadin reject this and hold instead—rightly in my opinion—that it refers to the sixth year of the Revolt, thus fixing the date of the document as October 71,[49] and they arrive at the following conclusions:

---

[47] On this document see the discussion of Falk, *Introduction, supra* n. 32, at 313ff., and the authors cited in notes 48-49 *infra*.

[48] In agreement with Milik, *supra* n. 45, at 106, see also Volterra, *supra* n. 45, at 43.

[49] R. Yaron, "The Meṣada Bill of Divorce", *Studi in onore di Eduardo Volterra* (Milan: Giuffrè, 1971), VI. 441ff.; Yaron had already arrived at this conclusion in a Hebrew article published in *Haʾumah* 10 (1964), 332ff.; Y. Yadin, *The Excavation of Masada 1963/64* (Jerusalem: Israel Exploration Society, 1965), 119 n. 112.

> It follows that at the time the Meṣadah bill of divorce was written the traditional *geṭ* had not yet arrived at its final and binding formulation. To sum up: we tend to hold that P. Mur. 19 was written in the autumn of A.D. 71. The Meṣadah *geṭ* is a typical Jewish bill of divorce, quite different from documents deriving from non-Jewish sources, e.g. papyri from Egypt or Dura Europos. The Meṣadah *geṭ* is very similar to the traditional *geṭ* of later times, even though there are a number of deviations, on matters of secondary importance.[50]

From *Eretz Israel* we come briefly to Egypt. A document prepared on the 10th of March 13 B.C.E. (= 17th year of Caesar Augustus) relates that "Apollonia and Hermogenes agree that they have dissolved their marriage by an agreement made through the same court in the 13th year of Caesar (Augustus) in the month Pharmounth" (= March-April 17 B.C.E.).[51] The editors of the *Corpus Papyrorum Judaicarum* held (on the basis that Sambation was the name of the father of the betrothed) that the document refers to Jews, and their interpretation was accepted by J. Modrzejewski,[52] who sought to deduce consequences from it relating to the Jews in Egypt (noting that it was against the traditional rule to speak of consent in the case of divorce).

In a study immediately afterwards, however, Yaron showed "reasonable doubt" on the Jewishness of the parties and consequently on the Jewishness of the document itself, observing also that "the prior agreement referred to is not an agreement concerning divorce, but the marriage contract";[53] thus it does not appear to be demonstrated that Egyptian Jews conducted themselves any differently from their brethren in *Eretz Israel.*

Such conclusions seem to be confirmed by Philo:

> Another commandment is that if a woman after parting from her husband for any cause whatever marries another and then again becomes a widow, whether this second husband is alive or dead, she must not return to her first husband but ally herself.....[54]

---

[50] "The Meṣada Bill of Divorce", *supra* n. 49, at 454f.

[51] V. Tcherikover and A. Fuks, *Corpus Papyrorum Judaicorum* (Cambridge Mass.: Harvard U.P., 1960), II.10-14 (no. 144), with text, translation and commentary by the editors.

[52] Modrzejewski, *supra* n. 35, at 162ff.; in agreement with Modrzejewski, see Falk, *Introduction, supra* n. 32, at II. 308 n. 1, who overlooks, however, Yaron's study cited *infra* n. 53.

[53] R. Yaron, "CPJud. 144 et alia", *IURA* 13 (1962), 170ff.; for the same view as Yaron see also D. Piattelli, "Alcune osservazioni su C.P.J. 144", *IURA* 18 (1967), 121ff. (without, however, any reference to Yaron's article), who harbours serious doubts as to whether the divorcing parties were Jewish.

[54] Philo, *De specialibus legibus* III.30: "Another commandment is that if a woman after parting from her husband for any cause whatever marries another and then again becomes a widow, whether this second husband is alive or dead, she must not return to her

To complete the picture, one must take account of the numerous arrangements of a pecuniary character, which came to limit the *practical* possibility of divorce, from which we can conclude with these words from Yaron:

> In the Talmudic period divorce was a unilateral, arbitrary act of the husband, but his pecuniary obligations incidental to divorce might impose restrictions upon his freedom of action. As a consequence of the dissolution of the marriage he is not only bound to restore all that the woman had brought with her as dowry (*neduniah*); he has also to pay all that he promised to her in her marriage contract (her *kethubah*). This arrangement reflects the metamorphosis of the biblical *mohar* (which had been a cash payment to the father of the bride, prior to marriage) into a fund designed to provide for the wife in case of the termination of the relationship (by the death of the husband, or by divorce, provided she did not bear the blame). Talmudic sources describe this postponement of payment until after the dissolution of the marriage as introduced on purpose, to make divorce more difficult. This development had been completed already in the time of Simon ben Shetah, at the beginning of the first century B.C. Whether the reason given in later sources was indeed present to the mind of those who gave the arrangement its final shape, one cannot know for certain. But what matters is that the need to pay up was felt as restricting the actual (not the theoretical) freedom of divorce.[55]

7. *Divorce of Jews in the Roman Empire in the light of Roman law and Jewish law*

From this exposition of the two systems we can appreciate that, in the period of classical Roman law, both Roman and Jewish law permitted divorce; there existed, however, numerous differences, both substantive and formal. In the first place, in Jewish law as opposed to Roman law, the woman could not renounce her husband directly: divorce remained a unilateral act, even if one accords importance to the fact that the *geṭ* had to be *accepted* by the woman. In some specific cases the wife could have had recourse to a Jewish tribunal (*bet din*) for a decision. However, such a decision could not of itself dissolve the marriage bond, but only

---

first husband but ally herself...." On the basis of the phrase "for any cause whatever", scholars have concluded that Philo has accepted the rule of the School of Hillel: B. Ritter, *Philo und die Halacha* (Leipzig: J. C. Hinrichs, 1879), 70 n. 1; S. Belkin, *Philo and the Oral Law* (Cambridge: Harvard U.P., 1940), 229ff. On p. 269 Belkin has noted that "Philo himself does not state in any place that a woman may demand a divorce".

The continuation of the passage has given rise to considerable scholarly discussion. See I. Heinemann, "Jüdisch-hellenistische Gerichtshöfe in Alexandrien?", *Monatsschrift für Geschichte und Wissenschaft des Judentums* 74 (1930), 364ff.; more generally, the recent study of R. D. Hecht, "Preliminary Issues in the Analysis of Philo's *De Specialibus Legibus*", *Studia Philonica* 5 (1978), 1ff.

[55] Yaron, "The Meṣada Bill of Divorce", *supra* n. 49, at 450. On the problem, see generally Falk, *Introduction, supra* n. 32, at 307ff. For the later period see M. Margaliot, *Hilkhot Erets Yisra'el min Hagenizah* (Jerusalem: Mosad Harav Kook, 1973), 118ff.

pressure on the husband to consent personally to a divorce; in case he declined, the Roman authorities could exercise pressure on the husband to convince him to concede the divorce. The *Mishnah* (*Gittin* 9.8) states the rule:

> A bill of divorce given under compulsion is valid if it is ordered by an Israelitish court, but if by a gentile court it is invalid; if the gentiles beat a man and say to him: "Do what the Israelites bid thee", it is valid.

The text demonstrates clearly that in the period under scrutiny[56] the Roman government recognised the decisions of the Jewish tribunals in matters of personal *status* and was ready to utilise mechanisms to give practical effect to such decisions.[57] The situation is further clarified in a passage of the Palestine Talmud that follows the Mishnah passage examined.

> R. Yirmiyah says in the name of Rav: A divorce given by a Jew under compulsion of gentiles is invalid. This refers to the case where the husband tells the wife: I do not wish to give you maintenance. R. Hiyyah taught: But if the gentiles issued their ruling in accordance with Jewish practice, it is valid even if the husband tells the wife: I do not wish to give you maintenance. R. Jose says: the Mishnah says so explicitly: the gentiles beat him and say to him "Do what the Israelites tell you to do". R. Hiyyah bar Ashi said in the name of Isi: In the case of one who says: I do not wish to give you maintenance, we compel him to give a divorce.

---

[56] According to Juster, *supra* n. 42, at II.57, this text goes back to the end of the 1st century C.E. and was still in force at the end of the 2nd century, the period of the redaction of the Mishnah, and still at the end of the third century, the period of the Sages who expressed opinions in conformity with that of the Mishnah, as reported in the Palestinian Talmud. G. Alon, *The History of the Jews in Palestine in the times of the Mishna and the Talmud* (Tel-Aviv: Hakibuts hameuḥad, 1961, Hebrew), II. 113, holds on the contrary that one ought to date it to the period of the Severi. It seems, however, that Alon did not take account of the study of V. Colorni, *Legge ebraica e leggi locali. Ricerche sull'ambito di applicazione del diritto Ebraico in Italia dall'epoca romana al secolo XIX* (Milan: Giuffrè, 1945), who observes, inter alia, in reference to the present text: "But the power exercised by the Jews was actual autonomous jurisdiction recognized by the State and binding upon a party even against the opponent's will. Consequently Jewish law was applicable not only by consent formerly given by the parties and within certain well-defined limits, but even where either party or even both parties did not consent to such application; and such application was not subject to any restriction wherever their personal status was affected, being a matter recognized by the State through the recognition given to this special jurisdiction.... The obvious conclusion is, that within the local limits wherein the Romans, until 398, recognized a Jewish jurisdiction concurrent with that of the State courts, they also recognized Jewish law as the exclusive source of substantive law in respect of the internal private relations among the Jews; and that they applied that law in their own courts wherever litigation between Jews was brought in their courts instead of in a Jewish court" (at 106). See also A. M. Rabello, "A Tribute to Jean Juster", *Israel Law Review* 11 (1976), 234ff.

[57] Thus also Juster, Colorni and Alon, cited n. 56 *supra*.

From these texts it appears that in the case of two Jewish *peregrini* in *Eretz Israel* and, almost certainly, in other parts of the Empire, the Jewish law was applied, whatever tribunal the parties had recourse to,[58] even if Roman law ignored the possibility of decisions which obliged the husband to divorce; for its part, Jewish law recognised only the decisions of Jewish tribunals, even if it was admitted that there could be external coercion to ensure their application.

Coming now to examine the situation of those Jews who were also Roman citizens, from the passages of Josephus which refer to the divorces of Salome and Herodias, we can assert that if the parties preferred to rely on their status as Roman citizens, they could do so, and in that case the divorce would be valid only according to Roman law and not Jewish law; it is clear therefore that in Roman law Salome and Herodias could have validly divorced their husbands—even against the will of the latter. Nonetheless, if the spouses preferred to conduct themselves according to Jewish law, normally, that is whenever the divorce was desired in agreement or by the husband, there ought to have been no difficulty in Roman law. Personally, I would not exclude the possibility that often, in order to avoid difficulties of interpretation, Jewish spouses would have preferred to have a "Jewish" and a "Roman" divorce, and thus satisfy the rather rigid Jewish norms, as well as the Roman ones which, after the *Lex lulia de adulteriis*, required the observance of various formalities in order to avoid penal sanctions laid down by law.

A more complicated case was when one dealt with a *iustum matrimonium romanum* in which the two spouses were Roman Jews or in which the husband was Roman and the wife a foreigner who desired a divorce. In such cases, in fact, the woman could have divorced freely according to Roman law, but it is difficult to suppose that the Roman authorities collaborated with a Jewish tribunal which decided that the husband *must* concede the divorce, according to Jewish rules; in the case where the woman was Roman and the husband foreign, on the other hand, one can suppose that the Roman authorities would have assisted; one can therefore agree with Juster when he maintains that "en matière de divorce le statut juif est facultatif pour le juif citoyen ro-

---

[58] On the problem of which Jewish courts could pronounce judgments recognised by the Roman authorities, see A. M. Rabello, "Sui Rapporti fra Diocleziano e gli Ebrei", *Accademia Romanistica Costantiniana* (Perugia: Libreria Universitaria, 1976), 157ff.

main; c'est-à-dire qu'il l'était pour tous après la *lex Antoniniana*, quand tous les Juifs étaient citoyens romains''.[59]

As far as the period of the Christian Roman empire is concerned, we do not have the sources which would enable us to reconstruct the legal situation; we can, however, presume that there were no changes worthy of mention, except to give—perhaps—greater importance to the reasons for a divorce.[60]

8. *The problem of the date in the geṭ*

A particular problem involves the dating of the Jewish divorce document. It is clear that the Sages of the Talmud were concerned that their acts be recognised as valid by the Roman government; on the other hand, it seems that the governors were particularly sensitive to the dating practice.[61] It was therefore necessary that the dates used should conform to Roman usage, and although the Romans were disposed to concede that the Jews could use their own calendar for strictly religious purposes,[62] they were not prepared to concede such use for acts with civil effects. *Mishnah Gittin* 8.5 establishes:

> (If) he wrote with reference to an unrecognised government (literally, a government that is not worthy), according to the era of the Medes, or the era of Greece, or as from the building of the Temple, or as from the destruction of the Temple...she shall go forth from this one and from that one and she has no (claim under her) marriage contract, no fruits, no aliments.....[63]

---

[59] Juster, *supra* n. 42, at II. 59. On the problem generally, from the viewpoint of Roman law, see E. Volterra, *Istituzioni di Diritto Romano* (Rome: Edizioni Ricerche, 1961), 654f.

[60] Juster, *supra* n. 42, at II. 59f.

[61] Juster, *supra* n. 42, at I. 362ff.

[62] M. D. Herr, "The Calendar", *Compendia Rerum Judaicarum ad Novum Testamentum* 2 (1976), 834ff.; A. M. Rabello, "L'Observance des fêtes juives dans l'Empire Romain", *Aufstieg und Niedergang der römischen Welt*, Bd. 2, 21 (in the press).

[63] On these last expressions, see, for a full comparative study in the light of the law of the papyri, A. Gulak, "*Haketubah perot mezonot ubala*ʾ*ot* in Mishnaic Law" (Heb.), *Tarbiz* 3 (1932), 249ff.

See also *T. Gitt.* 7:6 and the commentary of S. Lieberman, *Tosefta Ki-Fshuṭah* VIII (New York: Jewish Theological Seminary of America, 1973), 904f.; *cf. M. Yad.* 4:8 and the commentary of Albeck *ad loc.*; *cf.* also *P. Mur.* 18 and 115; see also H. I. Boornstein, "The Dates of Israel" (Heb.), *Hateḳufah* 8 (1930), 285ff.; Alon, *supra* n. 56, at I. 336ff., maintaining the need for a distinction between the opinions of the Pharisees, reported in our Mishnah, and that of the zealots who opposed the practice of recording the date in foreign style in a Hebrew document—possibly a further factor in favour of the view of Yaron and Yadin (*supra* n. 49) on the dating of *P. Mur.* 19; M. D. Herr, *The Roman Rule in Eretz Israel* (Jerusalem Ph.D. thesis, 1969), 77ff.; Yaron, "The Meṣada Bill of Divorce", *supra* n. 49, at 441f.; E. E. Urbach, "Halakha and History", *Jews, Greeks and Christians. Religious Cultures in Late Antiquity. Essays in Honour of W. D. Davies*, ed. R. Hamerton Kelly and R. Scroggs (Leiden: E. J. Brill, 1976), 112ff., 121.

The Palestine Talmud gives the explanation for such severity: Rabbi Yoḥanan says, on the authority of Rabbi Yanai (3rd century), that the reason for the rule must be sought in the desire to avoid the danger of persecution. This finds confirmation in the words of Ulla, another Palestinian Sage of the 3rd century, who in response to the question of why he had introduced Roman dating in the *geṭ* replied: to preserve the peace with the Empire![64]

It was the fruit of reciprocal concessions, permitting a *modus vivendi* in this sector too.[65]

---

[64] *Gitt.* 80a.

[65] The author acknowledges with thanks the helpful criticism of Prof. R. Yaron and the partial financial assistance of the Memorial Foundation for Jewish Culture.

X

IL PROBLEMA DEI MATRIMONI FRA EBREI E CRISTIANI NELLA LEGISLAZIONE IMPERIALE E IN QUELLA DELLA CHIESA (IV-VI secolo)

È forse opportuno premettere che anche per l'Ebraismo sussiste il problema dei cosiddetti «matrimoni misti», essendo permesso per il diritto ebraico soltanto il matrimonio fra Ebrei di nascita o fra Ebrei e proseliti.

Quello dei matrimoni misti non era stato considerato un problema per l'impero romano pagano, che non si interessava del problema religioso in campo matrimoniale[1]. Il problema suscitò, invece, fin dall'inizio, l'interesse della Chiesa e successivamente quello dello stesso impero romano cristiano.

Il primo intervento in materia lo abbiamo nel concilio di Elvira, in Spagna, riunitosi fra il 300 ed il 306[2]. Il canone 16 stabilisce:

> *De puellis fidelibus ne infidelibus coniungantur.*
> Haeretici si se transferre noluerint ad ecclesiam catholicam, ne ipsis catholicas dandas esse puellas; sed neque iudaeis neque haereticis dare placuit, eo quod nulla possit esse societas fideli cum infideli. Si contra interdictum fecerint parentes, abstineri per quinquennium placet.

Dal confronto fra questo canone e quello precedente (can. 15), che vieta le nozze fra fanciulle cristiane e pagani, possiamo notare

---

[1] Sul tema v. per tutti: E. Volterra, *Il matrimonio romano*, Roma 1961.

[2] Si consulti: A.M. Rabello, *Gli Ebrei nella Spagna romana e ariana visigotica* in

come in quest'ultimo caso non si imponga alcuna pena: evidentemente il matrimonio fra Cristiani, da un lato, eretici od Ebrei, dall'altro, costituiva agli occhi della Chiesa un pericolo più grave, in quanto che in tali matrimoni il marito non è, generalmente, indifferente alla religione della moglie; si comprende così anche perché il divieto sussista solamente per le fanciulle, dato che si suppone che il marito abbia una influenza maggiore sulla moglie, piuttosto che viceversa.

Il canone 78 si occupa di Cristiani che si prendano una concubina ebrea o una pagana:

> *De fidelibus coniugatis si cum iudaea vel gentili moechaverint.* Si quis fidelis habens uxorem cum iudaea vel gentili fuerit moechatus, a communione arceatur. Quod si alius eum detexerit, post quinquennium acta legitima poenitentia poterit dominicae sociari communioni.

È da osservare che la pena per l'adulterio di un Cristiano con una Cristiana è anch'essa cinque anni di scomunica (can. 69)[3].

Questa è quindi la prima presa di posizione ufficiale da parte della Chiesa, prima ancora che il Cristianesimo salisse al potere imperiale: tale posizione servirà come sfondo alla legislazione imperiale.

Nel 339 l'imperatore Costanzo[4] invia ad Evagrio, allora prefetto

---

Atti della Accademia Romanistica Costantiniana IV (= *Studi De Dominicis)*, Perugia 1981, 807 ss. e sp. 813 ss.

[3] Si confronti con il canone 14 del III Concilio di Toledo (del 589) su cui si veda J. JUSTER, *The Legal Condition of the Jews under the Visigothic King* (Brought up-to-date by A.M. RABELLO), Jerusalem 1976, 568, nt. 198; A.M. RABELLO, *La conversione di Reccaredo al Cattolicesimo e le sue ripercussioni sulla condizione giuridica degli Ebrei* in *Index*, 12, 1983-84, 373 ss., 380 s.

[4] Come è noto Seeck ha sostenuto che il nostro testo fa parte di un testo legislativo più ampio che comprendeva anche CTh. 16, 8, 1 e 16, 9, 2, proponendo soluzioni diverse per la datazione, il luogo d'emissione ed il nome dell'imperatore che avrebbe emesso la costituzione: si veda O. SEECK, *Regesten der Kaiser und Päpste*, Stuttgart 1919, 48; IDEM, *Die Zeitfolge des Gesetze Constantins* (rist. anast. a cura di M. SARGENTI), Milano 1983, XXI, XXXIII, 108, 117; G.G. ARCHI, *Teodosio II e la sua codificazione*, Napoli 1976, 65; A. LINDER, *Roman Imperial Legislation on the Jews*, Jerusalem 1983 (in ebraico) 105, fa propria l'opinione che si tratti di Costantino II; la facilità con cui un amanuense poteva confondere i nomi Costanzo, Costantino e Costante è evidente; si confronti per es. un autore moderno CH. VOGLER, *Les Juifs dans le Code Théodosien* in *Les Chrétiens devant le fait juif*, Paris 1979 (= *Le Point Théologique*, No. 33), in cui l'a. scrive a p. 52: «Il s'agit d'une loi promulguée par l'empereur Constant en Occident, en 339 peu après la mort de Constantin le

del pretorio dell'Italia, una costituzione in cui viene esaminato il problema dei matrimoni misti, prendendo spunto da un caso particolare che doveva aver destato la preoccupazione imperiale. Ci troviamo a pochi anni di distanza dalla decisione di Elvira e la costituzione è dello stesso tenore, cioè il divieto è sempre rivolto al matrimonio di una fanciulla cristiana con un Ebreo: *ne mulieres suis iungant flagitiis*. La disposizione fa intravedere chiaramente il timore della conversione, dell'influsso dei *flagitia*. La pena per i trasgressori sarebbe stata quella capitale. Precede questa disposizione — quella per cui la norma in esame viene normalmente richiamata a proposito dei matrimoni misti — un'altra disposizione con effetto retroattivo: nel caso che la fanciulla cristiana sia stata tratta dal gineceo imperiale e condotta *in turpitudinis suae consortium*, tale donna avrebbe dovuto essere resa al gineceo[5]. È un caso interessante, in cui al fattore religioso si unisce quello economico: per quanto riguarda il significato dell'espressione, anche se è stata avanzata l'ipotesi che ci si potesse riferire al concubinato (ipotesi che potrebbe essere, invero, rinforzata dato il livello sociale di tali fanciulle), la *communis opinio* è giustamente convinta che si tratti di matrimonio fra Ebreo e Cristiana[6].

Grand», attribuendo poi, nella *inscriptio* di CTh. 16, 8, 1; 16, 8, 6 la costituzione a «L'empereur Constantin Auguste à Evagrius» (pp. 63, 64), mentre CTh. 16, 9, 2 è attribuita a «L'empereur Constance Auguste» (p. 73); la confusione permane anche per quanto riguarda la datazione: mentre a p. 52 n. 36 si sostiene che CTh. 16, 8, 1; 16, 8, 6 e 16, 9, 2 «faisaient problablement partie à l'origine d'une même constitution», datata 339, nella traduzione tale data è mantenuta soltanto per CTh. 16, 8, 6 e 16, 9, 2 mentre CTh. 16, 8, 1, è anticipata al 315 (p. 63).

[5] Osserva J. JUSTER, *Les Juifs dans l'Empire Romain*, Paris 1914, II, 47 nt. 2: «C'est donc une mesure d'intolerance religieuse et d'interêt pecuniaire»; sul gineceo si veda J.P. WILD, *The Gynaeceum at Venta and its Context* in *Latomus*, 26, 1967, 648 ss.; sulla posizione delle persone obbligate a prestazioni personali di lavoro, con espresso riferimento ai *gynecia*, v. A.H.M. JONES, *L'economia romana*, Torino 1984, 303; riportiamo anche l'osservazione di M. AVI-YONAH, *The Jews under Roman and Byzantine Rule*, Jerusalem 1984, 175:

> «Another paragraph of the same law is more interesting. It annuls the mixed marriages of women who had once formed part of the imperial *gynecaeum*; such women were ordered to return at once to their former place. It seems that cases of this kind, which could not have been very numerous, were the real motive behind the provision against mixed marriages. We notice the economic motivation of this law. The imperial *gynecaeum* was a spinning and weaving factory. Women who left it to marry Jews enabled the latter to compete with the imperial manufactures, and thus aroused the wrath of the Treasury».

[6] Si veda, per es. P.M. MEYER, *Der römische Concubinat nach den Rechtsquellen und den Inschriften*, 1895, 127 ss., 129 nt. 268, che esamina la possibilità che *consor-*

La Costituzione verrà inserita da Teodosio II nel suo Codice, CTh. 16, 8, 6:

> IMP. CONSTANTIVS A. AD EVAGRIVM. POST ALIA: Quod ad mulieres pertinet, quas Iudaei in turpitudinis suae duxere consortium in gynaeceo nostro ante versatas, placet easdem restitui gynaeceo idque in reliquum observari, ne Christianas mulieres suis iungant flagitiis vel, si hoc fecerint, capitali periculo subiugentur. DAT. ID. AVG. CONSTANTIO A. II CONS.

Nel Codice Teodosiano possediamo un'altra costituzione di Valentiniano, Teodosio e Arcadio: CTh. 3, 7, 2:[7]

---

tium significhi concubinato, respingendola per il testo in esame; per *consortium* col significato di matrimonio si veda J. JUSTER, *Les Juifs dans l'Empire* (supra, nt. 5), II, 47 nt. 1; E. BERGER, *Encyclopedic Dictionary of Roman Law,* Philadelphia 1950, 409; B. BIONDI, *Il Diritto Romano cristiano*, I, Milano 1952, 281 e III, 1954, 91 s.; A. LINDER, *Roman Imperial Legislation (op. cit.*, nt. 4), 108 nt. 1; F. BLANCHETIÈRE, *L'Evolution du statut des Juifs sous la dynastie constantinienne* in *Crise et redressement dans les provinces européennes de l'Empire* (par E. FRÉZOULS), Strasbourg 1983, 127 ss., 134 s. Per CH. VOGLER, *Les Juifs dans le Code Théodosien*, non vi è un chiaro riferimento al matrimonio: «la formule employée désigne peut-être l'effet du prosélytisme juif dans ce milieu féminin ouvrier»: anche Blanchetière pensa che sia da vedere qui soprattutto il timore di un proselistimo ebraico, ed in effetti, se si tiene presente anche CTh. 16, 9, 2, il timore dell'influenza esercitata dal padrone ebreo sullo schiavo risulta evidente; tuttavia non vi è da vedere in questo una motivazione contrastante con quella da noi sostenuta (e, *in primis*, dal Juster); infatti a nostro avviso già la proibizione dei matrimoni misti da parte di ragazze cristiane, stabilita nel concilio di Elvira, trovava la sua giustificazione nella «presunzione che la donna fosse più facilmente soggetta all'influenza del marito»: A.M. RABELLO, *Gli Ebrei nella Spagna Romana*, (cit. nt. 2) 814.

[7] Cfr. J. JUSTER, *Les Juifs dans l'Empire Romain*, II, 48 nt. 1; sul *ius accusandi* v. E. VOLTERRA, *Per la storia della accusatio adulterii iure maritis vel patris* in *Studi economico-giuridici dell'Università di Cagliari*, 17, 1929, 40 ss.; A.M. RABELLO, *Effetti personali della «Patria Potestas»*, I, Milano 1979, 210 ss.

Su questa legislazione si veda in particolare: S. SOLAZZI, *Le unioni di cristiani ed ebrei nelle leggi del Basso Impero* in *Atti Acc. Pontan. Scienze mor. e pol.*, 59, 1939; 64 ss. (riprodotto ora in IDEM, *Scritti di Diritto Romano*, IV, Napoli 1963, 49 ss., da cui sono tratte le citazioni); M. SIMON, *Verus Israël. Etude sur les Rélations entre Chrétiens et Juifs dans l'Empire Romain (135-425)*, Paris 1964[2], 157 s., 339 ss.; M. PAVAN, *I Cristiani e il mondo ebraico nell'età di Teodosio «il grande»*, Perugia 1965, 157 s.; B. BLUMENKRANZ, *Juifs et Chrétiens dans le monde occidental (430-1096)*, Paris 1960, 319 ss.; L. DE GIOVANNI, *Chiesa e Stato nel Codice Teodosiano. Saggio sul libro XVI*, Napoli 1980, 130 nt. 50.

Si tenga presente anche la posizione di Ambrogio, espressa in una lettera ad un vescovo, del 385: «quomodo potest coniugium dici, ubi non est fidei concordia?»; si veda in particolare J. GAUDEMET, *L'Église dans l'Empire Romain* (IV-V siècles), Paris 1958, 623 ss. 631 e B. BIONDI, *Il Diritto Romano Cristiano (supra* nt. 6), III, 82.

IMPPP. VALENT(INIANVS), THEOD(OSIVS) ET ARCAD(IVS) AAA. CYNEGIO P(RAEFECTO P(RAETORI)O. Ne quis Christianam muliere in matrimonio Iudaeus accipiat, neque Iudaeae Christianus coniugium sortiatur. nam si quis aliquid huiusmodi admiserit, adulterii vicem commissi huius crimen obtinebit, libertate in accusandum publicis quoque vocibus relaxata. DATA PRID. ID. MART. THESSAL(ONICA) THEOD(OSIO) A. II. ET CYNEGIO V̄.C̄. CONSS.
INTERPRETATIO. Legis huius severitate prohibetur, ut nec Iudaeus Christianae matrimonio utatur, nec Christianus homo Iudaeam uxorem accipiat. Quod si aliqui contra vetitum se tali coniunctione miscuerint, noverint se ea poena, qua adulteri damnantur, persequendos, et accusationem huius criminis non solum propinquis, sed etiam ad persequendum omnibus esse permissam.

CTh. 9, 7, 5:

IMPPP. VAL(ENTINI)ANVS, THEOD(OSIVS) ET ARCAD(IVS) AAA. CYNEGIO P(RAEFECTO) P(RAETORI)O. Ne quis Christianam mulierem in matrimonio Iudaeus accipiat neque Iudaeae Christianus coniugium sortiatur. Nam si quis aliquid huiusmodi admiserit, adulterii vicem commissi huius crimen optinebit, libertate in accusandum publicis quoque vocibus relaxata. DAT. PRID. ID. MAR. THESSAL(ONICAE) THEOD(OSIO) A. II ET CYNEGIO CONSS.

INTERPRETATIO. Nec Iudaeus Christianam nec Christianus Iudaeam ducat uxorem. Quod si fecerit, cuiuslibet accusatione velut in adulteros vindicetur.

La norma del Teodosiano è stata ripresa nel *Breviarum Alaricianum* (3, 7, 2 e 9, 4, 4), nella *Lex Romana Burgundionum* ed anche nella *Lex Raetica curiensis* (3, 7, 2)[8].

È anche da tener presente che un interventismo in senso limitativo dello Stato romano in campo matrimoniale non era nuovo nella tradizione imperiale: si veda P. BONFANTE, *Corso di Diritto Romano*, I, *Il Diritto di famiglia*, rist. a cura di G. Bonfante e G. Crifò, Milano 1963, 231; cfr. anche CTh. 3, 14, 1; E. ALBERTARIO, *La definizione di matrimonio secondo Modestino* in *Studi di Diritto Romano*, I, Milano 1953, 189 ss.

[8] Sul problema di quale delle due costituzioni geminate in CTh. 3, 7, 2 e 9, 7,

Infine la costituzione verrà ripresa nel Codice giustinianeo, C. 1, 9, 6:

IMPPP. VALENTINIANUS THEODOSIUS ET ARCADIUS AAA. CYNEGIO PP. Ne quis Christianam mulierem in matrimonium Iudaeus accipiat neque Iudaeae Christianus coniugium sortiatur. nam si quis aliquid huiusmodi admiserit, adulterii vicem commissi huius crimen obtinebit, libertate in accusandum publicis quoque vocibus relaxata. D. PRID. ID. MART. THESSALONICA THEODOSIO A. II ET CYNEGIO CONSS. [a. 388].

La costituzione vieta dunque all'Ebreo di prendere in moglie una donna cristiana ed al Cristiano di sposare un'Ebrea; i contravventori del divieto vengono considerati come adulteri ed il *ius accusandi* sarà riconosciuto ad ognuno.

La *disparitas cultus* fra un Ebreo e una Cristiana, o un Cristiano e una Ebrea, era considerata particolarmente pericolosa nei primi secoli della Chiesa, dato che la stessa Chiesa non si era ancora completamente liberata da influssi ebraici[9]; è inoltre evidente che la diversità di religione non contribuisce all'unità della famiglia, specie per persone presso le quali il fattore religioso esercita influenza degna di rilievo. Tenendo presente che anche l'Ebraismo non ammette «matrimoni misti», possiamo comprendere come l'Ebraismo stesso non doveva sentirsi particolarmente colpito da tale costituzione; tuttavia dobbiamo notare alcuni particolari che assumono una certa gravità: il considerare il matrimonio misto fra Ebrei e Cristiani come adulterio, implicava il comminare per tali unioni la massima pena, cioè la morte[10], con il diritto concesso a chiunque di promuovere l'azione pe-

---

5 sia stata scelta dai compilatori v. G. ROTONDI, *Studi sulle fonti del Codice giustinianeo* in *Scritti*, I, Milano 1922, 182 ss.; J. GAUDEMET, *Un problème de la codification théodosienne: les constitutions géminées* in *RIDA*, III s., 4, 1957, 253 ss.; R. BONINI, *Ricerche di Diritto Giustinianeo*, Milano 1968, 121 nt. 87.

[9] Si veda per tutti M. SIMON, *Verus Israel* (op. cit. a nt. 7).

[10] Per le pene previste per gli adulteri si veda J. JUSTER, *Juifs*, II, 47 s.; S. SOLAZZI, *Le unioni di cristiani ed ebrei* cit. (supra, nt. 7), 49 ss. e 50 nt. 1: «per il codice giustiniano la pena dell'adulterio è la morte» e prosegue osservando che tale pena doveva essere sussistita anche dopo la legislazione delle Novelle. Si veda anche A. GUARINO, *Studi sull'incestum* in *ZSS*, 63, 2943, 229 s.; L. CHIAZZESE, *Adulterio* in *NNDI*, 1, 1958, 322 s.; A.M. RABELLO, *Effetti personali della Patria Potestas* (supra nt. 7) 210 ss.

nale. Vi è inoltre da tener presente il problema che poteva sorgere con la conversione di una delle parti. Nel caso che il Cristiano, o la Cristiana, si fosse convertito all'Ebraismo, non doveva sussistere, generalmente, problema alcuno per l'Ebraismo, mentre è evidente che il Cristianesimo avrebbe visto in tale fenomeno un aggravamento della situazione, uno dei motivi essenziali della legislazione contro i matrimoni misti essendo appunto il pericolo della conversione del coniuge cristiano; pertanto è probabile che in tal caso anche il legislatore avrebbre proseguito a considerare il convertito all'Ebraismo come Cristiano, in conformità alla legislazione canonica che stabiliva la perpetuità del valore del battesimo[11], con la conseguenza che l'unione avrebbe continuato ad essere considerata come adulterio.

Differente doveva essere invece la soluzione qualora la parte ebrea si fosse convertita al Cristianesimo; la cosa era ovviamente condannata dall'Ebraismo, mentre doveva essere gradita al Cristianesimo: si può pertanto ritenere che in tal caso l'unione cessasse di venire considerata adulterio; se si fosse trovato chi avesse accusato i coniugi di adulterio, dopo che la parte ebrea si era convertita al Cristianesimo, vi è da presumere che tale accusa sarebbe stata facilmente respinta.

Si pone il problema di quale fosse il significato della frase: *adulterii vice commissi huius crimen obtinebit*. Siro Solazzi, in un articolo scritto durante il periodo della legislazione razziale in Italia[12], sottolinea che la costituzione, a differenza della *interpretatio* visigotica, stabilisce non già che i coniugi *siano puniti* come adulteri, bensì che *siano considerati come adulteri*: il risultato sarebbe che la costituzione avrebbe voluto punire non solo il matrimonio, ma anche il concubinato fra Ebrei e Cristiani.

È probabile che l'interpretazione del Solazzi sia stata influenzata dall'interesse che la Chiesa dimostrava per il concubinato[13], tuttavia

---

[11] La cosa trova espressione, per esempio, in can. 57, IV Concilio di Toledo (633), su cui si veda A.M. RABELLO, *The Jews in Visigothic Spain in the Light of the Legislation*, Jerusalem 1983 (in ebraico), 180 s.

[12] Ci sia concesso di rendere omaggio al coraggio civico del Solazzi che in pieno regime fascista non esitava ad esprimere la propria opinione; si veda l'inizio dell'articolo *Le unioni di cristiani ed ebrei* (cit. nt. 7) a p. 49 e la nota 16 a p. 54, in cui fa presente la differenza fra il divieto del matrimonio misto per motivi religiosi ed il divieto per motivi razziali. In senso difforme B. ALBANESE, *Le persone nel diritto privato romano*, Palermo 1979, 424, parla di «divieto di chiaro valore razzista e apertamente vessatorio».

[13] Si veda per esempio il canone 17 del I Concilio di Toledo (397-400), su cui

tale interpretazione non mi pare esatta; leggiamo infatti nell'interpretazione visigotica: *noverint se ea poena qua adulteri damnantur persequendos*[14]. È ben vero che il Solazzi sottolinea proprio qui la differenza tra l'*Interpretatio* e la costituzione, ma sembra strano che i compilatori giustinianei, di fronte alla possibilità di una interpretazione più «blanda», non abbiano incluso espressamente anche i concubini, interpolando il testo, tanto più che lo stesso Giustiniano si era interessato del problema dei concubini[15]; in ogni caso la costituzione continuò ad essere interpretata come riferentesi alla pena, come possiamo apprendere dal corrispondente passo dei Basilici, 1, 1, 38:

ἐν τῇ τῆς μοιχείας ποινῇ ὑποβαλλόμενος

(*poena adulterii obnoxius*... trad. Heimbach).

A mio avviso, quindi, la costituzione non doveva comprendere anche il concubinato: essa ribadisce il divieto dei matrimoni misti, stabilendo che verranno puniti come adulterio, e che verrà concesso a chiunque di promuovere l'accusa.

La legislazione imperiale è stata, quindi, decisamente influenzata dalla posizione della Chiesa, che ha trovato espressione nei Canoni del Concilio di Elvira ed in varii scritti dei padri della Chiesa; è interessante notare come in un periodo successivo sarà questa legislazione a dare l'incentivo ad altri concilii locali della Chiesa ad intervenire, imponendo ai renitenti la cessazione del rapporto matrimoniale, oltre all'uso di una pena religiosa, la scomunica a tempo indeterminato[16].

---

v. G. Caselli, *Concubina pro uxore. Osservazioni in merito al can. 17 del primo Concilio di Toledo* in *Rivista di Storia del Diritto Italiano*, 37-38, 1964-65, 163 ss.; si consulti anche il can. 14 del III concilio di Toledo, su cui A.M. Rabello, *La conversione di Reccaredo* (cit. nt. 3), 380.

[14] Si veda anche l'*Interpretatio* a CTh. 9, 7, 5.

[15] Si veda R. Danieli, *Sul concubinato in diritto giustinianeo* in *Studi Arangio Ruiz*, Napoli s.d., III, 175 ss.

[16] Per ragioni di completezza dobbiamo ricordare anche il canone 14 del concilio di Calcedonia del 451; tale canone riguarda però un caso particolare.

Riporto qui il testo del canone 14, nella traduzione curata dalla mia assistente, Dott. Lia Di Segni: «Poiché in alcune provincie è permesso ai lettori e cantori di sposarsi, il santo concilio ha deciso che non sia permesso ad alcuno di loro di prendere in moglie una donna eterodossa; e quanto a quelli che hanno già figli da tali nozze, se hanno già portato a battesimo presso gli eretici figli nati loro da tali

Il secondo concilio di Orléans, in Gallia, del 533, stabilisce nel suo canone 19:

> Placuit ut nullus Christianus Iudaeam, neque Iudaeus Christianam in matrimonium ducat uxorem, quia inter huiusmodi personas illicitas nuptias censemus. Qui si commoniti a consortio hoc se separare distulerint, a communionis gratia sunt sine dubio submovendi[17].

Si noti che non bisogna necessariamente interpretare questo canone come più severo, come crede Blumenkranz[18], di quello di Elvira; è vero che quest'ultimo non puniva la fanciulla cristiana che avesse sposato un Ebreo, e soprattutto non imponeva la separazione dei coniugi, ma è anche vero che la mancata punizione era dovuta alla concezione che non la sposa è responsabile del suo matrimonio, bensì i genitori, i quali erano puniti con ben cinque anni di esclusione dalla comunione, come gli adulteri[19]. Invece il canone di Orléans impone l'allontanamento dai sacramenti solo fino al momento in cui il coniuge non accetti la separazione, come è chiaro dal tenore del canone nella sua seconda ripetizione nel concilio di Orléans III[20]. Resta

---

donne, che li introducano nella comunione della Chiesa cattolica; se invece non sono stati battezzati, che non possano più portarli a battesimo presso gli eretici; e che assolutamente non li diano in matrimonio a persona eretica, ebrea o pagana, a meno che la parte che contrae matrimonio con la persona ortodossa non prometta di abbracciare la fede ortodossa. Chi trasgredisce questo divieto del santo sinodo, sia soggetto alle pene canoniche».

I chierici sposati a donne eretiche devono battezzare nel cattolicesimo, o se già battezzati nell'eresia, trasferire alla comunione cattolica i figli già nati da tale matrimonio; in più sono ammoniti a non darli in matrimonio a eretici, pagani o Ebrei; poiché questa ammonizione sembra superflua, nel caso che il precedente ordine sia stato eseguito, sembra che possa essere motivata dal sospetto che il genitore cattolico, di fronte all'opposizione della moglie e madre eretica, cercasse di aggirare il canone allontanando il figlio dalla propria casa col darlo in matrimonio, e naturalmente a un non cattolico, in modo che non potesse essere forzato, o forzata, a passare alla comunione cattolica.

[17] J.D. MANSI, *Sacrorum Conciliorum nova et amplissima collectio*, Venezia 1758-1798 (Graz 1960-1962), VIII, 835 ss.; K.J. HEFELE-H. LECLERCQ, *Histoire des Conciles après les documents originaux*, Paris 1907-31; C. DE CLERCQ, *Concilia Galliae A. 511-A. 695*, Turnhout 1963, 99-103.

[18] B. BLUMENKRANZ, *Juifs et Chrétiens* (cit. nt. 7), 321 nt. 128.

[19] Cfr. can. 69; MANSI, *Sacrorum conciliorum* (cit. nt. 17), II, 17.

[20] Il canone è ripetuto a Clermont (535), can. 6; DE CLERCQ, *Concilia Galliae*,

quindi un solo aspetto in cui il canone del VI secolo è più severo di quello del IV, cioè l'interruzione del rapporto matrimoniale, che non è dovuta tanto ad una impostazione più rigorista, quanto alle mutate circostanze storiche e all'esistenza di una normativa civile in proposito.

Nel 535 un nuovo concilio franco riunitosi a Clermont riprende in esame anche il problema dei matrimoni misti, nel canone 6:

> Si quis Iudaicae pravitati iugali societate coniungitur, et seu Christiana Iudaeo, seu Iudaeus Christianae mulieri carnali consortio misceatur, quicumque horum tantum nefas admisisse dignoscitur, a Christianorum coetu atque convivio, et communione ecclesiae, cuius sociatur hostibus, segregetur[21].

Si noti che la formulazione è qui molto più aspra che nel canone 19 di Orléans II: evidentemente il divieto di due anni prima non aveva conseguito il risultato desiderato e si sentiva bisogno non solo di usare un linguaggio più violento, ma anche di aggravare la pena: il colpevole è escluso non solo dalla comunione, ma anche dal *coetum et convivium* dei Cristiani, in altre parole è dannato all'interdetto. In questa forma il canone passerà in collezioni canoniche del VII e IX secolo e nel concilio di Meaux e Parigi dell'845-846[22].

Il problema verrà riesaminato nel III Concilio di Orléans, del 538, nel canone 14 (13) in cui, fra l'altro, è stabilito:

> ... Christianis quoque omnibus interdicimus, ne Iudaeorum coniugiis misceantur. Quod si fecerint, usque ad sequestrationem, quisque ille est, communione, pellatur[23].

Il matrimonio misto è vietato, quindi, sotto pena di scomunica, che rimarrà in vigore fino allo scioglimento del legame.

---

106 s., e ad Orléans III (538), can. 14 (13): *ibid.*, 120, dove il termine dell'esclusione dalla comunione è precisato con le parole *usque ad sequestrationem*.

[21] De Clercq, *Concilia Galliae*, 106; Mansi, *Sacr. conc.*, VIII, 861.

[22] Ps. Isidoro, *Hispana*, XXXV, 4, PL. 84, 291; Floro di Lione, *De Fugiendis*, 3; B. Blumenkranz, *Deux compilations canoniques de Flours de Lyon et l'action antijuive d'Agobard* in *RHD*, 33, 1955, 575; Agobardo, *De superstitionibus iudaicis* 8, PL 104, 85; Amolone, *Liber contra Iudaeos* 58, PL. 116, 183; Concilio di Meaux e Parigi, can. 73, Mansi, XIV, 839. Cfr. B. Blumenkranz, *Juifs et Chrétiens* (supra nt. 7), 321 s. e note 128 bis e 130.

[23] De Clercq, *Concilia Galliae*, 120; Mansi, IX, 15.

Il divieto dei matrimoni misti torna in Spagna alla fine del VI secolo e poi nel VII, ed è interessante notare la differenza che intercorre fra i canoni francesi e quelli spagnoli. Il canone 14 del III Concilio di Toledo del 589[24] vieta che gli Ebrei abbiano mogli o concubine cristiane, senza imporre alcuna penalità alla parte cristiana, ma intervenendo invece duramente contro la parte ebraica, che viene privata in parte della patria potestà con l'imposizione del battesimo dei figli nati da tale unione[25]. Nel IV concilio di Toledo (633) il canone 63[26] impone la separazione dei coniugi, il battesimo dei figli e il loro allontanamento dal genitore ebreo. La mancanza di sanzione religiosa per la parte cristiana può dipendere dal fatto che i matrimoni erano *diventati* misti, per la conversione di uno dei coniugi al Cattolicesimo[27]; in ogni caso è degna di nota la maggior virulenza dei canoni spagnoli, che tendono in maniera evidente ad annientare fisicamente la comunità giudaica, mediante la cristianizzazione forzata di intere famiglie, in cui un solo coniuge era stato guadagnato al Cristianesimo[28]; mentre in Francia, anche se si tenta di innalzare una barriera fra le due comunità, resta intatto il rispetto per i diritti naturali dell'individuo. È evidente che il passaggio al Cattolicesimo della monarchia franca non ha avuto come risultato, in Gallia, la violenta reazione antigiudaica che ha avuto in Spagna la conversione dei re visigoti[29].

---

[24] De iudaeis. «Suggerente concilio id gloriosissimus dominus noster canonibus inserendum praecipit, ut iudaeis non liceat christianas habere uxores vel concubinas neque mancipium christianum in usus proprios conparare; sed et si qui filii ex tali coniugio nati sunt adsummendos esse ad babtisma; nulla officia publica eos opus est agere per qua eis occasio tribuatur poenam christianis inferre. Si qui vero christiani ab eius iudaismo ritu sunt maculati vel etiam circumcisi, non reddito pretio, ad libertatem et religionem redeant christianam»; Vives, *Concilios*, 129.

Il canone è stato da me esaminato di recente nel mio articolo *La conversione di Reccaredo* (supra, nt. 3), 379 ss. e note 17-22 e 387 ss.

[25] Bisogna tuttavia tener presente che per la legge ebraica i figli di una donna non-ebrea non erano comunque ebrei ed era necessario, quindi, per renderli tali praticare la conversione, il che era già stato proibito dal Codice Teodosiano e dal Breviario Alariciano.

[26] Mansi, X, 634.

[27] B. Blumenkranz, *Juifs et Chrétiens* (cit., nt. 7), 321, nt. 128.

[28] E magari non per convizione: la conversione infatti poteva essere usata come un espediente per ottenere facilmente il divorzio e la custodia dei figli.

[29] Sull'argomento si veda J. Juster; A.M. Rabello, *The Legal Condition* (cit. nt. 3); A.M. Rabello, *The Jews in Visigothic Spain* (cit. nt. 11).

Può essere utile, infine, una osservazione «negativa» riguardante il periodo giustinianeo: dall'esame delle sedi dei concilii possiamo osservare, infatti, che essi si svolgono tutti nella parte occidentale, in quella zona che ormai non faceva più parte dell'Impero Romano: evidentemente era questa la zona che più aveva bisogno delle direttive della Chiesa; per l'impero bizantino ci si poteva, o ci si doveva, fidare senz'altro di Giustiniano; la riunione in tale sede di un concilio sarebbe stata assolutamente senza scopo, che non fosse voluto da Giustiniano stesso[30].

[30] A tale conclusione ero già giunto al termine del mio studio su «Gli Ebrei nella legislazione della Chiesa fino alla fine del periodo giustinianeo (565)», parte di uno studio più vasto su «Giustiniano, gli Ebrei ed i Samaritani», in corso di pubblicazione dall'editore Giuffrè, in una collana di studi giustinianei diretta da M. Amelotti. Mi è gradito cogliere l'occasione per ringraziare la dott.ssa Lia Di Segni per la sua preziosa collaborazione.

XI

THE SAMARITANS IN JUSTINIAN'S CORPUS IURIS CIVILIS

Introduction

Justinian, in his *Corpus Iuris Civilis*, showed great interest in the Samaritans,[1] in the context of his lifelong effort to make Orthodox Christianity the prevailing faith of the Roman empire. In general, Justinian's relationship to non-Catholic religions was one of discrimination and degradation. The Samaritans were subjected to especially harsh treatment and repressive legislation, due to their sanguinary rebellions. This cycle of repression and rebellion had dire economic consequences in Palestine for the entire general population, including Christians, and contributed to the general population's dissatisfaction with Imperial policy.

In the Theodosian Code, the first official collection of Imperial constitutions, Samaritan-related legislation was grouped together with legislation related to Jews and Caelicolae, in the general context of the relationship between the Empire and the Church.[2]

* Montesquieu Professor of Comparative Law and Legal History, The Hebrew University of Jerusalem.

1 On the Samaritans see A.D. Crown, *A Bibliography of the Samaritans*, (Metuchen, N.J., 1984); A.M. Rabello, "On the Relations between Diocletian and the Jews" (1984) 35 Journal of Jewish Studies 147ff.; R. Pummer, *The Samaritans* (Leiden, 1987); A.M. Rabello, *Giustiniano, Ebrei e Samaritani alla luce delle fonti storico-letterarie, ecclesiastiche e giuridiche*, vol. I, (Milano, 1987), vol. II (Milano, 1988); A.D. Crown, ed., *The Samaritans*, (Tuebingen, 1989); P.T.R. Gray, "Palestine and Justinian's Legislation on Non-Christian Religions", in B. Halpern and D.W. Hobson, eds., *Law, Politics and Society in the Ancient Mediterranean World* (Sheffield Academic Press, 1993) 241-270.

2 *De Iudaeis, Caelicolis et Samaritanis* ("On the Jews, *Caelicolae* and the Samaritans."), Chapter VIII of Book XVI. See L. De Giovanni, *Il libro XVI del Codice Teodosiano. Alle origini della codificazione in tema di rapporti Chiesa-Stato* (Napoli, 1985); B.S. Bachrach, "The Jewish Community of the Later Roman Empire as seen in the *Codex Theodosianus*", in J. Neusner-E.S. Frerichs, eds., *"To see ourselves as others see us"* (Chico, 1985) 399ff. (at pp. 416ff. on the Samaritans); C. Capizzi, *Giustiniano I tra politica e religione* (Napoli, 1994) 41ff.

In the second edition of Emperor Justinian's Code of 534 CE.,[3] religious problems found their place in the first book, reflecting the importance Justinian attributed to Religion. Here, in the chapter parallel to C.Th.16.8, i.e. Justinian's Code 1,9, we find mention only of Jews and Caelicolae (*De Judaeis et Caelicolis*), while the constitutions regarding Samaritans are relegated to chapter five of the first book, along with those relating to Heretics (*De Hereticis, et Manichaeis et Samaritis*).

This change could not have been unintentional; it seems obvious that the implied comparison between *Samaritans* and *Heretics* was a consequence of the intention to regulate Samaritans more severely than Jews.[4] Nevertheless, it is not clear that introducing the Samaritans into the legislation against the Heretics imposed itself automatically, since these texts are not unequivocal ones.[5] Therefore, in this article we shall examine only those Justinian Constitutions of Book I, Chapter V which refer *expressly* to Samaritans. As we will see, their legal situation was sufficiently bad that it was unnecessary to impose on them the regulations imposed against *Heretics*.

A) *The Samaritans in Justinian's Code, I,5.*

1) *C.J.1.5.12 - Policy Towards Heretics, Jews and Samaritans*

The decree's definition of heretic is interesting, comprising all those not loyal to the Catholic (Orthodox) Church,[6] but expressly adding

3 *Const. Cordi*, (16.XI.534).

4 A. Berger,"La concezione di eretico nelle fonti giustinianee", in *Atti della R.Accademia Nazionale dei Lincei*, s. 8, vol. 10, (1955) 354f.; P.T.R. Gray, *The Defense of Chalcedon in the East (451-553)* (Leiden: Brill, 1979) 44-79; S. Pietrini, "La Novella 18 di Valentiniano III nel quadro dei rapporti tra Stato e Chiesa" (1989) 101 *Studi Senesi*, 425ff.; S. Puliatti, *Ricerche sulle Novelle di Giustino II. La legislazione imperiale da Giustiniano I a Giustino II*, vol. II (Milano, 1991) 161ff., 249 n. 32; F. Zuccotti, *"Furor Haereticorum". Studi sul trattamento giuridico della follia e sulla persecuzione della eterodossia religiosa nella legislazione del tardo impero romano* (Milano, 1992) 196; R. Maceratini, *Ricerche sullo status giuridico dell'eretico nel diritto romano cristiano e nel diritto canonico classico* (Padova, 1994); E. Dovere, *"Ius principale" e "Catholica Lex". Dal Teodosiano agli Editti su Calcedonia* (Napoli, 1995) 150, 202, 268.

5 A.M. Rabello, *Giustiniano, Ebrei e Samaritani, op. cit., supra* n. 1, at vol. II, pp. 716ff.

6 B. Biondi, *Il Diritto Romano Cristiano*, vol. 3 (Milano, 1957) 352ff.; S. Puliatti, "La legislazione antisamaritana di Giustiniano e di Giustino I", in *Studi in onore di A. Falzea*, vol. IV (Milano, 1991) 323ff.

pagans, Jews and Samaritans, as if to emphasize that their inclusion among the heretics was not to be taken for granted.[7]

The first section of this decree reflects the fact that there had been an easing in Roman policy towards heretics, particularly Arians, during the beginning of the common reign of Justin and Justinian (April-July 527). During that period, some heretics had managed to gain access to public positions. The decree confirms the prohibition against Heretics holding public, honorific, civil or military positions, the only exception being decurion, a particularly onerous job.[8]

The decree continues with prohibitions linked to judicial activity, e.g. against the compulsory execution of sentence against orthodox Christians in cases involving Heretics, Samaritans or Jews, and confirms the prohibition against these people becoming *defensor civitatis* or *pater civitatis*, in order to avoid possible offence against bishops and other Christians. Heretics are forbidden to judge or pass sentences.[9] Advocacy[10] was also forbidden to them, as it was commonly linked to the study of law.[11] Whoever manages — in spite of the prohibition — to achieve such positions, was to be dismissed, if only on the basis of violation of these

7 B. Albanese, *Le Persone nel Diritto Privato Romano* (Palermo, 1979) 425ff.

8 On the expulsion from public services B. Biondi, *Il Diritto Romano Cristiano, supra* n. 6, vol. 3, pp. 371ff.; A. Sharf, "Byzantine Jewry in the Seventh Century" (1955) 48 *Byzantinische Zeitschrift*, 21; A.M. Rabello, "The Legal Condition of the Jews in Roman Empire", *Aufstieg und Niedergang der Roemischen Welt* (Berlin-New York, II, 13, 1980) 662ff., at 742f.; A. Linder, *The Jews in Roman Imperial Legislation* (Detroit, 1987, English transl. of the original Hebrew, Jerusalem, 1983), No. 56. On the office of the *decuriones* see A. Berger, *Encyclopedic Dictionary of Roman Law* (Philadelphia, 1950) 426 with the definition: "Members of a municipal senate elected for life . . . The *decuriones* decided about all matters involving the interests of the community, appointed local magistrates, and functioned as a court of appeal of fines imposed by municipal officers". See also M. Nuyens, *Le statut obligatoire des decurions dans le droit constamtinien* (Louvain, 1964).

9 B. Biondi, *Il Diritto Romano Cristiano, supra* n. 6, vol. 3, p. 377: "...gli eretici non possono esercitare la funzione di giudici appunto perchè ignorano i precetti divini"; S. Puliatti, *Ricerche, op. cit., supra* n. 4, at 253. On the *defensor civitatis* see V. Mannino, *Ricerche sul defensor civitatis* (Milano, 1984) 95.

10 On the advocates in Roman Law see P. Rasi, "Avvocato", in *Novissimo Digesto Italiano*, I, 2 (Torino, 1958) 162ff.; Y. Dan, "The Legal Profession in Palestine during the Byzantine Period" (1982) 17 Is. L.R. 279ff.

11 J. Juster, *Les Juifs dans l'Empire Romain* (Paris, 1914) vol. 2, pp. 263f.; Y. Dan, "Cultured Liberal Professions in the Cities of Eretz Israel in the Byzantine Period", (1978) 8 *Cathedra* 95ff.

positions' oaths of office, which explicitly demanded that the candidate be orthodox and pronounce the Christian creed.[12]

Justinian threatens with punishments all those who might infringe upon the decree, and those who, in spite of being obliged to guard the law, had neglected their duty.

The final section of the decree relates to those problems of family law connected with religious situations. It was the wish of the emperors that in cases of litigation between parents regarding the religious education of their child, or in disputes between parents and children regarding choice of religious education, the side wishing to be closer to orthodox Christianity should prevail. Thus, Biondi writes: "Professing the true faith is a legal duty of the citizens, as much as it is the duty of the state to protect the orthodox faith, repressing heresies or doctrines which are contrary to the Apostolic Catholic Church and which have repeatedly been shown to be errors, insanity, madness. Thus, the heretics are banned from public life".[13] It is thus obvious, that all normal juridical principles, even important ones such as *patria potestas*,[14] would have to cede before the principle of the supremacy of (the orthodox Christian) faith.

From the decree itself, we can learn that similar, previous norms had not been applied effectively. This was not to be repeated: the emperors proposed to apply the law strictly and appointed an apparatus of men of the church for the enforcement of the decree in Constantinople and throughout the Empire.

We are in fact in the year 527: the year of persecutions against the Manichaeans, on the eve of the revolt and persecution of the Samaritans.[15]

12 *Cf. Novella* 8 of Justinian; B. Biondi, *Diritto Romano Cristiano*, *supra* n. 6, vol. I, pp. 145ff., 350f.; see the observation of K.G. Holum, "Caesarea and the Samaritans", in Hohlfelder, ed., *City, Town and Countryside in the Early Byzantine Era* (New York, 1982) 72 n. 19: "Presumably recruiting among Samaritans had continued despite Zeno's measure". *Cf.* also R. Bonini, *Ricerche sulla legislazione giustinianea dell'anno 535*. (Bologna, 1976).

13 B. Biondi, *Giustiniano primo principe e legislatore cattolico* (Milano, 1936) 32.

14 A.M. Rabello, *Effetti personali della patria potestas* (Milano, 1979).

15 See J.A. Montgomery, *The Samaritans. The Earliest Jewish Sect. Their History, Theology and Literature* (New York, 1907) (repr. 1968), 113: "The tragedy seems to have received its impulse from an edict of Justinian found under the title De Haereticis et Manichaeis et Samaritis, issued in 527 (C.1.5.12)". We are in a period of religious reaction; see Malalas, *Chron.* XVIII, p. 451 (ed. Bonn) and A. Cameron,

2) *C.J.1.5.13 — Orthodox Heirs of Heretics, Jews and Samaritans*

In a certain sense, this decree supplements the former one, adding prohibitions relating to norms of legacy (relating to the years 527-528). In a society where religion was of great importance, it is understandable that parents belonging to a minority might disinherit apostate children, in an attempt to protect their religion. Justinian, who was interested not in religious freedom *lato sensu*, but in conversion to orthodox Christianity,[16] decreed invalid a testament in which an orthodox Christian child of a heretic, Jew or Samaritan, had been disinherited; the apostate would inherit at least that part of the inheritance to which he would be entitled *ab intestato*.[17]

Such a decree must have provoked the indignation of Jews and Samaritans, and must have been one of the reasons for the latter's revolt.[18]

"The Last Days of the Academy of Athens", in *Proceedings of the Cambridge Philological Society*, n.s., 15 (1969) pp. 7ff.; J. Glucker, *Antiochus and the Late Academy* (Goettingen, 1978) 322ff.; M. Stern, *Greek and Latin Authors on Jews and Judaism*, (Jerusalem 1980) vol. II, p. 671; O. Bucci, "La politica culturale di Cosroe Anusirvan (531-579), la chiusura delle scuole di Atene (529) e l'esilio degli ultimi Maestri pagani in Persia", in *Studi Biscardi*, vol.VI, (Milano, 1987) 507ff.; A.M. Rabello, *Giustiniano, op. cit., supra* n. 1, at 721ff.; S. Puliatti, *Ricerche, supra* n. 4, at 279.

16 B. Biondi, *Giustiniano, supra* n. 13, at 21.

17 *Cf.* J. Juster, *Les Juifs, supra* n. 11, vol. 2, p. 91; and *cf.* Mishna, Baba Batra 8,5; R. Yaron, *Gifts in Contemplation of Death in Jewish and Roman Law* (Oxford, 1960) 37ff.; E.E. Urbach, "Laws of Inheritance and After Life", now in E.E. Urbach, *The World of the Sages. Collected Studies* (Jerusalem, 1988, in Hebrew) 229ff.; Z. Falk, "Testate Succession in Jewish Law" (1961) Journal of Jewish Studies 67; O. Irshai, "The Apostate as an Inheritor in Geonic Responsa", in *Shenaton Hamishpat Haivri*, XI-XII, (1984-1986) pp. 435ff. (in Hebrew).

18 See S. Winkler, "Die Samariter in den Jahren 529-530", (1965) 43-45 *Klio* 450; A. Linder, *Roman Imperial Legislation, supra* n. 8, (1987) No. 56; P.T.R. Gray, "Palestine and Justinian's Legislation on Non-Christian Religions", *supra* n. 1, at 253 notes: "This law was of crucial importance to Samaritans. Largely self-sufficient agricultural communities, the Samaritan villages must have depended for their long-term survival on the passing of Samaritan land to Samaritan heirs. If sons who converted were entitled to inherit real property, the break-up of the Samaritan communities was possible".

3) *C.J. 1.5.17 — Samaritan Synagogues and the Right of Ownership of the Samaritans*

We now find ourselves in the presence of one of Justinian's particularly harsh decrees related to the great Samaritan revolt of 529 C.E. As the decrees of C.J. 1.5. 14-18 are not dated, we do not know with precision, whether they precede, are contemporary with, or follow the revolt.[19] Here it is decreed that the Samaritan synagogues be destroyed, and any attempt to rebuild them be punished. Obviously, Justinian was trying to definitively extirpate the Samaritan religion and oblige the Samaritans to convert to Christianity, as is attested by Procopius.[20] *Testamenti factio* is denied to the Samaritans, and so is the possibility to have heirs *ab intestato*; the only exception is in favour of orthodox Christian heirs. Thus, Samaritans are able to make donations or sell only to an orthodox Christian, and the rest of their estates were to be confiscated and put in the care of bishops.

The first part of the decree was meant to punish the Samaritans religiously, given the great importance which the synagogue had in Samaritan life. Like the Jewish synagogue, the Samaritan synagogue was a place of communal gatherings, and in particular the place for reading the Bible and for prayer. It facilitated the transmission of Samaritan teaching and tradition.[21]

19 *Cf.* F.M. Abel, *Histoire de la Palestine depuis la conqête d'Alexandre jusqu'à l'invasion arabe* (Paris, 1952) vol. II, p. 358; according to Stein and Puliatti this constitution must have been promulgated in 528, before the revolt: E. Stein, *Histoire du Bas Empire*, vol. II (Paris, Bruges, 1949) (= Amsterdam 1968) p. 373 n. 2: S. Puliatti, *Ricerche, op. cit., supra* n. 4, at 260: this thesis is based on the order of the constitutions in the Code and on its quotation in the next constitutions.

20 See A.M. Rabello, *Giustiniano, Ebrei e Samaritani, supra* n. 1, vol. I, pp. 237ff. and p. 246, n. 19; S. Puliatti, *Ricerche, supra* n. 4, at 260ff.

21 "While the true Jews were subjected to the hatred of Byzantine rulers, the petty community of the Samaritans on Palestinian soil, thanks to their frequent revolts, suffered almost the total extirpation of their whole sect and their sanctuaries were burnt down and converted into chapels and churches", S. Kraus, "The Christian Legislation on the Synagogue", in *I. Goldziher Memorial Volume II* (Jerusalem, 1958) 19; see also: Z. Safrai, "Samaritan Synagogues in the Roman Byzantine Period", (1977) 4 *Cathedra* 84ff. (in Hebrew); A. Kloner, "Ancient Synagogues in Israel: An Archaeological Survey", in L.I. Levine, *Ancient Synagogues Revealed*, (Jerusalem, 1981) 11; A.M. Rabello, "Le sinagoghe samaritane in Palestina", in *idem., Giustiniano, supra* n. 1, vol. II, pp. 846ff.

The second part of the decree punishes Samaritans economically, preventing them from executing any form of property transfer, except to orthodox Christians; Justinian intends to promote the conversion of the Samaritans and for this purpose grave sanctions are set against them.[22] The decree is basically an attempt to eliminate any Samaritan property, but, as Baron observes, "the very continuity of existence of the Samaritan denomination was now severely threatened".[23]

4) *C.J. 1.5.18 — Heretics and Samaritans Excluded from Teaching*

After opening solemnly with the profession of the Christian faith, this decree extends prohibitions established previously against Samaritans to some other categories of heretics, probably as in decree C.J.1.5.17, *inter alia* the prohibition to build synagogues. This decree defines heretic in a wide sense, to include all those not belonging to the Apostolic Church. Thus, the prohibition of holding any honour, military office or profession which might cause offence to the orthodox faith, is extended also to Samaritans. In particular, this decree extends to pagans and Samaritans the prohibition of receiving food distributions and of teaching. Since teaching can corrupt the soul, only orthodox Christians would be allowed to teach.[24] Punishments are prescribed for those who, in order to accede to public positions or advocacy, pretend to be orthodox Christians. The inability of non-orthodox children to inherit from Catholic parents is reconfirmed.

It is unclear from the language of this constitution whether its prohibitions extended to Jews as well. Juster's research led him to conclude that the term heretic in this decree was interpreted in its narrow sense, to exclude Jews.[25] Had the legislator wanted to include

22 B. Biondi, *Giustiniano, supra* n. 13, at 20, 32f.; B. Albanese, *Le Persone, supra* n. 7, at 423 n. 351.

23 S.W. Baron, *A Social and Religious History of the Jews* (Philadelphia, 1957) vol. 3, pp. 9f. and see the articles of Z. Safrai and Y. Dan in Z. Baras, S. Safrai, M. Stern, Y. Tsafrir, eds., *Eretz Israel from the Destruction of the Second Temple to the Muslim Conquest* (Jerusalem, 1982, in Hebrew) 127ff., 284ff.

24 B. Biondi, *Il Diritto Romano Cristiano, supra* n. 6, vol. I, pp. 138, 146, 150, 353; vol. III, p. 371; A. Segre', "Essays on Byzantine Economic History, I, The annona civica and the annona militaris", (1942-43) 16 *Byzantion* 393ff.

25 J. Juster, *Les Juifs dans l'Empire Romain, supra* n. 11, vol. I, pp. 177ff.; in the same direction J. Parkes, *The Conflict of the Church and the Synagogue* (New York, 1974) 256.

Jews within the scope of the decree, he would have added *Judaei* (Jews), in order to be consistent with his explicit reference to *pagans* and *Samaritans*. Berger came to an opposite conclusion: in his opinion, "even were, in C.J. 1.5.18.4, Jews not specifically mentioned, they were however affected by the restrictions against the non-orthodox":[26] furthermore, he asks, would it ever have been admissible for a Jew to teach?

In my opinion, given the clear inconsistency in the use of the term "heretic", it is impossible to generalize. For instance, I cannot imagine that the decree would have forbidden Jews from teaching other Jews. Similarly, it seems unlikely that Christian scholars would have been prohibited from learning the *hebraica veritas* from some rabbi. It would seem to me that Jews would not be *automatically* included in the decree, though they *might be* included in a specific case, based upon the discretion of the sitting judge.[27] If such was the case, the legal position of Samaritans was clearly inferior to that of Jews.

5) *C.J.1.5.21 — Jews and Samaritans as Witnesses in Courts of Law*

On July 28th, 531, Justinian discusses the admissibility of testimony of non-orthodox Christians, in order to settle a question which had been repeatedly submitted to him by the judges.[28] It will be of a particular interest to us to examine the rule established regarding Samaritans.

Prior to Justinian, no imperial decree had been issued regarding the admissibility of a *Jew*'s testimony in a trial involving a Christian,[29]

26 A. Berger, "La concezione di eretico", *supra* n. 4.

27 This constitution too refers to the prohibition of pagan teaching and Justinian's decision about the Academy of Athens; see *supra* n. 14 and see also M. Luz, "Marinus: A Neo-Platonic Eretz-Israeli in Athens", in *Greece and Rome in Eretz Israel* (Jerusalem, 1989, in Hebrew) 36ff.; M. Amelotti-L. Migliardi Zingale, *Le costituzioni giustinianee nei papiri e nelle epigrafi* (Milano, 1985) 17ff., 136f.; in general see: A.D. Crown, "The Samaritan Diaspora to the End of the Byzantine Era" (1972) 2 Australian Journal of Biblical Archaeology 107ff.

28 On the problem of reference of the judges to the Emperor (*referé au legislatif*) for the solution of a juridical question, see A.M. Rabello, "Non Liquet: from Modern Law to Roman Law" (1974) 9 Is. L.R. 963ff.; G. Bassanelli Sommariva, *L'imperatore unico creatore ed interprete delle leggi e l'autonomia del giudice nel diritto giustinianeo* (Milano, 1983).

29 On this legislation see A. Berger, "Studi sui Basilici, VI, Bas, 21.1.45 e CI.1.5.21" (1955) 6 *IURA* 104ff.; Parkes, *Church and Synagogue, supra* n. 25, pp. 177ff.

though the subject had been treated previously by the Church councils.[30] The rulings of the Church councils, however, did not address the admissibility of a *Samaritan*'s testimony. Justinian ruled inadmissible any trial testimony given by a Jew against an orthodox Christian, even where all the disputants were Christian (in which case the testimony would invariably damage at least one Christian disputant). Such testimony would be admissible only when both parties were not Orthodox Christians, or when the testimony would damage only non-Orthodox Christians. In such cases, a Jew's status was comparable to that of a heretic.

In cases of extra-judicial testimony, and in particular in cases of inheritance and contracts, the testimony of Jews (or heretics) is expressly admissible.

The *Samaritans*, however, are given a status similar to that of the same group as Manichaeans, Borborites, Pagans, Montanists, Tascodruges and Ophites: their judicial or extra-judicial testimony is forbidden. This more severe attitude towards the Samaritans may be explained as a reaction to the recent revolts.

Such a situation was to continue for six years, until *Novella* 45 of Justinian was to replace the aforementioned norms.[31]

6) *Partial Conclusions*

Scholars disagree as to whether each of the constitutions discussed above were issued before or after the Samaritan revolt of 529. We think that the strong legislation against the Samaritans preceded the revolts and contributed to provoking them. However, Justinian's Code itself was issued five years after the repression of the revolt (534). Perhaps the continuation of the severe legislation against the Samaritans, more severe that that issued against other religious minorities, was justified by the continuing rebellions and by the fear of an alliance between the Samaritans and the Persians, Justinian's major external enemy. However, it should not be forgotten that Justinian's rule was marked by general religious intolerance and persecutions.[32] The legislation hurt

30 See the canon 196 of the Council of Carthage of 419 and our comments in *Giustiniano, Ebrei e Samaritani, supra* n. 1, at 537ff. and *cf.* the *Novella* 45 of Justinian (537).

31 On this constitution see J. Juster, *Les Juifs dans l'Empire Romain, supra* n. 11, vol. I, p. 179; A.M. Rabello, *Giustiniano, supra* n. 1, at 802ff.

32 *Cf.* M. Avi-Yonah, *The Jews of Palestine. A Political History from the Bar Kochba War to the Arab Conquest* (Oxford, 1976) 247.

Samaritans in their private lives, in their religious and communal lives and excluded them from Imperial public life; the repression of the Samaritans was very real, and worse that that of the Jews,[33] though the Jews suffered from more detailed and specific repressive legislation. The difference in the form of repression against the Jews devolved from Judaism's historical links to Christianity, the relatively great and deep Christian interest in Jews and Judaism, and the large and widespread Jewish diaspora throughout the Empire.

B) *The Samaritans in Justinian's Novellae*

1) *Introduction*

In the second part of our article we will focus on the new Constitutions (*Novellae*) that Justinian devoted to the Samaritan problem, and we will examine their content.

It should be recalled that, generally, the purpose of a *Novella* was to deal with a particular topic which had not been sufficiently addressed in the *Codex* or to explicitly rule how a constitution of the *Codex* was to be interpreted. For this reason, we can not expect to be able to draw from the *Novellae* a complete picture of the Samaritans' situation during this period. Only after first closely examining *all* the texts of the period may one be able to attain a more complete picture of the Samaritans' legal situation during the Justinian era.

We shall now start our examination of the Samaritan-related Novellae.

2) *Novella 45: Jews and Samaritans as Decuriones or as Witnesses (537)*

During the Justinian era the problem of the Decurions[34] was generally perceived: "Upon reviewing the civic councils of our time, we see that

33 On the situation of Judaism in the Roman Empire and in particular in the time of Justinian see A.M. Rabello, *Giustiniano, op. cit., supra* n. 1; *idem*, "The Legal Condition, *op. cit., supra* n. 8; on the problem of the Jurisdiction, *idem*, "Jewish and Roman Jurisdiction" in *An Introduction to the History and Sources of Jewish Law*, B. Jackson, et al. eds., (Oxford, 1996) 141-167.

34 Regarding the particularly onerous nature of the office of *decurion*, see *supra* our Comment on C.J. 1.5.12 and see n. 8.

they are very small, some of them in a bad condition in terms of their number and resources. Even in councils that might have more members, no member would owned property" (so Justinian himself in his Preface to Novella 28). "Undoubtedly, however, a considerable number of decurions — particularly the influential and rich ones, who could bribe the officials and intimidate their colleagues — were able to avoid the office".[35]

It is evident that everyone tried to avoid the difficult task of Decurion. Since the *decurio* was a public office, it is not surprising that Jews, Samaritans and Heretics tried their best to free themselves from the job under the pretext that access to public office had been prohibited to them.[36]

In reality, previous Constitutions[37] already made clear that Jews or Samaritans were subjected to the burden of the office, though they were to be deprived of the honor associated with it. As a consequence, it is understandable that the Emperor was "amazed" at the readiness of the praetorial prefect to deliberate on the question of whether Jews and Samaritans, forbidden from holding public office, were to be exempt from the *decuriat*, a public office. Justinian repeatedly explained that Jews and Samaritans had to be subjected to all duties and burdens (*onera*) of the *decuriat*, without enjoying its honors (*honores*). Justinian's response reflects his indignation at being asked such a simple question; he explicitly threatened to make the petitioners regret their indiscretion in submitting the question.

Our interpretation is very different from that of Ferrari Dalle Spade, who considers Novella 45 "one of the most interesting documents proving that over the course of several centuries, Jews, Samaritans and

35 A.H.M. Jones, "Il sistema delle caste nel tardo impero romano", in A. Vera, ed., *La Società del Basso Impero. Guida storica e critica* (Bari, 1983) 49.

36 Regarding this *Novella* see J. Juster, *Les Juifs dans l'Empire Romain, op. cit., supra* n. 11, vol. II, p. 123f. P. Browe, "Die Judengesetzgebung Justinians", (1935) 8 *Analecta Gregoriana* 109 ff., at 129; A. Berger, "Studi sui Basilici, VI, Bas. 21.1.45 e CI.1.5.21", *supra* n. 29; N. Van Der Wal, *Manuale Novellarum Justiniani. Aperçu systematique du contenu des Novelles de Justinien* (Groningen, 1964) 56ff., 136; A.M. Rabello, "The Legal Condition, *op. cit., supra* n. 8, at 742 f.; A. Linder, *Roman Imperial Legislation, op. cit., supra* n. 8, No. 64; A.M. Bartoletti Colombo, *Lessico delle Novelle di Giustiniano* (Roma, 1981-86); Eadem, *Legum Iustiniani Imperatoris Vocabularium — Novellae, pars latina, i-x and Indices* (Milano, 1977-79); *pars graeca* (Milano, 1984).

37 See e.g., C.J. 1.9.5; 1.9.10; 1.5.7; 1.5.12 etc.

Montanists enjoyed ample immunity. This immunity was removed by Justinian, who was under the influence of the Church of Byzantium, which was able to dominate him".[38]

Novella 45 was issued in the year 537. We think that these reforms, which on one hand denied Jews and Samaritans access to public office, yet on the other hand obliged them to undertake the position of decurion, dates back to a previous period. In this same Novella, the Emperor simply confirms an already established principle in order to ensure that Jews, Samaritans and Heretics were unable to escape this task.[39]

The second part of the Novella concerns a practical contemporary development: the problem of Jewish and Samaritan testimony. We have already seen[40] that Justinian's position was to exclude all possibility that Jews or Samaritans could bear witness against Orthodox Christians. Jews or Samaritans could not bear witness in any litigation between two Orthodox Christians, as any testimony in favor of one meant testimony against the other! If only one side in a litigation was an Orthodox Christian, testimony by a Jew or Samaritan against that side was prohibited.

However, Jews or Samaritans could bear witness in favor of an Orthodox Christian or in a trial between parties who were not Orthodox Christians. This raised the problem of the admissibility of Jewish or Samaritan testimony in favor of the Public Administration. Would a Jew or Samaritan be allowed to testify that an Orthodox Christian was a member of the order of decurions? According to Justinian's own general principles, the answer would have to be *negative*, because no testimony of a Jew or Samaritan against an Orthodox Christian could be valid. However, Justinian answered *affirmatively*: testimony in favor of the Roman Catholic State would be admissible. This example of defending an interest of State ("is he not acting to our State's benefit?") on theological grounds, in this case the 'Catholic' nature of the State, is

38 G. Ferrari Dalle Spade, "Privilegi degli Ebrei nell'impero romano-cristiano", in *Festschrift L. Wenger*, vol. II, (1944) pp. 102ff. (= *Scritti giuridici*, III, p. 277).

39 See e.g., the constitutions quoted in n. 3; In general, see J. Juster, *Les Juifs dans l'Empire Romain, op. cit. supra* n. 11, vol. II, p. 261; V. Colorni, *Gli Ebrei nel sistema del Diritto comune fino alla prima emancipazione* (Milano, 1956) 21; A.M. Rabello, "The Legal Condition", *op. cit., supra* n. 8, at 742f.

40 See our discussion of C.J. 1.5.21, *supra* text at nn. 28-31 and see J. Juster, *Les Juifs dans l'Empire Romain, op.cit., supra* n. 11, vol. II, p. 123 n. 4 regarding an "interpretation apportée par la Nov.J. 45 cap. 1".

particularly interesting in light of the non-ecclesiatical nature of the Novella.[41]

We would like to point out two peculiar aspects of Novella 45. First, we feel that it reveals a sarcastic, almost mocking public attitude towards the government, prevalent during the Justinian era. The oppressed would compete amongst themselves in displays of disdain of their oppressors, defending themselves in any way they can, laughing at all, in the face of all. It is within this psychological climate that literary works such as the *Secret History* of Procopius or some passages of the *Targum Sheni'* to the Book of Esther originated.[42] Justinian, an Emperor who forbade all from commenting on his laws, was confronted by a *vulgar*, popular comment that took into account only one aspect of the legislation, ignoring all others, *and making his prohibition absurd* (for Jews, Samaritans and Heretics to be denied access to public office and as a consequence . . . be exempted from the decurionate obligation!). It almost appears that a significant part of the bureaucracy intentionally misinterpreted the constitution: "*they think that they have freed themselves from the decurionaes' charges*", not due to special privilege, but just because of the great loathing Justinian nourished against Heretics, Jews and Samaritans . . . This was too much; the Emperor could hardly believe his eyes. How could his praetorian prefect have believed such things! His astonishment knew no limits . . . unless we presume that the bureaucrat at the Imperial Chancellory who wrote Justinian's answer had himself somewhat fallen prey to the same inclination to sarcasm: how is it possible to reach such a high position and be unable to understand certain things . . . This amazement caused E. Stein to see in this constitution an indication of the non-orthodox ideas of John of Cappadocia,[43] "perhaps the most prominent figure of

41 See A.M. Rabello, *Giustiniano, Ebrei e Samaritani, op. cit., supra* n. 1, vol. I, pp. 157ff. (on Procopius), pp. 237ff. regarding the *Secret History* of Procopius and pp. 456ff. (on *Targum Sheni*), and the Bibliography quoted there.

42 This explanation seems incongruous to J. Juster, *Les Juifs dans l'Empire Romain, op. cit., supra* n. 11, vol. II, p. 124; A. Linder, *Roman Imperial Legislation, op.cit., supra* n. 8, No. 64.

43 E. Stein, *Histoire du Bas Empire, op. cit., supra* n. 19, vol. II, p. 435.

Justinian's reign".[44] With all his intelligence (SUNESYS) and sagacity, with all his acumen (OXUTES), John of Cappadocia was duped by a group of Heretics, Jews and Samaritans. It seems as if Tribonian, John's great rival, would have liked this very much!

A second peculiar aspect of Novella 45, this one strictly juridical, is its nature and purpose of serving as an *authentic interpretation* of the Emperor's will, as expressed in his prior Constitution C.1.5.21.[45]

3) *Novella 129 of Justinian (551) and Novella 144 of Justin II (De Samaritis) (572)*

We detect in Justinian's Novella 129[46] some remaining spirit of toleration,[47] a spirit which would remain reflected in the law until the

44 R. Bonini, *Introduzione allo studio dell'età giustinianea* (Bologna, 4th ed., 1985) 105. According to Bonini (p. 108), Novella 45 is an example of "atteggiamenti di netta critica" of the Emperor towards his *praefectum praetorio*. Regarding the circumstances of the transmission of this Novella to the *praefectum praetorio*, see F. De Martino, *Storia della Costituzione Romana*, vol. V (Napoli, 1967) 260f., n. 23.

45 Regarding this phenomenon, see A.M. Rabello, "Non Liquet", *op. cit., supra* n. 28, at 63ff.; G. Bassanelli Sommariva, *L'imperatore unico creatore ed interprete delle leggi e l'autonomia del giudice nel diritto giuistinianeo* (Milano, 1983); G. Lanata, *Legislazione e natura nelle Novelle giustinianee* (Napoli, 1984) 134ff., 135 n. 97.

46 Regarding Novella 129, see, in particular, J. Montgomery, *The Samaritans, supra* n. 15, at 120ff.; N. Van Der Wal, *Manuale Novellarum, supra* n. 36, index; R. Bonini, *Introduzione, supra* n. 44, at 99; S. Puliatti, *Ricerche sulle Novelle di Giustino II. La legislazione imperiale da Giustiniano I a Giustino II*, vol. I, *Problemi di diritto pubblico* (Milano, 1984) 20 and 40; regarding the linguistic characteristic of this Novella, see G. Lanata, "Le Novelle giustinianee e la traduzione dell'Autentico. A proposito del Legum Iustiniani Imperatoris Vocabularium" (1979) 49 *Byzantion* 261 and n. 85; regarding the character of retroactivity of some norms, see G. Lanata, *Legislazione e natura, supra* n. 45, at 63; regarding the publication of Novella 129, see Eadem, *ibidem*, p. 119; regarding the international political situation, with reference to Palestine too, see P. Brown, *The Making of Late Antiquity* (Harvard University Press, Cambridge, Mass., 1978); regarding the relations between Rome and Iran during this period, see M.G. Angeli Bertinelli, *Roma e l'Oriente. Strategia, economia, societa' e cultura nelle relazioni fra Roma, la Giudea e l'Iran* (Roma, 1979) 146ff.; regarding the situation in Palestine, see A.M. Rabello, *Giustiniano, supra* n. 1, 42ff.; 149ff.; 237ff.; regarding the situation in Çesarea, see L.I. Levine, *Caesarea under Roman Rule* (Leiden, 1975) 60, 136f.

47 This word is preferred by Puliatti, *Ricerche, op. cit.*, in place of liberality.

re-deterioration that may be associated with Novella 144 of Justin II, Justinian's successor.[48]

It seems that the same Justinian realized that the Empire's state of relations with the Samaritans was unsustainable. It was thus, that when Sergius, bishop of Caesarea, addressed the Emperor and called upon him to have mercy upon the Samaritans, who remained a wealthy and large constitutency in Caesarea, the Emperor immediately consented. The preface expresses highest praise for the clemency to which every act of criminality is subject:

> *Nullum ita magnum subiectorum nostrorum delictum est, quod non nostra clementia medeatur. Licet enim eorum facta odio habentes ad vindictam pro eis insurgamus, tamen tempus medentes et commonentes modis competentibus delinquentes rursus ad nostram clementiam remeamus, iustitiam iracundiae benignitatis reconciliantes rationibus* . . .

The Samaritans, moreover, well knew that they were the cause of the enactment of the legislation against them, the Emperor said.[49]

The *first chapter* makes clear reference to Sergius and his request. Founded on the hope of future Samaritan loyalty, the Novella restored to Samaritans the competence to make a testament (*testamenti factio*), the application of the rules on inheritance *ab intestato*, and the ability to negotiate and to give donations.

However, the *second chapter* limited such freedoms; in the case of Christians and Samaritans heirs, only the former could claim the inheritance *ab intestato*.

Nevertheless, the *third chapter* established that one so excluded from an inheritance who would convert to Christianity could obtain his

48 Regarding Novella 144, see especially J. Montgomery, *The Samaritans, supra* n. 15, 122ff.; N. Van Der Wal, *Manuale Novellarum, supra* n. 36, index; Y. Dan, "Eretz Israel in the IV and V Century" in *Eretz Israel from the Destruction of the Second Temple to the Muslim Conquest*, vol. I (Jerusalem, 1982, in Hebrew) 288f.; S. Puliatti, *Ricerche, supra* n. 46, at 3ff., 15ff.; 33ff.; 48; 125; G. Lanata, *Legislazione e natura, supra* n. 45, at 120, 128ff.

49 Nevertheless, we would not claim that the Samaritan legislation was a consequence of the revolt. We have confined ourselves to quoting the arguments reported in the Novella itself. Personally, we think the opposite; we believe that the revolt was a result of the legislation. Jones shares this opinion, see *infra* n. 53. See also the observations of R. Bonini, "L'ultima legislazione pubblicistica di Giustiniano (543-567), in *Idem, Studi sull'eta' giustinianea* (Rimini, 1987) 57ff.

hereditary share, though he could not sue for retroactive usufructuary rights. In any case, a testator could leave to Samaritan descendants no more than one-sixth of his estate.

The final, *fourth chapter* prevented tax-collectors from taking advantage of the previous legislative situation, thus giving this Novella a retroactive quality.

The limited reform proved to be too little, too late. The Samaritans were not appeased, and rebelled once more, in 556. This rebellion, like the preceding one, was repressed only after tremendous bloodshed. The legislative response can be discerned in Novella 144, promulgated by the Emperor Justin II, in 572,[50] which was, to some extent, a reaction to the rebellion. The Novella was specifically addressed to Diomedes, responsible for the prefecture of the Orient.

Justin opens Novella 144 by recalling his father's benevolence to the Samaritans, as reflected in Novella 129. Justin expresses his anger at Justinian's benevolent position being misunderstood by the Samaritans.

Novella 144 would once again deprive Samaritans of the ability to bequeath, inherit, donate, receive donations, or take part in contractual negotiations. Samaritans might bequeath their property only to Orthodox Christian heirs; in other instances, their property would be confiscated.

However, the second chapter establishes an exception in favor of *coloni* (farmers on land taken on lease), who might dispose of their farmland *mortis causa* and *inter vivos*, mostly for tax reasons. Abandonment of farmland by the Palestinian agricultural population, this during a very difficult period for agriculture, would lead to a devaluation of land prices and a consequent reduction of property taxes. The exception also safeguarded the continuation of agricultural activities in Palestine. If there were no heirs by will or *ab intestato*, possessions of free Samaritan *coloni* would go to the landowner, who acted in place of the *fiscus* (tax-collector), "since he pays the *colon*'s land-tax".

The Novella excluded Samaritans from all public, military and civil service and denied them the right to practice law, to study law or to teach the youth. This last restriction should be viewed in light of the presence of Samaritans among members of the Academy of Athens.[51]

50 Regarding the dating, see P. Marc, *Plan eines: der griechischen Urkunden des Mittelalters und der neueren Zeit* (Munchen, 1903) 36; S. Puliatti, *Ricerche, supra* n. 46, at 33, n. 65f.

51 M. Stern, *Greek and Latin Authors, supra* n. 15, at 671ff.; Y. Dan, "Eretz Israel in the IV and V Century", *supra* n. 48, at 48 ff.; O. Bucci, "La politica culturale di Cosroe Amsirvan (531-779), in *Studi Biscardi*, vol. VI (Milano, 1987) 507ff.

A Samaritan convert to Christianity caught observing the Samaritan Sabbath or Festivals was to have his property confiscated and be condemned to everlasting exile. In order to be certain that conversions were genuine, the Novella established a two-year period of 'catacumenate',[52] a religious study program under the supervision of Christian teachers expert in the Bible, as a pre-requisite for conversion of adult Samaritans (children could be converted without this pre-requisite).

Finally, it was established that Samaritans could not have Christian slaves: a slave who was a Christian at the time of his being purchased by a Samaritan would become free at the moment of purchase; a non-Christian slave of a Samaritan would become free immediately upon converting to Christianity.[53]

52 J. Juster, *Les Juifs dans l'Empire Romain, supra* n. 11, vol. I, pp. 113 and 114 n. 2. Juster explains that originally this period was established for Samaritans, and not for Jews as, for the moment, only Samaritans were being forced to convert to the State religion, and only Samaritan converts to Christianity were being suspected of secretly continuing to practice their former faith. See A.M. Rabello, *Giustiniano, supra* n. 1, at 619.

53 We report the conclusive words of A.H.M. Jones, *The Later Roman Empire, 284-602*, vol. 1 (Baltimore, 1986) 296, "Justinian became increasingly religious with advancing years. He continued to issue laws regulating minutely the internal affairs of the church, and he even extended his interest to the Jewish cult, laying down rules for synagogue services. The penal laws against pagans, Jews, Samaritans and heretics were not relaxed, and there was a renewed drive against pagan practices in 562. Justinian also continued untiringly his efforts to reconcile the monophysites to the true faith." In vol. 2., pp. 948, Jones adds, "The Eastern government followed suit in 438 with a severer law, debarring Jews and Samaritans from all *dignitates* and *militiae*, including even the lowly post of *defensor civitatis*; they were not, however, relieved of the onerous service of the *cohortalini*, nor yet from the *curia*. By the law of Leo, which declared that only orthodox Christians might be barristers, Jews were also excluded from the legal profession. This remained the law under Justinian, who sharpened it by adding to the list of prohibited posts that of *curator* or *pater civitatis*, and by depriving Jews and Samaritans of the meagre privileges which still sttached to curial rank while holding them to its onerous obligations. Except for their exclusion from the public service and the bar the Jews thus incurred no serious civil disabilities until the reign of Justin. He applied to them (and to Samaritans) the same penal laws which he enacted against pagans and heretics. Like them they were debarred from making wills or receiving inheritances, from giving testimony in a court of law, or indeed from performing any legal act. In the relative toleration accorded to Jews down to the reign of Justinian the imperial government was undoubtedly fighting a rearguard action against the mounting pressure of public opinion".

4) *Novella 131, 14: Lands Where Churches are Erected (545)*

The long Novella 131 (545) deals with *de ecclesiasticis canonibus et privilegiis*,[54] of which only chapter 14 is relevant to our discussion. The chapter begins by establishing that heretics cannot obtain by any means (e.g. purchase, long-term lease or tenancy) real estate belonging to a Holy Church, or any venerable place. This is a broad prohibition, that includes all ecclesiastical property.

Juster rightly found reason to think that this provision did not apply to Jews.[55] We concur, and would suggest also that neither was it applied to the Samaritans. We base our opinion on the fact that Jews and Samaritans are explicitly cited only later in the chapter, in its first paragraph, regarding the right of a local church to claim the land on which a church was erected, should the orthodox Christian owner of such land sell, lease for a long term, or rent such land to a Jew, Samaritan, pagan or heretic.[56]

Therefore, it was prohibited for Jews and Samaritans to possess the lands on which a church was *erected*, but not, in our opinion, the lands belonging to the Church. Evidently, the reason for this was the desire

54 The first chapter of this Novella is significant as it gives legal force to the canons approved by the councils of Nicaea, Constantinople, Ephesus and Chalcedon. R. Bonini points out that this reflected "not expansion in the sphere of the church's influence, but rather, on the contrary, the establishment of a presupposition for State intervention and interference in the internal life of the Church and for the assertion of a more oppressive protectorate". See "L'ultima legislazione pubblicistica di Giustiniano" (543-567), *supra* n. 49, at 83. This event did not have a great effect on either Jews or Samaritans, because there was no disagreement between the Church and Justinian regarding them.

55 J. Juster, *Les Juifs dans l'Empire Romain, supra* n. 11, vol. II, p. 69 n. 3.

56 M. Avi-Yonah, *The Jews of Palestine, supra* n. 32, at 249; J. Parkes, *The Conflict of the Church and the Synagogue, supra* n. 25, at 247.

not to damage agriculture. This exception would have been very important, had the Novella become general law,[57] for Palestine.[58]

Paragraph 2 reiterates the prohibition against building synagogues, a prohibition in force since the rule of Theodosius II (Novella 3) and reiterated by Justinian (C.1.9.18).[59] We believe that punishment for violating this provision would be the sanctions established in C.1.9.18.[60]

57 See the conclusion of the Novella, where the Emperor, after publishing the Novella in Constantinople, delayed its publication in the provinces. F.A. Biener, *Geschichte der Novellen Justinians* (Berlin, 1824, = repr. Aalen, 1970) 33; Juster, *Juifs*, *supra* n. 11, vol. I, p. 238, stated that they did not understand such reserve. Yet, one must recall that during this period the Emperor wanted to avoid the expenses entailed in publishing constitutions. Regarding this, see Van Der Wal, *Manuale Novellarum*, *supra* n. 36, at 13, no. 4. From this, we conclude that the Novella was in universal force, even though its publication was limited. As far as the expenses of publication are concerned, without reference to the Novella, see M.F.F. Von Schwind, *Zur Frage der Publikation im Römischen Recht* (Muenchen, 1940).

58 Regarding Palestinian real estate, see A. Gulak, *History of Jewish Law in Talmudic Times: The Law of Real Property* (Jerusalem, 1939, in Hebrew); D. Sperber, *Roman Palestine, 200-400, The Land* (Ramat Gan, 1978).

59 Juster, *Juifs*, *supra* n. 11, vol. I, p. 472, n. 3; S. Kraus, "The Christian Legislation on the Synagogue", *supra* n. 21; M. Avi-Yonah, *The Jews under Roman and Byzantine Rule. A Political History of Palestine from the Bar Kokhba War to the Arab Conquest* (Jerusalem-New York, 1984) 250. Note that from this point of view, Jews were in a better position than Samaritans, who were not able to maintain any synagogues.

60 S.W. Baron, *A Social and Religious History of the Jews*, vol. 3, (Philadelphia, 2nd ed., revised and enlarged, 1967) 9 "Nevertheless, the basic continuity in the Empire's general toleration of Judaism becomes doubly evident when one considers Justinian's contrasting treatment of the Samaritans. We shall see in another context how troublesome these sectarians, after their great religious revival under Baba Rabba, had become to the Byzantine administration. Justinian thought that he could settle the problem by a sleight of hand. By declaring the Samaritans a Christian rather than a Jewish sect, in 529, he removed from under their legal status whatever props had been lent them by their traditional toleration as a *religio licita*. Not only was their temple on Gerizim to be permanently replaced by a church, but their synagogues were to be destroyed everywhere. In the subsequent legislation, too, their faith appears as merely part and parcel of the Christian heretical movements. While heresies were much too widespread throughout the empire and embraced too large and influential segments in the population to be placed under the sanction of capital punishment as they later were in Western laws, the very continuity of existence of the Samaritan denomination was now severely threatened": pp. 230, footnote no. 4 "... Justinian's *Novella* 131, XIV. 1 in CJ, III, 663. *Cf.* Arcadius' statement quoted by H. Gregoire in his chapter on "The Byzantine Church," in N.H. Baynes and H. St. L.B. Moss, *Byzantium: An Introduction to East Roman Civilization* (Oxford, 2nd ed., 1961) 131; Juster, *Juifs, supra* n. 11, vol. I, p. 251, n. 1. Justinian's combination of

Conclusions

We have briefly examined Novella 45. on the *decuriones* (537), Novella 129 of Justinian (551) and Novella 144 of Justin II (572), which are completely dedicated to the Samaritan problem, and Novella 131, 14 (545). This legislation was a continuation of the more comprehensive legislation regarding Samaritans, Jews and Heretics, which we have seen in the Justinian Code of 534.

During Justinian's reign, the Samaritans suffered discrimination and infringements of civil, religious and political rights in public and private life. Our study of both Codex and Novellae give us a more complete picture of the Samaritan's difficult juridical situation in the Justinian Empire. The available documentation illustrates how, during this period of intolerance and persecutions, legislation was used as one of the instruments of persecution in the comprehensive effort to repress the Samaritans. For Justinian's regime, as for other regimes throughout history, religion and the law served as, among other things, a convenient means of covering socio-economic conflicts.[61] This would be a harsh and difficult inheritance for the Samaritans to bear as they passed from the Roman-Byzantine period and entered the Middle Ages.[62]

the prohibition of new synagogues with that of the acquisition of church property by Jews in that Novella of 545 was not merely coincidental. In at least one case, we are told, a fanatical Christian monk, Sergius of Mesopotamian Amida, was long thwarted by the local clergy in his efforts to destroy the synagogue and to eliminate the Jewish community. The Jews were "settled in the territory of the Church of Amida", John of Ephesus reports, "and used to pay many contributions to the members of the Church; out of the desire for the abundance of their gold all the members of the Church became their supporters, threatening the blessed Sergius and saying, 'This man wishes to destroy the property of the Church'. *Cf.* his *Lives of the Eastern Saints*, v. ed. and trans. by E.W. Brooks, vol. I, p. 70ff." pp. 231, footnote no. 6, "... The undated edict, 1.5.17 (II, 56), especially, not only ordered all Samaritan destroyed, but also disqualified these sectarians from testimony in courts even in their own affairs, and removed from them all rights of testamentary disposition".

61 See S. Puliatti, *Ricerche, II, supra* n. 4, at 237ff.

62 See P. Brown, *The World of Late Antiquity, from Marcus Aurelius to Muhammad* (London, 1971) 172ff.

Abbreviations: C.I.C. - *Corpus Iuris Civilis;* C.Th. - *Codex Theodosianus* (Theodosian Code of Theodosius II, 438 C.E.); C.J. - *Codex Justinianus* (Justinian Code, the second edition of Justinian's Code, *Codex repetitae praelectionis*, of 534); N.J. - *Novellae Justiniani* (New constitutions of the Emperor Justinian).

XII

JEWISH AND ROMAN JURISDICTION*

1. *Introduction*

In this chapter we shall discuss the extent to which the Roman authorities (who conquered all the Mediterranean lands, including Palestine — known to the Jews as *Erets Yisrael*, 'the Land of Israel') permitted the Jews to keep their own civil law as the binding law in their relations amongst themselves. From the perspective of the Roman sources, it is a question of jurisdiction.[1]

The problem of jurisdiction is a particularly complex one; its difficulties vary according to the different sources and the different periods. There is a distinction between the problems of civil jurisdiction — which deals with private law (e.g., family law, contract law or property law) — and those of public jurisdiction which includes criminal law. Moreover, what were the characteristics of the court which exercised jurisdiction over Jews in civil and criminal matters? Was it a Jewish court or a Roman court? Did Jewish courts and Roman courts have any kind of contact with one another? According to which legal system were the Jews judged? Other questions concerning this issue emerge: did Roman law give the Jews the right to hold their own courts with legal authority to judge matters between Jews? Could these Jewish courts give judgments which would be recognized by the Roman Government as judgments that could turn into a *res iudicata*, so that these cases would not be brought again before a Roman court? Were the judgments of the Jewish courts executable and who was to implement

* This study is dedicated to the blessed memory of the great Talmudist, Scholar, Teacher and Friend, Professor Ephraim Urbach ז"ל with gratitude and love.

them — the Jewish authorities or the Roman authorities?

Closely implicated in these questions is the issue of citizenship. What was the civil status of the Jews under Roman rule? Did they continue to have a recognized citizenship, or was their status so reduced that they no longer enjoyed any civil rights? If the answer to this latter question is affirmative, it will have a major impact on the question of jurisdiction, because it is not possible that people with low civil status will enjoy high jurisdictional status and other privileges. Our treatment of each period therefore commences with some remarks on *status civitatis.*

The problem of civil status arises also in respect of Diaspora Jews. In many places these Jews received political rights locally; in others they acquired Roman citizenship. Any serious discussion of this subject must draw distinctions according to the various provinces and the different periods.

Here, we shall discuss principally those questions which relate specifically to Jewish civil jurisdiction[2] in Palestine, reviewing the evidence for each major period in turn (sections 2-5); we then turn to the Diaspora (section 6), and conclude with some questions concerning family law (section 7).

2. *Jewish Jurisdiction in Palestine until the End of the First Jewish War (63 B.C.E.-70 C.E.)*

Those Jews who had local citizenship in Palestine were considered by Roman law as *peregrini* in consequence of treaties between Judaea and Rome. As far as Greek cities were concerned, Jews were aliens of Jewish nationality. They could become either 'aliens without the right of local residence' (ξένοι) or, the more common case 'aliens with the right of domicile' (*incolae*).[3] In neither case, however, could they obtain the right of citizenship.

Furthermore, a large number of Jews enjoyed some local civic rights.[4] Those possessing Greek citizenship were exempt from having to worship the local gods, a circumstance which often led to riots on the part of the local population. There were in addition Jews who were Roman citizens (*cives Romani*). Such were either slaves freed by a master who was himself a Roman citizen (by *manumissio*), or freemen who had won Roman citizenship as a grant from the Government. Finally, there were Jewish slaves (*servi*).

We have many sources — both documents and the Palestinian rabbinic sources — which show that Jews regularly used to arrange their own affairs before Jewish judges. But was this practice accepted legally?

At the beginning of the occupation, Rome was well aware of how highly the Jews of Palestine valued their traditions (the customs of the fathers), which were, above all, of religious importance. Rome had no desire to involve itself in internal institutions, other than the determination of who would be responsible to Rome for providing internal order. More extreme intervention would have brought negative reactions and could, they realized, lead to a revolt. Thus Pompey (who in 63 B.C.E. overthrew the Hasmonean kingdom and established a new order in Palestine[5]) left Judea under the rule of Hyrcanus II (the last member of the Hasmonean dynasty), as Ethnarch (the highest Jewish official in Palestine) and High Priest;[6] after the difficult governorship of Gabinius, Julius Caesar restored Hyrcanus II to his position (47 B.C.E.). His duties were primarily religious, and related to the Temple in Jerusalem. Hyrcanus was subordinated to the supervision of the Roman ruler of Syria. What is worthy of note is that Hyrcanus retained the right to administer justice to the nation on an internal basis according to the 'customs of the fathers';[7] the principle of judicial autonomy was thus preserved.[8]

In general, as far as civil law goes, King Herod (37-4 B.C.E.) too did not interfere overtly by changing the 'laws of the fathers'. Local courts continued to function in accordance with traditional norms.[9] Clearly the internal conflicts between classes and sects, particularly between Sadducees and Pharisees, bear no connection at all to the question of whether Rome allowed autonomy of civil justice to remain, as it apparently did.

In the year 6 C.E., Judaea became a Roman *provincia*,[10] and the Roman ruler became the highest authority in both criminal and civil law. The same rules which were applied in other countries subordinated and attached to the Roman Empire by alliance, appear to have applied also in Palestine. Jewish courts (i.e. 'local courts') had the authority to execute judgments in civil cases involving Jews (*iudaei*), whether they were cases of conflicts among Jews or cases involving Jews and non-Jews. However, a case involving a Roman citizen could be brought before a Roman magistrate.

One of the responsibilities of the Jewish court was the appointment of guardians, at least when the matter concerned a non-Roman citizen. In the case of Roman citizens, members of the family were automatically appointed, in the absence of guardians appointed by will. Roman law required both children under 14 and women to have their dealings, including litigation, authorized by guardians. The Jewish practice may have been prompted by the needs of Jews who were non-citizens to seek access to Roman courts in property matters (as in the case of Babatha, ssee p.146 below). The very term for guardian, *apotropos*, suggests a Hellenistic source for the institution in Jewish law.

Alongside the courts, it seems that archives existed in Greek towns (i.e. the towns with a longstanding population of Hellenistic origin, such as Caesarea, Gaza and Scytopolis[11]) and other places; these archives helped in confirming and validating various kinds of legal document.

Roman provincial governors also had in theory authority to involve themselves in civil judgments; however, following the custom of Rome, they preferred, in this period, not to intervene. There was, however, no universal practice in such matters throughout the Empire.[12] Yet even after Judea became a Roman *provincia*, the governor maintained the principle of leaving civil justice to the local Jewish institutions. Rome defined autonomy as the right to live according to independent laws (*suae leges*), 'autonomy in the broad sense of independent civil justice'.[13]

I believe that Judaea was among those states that had their own law restored to them — *leges suas reddere*.[14] The residents had the status of foreigners enjoying their own law (*peregrini qui suis legibus utuntur*), and thus living 'in accordance with local law' (*secundum propriae civitatis iura*). Thus it is possible to establish that Jewish courts in Palestine were able to judge conflicts between Jews, just as in other places conflicts between local residents were decided by local courts or by *iudex peregrinus.*

As for criminal law, we cannot be certain as to the limits which Rome placed on the competence of Jewish courts to enjoy jurisdictional autonomy. The issue is discussed in an earlier chapter, in the context of the trial of Jesus (ch.2, p.38, above). One special problem relates to the capital punishment of a stranger who entered the Temple of Jerusalem. Jean Juster believed that the Sanhedrin had the authority, with the backing of the Roman law, to execute every stranger (even if he were a Roman citizen) who had entered the forbidden grounds of the Temple. His belief was based on a dubious paragraph in Josephus' *War*, 6,2,4, which stands in contradiction to other sources. There is no other source, either Jewish or Roman, that can verify the assumption that the Roman administration recognized the Sanhedrin's power to pronounce death verdicts on Roman citizens. In fact, the 'capital punishment' here may well be extra-judicial, a form of popular justice (or self-help) rather than an act of government or the judicial system.[15]

3. *Between the Two Jewish Revolts (70-135 C.E.)*

A. Citizenship

According to the theory of Mommsen,[16] after the war which ended in the destruction of their State in 70 C.E., all the Jews in the Empire lost the autonomy they had formerly enjoyed. Those who had remained free became *peregrini dediticii*:[17] According to Mommsen Judaism was no longer the national cult of the Jewish people. It became a 'tolerated cult', a *religio licita*. Juster vehemently rejects this view. In his opinion, the war which destroyed the Jewish State had no effect on the *status civitatis* of the Jews in the Empire. They continued to be regarded as a people (*natio*) even after 70 C.E., and in a certain sense they enjoyed a number of privileges. This was due to the respect for religion which the Romans had acquired and to the close link which existed between the Jewish religion and the Jewish Law.[18] Juster's criticism of Mommsen's theory opened the door for recent studies, which proved that the legal status of the Jews was much more diversified, not only in different places but also at different periods; therefore, it would be wrong to generalize. In particular with regard to the Jewish community in Palestine, one must make distinctions according to the different types of relationship which could exist with Rome. In theory, conquered communities could be deprived of all civil rights, being relegated to the status of *dediticiae*. This does not appear to have occurred in Palestine;[19] rather, it appears that here as elsewhere there is 'decisive proof that local laws were applied in the Roman provinces for regulating the relations between private persons' (Volterra).[20]

B. Roman Courts

i. The application of Jewish Law by Roman courts in Palestine (70-132 C.E.)

Each province had its own special law (*lex provinciae*); we do not however have any evidence concerning the special law of Syria-Palestine. Therefore, we must try to draw a picture of the situation from what evidence we do have, which are rabbinic sources on the one hand, and Roman sources from other provinces on the other hand.

In civil cases involving Jews only,[21] the Jewish courts had authority to pass judgments, but this authority was no longer exclusive, as it had been before the War; it was concurrent with the authority of Roman courts. But even these Roman courts might apply Jewish Law, as the Jewish sources themselves indicate. Rabbi Eleazar ben Azariah (end of the first century and one of the greatest Sages of Yavneh), reports:[22]

> Now suppose the gentile courts judge according to the laws of Israel. I might

> understand that their decisions are valid. But Scripture says: 'And these are the ordinances which thou shalt set before them.' You may judge their cases but they are not to judge your cases.

On the basis of this interpretation of 'And these are the ordinances which thou shalt set before them' (*Ex.* 21:1), the Rabbis argued (*ibid.*):

> A bill of divorce given by force, if by Israelitish authority, is valid, but if by gentile authority, it is not valid. It is, however, valid if the Gentiles merely bind the husband over and say to him: 'Do as the Israelites tell thee'.

Thus we understand from Rabbi Eleazar's words that non-Jews (i.e. Roman courts) were indeed allowed to judge Jews. According to which law did the Roman courts judge the Jews? The answer to this question can also be found in Rabbi Eleazar ben Azariah's words: generally they had to pass judgments according to the local law, i.e. in this case the national laws of the Jews (*iudaei*): 'The non-Jews passed judgments according to the laws of Israel'.

There is a great importance in Rabbi Eleazar's words, since we know that at a certain period he served as Patriarch (*Nasi*) instead of Rabban Gamliel (after the latter's temporary expulsion): the Patriarch, as Head of the Sanhedrin (see pp.44f., 127ff., above) was the Jewish leader of *Eretz Yisrael*, and was regarded by the Diaspora Jews as the leader of all Jewry, a sort of a national leader. According to the Jerusalem Talmud, Rabbi Eleazar was appointed President of the Court (*Av Bet Din*) after the return of Rabban Gamliel to his previous position of Patriarch; moreover, Rabbi Eleazar was in Rome with the delegation of Rabbis from Yavneh.[23]

ii. The application of Roman Law to Romans and non-Romans in Roman courts: the case of Babatha

It is clear that in Palestine, as in other provinces, the Roman governor had judicial authority concurrent with that of the local courts. The authority of justice (*iurisdictio*)[24] — both civil justice[25] and criminal justice — was among his most important responsibilities. He exercized this authority in the courts that were established in various areas, the *conventus*. The governor judged civil cases primarily between Roman citizens, with authority similar to that of the *praetor urbanus* at Rome. He upheld the norms of provincial decrees (*edicta*) and the norms established by the law of the province (*lex provinciae*). We must not forget that at this time there were many Roman citizens in Palestine. They were members of the provincial government, soldiers, newly created Roman citizens (such as Herod's family), former slaves who were freed by Roman masters,[26] or non-Jewish citizens living in Palestine. The Roman Judge had to judge cases involving Roman citizens, at least when the citizens were the defendants.

Recently, in 'the Cave of Letters' at Ein Gedi (near the Dead Sea) the Archive of Babatha, the daughter of Simon, was discovered. It includes documents of great interest.[27] Babatha, who lived in Maoza (in the recently established province of Arabia [Petraea]) preserved documents from the period between 93-94 and 132 C.E.;[28] three of the papyri discovered, from 124-125, directly concern our problem: they deal, for example, with her dispute with the guardians of her orphan son, Yeshua Ben Yeshua. Though Babatha does *not* appear to have had Roman citizenship, she sues in the court of the Roman governor at Petra. Some deeds of gift in the archive, designed to advance the financial interests of daughters and wives, appear to presuppose a law of succession in some respects different from that of Jewish law.[29] There is also evidence of Jews registering their ownership of land in Greek declarations which include oaths by the Roman Emperor.[30]

One of the Greek texts is a translation of the praetor's formula reported in Gaius' *Institutes*, IV.7.[31] A non-Roman citizen was thus submitting to a Roman jurisdiction applying Roman law, and the Roman jurisdiction was available to such a non-citizen. But in order to get a more balanced picture it should be remembered that the period concerned was a particularly hard one (between the revolt which had just ended in 117 and the revolt which was about to occur in 132). It should also be taken into account that Babatha was a widow who wanted to secure her position and that of her son, and who wanted her document to be recognized throughout the land, e.g. in the new province of Arabia. I would not therefore derive from this any general conclusion regarding the extent of exercise of Roman jurisdiction over Jews, although the phenomenon of the use of Roman, or Roman-Hellenistic, Law in different aspects of Jewish life could not have been marginal. The Jews were well aware of all the dangers to Jewish Law concealed in the power of the laws of the conquerors.

C. Jewish Courts

i. Jewish courts in Palestine before Bar Kochba's revolt, 132 C.E.

We have noted already the comments of Rabbi Eleazar on the possibility of Roman application of Jewish Law (pp.145f., above). The comment indicates the possibility that a Jew would not wish to be judged according to a completely unfamiliar law (Roman Law), but might agree to be judged in a

Roman court if it were to pass judgments according to the 'Jewish Law'. On account of this potential danger to the integrity of the Jewish system, Rabbi Eleazar forbids Jews to have recourse to Roman courts. It must follow that in this period — between the First Jewish Revolt and that of Bar Kochba's— the Jews of Palestine did have (concurrent) juridical autonomy.

Other Rabbinic sources lead to similar conclusions. For example, *B. Gitt.* 88b:[32]

> Rabbi Tarfon used to say: in any place when you find Heathen law courts (*Agoraiot*), even though their law is the same as the Israelites', you must not resort to them ...

Attention should be paid to the word *Agoraiot*: the *agora* was the place where public meetings and trials took place, but here the Greek term is the translation of the Latin term *conventus*, and refers to public meetings in provinces for the purpose of passing judgments.

Recent research on the Roman provinces helps us to understand better the Sages' fears. In the provinces there was a juridical system which was divided into three: first, there was the Roman Law, the one which was implemented in Rome, and which was also applied to Roman citizens in the provinces; second, there was the local law, the national law which existed in the area prior to the Roman occupation (including Jewish Law, Greek Law and Egyptian Law); third, there was the Provincial Law — in reality the local law, but subject to such changes as the rulers wished to introduce as a part of the local law according to the Roman spirit. This triple juridical system meant that judgment varied from place to place. Thus, even where Roman courts purported to apply 'local' (here, Jewish) law (pp.145f., above), it would be in the sense of 'Provincial Law', and thus subject to modification in the light of Roman directives and principles.

Greek writers from the Flavian period such as Dio Chrysostomus (from Bytinia) and Plutarch also considered legal autonomy as a serious problem.[33] These writers emphasize the subordination of the Greek magistrate to the Roman magistrate. They also stress the importance of bringing their cases before local judges (i.e. in this case Greek judges) and not before the Roman proconsul. If we take into account the fact that these sentiments were uttered by writers who thought that the cultures of Greek and Rome could coexist, we will be able to understand better the Jewish Sages' position on this matter. It was in the very procedure which apparently made Jewish Law applicable in Roman courts that the Sages of Palestine foresaw the greatest danger to the independence of the Jewish Law.

The Sages of Israel understood that the common people could have innocently thought that they were presented with a *Torah* judgment in Roman courts too, because that could have been the way matters appeared. But they realized that *Torah* judgment could not possibly remain autonomous if it was applied by non-Jewish judges and mixed with other laws which could have appeared as 'more human' or more correct in the view of Roman judges. The integrity of Jewish Law depended not merely on its being applied as law, but also on its being applied by its own justices.

Indeed, just as we hear of a Roman judge in Egypt who negated the local law because it appeared 'inhuman' to him,[34] so too do we hear in *Erets Yisrael* of delegations that came from Rome to Yavneh in order to check the laws of the Jews. The Romans thus sought to control local legislation in addition to the local courts. They noted with disapproval the existence of a number of laws which discriminated against foreigners in matters concerning tortious responsibility for animals, although it seems that this inspection never brought practical results.[35]

The presence of Roman rule was already profoundly felt in Palestine and several ways of opposing it were considered, but the Sages and the Patriarch could not always agree on which to choose. The Patriarch wished to strengthen his institution in order to create a spiritual and political centre which could guide the people both in domestic and in foreign affairs. 'The Patriarchate institution saw itself,' writes Urbach, 'as an institution which was to organize the jurisdiction in towns and provinces and to create an attachment between the towns and the centre.'[36] The story of Rabban Gamliel, who went 'to ask permission from the *hegemon* of Syria',[37] may be understood against this background. Hence, too, the strictness of the rule the Patriarch established, in his relations with the Sages, which allowed him to make nominations of judges on his own, and furthermore to prevent courts from making such nominations unless they had his permission.

In this period there were clearly elements in the community who were not satisfied with the system of Jewish jurisdiction. They used to approach the authorities and complain about certain legal proceedings, as in the case of the denunciation of the 'too simple judgment' of Rabbi Bana'a,[38] but the authorities allowed him to carry on passing judgments. It is obvious that the judges of Israel had to pass fair judgments and to do their jobs the best way they could; they not only had to consider the amount of evidence, but also had to make sure that no one would suspect them of light-mindedness or judging for reward. We can now understand Yossi Ben-Elisha's words: 'If you saw a generation which suffered great distress, go and check the cause for it with the judges of Israel.'[39]

ii. Jew and gentile before a Jewish court

A particular problem was that of a civil judgment involving a non-Jew before a Jewish court. A passage reported in the Babylonian *Talmud* introduces us to the problem:[40]

> Our Rabbis taught: The Government of Rome had long ago sent two commissioners to the Sages of Israel with a request to teach them the Torah. It was accordingly read to them once, twice and thrice. Before taking leave they made the following remark: We have gone carefully through your Torah, and found it correct ['*ve'emet hu*'] with the exception of this point, viz. your saying that if an ox of an Israelite gores an ox of a Canaanite there is no liability, whereas if the ox of a Canaanite gores the ox of an Israelite, whether *Tam* [uncertified as dangerous] or *Mu'ad* [certified as dangerous], compensation has to be paid in full ... We will, however, not report [*modi'im*] this matter to the Government.

The problem is examined also in another passage from the tannaitic period:[41]

> Listen to your brothers: This was the practice of R. Ishmael: when a Jew and a Gentile came to him for judgment, if it was according to the laws of Israel, he would justify the Jew, and if it was according to the laws of the heathen, he would justify the Jew. He said: What is it to me, did not the Torah say, Listen to your brothers? R. Simon b. Gamliel said — it is not so — if they came to be judged according to the laws of Israel, he judged according to the laws of Israel; if according to the laws of the heathen, he judged according to heathen law.[42]

I think that for a better understanding of this problem we have to compare the situation with the principles of Roman Law in other provinces. In a case of judgment between a local resident and a Roman citizen it would seem that the *lex Rupilia* applied. This law from 111 B.C.E. required that the judge and the defendant be of the same nationality, and that the law in effect be that of the plaintiff.[43] A letter from Octavius to Rhosos apparently refers to this principle: in it citizenship is granted to Seleucus and his relatives along with the right to choose the manner of justice should he be a defendant; however, as a plaintiff he would be required to follow the local law.[44] Thus, the principle of choosing the better law for the citizen was not strange to Roman Law either!

4. *Palestine from Bar Kochba's Revolt (135 C.E.) to the Christianization of the Empire*

The abolition of Jewish jurisdiction in Palestine may be regarded as one of the many terrible consequences of the Bar Kochba revolt.[45] Roman authorities probably continued to deny recognition of rabbinic jurisdiction for years after the end of the revolt. This may explain the dark picture painted by some contemporary scholars.[46] But Roman policy changed soon after, during the second half of the second century, at the end of the Antoninian dynasty and the beginning of the Severian dynasty (second half of the second cent C.E.), when the Emperor and the Patriarch reached a *modus vivendi* which included, *inter alia*, the permission for Jews to pass judgments according to their own laws. This period was blessed by the exceptional character of Rabbi Judah the Patriarch, the compiler of the *Mishnah*. The bitter experience of severe persecution in the Hadrianic period and the desire of several Sages not to be totally subordinated to the Patriarch, prompted the Sages to decide to develop the institution of arbitration and compromise, an institution which was recognized by Roman law too.

A major change in citizenship occurred in the middle of this period, close to the time of the compilation of the *Mishnah*. In the year 212 C.E. the *Constitutio Antoniniana* of the Emperor Antoninus Caracalla granted Roman citizenship to all inhabitants of the Empire by the *Constitutio Antoniniana de civitate*.[47] A question to which no agreed solution has yet been reached is whether the Jews — now Roman citizens — also retained citizenship of the political communities to which they had previously belonged? Scholars are divided on this issue. Luzzatto and Arangio-Ruiz maintain that there is no basis in the sources for 'dual citizenship'. They claim that foreigners, after receiving Roman citizenship, remained under the jurisdiction of their local law, under the principle of 'the personality of the laws'. Local officeholders, in practice, applied both Roman law and local law to such citizens: this practice led to the formation of 'Vulgar Law', a composite legal system which ultimately came to be regarded as normative Roman Law.

It seems that this new political reality did not have a major impact on the status of Jewish Law, since the basis of adherence to Jewish Law had always been national-religious, rather than a matter of citizenship. Nevertheless, at a time when the Roman Empire was striving for centralization, it is clear that there was always a danger that the autonomy of a local legal system could be cancelled.

Let us sum up the situation with the words of Juster:

> After the fall of Jerusalem, as before it, the Jews brought their law suits not only before Jewish judges — who might possibly be considered as arbitrators — but also before true Jewish courts empowered to dispense justice in accordance with Jewish law, and they were authorized by the Romans to do so. That is to say, a Jewish court of law was constituted [as a

> recognized tribunal]; this court then had authority over the defendant; it could summon and compel him to appear before it or convict him by default, subsequently carrying out the sentence by whatever means it had. The Roman government recognized that the verdict was founded on legitimate judicial authority. Nevertheless, as in other parts of the Empire, it seems that Roman rule provided some kind of supervision over the moral standards and professional competence of the Jewish Judges.[48]

With regard to the period in which the Jewish jurisdictional autonomy was still recognized, the following question must be asked: who exercised this jurisdiction which was recognized by the Roman Government? It is possible that we may be able to find the answer to this question in a rescript by Diocletian (Emperor from 284-305 C.E.) which was included in Justinian's Code (C.3.13.3). The Emperor's answer was sent to one Iuda[49] — the only time that this name appears in Roman legal sources. He says:

> The agreement of the private [people] (*privatorum consensus*) cannot appoint as a judge a person who does not hold the position of Head of a court, and whatever judgment he makes, it will not have the effect of a court judgment (*res iudicata*).

I believe that this rescript was composed as Diocletian's response to the Patriarch regarding the Patriarch's conflict with the Rabbis regarding the power of judicial ordination. I interpret the rescript as a reaffirmation by Diocletian to the Patriarch that the Rabbis hold the status of *privati*, that though they play an important role in the public life of the Jewish people, they have no recognized standing in Roman Public Law.[50] Only the Patriarch, recognized as an institution by Roman Public Law, may appoint Judges.

From the historical perspective, the meaning of the rescript would be as follows: Roman Law does not recognize a judge appointed by private individuals (note the distinction between *privati*, private individuals, and *partes*, parties to a dispute). To be a judge, that person must stand at the head of a court of law. For that purpose a judge must be appointed by the competent authority — in our case, the Patriarch, who, after the destruction of the Temple and the loss of Judean political independence, assumed ever-increasing importance as a political leader, until he was eventually recognized as such by the Roman administration. Moreover, whenever the parties turned to judges appointed only by the Rabbis (private individuals by the Roman Law), the decisions of these judges would not have been recognized in Roman Law as *res iudicata* (a judgment passed by a judge). This reality represented a threat to the integrity and independence of Jewish Law, since all judicial appointments would be in the hands of an official himself requiring the recognition of the Roman power.

Only after the Roman Emperor had explained the position of Roman Law was a compromise reached between the Patriarch and the Sages, namely that judges ought to be appointed with the agreement of both the Patriarch and the Rabbis. An echo of these disputes and of the subsequent agreement can be found in a passage of the Palestinian *Talmud, Sanhedrin* 1, 4(5), 19a:

> Rabbi Abba said: At first everyone used to ordain his own students like Rabban Yoḥanan ben Zakkai (who) ordained R. Eliezer and R. Joshua, and R. Joshua (who ordained) Rabbi Akiva, and Rabbi Akiva (who ordained) Rabbi Meir and R. Simeon. He (R. Akiva) said: Let R. Meir sit first. R. Simeon became distraught. Said R. Akiva to him: Enough — I and your creator recognize your worth. They returned to their original practice of honouring the Patriarchate (granting honour to this house, i.e. Patriarchate). They said: A court which ordains against the will of the Patriarch — its ordination is invalid. A Patriarch who ordains against the will of the court — his ordination is valid. Once again they changed their position and laid down that a court should not ordain against the will of the Patriarch and that the Patriarch should only ordain in accordance with the will of the court.

In any event, the decisions of the Sages accepted by the parties were recognized by the Roman authorities as valid arbitrations.

5. *The Christian Period (313-565)*

The Christian Emperors treated the Jews harshly in matters of political and civic status, but the Jews still continued to be *cives Romani*: *Iudaei Romano et communi iure viventes,* as the fifth century Theodosian Code, 2.1.10, put it. However, there was a real change in jurisdiction: with the promulgation of Arcadius' and Honorius' famous Constitution of 398, Jewish jurisdictional autonomy was abolished and the recognition of its courts was withdrawn. The constitution reported in the Theodosian Code (*C.Th.* 2,1,10) thus:

> The same Augustuses to Eutychianus, Praetorian Perfect. Jews who live under the Roman and common law shall approach the courts in the customary manner in those cases which concern not so much their superstition as their forum, the statutes and the law; and they shall bring and defend all actions according to Roman law; in fine, they shall be subject to Our laws. Certainly, in the case of civil suits only, if any Jews should suppose that, by a mutual promise to abide by the decision in accordance with the agreement of both parties, they should litigate before Jews or Patriarchs as though before arbitrators, they shall not be prohibited by public law from choosing the judgment of such men. The judges of the provinces shall execute their

> sentences as if such arbitrators had been assigned by a judge's decision. — Given on the third day before the nones of February at Constantinople in the year of the fourth consulship of Honorius Augustus and the consulship of the most Noble Eutychianus. — 3 February, 398. (Pharr's translation)

As we can see, in this Constitution jurisdictional distinctions were made relating to subject-matter: purely religious matters remained in the authority of the Jewish (rabbinic) courts alone; criminal cases were to be dealt with in Roman courts alone; civil matters were also passed on to Roman courts, but the litigants — through a mutual agreement (*compromissum*) — were permitted to bring their cases before rabbinic courts acting as arbitrators. Nevertheless, as far as the Roman administration was concerned, Jewish jurisdictional autonomy ceased to exist. Jewish jurisdiction had changed its status from that of a recognized jurisdiction in competition with Roman jurisdiction, to that of arbitration, whose existence was now dependent upon the good will of the parties to settle their disputes.

Even the autonomy of the rabbinic courts in religious matters ceased to exist in the days of Justinian (early sixth cent C.E.), — who changed the meaning of the constitution by the simple expedient of omitting the word *non* (Justinian Code 1,9,8, cf. also Novella 146 of Justinian, 553 C.E.). Nevertheless, even during the Christian period the Jews retained the right to keep the Shabbat and not to be judged on that day (*C.Th.* 2.8.26), a right that was confirmed also by Justinian (Justinian Code 1.9.13).

6. *The Diaspora*

A. Egypt and Other Provinces

The information we have from other provinces helps us to confirm that Palestine (pp.145ff., above) was not exceptional in having local law applied by Roman officials. We have protocols of several trials which took place in the Roman province of Egypt, preserved in Greco-Egyptian papyri. In these trials, the Roman official (*procurator*) refers to *Nomos ton Aiguptíon* (literally, the custom of the Egyptians[51]); in his judicial role he was assisted by the *Nomikoi* (*iurisprudentes*) who were, it seems, experts in local laws (mainly unwritten laws).[52] In Egypt 'local law' means, of course, Greek and Egyptian Law. According to Lieberman, Moses appeared as *Nomike* in some Jewish and Samaritan sources, and this proves that such a role (i.e. an expert on local law) existed in Palestine too (where, of course, the expert had to be familiar with Jewish Law).[53]

From the exchange of letters between the Roman writer Pliny, who was Governor of the Roman Province of Bitynia, and the Emperor Trajan, we learn much about the normal procedure in another province and in Roman provinces in general.[54] From them, it appears that in the provinces, Roman magistrates and local officers did not apply the Roman Law (i.e. the law valid in Rome and Italy) to private individuals; they applied only the local laws (those which existed before the Roman occupation) of that province, with such specific changes as were made for each province by governors or Emperors.

B. Jewish Jurisdiction in the Diaspora

The problem of Jewish jurisdiction was common also in the Diaspora. Some scholars have maintained that a distinction should be drawn between the Eastern part of the Empire, where autonomy of Jewish jurisdiction did exist, and the Western part, where it did not. Others dispute this. In my view, each place in the Empire ought to be thoroughly examined independently. Nevertheless, there seems to be an agreement on one fact: many Jews continued to bring their cases before local Jewish judges. It is also clear that *C.Th.* 2.1.10 (pp.153f., above) refers also to the Jews of the Diaspora, and thus that from 398 the Jews had to bring their cases before Roman courts — unless they agreed that their cases be brought before a rabbinic court recognized by the Roman authorities as an arbitration institution.[55]

Among the privileges which the Jews enjoyed during the Christian period was the right not to appear in court on Shabbat, Shabbat Eve or holidays; even Justinian did not deny the Jews this privilege. However, it was in the days of Justinian that the position of the Jews worsened: while it was forbidden for a Jew to testify *against* an Orthodox Christian, a Jew's testimony would count if he testified in *favour* of a Christian. There was discrimination against Jewish testimony in most cases — apart from cases in which he testified in favour of the Government.[56]

7. *Some Questions Concerning Family Law*

Many questions arise concerning the application of family law by the Jews under the Roman Empire.[57] We shall discuss a few relating to marriage and divorce.

(1) There is the question of the validity of marriages between Jews of a

different civil status (*status civitatis*): does legal competence for marriage (*connubium*) exist between them? It seems that a positive answer would have been given according to Roman Law. Take, for example, a Jew from Palestine who has the status of *peregrinus* (a foreigner, a citizen of a State other than Rome) who wants to marry a Jew from Rome who has the status of Roman citizen (*civis romana*): it is clear that this kind of marriage is permitted according to Jewish Law, but I believe that the man has the competence to marry the woman legally according to Roman Law too.

(2) Are Jews allowed to be married to two or more wives though Roman Law forbids and punishes bigamy? It appears that originally the Roman authorities tolerated Jewish polygamy *de facto*, especially in Palestine, but from 393 C.E. it was explicitly forbidden.[58]

(3) What authority does a father who is a Jewish Roman citizen have over his sons: does he enjoy the father's authority (*patria potestas*) as a Roman father or must he go by Jewish Law? I believe that in cases of *iustum matrimonium*, a father may exercise his Roman *patria potestas*. Generally, in Roman Law a father had a dominant position in his family, but in cases of mixed marriages (i.e. a marriage between a Jew and a Christian), the Christian Empire always preferred the Christian parent, despite the *patria potestas* rules.

(4) In inheritance matters there was special legislation in the days of Constantine which maintained the right of a Jew who was converted to Christianity to succeed his Jewish parents, even against their will (the Christian faith thus being accorded priority over general rules of freedom of testation); additionally, a law was passed guaranteeing the freedom of worship of Christian slaves inherited by Jews.

(5) As for divorce, we know that in the period of classical Roman Law (first-third centuries C.E.) both Roman and Jewish Law permitted divorce; there existed, however, numerous differences between them, both substantive and formal. In the first place, in Jewish Law, as opposed to Roman Law, the woman could not renounce her husband directly: divorce remained a unilateral act, even if one accords importance to the fact that the *geṭ* (*libellus repudii*) had to be accepted by the woman. In some specific cases the wife could have recourse to a Jewish tribunal for a decision. However, such a decision could not of itself dissolve the marriage bond. That could have been done only by pressure on the husband to consent personally to a divorce; if he declined, the

Roman authorities could exert pressure to convince him to grant the divorce. *M. Gitt.* 9:8 states the rule:

> A bill of divorce given under compulsion is valid if it is ordered by an Israelitish court, but if by a gentile court it is invalid; if the gentiles beat a man and say to him: 'Do what the Israelites bid thee', it is valid.

The text demonstrates clearly that in this period the Roman Government recognized the decisions of Jewish tribunals in matters of personal status and was ready to utilise enforcement mechanisms in order to give practical effect to such decisions. This assumes that the wife has approached a Jewish court first; perhaps 'if by a gentile court' refers to a woman who approaches the Roman court directly (Babatha-like!, but in a different case). The situation is further clarified in a passage of the Palestine *Talmud* which follows the above *Mishnah* passage:

> R. Yirmiyah says in the name of Rav: A divorce given by a Jew under the compulsion of gentiles is invalid. This refers to the case where the husband tells the wife: I do not wish to give you maintenance. R. Ḥiyyah taught: But if the gentiles issued their ruling in accordance with Jewish practice, it is valid even if the husband tells the wife: I do not wish to give you maintenance. R. Jose says: the *mishnah* says so explicitly: the gentiles beat him and say to him 'Do what the Israelites tell you to do.' R. Ḥiyyah bar Ashi said in the name of Isi: In the case of one who says: I do not wish to give you maintenance, we compel him to give a divorce.

From these texts it appears that in the case of two Jewish *peregrini* in *Erets Yisrael* and, almost certainly, in other parts of the Empire, Jewish Law was applied, whatever tribunal the parties had recourse to, even if Roman Law ignored the possibility of decisions which obliged the husband to divorce; for its part, Jewish Law recognized only the decisions of Jewish tribunals, even if it was admitted that there could be external coercion to ensure their application.

Coming now to examine the situation of those Jews who were also Roman citizens, based on some passages of Josephus (*Vita*, 75, 414-15), we can assert that if the parties preferred to rely on their status as Roman citizens, they could do so, and in that case the divorce would be valid only according to Roman Law and not Jewish Law; it is clear therefore that in Roman Law Jewish Roman women could have validly divorced their husbands — even against the will of the latter. Nonetheless, if the spouses preferred to conduct themselves according to Jewish Law, then whenever the divorce was desired either by both parties or by the husband alone, there ought to have been no difficulty in Roman Law. Very likely, in order to avoid difficulties of interpretation, Jewish spouses would have preferred to have both a 'Jewish' and a 'Roman' divorce and thus satisfy the rather rigid Jewish norms, as well as the Roman ones.[59]

A more complicated case arises with a *iustum matrimonium* (marriage valid according to Roman civil law) in which the two spouses were Roman Jews or in which the husband was Roman and the wife a foreigner. What if, in such a case, it was the wife who desired a divorce? In such cases the woman could have divorced freely according to Roman Law, but it is difficult to assume that the Roman authorities would collaborate with a Jewish tribunal which decided that the husband must concede the divorce according to Jewish rules. In cases of a Roman woman married to a foreigner, one may assume that the Roman authorities would have assisted the woman seeking divorce;[60] this would be consistent with the Roman principle of freedom of marriage and divorce. The situation changed, probably during the Christian period.

In general, we may conclude that Jewish private law remained in effect for the Jews in the Roman Empire, even after they were granted Roman citizenship. Roman Law was willing to tolerate a number of exceptions in the field of marriage and divorce. In this field too the important limitations appeared only when Christianity became the recognized and preferred religion, and especially in the days of Justinian.

8. *Bibliography*

Albeck, S., *Law Courts in Talmudic Times* (Jerusalem: Bar-Ilan University Press, 1980, in Hebrew).

Alon, G., *Jews, Judaism and the Classical World* (Jerusalem: Magnes Press, 1977).

Alon, G., *The Jews in their Land in the Talmudic Age* (Jerusalem: Magnes Press, 1980-1984, 2 vols.).

Bammel, E., 'The Organisation of Palestine by Gabinius', *Journal of Jewish Studies* 12 (1961), 159-162.

Colorni, V., *Legge ebraica e leggi locali* (Milano: Giuffrè, 1945).

Daube, D., 'Jewish Law in the Hellenistic World', in *Jewish Law in Legal History and the Modern World*, ed. B.S. Jackson (Leiden: E.J. Brill, 1980), 45-60.

Elon, M., ed., *The Principles of Jewish Law* (Jerusalem: Encyclopaedia Judaica, 1975).

Friedman, M.A., *Jewish Marriage in Palestine — A Cairo Geniza Study* (Tel Aviv and New York: Jewish Theological Seminary of America, 1980, 2 vols.).

Jackson, B.S., 'On the Problem of Roman Influence on the Halakhah and Normative Self-Definition in Judaism', in E.P. Sanders, ed., *Jewish and Christian Self-Definition* (Philadelphia: Fortress Press, 1981), II, 157-203 (text), 352-79 (notes).

Jolowicz, H.F., *Historical Introduction to the Study of Roman Law* (Cambridge: Cambridge University Press, 1961).

Juster, J., *Les Juifs dans l'Empire Romain. Leur condition juridique, économique et sociale* (Paris: P. Geuthner, 1914, 2 vols.).

Katzoff, R., 'Responsa Prudentium in Roman Egypt', in *Studi in onore di Arnaldo Biscardi* (Milano: Giuffrè, 1968), II, 523-535.

Levine, L.I., *Caesarea under Roman Rule* (Leiden: E.J. Brill, 1975).

Levine, L.I., *The Rabbinic Class in Palestine during the Talmudic Period* (Jerusalem: Yad I. Ben-Zvi Institute, 1985), in Hebrew.

Lieberman, S., *Hellenism in Jewish Palestine* (New York: The Jewish Theological Seminary of America, 1962, 2nd ed.).

Lieberman, S., 'Palestine in the Third and Fourth Centuries', *Jewish Quarterly Review* 36 (1946), 329-370; 37 (1947), 31-54.

Lieberman, S., *Studies in Palestinian Talmudic Literature*, ed. D. Rosenthal (Jerusalem: Magnes Press, 1991), in Hebrew.

Lifshitz, B., 'The rules governing conflict of Laws between a Jew and a Gentile according to Maimonides', in *Mélanges M.H. Prévost* (Paris: Presses Universitaires de France, 1982), 179-89.

Rabello, A.M., 'The Lex de Templo Hierosolymitano prohibiting gentiles from entering Jerusalem's Sanctuary', *Christian News from Israel* XXI/3 (1970), 28-32; XXI/4 (1970), 28-32.

Rabello, A.M., 'On the paternal power in Roman and Jewish Law', *Diné Israel* 5 (1974), 85-153 (in Hebrew).

Rabello, A.M., 'The Responsibility of Minors in Jewish Criminal Law', *Acta Juridica* (1977), 309-36 (Essays in Honour of Ben Beinart).

Rabello, A.M., *Effetti personali della Patria Potestas* (Milano: Giuffrè, 1979).

Rabello, A.M., 'The Legal Condition of the Jews in the Roman Empire', *Aufstieg und Niedergang der Römischen Welt* (Berlin-New York: de Gruyter, 1980), II, 13, 662-762.

Rabello, A.M., 'Divorce of Jews in the Roman Empire', *The Jewish Law Annual* 4 (1981), 79-102.

Rabello, A.M., 'Les Effets personnelles de la puissance paternelle en droit hébraïque, à travers la Bible et le Talmud', in *Mélanges M.H. Prévost* (Paris: Presses Universitaires de France, 1982), 85-101).

Rabello, A.M., 'On the Relations between Diocletian and the Jews', *Journal of Jewish Studies* 35 (1984), 147-67.

Rabello, A.M., *Giustiniano, Ebrei e Samaritani alla luce delle fonti storico-letterarie, ecclesiastiche e giuridiche* (Milano: Giuffrè, 1987-88, 2 vols., Monografie del Vocabolario di Giustiniano).

Rabello, A.M., 'Herod's Domestic Court? The Judgment of Death for Herod's Sons', *The Jewish Law Annual* 10 (1991), 39-56.

Rabello, A.M., 'Civil Justice in Palestine from 63 B.C.E. to 70 C.E.', *Classical Studies in honor of David Sohlberg*, ed. R. Katzoff, J. Petroff and D. Schaps (Ramat Gan: Bar- Ilan University Press, 1996, forthcoming).

Schürer, E., *The History of the Jewish People in the Age of Jesus Christ (175 B.C.- 135* C.E.*)*, ed. G. Vermes & F. Millar (Edinburgh: T. & T. Clark, 1973), Vol. I.

Smallwood, E.M., *The Jews under Roman Rule from Pompey to Diocletian* (Leiden: E.J. Brill, 1981).

Urbach, E.E., *The Halakhah: Its Sources and Development* (Ramat-Gan: Massada, 1986).

Urbach, E.E., *The Sages, Their Concepts and Beliefs* (Jerusalem: Magnes Press, 1975).

Urbach, E.E., *The World of the Sages. Collected Studies* (Jerusalem: Magnes Press, 1988), in Hebrew.

Notes:

1 On the legal situation of the Jews in the Roman Empire and the problem of jurisdiction, see A.M. Rabello, 'The Legal Condition of the Jews in the Roman Empire', *Aufstieg und Niedergang der Römischen Welt* (Berlin-New York, de Gruyter, 1980), II, 13, 662ff.; see also A.M. Rabello, *Giustiniano, Ebrei e Samaritani alla luce delle fonti storico-letterarie, ecclesiastiche e giuridiche, Monografie del Vocabolario di Giustiniano* (Milano: Giuffrè, 1987-88), 2 vols., and see the bibliography in section 8, above; J. Juster, *Les Juifs dans l'Empire Romain. Leur condition juridique, économique et sociale* (Paris: Geuthner, 1914), II.94; B.S. Jackson, 'On the Problem of Roman Influence on the Halakhah and Normative Self-Definition in Judaism', in E.P. Sanders, ed., *Jewish and Christian Self-Definition* (London: SCM Press, 1981), vol.II, 157-203 (text), 352-79 (notes), at 159ff.

2 A. Berger, *Encyclopedic Dictionary of Roman Law* (Philadelphia, The American Philosophical Society, 1953), s.v. '*Iurisdictio*'.

3 See *Digesta* 50.16.239.2. See V. Colorni, *Legge ebraica e leggi locali* (Milano: Giuffrè, 1945), 13ff.; S. Applebaum, 'The Legal Status of the Jewish Communities in the Diaspora', in *Compendia Rerum Judaicarum ad Novum Testamentum*, ed. S. Safrai and M. Stern (Assen: van Gorcum, 1974), Vol. I, Pt.1, 455ff.

4 It is not possible to deal here with the many places which have been treated in great detail (in Asia and especially Antioch, Caesarea, Tiberias; in Africa and especially Alexandria and Cyrene). For a detailed discussion see Applebaum, *supra* n.3, at 420ff.; and E.M. Smallwood, *The Jews under Roman Rule from Pompey to Diocletian* (Leiden: E.J. Brill, 1981), *passim*.

5 This was not the first appearance of the Romans in Jewish political history. A treaty of friendship had been signed between Rome and Judah the Maccabee: *I Mac.* 8, Josephus *Ant.* xii, 414-19; see further E. Schürer, *The History of the Jewish People in the Age of Jesus Christ* (175 B.C.- A.D. 135), ed. G. Vermes & F. Millar (Edinburgh: T. & T. Clark, 1973), Vol.I, 171. Perhaps it was the memory of this that later prompted the Romans (with the notable exception of the period of Hadrian) to permit the Jews to use their own laws (*suis legibus uti*).

From a legal perspective the new order established by Pompey cannot be called a *provincia*, as did Ammianus Marcellinus, in his *Res gestae*; see M. Stern, *Greek and Latin Authors on Jews and Judaism*, (Jerusalem: Israel Academy of Sciences and Humanities, 1976-1984), Vol. II, No. 505. Rather it constituted an intermediate situation, differing both from a *provincia* and from a state in alliance with Rome. On the basis of statements of Josephus, it may have been incorporated into the Roman province of Syria, under Gabinius' governorship of that province (57-55 B.C.E.): see Schürer, *supra* n.5, at Vol.I, 267. In any event, institutions of government and national laws were preserved. See A.M. Rabello, 'Civil Justice in Palestine from 63 B.C.E. to 70 C.E.', *Classical Studies in honor of David Sohlberg*, ed. R. Katzoff, J. Petroff and D. Schaps (Ramat Gan: Bar-Ilan University Press, forthcoming).

6 Smallwood, *supra* n.4, at 32ff.; Schürer, *supra* n.5, at Vol.I, 267-80 (on Hyrcanus II, 63-40 B.C.E.).

7 Z.W. Falk, *Introduction to Jewish Law of the Second Commonwealth* (Leiden: E.J. Brill, 1972), I, 88ff.('The Town Court').

8 One possible objection may be derived from a text of the Palestinian Talmud, *Sanhedrin* 1:1:

> It was taught: Forty years before the destruction of the Temple the right to judge capital cases was withdrawn, and it was in the days of Shimon b. Shetaḥ that the right to judge property cases was withdrawn. Said R. Shimon b. Yoḥai, 'Blessed be the All merciful that I am not a sage required to make court decisions' (translation of J. Neusner, *The Talmud*

of the Land of Israel, vol. 31 Sanhedrin 1,1 p.12, III [A], [B].) Shimon b. Shetaḥ dates from the 1st century B.C.E. and is thought to have been a contemporary of Alexander Jannaeus, while Rabbi Shimon b. Yoḥai was a scholar from the 2nd century C.E. Although, the period in the days of King Jannaeus and Shimon b. Shetaḥ (before Pompey's conquest) was complicated, I do not believe that traditional Jewish civil law was cancelled. We should notice that the reading is not certain; in the parallel text in *Sanhedrin* 7:2 instead of Shimon b. Shetaḥ, Shimon b. Yoḥai appears. Neusner ignores this difference. The reading Bar Yoḥai corresponds with the continuation of the talmudic text and it seems to correspond with the historical period (in the days of the Emperor Hadrian and Bar-Kochba's Revolt). This reading is accepted by A. Büchler and G. Alon; see also Jackson, *supra* n.1, at 159ff.

9 B. Cohen, 'Arbitration in Jewish and Roman Law', in his *Jewish and Roman Law* (New York: Jewish Theological Seminary of America, 1966), II, 651ff.

10 A. Momigliano, 'Judaea becomes a Roman Province', *Cambridge Ancient History*, X, p.337ff.; M. Stern, 'The Province of Judaea', in *Compendia*, *supra* n.3, at Vol. 1 Pt. 1, 308ff.

11 A.H.M. Jones, *The Cities of the Eastern Roman Provinces* (Oxford: Clarendon Press, 1937), 227ff.; Z.G. Downey, The Later Roman Empire (New York: Holt, Rinehart and Winston, 1969); Y. Dan, *The City in Eretz-Israel During The Late Roman and Byzantine Periods* (Jerusalem: Yad Ben-Zvi, 1984, in Hebrew); on Caesarea, see L.I. Levine, *Caesarea under Roman Rule* (Leiden, E.J. Brill, 1975); on Gaza: M. A. Meyer, *History of the City of Gaza* (New York: Columbia University Press, 1907); G. Downey, *Gaza in the Early Sixth century* (Norman: Oklahoma University Press, 1963); on Scytopolis: G. Fuks, *Scytopolis — a Greek City in Eretz-Israel* (Jerusalem: Yad Ben-Zvi, 1983, in Hebrew).

12 Like Judea, other nations sought autonomy. Cicero tells us of the decree he made as ruler of Cilicia, in which he permitted local judges to continue to perform their function: *Ad Atticum*, VI, 1.15. F. De Martino, *Storia della Costituzione Romana*, Napoli, Jovene, 1960, Vol. II, 316ff., observes: 'There was no firm standard principle requiring preservation of national norms ... We must remember that Roman policy adapted itself to different situations. In a few cases local law and national institutions were indeed preserved with unsure status, always subject to suspension by the ruler. In other cases even these were changed, or otherwise, national institutions were changed fundamentally, Roman judges and Roman courts were imposed, and the traditional norms of the subjugated people were not honoured.' (Translation of AMR.)

13 See R. Martini, *Ricerche in tema di Editto provinciale* (Milano: Giuffrè, 1969), 48: 'This recognition in the autonomy of the citizens had seemed to the citizens of the provinces, first of all, as a possibility, which was derived

from this autonomy, to use the local judges'. See my examination of the situation in 'Civil Justice ...', *supra* n.5.

14 Inferred from Cicero, *Ad Atticum*, VI, 1.15.

15 See further A.M. Rabello, 'The *Lex de Templo Hierosolymitano* prohibiting gentiles from entering Jerusalem's Sanctuary', *Christian News from Israel* XXI/3 (1970), 28-32; XXI/4 (1970), 28-32.

16 Th. Mommsen, 'Der Religionsfrevel nach roemischen Recht', *Historische Zeitschrift* 64 (1890), 389ff.; *idem*, *Römisches Strafrecht* (Leipzig: Duncker, 1899), 573.

17 Berger, *supra* n.2, at 427: 'The citizens of a foreign state or community, who were vanquished in a war with Rome, surrendered to the power and protection of Rome (*deditio*). They constituted a specific group of the Roman population; they were free but lacked any public rights and citizenship (*nullius civitatis*). Their legal status as *peregrini dediticii* could be improved by unilateral concessions granted by Rome to individuals or groups. But even the general grant of Roman citizenship to peregrines by the constitution of the Emperor Caracalla excluded the *dediticii*. The status of *dediticii* termed by Justinian *dediticia libertas*, was abolished by him (C.J. 7.5.1).' *Dediticii* were not allowed to reside within 100 miles of Rome.

18 Juster, *supra* n.1, at II, 19-23: 'Since the Jews continued to enjoy their privileges ... they could do so as members of a nation ... The exercise thereof was therefore permitted only to the members of the Jewish nation.'

19 See also Colorni, *supra* n.3, at 16: '... in whatever way the question should be solved as regards Palestine, scholars agree with Juster's certain belief that the Jews of the Diaspora were subjected to no reprisals for the events of the year 70.' See also Applebaum, *supra* n.3, at 420ff.

20 This is on the basis of documentation discovered at Murabba'at. See E. Volterra, 'Nuovi documenti per la conoscenza del diritto vigente nelle provincie romane', *IURA* 14 (1963), 29ff.; E. Volterra, 'I diritti locali', in *I diritti locali nelle provincie romane con particolare riguardo alle condizione giuridiche del suolo* (Rome: Accademia Nazionale dei Lincei, 1974), 55ff.: '... it must have been extremely difficult for the Roman authorities to abrogate these norms and institutions as well as local customs. And yet, it is most likely that, in Palestine, the local laws and customs, especially in certain matters, must have been preserved for a long time ... The victorious nation did not impose its private law upon the vanquished, but allowed them to keep their own local law, customs and often even their own local administration. In contrast to the modern idea of unity of private law in every State, it was considered quite normal in the ancient world, that, among the subjects submitted to the same sovereignty, there could be different laws applicable simultaneously' (at 64).

21 Ultimately, in 398 C.E., Jewish legal autonomy was drastically limited by the famous Imperial Constitution of Theodosius II (reported in the Theodosian Code, 2.1.10). In 1899, Chajes argued that during the whole period from 70-

398, Jewish courts functioned merely as arbitral bodies, but most scholars now think that the Jewish courts did have authority to pass judgments. See H.P. Chajes, 'Les Juges Juifs en Palestine de l'an 70 à l'an 500', *Revue des Etudes Juives* 39 (1899), 39ff.; see also Sh. Albeck, *Law Courts in Talmudic Times* (Jerusalem: Bar-Ilan University Press, 1980, in Hebrew). See further section 3Ci.

22 *Mekhilta deRabbi Ishmael* ('Mishpatim' section, Exodus, 21), quoted from the English translation of Jacob Z. Lauterbach, *Mekilta de-Rabbi Ishmael* (Philadelphia: Jewish Publication Society of America, 1933), Vol. III, 1-2.

23 Groups of Sages used to come from Palestine to Rome to discuss the relations between the Jews of Palestine and the Roman Government. On the delegation to Rome see G. Alon, *The Jews in their Land in the Talmudic Age*, (Jerusalem: Magnes Press, 1980), I, 124ff.; M.D. Herr, 'The Historical Significance of the Dialogues between Jewish Sages and Roman Dignitaries', *Scripta Hierosolymitana XXII* (Jerusalem: Magnes Press, 1971), 123ff.

24 Stern, *supra* n.10, at 336ff.; S. Safrai, 'Jewish Self-Government', in *Compendia Rerum Judaicarum ad Novum Testamentum*, ed. S. Safrai and M. Stern (Assen: van Gorcum, 1974), Vol. 1 Pt. 1, 397ff.

25 Justinian *Digest*, 1.16.7.2; 1.18.10.12.

26 Rabello, 'Legal Condition', *supra* n.1, at 725ff.

27 See the text of these documents in N. Lewis, Y. Yadin and J.C. Greenfield, eds., *The Documents from the Bar Kochba Period in the Cave of Letters. Greek Papyri and Aramaic and Nabatean Signatures and Subscriptions* (Jerusalem: Israel Exploration Society, 1989); the texts to which we refer are at 118ff. See also N. Lewis, 'The World of P. Yadin', *Bulletin of the American Society for Papyrology* 28 (1991), 35-41; H. Cotton, 'The Guardianship of Jesus Son of Babatha. Roman and Local Law in the Province of Arabia', *Journal of Roman Studies* 83 (1993), 94-108; B. Isaac, 'The Babatha Archive. A Review Article', *Israel Exploration Journal* 42 (1992), 62-75.

28 The archive (mostly in Greek) of a second Jewish woman, also from Maoza, dating from between 125 and 131, has also now been published. See H. Cotton, 'The Archive of Salome Komaise Daughter of Levi: Another Archive from the "Cave of Letters"', *Zeitschrift für Papyrologie und Epigraphie* 105 (1995), 171-207. She concludes that the marriage contract in it (*P. Yadin* 37) reflects the Hellenistic *agraphos gamos*.

29 See H.M. Cotton and J.C. Greenfield, 'Babatha's Property and the Law of Succession in the Babatha Archive', *Zeitschrift für Papyrologie und Epigraphie* 104 (1994), 211-224, esp.220. Cotton takes the view, in general, that the papyri from such Jewish archives show little awareness of Jewish law, but indicate considerable assimilation into a Roman-Hellenistic legal environment not dissimilar from that of Egypt. See H. Cotton, "A Cancelled Marriage Contract from the Judaean Desert (*XHev/Se Gr.2*)", *Journal of Roman Studies* 84 (1994), 65-86, esp. 81-85, reviewing evidence

from eight marriage contracts (including two written in Greek) from various sites in the Judaean desert;

30 H.M. Cotton, 'Fragments of a Declaration of Landed Property from the Province of Arabia', *Zeitschrift für Papyrologie und Epigraphie* 85 (1991), 263-267; *idem*, 'Another Fragment of the Declaration of Landed Property from the Province of Arabia', *Zeitschrift für Papyrologie und Epigraphie* 99 (1993), 115-121.

31 See the following studies: H. J. Polotsky, 'Three Greek Papyri from the Cave of Letters', *Israel Exploration Journal* 12 (1962), 258ff.; *idem*, 'Three Greek Documents from the Family Archive of Babatha', *Eretz Israel* 8 (1967), 46ff.; M. Lemosse, 'Le procès de Babatha', *The Irish Jurist* 3 (1968), 363ff.; A. Biscardi, 'Nuove testimonianze di un papiro arabo-giudaico per la storia del processo provinciale romano', *Studi in onore di G. Scherillo* (Milano: Giuffrè, 1972), I, 111ff.; *idem*, 'Sulla identificazione degli "Xenokritai" e sulla loro attività in P.Oxy. 3016', *Festschrift für E. Seidl*, ed. Huebner (Cologne: P. Hanstein, 1975), 15ff.; Jackson, *supra* n.1, at 164f.

32 In parallel texts we find the names of Rabbi Shimon and Rabbi Meir (from a later period than Bar-Kochba's revolt). See Alon, *supra* n.23, at II, 537f.

33 See Dio Chrysostomus, *Orationes* 40, 509-12 and Plutarch, *Moralia, De reipublicae gerenda*, 19.

34 P. Oxy. II, 237; see J. Mélèze-Modrzejewski, "La loi des Egiptiens: le droit grec dans l'Egypte romaine", in *Droit impérial et traditions locales dans l'Egypte romaine* (Aldershot: Variorum, 1990), 383-399.

35 *B.B.K.* 38a, quoted below at n.37, in the discussion of Jew and Gentile before a Jewish court, section Cii *infra*.

36 E.E. Urbach, *The World of the Sages. Collected Studies* (Jerusalem: Magnes Press, 1988), 306ff. (in Hebrew).

37 *M. Eduy.* 7:7. According to Alon, *supra* n.23, at I, 121: 'Rabban Gamaliel went to get an official appointment as Patriarch and leader of the Jews.'

38 A Palestinian *Tanna* from the 3rd century, *B.B.B.* 58a. See Alon, *supra* n.23, at I, 216.

39 *B. Shab.* 139a. Cf. Alon, *supra* n.23, at II, 674. See also n.8, *supra*.

40 *B.B.K.* 38a, Soncino translation. Other versions are found at *Y.B.K.* 4.3 (4b) and *Sifre Deut* 344 (Finkelstein, 401). See recently: Jackson, *supra* n.1, at 168; B. Lifshitz, 'Conflict of Laws between a Jew and a Gentile', *Mélanges M.H. Prévost* (Paris: Presses Universitaires de France, 1982), 179ff.

41 *Sifre Deut.* 16 (Finkelstein, 26).

42 This dispute appears in a somewhat different format in Babylonian *Talmud*, *B.K.* 113a: 'Where a suit arises before you between an Israelite and a heathen, if you can justify the former according to the laws of Israel, justify him and say: "This is our law"; so also if you can justify him by the laws of the heathens justify him and say (to the other party): "This is your law"; but if this cannot be done, we use subterfuges to circumvent him. This is the view

of R. Ishmael, but R. Akiba said that we should not attempt to circumvent him on account of the sanctification of the divine Name.' See also *T.B.K.* 4:2, *Y.B.K.* 4:3 (4b); Lifshitz, *supra* n.40, at 184.

43 In other cases, the case could be tried before a Roman court (*ex conventu civium romanorum*) or a local court.

44 CIL, XVI, No. 11; S. Riccobono, *Fontes iuris romani antiqui* (Florence: Barbera, 1941), I, 308ff., line 53ff.

45 *Y. Sanh.* 1:1, and see n.6 above.

46 M. Goodman, *State and Society in Roman Galilee A.D. 132-212*, (Totowa, New Jersey: Rowman and Allenheld, 1983), esp. pp.93ff., 119ff., 155ff. (note that this study is limited to Galilee); see also D.M. Goodblatt, *Rabbinic Instruction in Sasanian Babylonia* (Leiden: Brill 1975).

47 See Berger, *supra* n.2, at 409: 'A constitution of the emperor Caracalla by which all inhabitants of the Empire, organized in *civitates* with local autonomy, were granted Roman citizenship, except the so-called *peregrini dediticii*.' On the other hand, Colorni, *supra* n.3, at 17ff., maintains that citizenship was extended without any discrimination (i.e. even to *peregrini dediticii*). On the effect of the constitution, H.F. Jolowicz and B. Nicholas, *Historical Introduction to the Study of Roman Law* (Cambridge: Cambridge University Press, 1972, 3rd ed.), 347, comment: 'From the point of view of private law, however, it was more important, though rather for its indirect effect on the character of the law itself than for its direct impact on the new citizens. For though, on the generally accepted view, large numbers of provincials who previously had lived by their own laws, were now expected to adapt themselves to Roman law, the immediate result, as we shall see, was often no more than the adoption of the forms of Roman law as clothing for the unchanged substance of local law.'

48 *Supra* n.1, at vol.II, p.96.

49 Perhaps Rabbi Judah III, who was the Patriarch from 290 to 320, i.e. at the time of Diocletian. If so, we may assume that he himself petitioned the Emperor. For a full discussion, including the implications of the passage for the jurisdictional situation after 70 C.E., and its relationship to *C.Th.* 2,1,10 (discussed below), see A.M. Rabello, 'On the Relations between Diocletian and the Jews', *Journal of Jewish Studies* 35 (1984), 147-167.

50 See further Rabello, *ibid.*, at 164-65 and sources there quoted.

51 Actually, Greek law practiced by the "*Aegyptii*": peregrines who are neither Roman citizens nor citizens of a Greek city of Egypt (Alexandria, Ptolemais, Neucratis). See Méléze-Modrzejewski, *supra* n.34.

52 On the *nomikos* in Egypt see R. Katzoff, 'Responsa Prudentium in Roman Egypt', *Studi in onore di Arnaldo Biscardi* (Milano: Giuffrè, 1968), II, 523ff.

53 On the *nomikos* in Palestine, see S. Lieberman, *Hellenism in Jewish Palestine* (New York: Jewish Theological Seminary of America, 1962), 81f

54 On Pliny's letters see A.N. Sherwin-White, *The Letters of Pliny. A Historical*

and Social Commentary (Oxford: Clarendon Press, 1966).

55 Rabello, *Giustiniano*, *supra* n.1, at Vol. II, pp.751ff.

56 A.M. Rabello, 'L'Observance des fêtes hébraïques dans l'Empire Romain', *Aufstieg und Niedergang der Römischen Welt* (Berlin-New York: W. de Gruyter, 1984), Vol. II, 21, 2, pp.1288-1312.

57 See further A.M. Rabello, 'Divorce of Jews in the Roman Empire', *The Jewish Law Annual* IV (1981), 79ff.

58 In a constitution reported in Code of Justinian, 1.9.7

59 After the *Lex lulia de adulteriis*, Roman law required the observance of various formalities in divorce, in order to avoid penal sanctions.

60 Juster, *supra* n.1, at II.59. On the problem in general from the point of view of Roman Law see M. Kaser, *Roman Private Law* (London: Butterworths, 1968), 238ff. On problems of citizenship, see A.N. Sherwin-White, *The Roman Citizenship* (Oxford: Oxford University Press, 1939). See also A. Linder, *The Jews in Roman Imperial Legislation* (Jerusalem: The Israel Academy of Sciences and Humanities, 1987).

XIII

CIVIL JEWISH JURISDICTION IN THE DAYS OF EMPEROR JUSTINIAN (527-565): CODEX JUSTINIANUS 1.9.8.

A. *The State of the Jewish Judiciary Before Justinian*

The extent to which the Roman government which had conquered the Land of Israel (*Palaestina)* as well as large areas outside of it (collectively termed the Roman Empire) permitted Jewish courts to rule in matters regarding Jews is a question which has attracted relatively little attention.[1] In his fundamental book *Les Juifs dans l'Empire Romain*[2] the renowned scholar Jean Juster sums up the situation of the Jewish judiciary as such: "After the fall of Jerusalem, the Jews continued to bring their cases not only before Jewish judges (whom it was possible to define as arbiters) but even before actual Jewish courts authorized to judge according to Jewish law and granted authority to do so by the Romans. The Jewish court received the status of a regular court the moment one of the Jewish sides submitted a claim to it, thereby effectively preventing the submission of the case to a rival non-Jewish court. The Jewish court thus received the authority to summon the defendant, to force him to appear, and to ensure that its rulings would be enforced. Its rulings would be recognized by the Roman authorities as coming from legitimate judicial authority".[3]

1 See A.M. Rabello, "Civil Justice in Palestine from 63 BCE to 70 CE", in R. Katzoff, ed., *Classical Studies in honor of David Sohlberg* (Ramat Gan, 1996) 293ff.; *Idem*, "Jewish and Roman Jurisdiction", in N.S. Hecht, B.S. Jackson, S.M. Passamaneck, D. Piattelli and A.M. Rabello, eds., *An Introduction to the History and Sources of Jewish Law* (Oxford, 1996) 141ff.

2 "Great work", as defined by Menachem Stern in the introduction to his book *Greek and Latin Authors*, (Jerusalem, vol. I, 1974) 7.

3 Jean Juster, *Les Juifs dans l'Empire Romain*, (Paris, vol. 2, 1914) 96 (cited hereafter as: Juster, *Juifs*). Colorni claims that this authority was recognized only in the land of Israel and in some of the Eastern Provinces, but not in the Empire as a whole: V. Colorni, *Legge ebraica e leggi locali*, (Milano, 1945) 115ff. (cited hereafter as: Colorni: *Legge ebraica*).

A change in the situation described above, that is to say a cancellation of Jewish judicial autonomy, occurred, it seems,[4] only in the Later Empire. In the year 398 the law of Arcadius and Honorius, as published in the *Codex Theodosianus* (C.T.) 2.1.10 established that:

> The Jews, who live under the Roman common law, shall address the courts in the usual way in those cases which do not concern so much their superstition as court, laws and rights, and all of them shall bring actions and defend themselves under the Roman laws; in conclusion, they shall be under our laws. Certainly, if some shall deem it necessary to litigate before the Jews, or the patriarchs through mutual agreement, in the matter of arbitration, with the consent of both parties and in civil matters only, they shall not be prohibited by public law from accepting their verdict; the governors of the provinces shall even execute their sentences as if they were appointed arbiters through a judge's award.
> Given this Third Day before the Nones of February at Constantinople, In the Consulate of Honorius Augustus For the Fourth Time and of Eutychianus.[5]

4 In our estimation the change did not occur prior to this, and certainly not in the days of Emperor Diocletian. See A.M. Rabello, "On the Relations between Diocletian and the Jews", (1984) 35 J. Jewish Studies 147ff., esp. at 157ff.

5 In the translation of A. Linder, *The Jews in Roman Imperial Legislation, Edited with Introductions, Translations, and Commentary* (Detroit, 1987) 208. The original text has:
Idem AA. (= Impp. Gratianus Valentinianus et Theodosius AA.) ad Eutychianum P(raefectum) P(raetorio)
Iudaei Romano et communi iure viventes in his causis, quae non tam ad superstitionem eorum quam ad forum et leges ac iura pertinent, adeant sollemni more iudicia omnesque Romanis legibus inferant et excipiant actiones: postremo sub legibus nostris sint. Sane si qui per compromissum ad similitudinem arbitrorum apud Iudaeos vel patriarchas ex consensu partium in civili dumtaxat negotio putaverint litigandum, sortiri eorum iudicium iure publico non vetentur: eorum etiam sententias provinciarum iudices exsequantur, tamquam ex sententia cognitoris arbitri fuerint adtributi.
Dat. III Non. Febr. Constant(ino)poli Honor(io) A. IIII et Eutychiano V Conss. (a. 398).
See A.M. Rabello "The Legal Condition of Jews in the Roman Empire", (1980) II, 13 ANRW 731ff; *cf.* the situation of the *episcopalis audientia* and see M.R. Cimma, *L'Episcopalis Audientia nelle costituzioni imperiali da Costantino a Giustiniano* (Torino, 1989); G. Crifó, "A proposito di episcopalis audientia", in *Institutions, Societe' et vie politique dans l'empire Romain au IVe siècle après J.C.* (Rome, 1992) 397ff., at 408. See *infra* n. 26.

In this constitution it was established that the issue of judicial authority would be determined according to the category of the dispute: matters that were purely religious in substance would remain in the sole jurisdiction of the Jewish courts; criminal matters would be placed under the sole jurisdiction of the Roman courts; and civil matters would be placed in the jurisdiction of the Roman courts with a provision allowing the parties to bring their case before the Jewish court in the form of arbitration should they mutually agree to do so (*compromissio*). In any event, its clear that with the cessation of Jewish judicial autonomy, the status of the Jewish judiciary itself changed from that of a competitor independent of the Roman judiciary, to that of an arbitrator whose very existence as a viable source of law would be dependent upon the good will of the parties to the disputes that might be brought before it. It is Juster's assertion that the text before us contains hints to the effect that the authority of the Jewish courts when chosen enjoyed a position superior to that which it had held when it was forced upon the parties. However, to the court of the Jewish judiciary's chief magistrate, and more generally to every Jewish court, there only remained, according to this constitution, the authority to deal with religious matters.

It is appropriate to mention that in the Christian period Jews were permitted to honour the Sabbath, and court sessions in which they were involved were not convened on that day. This rule appears in the Theodosian Code 2.8.26, which states:

> We order, that no one shall be obliged to do anything or be summoned in any way whatsoever, on the Sabbath day or on the other days on which the Jews keep the reverence of their cult, for it is clear that the remaining days could suffice for the fiscal revenues and for private litigation.
> Given on the Seventh Day Before the Calends of August at Ravenna, in the Consulate of our two Masters and Augusti, Honorius for the eighth time and Theodosius for the third.[6]

6 In Linder's translation, *supra* n. 5. See A.M. Rabello, "L'observance des fêtes juives dans l'Empire Romain", (1983) II, 21, 2, ANRW 647ff.

B. The State of the Jewish Judiciary in the Days of Justinian (Codex Justinianus 1.9.8)

The constitution which we examined above (in the form in which it appeared in the Theodosian Code) was published a second time in the Code of the Emperor Justinian (C.J.1.9.8) in the year 534[7] — after having undergone several changes. Some of these changes were of a purely administrative nature while others were, in our opinion, qualitatively significant.[8]

IMPPP. GRATIANUS VALENTINIANUS ET THEODOSIUS AAA. EUTYCHIANO PP.
Iudaei Romano communi iure viventes in his causis, quae tam ad superstitionem eorum quam ad forum et leges ac iura pertinent, adeant solemni more iudicia omnesque Romanis legibus conferant et excipiant actiones. Si qui vero ex his communi pactione ad simililtudinem arbitrorum apud Iudaeos in civili dumtaxat negotio putaverint litigandum, sortiri eorum iudicium iure publico non vetentur. Eorum etiam sententias iudices exsequantur, tamquam ex sententia cognitoris arbitri fuerint attributi.

On first reading the text of this imperial constitution, one is liable to conclude that it is identical with that which we cited above (C.T.

7 On Justinian's attitude to Jews, Samaritans and heretics see: B. Biondi, *Il Diritto Romano Cristiano* (Milano, vol. I, 1952) 253ff.; M. Amelotti, "Giustiniano tra teologia e diritto", in *L'imperatore Giustiniano. Storia e mito.* (Milano, 1978) 133ff.; M. Simonetti, "La politica religiosa di Giustiniano"; in *Il mondo del diritto nell'epoca giustinianea. Caratteri e problematiche,* (Ravenna, 1985) 91ff.; A.M. Rabello, *Giustiniano, Ebrei e Samaritani alla luce delle fonti storico-letteraerie, ecclesiastiche e giuridiche,* (Milano, vol. I, 1987/vol. II, 1988); M. Amelotti, "Giustiniano e gli Haeretici", in *idem, Scritti Giuridici* (a cura di L. Migliardi Zingale), (Torino, 1996) 640ff.

8 Several scholars are of the opinion that the text was introduced into the C.J. from the C.T. "without the effecting of substantive changes"; see M. Talamanca, *Richerche in tema di compromissum*, (Milano, 1953) 141, and from a different perspective, Jean Gaudemet in his book *L'Eglise dans l' Empire romain*, p. 627, note 5 commenting: "in C.J. 1.9.8 the text appears with insertions which indicate a negative attitude regarding the Jewish judiciary", ("au CI.1.9.8 le texte figure avec des interpolations qui marquent la défaveur à l' égard des jurisdictions juives").
Concerning iura and leges in the body of the constitutio as brought in C.Th. 2.1.10 see the comments of G.G. Archi, *Giustiniano legislatore*, Bologna, 1970. p. 59.

2.1.10). After presenting the translation of C.J. 1.9.8 we shall examine the text more closely:

> THE THREE EMPERORS AND AUGUSTI GRATIAN VALENTIAN AND THEODOSIUS TO EUTYCHIANUS, PRAEFECTUS PRAETORIO
> Jews, who live under the Roman common law shall address in the usual way the courts in those cases which concern their superstition as well as those that concern court, laws and rights and all of them shall accuse and defend themselves under the Roman laws. Indeed, if some of them shall deem it necessary to litigate before the Jews in a common agreement in the manner of arbitration and in civil matters only, they shall not be prohibited by public law from accepting their verdict. The governors shall even execute their sentences as if arbiters were appointed through a judge's award.
> Given on the Third Day before the Nones of February at Constantinople, in the Consulate of Honorius Augustus for the Fourth Time, and of Eutychianus.[9]

The introductory section of the law (the *inscriptio)* as it appeared in Codex Justinianus (C.J.) reads "*Imppp.* (the Emperors) *Gratianus Valentinianus et Theodosius AAA*" whereas in C.T. 2.1.10 the text reads "*Iidem (*"them"*)* as though to say "Arcadius et Honorius AA Impp". It is clear that the in*scriptio* of C.J. is incorrect, for the Empire's rulership was not in the hands of Gratian, Valentinian and Theodosius in the year 398 which, according to the end of the text (the *subscriptio*) was the year of the constitution's publication; from the year 395 and onward Arcadius and Honorius controlled the Empire. Apparently the mistake[10] in the authorship's assignation was caused by confusion regarding the meaning of "Iidem" which had appeared in the earlier Theodosian version of the constitution.

9 In Linder's translation, *supra* n. 5.

10 Solazzi defines this "a mystery", "Ancora glossemi," in SDHI, 13-14, 1948, p. 204 note 1. Similarly, see: J. Gaudemet in IURA, 2, (1951) 265. It appears that L. Wenger is of the opinion that the *constitutio* as originally presented by Honorius and Arcadius was published a second time in the days of Gratian Valentinian and Theodosius; *Institutes of Roman Law of Civil Procedure*, (1940) 340.

The constitution opens with the words "Jews who live under the Roman common law" — *Judaei romano communi iure viventes;* the Theodosian version is: "Jews who live under the Roman and common law" — *Judaei romano et communi iure* ; whereas the Visigothic interpretation is: "All of the Jews, who are known to be Romans — *Judaei omnes qui Romani esse noscuntur*". The opinion of Godefroy is that the constitution distinguishes between two categories of Jews: those who live (*viventes*) according to the Roman law *(romano iure)*, and those who do not live according to the Roman law, while Jews of both categories are considered Roman citizens.

The Italian scholar G. Ferrari Dalle Spade rejects Godefroy's interpretation and claims instead that alongside those Jews who were Roman citizens (*cives romani*) there lived Jews who were not citizens, and that the constitution does not deal with the latter group at all.[11]

The explanation of Dalle Spade is to our mind, entirely acceptable and yet we are of the opinion that at least as far as the constitution of Justinian is concerned the legislator intended only to emphasize that in the majority of the Empire's domain Jews were automatically subject to Roman law.[12]

The constitution deals, then, with those Jews who were citizens of the Empire who lived subject to the Roman law which fell upon all citizens (*Romano communi iure*) and who, according to the Visigothic interpretation were recognized as Romans (*qui Romani esse nonscuntur*).[13] The

11 G. Ferrari Dalle Spade,"Giurisdizione speciale ebraica nell'Impero romano-cristiano", *Scritti Beatificazione C.Ferrini*, I, (Milano, 1947) 239 ss. = G. Ferrari Dalle Spade, *Scritti Giuridici* III, pp. 279ff. at 281. Indeed S. Solazzi writes: "In the Roman Empire lived Jews who were forced to live by the Roman law which applied to everybody, and there were Jews who lived according to a Roman law which was unique to them. However, it is doubtful whether it is possible to establish with certainty that in the days of Justinianus there existed at the same time as a generally applied Roman law special rights given to subgroups within the Empire"; S. Solazzi, "Ancora glossemi", in *Scritti di Diritto Romano,* (Napoli, vol. V, 1960) 47 (in our translation). .

12 This approach (at least in its summary part) is similar to the reconstruction presented by V. Colorni the essence of which appears in his work: "Autonomie ebraiche in Italia nel Medioevo e nel Rinascimento" in *Idem*, *Iudaica minora.Saggi sulla Storia dell'Ebraismo italiano dall'Antichita' all'eta' moderna,* (Milano, 1983) 492ff. Reinach translates (in opposition to this) the Theodosian text as follows: les Juifs vivant à la foi selon le droit romain et le droit (qui leur est) commun ...", J. Reinach," Controversie, et litige,comparaison de C.Th.2.1.10 et de C.1.9.8", (1960) 2 IURA 186. Indeed this is an interesting interpretation, however, we don't agree with it.

13 On this *interpretatio* see A.M. Rabello, *The Jews in Visigothic Spain in the Light of the Legislation* (Jerusalem, 1983) 101ff. (in Hebrew).

obligation was placed upon these Jews to bring their legal concerns before the Roman courts "in those cases which concern their superstition as well as those that concern court, laws and rights" (*in his causis quae tam ad superstitionem eorum quam ad forum leges ac iura pertinent.*)

In contrast to this reading, the Theodosian version of the constitution reads as such: "in those cases which do not concern so much their superstition as court, laws and rights" (*in his causis, quae non tam ad superstitionem eorum quam ad forum et leges ac iura pertinent*).

The Visigothic interpretation of the text establishes:

> ... *hoc solum apud religionis suae maiores agant, quod ad religionis eorum pertinent disciplinam, ita ut inter se, quae sunt Hebraeis legibus statura, custodiant.*
>
> *Alia vero negotia, quae nostris legibus continentur, et ad forum respiciunt apud iudicem proviniciae eo quo omnes iure confligant.*
>
> All of the Jews who are known to be Romans shall litigate before the heads of their religion only on what concerns the discipline of their religion, so that they shall observe among themselves what was established by the Hebrew laws. All other matters, however, which are covered by our laws and pertain to the court, shall be determined by the governor of the province according to the common law. Certainly, if the two parties shall consent and wish to litigate before the Heads of their law, in civil matters only, and the process shall be terminated by an arbitration award based on a mutual agreement, the award shall be recognized as if it was established by a judge's award.[14]

It seems clear then that, just as we saw from our examination at the beginning of this article, according to the Theodosian constitution, Jews were permitted to bring their religious disputes before the Jewish religious courts.[15]

14 In Linder's translation, *supra* n. 5.

15 For the sake of comparison see Juster, Juifs, Vol. 2, at 152: "quand Théodose apporta des restrictions à leur jurisdiction civile, il dit expressement que leur jurisdiction réligeuse ne sera point limitée."See also: G. Ferrari Dalle Spade, *Giurisdizione speciale* p. 281: "... Arcadius ceased to be interested and left the decisions to the authorized Jewish bodies, in the spirit of the Jewish law and according to their tradition".

The question which must be asked is — what importance are we to attach to the omission of the "*non*" from Justinian's constitution? Juster recognizes that the omission "changes the meaning of the text"; however, he is of the opinion that the omission originates in scribal error rather than in legislative intention and so arrives at the conclusion that Justinian — apart from Novel 146 of the year 553 — did not further narrow the limits of Jewish judicial autonomy.[16]

Contrary to this opinion, Ferrari Dalle Spade is of the view that "the omission of the negative 'non' by Justinius reverses the meaning of the legal instruction", meaning, "there is no longer a distinction between the categories of dispute and the constitution relates to them equally in declaring that both are to be referred to the regular Roman courts".[17]

Was the removal of the "non" then a scribal error, or an intentional omission meant to remove judicial authority in religious matters from the hands of the Jews? Scholars have exerted much effort in struggling with this question[18] and A. Berger even devoted an entire study to it,

16 Juster, *Juifs,* Vol. 2, at 152 and n. 2; in the note itself doubts regarding the correctness of this interpretation are expressed, particularly in light of the text of the *Basilica* 1.1.40: "Il se peut que dans les Basiliques il n'y a pas erreur, mais une mesure vexatoire de l' époque, auquel cas il faut supposer que même la jurisdiction réligieuse fut totalment enlevée aux Juifs et alors c'est le texte des Basil. qui aurait influence le texte du C.J." Agreement with the conclusion of Juster: P. Browe, "Die Judengesetzgebung Justinians", (1935) 8 *Analecta Gregoriana*, 110; and for comparison purposes see Colorni, *Legge Ebraica* p. 209 note 30 Basilica 1.1.36.

17 *Giurisdizione speciale* at 280.

18 It is proper to consider the opinion of G. Kisch on the subject "Zur Frage der Aufhebung judisch-religioeser Jurisdiktion durch Justinian, in (1960) 77 *ZSS* 395ff., esp. at 399 where he mentions his research from 1945. Later Kisch accepts the opinion of Berger that the deletion was intentional; Previously Solazzi claimed (in S. Solazzi, Fra norme romane antisemite p. 585 in Scritt*i di Diritto Romano*, III, (Napoli, 1960) 579ff., at 585 "Justinius, in C.1.9.8 deleted (the word) non" Solazzi reversed himself in his article *Ancora glossemi* p. 203 (Scritti V, at 47) " It is certain that the 'non' was erased by the hand of Justinian who in this way made equivalent the two types of judgement and directed that both must be brought before the regular Roman courts ... the requirement that cases which possess a religious or nationalist element of a particular people be brought before judges who are not of that people is anti-cultural and Justinian ..." S.W. Baron also claims that in the days of Justinian a substantive change took place, as does C.H. Vogler, "Les Juifs dans le Code Théodosien" in *Les Chrétiens devant le Point Juif,* (Paris, 1979) 56:

cet oubli volontaire du non aboutit à supprimer sans bruit la jurisdiction réligieuse des Juifs ....

The thesis of Berger was adopted also by A. Biscardi, "C.Th. 2, 1, 10 nel quadro della normativa giurisdizionale d'ispirazione religiosa," in *Atti dell'Accademia romanistica costantiniana*, (Perugia, 1986) 213ff.

reaching the conclusion that "the omission actually turns the meaning of the *constitutio* on its head".[19] In the opinion of Berger, there is a striking example here of what is actually a widespread pattern in which foreign material becomes assimilated into texts — *interpolatio* — by means of the addition or removal of the word "non". The addition or removal of the negative from a text contains the potential to completely reverse that text's meaning.

The Greek version of the Basilica proves that a change in the text was made. Berger claims, in contrast to Juster and in our opinion correctly, that the text of the Basilica accurately reflects Justinian's change and is not itself the origin of the change.[20] It is to be expected that Justinian, more than other Emperors, would revoke judicial authority in religious matters from the Jews — particularly since the exercise of such authority occasionally required the administration of corporal punishment.[21] Novel 146 is a good illustration of the change in policy that had taken place, and of its consequences: the revocation of judicial authority.[22]

19 A. Berger, C.Th. 2.1.10 and C. 1.9.8 pr "A perferct example of an interpolation through the cancellation of a NON" in (1959) 10 *Iura* 14.

20 The Basilica is a Byzantine codification of the Roman law. Modern-day historians generally ignore this source because of the late date at which it was authored; However, it is fitting to recall that legal historians have proven that the Basilica is a most important device, not only does it add to our knowledgeof the law in the days of Justinian and the emperors who succeeded him in Byzantium, but there is also material which is important to the Classic period as well. And here is the text of the Basilica 1.1.40, (in the Latin translation of Heimbach, 1, 27):
ludaei Romano communi iure viventes in his causis, quae ad superstitionem eorum et ad forum et leges et ius pertinent, adeant solemni modo iudicia et omnes Romanis legibus conferant et excipiant actiones. Qui autem horum communi pactione ad similitudinem arbitrorum apud ludaeos in pecuniaria tantum causa voluerint litigare, sortiri eorum iudicium iure publico non vetentur et sententias eorum ma gistratus exequantur, perinde ac si iudicio magistratus sententiae latae sint."
and for the sake of comparison also the *scholium* included in *Synopsis Basilicorum* 1,4,3 (=J.P). *Zepos*, V, 318.

21 A. Berger, C.Th. 2.1.10, *supra* n. 19, at 21.

22 Appropriate for special mention is the interpretation of J. Reinach, 'Controverse' et 'litige', *supra* n. 12, at 184ff — opposed in its purpose to the interpretation of Berger: in order to claim the existence of interposed material in the codex "il faudrait qu'on nous exhibe une constitution intervenue entre la publication des deux codes, qui aurait modifiée la règle que resulterait du premier". With all due respect, it does not

Therefore, from a legal point of view it was no longer possible for an obligation to settle religious issues judicially to continue to exist. At the same time, however, we must remember that parties to a dispute were permitted to turn to Rabbinical courts should they mutually agree to do so. Moreover, the settlement of disputes before religious courts and the acceptance of these courts' decrees, in and of itself, constitutes a religious commandment the observance of which was sometimes enforced by the imposition of various punishments upon those who sought to escape from it. Furthemore, it was also the right of the individual who was in transgression of a religious commandment to request that he be judged before the religious courts. This being the case, the judicial authority of rabbinical courts remained in force as far as the Jews were concerned, even if this was only because the Jews freely and expressly willed that this be so.[23]

appear to me that the need was felt ... by Justinian himself regarding his constitutio Cordi, *De emendatione codicis*: "... *si qua emendatione opus fieret, hanc facere non titubante animo, sed nostra autoritate fretos...*"

According to Reinach, the words *'non tamen'* which appear in the Theodosian Code "relève donc d'une appreciation du degré d'acuité de la controverse ... Le litige doit être né et actuel ... et dépasser le cadre d'une querelle sur l'interpretation de la Bible ou du Talmud ... (at 187)

The problem was, in his opinion, determining the moment in which a disagreement received the distinction of *'iudicium'* and it became possible to pass it over to the Roman courts. Justinian was satisfied, in his opinion, with a desire to simplify and established that "désormais les tribunaux pourront être saisis quel que soit l'état du conflit ... il n'est question que des causes mixtes, de causes qui d'origine réligieuse degenerent en litiges" (at 187). It does not seem to us that this forced explanation of the text is a possible one for it does not take the Visegothic 'interpretatio' into consideration. Apart from the fact that the Scriptures and the Talmud contain long section which are purely legal in nature the true nature of the *constitutio* of Justinian may be discerned from Novel 146 from the year 553 which was promulgated from the court of Justinian himself.

23 G. Kisch, *Zur Frage der Aufhebung, supra* n. 17, at 398, n. 9, brings the anecdote of the Bishop of Paris Garmanus (d. 576) who encountered a youth who was bound because he had refused to uphold Jewish law. Indeed, its possible that the incident must be explained allegorically: The ropes symbolize the adherence to Jewish law and the Christian grace the freeing from its bonds: This is a common topic in Christian anti-Jewish polemic; see Blumenkranz, *Les Auteurs chrétiens latins du Moyen Age sur les Juifs et le Judasme*, (Paris, 1963): "Venantius Fortunatus, Vita Germani", c. 65, at 66f. More than this, its possible that in this area the Theodosian Code was in force which as we noted above left the judicial autonomy of the Jews concerning religious matters undisturbed.

Let us now move from a discussion of religious law to that of the civil law. As regards the latter, there exists complete agreement between the Justinian and Theodosian texts; legal claims connected with the court of the Emperor and his laws (*ad forum et leges ac iura pertinent*) were to be decided in the usual fashion before the regular Roman courts.

Those scholars whose opinions differ regarding the existence or non-existence, between the years 70 CE and 398 (the date upon which the constitution of Arcadius and Honorius, in C.T. 2.1.10, was originally published)[24] of a Jewish judiciary whose decisions in civil matters were obligatory,[25] completely agree that in this matter no change took place: between the time of Arcadius until Justinian the Empire no longer recognized Jewish civil decisions as being obligatory.

Indeed, after the text revokes the force of Jewish law in both religious and civil matters,[26] it leaves open the possibility of presenting a claim to the religious courts in the form of arbitration ; "if indeed one of them" — *si quid vero ex his* — clarifies that this possibility is limited to the case in which both sides are Jews (for were it otherwise there would be a violation of the prohibition described in C.I. 1.9.10, which forbids a Jew from passing judgment on a non-Jew).[27]

"In a common agreement" (*communi pactione*): In the Theodosian version it was written "through mutual agreement" — closer to the meaning "compromise" (*per compromissum*). The change stems, appar-

24 It is enough at this point if we mention the central researches done on this topic: Juster, *Juifs*, II, at 29ff.; V. Colorni, *Legge Ebraica e leggi locali*, at 103ff.; G. Ferrari Dalle Spade, *Giurisdizione speciale ebraica cit.*

25 As can be seen in the above mentioned researches of Juster, Colorni, Ferrari Delle Spade, Berger and Kisch.

26 Regarding the similarity to the arrangement of *Episcopalis audientia* (bishop as judge) see G. Vismara, *Episcopalis audientia*, (Milano, 1937); L. Wenger, *Institutes*, at 339ff. (and the bibliography brought there); Colorni, *Legge ebraica*, at 127 ff.; Ferrari Dalle Spade, *Giurisdizione speciale ebraica*, at 296ff.; J. Jäger "Justinien et l'episcopalis audientia", (1960) 38 *RHD*, 214 ff. (and the survey of Kisch in Historia Judaica, 22 (1960) 131ff.) W. Selb, "Episcopalis audientia von der Zeit Konstantins bis zu Nov. XXXX Valentinianus III", (1967) 84 *ZSS*, 162ff. and see *supra* n. 5.

27 Ferrari Dalle Spade, *Giurisdizione speciale* at 287.

ently, from procedural reforms which had been instituted by Justinian in the year 529 (C.I.2.15.24).[28]

"As in the case of arbitration" (*ad simultudinem arbitrorum)*: Arbitration was available to every Roman citizen. It is in observing this that Ferrari Dalle Spade comments, justifiably, that "at this point the constitution not only grants the right of arbitration to Jews, but makes an announcement regarding that which public law (*ius publicum)* recognized as permitted to Roman citizens",[29] specifically that all arbitration required the making of an agreement (*pactio*) in order to be recognized.

"By the Jews" (*apud Iudaeos*), in the Theodosian version "by the Jews or their patriarchs" (*apud Iudaeos vel patriarchas*): It is possible that these words were added in order to refer to rabbinical courts, or at least to those Jews from whom such a court could be composed. In this way, it is possible to explain the remainder of the instruction; "the patriarchs" (*patriarchas*) was omitted following the cancellation of that group's status in the year 429 (compare with C.Th. 16.8.29).

"In a private dispute" (*In civili... negotio*) more strongly emphasizes the exclusion of criminal and public matters from the framework of arbitration; arbitration is recognized only in the realm of civic dealings, which is to say, private law.

This being the case, we must ask the following question: did the decisions of these arbiter-judges receive special recognition, or were they considered binding only to the same degree as every other arbitered decision? Here also it is possible to discern a similarity to the decisions which were rendered in the practice of "judgment before the bishop" (*episcopalis audientia*). The text declares that it is the task of the judges to carry out (*exsequantur)* the decisions of the arbitrators as if they were

28 P.F. Girard, *Manuel de droit romain*, (Paris, 1911) 609, n. 2; Juster, *Juifs*, II, at 103, n. 3; L. Wenger, *Institutes*, at 337ff.; M. Kaser, in *RPR*, 2, at 384, n. 93; *id.*, in *RZPR*, at 440, n. 18; 512, n. 3; 527, n. 8. On the *compromissum* see: M. Talamanca, *Ricerche in tema di 'compromissum'*, (Milano, 1958). On the *compromissum* and on the *pactio* see K.H. Ziegler, *Das private Schiedsgericht*, (München, 1971) 181f., 186, and the survey of G. Wesener in (1982) 23 *IURA* 215. Baron and Kisch claim that an agreement which contains an arbitration clause must be in writing (ZSS, at 549). On arbitration in Jewish law see: B. Cohen, "Arbitration in Jewish and Roman Law", in *id.*, *Jewish and Roman Law. A Comparative Study*, (New York, vol. II, 1966) 651ff. On use of the term *compromissum* see D. Sperber, *A Dictionary of Greek and Latin Legal Terms in Rabbinic Literature*, (Jerusalem, 1984) 171f. and see the comment of J. Modrzejewski, at 213.

29 Ferrari Dalle Spade, *Giurisdizione speciale*, at 287.

ex cognitoris arbitri; before us then is a situation in which the arbitrated decisions of Jewish clerics (made in civil matters that were brought before them with the mutual agreement of the litigants involved) received the privileged status of being considered as equal to the decisions of official judges and "they would be carried out by the usual bodies appointed to this task".[30]

The purpose of the constitution as it appeared in Justinian's Code, was to prevent all official recognition of Jewish law. With the abolition of the patriarchate (429) the religio-national center of the Jews crumbled; at the same time legislators sought, perhaps, to revoke the authority of the Jewish courts even in those cases where both litigants were Jews from birth but one had converted to Christianity or intended to do so. The constitution in its present form establishes clearly: Jewish civil law applies only with the mutual agreement of the parties to the judgment.

In order to better understand the background of the law under examination we must consider that — according to several scholars — during this period arbitration and compromise were the accepted manner of settling private disputes. The parties to a case preferred to turn to arbitration while the role of the governmental justice system was generally limited to questions of taxes and administration.[31] Though the situation in Egypt at that time demonstrates our point well, there were

30 *Ibid.*, at 294. See also at 296 — the distinction between thse types of arbitration which were once obligatory and those which were simply "of the people" is discussed. See also at 302 and on — a discussion of the possibility of appeal regarding an arbitrated decision. On the topic of force see: Talamanca, *Ricerche in tema di compromissum,* cited above in n. 28, at 141, n. 422: from the Italian: "In this situation the decision is as binding as in a situation in which the arbitrated decision was given by an iudex. In these situations, as emphasized regarding the *episcopalis audientia* the scholium ZEITI in *Bas.* 12.1.74, an arbiter's decision may be executed without the taking of a poena: This, it appears, is because the poena is unnecessary and it is possible to adopt sanctions as a right intrinsic to the decision itself"; see also G. Kisch, *Zur Frage* at 395 on *iudices provinciarum* for the execution of an arbited decision.

31 A.A. Schiller, "The Courts are No More", in *Studi Volterra* 1, (Milano, 1971) 469 and 498; *Idem*, "The Fate of Imperial Legislation in the Late Byzantine Egypt" in *Legal Thought in the U.S.A..*, (Brusselles, 1970) 41ff; and see the critical remarks of D. Simon, (1971) 18 *RIDA*, 623ff.

32 On this topic see the study by J.G. Kerman, The Case of Flavia Christodote: Observations on PSJ I 76", (1978) 29 *Zeitschr. f. Pap. u. Ep.*, 191ff.

times when the population would prefer the forum of government courts.[32] Even so, there is no serious doubt that the dominant approach in civil disputes was that of arbitration and compromise.[33]

In any event, since we are dealing with a period in which the practice of arbitration was widespread, we can well understand why, after recognition of Jewish law in the strict sense was revoked (in that parties were no longer obliged to submit themselves to it) the Code demonstrates a measure of tolerance: if, despite the freedom to turn to official courts, the parties insist on turning to a Jewish court, the law permits them to do so.[34] The scholar Guido Kisch claims that from the Jewish point of view the change included in C.I. 1.9.8 was not of practical significance since the Jews continued to bring their disputes before Rabbinical courts in the form of arbitration. We do not completely agree with this affirmation. Indeed, it is true that the Jews continued to bring their claims before Rabbinical courts and that they viewed the Rabbinical decisions as binding upon them; however, we must keep in mind that as well as those Jews for whom the fulfillment of religious commandments was an obligation, there were others for whom the religious tradition was completely uninteresting, or even an object of bitter rejection. In our opinion, this latter group also exerted its influence within the community. This article is not the proper place for an in-depth examination of these changes, or the influences, direct and indirect, of Imperial legislation upon the Jewish community. However, we are aware that at the end of a struggle which ranged over centuries, the Jews of Babylon exerted their cultural-halachic dominance over those in Israel. In the sphere of Jewish law, too, the influence of the Jews in

33 K.H. Ziegler, *Das private Schiedsgericht*, *supra* n. 28, at 263ff. Also L. Migliardi Zingale, in M. Amelotti and L. Migliardi Zingale,*Costituzioni giustinianee*, at 6ff., 9. It is very interesting to compare the case of the Samaritans, "Then upon Zeno's arrival in the land, he brought the Samaritans under the jurisdiction of the Christian courts", see J.A. Montgomery, *The Samaritans*, (New York, 1907) 112.

34 Kisch claims that the reason for this is not founded in religious tolerance, but rather in a willingness to absolve the parties from physical punishment for their action (as would no longer be the case with the enactment of Novel 146) in (1960) 77 *ZSS*, 399, with a quotation from E. Gans in which it is claimed that we are speaking of a *de facto* privilege.

Israel waned and flickered while that of the Jews in Babylon grew increasingly stronger. This constitution continues to leave its imprint upon the history of the Jews.[35]

We will end with a brief glance at Justinian's law and its proper meaning. Several years after the publication of his Code, Justinian once again became interested in the affairs of the Jews — this time in Novel 146, from the 8th of February 553.[36] The Novel deals with matters which are completely religious in nature, for instance, the language in which the Torah is to be read in synagogue, faith in resurrection and the day of judgment, and questions concerning the nature of angels. Regarding these questions, Justinian makes his stance known. In addition, he forbids Jewish rabbis from declaring a ban on those who refuse to heed their judicial decisions.

From the above we can see that the interpretation given to C.J. 1.9.8 was appropriate to the nature of an Emperor like Justinian — an Emperor who saw himself as God's representative on earth, authorized to rule in religious matters (and not only those of the Jews). With Justinian it would be logical to associate an intentional omission of the "non" and the consequent removal of religious authority.

As far as the Jews were concerned, the feeling that it was necessary to educate the people as to the importance of Tannaitic law grew among Jewish sages, as reflected in the Mechilta de Rabbi Ishmael (to Exodus 21):

> *'And these are the laws which you shall place before you': Rabbi Eleazar ben Azriah says, Behold. the nations are judging according to the laws of Israel, and so I think to myself that their rulings upon us will be acceptable. The Torah says 'These are the laws'—you judge your own affairs, it is not for them to judge your affairs.*[37]

35 On this subject and for a bibliography pertaining to it see: R. Bonfil, "Tra due mondi: prospettive di ricerca sulla storia culturale degli Ebrei nell'Italia Meridonale nell'alto Medioevo", in *Italia Iudaica*, (Roma 1983) at 135ff. For a discussion of this constitutio's interpretation in the Middle Ages see V. Colorni, *Legge ebraica* at 140ff. See R. Bonfil, *The Rabbinate During the Italian Renaissance*, (Jerusalem, 1979) 135ff.

36 On this Novel, see A. Linder, *The Jews and Judaism*, *supra* n. 5, at 295 and A.M. Rabello, *Giustiniano, Ebrei e Samaritani alla luce delle fonti storico letterarie, ecclesiastiche e giuridiche*, (Milano, vol. II, 1988) 814ff.

37 See A.M. Rabello, "Jewish and Roman Jurisdiction", *supra* n. 1, at 145ff.

In the Justinianic period the question "if the gentiles judge according to the laws of Israel" was no longer asked, and the emphasis changed to the fact that it was the obligation of every Jew involved in litigation with his fellow Jew to bring the case before Rabbinical courts. However, a discussion of the law's influence upon the Jews of the Middle Ages is outside the scope of this article, which concentrates on the days of Emperor Justinian, who limited the remnant of judicial autonomy which the Jews had held in regard to religious matters.[38] From then on, in the matter of purely religious issues as in all others, the life-blood of Jewish law would depend upon the willingness of Jews to prefer Rabbinical justice to that of the Emperors.

I am delighted to dedicate this study to my friend Professor Alan Watson: he visited us in Israel several times and published some important studies in our publications.[39] During his last visit, Alan seemed particularly interested in religious/legal problems.[40] Certainly, with his wisdom he will understand that my subject of study, which *prima facie* seems to take a very technical tone is, in reality, a very substantive problem, as it explores Jewish autonomy in religious and civic matters

38 On the religious politic of Justinian see *supra* n. 7.

39 See, e.g., A. Watson, "Illogicality and Roman Law", (1972) 7 Is. L.R. at 14 ff.; *Idem*, "The End of Roman Juristic Writing", (1995) 29 Is. L.R. at 228ff.; *Idem*, "Equity in the time of Cicero", in A.M.Rabello, ed., *Aequitas and Equity. Equity in Civil Law and Mixed Jurisdictions* (Jerusalem, 1997) 23ff.

40 See, e.g., A. Watson, *The State, Law and Religion: Pagan Rome* (Athens, 1992); *Idem*, *Jesus and the Jews. The Pharisaic Tradition in John* (Athens, 1995); *Idem*, *The Trial of Jesus* (Athens, 1995); *Idem*, *The Trial of Stephen. The First Christian Martyr* (Athens, 1996); *Idem*, *Jesus and Law* (Athens, 1996).

XIV

THE ATTITUDE OF ROME TOWARDS CONVERSIONS TO JUDAISM
(Atheism, Circumcision, Proselytism)

To Professor Avraham Wasserstein
in piam memoriam

Outline:

A) THE PAGAN PERIOD

1. Introduction
2. An Outline on Conversion to Judaism from the Jewish Point of View
3. Jewish Proselytism in Roman Literature
4. Proselytism and the Accusation of Atheism
5. Proselytism and the Prohibition of Circumcision

B) THE CHRISTIAN PERIOD

1. Introduction
2. The Crime of Apostasy to Judaism
3. Punishments for the Proselyte
4. Punishments for the Converter
5. Prohibition of Circumcising a Free Man
6. Prohibition of Circumcising a Slave
7. The Return to Judaism of Jews who had Converted to Christianity
8. Conclusions

1) Introduction

The problem which we would like to discuss in this article concerns the attitude of Rome towards individuals whose behavior excluded them from the societal norm. We will examine the particular case of Jews, with some mention of the case of early Christians.

The Jewish population in Roman Italy, composed partially of *peregrini* and partially of emancipated Roman citizens, required the concession of privileges in order to allow it to lead a way of life in accordance with its traditions. The first privileges granted to Jews were bestowed by Julius Caesar. He, who exempted Jews from military service, granted autonomy to judge their civil cases according to Jewish law, permitted forming themselves into congregations (notwithstanding the prohibition imposed by law against the *collegia*), and allowed money collection for the needs of the community and for the Temple in Jerusalem. Augustus, later, added privileges aimed at preventing the civic life of the Jews from being disturbed by impediments to their observance of the Sabbath.

It is worth noting the *national* character that was attributed to these privileges. Judaism appeared to the Romans not as an abstract philosophy, but rather as the religious customs of the Jewish Nation. Jewish customs were identified with the particular character of this Nation. The main purpose of the privileges was to allow the Jews *vivere suis legibus*. Significantly, these provisions applied to the *Iudaei*, not to Romans who became *Iudaei*.[1]

1 Cf. Scriptores Historiae Augustae, Ps. Lampridius, Alexander Severus, 22,4: *"Iudaeis privilegia reservavit, Christianos esse passus est"* and see Th. Mommsen, "Der Religionsfrevel nach Römischem Recht". in *Gesammelte Schriften*, 3, 1907, pp. 369 ff.; J. Juster, *Les Juifs dans l'Empire romain. Leur condition juridique, économique et sociale*, Paris, 1914, vol. I, p. 226 and p. 259; M. Stern, *Greek and Latin Authors on Jews and Judaism*, Jerusalem, 1980, vol. II, No. 520; A.M. Rabello, "The Legal Condition of the Jews in the Roman Empire", *Aufstieg und Niedergang der Römischen Welt* (= ANRW), Berlin-New York, II, 13, 1980, pp. 662 ff. nt. 93 and nt. 148.; C. Saulnier, "Lois romaines sur les Juifs selon Flavius Josephe", *Revue Biblique*, 88, 1981, pp. 163 ff.; T. Rajak, "Was there a Roman Charter for the Jews?", *Journal of Roman Studies*, 74, 1984, pp. 110 ff.; *eadem*, "Jewish Rights in the Greek Cities under Roman Rule: A New Approach", *Approaches to Ancient Judaism* vol. 5 *Studies in Judaism and Its Graeco-Roman Context* (ed. W.S. Green), Atlanta, 1985, pp. 33 ff.; L.H. Feldman, "The Omnipresence of the God-Fearers", *Biblical Archaeology Review*, 12.5, Sept.-Oct. 1986, pp. 58 ff.; Sh. J.D. Cohen, "Respect for Judaism by Gentiles according to Josephus", *Harvard Theological Review*, 80, 1987, pp. 409 ff.; A.M. Rabello, *Giustiniano, Ebrei e Samaritani alla luce delle fonti storico-letterarie, ecclesiastiche e giuridiche*, Milano, 1987-1988, s.v. "privilegi"; M. Pucci Ben-Zeev, "Jewish Rights in the

The Romans believed that the Jewish cult must be tolerated in a manner similar to the customs of every other friendly population, which were at the beginning allied - and later annexed - to the Empire. But the Jews, were not satisfied with a policy of passive tolerance. To put into practice the principle of religious tolerance for the Jews, it was necessary to introduce rules that allowed the infringement of the general Roman norms. This was accomplished by establishing privileges. In fact, it can be said that the history of Judaism in the Roman Empire is one of granted or denied privileges.

From the point of view of Roman law, only foreign Jews might benefit from privileges; those who were Roman citizens were subject to general laws and were obliged to honour the Roman gods. Nevertheless, in practice, Jewish Roman citizens enjoyed the same privileges. Under the Emperors of the first and second century, the relations between Rome and the Jews were disturbed by periodical crises, which provoked riots, on the one hand, and expulsions and deportations, on the other. Some of this turmoil probably broke out because of disagreements among Jews themselves or between Jews and early Christians. Suetonius, for example, relates that Claudius expelled the Jews from Rome *"impulsore Chresto assidue tumultuantes"*,[2] which appears, however, to have had a very limited effect.

It appears that even the 66-70 war had no repercussions in Italy, and Jews enjoyed a period of relative quiet under Nero, Vespasian and Titus. Certainly, the terrible events that took place in Palestine caused the Jews of Rome a great deal of grief, but they themselves, were not subjected to direct persecutions. On the other hand, Domitian undertook harsh and shameful measures to impose the payment of the *Fiscus Judaicus* - on

Roman World: New Perspectives", in Te'uda n. XII, *Studies on the Jewish Diaspora in the Hellenistic and Roman Periods* (eds. B. Isaac & A. Oppenheimer), Tel-Aviv, 1996, pp. 39 ff. On the national character of the privileges at the time of Diocletian, a period of persecutions against Christians and of relative peace for the Jews, see A.M. Rabello, "On the Relations between Diocletian and the Jews", in *Journal of Jewish Studies*, Oxford, 35, 1984, pp. 147 ff. On the laws against Christians see: T.D. Barnes, "Legislation against the Christians", *Journal of Roman Studies*, 58 (1968), 32 ff.; E.Bickerman, "Trajan, Hadrian and the Christians", *Rivista di Filologia e di Istruzione classica*, 96 (1968), 290 ff.; G. Lanata, *Gli atti dei Martiri come documenti processuali*, Milano, 1973.

2 Suetonius, *Divus Claudius*, 25,4: *"Iudaeos impulsore Chresto assidue tumultuantes Roma expulit"*. On the text, with bibliography and commentaries, see M. Stern, *Greek and Latin Authors* (*op. cit. supra* nt. 1) vol. II, Nr. 307, pp. 113 ff..

both Jews and proselytes[3] - and persecuted proselytes[4].

Generally speaking, notwithstanding the two major wars fought by the Flavians and later by Hadrian, the balance of the relationship between Rome and the Jews in Italy was positive: Jews enjoyed relative peace and were granted new privileges; they were exempted (themselves and their own children only) from the prohibition to practice circumcision[5] as well as from the obligation to take part in the cult of the Emperor, a cult opposed to their religious principles. Here, too, we must remember that these privileges were in force only for Jews by birth, as opposed to those Roman citizens who became Jews.

Nevertheless, according to the opinion that seems to us to be the most correct, during the pagan age, conversion to Judaism did not consitute a *crimen sui generis*. Rather, the *crimen* consisted of atheism, i.e., not worshipping Roman gods without having a privilege exempting one from such duty. Similarly, the *crimen* in undergoing circumcision without a special privilege allowing it was based upon a charge of atheism.[6]

2) An Outline on Conversion to Judaism from the Jewish Point of View

At this point, we believe it would be useful to present some very brief information on conversion to Judaism, from the Jewish point of view, considering, in particular, the procedure. The will to become a Jew means to become part of the Jewish people and to accept complete submission to God and to His precepts. The classic example of a proselyte is the Biblical one of Ruth the Moabite who, addressing Naomi, declares (Ruth 1, 17): "Your people are my people, your God is my God".

For an individual who wished to be converted, the following steps were therefore necessary:

3 On the duty of proselytes to pay the *fiscus iudaicus* see M. Stern, *Greek and Latin Authors*, (*op. cit. supra nt.* 1) vol. I, p.198.

4 Suetonius, *Domitianus*, 12,2 (the passage is quoted *infra*, in the text near footnote 34). On the text, with bibliography and commentary, see M. Stern, *Greek and Latin Authors* (*op. cit. supra* nt. 1) vol.. II, Nr. 320, pp. 128 ff.

5 Cf. A.M. Rabello, "The Ban on Circumcision as a cause of Bar Kokhbah Rebellion", in *Israel Law Review*, vol. 29, 1995, pp. 176 ff.

6 Regarding this, we adhere to the opinion of J. Juster, *Les Juifs dans l'Empire Romain*, vol. I, pp. 254 ff.; Mommsen believes, on the contrary, that a *crimen* of apostasy to Judaism existed, as well: Th. Mommsen, *Römisches Strafrecht*, Leipzig, 1899, pp. 573 f.

a) Submitting to what is called in Rabbinic literature "the yoke of the Kingdom of Heaven", i.e., committing to fulfil all Biblical precepts, as interpreted by the Rabbinic tradition. One of these precepts, the Second Commandment of the Decalogue, demands: "Thou shalt have no other gods before Me". This commandment imposes an absolute prohibition against taking part in any other cult, in the worship of anything, including the cult of the Roman Emperor. We can hence understand how being Jewish could lead to a charge of atheism for one who had no privilege exempting him from the duty of the Roman pagan cult.

b) If the prospective convert is male, he must consent to being circumcised and be circumcised in accordance with Biblical law. Circumcision is considered the tangible sign of the covenant between God and the People of Israel, since Abraham, and is a requirement made of all Jewish males: "And God said unto Abraham, But thou, for thy part, shalt keep my covenant, thou and thy seed after thee, in their generations. This is my covenant, which ye shall keep, between me and between you, and between thy seed after thee: Every man-child among you shall be circumcised. And ye shall circumcise the flesh of your foreskin; and this shall serve as the token of the covenant between me and you. And at eight days old shall every man-child in your generations be circumcised among you, he that is born in the house, or bought with money of any stranger, who is not of thy seed. He that is born in thy house, and he that is bought with thy money, must be circumcised; and my covenant shall be in your flesh for an everlasting covenant. And any uncircumcised male, who circumciseth not the flesh of his foreskin, that soul shall be cut off from his people; he hath broken my covenant".[7]

Therefore, we can well understand the direct relationship between the legislation of Roman laws against circumcision (at first in the form of general prohibitions, and later directed particularly at non-Jews) and the *conversion* rate. The absence of a similar requirement made of female converts is one factor in the explanation why, in Rome, female proselytes to Judaism outnumbered males ones.

c) Immersing onself in a ritual bath of purification during a ceremony in the presence of a rabbinical tribunal. Such an immersion is called by some Graeco-Roman authors "baptism".

7 Genesis 17, 9-14, in the translation by I. Leeser, Hebrew Publishing Company, New York 1923.

d) When the Sanctuary in Jerusalem was functioning, the final ritual to be performed was the offering of a sacrifice. After the destruction of the Sanctuary in the 70 C.E. war, this requirement was waived.[8]

At the conclusion of this procedure, a non-Jew is considered to have properly become a Jew and, as one of them, is subject to rights and duties of a Jew by birth.

Generally speaking, Judaism quite never considered as one of its tasks that of looking for new adepts: every non-Jew is considered by the Jewish tradition to be subject only to the so-called "seven Noahides precepts", which can be defined as basic moral precepts, or laws of nature, such as "Thou shalt not kill". Jewish tradition does not request from a non-Jew to become a Jew, but simply to observe those precepts of the sons of Noah.

The attitude of the Sages of Israel towards the acceptance of proselytes was not unequivocal.[9] There were those who believed that the very purpose of Israel's exile was to divulge knowledge of the Lord's Torah and to receive under the wings of heavenly protection a great number of proselytes. Others admired the proselytes' very scrupulous allegiance to

8 See Mishnah Pesachim, VIII,8; Mishnah 'Eduiot v. 2; Talmud Bab. Keritot 9a; Talmud Bab. Yevamot 46 a-b.

9 On the problem of the choice of Israel and of conversion to Judaism, see the in-depth analysis by E.E. Urbach, *The Sages. Their Concepts and Beliefs*, Jerusalem, 1979, pp. 541 ff.; see also B.J. Bamberger, *Proselytism in the Talmudic Period*, Cincinnati, 1939; W.G. Braude, *Jewish Proselytism in the First Five Centuries of the Common Era: the Age of the Tannaim and Amoraim*, Providence, 1940; M. Simon, *Verus Israel, Etude sur les relations entre Chrétiens et Juifs dans l'Empire Romain (135-425)*, Paris, 1964, pp. 316 ff.; M. Hengel, *Judaism and Hellenism: Studies in Their Encounter in Palestine during the Early Hellenistic Period*, Philadelphia, 1974, I, pp. 307 ff.; II, p. 204; M. Avi-Yonah, *The Jews under Roman and Byzantine Rule. A Political History of Palestine from the Bar Kokhba War to the Arab Conquest*, Jerusalem – New York, 1984, pp. 81 ff.; S. McKnight, *A Light among the Gentiles. Jewish Missionary Activity in the Second Temple Period*, Minneapolis, 1991; M. Goodman, "Proselytising in Rabbinic Judaism", JJS 40, 1989 pp. 175 ff.; idem, "Jewish Proselytising in th First Century", in J. Lieu, J. North and T. Rajak (eds.), *The Jews among Pagans and Christians in the Roman Empire*, London and New York, 1992, pp. 53 ff. E. Will, C. Orrieux, *Proselytisme Juif? Histoire d'une Erreur*, Paris, 1992; L.H. Feldman, *Jew and Gentile in the Ancient World. Attitudes and Interactions from Alexander to Justinian*, Princeton, 1993; and the observations of D. Rokeach, "Conversion to Judaism in Ancient Times according to Jewish law and in practice", *Bet Mikra*, 141, 1995, pp. 135 ff. (Hebrew). M. Goodman, *Mission and Conversion. Proselytising in the Religious History of the Roman Empire*, Oxford, 1994 (and the Review of D. Mendels, in *Scripta Classica Israelica*, XV, 1996, pp. 303 ff..

Tradition. For example, during the second half of the second century, Rabbi Eleazar declared: "The Saint, Blessed be He, did not exile Israel among the nations but to allow proselytes to join it".[10]

On the other hand, there were also those who pointed out, with sorrow, that the number of proselytes who did not observe the Torah was great and that they had brought about an internal weakening of the Jewish people. We cannot exclude the possibility that many of these discussions took place in reaction to the Roman legislation regarding circumcision and proselytism. With this we shall suffice, as the Jewish attitude regarding proselytism during this period is beyond the scope of this work,[11] the aim of which is to examine the flip side of the coin, i.e., Rome's attitude towards this phenomenon.

3) Jewish Proselytism in Roman Literature

We think it could be useful, for a better understanding of the topic, to examine briefly how Jewish proselytism was seen by some Roman authors.

Horatius (65 - 8 B.C.E.) makes one allusion to the missionary zeal of Jews: *"... nam multo plures sumus, ac veluti te Iudaei cogemus in hanc concedere turbam"*.[12] This comparison makes us presume that there was Jewish missionary activity in Rome.

At the beginning of the first century C.E., Valerius Maximus referred to the banishment of astrologers and Jewish missionaries from Rome in 139 B.C.E. by the *praetor peregrinus*. This act emphasizes the fear exhibited by the upper classes due to the spreading influence of oriental ideas on Romans. There are those who connect such missionary activity to the enthusiasm among the Jews of Rome which followed the victory of the Maccabees over Antiochus IV Epiphanes. Though original texts have not reached us, we do have the texts of two epitomists, Nepotianus

10 Talmud Bab. Pesachim, 87 b.

11 On the opposite problem of apostasy during this period see: S. Zeitlin, "Mumar and Meshumad", *Jewish Quarterly Review*, N.S. 54 (1963-64), pp. 84 ff. = *Studies in Early History of Judaism*, vol. 3: *Judaism and Christianity*, N.Y. 1975, pp. 246 ff; S.M.Wagner, "The Meshumad and Mumar in Talmudic literature", *Memorial vol. Dolnitsky*, 1982, pp. 198 ff.

12 Sermones I,4, 142-143; for text see: M. Stern, *Greek and Latin Authors*, vol. I, Nr. 127, pp. 321 and 323.

(probably 4th-5th century) and Iulius Paris (probably 4th century). The latter's epitome appears to be more accurate:

> *Chaldeos igitur Cornelius Hispalus urbe expulit et intra decem dies Italia abire iussit, ne peregrinam scientiam venditarent. Iudaeos quoque, qui Romanis tradere sacra sua conati erant, idem Hispalus urbe exterminavit, arasque privatas e publicis locis abiecit.*[13]

> *Cn. Cornelius Hispalus praetor peregrinus M. Popilio Laenate L. Calpurnio coss. edicto Chaldeos citra decimum diem abire ex urbe atque Italia iussit, levibus et ineptis ingeniis fallaci siderum interpretationem quaestosam mendacis suis caliginem inicientes - Idem Iudaeos qui Sabazi Iovis cultu Romanos inficere mores conati erant, repetere domos suas coegit.*[14]

The name *Iupiter Sabatius*, which certainly does not exist in this way in Jewish literature (although there are those who saw in it a translation into Latin of the name *Ado-nai Zevaot*), gives us a clear glimpse of a Judeo-pagan syncretism, which certainly was not Judaism, though to Romans it might appear to be such, and which was considered dangerous because of its potential popularity.

During approximately the same period, the philosopher Seneca (end of the first century B.C.E. - 65 C.E.) refers to the movement of the spreading of Jewish customs across the entire Mediterranean:

> *De illis sane Iudaeis cum loqueretur, ait: consuetudo convaluit, ut per omnes iam terras recepta sit; victi victoribus leges dederunt. Ait enim: "Illi tamen causas ritus sui noverunt; maior pars populi facit, quod cur faciat ignorat".*[15]

We accept the interpretation proposed by Reinach and shared by Stern, that *illi* refers to Jews, while *maior pars populi* refers to non-Jews who

13 Facta et dicta memorabilia, I,3,3, Ex Epitoma Ianuarii Nepotiani.

14 Facta et dicta memorabilia, I,3,3 Ex Epitoma Iulii Paridis. For text see: M. Stern, *Greek and Latin Authors*, (*op. cit. supra* nt. 1) vol. I, Nr. 147a, Nr. 147b, pp. 357 ff.

15 De Superstitione, apud August. D-i civitate D.,VII, 11; for text see: M. Stern, *Greek and Latin Authors*, vol. I, Nr. 186, pp. 429 ff.

adopted Jewish customs. We must also keep in mind that only at the end of Seneca's life did the Roman government begin to make a distinction between Jews and Christians.

Between 50 and 130 C.E., another stoic philosopher, Epictetus, refers to Jews in a more objective tone, without the hostility with which Seneca did. Epictetus refers to the difference between various peoples - Jews, Syrians, Egyptians - maintaining that one who adopts Judaism and is "baptized" feels himself to be a Jew, as if he were a Jew by birth. Epictetus' use of the term 'baptism' might be semantic and doesn't indicate that he confused Jews with Christians: a convert's requirement to immersion himself in a ritual bath during a special ceremony might easily be called, *tout-court*, "baptism".[16]

Tacitus (56-120) expressly refers to proselytes apropos circumcision:

> *"(Iudaei) Circumcidere genitalia instituerunt, ut diversitate noscantur. Transgressi in morem eorum idem usurpant, nec quidquam prius imbuuntur quam comtemnere deos...".*[17]

In his Annals, Tacitus reports the banishment of Egyptians and Jews to Sardinia, in 19 C.E.; this *senatusconsultum* was also applied to proselytes to Judaism, probably on the basis of their being *"quattuor milia ... ea superstitione infecta".*[18]

Additionally, the edict includes "God fearers" and sympathizers: *"Quidam sortiti metuentem sabbata patrem ...".*[19]

Cassius Dio (160-230) expressly affirms that among the IOUDAIOI are included also those who joined the Jewish religion/ nation; such a remark is considered proof that Jewish proselytism continued during the period

16 For text see: M. Stern, *Greek and Latin Authors*, (*op. cit. supra* nt. 1) vol.1, Nr. 254, p. 543 f.

17 Historiae V,2. For text see: M. Stern, *Greek and Latin Authors*, (*op. cit. supra nt.* 1), vol. II, Nr. 281, pp. 19 and 41.

18 For text see: M. Stern, *Greek and Latin Authors*, (*op. cit. supra* nt. 1) vol. II, Nr. 284, pp. 70 ff.

19 Juvenalis, Saturae XIV, 96. On this phenomenon see explication and bibliography in M. Stern, Greek and Latin Authors, vol. II, pp. 103 ff.

of the Severi.[20] Cassius Dio connects the banishment of the Jews from Rome during the reign of Tiberius with their proselytic activities (Hist. LXVII, 18, 5). This interpretation is supported by Josephus Flavius' report of the activity of the Roman matrona Fulvia, who became a proselyte.[21] In other passages, Cassius makes express reference to the accusation of atheism against the proselytes. We will examine these passages in the next section and here want only to stress the expansion of the phenomenon among the senatorial class and the imperial family.

4) Proselytism and the Accusation of Atheism

The first clash between Judaism in Italy and the order and laws of Rome surrounded the issue of proselytsim. As we have seen, Jews have always accepted new members to their religion, and conceive of conversion as a form of adoption to the bosom of the Judaic nation.

Rome, for its part, though in principle tolerant of the religions of all foreigners, was hostile to having its own citizens adopt cults whose customs could conflict with those of Rome. The authorities feared that the spread of esoteric and conflicting rites among Roman citizens might eventually fan political and social dissatisfactions and lead to unrest. During the pagan period, when proselytism was not a criminal offence, the authorities reacted to this perceived threat by expelling the adherents of the feared cults. This form of collective administrative punishment was imposed upon Jews and members of other oriental cults without discrimination, in 139 B.C.E., and during Tiberius' reign.[22]

20 M. Simon, *Verus Israel op. cit.* (*supra* nt.9), pp. 315 ff.; M. Stern, *Greek and Latin Authors*, vol.II, pp. 348 ff., p. 353 and text Nr. 406.

21 Josephus Flavius, *Ant.* XVIII, from 81; on the passage from Cassius see: M. Stern, *Greek and Latin Authors*, (*op. cit. supra* nt. 1), vol. II, p. 365.

22 Val. Max. I, 3, 3; Jos.Fl. *Ant.* XVIII, 3, 5 (81-84); Tac. *Ann.*, II, 85,5; Suet. Tiberius, 36; Cassius Dio, LVII, 18,5a. The cause of the measure under Tiberius was, according to Josephus Flavius, a fraud some Jewish swindlers perpetrated against a proselyte noble woman; but the real reason for such a severe punitive measure most probably was the success of Jewish proselytism in Rome; E.M. Smallwood, *The Jews under Roman Rule from Pompey to Diocletian*, Leiden, 1981, pp. 201 ff.; A.M. Rabello, *Giustiniano, Ebrei e Samaritani, (op. cit. supra* nt. 1*)*, vol. II, p. 671 nt .1.

Proselytes, however, were subject to criminal sanction, for being in violation of the Roman prohibition against atheism, which included refusal to worship domestic gods and gods dear to Rome. As mentioned above, proselytes to Judaism by definition must so refuse because of Judaism's exclusive monotheistic nature.[23] It was only by virtue of a privilege bestowed upon them that Jews from birth were exempted from participation in the public cult and so avoided criminal charges.

Without the benefit of such a privilege, a woman could be convicted for refusing to participate in rites of her husband's domestic cult,[24] and state functionaries or court personages could be convicted for refusal to participate in the cult of the emperor or the cult of the state gods.

Over time, as the attitude of Rome's ruling class changed toward oriental religions in general, and toward Judaism in particular, Rome's attitude towards proselytes became ambivalent and more complex. Parallel to the Jewish community earning the favor of the authorities and of the ruling class, occasional personages from the ruling class, and even from the Imperial family, such as Poppaea and Flavius Clemens, would dally with Judaism, although without being formally converted.[25]

Of course, Domitian, a conservative emperor who maintained Rome's traditonal attitutde of suspicion, put Flavius Clemens to death for atheism. Under Domitian's reign, accusations of atheism in connection with the cult of the Emperor *numen* were relatively common; Cassius Dio states that Clemens and his wife Domitilla were accused together with many

23 J. Juster, *Les Juifs dans l'Empire romain*, vol. I, p. 256: "Ce crime – Juster explains in his masterly work – est une infraction par omission, punie indépendémment des motifs qui la font commettre que ce soit une convinction philosophique ou l'adoption du judaïsme. Le prosélyte juif ne sera donc pas puni comme tel, mais en tant qu'athée. Car l'athéisme n'est pas puni comme opinion, mais comme non-accomplissement d'un acte, c'est a dire en tant qu'il se manifeste extérieurement par un refus d'adorer les dieux".

24 To recall the case of Pomponia Graecina under Nero, see Tacitus, *Ann.*, XIII, 32.

25 The Talmud notes more than once the honourable behaviour of Roman governors, some of whom received a philosophic or religious education which helped them to be more open-minded towards Judaic mentality. See also M. Stern, "Sympathy for Judaism in Roman Senatorial Circles in the Period of the Early Empire", in Zion, 29, 1964, pp. 155 ff., (in Hebrew).

others who joined Judaism: ες τα των 'Ιουδαιων ηση εξοκελλοντες.[26]

Did the enlargement of the fiscal base increase also the number of those who had the right to enjoy Jewish privileges? Or, in other words, could those people who were included in the list of the *Fiscus Iudaicus* to appeal for this reason to exemption from military service, from appearing before the Court on Saturday, from worshipping the State gods and the divinity of the Emperor, even if they were not formally converted? The policy of Domitian appears, in this case, to be lacking in consistency: in the last years of his empire, in fact, the charge of atheism was raised against Judaizers, when the Emperor, worried about his own divinity, initiated a series of trials against high ranking Judaizers who were sentenced, as we saw in the passage from Cassius Dio, to exile and to death. Domitian's worries seem to be politically justified, if it is true that the senatorial class adopted Judeo-Christian ideas as a form of protest against absolutism.[27] M. Smallwood believes that only professed converts were punished for atheism and that for this reason a great number of men abstained from openly professing Judaism and exposing themselves to the risk of sanctions.[28] But the sentence against Clemens dates back to 95 C.E., while the persecution of Judaizers has to be placed in the period of Suetonius' youth, before 90 C.E. From the words of Cassius Dio we cannot draw the conclusion that those who were condemned were professed converts; besides, Suetonius emphasizes, as we saw, that Clemens was condemned *"ex tenuissima suspicione"*, therefore not owing to an open admission or profession of Judaism. Smallwood, too, admits that Clemens, as well as Keti'ah bar Shalom (the Roman senator converted to the Judaic faith, but was uncircumcised until his death[29]), was not a proselyte but a Judaizer.[30] Since we know, however, that formal adherence to Judaism represented for Christians a way out of persecution, the result was that Domitian's policy was indeed incoherent – putting

26 Cassius Dio, *Historia Romana*, XLVII, 14, 1-2. On the text, with bibliography and commentary, see: M. Stern, *Greek and Latin Authors*, (*op. cit. supra* nt. 1), vol. II, Nr. 435, from pp. 379 ff., referring also to the relationship with the Emperor and to the phenomenon of conversions and sympathizers for Judaism within the higher classes of Roman society.

27 S. Applebaum, *Prolegomena to the Study of the Second Jewish Revolt (A.D. 132-135)*, in BAR (=British Archaeological Reports) Supplementary Series, 7, Oxford, 1976, p. 2.

28 E.M. Smallwood, *The Jews under Roman Rule*, *op. cit.* pp. 280 ff.

29 Mentioned in Talmud Bab.,'Avodah Zharah 10 b; Midrash Devarim Rabbah, II, 24.

30 E.M. Smallwood, *The Jews under Roman Rule*, p. 382 f.

Judaizers in the same category, in relation to economic matters, with Jews and proselytes, and at the same time excluding them from the liberty of conscience granted to the latter. Domitian struck out at those who assumed Judaizing religious attitudes without identifying themselves with the People of Israel, which was considered to be identical to the enrolling into the lists of the *Fiscus Iudaicus,* the only thing that gave one the right to live in conformity with the Jewish customs. We can therefore assume that enrollment into the *Fiscus Iudaicus* could constitute a shelter from the charge of atheism; but the truth is that on some level Domitian must not have been ready to accept conversions to Judaism (those which were politically suspect) in the upper classes. It is also unlikely that the Roman nobility wished to submit to the payment of such a humiliating tax, imposed only twenty years earlier as a punishment to a defeated people.

Nerva put an end to the practice of punishments against the ASEBEIA and the customs of the Judaizers.[31] This privilege of the Jews remained in force every time that persecutions began again against those who refused to offer sacrifices, which resulted in the Jews offering to the Christians the protection of the synagogue - in order to avoid persecutions - an offer that was considered by the latter as an enticement to apostasy.[32]

5) Proselytism and the Prohibition of Circumcision

In the Roman Empire circumcision was not forbidden, at least until the time of Hadrian; we can thus understand how Herod could require that Sillaeus the Arab undergo circumcision, as a condition to marry his sister Salome, a marriage which actually never took place because of Sillaeus' refusal to be circumcised. The same happened again in the case of the daughter of Agrippa I and Epiphanes, son of the King of Commagene. However, Arizus, King of Emesa in 52 C.E. as well as Polemos, King of

31 Cassius Dio, *Historia Romana*, LXVIII, 1-2; on the text, with bibliography and commentary, see: M. Stern, *Greek and Latin Authors on Jews and Judaism*, (*op. cit. supra nt.* 1) vol. II, Nr. 436 p. 384 f. Note too, the coinage of a special coin of Nerva with the inscription: *"Fisci Iudaici calumnia sublata"*. Cf. also A.M. Rabello, *Giustiniano, Ebrei e Samaritani* (*op. cit. supra* nt. 1) vol. I, p. 51, nt. 10.

32 Hieronymus, *Comm. Ad Galatas*, 6.12.

Pontus and Cilicia, in 63[33], underwent cicrumcision.

Domitian punished castration, but not circumcision, regulating at the same time the trade of eunuchs. Based on the consideration that the trade of eunuchs had to continue, nevertheless, due to import, Dalla mentions the passage of Marcianus (D.39.4.16.7) from which we learn that among the articles subjected to tax were also Indian broadswords and lions:

"We cannot exclude with certainty, besides for the purpose of restraining a society more and more addicted to luxury and corruption, the motivation to introduce a taxation on a trade in order to secure an undoubted profit to the Treasury. The prohibition compels the interested party to turn to the import channel if he wants to avoid tax-evasion".[34]

We agree with Dalla's observations and it even seems to us that one can find evidence for the terrible and merciless tax collection of the Fiscus Iudaicus; as already quoted, Suetonius tell us that under the same Domitian:

"Praeterea ceteros Iudaicus Fiscus acerbissime actus est; ad quem deferebantur cui vel ut improfessi Iudaicam viverent vitam vel dissimulata origine imposita genti tributa non pependissent. Interfuisse me adulescentulum memini, cum a procuratore frequentissimoque consilio inspiceretur nonogenarius senex, an circumsectus esset".[35]

It is plain that here it was not a matter of prohibiting circumcision but, on the contrary, of minutely examining those who were circumcised to

33 Josephus Flavius, *Antiquitates Judaicae* 16,7,6 (225); 19, 9, 1 (335); 20,7,1 (139); 20, 7, 3 (145); see: J. Juster, *Les Juifs dans l'Empire Romain,* I, p. 264; A. Schalit, *King Herod, Portrait of a Ruler*, Jerusalem, 1964 (in Hebrew), p. 227; A.M. Rabello, "The Ban on Circumcision", *op. cit. (supra* nt. 5), pp. 176 ff.

34 D. Dalla, *L'Incapacità Sessuale in Diritto Romano*, Milano, 1978, p. 78. On relations between Domitian and the Jews see: M. Smallwood, "Domitian's attitude towards Jews and Judaism", *Classical Philology*, 51, 1956, pp. I ff.; A.M. Rabello, "Domitian", *Enc. Judaica,* Jerusalem, 6, 1971, col. 164; S. Applebaum, "Domitian's Assassination: the Jewish Aspect", *Scripta Classica Israelica*, 1, 1974, pp. 116 ff.

35 Suetonius, *Domitianus*, 12,2; see also the passage in Cassius Dio, *Historia Romana*, XLVII, 14, 1-2, according to which the motivation could be found in Domitian's contempt towards the memory of Titus; on the passage Dalla, *op. cit.* p. 82 and nt. 28.

subject them to the payment of the *Fiscus Iudaicus*. We have here a confirmation that conversion and circumcision were not punished as such, but, at least in this case, the intention was to increase, in this way, the State revenue.[36] The intervention of Domitian against castration took place by the extension (we do not know to what extent), of the penalties against homicide contained in the *Lex Cornelia de sicariis et veneficis*.[37]

Domitian's successor, Nerva, with a *Senatusconsultum* in 96 C.E. had the system of collecting the *Fiscus Iudaicus* abolished, but not the tax itself;[38] he, too, dealt with the prohibition of castration and in 97 C.E. had a legislative measure approved, according to which those who had their slaves castrated, would be deprived of half of their property (Dig. 48.8.6).

Keeping in mind other passages of Marcianus referring to Nerva (Dig. 48.8.3.4 e5), we can, in this context, point out that with Domitian started a legislative movement directed to avoid castration, punishing it with the penalties provided by the *Lex Cornelia de sicariis*. This movement continued with Nerva, who brought integrations and some changes, keeping, however, the prohibition as regulated by the *Lex Cornelia de sicariis*.[39]

All through the period before Hadrian, circumcision appears to remain lawful; the empire did not yet regulate it, thus even allowing some New Christians to escape persecution, passing themselves off as circumcised Jews, who therefore could enjoy the same Jewish privileges, among which, primarily, was the one exempting them from the obligation to

36 See the comment in M. Hengel, *Judaism and Hellenism. Studies in their Encounter in Palestina during the Early Hellenistic Period*, Philadelphia, 1974, vol. 2, p. 204 nt. 303: "After A.D. 70 the *fiscus Judaicus* was levied from every circumcised Jew, even the proselytes. Intrinsically a punitive tax for the rebellion as 'ethnos' of the Jews.". According to Juster, *Les Juifs*, 2, p. 284 nt. 3 the accusations against wealthy men were more severe, so that Domitian was able to confiscate their wealth.

37 For an essential bibliography on the Lex Cornelia de sicariis see A.M. Rabello, *Effetti personali della Patria Potestas. Dalle origini al periodo degli Antonini*, Milano, 1979, pp. 144 ff.; to set Domitian's measure against the background of his general politics, see F. Grelle, "La correctio morum nella legislazione flavia", *ANRW*, 2, 13, pp. 340 ff. (see particularly footnotes 18 and 19).

38 See I. A.F. Bruce, "Nerva and the Fiscus Iudaicus", *Palestina Exploration Quarterly*, 96,1964. pp. 34 ff. A.M. Rabello, "Nerva", *Encyclopaedia Judaica*, Jerusalem, 1971; M. Goodman, "Nerva, the Fiscus Judaicus and Jewish identity", JRS 79, 1989, pp. 40 ff.

39 A.M. Rabello, "The Ban on Circumcision", (*op. cit. supra* nt. 5), pp.176 ff.

worship the Emperor as a god. Although there was no juridical value, in fact, it was not always easy to differentiate between circumcised Jews and circumcised Christians; this is pointed out very well by Hieronymus in his commentary to the Epistle to Galatians[40] and this came to confirm that pagans who were converted to Judaism and circumcised could also find, in fact, a way to avoid the duty of participating in pagan cults.

With his provision quoted in Dig. 48.8.4.2 (Ulpianus, seventh book *de officio proconsulis*), Hadrian renewed the prohibition of castration, which was still punished by the *Lex Cornelia de sicariis*; but he used the more general term *excidere* which could be interpreted as a prohibition of castration as well as a prohibition of circumcision. In Palestine the provision was interpreted as including circumcision, as it is asserted by Jewish sources, too; this provision, probably dated 129 C.E.-130 C.E., is considered to be one of the direct causes of the Bar-Kokhba revolt which broke out in Palestine against Hadrian.[41]

In the matter of the punishments, we can observe that the following individuals were liable to death penalty:

a) Those who underwent circumcision voluntarily;

b) The physician who performed circumcision;

c) The slave who performed circumcision;

d) It is probable that, already during that period, those who performed circumcision against the will of the circumcised (excised, castrated) were also subject to this penalty (Dig. 48.8.4.2 and Pauli Sententiae 5,23,13). The free man who had performed circumcision (excision, castration) was liable to deportation to an island (Dig. 48.8.3.5) and to the confiscation of his property.[42]

With Hadrian, the problem of proselytism was based, therefore, on the prohibition of circumcision, so that, most probably, conversion of women was tolerated, when conversion of men brought with it penalties for the

40 *Ad Gal.* 6,12 in Migne, *Patrologia Latina*, 26, 435. It must be kept in mind, however, that the opposing phenomenon also existed, that is Judeo-Christians or very assimilated Jews generally preferred to undergo an operation which effaced the signs of the circumcision *(epispasmos)* in order to avoid payment of the *Fiscus Iudaicus*.

41 A. M. Rabello, "The Ban on Circumcision", (*op. cit. supra* nt. 5), pp. 176 ff. with an examination of the sources and a discussion of the different opinions.

42 *Ibid.*

proselyte as well as for the converter.

However, in this case too, a *modus vivendi* was reached with the rescript of Antoninus Pius, referred to Dig. 48, 8, 11,pr.:

> *Modestinus, l.6 regularum: Circumcidere Iudaeis filios suos tantum rescripto divi Pii permittitur: in non eiusdem religionis qui hoc fecerit, castrantis poena irrogatur.*

The rescript confirms again the prohibition of circumcision, which is still punished according to the rules of the *Lex Cornelia de sicariis*. Yet, Antoninus Pius granted to the Jews alone the privilege to circumcise their own sons, while they were forbidden to circumcise others, including their slaves.[43] In the repetition of the edicts on this subject and in the infliction of the penalties on the transgressors, we can see an indication of the fact that proselytism continued to exist, though, as we will see further on, this is an argument that must be used with great caution.

Severus renewed the prohibition of circumcision, and according to the historian Spartianus:*"Iudaeos fieri sub gravi poena vetuit. Idem etiam de Christianis sanxit"*; some scholars explain this passage in the sense that the Emperor prohibited proselytism without distinction between Jews and Christians, but Juster maintains, on the contrary, that Spartianus refers to the renewal of the decree against circumcision and that only for the sake of parallelism, that was a common literary style, Spartianus mentioned together Jews and Christians.[44]

43 I accept this interpretation, on the basis of the two Scholia of the corresponding passage of the Basilica; scholars hold different opinions on the interpretation of D. 48.8.11: for some, the *tantum* refers to *Iudaei*, therefore excluding from the privilege those who were not Jews by birth and thus forbidding circumcision to non-Jews; on the contrary for others, the *tantum* refers to *filios suos*, that is forbidding Jews to circumcise others than their own children, for example, their slaves. See A.M. Rabello, "The Legal Condition of the Jews", (*op. cit. supra* nt. 1), pp. 700 ff.

44 Scriptores Historiae Augustae, *Vita Severi*, 17,1; see M. Stern, *Greek and Latin Authors*, (*op. cit. supra* nt. 1), II, Nr. 515.; see also the opinion of Juster, *Les Juifs*, p. 259 nt. 1; p. 267 nt. 1. As a matter of fact, we have no information that the charge of atheism was ever again brought against proselytes to Judaism, while it was lodged against Christians; see A.M. Rabello, "On the relations between Diocletian and the Jews", (*op. cit. supra* nt. 5), pp. 147 ff.

B) THE CHRISTIAN PERIOD

1) Introduction

With the advent of the Christian Empire, the specific crime of apostasy to Judaism was defined. While the punishment for those who infringed upon the prohibition of the circumcision remained firmly in force, Christians were prohibited to convert to Judaism, under penalty of confiscation of their properties and deprivation of the right to draft their wills.[45]

The Empire, also became more intolerant towards Jewish propaganda, and openly joined with the efforts of the Church to stamp out Jewish proselytism; in the fourth and fifth centuries, indeed, Judaism still continued to attract proselytes and sympathizers. This is the background for the numerous imperial interventions in the legislative field against conversions, especially to Judaism.[46]

Probably, in various cases, Jews succeeded in eluding the observance of those imperial constitutions, but for this consideration alone we cannot

45 Essential also for this subject remains the study of Juster, *Les Juifs dans l'Empire Romain*, I, p. 260 ff. In general, on the attitude of the Roman Christian Empire towards Judaism, with some mention of the problem of conversions, see: B. Biondi, *Il Diritto Romano Cristiano*, vol.1-3, Milano, 1952-1957; J. Gaudemet, *L' Église dans l'Empire Romain (IV-V Siècles)*, Paris, 1958; G.G. Archi, *Giustiniano Legislatore*, Bologna 1970; *idem*, *Teodosio II e la Sua Codificazione*, Napoli, 1976; L.De Giovanni, *Chiesa e Stato nel Codice Teodosiano. Saggio sul Libro XVI*, Napoli, 1980; A.M. Rabello, "The Legal Condition of the Jews in the Roman Empire", (*op. cit. supra* nt. 1), pp. 662 ff; J. Gaudemet, *Eglise et Société en Occident au Moyen Age*, London, 1984; A.M. Rabello, *Giustiniano, Ebrei e Samaritani* (*op. cit. supra* nt. 1). The change from paganism to Christianity is described as follows by B. Biondi: "Dalla libertà religiosa pagana si passa all'apostolato; dall'apostolato, con crescendo spaventoso, all'intolleranza e alla persecuzione... Liberta` religiosa e agnosticismo tramontano. L'impero diventa apertamente confessionista: prospetta una precisa formula di fede, ne impone l'osservanza ai sudditi e mira a reprimere tutto ciò che non sia conforme ad essa." *Il Diritto Romano Cristiano*, I, pp. 236 and 306.

46 See S.W. Baron, *A Social and Religious History of the Jews*, New York/Philadelphia, 1952 and the article by L.H. Feldman, "The Contribution of Professor Salo W. Baron to the Study of Ancient Jewish History: his appraisal of anti-Judaism and Proselytism", *AJS Review*, 18, 1993, pp. 1 ff.; see also idem, "The Omnipresence of the God-Fearers", *Biblical Archaeology Review*, 12.5, Sept.-Oct. 1986, pp. 58 ff.

claim that the laws did not, for the most part, have significant influence. In fact, the need to try to elude the law by appealing to corrupt Province governors and continuing to bribe them, created a situation which required intense efforts, thereby disturbing the daily life of the Jew.[47]

47 See e.g,. the observations by L.H. Feldman: "Professor Baron remarks that, on the whole, after Constantine, the legal situation of the Jews was much more favorable in the Persian than in the Roman Empire" (2.180). This is undoubtedly true, but we may perhaps qualify this remark by noting that *de facto* even in the Roman Empire the Jews were not so badly off, inasmuch as there is much evidence that the laws were simply not enforced, *op. cit.* p.11 and nt. 34; see also *idem*, "Proselytism by Jews in the Third, Fourth and Fifth Centuries" in *Journal for the Study of Judaism*, XXIV, 1993, pp. 1 ff. Among my various studies dedicated to the subject, almost all of them in Italian, Feldman refers only to my contribution in English published in ANRW, II, 13, 1988. Among other things, Feldman accuses me of underestimating the fact that the imperial constitutions come back persistently to the prohibition of proselytism; this is an indication, he maintains, that Jewish proselytism continued actively also during the Christian period, in a way that justified the continuous legislative intervention. It is interesting to note that on my very point of there having been Roman intervention, a position opposite to that of Feldman is developed by Giorgio Barone Adesi- who thought that, on the contrary, I had attached too much importance to the sources. This scholar pointed out that there existed a problem of repetition as a "topos" of various norms, including those referring to proselytism, therefore, indeed, we must not attach too much importance to the fact of the repetition itself. The phenomenon of the normative reiterations is now studied by F. Zuccotti, *"Furor Haereticorum". Studi sul trattamento giuridico della follia e sulla persecuzione della eterodossia religiosa nella legislazione del Tardo Impero Romano*, (Milano, 1992), particularly pp. 145 ff. I think I can come to the conclusion that, between these two polar positions, I maintained the one that, a posteriori, seems to be the middle course; that is, I tried to assign the corect emphasis (or what seems to me to be the correct weight) to each of the sources examined.
Among other prominent studies, recently published, worthy of mention: M.P. Baccari, "Gli apostati nel Codice Teodosiano", Apollinaris, 54, 1981, pp.538 ff.; Eadem, "Comunione e cittadinanza. (A proposito della posizione giuridica di Eretici, Apostati, Giudei e Pagani secondo i Codici di Teodosio II e Giustiniano I)", *Studia et Documenta Historiae et Iuris*, 57, 1991, pp. 264 ff.; B.S. Bachrach, "The Jewish Community of the Later Roman Empire as Seen in the *Codex Theodosianus*", *'To See Ourselves As Others See Us': Christians, Jews, 'Others' in Late Antiquity* (eds. J. Neusner and E.S. Frerichs), California, 1985, pp. 399 ff.; G. Barone Adesi, *Monachesimo Ortodosso d'Oriente e Diritto Romano nel Tardo Antico*, Milano, 1990; A. Di Mauro Todini, *Aspetti della legislazione religiosa del IV secolo*, Roma, 1990; C. Capizzi, *Giustiniano I tra politica e religione*, Perugia 1994; E.Dal Covolo, *I Severi e il Cristianesimo. Ricerche sull' ambiente storico-istituzionale delle origini cristiane tra il secondo e il terzo secolo*, Roma, dateless. What I maintain is that, even if argumentations like the ones Feldman brings could be true, we must not forget that every new constitution surely caused worries among the Jews as well as among those who intended to be converted to Judaism, and surely a great deal of activity was exerted and great expenses requested to paralyze the aforesaid consitutions: only taking into account those efforts too, we could have a more correct picture of the situation. This thesis I happened to support already when I examinated the juridical position of the Jews in Visigothic Spain: A.M. Rabello, *The Jews in Visigothic Spain in the Light of the Legislation*, Jerusalem, 1983 (in Hebrew).

All this created, in a word, a spiritual ghetto, before the material one was established. Finally, we must keep in mind that the deprivation of a state power was, for the most part, probably more detrimental than favorable for the Jews, as stronger and better organized forces knew how to use this deprivation to their own advantage.

2) The Crime of Apostasy into Judaism

The consitutions which deal with this problem are various. There are constitutions whose purpose was to punish the adherence to Judaism by *formal adhesion* to the Jewish Community; the Jewish doctrine is defined in an unfavourable way, in order to prevent its adoption. In chronological order, we have:[48]

C.Th. XVI.8.1 (315 but 329[49]): *Si quis vero ex populo ad eorum nefariam sectam accesserit et conciliabulis eorum se adplicaverit...*

C.Th. XVI.8.7 (352[?], 357): *Si quis lege venerabili constituta ex Christiano Iudaeus effectus...*

C.Th. XVI.7.3 (383): *Qui Christianae religionis et nominis dignitate neglecta Iudaicis semet polluere contagiis acrilegis cetibus adgregetur...*

48 J. Juster, *Les Juifs dans l'Empire Romain*, 1, pp. 260 ff.; A. Linder, *The Jews in Roman Imperial Legislation*, Detroit-Jerusalem, 1987. See the observations of L.H. Feldman, "*The Contribution of Prof. Salo W. Baron*", *op. cit.* p. 23: "One of the most striking indications that proselytism continued to be practiced by Jews during these centuries is that, of the sixty-six laws in the *Codex Theodosianus* pertaining to Jews, fourteen (21 percent) deal with proselytism of free men amd twelve (18 percent) deal with the conversion of slaves". I think, too, that the phenomenon of proselytism anyhow continued to exist during this period; nevertheless, in my opinion, we must keep in mind, here too, that there was a large part of the legislation which was transmitted which nobody wished to waive, perhaps because of their relationship with the Church, or perhaps to prevent any negative eventuality.

49 See the "Chronological Table of Roman Laws on Jews" in A.M. Rabello, "The Legal Condition", (*op. cit. supra* nt. 1), pp. 748 ff.

Here (C.Th. XVI.7.3) Judaism is defined: *error.*
Here

C.Th. XVI.8.19 (409): *Si quis ex Christiana fide incredulitate Iudaica polluatur...*
Here (C.Th. XVI.8.19) Judaism is defined: *perversitas iudaica.*

Nov.Th. III, 4 (438): *...ex cultu Christianae religionis in nefandam sectam ritumve (transduxerit)...*
(Nov. Th., III, 5) Judaism is defined: *perversa doctrina.*
In this Novella

A more complicated problem was the one of adopting the *name* of Jew. On the one hand, Christianity itself had, under the pagan Empire, undergone persecutions precisely for the use of the *nomen Christianum.* Therefore, it would seem to be logical that the Christian Empire - which seized the old accusations that the pagan empire once brought against Christians, now making use of them against non-Christians and particularly Jews - would transfer this kind of crime to *nomen Hebraicum.* On the other hand, there was a theological problem, since the Church mantained that, after the advent of Jesus, Christians, and not traditional Jews, were the *Verus Israel,*[50] the real "Jews", bearers of the revealed truth. This is not to be considered a simple play on words: this item is one of the main reasons for the division between Judaism and Christianity, and Augustine refers in his epistles to the case of a Christian who used to go around having himself called a Jew.[51] As far as we know, those who defined themselves as Jews because of their being Christians were not liable to be punished; however, *propter ambiguitatem vocabuli* (using Augustine's expression), Christians, at least those who were "normal"

50 M. Simon, *Verus Israel* (*op. cit., supra* nt. 9).

51 Augustinus Ep. 196,9 ff. (=Migne, *Patrologia Latina*, 33, 894 ff.); I quote from Juster, *Juifs*, I, p. 260 nt. 5. Cf. B. Blumenkranz, *Die Judenpredigt Augustins. Ein Beitrag zur Geschichte der Judisch-Christlichen Beziehungen in den Ersten Jahrhunderten*, Basel, 1946.

ones, ceased very soon to use the name of 'Jew' to identify themselves.[52] The use of the name 'Jew' as a crime punished by Roman-Christian law refers then, evidently, to Christians who used it because of their conversion to Judaism. Imperial texts deal with this problem and it is symptomatic that the first constitution just refers to the *nomen Christianum:*

C.Th. XVI.7.3 (383): *Qui Christianae religionis et nominis dignitate neglecta.*

At the beginning of the fifth century, the *nomen Iudaicum* appears:

C.Th. XVI.8.19 (409): *taetrumque Iudaeorum nomen induere.*

The first constitution on this subject was issued in the West by Constantius in 357 (C.Th. XVI.8.7), but it is unlikely that Julian the Apostate promoted its extension to the East, when he ascended to power, so that we must wait until Theodosius in order to see a renewal of the condemnation of the crime of apostasy. This was not due to the authorities being acquiescent to the phenomenon. Rather, it seemed to them that the laws against circumcision were sufficient to stem apostasy, all the more since the atmosphere of the time must not have encouraged the passage from a triumphant Christianity to a Judaism attacked, by them, both by the Church and by the State, which had become a Christian one. Yet we know, on the other hand, that the phenomenon of conversion to Judaism continued to exist. In a number of sources, as in C.Th. XVI.8.13 by

52 This happened all the more once the phenomenon of "Judaizare" existed among Christians, that is, one who behaved, in any way, like Jews, a phenomenon which was particularly widespread in Africa, as we can learn from historical and epigraphic testimonies. The phenomenon went so far as the establishment of real Jewish-Christian sects, such as the Coelicoli or the disciples of Actus (about them see Augustinus, Ep. 196; P.L. 33, col. 891 ff. and about Actus col. 898). On Coelicoli, see C. Th. XVI. 5.43 and XVI.8.19; the condemnation of the sect pronounced by Honorius and Theodosius, with the above mentioned constitutions from 408 and 409, was repeated in the *Codex Iustinianus* I, 9, 12. In the times of Augustinus, the "Judaizing" customs of the Jews who were converted to Christianity were regarded with a certain tolerance (P.L. 33, 892), but Hieronymus warned the African bishop against an excessive acquiescence to such a situation (P.L. 22,916 ff.). The African Church seems still to continue struggling with the problem of Judaizers in the sixth century, as the deacon of Carthago, Fulgentius Ferrandus, deemed it necessary to insert in his *Breviatio Canonum* the Canons of Laodicea and Antioch from the fourth century against the "Judaizing" Christians. On this phenomenon see A.M. Rabello, *Giustiniano, Ebrei e Samaritani* (*op. cit. supra* nt. 1), I, pp. 75 ff. and, on the problem of Celicoli, *ibidem,* II, pp. 787 ff.

Arcadius and Honorius (397) we have an implicit prohibition of proselytism; in fact, they write that Jews had to perform religious ceremonies in private: *Iudaei sint obstricti caerimoniis suis*, i.e., without having the possibility of attracting new adherents.[53]

The Theodosian Novella III, of Theodose II and Valentinian, collects in one text the greater part of the provisions regarding Jews, renewing the prohibition of proselytism to Judaism, applying to Christian free men as well as to slaves. The transgression of this prohibition was punishible by death penalty.[54]

3) Punishment for the Proselyte

The Roman-Christian legislation did not immediately fix a precise punishment for the proselyte; it left this entirely to the discretion of the judge: C.Th. XVI.8.1 from 315 refers to *poenas meritas.*

Constantine restored the prohibition of Antoninus Pius and Septimius Severus with a constitution in 335 (C.Th. XVI.9.1) establishing, however, that the circumcised slave of a Jewish master must be set free. This edict

53 A. Linder, *The Jews in Roman Imperial Legislation*, Nr. 54.

54 G. Stemberger, *Juden und Christen im Heiligen Lande: Palaestina unter Konstantin und Theodosius*, München, 1987; according to this author, not even was the Novella III of Theodosius aimed to create a systematic policy towards Judaism; it limited itself to protecting Jew who was converted to Christianity and to confirming the prohibition of circumcising slaves belonging to a Jew. See, however, the right observations of B. Blumenkranz, with regard to the Theodosian legislation: "Le besoin d'un statut codifié ne s'était pas fait sentir dans l'Empire Romain à l'époque païenne. Mais le principe est acquis que seuls les Juifs parmi les citoyens gardent le droit de ne pas adorer les dieux romains. Bien mieux, leur religion étant licite, les Juifs jouissent dans son exercise de la protection de l'état, sauf le droit au prosélytisme qui leur reste refusé. La situation change avec l'adoption du Christianisme comme religion d'état. Ce n'est pas la production pléthorique des lois au sujet des Juifs qui nous intéresse ici, mais leur réunion ene une masse compacte lors de la rédaction du Code Theodosien. Les titres 8 et 9 du livre 16 qui contiennent trente-trois lois sur les quarante neuf, a côté de restrictions, d'écheances et interdictions, notamment en matière des fonctions publiques, des mariages mixtes, de la possession d'esclaves, de toute forme de prosélytisme, énoncent également les normes de l'administration juive interne, la licéité du culte, et sa protection..." (B. Blumenkranz, *Juifs et Chrétiens dans le Monde Occidentale* 430-1096, Paris, 1960, p. 300); we must also note that a "De Iudaeis" rubric does not appear in the Hermogenian Code; see A. Cenderelli, *Ricerche sul "Codex Hermogenianus"*, Milano, 1965, pp. 263 ff. and A.M. Rabello, *Giustiniano, Ebrei e Samaritani*, (*op. cit. supra nt.* 1), II, 734 ff.

did not restore the death penalty enacted by Severus, nor the banishment and the confiscation of the properties instituted by Antoninus Pius.[55]

A few years later, we find the following enactment in the constitution C.Th. XVI.8.7, of 357, the penalty of the confiscation of the property is established: *Facultates eius dominio fisci iussimus vindicari.* The prohibition to make a will was added to this penalty a few years later: C.Th. XVI.7.3, of 383, *negata testandi licentia.*[56]

However, it was not always easy to discover the apostate during his life. He could have been able to keep his change of religion a secret until the end of his life, arousing suspicions only at his death. It was possible then to open a trial against the deceased[57] suspected of having joined paganism or Judaism during his lifetime.

Who had the right to bring the action? Only a *proximus suus* (legitimate heir), since the text expressly mentions a private action. Therefore, it is probable that the accuser suspected the apostasy of the deceased because he did not receive the inheritance he had expected; the punishment, if the charge was accepted, consisted of decreeing the invalidity of the will to allow for the opening of the succession *ab intestato*, thus safeguarding the rights of those who followed the Christian way *...totumque ab intestato Christianitatem sectantibus propinquis*, according to the term found in C.I. 1.7.4.[58] It was also necessary that the accuser did not know the apostasy of the *de cuius* when he was still alive: this had to be proven at the beginning of the trial; for if it turned out that the accuser knew about the apostasy, he was punished with the rejection of the action for having not denounced it. The action was invalidated by prescription after five years.[59]

It is probable that this penalty applied as well to Gentiles who were converted to Christianity and converted afterwards to Judaism, also to the

55 Dig. 48.8.3.5; Pauli Sententiae 5.22.3; Script. Hist. Aug., *Vita Severi*, 17, 1.

56 J. Juster, *Juifs*, I, pp. 260-262; M. Pavan, *I Cristiani e il mondo ebraico nell'eta` di Teodosio il grande*, Perugia, 1965, p. 118 f.: Pavan sees in the expression, *Iudaici semet polluere contagiis,* a reference to circumcision; A.M. Rabello, *Giustiniano, Ebrei e Samaritani* (*op. cit. supra* nt. 1), II, p. 731.

57 E.Volterra, "I processi contro i defunti in diritto romano", *RIDA*, III, 1949, pp. 485 ff.

58 A. M. Rabello, *Giustiniano, Ebrei e Samaritani* (*op. cit. supra* nt. 1), II, p. 732.

59 C. Th. XVI. 7.3, from 383; C.I. 1.7.2, on which *ibid.* p. 731; G. Stemberger, *Juden und Christen im Heiligen Lande* (*supra,* nt. 52)

Catechumens, as it is specified in the case of apostasy to paganism (C.Th. XVI. 7.2. of 383).

The constitution we find in C.Th. XVI.8.1, which decrees the death penalty to those Jews who attacked former co-religionists who had converted to Christianity, threatens the same penalty also to the one who *ex populo ad eorum nefariam sectam accesserit et conciliabulis eorum se adplicaverit.*

It is possible that this codicil does not concern the crime of apostasy as such, but only levels the threatened punishment against those who, although they are not Jews by birth but only proselytes or sympathizers to Judaism, join the Jews in attacking the converts: *cum ipsis poenas meritas sustinebit.*

This interpretation is based on the fact that, firstly, this category states the penalties not for apostates, but rather, a penalty in common with Jews; and second, this paragraph disappears when the constitution is inserted in the *Codex Justinianus*, since in the juridical situation of the sixth century the category of proselytes and Judaizers probably did not overly trouble the imperial authorities.

In the Theodosian Novella III, a death penalty is provided for those who infringe upon the prohibition of proselytism.

4) Punishments for the Converter

Imperial constitutions contemplated and punished not only the proselyte, but also those who cooperated in the conversion to Judaism[60]: *auctores vero persuasionis huius*, (C.Th. XVI.7.3), establishing a penalty which is similar to the one for the convert. Thus in C.Th. XVI.8.1 we find an arbitrary punishment that is left to the discretion of the judge; although later, with the C.Th. XVI.7.3. from 383, the Emperors added to the penalty of the prohibition of being able to make a will, and provided for the convert, too, a penalty *extra ordinem:*

> *quin etiam graviora plerumque pro motibus iudicum et qualitate commissi extra ordinem promi...*(ibid).

60 J. Juster, *Les Juifs*, I, 262.

In 409, with the constitution C.Th. XVI.8.19 of Honorius and Theodose the crime of lese-majesty was established:

> *...si quis ex Christiana fide incredulitate Iudaica polluatur... si quisquam contra hanc legem venire temptaverit, sciat, se ad maiestatis crimen esse retinendum.*

And finally, in 438, with the Novella Theodosiana III of Theodose II and Valentinian,[61] the death penalty is established for those who converted a slave or a free-by-birth man:

> *Quicumque servum seu ingenuum, invitum vel suasione plectenda, ex cultu Christianae religionis in nefandam sectam ritumve transduxerit, cum dispendio fortunarum capite puniendum (N.Th. III,4).*
> *Cernat praeterea bona sua proscripta poenae mox sanguinis destinandus qui fidem alterius expugnavit perversa doctrina (N.Th.III.5).*

This was to be the inheritance of Justinian, as well.[62]

5) The Prohibition of Circumcising a Free man

As we have seen, already in the pagan period the prohibition against circumcision was used to stem and punish conversions to Judaism. The issue of circumcision certainly remained very problematic for the Church itself, which even until a few years ago mentioned in its calendars the first of January as the day of the "Circumcision of Our Lord"; it is also known that in our day Franciscan scholars in Israel maintain that the *Church from the circumcision* continued during a period much longer than generally thought.[63] The free men who underwent circumcision were punished already in the pagan period with banishment and confiscation of their properties. In *Pauli Sententiae* 5.22.3, it is established:

"Cives romani, qui se Iudaico ritu vel servos suos circumcidi

61 G. Stemberger, *Juden und Christen im Heiligen Lande*: *op. cit.*

62 Cfr. c. j. 1.7.1 and see A.M. Rabello, *Giustiniano, Ebrei e Samaritani*, (*op. cit. supra* nt. 1), vol. II, p. 730.

63 B. Bagatti, *The Church from the Circumcision. History and Archaeology of the Judaeo-Christians*, Jerusalem, 1971.

patiuntur bonis ademptis in insulam perpetuo relegantur; medici capite puniuntur.".

This was, pratically, the rule established by Hadrian and re-established by pagan Emperors; it does not discriminate between Roman citizen and foreigners. Therefore, it stands to reason that Christian Emperors had to do nothing but renew the prohibition for Jews to circumcise Christians, under penalty of banishment and death.[64] We should mention here C.Th. XVI.8.26 which threatens to sentence to the confiscation of this property and to perpetual exile[65] the Jew who circumcised a Christian or made him be circumcised. The interesting thing, from a legal point of view, is the equalization of the punishment both for the material executor of the action and for the instigator.[66]

6) THE PROHIBITION OF CIRCUMCISING A SLAVE

Particular importance was assigned to the problem of circumcising a slave owned by Jews. The slave was considered as not having really consented to being circumcised, that is, he was considered as having been coerced, and for this reason he was not punished for having undergone circumcision. We already saw that the rescript of Antoninus Pius quoted in Dig. 48.8.11 specifically applied, in all likelihood, to the issue of circumcising a slave.[67]

This problem became very acute during the Christian period. From a Jewish point of view, circumcising a slave, more than an act of religious proselytism (praised, incidentally, by the Sages of Israel), represented a

64 J. Juster, *Les Juifs*, I, pp. 226 ff.

65 V. De Villa, "Exilium perpetuum", in *Studi Albertario*, I, 1953, pp. 293 ff. and p. 307 nt.1.

66 Cf. the corresponding passage, C.I. I,9,16 and Basilica I.1.46 and see particularly Th. Mommsen, *Römisches Strafrecht, op.cit.*, (*supra* nt.6 I; J. Juster, *Les Juifs*, 1, p. 267 f.; A.M. Rabello, "Legal Condition",(*op. cit. supra nt.* 1), pp .699 ff.; Idem, "The Ban on Circumcision" *op. cit.* (*supra* nt. 5), pp. 176 ff.; A. Linder, *The Jews in Roman Imperial Legislation*, Nr. 48.

67 Modestinus, 1. VI Regularum; the point at which Modestinus deals with the question is the chapter *De potestate dominorum*: cf. P. Lenel, *Palingenesia Iuris Romani*, I, Leipzig, 1889, p. 136, N. 230. The privilege of Antoninus Pius represents most probably only a formulation by law of an exemption that was already granted *de facto* under Hadrian in certain zones of the Empire; see A. M. Rabello, *Giustiniano, Ebrei e Samaritani*, (*op. cit. supra* nt. 1), II, p. 674 nt. 22.

way of admitting the slave into the family, and of letting him receive a number of benefits, among them the liberation from slavery. It was also a matter of convenience, because a non-Jewish slave could not participate in the preparation of food, nor in the making of wine, oil and bread which must be ritually pure.[68]

On the other hand, it is understandable that also for the Church, the relatively easy religious influence that could be exerted on the slave aroused some concern, which required the intervention of the Roman Christian Empire. On this subject Jean Gaudemet writes: "Plus que le mariage, la servitude auprés d'un maître juif risquait de mettre la foi chrétienne en péril. Maître du corps et de la vie de l'esclave, le maître ne pouvait-il le contraindre à abjurer? L'importance sociale de ce problème explique qu'un titre lui ait été consacré au Code Théodosien".[69]

In the case of a slave, Christian or pagan, whom the Jewish master had circumcised, the slave obtained, according to an edict of Constantine of 335, the right to be taken away from his master and set free; a second edict decreed, more severly, that the slave was to be handed over to the public treasury and his master punished with the death penalty.[70]

Justinian adopted a *contaminatio* between the two laws, which combined the freedom promised to the slave with the death penalty

68 See, in general, the Talmudic treatise of *'Avoda Zhara'* and E.E. Urbach, "The Laws regarding Slavery as a Source for Social History of the Period of the Second Temple, the Mishnah and Talmud", in *Papers of the Institute of Jewish Studies*, London, I, 1964, pp. 1 ff.

69 J. Gaudemet, *L' Église dans l'Empire romain (IV-V siécles)*, Paris, 1958, p. 629: (La protection des esclaves chrétiens). We must note that, while the title in the Codex Theodosianus is only "Ne Christianum mancipium Iudaeus habeat", the Justinian Code (C.I. I,X) is more specific: "...vel possideat vel circumcidat". About the influence that this legislation had on the economic life of the Jews, as one of the reasons that caused the neglect of agricultural labour, see A.M. Rabello, *Giustiniano, Ebrei e Samaritani*, (*op. cit. supra* nt. 1), II, p. 785 and nt. 3; see also G. De Bonfils, *Gli schiavi degli Ebrei nella legislazione del IV secolo. Storia di un divieto*, Bari, 1992, and F. Lucrezi," CTh. 16.9.2: Diritto romano-cristiano e antisemitismo", *Labeo*, 40, 1994, pp. 220 ff.

70 The date of this second intervention is uncertain: if, as many are inclined to think today, this edict precedes the one of 335, we cannot see in the mitigation of the punishment the wish to exert less severity towards those Jews who wanted to circumcise their slaves, but simply a device to make the denunciation of the fact easier. It is obvious that a slave, who could expect to be set free as a consequence of the denunciation of the undergone operation, without prejudice for the life of the master, was more willing and had less trouble to do so than one who could expect only to be passed on to the much harsher public property, and moreover, to cause the death of his ex-master. About the attitude of the Christian emperors towards the Christian slaves in the hands of the Jews, see Rabello, *Giustiniano, Ebrei e Samaritani*, (*op. cit. supra* nt. 1), II, p. 676 nt. 28.

sentenced to the master who performed the circumcision; it did not matter if the slave was Christian or pagan (C.I.1.10.1).[71]

7) The Return to Judaism of Jews who had Converted to Christianity

Title VII in the first book of the Code of Justinian is dedicated to apostasy, *de apostasia*. The first constitution (C.I. 1.7.1 = C.Th. XVI.8.7. of 357) concerns the case of a Christian who is converted to Judaism. The penal provision *(cum accusatio fierit comprobata)* takes into consideration the case, which was surely infrequent in the sixth century, of a Christian who became a Jew, joining *sacrilegis coetibus*. Here, the prohibition to be converted is confirmed, which was particularly serious for Judaism, eliminating the possibility of new elements joining the original stock. Particularly problematic, however, was the case of the Jew who, having been converted to Christianity, wished to return to his original religion. Those Jews had been converted to Christianity mostly due to their opportunism or in order to escape difficult situations. The phenomenon of insincere conversions to Christianity was openly recognized by Emperors Honorius and by Theodosius II in 416, and the constution is brought in C.Th. XVI.8.23. It stated that those Jews who had been converted *...non id devotione fidei sed obreptione simulandum* could be brought back to their original religion *quia magis Christianitati consulitur*. It was a wise decision which, if adopted, could have been able to spare the painful problems created by the ultimate decision, which, on the contrary, affirmed the validity of the baptism, even against the wish of the person who had been christened.[72] Indeed, this last decision was the

71 A. M. Rabello, *ibidem*, p. 676 nt. 29 and p. 786 with bibliography.

72 It is also interesting to note that C.Th. XVI.8.23 limits itself to permit the Jew who had converted to return to Judaism: "*Et veteribus et nostris sanctionibus constitutum est, cum propter evitationem criminum et pro diversis necessitatibus Iudaicae religionis homines obligatos ecclesiae se consortio sociare voluisse didicerimus, non id devotione fidei, sed obreptione simulandum fieri. Unde provinciarum iudices, in quibus talia commissa perhibentur, ita nostris formulatam statutis deferendum esse cognoscant, ut hos, quos neque constantia religiosae confessionis in hoc eodem cultu inhaerere perspexerint neque venerabilis baptismatis fide et mysteriis inbutos esse, ad legem propriam, quia magis Christianitati consulitur, liceat remeare*". Juster points out that in the *Antiqua summaria*, on the contrary, the constitution is summarized as if it obliged those Jews to return to Judaism: "*Iudaeos, si oro necessitate non devotione mentis vel religionis per subreptionem dispendia cupiunt evitare propria religionis reddantur*".

one the Church adopted in the Fourth council of Toledo, following the opinion of its Chairman, Isidorus from Seville.[73]

C.Th. XVI.8.23 exonerated Christians ex-Jews from the crime of apostasy and allowed their return to their ancient religion, but this rule was not transferred to the Code of Justinian, which complied in this way with the will of the Church. Therefore, we must presume that, in the times of Justinian, even the properties of the ex-Jew who returned to Judaism from Christianity must have been confiscated, just as in the case of any other Christian who was converted to Judaism.[74]

8) Conclusions

Coming to the end of this brief examination of ours, we think it could be useful to quote here the words with which Jean Juster concludes his examination of the problem: "Les Empereurs chrétiens ont donc créé le crime du judaïsme, mais ils sont conservé en même temps les mesures dont se servirent contre lui les empereurs paiens. Toutes ces peines nouvellement edictées ne frappent le convertisseur ou le converti qu'autant que le prosélyte était chretien. Elles ne concernent pas les païens qui n'encourent de peine qu'en cas de circoncision".[75]

This is more or less the situation we find at the time of Justinian, as well.

Examining the significant change in the behaviour of the Roman Empire towards Jews after the advent of Christianity, and the slow progression with which, from an attitude still bound by scruples of legality and impartiality, the legislator progresses to the unabashed execution of a program of isolation, devaluation and delegitimization of the Jewish element in the social context of the Empire, in the spirit of Ambrose, John Chrysostomus and Cyril of Alexandria, the role played by

73 See A.M. Rabello, "Sisebuto re di Spagna (612-621) e il battesimo forzato", *Rassegna Mensile di Israel*, LI, 1985, pp. 33 ff.

74 The examination of the Roman legislation aimed to repress the punitive attitudes of the Jews against other Jews who had been converted to Christianity, is beyond this study; cf., f.e., C.Th. XVI.8.5 (from 335).

75 Juster, *Les Juifs*, I, p. 252 f. As already pointed out, we believe that, on the contrary, also the Pagans who adopted Judaism were liable to punishment.

the Church in this process is evident. Nevertheless, it would be wrong to simply interpret this motivation as being a natural consequence of the influence exerted by the Church on the State, borne of vengeance, aimed at the glorification of the victory of the "New Testament" over the "Old" one, and convincing the Jews, by way of oppression, to give up their abstention from recognizing Jesus as the Messiah. First of all, the Empire had chosen the Church of Jesus, above all, in order to achieve unification, and in the arduous process of unification-Christianization, it could not avoid co-opting the prejudices of the Church against the alien and the autonomous. Secondly, the Church, being challenged by heresies, defended itself by striking what was easily identifiable as non-Church. A thousand years after, Rome, menaced by the Reformation, renewed it anti-Jewish law-making. Having struck at Judaism, it was later easier to denounce those who were out of line, calling them *Iudaei* – a custom that the Fathers of the Church meticulously followed. Therefore it seems that we can perceive a real fear, a genuine defensiveness on the part of the Christian Empire and a desire to safeguard itself against Jewish influence.[76]

It is worth mentioning that despite the new balance reached in the legislation to the full detriment of the Jews, their enemies in the Church did not use the Code in order to strike at them, but were content with doing so by illegal means, taking advantage of the lack of state power, which left the interpretation of the law in the hands of the bishops.

We must also keep in mind that other areas of the law, for instance the prohibition of mixed marriages between Jews and Christians, the laws concerning slavery, and the ban against Jews from holding public office, had the definite aim to avoid the advent of new proselytes. We did not examine in this context the problem of half-proselytes, of *metuentes* or God-Fearers, as a most interesting phenomenon, yet requires a rather in-depth examination.[77]

76 Yet we must not overestimate, as L. H. Feldman inclines to in his recent studies quoted above, the value of these texts as a testimony of a large phenomenon of continued proselytism; I agree that the phenomenon existed, but we must keep in mind that also a small number of conversions could be sufficient to justify the imperial intervention, so much the Church considered it insulting.

77 L.H. Feldman dedicated various studies to this phenomenon: see, among others: "The Omnipresence of God-Fearers", *Biblical Archeology Review*, 12.5, 1986, pp. 58 ff.; "Proselytes and 'Sympathizers' in the Light of the New Inscriptions from Aphrodisias", *Revue des Etudes* Juives, 148, 1989, p. 297.

The anti-Jewish legal system which developed under Justinian, having been prepared by the Christian emperors who preceded him, appeared to the prevailing Christian mentality, not so much as a brute instrument of oppression, but more as an experiment of a new balance. This is extremely unsatisfactory from the point of view of natural justice, but most satisfactory from that of stability. We could say that this balance was a reflection of the Byzantine Empire itself, whose tormoils and problems it mirrors more than its triumphs. However, the sad fact is that the Jews were those who paid a painful price for those turmoils, for those problems, and for those triumphs...*

List of Constitutions

C.Th. XVI.7.3 = C.I. 1.7.2
C.Th. XVI.8.1 = C.I. 1.9.3
C.Th. XVI.8.7 = C.I. 1.7.1
C.Th. XVI.8.13 does not appear in C.I.
C.Th. XVI.8.19= C.I. 1.9.12
C.Th. XVI.8.23 does not appear in C.I.
C.Th. XVI.8.26= C.I. 1.9.16
C.Th. XVI.9.1 = C.I. 1.10.1
C.Th. XVI.9.2
Nov.Th.III, 4-5 = C.I. 1.7.5

The constitutions in chronological order

C.Th. XVI.8.1 Constantinus, 329 (315, Juster)
C.Th. XVI.9.1 Constantinus, 335 (336, Juster)
C.Th. XVI.8.7 Constantinus et Iulianus, 353 (352,357)
C.Th. XVI.7.3 Gratianus, Valentinianus, Theodosius, 383
C.Th. XVI.8.13 Arcadius et Honorius, 397
C.Th. XVI.8.19 Honorius et Theodosius, 409
C.Th. XVI.8.23 Honorius et Theodosius, 416
Nov.Th.III,4-5 Theodosius et Valentinianus,438

* I would like to thank my friend Prof. Izhak Fikman for having read this article and for his helpful comments

XV

A TRIBUTE TO JEAN JUSTER*

I. *BIOGRAPHICAL NOTE*

The Faculty of Law of the Hebrew University of Jerusalem and the *Israel Law Review* wish to honour the memory of a brilliant young Jewish scholar who was killed in action while fighting for France in the First World War.

Jean Juster[1] born in 1881[2] at Piatra-Neamtz[3], in Rumania (Moldavia), was of a family well-known in the region. His grandfather, Abraham Lipa Juster, one of the leaders of the Jewish community, was erudite and active in public affairs.[4] His father, Moshe, was also learned in Jewish studies and active in the promotion of the well-being of the community.

Jean probably received his Jewish education at Piatra. In that town, which N. Sokolow called "the Moldavian Jerusalem", a branch of the *Hovevei Zion* movement was created in 1894 and from 1897 groups of supporters of Zionism were active. Jean Juster studied at the local high school while con-

* The assistance of Prof. S. Ginossar, throughout the preparation of this work is acknowledged with gratitude. The author also acknowledges with thanks the helpful criticism of Prof. R. Yaron, and the assistance of Mrs. P. Mizrahi, A. Feller, Prof. S. Z. Feller (Jerusalem) and Prof. J. Modrzejewski (Paris) in tracing personal data concerning Juster.
For (1) Dates of Visigothic Spain, (2) Abbreviations, and (3) Juster's bibliography and source material, see *infra* p. 254.

1 On Jean Juster see *Jüdisches Lexicon* (1927) vol. 3, col. 500; *Pinkas Ha-Kehilot: Rumania* (Jerusalem, 1969–70, in Hebrew) 213; A. L. Mizrahi, *'Im Dori u-Ma'avakav* (With my Generation and its Struggles) Zionist and National Battles of the Rumanian Jews (Tel-Aviv, 1970, in Hebrew) 178 ss.; S. L. Guterman, "J. Juster" *Judaica,* vol. 10, col. 475.

2 In most of the works quoted in the preceding note the year of birth is said to be 1886, while Mizrahi gives the date 1881: the latter date seems to be the correct one, as held by those closely related to the Juster family and it also fits better into the dates of his studies. Despite a thorough inquiry, no trace could be found at the University of Paris, as stated by Mr. Horowitz in his letter.

3 On this community see *Pinkas Ha-Kehilot: Rumania, op. cit.,* at p. 208; "Piatra-Neamt" *Judaica,* vol. 13, col. 493 ss.

4 According to Mizrahi (*op. cit.,* at p. 494) the writer A. L. Zissu mentioned Jean's grandfather in his works.

tinuing to receive his traditional Jewish education. He soon adhered to the Zionist movement, in which he for some time played an active role.[5]

He then studied law at the University of Bucharest and graduated in 1903. His final dissertation, entitled *Adulterul,* was published in its original Rumanian version in 1904. After a short period of advanced studies in Germany, he proceeded to Paris. There he completed his doctoral thesis, a critical discussion of the sources concerning the legal condition of the Jews in the Roman Empire, *Examen critique des sources relatives à la condition juridique des juifs dans l'Empire Romain* (Paris, 1911).

A year later Juster published his book on the political rights of the Jews in the Roman Empire *Les droits politiques des juifs dans l'empire romain* (Paris, 1912); and, in the same year, his research on the legal status of the Jews under the Visigothic kings, *La condition légale des Juifs sous les Rois Visigoths* (Paris, 1912). The latter article has been selected for publication *in extenso* in English, to be accompanied with remarks designed to bring it up to date in the light of more recent research.

On the eve of World War I the two volumes of Juster's monumental work were published in Paris, describing the legal, economic and social condition of the Jews in the Roman Empire, *Les juifs dans l'empire romain: leur condition juridique, économique et sociale* (Paris, 1914). This has remained the main authority on the subject to this day, and its intrinsic importance is sufficient to justify the summary we now propose to give of its contents, with some comment on subsequent scientific developments. Such a summary may be especially opportune for the readers of the article on the Jews in the Visigothic kingdom. Although that article was published before his *magnum opus,* it is substantially a sequel to it.

The outbreak of war found Juster in the midst of his family in Rumania. But determined as he was to take part in France's struggle with Germany, he returned to France and enlisted as a volunteer. He fought in the offensives which preceded the Battle of Verdun and there, on the front-line of Givenchy, he met his death. The great scholar who paved the way for so wide a field of research was aged only 34.

5 A. L. Mizrahi (*ibid.,* at p. 179) writes: "In his youth he adhered to the Zionist ideal, was active in the movement and twice served as a delegate to Zionist Congresses." On what elements was this latter assertion based? A search made at my request by Mr. I. Philip, assistant director of the Central Zionist Archives (and for which I acknowledge my thanks) revealed no further information. Juster's name could not be found on the list of delegates; neither does it appear in *Die Welt*'s report of Congress proceedings nor on the list of obituaries at the 12th Congress (1921) in memory of active Zionists deceased since the 8th Congress (of 1907). See also the *Index to the Minutes of the First Zionist Congress* (Tel-Aviv, 1966), where J. Juster's name is also absent. He may have been a delegate to the local Zionist Federation, and his non-participation in the World Congress can be explained by his age.

II. *SUMMARY-REVIEW OF "THE JEWS IN THE ROMAN EMPIRE" BY J. JUSTER*

This is rightly considered as the fundamental work on the subject,[6] and no further research can be attempted without reference to it and to the impressive collection of sources compiled and quoted in its numerous footnotes.

Nevertheless, and although many of his views are still accepted as representing the *communis opinio,* there are inevitably a few which have since been abandoned. This, of course, does not in the least detract from Juster's merit: it was he who, by his scientific method, laid the very foundation for the criticism against his own views and for a fruitful rethinking of those which may have been found faulty.

After a long biographical list, an Introduction (pp. 1–212) is devoted to a survey of the primary sources where the relevant material may be found. These comprise: *literature,* whether Jewish (in Greek, Hebrew or Aramaic, written by Rabbinical or sectarian authors);[7] pagan (Greek and Roman);[8] or Christian (the New Testament, Christian polemics against the Jews, ca-

6 "Fondamentale lavoro", V. Colorni, *Gli Ebrei nel sistema del diritto comune fino alla prima emancipazione* (Milan, 1956); "fundamental work", A. Berger, (1957) 8 *IURA* 75 n. 1; *"rappresenta tuttora una guida assai valida e che difficilmente potrebbe essere sostituita",* G. I. Luzzatto, review of *Corpus Papyrorum Judaicarum* by Tcherikover, (1961) 27 *SDHI* 373; "great work", M. Stern, *Greek and Latin Authors on Jews and Judaism* (Jerusalem, 1974) vii; "the masterly work by J. Juster", A. D. Momigliano, *Judaica,* (Suppl., 1974) 224. See also the reviews that appeared at the time the book was published: N. Bentwich "The Rightfulness of the Jews in the Roman Empire" (1915–16) 6 J.Q.R. 325 ss. "It is distinguished by two admirable qualities: (1) a mastery of the whole literature bearing upon the subject ancient and modern, permanent and periodical, Jewish and Gentile; and (2) a very clear and definite point of view, which gives unity and a plan to his mass of material ..."; Th. Reinach, (1920) 70–71 *REJ* 93 ss.; when Juster's book was reprinted in photocopy (New York, 1965) the following note appeared: A. M. Rabello (1967) 18 *IURA* 307 ss.

7 See U. Rapaport "Bibliography of Works on Jewish History in the Hellenissic and Roman Periods, 1946–1970" in *Studies in the History of the Jewish People and the Land of Israel* (Haifa, 1972) vol. 2, p. 247 ss. See also the most recent publication of G. Vermes, "Ancient Rome in Post-Biblical Jewish Literature" in *Post-Biblical Studies* (Leiden, 1975) 215 ss.

8 M. Stern, *Greek and Latin Authors on Jews and Judaism,* edited with Introductions, Translations and Commentary (Jerusalem, 1974) vol. I; see also M. Stern, "Roman Literature" *Judaica,* vol. 14 col. 232 ss.; Safrai-Stern, *Jewish People* 1–77; J. N. Sevenster, *The Roots of Pagan Anti-Semitism in the Ancient World* (Leiden, 1975).

non law, liturgy, formulas of abjuration);[9] *documentary* sources: pictorial, numismatic,[10] epigraphic,[11] papyrus;[12] and *legal* sources: writings in the Book of the Maccabees,[13] the official records of Josephus,[14] Emperor Julian's letter to the Jews,[15] books of jurists and collections of statutes (*codices*);[16]

9 Parkes, *Church and Synagogue* (2nd ed.); M. Simon, *Verus Israel. Etude sur les relations entre Chrétiens et Juifs dans l'Empire Romain (135–425)* (Paris, 2nd ed., 1964); Blumenkranz, *Juifs et Chrétiens.*

10 E. Goodenough, *Jewish Symbols in Greco-Roman Period* (New York, 1953–1968) and see E. Bickerman's review in (1967) 44 *Syria* 131 ss.; *Corpus nummorum Palaestinensium* (Jerusalem, 1956); J. Meshorer, *Jewish Coins of the Second Temple Period* (Tel Aviv, 1967, in Hebrew).

11 S. Klein, *Jüdish-palästinisches Corpus Inscriptionum* (Ossuar... Grab... und Synagogeninschriften) (Wien-Berlin, 1920); J. B. Frey, *Corpus Inscriptionum Iudaicarum, Recueil des inscriptions juives qui vont du IIIe siècle avant Jésus-Christ au VII siècle de notre ère* (Città del Vaticano, 1936) vol. 1 (1952) vol. II; M. Cassuto-Salzman, "Selected Bibliography" Publications on Archaelogical Excavations and Surveys in Israel (1969) 8 'Atiqot, English Series Suppl.), (1973) 9–10 *ibidem* (suppl.); M. Cassuto-Salzman, "Hebrew Inscriptions of the End of the First Temple Period Discovered in Jerusalem", *David Kotlar Jubilee Volume* (Studies in Judaism, Tel Aviv, 1975) 123 ss.

12 V. Tcherikover—A. Fuks—M. Stern-Lewis, *Corpus Papyrorum Judaicarum,* in 3 vols. (Cambridge-Jerusalem, 1957–1964); M. Stern "Papyri" in Safrai-Stern, *Jewish People* 43 ss.

13 E. S. Artom, "Sull'alleanza tra Giuda Maccabeo e Roma" (1909) 5 *Rivista Israelitica* 192 ss.; E. S. Artom, "Sulle relazioni tra Simone Maccabeo e Roma" (1912) 8 *ibidem* 43 ss.; A. Momigliano, *Prime linee di storia della tradizione maccabaica* (1930); Ginsburg, *Rome et la Judée. Contribution à l'histoire de leurs relations politiques* (Paris, 1938); E. Bikerman, *Institutions des Séleucides* (Paris, 1938); F. M. Abel, *Les livres des Maccabées* (1949); Sordi, "Il valore politico del trattato tra i Romani ed i Giudei nel 161 A.C." (1952) 5 *Acme* 3 ss.; J. Liver, *Chapters in the History of the Priests and Levites* (Jerusalem, 1968, in Hebrew); T. Liebman Frankfurt, "Rome et le conflict judéo-syrien 164–161 a.l." (1969) 38 *L'Antiquité Classique* 16 ss.; M. Stern, *The Document on the History of the Hasmonean Revolt* (Tel Aviv, 1972, in Hebrew); D. Piattelli, "Ricerche intorno alle relazioni politiche tra Roma e l'ETHNOS TON IOUDAION dal 161 a.C. al 4 a.C." (1971) 74 *Bullettino dell' Instituto di Diritto Romano* 219 ss.

14 Thackeray, *Josephus, the Man and the Historian* (New York, 1929); M. Stern, *Flavius Josephus' Method of Writing History* (Jerusalem, 1962, in Hebrew); Schrockenberg, *Bibliographie zu Flavius Josephus, Arbeiten zur Literatur und Geschichte der Hellenistischen Judentums,* Suppl. I; E. Volterra, "Senatus consulta" (1969) 16 *NNDI* 1047 ss.

15 J. Levy, "The Emperor Julian and the Rebuilding of the Sanctuary" in *Olamot Nifgashim, Studies in Jewish Hellenism* (Jerusalem, 1969, in Hebrew) 221 ss. (=*Zion,* 6, 1941, 1 ss.); S. Lieberman, "The Martyrs of Caesarea" (1939–44) *Annuaire de l'Institut de Philologie et d'Histoire Orientales et Slaves*

the latter being the most important source to date. No legal sources concerning Jews have come to light subsequent to Juster's work. On many points Juster's remarks have served as a starting-point for deeper research.[17] Most useful is the chronological table of statutes affecting the Jews and contained in the Codex of Theodosius and in that of Justinian. The Introduction concludes with the dispersion of the Jews and their numerical distribution.[18]

Chapter I (pp. 213–242) deals with *privilegia* granted to the Jews or imposed upon them (*odiosa privilegia*). In Roman law a *privilegium* is a "legal enactment concerning a specific person or case and involving an exemption from common rules".[19] The chapter discusses the nature, creation and development of privileges affecting Jews. Indeed the Jewish people were, because of their character, in need of a special status: their Deity could not be inserted into the pagan Pantheon and the normal principle of religious toleration could not operate. The Jews, therefore, only had the option between persecution and privileged status; and the same dilemma confronted every successive ruler.[20]

The Roman *privilegia* were created by the *edicta* of Roman office-holders, by international treaties concluded between Judaea and Rome, by the military assistance offered to Rome at the time of Julius Caesar, and by the links established between the Jewish people, on the one hand, and, on the other, the Roman authorities and Emperors. Another factor was the fear of Jewish revolt.

195 ss.; S. Lieberman, "Palestine in the Third and Fourth Centuries" (1945–46) 36 J.Q.R. 239 ss.; (1946–47) 37 *ibidem* 329 ss.; M. Simon, *Verus Israel, op. cit.* at p. 139 ss.; A. Momigliano (ed.), *The Conflict Between Paganism and Christianity in the Fourth Century* (Oxford, 1963); D. Rokeah, "Julian the Apostate" *Judaica,* vol. 10, col. 467 ss.

16 Ulpian, Paul, Modestine, *Codex Gregorianus* and *Hermogenianus, Codex Theodosianus, Codex Justiniani* etc.

17 See, for example, Juster's observations on the *Collatio legum Mosaicarum et Romanarum;* they serve E. Volterra in his fundamental work: *Collatio legum Mosaicarum et Romanarum,* Accademia Nazionale dei Lincei, Serie VI, (Rome, 1930) vol. 3; see also A. M. Rabello, "On the 'Collatio legum Mosaicarum et Romanarum'" *Shenaton ha-Mishpat ha-ivri* (Annual of the Institute for Research in Jewish Law) (Jerusalem, 1974, in Hebrew) 231 ss. with bibliography.

18 D. Askowith, *The Toleration of the Jews Under Julius Caesar and Augustus* (New York, 1915); N. Ferorelli, *Gli Ebrei nell'Italia meridionale dall'età romana al secolo XVIII,* (Turin, 1915); C. Roth, *The History of the Jews in Italy* (Philadelphia, 1946); Baron, *History,* vol. II; H. J. Leon, *The Jews of Ancient Rome* (Philadelphia, 1960); V. Tcherikover, *The Jews in Egypt in the Hellenistic-Roman Age in the Light of the Papyri* (Jerusalem, 2nd ed., 1963, in Hebrew); S. Applebaum, *Greeks and Jews in Ancient Cyrene* (Jerusalem, 1969, in Hebrew).

19 Berger, "Privilegium" *E.D.* 651.

20 See also A. Milano, *Storia degli Ebrei in Italia* (Turin, 1963) 10 s.

Privileges have the character of Roman legal norms. Their object is to make it possible for the Jews "to live according to their own laws".[21]

The author describes the fate of these privileges at the time of the Jewish Revolt and the changes that took place during the pagan period and under Christian rule.[22] Christian theology sees the Jews as *testes veritatis,* a living testimony of the true faith, and Christianity is therefore determined to keep the Jewish nation alive. But, at the same time, it desires that that nation be kept in a miserable and humble condition: while there may be some degree of toleration for the Jewish cult, there is no lack of persecution of Jews aimed at persuading them to embrace Christianity.[23]

Until the year 70, the date of the destruction of the Temple, the privileges were conditional upon (a) Jewish origin; and (b) observance of the Jewish commandments (*mitsvoth*). After that date a third condition was added, being the payment of the Jewish tax (*fiscus iudaicus*);[24] and these same three conditions were perpetuated under Christian rule.

Juster does not refer to the local status of Palestine, since the rights of the Jews in that territory were regulated by the provincial bye-laws and did not amount to privileges.[25] Juster believes that, in the matter of Jewish

21 "These religious privileges were, however, not respected by all Emperors (e.g., Tiberius, Caligula, Vespasian, Hadrian)." Berger, *E.D.* 517.

22 The contrast between pagan and Christian thinking, has been well described by Biondi: *"Dalla libertà religiosa pagana si passa all'apostolato, dall'apostolato, con crescendo spaventoso, all'intolleranza e alla persecuzione",* B. Biondi, *Il Diritto Romano Cristiano* (Milan, 1952) vol. 1, p. 256. See also V. Colorni, "Israeliti" (1963) 9 *NNDI* 203 ss.

23 See: G. Ferrari dalle Spade, "Privilegi degli Ebrei nell'Impero romano-cristiano" *Festschrift für L. Wenger* (1944) vol. 2, p. 102 ss.; J. Gaudemet, *L'Eglise dans l'Empire romain (IV–V siècles)* (Paris, 1958) 624 ss.; E. Simon, *Versus Israel, op. cit.*

24 "A central fund in Rome for revenues from the poll-tax paid by the Jews in the whole empire" Berger, *E.D.* 473 (see also *infra*).

25 A. Momigliano, *Ricerche sull'organizzazione della Giudea sotto il dominio romano (63 a.C.–70 d.C.)* (Bologna, 1934, reprinted Amsterdam, 1967); A. Schalit, *Roman Administration in Palestine* (Jerusalem, 1937, in Hebrew); E. Bammel, "Die Bruderfolge im Hochpriestertum der herodianisch-römischen Zeit" (1954) 70 *Zeitschrift des Deutschen Palästina-Vereins* 147 ss.; H. Hart, "Judea and Rome, the Official Commentary" (1952/53) 3 Journal of Theological Studies 172 ss.; Th. Frankfort, "Présence de Rome en Israel" (1960) 19 *Latomus* 708 ss.; S. Safrai, "The Status of Provincia Judaea after the Destruction of the Second Temple" (1962) 27 *Zion* 216 ss.; H. G. Pflaum, "Remarques sur le changement de statut administratif de la province de Judée: à propos d'une inscription récemment découverte à Sidé de Pamphylie" (1969) 19 Israel Exploration Journal 225 ss.; G. I. Luzzatto, "Sul regime del suolo nelle provincie romane" (1974) 194 *Accademia Nazionale dei Lincei* 43 ss.; M. Stern, "The Province of Judea" in Safrai-Stern, *Jewish People* 308 ss.; see also, the new edition of Schürer's

privileges, there was legal uniformity; but this question seems to have been more complicated.[26]

The chapter concludes with a description of the sanctions and of the judicial powers competent to adjudicate in matters of *privilegia,* including *odiosa privilegia.*

The subject of Chapter II (pp. 243–390) is the Jewish cult and the religious policy of the Roman Empire, both under pagan and later, under Christian rule.[27] Juster marks the contrast between the two attitudes and the reason therefor:

> The pagan Emperors were free from religious intolerance because the State religion consisted only of rites, of the fulfilment of acts and ceremonies, and left the individual complete liberty of opinion. In view of the legal principle of liberty which had its roots in the tolerance of the deities between themselves, they sacrificed for the benefit of the Jews and their jealous God the requirements of the official religion by dispensing them from the accomplishment of the rites. The Christian Emperors, on the other hand, dissociating religion and nationality, made it a cardinal principle to pay no respect to the national customs of the peoples of the Empire when they were religious customs. Outside Christianity, every other religion or even religious doctrine is more or less criminal, and its adherents are to be visited with penalties. Such a minimum of tolerance as was conceded for theological reasons to the Jews was exclusively for those born in the faith.[28]

Special attention is devoted to the problem of conversion to Judaism: contrary to the opinion of Mommsen,[29] Juster holds the view that conversion never constituted a crime *sui generis:* the only crime was that of *atheism.*

History: Schürer, Vermes, Millar, *The History of the Jewish People in the Age of Jesus Christ* (1973) vol. 1, pp. 357–427; 455–470; 514–528.

26 See Momigliano's observations: *"ma il difetto, o, se si vuole, il limite della costruzione del Juster è un po'quello di tutta la sua opera, la quale non sa differenziare abbastanza gli Ebrei nel tempo e nello spazio e considera il Giudaismo nell'impero romano come un blocco unico, che si possa scomporre nei suoi elementi."* A. Momigliano, "I nomi delle prime 'Sinagoghe' romane e la condizione giuridica delle comunità in Roma sotto Augusto" (1931) 6 *La Rassegna Mensile di Israel* 287. On the problem of the effectiveness of the imperial constitutions, see the works quoted by G. I. Luzzatto, "Rassegna epigrafica greco-romana IV" (1957) 8 *IURA* 292; see also C. Dupont "La domaine géographique d'application des textes constantiniens. Procédés de détermination" (1967) 18 *IURA,* 28 ss.

27 Parkes, *Church and Synagogue;* S. E. Seaver, *Persecution of the Jews in the Roman Empire (300–438)* (Lawrence, 1952).

28 N. Bentwich, "The Rightfulness of the Jews" *op. cit.,* at p. 328 s.

29 Th. Mommsen, "Der Religionsfrevel nach römischem Recht" (1890) 64 *Historische Zeitschrift* 389 ss. (= *Gesammelte Schriften, III,* 389 ss.); Th. Mommsen "Christianity in the Roman Empire (1893) 8 The Expositor 1 ss.(=*Ges. Schr.* 6, 540 ss.); Mommsen, *Le droit pénal romain,* (Paris, 1907) vol. 2, p. 269 ss.

The dispute arises around the following passage of Spartianus: *Iudaeos fieri sub gravi poena vetuit; idem etiam de Christianis sanxit* (*Vita Severi,* 17, 1).[30] Juster construes this as prohibiting only the rite of circumcision and not conversion; and, in his opinion, a full-fledged prohibition of conversion to Judaism cannot be based on such a short passage. In spite of the numerous arguments on this point,[31] it is the opinion of the author that Juster's version is the correct one.[32] It is anyway clear that the legislation against circumcision turned out to be, in fact, a serious obstacle to Jewish proselytism.

Another problem, connected with the preceding one, is that of circumcision.[33] Permissible until the reign of Hadrian, it was proscribed by the latter

30 On Emperor Lucius Septimius Severus and the Jews see A. M. Rabello "Severus, Septimius" *Judaica,* vol. 14, col. 1200 s. (with bibliography).

31 On Jewish proselytism see: B. J. Bamberger, *Proselytism in the Talmudic Period* (Cincinnati, 1939); W. G. Braude, *Jewish Proselytizing in the First Five Centuries* (Providence, 1940) and see G. Allon's review, *Studies in Jewish History in the Times of the Second Temple, the Mishna and the Talmud* (Tel Aviv, 2nd ed., 1970, in Hebrew) vol. 2, p. 278 ss.; S. Lieberman, *Greek in Jewish Palestine* (New York, 1942) 58 ss.; M. Simon, *Verus Israel, op. cit.,* at p. 316 ss.; E. E. Urbach, "Gher" *Enz. Ivrit* (1957, in Hebrew) vol. 11, p. 172 ss.; E. E. Urbach, *The Sages, Their Concepts and Beliefs* (Jerusalem, 1975) 541 ss. For the articles of D. Rokeah and Z. Falk see A. M. Rabello, "Israele" (1972) 3 *Index, International Survey of Roman Law* 66.

32 *Contra* Juster, see (following Mommsen's view) V. Colorni, *Gli Ebrei nel sistema del diritto comune fino alla prima emancipazione* (Milan, 1960) 4 n. 10 and A. M. Rabello, "Review of Juster" (1967) 18 *IURA* 309.

33 On circumcision see: Z. Zmigryder-Konopka, "Les Romains et la Circoncision des Juifs" (1931) 33 *Eos* 334 ss.; S. Lieberman, "The Martyrs of Caesarea" *op. cit.,* at p. 423 ss.; E. M. Smallwood, "The Legislation of Hadrian and Antoninus Pius against Circumcision" (1959) 18 *Latomus* 334 ss., and 'Addendum' (1960–61) 20 *ibidem* 93 ss.; D. Rokeah, "Comments on the Revolt of Bar Kohba" (1966) 35 *Tarbiz* 127 ss.; A. Linder, "The Roman Imperial Government and the Jews under Constantine" (1975) 44 *Tarbiz* 126 ss. (and nn. 180 ss.). It is regrettable that the scholars who have discussed the problem have entirely ignored the text of the *Basilica,* a Byzantine codification, *Bas.* 60.39.7 (Heimbach, vol. 5, (Lipsiae, 1850) 766). The suspicion arises that these scholars have taken no genuine interest in the *Basilica* because of their belated enactment; but the historians of the law agree that "the *Basilica* constitute a legal monument of the highest importance for our knowledge of Justinian and post-Justinian law in the Byzantine Empire, and for the criticism of some texts of Justinian's *Digest* and *Code* in instances in which the Greek text of the *Basilica* and their scholia is better preserved than in the Latin manuscripts of Justinian's legislation". (Berger, *E.D.* at p. 372). It will also be remembered that, as stressed by Solazzi, the text of Modestinus (*D.* 48.8.11) explicitly prohibits the circumcision of the *slaves* (in contradistinction to that of the *sons,* which was permitted). This interpretation is corroborated by Lenel's *Palingenesia,* I, 736, No. 230. A problem connected with that of circumcision is probably that of the Sikarikon: in the opinion of Graetz and Safrai, this term is derived from

Emperor;[34] and this was probably one of the causes of Bar-Kochba's rebellion.[35] Antoninus Pius then allowed the Jews to circumcise their own sons; while the penalty remained effective against the non-Jew submitting to circumcision, and against the person performing such a rite on a non-Jew, even where the latter was his own slave.[36]

The problem of conversion also leads to that of the baptized Jew reverting to Judaism, a problem of special importance to the Christians; to that of the "half-converted", of Judaism and Jews in missionary propaganda and in Christian liturgy; all these points are discussed.[37]

sicarii and is more specifically related to the *Lex Cornelia de Sicariis,* in that it refers to those who have violated the prohibition of circumcision. H. Graetz, "Das Sikarikon-Gesetz" (1892) *Jahresbericht des jüd. theol. Seminars* (Berlin); F. Rosenthal, "Das Sikarikongesetz" (1893) 37 *MGWJ* 1 ss.; J. Elbogen, "Siqarikon" (1925) 69 *MGWJ 249* ss.; A. Gulak, "Siqariqin" (1934–35) 5 *Tarbiz* 23 ss.; E. E. Urbach, "Halakhot Regarding Slavery as a Source for the Social History of the Second Temple and the Talmudic Period" (1960) 25 *Zion* 176; S. Safrai, "Siqariqon" (1952) 17 *Zion* 56 ss.; M. Gil, "Land Ownership in Palestine under Roman Rule" (1970) 17, 3rd series *RIDA* 11 ss., 45 ss.; S. Shilo, *Dina de-Malkhuta Dina* (The Law of the State is Law) (Jerusalem, 1974, in Hebrew) 41 s.; A. Linder, "The Roman Imperial Government", *op. cit.,* at p. 127, n. 183.

34 The legislation of the early Empire tried to suppress castration: Domitian prohibited that practice by the *Lex Cornelia de Sicariis* (see Berger, *E.D.* 382, 550, 706), and Hadrian extended the prohibition to circumcision. This prohibition was probably general; and Samaritans, Egyptians and Arabs also suffered from it. See, M. Gaster, *The Samaritans* (London, 1925) 37 s.; J. A. Montgomery, *The Samaritans* (Philadelphia, 1907, 2nd ed., 1968) 90 ss.; P. Foucart, "Rescrit d' Antonin relatif à la circoncision (D. 48.8.11. pr.) et son application en Egypte" (1911) *Journal des savants* 5 ss.; N. Hohlwein, "Papyrus choisis (Traduction et commentaire)" (1913) 17 *Musée Belge* 27 s.; J. Schwarz, "Sur une demande de prêtres de Socnopéonèse" (1944) 44 *Annales du Service des Antiquités de l'Egypte* 235 ss.; M. Pillet, "Les scènes de naissance et de circoncision dans le temple nord-est de Mont. à Karnak" (1952–54) 52 *ibidem* 77 ss.

35 There is some argument as to whether the prohibition of circumcision should not be considered to have been one of the direct causes of Bar-Kochba's revolt (as would appear from Spartianus, *Vita Hadriani*), or rather a consequence thereof (as was recently held by H. Mantel, see *infra*). I believe that this prohibition preceded the revolt, and in favour of this view see, among others: E. Schuerer, Th. Mommsen, G. Allon, S. Lieberman, S. Mazzarino, M. Smallwood, S. Safrai, M. D. Herr, Sh. Applebaum, A. Linder.

36 On Antoninus' policy toward proselytism and the circumcision of slaves, see: E. E. Urbach, "Halakhot Regarding Slavery", *op. cit.,* at p. 166 ss.; M. Simon, *Verus Israel, op. cit.,* at p. 127 ss.; A. Linder, "Roman Imperial Government", *op. cit.,* at p. 128 ss.

37 On Jewish sympathizers see: L. H. Feldman, "Jewish Sympathizers in Classical

A special problem is that of exempting the Jews from the religious cult due to the Emperor. It seems that there was no such exemption; but the authorities did agree to reduce the cult to certain forms, such as: an oath of allegiance to the Emperor, specially devised, or the offering of sacrifices and prayers to *the Almighty in favour of the Emperor,*[38] instead of to the Emperor himself. But such forms obviously deprived of all its "fervour" the pagan and the Christian cult of the Emperor, and this gave substance to the charge that the Jews refused to pay the Emperor the full tribute of respect to which he was entitled.

Observance of the Sabbath and the Jewish holidays was generally allowed; but beginning with the Christian rulers we witness a growing interference of the authorities in religious matters.[39]

As regards language, Juster is probably right in saying that the Jews were free to use the Hebrew tongue (contrary to Mommsen's opinion, that this was prohibited). Special attention is drawn to *Novella* 146 of Justinian (year 553), by which the Emperor, interfering in an internal dispute, actually regulates the *credo* of the Jews. For Juster, the *Novella* is tantamount to a flagrant interference in the internal affairs of the Jewish community; and this appreciation seems correct in spite of the doubts expressed by Vol-

Literature and Inscriptions" (1950) 81 Transactions Am. Phil. Assoc. 200 ss.; L. Robert, *Nouvelles Inscriptions de Sardes* (Paris, 1964) vol. 1, p. 37 ss.; M. Simon, *Verus Israel, op. cit., passim;* E. E. Urbach, *The Sages, op. cit.,* at p. 541 ss.

38 On the dedication *Deo Aeterno pro salute Augusti* (or similar) see: J. B. Frey, *Corpus Inscriptionum Iudaicarum, op. cit.,* II, nn. 972, 1432, 1433, 1440–1444; F. Fülep, "New Remarks on the Question of the Jewish Synagogue at Intercisa" (1966) 18 *Acta Archaeologica Academiae Scientiarum Hungaricae* 93 ss.; M. Floriani Squarciapino, "Plotius Fortunatus Archisynagogus," *Scritti Milano, Rassegna Mensile di Israel* (1970) 184; F. Zevi, "The Synagogue at Ostia" *Scritti Sereni* (Jerusalem, 1970, in Hebrew) 73.

39 The Jews were exempted from appearing in a law court on the Sabbath and other Jewish festive days (*C.I.,* 1.9.2.; 1.9.13); the Council of Nicaea threatened punishment for Christians who celebrated Easter coincidentally with Passover. According to Eusebius and other Church Fathers, Constantine made the decisions of the Council binding in the law of the State. But it appears that these measures were ineffective, since the problem still persisted at the time of Justinian. According to Procopius (*Historia Arcana,* 128, 16–18), Justinian decreed that Jews must celebrate Passover only after Easter. But, three years later, Justinian himself postponed Easter and failed to act in accordance with his own Law. On this point, see Baron, *History,* vol. 3, p. 4 ss.; M. Simon, *Verus Israel,* 361 ss. The observance of Purim was allowed, with numerous restrictions in order not to offend the Christian religion by the "crucifixion" of Haman *(C.Th.* 16.8.18). On this law see: A. M. Rabello, "The First Law of Theodosius II and Celebrations of Purim" (1974) 24 Christian News from Israel 159 ss.

terra:[40] the question in dispute was that of the language in which the Tora should be read in the synagogues, whether in Hebrew or in Greek.[41]

The Emperor ruled that the Bible may be read in any language, provided it is understandable to the listeners; he recommended the Septuagint (preferred by the church), but also tolerated Aquila's version which was preferred by the synagogue. He forbade the reading of the Mishnah, which he considered a human law that distorted rather than interpreted the Scriptures. The Jewish religious authorities were forbidden to punish, by excommunication or penalties, anyone who read the Bible in Greek or in any other language; anyone who did so was subject to corporal and monetary punishment. The Jews who denied the resurrection of the dead, the final judgment and the divine nature of the angels were to be exiled. Justinian finally expressed the hope that the correct understanding of the Scriptures might lead the Jews to the "truth", i.e., to Christianity. The enforcement of these rules was entrusted to the governors and bishops who had to report directly to the Emperor in case of any failure to comply.

Chapter II closes with a discussion of the problems of taxation.[42]

As long as the Second Temple stood, the Jews enjoyed the privilege of sending contributions to Jerusalem in support of maintenance and ceremonies of the cult (*half a shekel*). This transfer of funds also served as an opportunity to make a pilgrimage to the Holy City;[43] and a famous trial was held when a high Roman official named Flaccus confiscated the funds prepared for that purpose and when the greatest of Roman orators, Cicero, delivered the speech for his defence *Pro Flacco.*[44] But after the Temple was destroyed, the defeat of the Jewish Government by its Roman rivals was symbolized by converting that privilege into the imposition of the Jewish tax (*fiscus iudaicus*).[45]

40 *Collatio legum, op. cit.,* at p. 112.

41 On *Novella 146* see V. Colorni, "L'uso del greco nella liturgia del Giudaismo ellenistico e la Novella 146 di Guistiniano" (1964) 8 *ASD* 19 ss.; see also the Reviews of G. I. Luzzatto (1935) 31 *SDHI* 433 ss., and of A. M. Rabello (1966) 12 *Labeo* 140 ss.; see also A. M. Rabello, "Alcune note sulla Collatio legum Mosaicarum et Romanarum e sul suo luogo d'origine" *Scritti Bedarida* (Florence, 1966) 184 ss. and n. 22.

42 A. Gulak, "The Method of Collecting Roman Taxes in Palestine" *Magnes Anniversary Book,* (Jerusalem, 1938, in Hebrew) 97 ss.; C. Roth, "Taxation" *Judaica,* vol. 15, col. 838 ss.; M. Elon, "Taxation", *Judaica,* vol. 15, col. 840 ss.; S. Shilo, *Dina de-Malkhuta Dina, op. cit.,* at p. 202.

43 S. Safrai, *Pilgrimage at the Time of the Second Temple* (Tel Aviv, 1965, in Hebrew); S. Safrai, "Relations between the Diaspora and the Land of Israel" in Safrai-Stern, *Jewish People,* 184 cc.

44 J. Lewy, "Cicero and the Jews in the 'Pro Flacco' ", *Olamot Nifgashim, Studies in Jewish Hellenism* (Jerusalem, 1960) 79 ss.; A. M. Rabello, "Pro Flacco" (1968) 14 *Labeo* 117 ss.; M. Stern, *Greek and Latin Authors, op. cit.,* at p. 193 ss.

45 M. S. Ginsburg, "Fiscus Iudaicus" (1930–31) 21 J.Q.R. 281 ss.; V. Tcheri-

A final section describes the *aurum coronarium,*[46] that is to say, the contributions payable to the Patriarch and messengers of the community.

A third chapter (pp. 399–408) is devoted to the central organization of the Jews in the Roman Empire, comprising the Patriarchate,[47] and its place in the public law of Rome until its extinction (*C. Th.* 16.8.29);[48] the *sanhedrin;*[49] the regional patriarchs[50] and the messengers. The privileges

kover, *The Jews in Egypt in the Hellenistic-Roman Age in the Light of the Papyri* (Jerusalem, 1963, in Hebrew) 86 ss.; V. Tcherikover, *Corpus Papyrorum Iudaicarum, op. cit.*; E. M. Smallwood, "Domitian's Attitude Toward Jews and Judaism" (1956) 51 Classical Philology 1 ss.; A. M. Rabello, "Domitian", *Judaica,* vol. 6, col. 164; *Idem,* "Nerva", *Judaica,* vol. 12, col. 965 ss.

46 'Gold for the crown'; Baron, *History,* vol. 2; G. Allon, *Toldot . . . A History of the Jews in Palestine During the Period of the Mishnah and Talmud* (Tel Aviv, 1961, in Hebrew) vol. 1, p. 147, 156 ss.; I. Gafni, "Aurum coronarium" *Judaica,* vol. 3 col. 854. In 429 the *aurum coronarium* was converted into a special Jewish tax to the state's Treasury (see also n. 48); I. S. Zuri (Rzezak), *History of Hebrew Public Law, The Reign of the Patriarchate and the Sanhedrin,* in 3 vols., (London, 1933, in Hebrew); A. Swiderek, "Ioudaikos Logos" (1971) 16–17 The Journal of Juristic Papyrology 45 ss.

47 On the Patriarch (*Nasi*) see: B. Z. Dinur, "Diocletian's Rescript to the Jews", *Memorial Volume in Honor of A. Gulak and S. Klein* (Jerusalem, 1942, in Hebrew) 76 ss.; G. Allon, *Studies in Jewish History* (Tel Aviv, 1957, in Hebrew) vol. 2, p. 55 ss.; S. Safrai, "Land of Israel, History" *Judaica,* vol. 9, col. 240 ss.; A. Linder, "Roman Imperial Government", *op. cit.,* at p. 117 ss., and nn. 136–166.

48 In 415 Patriarch Gamliel was deposed *(C. Th.* 16. 8. 22; the office of Patriarch disappeared in subsequent years, and in 429 Emperor Theodosius II took advantage of this by imposing a new tax which was to be paid by the community (*C. Th.* 16. 8. 29); J. Gaudemet, *L'Eglise dans l'Empire Romain* (Paris, 1958) 623 ss.; Parkes, *Church and Synagogue* 235; A. M. Rabello, "Honorius Flavius" *Judaica,* vol. 8, col. 968; A. M. Rabello, "Theodosius II" *Judaica,* vol. 15, col. 1101–2.

49 M. Schwabe, "Mikhtavé Libanius el ha-Nasi b'Eretz Israel" (1929–30) 1 *Tarbiz* part 2, 85 ss.; *id.,* "Dokument Hadash le-Toldot ha-Yehudim b'Meah haRevi'it (1929–30) 1 *Tarbiz* part 3, 107 ss.; B. Dinur, "Diocletian's Rescript" *op. cit.,* at p. 76 ss.; H. Albeck, "Semikha and Minnui and Beth Din" (1943) 8 *Zion* 85 ss.; *Id.,* "The Sanhedrin and its President" (1943) 8 *Zion* 165 ss.; I. F. Baer, "The Origins of the Organization of Jewish Community of the Middle Ages" (1950) 15 *Zion* 1 ss.; G. Allon, *A History, op. cit.,* at vol. 2, p. 38 ss.; S. Hoenig, *The Great Sanhedrin* (Philadelphia, 1953); H. Mantel, *Studies in the History of the Sanhedrin* (Harv. U.P., 1961) 175 ss.; E. E. Urbach, *Class Status and Leadership in the World of Palestinian Sages* (The Israel Academy of Science and Humanities, Jerusalem, 1966) vol. 2; H. Mantel, "Sanhedrin" *Judaica,* vol. 14, col. 836 ss.; I. Efron, "The Sanhedrin in Vision and Reality of the Second Temple" in *The Roman Period in Palestine* (Tel Aviv, 1973, in Hebrew) 55 ss.; S. Safrai, "Jewish Self-Government" in Safrai-Stern, *Jewish People* 377 ss.

enjoyed by the holders of these offices are described, and in particular their liberty of action and their exemptions from compulsory labour.

Chapter IV (pp. 409–496) describes in greater detail the local organization of the Jews.

50 H. Mantel, *Studies in the History of the Sanhedrin, op. cit.*, at p. 205: "The Roman government took full cognizance of these deputies of the Nasi, and the Code of Theodosius refers to them as "primates" or "[little] patriarchs". It may well be that the Nasi's representatives governed the Jewish communities throughout the Roman Empire". *Ibid.*, at n. 219: "*Cod. Theod.*, 16, 8, 8 and 29, also *The Justinian Code,* I, 9, 7, Juster is right in defining "primates" and "patriarchs" as "chiefs of provinces" (Juster, *Les Juifs,* I, 402–403). The historians who reject this definition have produced nothing better or even as satisfactory. Krauss equates the "little patriarch" with the archisynagogues (Krauss, *Synagogale Altertümer,* pp. 155–156), and identifies both with the apostles (Krauss, "Die jüdischen Apostel", p. 374), despite the fact that the Code of Theodosius distinguishes between archisynagogues and apostles (*Cod. Theod.*, 16, 8, 14). Baron rejects Juster's definition of "little patriarchs" as single, regional leaders (Baron, *The Jewish Community,* I, 107), but Juster's view is confirmed by a letter of Libanius (no. 1251, ed. Förster, p. 327), which speaks of a ruler of Antioch sent by the Nasi (see Schwabe, "Dokument", pp. 107ff.). Frey believes that the reference to the patriarch in the Stobi inscription was to a provincial "little" patriarch, but Baron thinks that the existence of such an official cannot be assumed at so early a date as 165 C.E. (Baron, *The Jewish Community,* III, 28, n. 24). Both views are necessarily speculative. On the one hand, we do not know whether there ever was a "little" patriarch in Stobi; and on the other, the date 165 C.E. need not be too early, given the fact that Todos (*Pes.* 53a) and Mathia b. Heresh (*Sanh.* 32b) had taught and ruled the Jews of Rome for the last two generations. Actually, Sukenik (*Ancient Synagogues in Palestine and Greece,* p. 79) infers from the style of the Stobi synagogue that the inscription found there could not be earlier than the end of the fourth century C.E.".
See also V. Colorni, *Legge ebraica e leggi loali, op. cit.*, at p. 109, n. 22: "Since the text of the statute mentions the patriarchs, in the plural, it clearly does not refer to the single Supreme Patriarch, whose seat was in Palestine, but to the lower-ranking patriarchs being the leaders of the Jews in every province. In the text of the law as compiled by Justinian these patriarchs are no longer mentioned, and this gives substance to the assumption that they no longer existed on the same level as the Supreme Patriarch." G. Ferrari dalle Spade, "Giurisdizione speciale ebraica nell'impero romano-cristiano" *Scritti Beatificazione Ferrini* (Milan, 1947) vol. 1, p. 239 ss. (especially at p. 244 ss.); G. Allon, "On Diocletian's Rescript, C.J. 3. 13.3" *Studies, op. cit.*, at vol. 2, p. 55 ss.; I. F. Baer, "The Origins of the Organization" *op. cit.*, at p. 16, n. 46 (the author supposes that 'little patriarchs' were invented by Juster; but see already Gothophredus' Commentary on *C.Th.* 2. 1.10!); A. Linder, "The Roman Imperial Government" *op. cit.*, at p. 123 and n. 162; A. M. Rabello, "Sui rapporti fra Diocleziano e gli Ebrei" *Atti del secondo Seminario Costantiniano,* (Perugia, in press).

In the first place the right of assembly is discussed, both under pagan and Christian rule. Contrary to Mommsen's opinion, Juster holds (p. 420, n. 4) that there did exist a "Head of the Roman Jewish Community" and considers that Rabbi Mattia Ben Heresh, for example, held such an office; but this view was not accepted by the specialists and was criticized by Frey and Momigliano[51] who believe there were several communities in Rome itself. I venture to submit that this is no reason to exclude the possibility of a personality such as Rabbi Mattia Ben Heresh being considered *de facto* as Chief of the Jews of Rome.[52]

The Jewish community was recognized as a legal person, having its own funds, capable of owning property and of entering into legal transactions. At pp. 423–4 Juster raises the question of its capacity to accept a legacy. On the authority of the Digest (D. 34.5.20.12) he adopts Waltzing's affirmative solution (again opposed to that of Mommsen), at least during the reign of Aurelius; but he has to overcome the objection arising from the Justinian Code (*C.J.*1.9.1.) containing the well-known *rescriptum* of Emperor Antoninus Caracalla, dated 213, refusing the *universitas iudaeorum* of Antioch permission to accept a legacy left by Cornelia Salvia. Juster rightly rejects the theory that the Jewish community was regarded as an illegal association (a theory accepted by eminent Romanists, such as Cujas, Dirksen, Gierke, Savigny, Zimmernius) or even that such was the condition vitiating the Jewish community of Antioch.[53] His conclusion, which had already been reached by Heineccius, is that the point was decided under some special statute. I have serious doubts on this, and would prefer the explanation proposed by Berger (and approved by Yaron),[54] that in this con-

51 J. B. Frey, "Les communautés juives à Rome aux premiers temps de l'Eglise" (1930) 30 *Recherches de science religieuse* 269 ss. and (1931) 31 *ibidem* 129 ss.; *id.* "Le Judaïsme à Rome" (1931) 30 *Biblica* 129 ss. and now *Corpus Inscriptionum, cit.* vol. 1, p. CVI; A. Momigliano, "I nomi delle prime Sinagoghe romane e la condizione giuridica della Comunità di Roma sotto Augusto" (1931) 6 *La Rassegna Mensile di Israel* 223 ss.; H. J. Leon, *The Jews of Ancient Rome, op. cit.,* at chap. 8: "The Organization of the Roman Jewish Community" 167 ss.; A. Toaff, "Matià ben Cheresh e la sua accademia rabbinica di Roma" *Annuario di Studi Ebraici* (Rome, 1966) 79; M. Simon, "Les Juifs de Rome au debut de l'ère chrétienne" (1967) *Bible et Terre Sainte* 94.

52 See my observation on Toaff's and Simon's articles in (1968) 14 *Labeo* 117 ss. and (1969) 15 *Labeo* 109 ss.

53 On the Jews at Antioch, see: C. H. Kraeling, "The Jewish Community at Antioch" (1932) 51 Journal of Biblical Literature 130 ss.; V. Tcherikover, *Hellenistic Civilization and the Jews* (Philadelphia, 1959) 30, 289, 328 s.; D. Flusser, "Antiokhyah" *Enz. Ivrit,* vol. 4, p. 458 ss.; G. Downey, *A History of Antioch in Syria from Seleucus to the Arab Conquest* (New Jersey, 1961). See also P. B. Bagatti, *L'église de la circoncision* (Jerusalem, 1965).

54 A. Berger, "Some Remarks on Caracalla's Rescript CI 1. 9.1. and its 'Universitas Iudaeorum' " (1957) 8 *IURA* 75 ss.; "A quite different importance as-

text the term *universitas* in relation to the Jewish community is not meant in its technical sense: the Emperor's decision is simply a logical application of the rule precluding the giving of a legacy to *incertae personae,* the uncertainty as to the identity of the legatee having been caused by the vague manner in which the will had been drafted, so that there is nothing to contradict the basic rule in the *senatus-consultum* reported in D. 34. 5. 20.12.

The internal management of the communities is also explained in detail, including the role of the general assembly, of the council and of the holders of administrative and spiritual offices.

With great hesitation Juster adheres to the view that the synagogue premises were in the nature of a holy site (*aedes sacra*) by virtue of some special *privilegium.* But Berger, while admitting the existence of such privileges, has shown that their effect was simlpy to give synagogues the status of places of worship (*loca religionum*): no place can be recognized as *aedes sacra* unless by special consecration by the Roman people (*consecratio populi romani:* Gaius 2, 4; 2, 5); and this is why the State did not inspect the synagogues or care for their maintenance.[55]

The chapter concludes with a survey of legislation concerning synagogues until the reign of Justinian, when the synagogues of Africa were turned into churches;[56] and also concerning schools, libraries, market-places, hospitals, ritual baths (*mikvahot*) and burial grounds. In all these matters the influence of the Catholic church is noticeable: the church sought to ensure the survival of the Jews as a separate nation, in a condition of misery.[57]

sumed the rescript in Justinian's Code through the insertion into the title *De Iudaeis* and the more developed significance which the term *universitas* assumed in Justinian's legislative work: the imperial decision sounds like a general exclusion of Jewish organized groups from claiming legacies altogether." (p. 86); R. Yaron, "Reichsrecht, Volksrecht und Talmud" (1964) 11 *RIDA* 284 ss.; A. M. Rabello (1967) 18 *IURA* 310; A. Linder, "The Roman Imperial Government", *op. cit.,* at p. 116, n. 121.

55 A. Berger, "The Jewish Synagogue and the *aedes sacrae* in Roman Law" in *Studi Biondi* (1965) vol. 1, p. 143 ss. "... the synagogue might be granted a special privilege through a particular statute in earlier times or an imperial enactment depending primarily upon the attitude of its imperial author towards the Jews and Judaism".

56 On the legislation on synagogues see J. E. Seaver, *Persecution of the Jews in The Roman Empire (200–438)* (Lawrence, 1952) 30 ss,; M. Avi-Yonah, *In the Days of Rome and Byzantium* (Jerusalem, 1962, in Hebrew).

57 See Y. Baer, "Israel, The Christian Church and The Roman Empire" in *Scripta Hierosolymitana,* (1961) vol. 7, p. 79 ss.; S. Grayzel, "The Jews and Roman Law" (1968) 59 J.Q.R., 93 ss. See also E. E. Urbach, *The Sages, op. cit.,* at p. 545 s.: "For about a hundred and fifty years, from after the Revolt of Bar Kokhba until Christianity became dominant in the Roman Empire, the Sages of Israel stood embattled on two fronts: one facing them and the other at the rear. They joined issue with the pagans, who proceeded to negate Israel's elec-

The 2nd volume opens with a chapter (V, pp. 1–27) on the political status (*status civitatis*) of the Jews in the Roman Empire. Any discussion of this subject must distinguish ,among the various provinces and take into account the fact that different periods of time are involved.

Before the year 70 C.E., those Jews who had the rights of citizens in Palestine were considered foreigners (*peregrini*) by Roman law, as were also the Jews of the Diaspora, who had settled in and become citizens of various other provinces of the Empire. Those Jews who lived in Rome, however, or in the Roman State, became Roman citizens (*cives romani*), either through enfranchisement (*manumissio*) by their masters, themselves Roman citizens, or by governmental concession. On the other hand, there were also Jewish slaves.

Theodor Mommsen's theory on the subject is well-known:[58] After the destruction of the Temple in the year 70, all the Jews in the Empire are supposed to have been deprived of their former autonomy; and those who were lucky enough to remain free men became *peregrini dediticii*.[59] Judaism was transformed from a national cult into a licit religion (*religio licita*). This theory gained the approval of eminent Romanists, such as Mitteis, Girard and P. M. Mayer.

Juster, however, rejects it resolutely. In his opinion the Jewish War had no influence on the *status civitatis* of the Jews: after the year 70, as before,

tion with politico-territorial arguments: a subjugated people, which had neither independence nor Temple, could not be regarded by them as a chosen but as an inferior people; and they polemized against the Christians, who boasted that they had inherited the election-birthright of the Jewish people and its covenant with its God, as well as the accompanying spiritual attributes, precisely because they were not a people but a church of the peoples".

58 Th. Mommsen, "Der Religionsfrevel nach römischen Recht" (1890) 64 *Historische Zeitschrift,* 389 ss. (= *Gesammelte Schriften,* III, 389 ss.); *Idem, Le Droit pénal romain,* (Paris, 1907) vol. 2 p. 276 n. 3.

59 See Berger, *E.D.*, 427: "The citizens of a foreign state or community, who, vanquished in a war with Rome, surrendered to the power and protection of Rome (*deditio*). They constituted a specific group of the Roman population; they were free but lacked all public rights and citizenship (*nullius civitatis*). Their legal status as *peregrini dediticii* could be improved by unilateral concessions granted by Rome to individuals or groups. But even the general grant of Roman citizenship to peregrines by the constitution of the emperor Caracalla excluded the *dediticii*. The status of *dediticii,* termed by Justinian *dediticia libertas,* was abolished by him (C. 7.5.1)". See also Jolowicz and Nicholas, *Historical Introduction to the Study of Roman Law* (Cambridge, 3rd ed., 1972), 347: "On the other hand, the exception is grammatically more likely to be related to the reservation, and *dediticii* would then most naturally be understood in the wider sense. Many conjectures have been made as to the content of the reservation, the most attractive being those which suppose it to have concerned the local citizenship of those enfranchised: only the *dediticii* were excluded from local citizenship."

they continued to form a national community (*natio*) enjoying, in certain respects, a number of *privilegia*. This was the way in which the Romans showed their respect for religion and its close connection with Jewish law.[60]

Juster's criticism of Mommsen's theory paved the way for further research, as a consequence of which it was found that the legal status of the Jews was much more diversified, both in place and in time, so that it is better to refrain from generalizations. Thus, so far as the Jewish communities of Palestine are concerned, a distinction must be made according to their varying attitude towards Rome;[61] some of them may indeed be described as *dediticii*,[62] and it is possible to find conclusive proof that local laws were applied to relations between individuals in the different Roman provinces.[63]

Another problem, which is still the object of controversy, is linked with the grant of Roman citizenship to the entire population of the Empire, in-

60 Juster, *Juifs*, 19–23; "Since the Jews continued to enjoy their privileges ... they could do so as members of a nation ... The exercise thereof was therefore permitted only to the members of the Jewish nation." See also J. Juster, *Les droits politiques des Juifs dans l'Empire Romain* (Paris, 1912).

61 A. Momigliano, "Ricerche sull'organizzazione della Giudea sotto il dominio romano," (1934) 3 *Annali della R. Scuola Normale Superiore di Pisa*, serie II, (reprinted, Amsterdam, 1967); see also Luzzatto's review (1936) 2 *SDHI* 218 ss.; see also G. I. Luzzatto, "Peregrini" (1965) 12 *NNDI* 931 ss.

62 See also V. Colorni, *Legge ebraica e leggi locali op. cit.*, at p. 16 s.:"... in whatever way the question should be solved as regards Palestine, the scholars agree with Juster's certain belief that the Jews of the Diaspora were subjected to no reprisals for the events of the year 70". See also S. Applebaum, "The Legal Status of the Jewish Communities in the Diaspora" in Safrai-Stern, *Jewish People* 420 ss.

63 This is on the basis of documentation discovered at Murabba'ât. See E. Volterra, "Nuovi documenti per la conoscenza del diritto vigente nelle provincie romane" (1969) 14 *IURA* 29 ss.: *"Tale documentazione prova in modo irrefragibile l'applicazione nelle provincie romane dei diritti locali per quanto attiene ai rapporti fra privati"* (p. 34). See also E. Volterra," I diritti locali" in *I diritti locali nelle provincie romane con particolare riguardo alle condizioni giuridiche del suolo* (Rome, 1974) 55 ss.: "... it must have been extremely difficult for the Roman authorities to abrogate these norms and institutions as well as local customs. And yet, it is most likely that, in Palestine, the local laws and customs, especially in certain matters, must have been preserved for a long time ... The victorious nation did not impose its private law upon the vanquished, but allowed them to keep their own local law, customs and often even their local administration. In contrast to the modern idea of the unity of private law in every State, it was considered quite normal in the ancient world that, among the subjects submitted to the same sovereignty, there could be different laws applicable simultaneously". (p. 64). See also P. Benoit, J. T. Milik, R. De Vaux, *Discoveries in the Judean Desert: Les Grottes de Murabba'ât* (Oxford, 1961) vol. 2. Concerning certain propositions made by Milik, without reference to the results of Momigliano's research, see E. Volterra, "Nuovi docomenti" *op. cit.*, at p. 54 ss.

cluding Jews, by virtue of the *Constitutio Antoniniana*:[64] did the Jews, who thus became Roman citizens (*cives romani*) also keep the citizenship of the political communities to which they formerly belonged? To that question Schönbauer, Colorni, De Visscher and Tcherikover[65] give a positive reply, while Arangio Ruiz and Luzzatto[66] object that the sources contain nothing from which to infer the possibility of double citizenship: in this latter view, although the granting of citizenship was accompanied by the formal recognition of the principle of "personality of the law", the manner in which it was applied in fact by the authorities in the provinces was marked by a certain distortion of both Roman and local law, and this resulted in the creation of what came to be called "vulgar law" which prevailed and was applied as Roman law.[67]

64 See Berger, *E.D.*, 409: "A constitution of the emperor Caracalla by which all inhabitants of the Empire, organized in *civitates* with local autonomy, were granted the Roman citizenship, except the so-called *peregrini dediticii*". But see *supra*, n. 59 and also Jolowicz and Nicholas, *op. cit.*, at p. 347: "From the point of view of private law, however, it was more important, though rather for its indirect effect on the character of the law itself than for its direct impact on the new citizens. For though, on the generally accepted view, large numbers of provincials who previously had lived by their own law, were now expected to adapt themselves to Roman law, the immediate result, as we shall see, was often no more than the adoption of the forms of Roman law as clothing for the unchanged substance of local law".
The extension of citizenship, without any discrimination, is upheld by Colorni, *Legge ebraica e leggi locali, op. cit.*, at p. 17 ss., where the problem is discussed, with bibliographical references; while the opposite view is that of Arangio-Ruiz, "Editto di Caracalla" (1960) 6 *NNDI* 403: ". . . it may be taken for certain that only the so-called *dediticii* were excluded from the grant". This problem is generally discussed in every manual on the history of Roman law.

65 Naturally the problem of the Jews is merged into the general problem of citizenship in view of the principle of the 'personal' character of the law, as it was understood in the ancient world: Schönbauer, "Reichsrecht gegen Volksrecht?" (1931) 51 *ZSS* 277 ss. and several other studies (quoted by Arangio Ruiz; see next foot-note); V. Colorni, *Legge ebraica e leggi locali, op. cit.*, at p. 19; F. De Visscher, "La dualité des droits de cité et la mutatio civitatis" (1954) *Bull. Acad. Royal de Belgique* 49 ss.; V. Tcherikover, *Corpus Papyrorum Judiacarum, op. cit.*, at vol. 1. p. 100; *Idem, The Jews in the Graeco-Roman World* (Jerusalem, 1961, in Hebrew).

66 Arangio Ruiz, Review of Tcherikover, *Corpus Papyrorum Judaicarum* in (1969) 73 *Rivista di filologia ed istruzione classica; Id., Storia del Diritto Romano,* (Naples, 7th ed., 1964) 338 ss. and the updating note (w) at p. 424, with an ample discussion of the opposing thesis and, in particular, of the criticism of Schönbauer; G. I. Luzzatto, "Epigrafia giuridica Greca e Romana" (part 4) (1957) 8 *IURA* 192 s.; see also Luzzatto's reviews of Colorni, *Legge ebraica, cit.*, (1947–48) 13–14 *SDHI* 423, and of Tcherikover, *Corpus, op. cit.*, (1961) 27 *SDHI* 373.

67 On the *Constitutio Antoniniana* see also: L. Mitteis, *Reichsrecht und Volks-*

The Christian Emperors subjected the Jews to political and civil prohibitions, but the Jews continued to be considered *cives romani* (*Judaei romano et communi iure viventes, C. Th.* 2.1.10).

In Chap. VI, devoted to personal status (pp. 28–40), Juster stresses the persistence of private Jewish law, both before and after the Antonian Constitution of Emperor Caracalla, both before and after the coming into power of Constantine. It may even be admitted that, while under the Antonian Constitution the Jews who were Roman citizens were, generally and strictly speaking, subjected to Roman law, once Roman citizenship was awarded to all the *peregrini,* a concession, albeit never officially recognized *de jure,* was made in favour of all the Jews of the Empire, by which they were allowed to retain some of the institutions of Jewish law.[68] Thus, for example, in

recht in den östlichen Provinzen des römischen Kaiserreichs. Mit Beiträgen zur Kenntniss des griechischen Rechts und der spätrömischen Rechtsentwiklung (Leipzig, 1891, reimpr. 1963); V. Arangio Ruiz, "L'application du droit romain en Egypte après la Constitution Antoninienne" (1946–7) 29 *Bulletin de l'Institut d'Egypte* 83 ss.; R. Taubenschlag, *The Law of Greco-Roman Egypt in the Light of the Papyri (332 B.C.–640 A.D.)* (Warsaw, 2nd ed., 1955); H. J. Wolff, "Faktoren der Rechtsbildung im hellenistisch-römischen Aegypten (1953) 70 *ZSS* 20 ss.; Ch. Sasse, *Die Constitutio Antoniniana. Eine Untersuchung über den Umfang der Bürgerrechtsverleihung auf Grund des Papyrus Giss. 40 I* (Wiesbaden, 1958); J. Gaudemet, "L'autorité de la loi et de la coutume dans l'Antiquité" in *Rapports généraux aux VIe Congrès International de droit comparé* (Brussels, 1964) 9 ss.; D. Nörr, *Imperium und Polis in der hohen Prinzipatszeit* (Munich, 1966), J. Modrzejewski, "La règle de droit dans l'Egypte romaine (Etat des questions et perspectives de recherches)" (1970) 7 American Studies in Papyrology 317 ss.; M. Talamanca, "Su alcuni passi di Menandro di Laodicea relativi agli effetti della 'Constitutio Antoniniana" in *St. Volterra* (1974) vol. 5, p. 433 ss.; E. Volterra, "I diritti locali", *op. cit.* On vulgarization of Roman Law see M. Kaser, *Das Römische Privatrecht* (Munich, 1969) vol. 2, p. 13 ss. (with bibliography).

68 "But the power exercised by the Jews was actual autonomous jurisdiction recognized by the State and binding upon a party even against the opponent's will. Consequently Jewish law was applicable not only by consent formerly given by the parties and within certain well-defined limits, but even where either party or even both parties did not consent to such application; and such application was not subject to any restriction wherever their personal status was affected, being a matter recognized by the State through the recognition given to this special jurisdiction.... The obvious conclusion is, that within the local limits wherein the Romans, until 398, recognized a Jewish jurisdiction concurrent with that of the State courts, they also recognized Jewish law as the exclusive source of substantive law in respect of the internal private relations among the Jews; and that they applied that law in their own courts wherever litigation between Jews was brought in their courts instead of in a Jewish court." (V. Colorni, *Legge ebraica e leggi locali, op. cit.,* at p. 106). See also D. Piattelli, "Intorno al problema dell'organizzazione giuridica e del diritto

matrimonial matters, in the entire diaspora, some toleration was shown towards bigamy, marriage of uncle and niece, the levirate and, possibly, divorce. Even under the first Christian Emperors, Jewish law remained applicable in matters of marriage; but "the policy of unification followed by the Christian Emperors was bound, in the end to wipe out the last traces of these Jewish privileges".[69] This general proposition of Juster finds corroboration in the chapters that follow (VII–XIII), dealing with the various branches of private law.

The chapters that then follow are devoted to marriage (VII, pp. 41–56); to Divorce (VIII, pp. 54–61); to Legal Capacity (IX, pp. 62–4); to Contract Law (X, pp. 65–8); to Ownership (XI, pp. 69–70); to Slaves (XII, pp. 71–84); and to Wills and Inheritance (XIII, pp. 85–92).

We shall obviously have to take into account the latest conclusions reached by the numerous studies devoted to all these aspects of Roman law, such as: the validity of marriage between Jews having a different *status civitatis*, and the question of their *ius connubii*;[70] or the problem of relations between father and son, and the question of *patria potestas*;[71] on the problem of inheritance: as from the reign of Constantine, special legislation was in

applicabile dalle Comunità ebraiche viventi in Egitto nel periodo ellenistico-romano" (1968) 12 *Rivista Italiana per le Scienze Giuridiche* 309 ss. (with bibliography); S. Applebaum, "The Legal Status of the Jewish Communities in the Diaspora", in Safrai-Stern, *Jewish History* 420 ss. (especially at p. 455 ss.). This is not a suitable place for a discussion on Applebaum's observations on the theories of Mommsen, Juster and Colorni.

69 Juster, *Juifs* 2, 35.

70 The main authorities on the subject are the writings of De Visscher and Volterra; see bibliography reported by Volterra, "Connubium" (1959) 4 *NNDI* 786 s.; see also *id.* "Matrimonio, Diritto Romano" (1975) 25 *EdD* 726 ss. especially at p. 773 ss. and nn. 116–119; see also J. Modrzejewski, "Les Juifs et le droit hellénistique: divorce et égalité des époux (C.P.Jud. 144)" (1961) 12 *IURA* 162 ss.: R. Yaron, "C.P.Jud.144 et alia" (1962) 13 *IURA* 170 ss.; D. Piattelli, "Alcune osservazioni su C.P.Jud.144" (1967) 18 *IURA* 121 ss.

71 It seems remarkable to me that although Juster followed the then undisputed view, admitting that *"les juifs citoyens romains eurent sûrement le droit de constituer un tribunal domestique"*, he nevertheless did not so construe the passages of Josephus Flavius, *Antiquitates,* 16, 11, 2–3, 356 ss., where reference was made to the tribunal established by Herod for the trial of his own sons (see also *Bellum Judaicum,* 1, 1. 2–3), remarking: *"C'est un cas exceptionnel, qu'on peut expliquer autrement"*. It will further be noted that the text of Flavius has, on the contrary, been relied upon by Kunkel, "Das Konsilium im Hausgericht" (1966) 83 *ZSS* 219 ss. in his endeavour to refute Volterra's thesis as to the inexistence of domestic tribunals in Roman Law, "Il preteso tribunale domestico in diritto romano" (1948) *Rivista Italiana per le Scienze Giuridiche* 103 ss. and *id., Il matrimonio Romano* (Rome, 1961), 43 ss. On Kunkel's article see the critical remarks of Guarino (1967) 13 *Labeo* 124. See also A. M. Rabello, "On a Father's Power in Roman and Jewish Law" (1974) 5 *Dinei Israel* 85 ss. (with bibliography).

force regulating the right of a baptized Jew to inherit the estate of his Jewish parents;[72] or the right of a Christian slave towards a Jewish heir or legatee.[73]

A special chapter (XIV, pp. 93–214) is devoted to jurisdiction. Juster takes good care to distinguish between civil and criminal matters, between Jewish and Roman courts, between those established in Palestine and in the Diaspora.[74]

Juster believes that the jurisdiction of Jewish courts was recognized until the year 398.[75] The situation changed with the constitution of Emperors Arcadius and Honorius, dated 3 Feb. 398 (*C.Th.* 2.1.10)[76]—by which a

72 See M. Avi-Yonah, *In the Days of Rome and Byzantium, op. cit.,* at p. 139 ss.

73 See E. E. Urbach, "Halakhot Regarding Slavery", *op. cit.,* at p. 2 of English summary), "Conditions deteriorated considerably in the 4th century with the passage of anti-Jewish legislation which began with Constantinus' decree forbidding Jews to buy Christian slaves"; J. Gaudemet, *L'Eglise dans l'Empire Romain (IV–V siècles)* (Paris, 1958) 629 s.

74 On this problem see V. Colorni, *Legge ebraica e leggi locali, op. cit.,* at p. 103 ss., 311; *Id. Gli Ebrei nel sistema del diritto comune fino alla prima emancipazione,* (Milan, 1956) 1 ss.; G. Ferrari Dalle Spade, "Giurisdizione speciale ebraica nell'Impero romano-cristiano" in *Scritti Beatificazione Ferrini* (1947) vol. 1, p. 238 ss. (= *Scritti Giuridici,* III, 280 ss.): "Thus, under the Christian Emperors, the Jews had their own judges, and on account of their cult, their holidays and especially the Sabbath were recognized, in that they affected the rules of procedure (relying upon *C.Th.* 2. 8. 6; 8. 8. 8; 6. 8. 20)"; J. Gaudemet, *L'Eglise dans l'Empire Romain (IV–V siècles)* (Paris, 1958) 627 ss.; A. Linder, "The Roman Imperial Government" *op. cit.,* at p. 123 ss.; see also G. I. Luzzatto, "Giurisdizione" (1970) 19 *EdD.* 190 ss.

75 Colorni holds that this jurisdiction had been recognized only in Palestine and and in some of the oriental provinces, but not in the entire Roman empire (*Legge ebraica e leggi locali, op. cit.,* at p. 115 ss.).

76 *C.Th.* 2. 1. 10: "The same Augustuses to Eutychianus, Praetorian Prefect. Jews who live under the Roman and common law shall approach the courts in the customary manner in those cases which concern not so much their superstition as the forum, the statutes, and the law; and they shall bring and defend all actions according to the Roman law; in fine, they shall be subject to Our laws. I. Certainly, in the case of civil suits only, if any Jews should suppose that, by a mutual promise to abide by the decision in accordance with the agreement of both parties, they should litigate before Jews or patriarchs as though before arbitrators, they shall not be prohibited by public law from choosing the judgment of such men. The judges of the provinces shall execute their sentences as if such arbitrators had been assigned by the decision of a judge. *Given on the third day before the nones of February at Constantinople in the year of the fourth consulship of Honorius Augustus and the consulship of the Most Noble Eutychianus.—February 3, 398*". (Pharr's translation); see also *Brev. Alaric.* 2. 1. 10; *CJ.* 1. 9. 8. See also Gaudemet, *L'Eglise dans l'Empire, op. cit.,* at p. 627 n. 1: *"Au CJ, 1. 9. 8 le texte figure avec des interpolations qui marquent la défaveur à l'égard des juridictions juives"*; and see especially

distinction was made among the matters to which this jurisdiction applied: strictly religious matters remained within the exclusive competence of the Rabbinical tribunals, while criminal cases came within the exclusive competence of the Roman courts. As regards civil matters, these are henceforth within the competence of the Roman courts, but the litigants are allowed, by their joint assent (*compromissum*), to transfer the case to the Rabbinical tribunal. In Juster's view, the judgment of such tribunal is tantamount to an arbitration award, but it has inherently the effect of the *res judicata* of a Roman judge, and not merely that of an arbitrator. The scholars, however, are not all agreed on that point.[77] "It is clear," remarks Colorni, "that the

Berger's observations: "*C.Th.* 2. 1. 10 and *CJ.* 1. 9. 8 pr. A Perfect Example of an Interpolation through Cancellation of a 'non'" (1959) 10 *IURA* 14 ss. "Juster believes that a *compromissum* was only necessary to "connect" the controversy with Jewish authorities and that the judgment derived not from the *compromissum,* but from the right of jurisdiction of the Jewish judicial authorities. In a normal *compromissum,* when a private individual was appointed by the parties as an arbitrator (*arbiter ex compromisso*), his right to pass a judgment in that specific case arose from the mutual agreement of the parties who selected him as a judge. The same was the situation when a Jewish court, or Jewish authorities or a single dignitary were selected for arbitration. The fact that the selected arbitrator or arbitrators were chosen, did not bestow on them larger rights than those which were settled in the arbitration agreement. The Jewish authorities, which ever they were, acquired jurisdiction therefore only in a specific case when the parties selected them. Thus a general autonomous Jewish civil jurisdiction did not exist at all after 398 A.D." (p. 20), and also: "... the purpose of which was to establish whether Justinian wanted to eliminate the autonomous Jewish jurisdiction in religious matters—a measure which fits perfectly into the Emperors' general, certainly not favorable attitude towards the Jews—have been necessary to reject an opinion which excluded the conception of an interpolation in c. 8 pr. cit. and assumed instead that Justinian did not change the provision of the C.Th. cit.," (p. 17); and Berger concluded: "There remains no other solution of the problem of the authenticity of CI. 1.9.8pr. than that of an evident interpolation accomplished through cancellation of '*non*' in the text of the C.Th. All artificial efforts and farfetched arguments to restore the '*non*' in c. 8pr. and to save Justinian from the reproach of having suppressed the Jewish jurisdiction in religious matters, are—beyond any doubt—a failure" (p. 23).

77 V. Colorni, *Legge ebraica e leggi locali, op. cit.,* at p. 131 n. 77; J. Gaudemet, *L'Eglise dans l'Empire, op. cit,* at p. 628: "*... pour les matières civiles, mais dans ce cas, seulement à la suite d'un compromis. Pour être exécutoire, la sentence devait entre confirmée par le juge séculier*". In J. Oestersetzer's opinion there is a correlation between *C.Th.* 2. 1. 10 and the drafting of the *Collatio legum Mosaicarum et romanarum:* the author of the *Collatio* was a Jew, who, at the end of the 4th century, proposed to show the affinity between Roman and Jewish law, so as to prevent the latter's abrogation. ("La Collatio legum Mosaicarum et Romanarum, Ses Origines, Son But" (1934) 97 *REJ* 65 ss.); see A. M. Rabello, "Sull'ebraicità dell'autore della 'Collatio legum Mosaicarum

special jurisdiction had been abolished, to such an extent that the special rules of personal status themselves were removed . . . It was therefore for the very purpose of abrogating entirely the civil law of the Jews that the Roman Emperors deprived the Jews of the special jurisdiction which they had enjoyed until then: and actually such a provision is not surprising, being in harmony with the tendency towards legal unification of the Empire on the basis of Christian principles to which the Emperors aspired more and more after the triumph of the Catholic Church".[78]

Dealing with the jurisdiction of the Sanhedrin *ratione materiae,* he refers to the trial of Jesus,[79] a subject that has attracted a vast amount of research,

et Romanarum" (1967) 33 *Rassegna Mensile di Israel* 345 ss.; the *Collatio* was probably compiled in Rome between the years 294 and 313 C.E.; see also A. M. Rabello, "Collatio legum Mosaicarum et Romanarum," *Judaica,* vol. 5, col. 734 s.; See also F. Bossowski, "Suntne in iure romano, suadente usu forensi audientiae episcopalis, quaedam praecepta ad instar iuris privati hebraici introducta?" (1939) 10 *Racznik Prawniczego Wilenskiego* 1 ss. and Rabello's observations: "On the Collatio legum Mosaicarum et Romanarum" in *Shenaton Ha-Mishpat Ha-Ivri* (Annual of the Institute for Research in Jewish Law, Jerusalem, 1974) 244 ss. and n. 51 ss.

78 V. Colorni, *Legge ebraica e legge locali* 109 ss.

79 There is ample literature on the trial of Jesus, even within the limits of the most recent studies of its legal aspects. See especially: S. Zeitlin, *Who Crucified Jesus?* (New York, London, 1942); E. E. Urbach, "Homilies of the Rabbis on the Prophets of the Nations and the Balaam Stories" (1956) 25 *Tarbiz* 272 ss.; J. Klausner, *Jesus of Nazareth* (1957); H. Mantel,, *Studies in the History of the Sanhedrin* (Harv. U.P., 1961) 254 ss.; Winter, *On the Trial of Jesus* (Berlin, 1961); A. N. Sherwin-White, *The Trial of Christ in the Synoptic Gospel, in Roman Society and Roman Law in the New Testament* (Oxford, 1963) 24 ss. (in this lecture the author has taken a position opposed to that of Juster and of those who have followed his views, especially at p. 36 s.); on certain doubts on this point see, however L. Bove, "Nuovo Testamento e diritto romano" (1966) 12 *Labeo* 399 ss.; L. Bove, "A proposito del processo di Gesù" in *St. Volterra* (1968, reprint). Colin has discussed the problem in the ample introduction to his book, entitled: *Les villes libres de l'Orient gréco-romain et l'envoi au supplice par acclamations populaires* (Bruxelles, 1965) and also in "Sur le procès de Jésus devant Pilate et le peuple" (1965) 67 *Revue des Etudes Anciennes* 158 ss.: for some critical remarks see the review by G. I. Luzzato, in (1966) 106 *La parola del passato* 74 ss. (esp. 77); S. Pines, *Jewish Christians of the Early Centuries of Christianity According to a New Source* (Jerusalem, 1966); H. H. Cohn, "Reflections on the Trial and Death of Jesus" (1967) 2 Is.L.R. 332 ss. and, more extensively, *The Trial and Death of Jesus* (Tel Aviv, 1968, in Hebrew); D. Flusser, *Jesus* (Jerusalem, 1969); D. Flusser, "Jesus" *Judaica* vol. 10, col. 10 ss.; J. Imbert, "Le Procès du Christ. Essai de mise au point" (1972) 5, *Studi Grosso* 395 ss.; M. Stern, " The Province of Judaea" in Safrai-Stern, *Jewish People,* especially at pp. 338, 352. On the *Testimonium Flavianum* see S. Pines, *An Arabic Version of the Testimonium Flavianum and its Implica-*

on the part of theologians and historians as well as lawyers. This problem is also linked with the special status of Jerusalem: was that town a *polis?* Tcherikover reaches a negative conclusion.[80] Another aspect is that of the *ius*

tions (Jerusalem, 1971) (and A. M. Rabello's review in (1972) 3 *Index* 69 s.) On the question of the Law applicable in Palestine see R. Sugranyes de Franch, *Etudes sur le droit palestinien à l'époque évangelique. La contrainte par corps* (Fribourg, 1946) (reviewed by G. Furlani, (1946) 12 *SDHI* 195 ss.); Z. W. Falk, *Introduction to Jewish Law: The Period of the Second Temple* (Tel Aviv, 1969, in Hebrew) vol. 1 and (1971) vol. 2 (reviewed by A. M. Rabello (1969) 20 *IURA* 678 ss. and (1971) 22 *ibidem* 257 ss.); Z. W. Falk, "Jewish Private Law" in Safrai-Stern, *Jewish People* 504 ss.; H. J. Wolff, "Hellenistic Private Law" *ibidem,* 534 ss.; see also H. J. Polotsky, "Three Greek Documents from the Family Archive of Babatha" *Erez Israel, Sukenik Book,* (Jerusalem, 1967) 46 ss.; A. M. Rabello "Israele" (rapporto), (1970) 1 *Index* 24 ss.; Seidl, "Juristische Papyruskunde, 16. Bericht" (1967) 33 *SDHI* (appeared in 1968), 521, 550–552; *Id.* "Ein Papyrusfund zum klassischen Zivilprozessrecht" (1968) 2 *Studi Grosso* 343 ss.; Lemosse, "Le procès de Babatha" (1968) 3 The Irish Jurist 63 ss.; Hans Julius Wolff, *Romisches Provinzialrecht in der Provinz Arabia* (New York, 1972), (1971) 18 *RIDA* 774 s.; A. Biscardi, "Nuove testimonianze di un papiro arabo-giudaico per la storia del processo provinciale romano" *Studi Scherillo* (1971–72) vol. 1, p. 111 ss.; *Id.,* "Un remoto precedente storico del prontuairo bizantino 'de actionibus' " in *Atti del Seminario Romanistico Internazionale* (Perugia, 1972) 45 ss. See also B. Cohen, *Jewish and Roman Law* (New York, 1966) reviewed by A. M. Rabello, (1969) 20 *IURA* 551 ss. For general interest see D. Daube, *The New Testament and Rabbinic Judaism* (London, 1956) especially at p. 308 ss.

80 W. Tcherikover, "Was Jerusalem a 'Polis'?" (1964) 14 Israel Exploration Journal 61 ss.; also G. I. Luzzatto, "Sul regime del suolo" *op. cit.,* at p. 44: *"Per la stessa Gerusalemme che pure non era una Polis, il problema dell'autonomia è lungi dall'essere risolto"* and n. 142: *"Anche accogliendo le conclusioni dell'-Autore* (Tcherikover), *che sembrano in complesso sicure e per il quale Gerusalemme non sarebbe mai stata una Polis, rimane ugualmente aperto il problema delle autonomie delle città e del Tempio;"* in *Sul regime del suolo nelle provincie romane, op. cit.,* at p. 44; on this problem see M. Stern, "The Province of Judaea" in Safrai-Stern, *Jewish People* 340 ss. with bibliography; see especially at p. 344 s.: "It is clear on the other hand that we cannot simply affirm that Jerusalem really became a polis in all respects. Not only were the social and cultural institutions of a Greek polis not maintained there, but regular assemblies of the demos at a fixed time and place were not part of the city's constitution. Nor were the members of its boule elected in the Greek fashion. Furthermore, the boule was in effect identical with the traditional Sanhedrin of Jerusalem, which performed *inter alia* the function of city council. It may nevertheless be noted that changes had also taken place in the administration of the Greek cities of the East, departing from the original forms of the Greek polis, whereas the institutions of Jewish Jerusalem had adopted part of the terminology prevalent in the Hellenistic-Roman world. Thus the Sanhedrin began to be known as a boule and to bestow upon Jerusalem the external aspect of a normal polis."

gladii.[81] Juster believes that the Sanhedrin had the power, recognized by Roman law, to pronounce the capital sentence on any foreigner, and even on a Roman citizen, for trespassing and penetrating into the Temple premises.[82] This view is based on a passage of Josephus (*Bellum Iudaicum,* 6.2.4),[83] the authenticity of which seems doubtful and which clashes with other sources. Indeed there is no other source, whether Jewish or Roman, for the proposition that the Roman authorities ever recognized the Sanhedrin's power to sentence a Roman citizen to death. In a study devoted to this subject (the "Lex de Templo Hierosolymitano")[84] my own conclusion was as follows: ". . . the death penalty was not carried out by direct Divine intervention, as Derenbourg and Graetz thought, but by human hands. The executioners were not the Roman authorities, as Mommsen and many others thought, or the Sanhedrin, as Juster believed. It is maintained that, from the examination of the sources presented herein, the conclusion to be drawn is that the killing of

81 See Berger, *E.D.*, 529: " 'The power to punish criminal individuals' (D. 2. 1. 3) with all kinds of punishment, the death penalty included. In Rome it was the emperor himself who exercises the right in capital trials. He could delegate it to the supreme officials in the provinces (governors, *legati*) and to the prefects in Rome, at first only in a specific case, later generally". See C. Nardi, "Il ius gladii del procurator Caesaris nella Giudea" (1941) 1 *Rivista Internazionale di filosofia politica e sociale*; A. Biscardi, Introduction to Nardi, *Il Processo di Gesù* (Bari, 1966); see also: E. De Ruggero, "Ius gladii" *Dizionario Epigrafico* vol. 3, col. 532 ss.; H. G. Pflaum, *Les procurateurs équestres sous le Haut-Empire Romain* (Paris, 1950) 117 ss.; A. N. Sherwin-White, "Coercitio, cognitio and imperium in the First Century A.D." in *Roman Society, op. cit.,* at p. 1 ss. and Bove's observations, "Nuovo Testamento e Diritto Romano" *op. cit.,* at p. 402; A. H. M. Jones, *Studies in Roman Government and Law* (1960) 51 ss.; M. Stern, "The Province of Judaea" in Safrai-Stern, *Jewish People,* 339 s.

82 According to Juster "in countries and towns Roman public law made reservation (of the power to execute) only with regard to their own nationals. The Sanhedrin could exercise capital jurisdiction even over a non-Jew, even a Roman citizen, in the case, and only in the case, where he had presumed to pass beyond the Temple enclosure".

83 "Titus, yet more deeply distressed, again upbraided John and his friends. "Was it not you," he said, "most abominable wretches, who placed this balustrade before your sanctuary? Was it not you that ranged along it those slabs, engraved in Greek characters and in our own, proclaiming that none may pass the barrier? And did we not permit you to put to death any who passed it, even he a Roman?"

84 The inscription (discovered in 1871 by the French archaelogist C. Clermont-Ganneau, in Jerusalem, north of the Temple area) reads as follows: "No foreigner to enter within the balustrade and embankment around the sanctuary. Whoever is caught will have himself to blame for his death which follows." See C. Clermont-Ganneau, "Une stèle du Temple de Jerusalem" (1872) 23 *Revue Archéologique* 214 ss., 290 ss.

a Gentile who violated the ban was carried out by the people present who with their own eyes saw that deliberate breach."[85]

In an Annex to his work the author takes into account various revolts of Jews in the Diaspora and in Palestine, from the Jewish rebellion in Alexandria[86] to the War of 70 and its repercussions on the Diaspora.[87] Particular attention is devoted to the revolt of the Jews under Trajan in Egypt, Cyrenaica, Cyprus, Mesopotamia[88] and Palestine (the so-called War of Kitos mentioned in Talmudic sources).[89] The revolt of Bar Kochba is

85 A. M. Rabello, "The 'Lex de Templo Hierosolymitano', Prohibiting Gentiles from Entering Jerusalem Sanctuary" (1970) 21, 3 Christian News from Israel 28 ss. and (1971) 21, 4 *ibidem* 28 ss.; *Id.* in *Miscellanea di Studi in onore di Dario Disegni* (Turin, 1969) 199 ss.; with bibliography, 217 ss.; see also E. Bickerman, "The Warning Inscription of Herod's Temple" (1947) 37 J.Q.R. 387 ss.; M. Cassuto-Salzman, "Hebrew Inscriptions of the End of the Second Temple Period" *D. Kotlar Jubilee Volume* (Tel Aviv, 1975) 127 s.

86 A. Neppi-Modona, "La vita pubblica e privata degli Ebrei in Egitto nell'età ellenistica e romana" (1921) 2 *Aegyptus* 253 ss. and (1922) 3 *ibidem* 19 ss.; A. Momigliano, "Aspetti dell'antisemitismo alessandrino in due opere di Filone" (1930) 5 *Rassegna Mensile di Israel* 275 ss., V. Tcherikover, *The Jews in Egypt in the Hellenistic-Roman Age in the Light of the Papyri* (Jerusalem, 1963, in Hebrew); C. Kraus, *Filone Alessandrino e un'ora tragica della storia ebraica* (Naples, 1967).

87 See A. Momigliano, "The Jewish Rebellion", "The Campaigns of Vespasian", "The Siege and Fall of Jerusalem" in *Cambridge Ancient History* (1934) vol. 10; G. Allon, "The Burning of the Temple" in *Studies in Jewish History* (Tel Aviv, 1957, in Hebrew), vol. 1, p. 206 ss.; A. Schalit, *Roman Administration in Palestine* (Jerusalem, 1937, in Hebrew); M. Aberbach, *The Roman-Jewish War (66–70 A.D.): Its Origin and Consequences* (London, 1966).

88 For the Jewish revolt in Egypt see: J. Guttman, "The Jewish War in Trajan's Days" in *Sefer Asaf* (Jerusalem, 1953, in Hebrew) 149 ss.; V. Tcherikover, *Corpus Papyrorum Judaicarum, I, Prolegomena* (Jerusalem, 1957) vol. I, p. 85 ss.; A. Fuks, "The Jewish Revolt in Egypt (115–117 A.D.)" (1957) 22 *Zion* 1 ss.; A. Fuks, "Aspects of the Jewish Revolt in A.D. 115–117" (1961) 51 Journal of Roman Studies, 98 ss.; V. Tcherikover, *The Jews in Egypt in the Hellenistic Roman Age in the Light of the Papyri* (Jerusalem, 1963, in Hebrew) 160 ss.; On the Revolt in Cyrene see: S. Applebaum, "The Jewish Revolt in Cyrene in 115–7" (1951) 2 J.J.S. 177 ss.; S. Applebaum, *Greeks and Jews in Ancient Cyrene* (Jerusalem, 1969, in Hebrew) 175 ss.; on the Revolt in Cyprus and Mesopotamia see G. Allon, *A History of the Jews in Palestine During the Period of the Mishna and Talmud,* (Tel Aviv, 1961, in Hebrew) vol. 1, p. 241 ss., 250 ss.; S. Applebaum, *Greeks and Jews, op. cit.,* at p. 224 ss.

89 See E. M. Smallwood, *Documents Illustrating the Principates of Nerva, Trajan and Hadrian* (Cambridge, 1966); D. Rokeah, *Documenta Tumultus Iudaici tempora Traiani Imperatoris (A.D. 115–117)* (Jerusalem, 1970, in Hebrew); G. Allon, *A History of the Jews in Palestine, op. cit.,* at vol. 1, p. 255 ss.; A. Fuks, "Aspects of Jewish Revolt", *op. cit.;* E. M. Smallwood, "Palestine, c.A.D. 115–118" (1962) 11 *Historia* 550 ss.; D. Rokeah, "The War of Kitos:

also widely discussed; and this has not failed to attract the attention of scholars, whether historians, lawyers or archeologists.[90] What were the causes of the rebellion? In the early sources various causes were mentioned: according to Spartianus, it was the prohibition of circumcision;[91] while Dio

Toward the Clarification of a Philological-Historical Problem" in *Scripta Hierosolymitana,* vol. 23 (Jerusalem, 1972) 79 ss. Who exactly was the Kitos for whom the War of Kitos was named? Generally research-scholars agree that he was none other than Lusius Quietus, the Moorish general of Emperor Trajan's army, but Rokeah thinks that it was probably Quintus Marcius Turbo.

90 S. Lieberman, *Greek in Jewish Palestine* (New York, 1942) 15 ss., 144 ss.; S. Yeivin, *Milhemet Bar-Kokhba* (Jerusalem, 1946); S. Lieberman, *Hellenism in Jewish Palestine* (New York, 1950) 100 ss.; B. D'Orgeval, *L'Empereur Hadrien: Oeuvre législative et administrative* (Paris, 1950) 284 ss.; E. R. Goodenough, *Jewish Symbols in the Greco-Roman Period* (New York, 1952) vol. 1, p. 33 ss.; Baron, *History* at vol. 2, p. 67 ss.; L. Kadman, *The Coins of Aelia Capitolina, Corpus Nummorum Palestinensium* (Jerusalem, 1956) vol. 1, pp. 17 ss., 39 ss., 53 ss., 72 ss.; B. P. Benoit *et al., Les grottes de Muraba'at,* (1961); S. Abramsky, *Bar Kokhba, Nesi Israel* (Jerusalem, 1961); S. Mazzarino, *L'Impero Romano* (Rome, 1962) 195 ss.; Y. Yadin, *The Finds from the Bar Kokhba Period in the Cave of Letters* (1963); D. Daube, *Collaboration with Tyranny in Rabbinic Law* (London, 1965) and review by the author in (1968) 34 *Rassegna Mensile di Israel* 100 ss.; L. Huteau-Dubois, "Les sursauts du nationalisme Juif contre l'occupation Romaine: De Massada à Bar Kokhba" (1968) 127 *REJ* 133 ss.; M. D. Herr "The Historical Significance of the Dialogues between Jewish Sages and Roman Dignitaries", *Scripta Hierosolymitana,* vol. 22 (Jerusalem, 1971) 123 ss.; L. Moraldi, *I Manoscritti di Qumran,* (Turin, 1971); Y. Yadin, *Bar-Kokhba: The Rediscovery of the Legendary Hero of the last Jewish Revolt Against Imperial Rome* (Jerusalem, 1971); F. Grelle, *L'autonomia cittadina fra Traiano e Adriano* (Naples, 1972) 226 ss.

91 Spartianus (at the end of the third century); Scriptores Historiae Augustae, Spartianus, *De Vita Hadriani* XIV, 2, *"moverunt ea tempestate et Iudaei bellum, quod vetebantur mutilare genitalia"* ("mutilate their genitals" i.e. his prohibition on circumcision); see esp. E. Schürer, *Geschichte des jüdischen Volkes im Zeitalter Jesu Christi (Leipzig,* 1901) vol. 1, p. 674 ss.; G. Allon, *A History of the Jews op. cit.,* at vol. 2, p. 9 ss.; S. Lieberman, "The Martyrs of Caesarea" (1939–1944) 7 *Annuaire de l'Institut de philologie et d'histoire orientales et slaves*" 424: "We have seen above, that the prohibition of circumcision preceded the Jewish rebellion"; E. M. Smallwood, "The Legislation of Hadrian and Antoninus Pius against Circumcision" (1959) 18 Latomus 334 ss. and (1960–61) 20 *ibidem* 93 ss.; M. D. Herr, "Persecutions and Martyrdom in Hadrian's Days" in *Scripta Hierosolymitana* vol. 23 (1972) 85 ss. (esp. p. 93 ss.); S. Applebaum, "Some New Aspects of the Second Revolt", *op. cit.* at p. 39 ss.: "Talmudic evidence is definite that the prohibition of circumcision preceeded the rising" A. Grelle, *L'autonomia, op. cit.,* at p. 227; A. Linder, "The Roman Imperial Governement" *op. cit.,* at p. 126 ss. For another view see H. Mantel, "The Causes of the Bar Kokhba Revolt" (1968) 58 J.Q.R. 224 ss.; D. Rokeah, "Comments on the Revolt of Bar Kokhba" (1966) 35 *Tarbiz* 125 ss.; and *supra* n. 33.

Cassius believed that the revolt broke out as a result of Hadrian's order to rebuild Jerusalem as Aelia Capitolina, by dedicating a temple to Jupiter;[92] the Midrash relates that at an early stage Hadrian indeed wanted to rebuild Jerusalem with its Sanctuary, but was dissuaded from doing so by the Samaritans: the Jews were so disappointed that they rebelled;[93] and, lastly, Eusebius holds that the revolt broke out because of the madness of the Jews, i.e., their desire for independence: this latter view is the one to which Mantel[94] recently referred, considering the three formerly mentioned "causes" to be merely "effects" brought about by the war itself. It would be out of place to discuss this interesting problem here but, in the opinion of the writer the latter view does not sound convincing; that there was a latent desire for independence, an atmosphere of messianic expectation, is obvious; but it does not seem to exclude some more "immediate" cause, such as the prohibition of circumcision or the reconstruction of Jerusalem in the form of Aelia Capitolina.[95] Jewish rebellions continued into the reign of Justinian when, in 556, Jews and Samaritans united their forces against the Christians of Caesarea: the Emperor's reaction was a violent one.[96]

Chapter XV (pp. 215–220) deals with Custom.

Chapter XVI (pp. 221–234) discusses the names of the Jews. Juster distinguishes between Latin, Greek, Jewish and mixed names. It is worthwhile noting that precisely at the time when they came to be persecuted by the Christians, the Jews felt impelled to revert to typical Jewish names, mainly borrowed from the Bible.[97]

92 Dio Cassius (second-third centuries A.D.): "At Jerusalem he [Hadrian] founded a city in place of the one which had been razed to the ground, naming it Aelia Capitolina, and on the site of the Temple of the God he raised a new Temple to Jupiter" (*History,* 69, 12, transl. E. Cary, London, 1925) 447; see H. Strathmann (1927) 23 *Palästinajahrbuch* 92 ss.; G. Allon, *A History of the Jews, op. cit.,* at vol. 2, p. 14; H. Mantel, "The Causes..." *op. cit.,* at p. 226 ss. with A. Schalit's opinion; M. D. Herr, "Persecutions" *op. cit.,* at p. 94; F. Grelle, *L'autonomia, op. cit.,* at p. 227.

93 *Bereshit Rabbah,* chap. 64; G. Allon, *A History of the Jews, op. cit.,* at vol. 1, p. 272 ss.; H. Mantel, "The Causes..." *op. cit.,* at p. 274 ss.

94 Eusebius, (third-fourth centuries A.D.) *Ecclesiastical History,* 4, 6, 1–4; H. Mantel, "The Causes..." *op. cit.,* at pp. 225 and 277 ss.: "Our aim in this paper is to show that Eusebius is right. It was not the decrees of Hadrian that caused the Bar Kokhba revolt, but the reverse is true: Hadrian's decrees constituted a reaction of the Romans to the Jewish revolt".

95 See *supra,* n. 35.

96 Baron, *History,* 3, 4 ss.; J. A. Montgomery, *The Samaritans* (1968) 113 ss.; A. M. Rabello, "Justinianus," in Rabello (editor), *The Legal Status of the Jews in Roman Empire and in the Middle Ages* (Jerusalem, 1972) 251 ss.

97 On Jewish names see: V. A. Tcherikover, *Corpus Papyrorum Judaicarum, cit. passim*; H. J. Leon, *The Jews of Ancient Rome* (Philadelphia, 1960) 93 ss.; N. G. Cohen, *Jewish Names and their Significance in the Hellenistic and Roman*

Then follow a few chapters on miscellaneous subjects: the tribe (XVII, p. 235); participation in the free distribution of property (XVIII, pp. 236–238); the right to attend theatres and games (XIX, pp. 239–41); elections (XX, p. 242).[98]

Special mention should be made of chapter XXI (pp. 243–390) on public office i.e., the participation of the Jews in public functions. With the victory of Christianity, the Jews were separated by law from the faithful and relegated to an inferior legal position[99] although not to the same extent as heathens, heretics and apostates; the privilege of exemption from the office of a member of the municipal council (*decurio*)[100] was revoked; the heavy charge for that office had to be borne without receiving the honours attached to it *(curiam exerceant . . . indigni tamen curiali sunt honore, C.Th.* 16.8.3–4; 12.1.99; 16.8.24)[101]. Jews were excluded from the office of imperial commissars or inspectors (*C.Th.* 16.8.16; 16.8.24) and from the offices of court officials (*palatini*) and from military service. This exclusion began in the year 418 (*C.Th.* 16.8.24). After 425 Jews were excluded from legal practice. It is clear that these, and other interdictions, in their legal interpretation were particularly in the field of public law and impinged on the principle of equality. On 31 January 438 the Emperors Theodosius II and Valentinian

Periods in Asia Minor (Jerusalem, 1969) (doctoral thesis).

98 See M. Radin, *The Jews Among the Greeks and Romans* (Philadelphia, 1915); Berger, *E.D.* "Iudaei" 517 and "Theatrum" 736.

99 On the legal status of the Jews under the Roman Empire see also: M. Brücklmeier, *Beiträge zur rechtlichen Stellung der Juden in römischen Reich* (Diss., Munich, 1939); V. Colorni, "Israeliti" (1963) 9 *NNDI* 203 ss. with bibliography.

100 See Berger, *E.D.*, 426: *decuriones,* "Members of a municipal senate *(ordo decurionum)* elected for life. Vacant posts were filled at five-year intervals. Eligible were former municipal magistrates with a census of at least one hundred thousand sesterces. Persons of particular worth to the *municipium* and its protectors *(patroni municipii)* residing in Rome were honored by membership in the municipal senate. The *decuriones* decided about all matters involving the interests of the community, appointed local magistrates, and functioned as a court of appeal of fines imposed by municipal officers".

101 See Berger, *E.D.*, 422: *curiae municipiorum,* "The citizens of the municipalities *(municipes)* were organized in groups called *curiae* or *tribus. Curia* is also the council of administration, the senate, of a *municipium* (syn. *ordo decurionum*), and the building in which the council held its sessions". See also: J. Gaudemet, "Constantin et les curies municipales" (1951) 2 *IURA* 44 ss.; On *honor* see Berger, *E.D.*, 488: "The dignity and privileges attached to the power of a magistrate, both in Rome and municipalities; hence also the reverence, consideration due to him *(honorem debere, tribuere). Honor* is frequently syn. with *magistratus.* When both terms occur together, *magistratus* refers to the power and its exercise, whereas *honor* covers the dignity, rank and privileges connected with a magistracy. *Honor* was extended later to any honorific position occupied by a person in a municipality".

barred Jews from any employment and any administrative office (*N.Th.* 3). In the legislation of Justinian also Jews were excluded from holding administrative and distinguished offices (*C.* 1.9.19) as well as from municipal honours (*C.* 1.9.18). Legal practice was forbidden to them (*C.* 1.4.5; 2.6.8); the office of defender of a municipality (*defensor civitatis*) was also forbidden. This office was particularly important for the Jews of Palestine (*C.* 1.5.8); they were excused from military service but they were obliged to perform the duties of the *curia* (*C.* 1.9.5). Although Jews were subject to the numerous curial charges, they were deprived of curial honours ("Jews must never enjoy the fruits of office but only suffer its pains and penalties", *Novella* 45 of Justinian).[102] The work of Justinian was the last Roman attempt at unified Christian legislation affecting the Jews.[103]

On military service in the Pagan Empire, Reinach is probably right in saying that the author attributes too little importance to the edicts of Lentulus and of Dolabella by which the Jews were exempted from compulsory military service.[104]

Juster also describes the Jewish taxation, and especially the *fiscus iudaicus*,[105]

102 See Berger, *E.D.*, 589: *munera:* "Public services, charges, duties or offices which every individual living in the state is obliged to fulfill on behalf of the state or the city *(municipium)* in which he was born or has his domicile. The *munera* also embrace taxes whether paid in money or in kind. *Munera* have to be disguished from public offices *(magistratus)* which are a privilege, a dignity *(honos)* and not a burden. There was one public office which, originally a *honos,* later became the most burdensome *munus,* the *decurionatus munera patrimonii* which encumber property and are performed by the payment of money as a contribution to the costs of public works".

103 P. Browe, "Die Judengesetzgebung Justinians" (1935) 8 *Analecta Gregoriana* 109 ss.

104 T. Reinach (1920) 70–71 *REJ* 95; see also S. Applebaum, "The Legal Status of the Jewish Communities in the Diaspora" in Safrai-Stern, *Jewish People,* 458: "The problem of the relation of Jews to Roman military service, on the other hand, is much more complex and not a little obscure. There is no doubt that at least five specific exemptions from such service were accorded by Roman officials to the Jews of Asia; the most important of these was issued by Dolabella in 44 B.C.E. in response to the request of Hyrcanus II, as Ethnarch. The order appears to have related to the entire province, as it followed a similar exemption granted by L. Lentulus Crus in 49 B.C.E. M. Agrippa seems to have ratified the exemption for the Jews of Ionia, and while neither his ratification nor Hyrcanus' request refers specifically to the status of the Jews concerned, according to Josephus' text, all the other instructions given by Roman governors and officials of Asia direct the exemption specifically to Jews with Roman citizenship". (*Cf.* Josephus, *Ant.* 14, 230; 14, 240; 16, 27; 14, 225, 230, 231).

105 See *supra* n. 24; on *fiscus iudaicus* see: M. S. Ginsburg, 'Fiscus Judaicus" (1930–31) 21 J.Q.R., 281 ss.; G. Allon, *A History, cit.,* at vol. 1, p. 39 ss.; V. Tcherikover, *Corpus Papyrorum Judaicarum, op. cit.,* at pp. 60, 80 ss.; *Id., The Jews in Egypt, op. cit.,* at p. 86 ss.; E. M. Smallwood, "Domitian's Attitude Toward

the gold for the crown (*aurum coronarium*)[106] and Jewish *privilegia* on *munera patrimonii*[107].

The final chapter (XXII, pp. 291–326) describes the economic position of the Jews in the Empire and the extent to which it was influenced by law.[108] The most appropriate manner in which we can sum up the present note is by quoting the following comment of the late N. Bentwich:

"Our author also demonstrates clearly that agriculture was the dominant calling of the Jews as well in the Diaspora as in Palestine, till a harsh legislation drove them from the soil to commerce. They spread to the furthest limits of the Empire and beyond in their quest of liberty, and formed a kind of Jewish fringe colouring the life of every province. It was from these frontier Jewries that the communities of the Middle Ages in Western Europe derived their origin. Doctor Juster does well to show by abundant documentary evidence that (1) the Jews had no remarkable trend towards commerce till after the fifth century, when they were being consistently excluded from all liberal callings, and (2) that when Christian persecution began, the age-long harrying and hounding that has not ceased in our days, they were not noted for the number of their rich men but rather for their poverty. Jewish degradation as well as Jewish disabilities

the Jews and Judaism" (1956) 51 Classical Philology 1 ss.; S. Applebaum, *Greeks and Jews in Ancient Cyrene, op. cit.*, at pp. 204, 210, 230; H. J. Leon, *The Jews in Ancient Rome, op. cit.* at pp. 31 ss., 252; P. Baldacci, "*Patrimonium e ager publicus* al tempo dei Flavi" (1969) 128 *La Parola del Passato* 349 ss.; A. M. Rabello, "Domitian", *Judaica,* vol. 6. col. 164; *Id.,* "Nerva", *ibidem,* vol. 12, col. 965 ss. and *Id.* "Roman Emperors", *ibidem,* vol. 14, col. 229 ss.

106 See *supra* nn. 46–48.

107 See *supra* n. 102; see also G. Ferrari dalle Spade, "Privilegi degli Ebrei nell'impero romano-cristiano" *op. cit.,* at p. 271 ss.; *Id.,* "Immunità ecclesiastiche nel diritto romano imperiale" *Scritti* (1956) vol. 3, p. 125 ss.; C. Dupont, "Les privilèges des clercs sous Constantin" (1967) 62 *Revue d'Histoire ecclésiastique* 729 ss.; A. M. Rabello, "I privilegi dei Chierici sotto Constantino" (1970) 16 *Labeo* 384 ss. (with bibliography); A. Linder, "The Roman Imperial Government", *op. cit.,* at p. 124 ss.

108 A. Büchler, *The Economic Condition of Judaea after the Destruction of the Second Temple* (London, 1912); M. Rostovtzeff, *The Social and Economic History of the Roman Empire,* 2 vols. (Oxford, 1957); E. Volterra, "La base economica della elaborazione sistematica del Diritto Romano" (1967) 11 *Rivista Italiana per le Scienze Giuridiche* 239 ss.; D. Sperber, "On Social and Economic Conditions in Third Century Palestine" (1970) 38 *Archiv Orientální* 1 ss.; *Id.,* "Patronage in Amoraic Palestine (c. 220–400): Causes and Effects" (1971) 14 Journal of the Economic and Social History of the Orient 227 ss.; *Id.* "Flight and the Talmudic Law of Usucaption: A Study in the Social History of Third Century Palestine" (1972) *RIDA* 29 ss.; *Id.* "Laesio Enormis and the Talmudic Law of Ona'ah" (1973) 8 Is.L.R. 254 ss.; D. Sperber, *Roman Palestine (200–400): Money and Prices* (Bar Ilan Univ., 1974); L. I. Levine, *Caesarea under Roman Rule* (Leiden, 1975).

date from the union of the Church with the Roman State. We may hope that they may end with the dissolution of that union in the Empire which is the heir of the tradition and a large part of the dominions of Justinian. It is the principal lesson of Dr. Juster's work that the Jews have suffered from a false political idea that for fifteen hundred years has dominated European thought."[109]

Under the Christian Emperors, Judaism, unable to acquire converts, was compelled to withdraw into itself. Steadily extending prohibitions separated the Jews from the other citizens. The standpoint of the Church, with its tendency toward safeguarding the Jewish religion in its principal manifestations as *lumen veritatis,* whilst oppressing and inflicting sufferings on those who professed it, was also adopted within the realm of the law.[110]

109 N. Bentwich, "The Rightfulness of the Jews" *op. cit.,* at p. 336.

110 And these are the conclusive words of Juster, *Juifs,* 2, 325 ss.: "When the impoverished Jews came to the Church to seek asylum from their creditors, the law shut the gate before them even if they expressed their readiness to become Christians: they should have done so earlier, at a time when they were still wealthy—and that is what the cautious Jews were doing. And that is also what was done by those wishing to gain good reputation in literature or in the arts.

Christianity began to corrode and to subvert Jewish energy, to undermine Jewish spirit. There was no longer any quietness throughout the Empire. And as soon as the policy of persecution became constant, and some barbaric king took possession of the province where they lived, the Jews started to leave. This was the reason why they were so numerous in the new kingdoms.

But intolerance was to follow close upon their heels, and soon caught up with them . . .

With their instinct of self-preservation, for the sake of their collective survival, they began to settle close to the border, so that they might cross it when hate became too acute.

This situation was what henceforth induced the Jews to practice international trade, all the more since they were the natural middlemen between peoples belonging to different faiths.

. . . But these frontier-settlements of Jews, deprived of any fixed location, almost nomadic, mark the beginning of the history of the middle ages . . ."

ABBREVIATIONS

(i) *BOOKS*

Baron, *History:* S. W. Baron, *A Social and Religious History of the Jews* (New York, 1952).

Berger, *E.D.:* A. Berger, *Encyclopedic Dictionary of Roman Law* (Philadelphia, 1953).

Blumenkranz, *Juifs et Chrétiens:* B. Blumenkranz, *Juifs et Chrétiens dans le mond occidental (430–1096)* (Paris, 1960).

Grosse, *Fuentes:* R. Grosse, *Fontes Hispaniae Antiquae. IX: Las fuentes de la época visigoda y bizantinas* (Barcelona, 1947).

Katz, *Jews:* S. Katz, *The Jews in the Visigothic and Frankish Kingdoms of Spain and Gaul* (Cambridge, 1937).

King, *Law and Society:* P. D. King, *Law and Society in the Visigothic Kingdom* (Cambridge, 1972).

Juster, *Juifs:* J. Juster, *Les Juifs dans l'Empire Romain* (Paris, 1914).

Mansi, *Conc.:* G. D. Mansi, *Sacrorum conciliorum . . . amplissima collectio* (Florence, 1759 . . .).

Parkes, *Church and Synagogue:* J. Parkes, *The Conflict of the Church and the Synagogue* (London, 1934 and Philadelphia, 1961).

Safrai-Stern, *Jewish People:* S. Safrai and M. Stern (in co-operation with D. Flusser and W. C. van Unnik), *The Jewish People in the First Century (Compendia Rerum Iudaicarum ad Novum Testamentum)* (Assen, 1974), vol. 1.

Thompson, *Goths:* E. A. Thompson, *The Goths in Spain* (Oxford, 1969).

Vives, *Concilios:* J. Vives, ed. *Concilios visigóticos e hispano-romanos. España Cristiana,* textos (Barcelona-Madrid, 1963) vol. I.

Vives-Ferrua, *Inscripciones:* J. Vives, *Inscripciones cristianas de la España Romana y visigoda* (Barcelona, 1942). MHS, serie patrística, II, 2nd ed., 1969), with appendix 1° by A. Ferrua, *Inscripciones griegas y judías.*

Ziegler, *Church and State:* A. K. Ziegler, *Church and State in Visigothic Spain* (Washington, 1930).

(ii) *PERIODICALS AND LEGAL SOURCES*

AHDE: Anuario del historia del derecho español.
ALMA: Archiuum latinitatis medii aeui (Bulletin Du Cange).
ASD: Annuario di Storia del Diritto Italiano.
AST: Analecta Sacra Tarraconensia.
Brev. Alaric.: Breviarium Alaricianum (= Lex Romana Visigothorum).
C.J.: Codex Justiniani.
C.Th: Codex Theodosianus.
Coll.: Collatio legum Mosaicarum et Romanarum.
EdD.: Enciclopedia del Diritto.
EV: Estudios Visigodos (Madrid-Rome).
FIRA: Fontes Iuris Romani Anteiustiniani (3 vols., Florence, 1940).
HUCA: Hebrew Union College Annual (Cincinnati).
J.J.S.: Journal of Jewish Studies.
J.Q.R.: Jewish Quarterly Review.
IRMAE: Ius Romanum Medii aevi.
Judaica: Encyclopaedia Judaica (Jerusalem, 1971).
Leg. Visig.: Leges Visigothorum.
MGH: Monumenta Germaniae Historica.
MHS: Monumenta Hispaniae Sacra.
NNDI: Novissimo Digesto Italiano.
NTh: Novellae Theodosianae.
PL: Patrologia, series Latina, ed. Migne (Paris, 1844 ...).
PS: Pauli Sententiae.
PW-RE: Pauly-Wissova, Real-Encyclopädie.
REJ: Revue des études juives.
RIDA: Revue Internationale des Droits de l'Antiquité.
SDHI: Studia et Documenta Historiae et Iuris.
Tarbiz: Tarbiz (A Quarterly for Jewish Studies, in Hebrew).
Tol: Council of Toledo.
Zion: Zion (A Quarterly for Research in Jewish History, in Hebrew).
ZSS: Zeitschrift der Savigny-Stifung für Rechtsgeschichte, Romanistische Abteilung.
[..] Additions by A. M. Rabello.

ADDENDA

II Herod's Domestic Court? The Judgement of Death for Herod's Sons

J. Jeremias, *Jerusalem in the Time of Jesus. An Investigation into Economic and Social Conditions during the New Testament Period* (London, 1969); F. Serrao, *Diritto Privato, Economia e Società nella Storia di Roma*, I (Naples, 1984), pp. 199 ff.; L.H. Feldman, *Josephus and Modern Scholarship (1937–1980)* (Berlin–New York, 1984), pp. 296 and 925; and *idem*, *Josephus, A Supplementary Bibliography* (New York–Leiden, 1986), p. 409; J.C. Dumont, *Servus. Rome et l'esclavage sous le République* (Rome, 1987), p. 126; G.. Franciosi, *Famiglia e Persone in Roma Antica. Dall'età arcaica al principato* (Turin, 1989), pp. 49 ff., p. 55 f.; D.R. Schwartz, *Agrippa I, The Last King of Judea* (Tübingen, 1990), pp. 130 ff., esp. p. 134; on the reconquest of Judea by Herod, see J. Shatzman, *The Armies of the Hasmoneans and Herod. From Hellenistic to Roman Frameworks* (Tübingen, 1991), pp. 150 ff.; I. Ben-Shalom, *The School of Shammai and the Zealots' Struggle against Rome* (Jerusalem, 1993), in Hebrew.

IIIa-IIIb The 'Lex de Templo Hierosolymitano' prohibiting Gentiles from entering Jerusalem's Sanctuary

V.R.I. Fry, *The Warning Inscription from the Herodian Temple*, Dissertation, The Southern Baptist Theological Seminary (Louisville, Kentucky, 1974), (*non vidi*, cit. in Feldman, *infra*, p. 446); S. Safrai, 'The Temple', in S. Safrai and M. Stern (eds),*The Jewish People in the First Century. Historical Geography, Political History, Social, Cultural and Religious Life and Institutions*, vol. II (Assen, 1976), pp. 865 ff.; H. Schreckenberg, *Bibliographie zu Flavius Josephus Supplementband mit Gesamtregister* (Leiden, 1979), p. 113; B. Bar-Kochva, *The Battles of the Hasmoneans. The Times of Judas Maccabaeus* (Jerusalem, 1980), in Hebrew; T.A. Busink, *Der Tempel von Jerusalem. Von Salomo bis Herodes. Eine archäologisch-historische Studie unter Berücksichtigung des Westsemitischen Tempelbaus II* (Leiden, 1980), pp. 1062–1200; J.P. Lémonon,

Pilate et le gouvernement de la Judée. Textes et monuments (Paris, 1981); J.M. Baumgarten, 'Exclusion from the Temple: Proselytes and Agrippa I', *Journal of Jewish Studies* 33, *Essays in Honour of Y. Yadin* (1982), pp. 215 ff.; L.H. Feldman, *Josephus and Modern Scholarship (1937–1980)* (Berlin–New York, 1984), pp. 444 ff.; *idem*, *Josephus, A Supplementary Bibliography* (New York–Leiden, 1986), p. 408; K.L. Ritmeyer, 'Reconstructing Herod's Temple Mount in Jerusalem', *The Biblical Archaeology Review* 15 (1989), pp. 23–42; H. Schwier, *Tempel und Tempelzerstörung. Untersuchungen zu den theologischen und ideologischen Faktoren im erster jüdisch-römischen Krieg (66–74 n.Chr.)* (Göttingen, 1989), pp. 55–74; P. Segal 'The Penalty of the Warning Inscription from the Temple of Jerusalem', *Israel Exploration Journal* 39 (1989), pp. 79–84; D.R. Schwartz, *Agrippa I, The Last King of Judea* (Tübingen, 1990), p. 128 ff.; M. Hengel, *The Zealots. Investigation into the Jewish Freedom Movement in the Period from Herod I until 70 AD* (Edinburgh, 1991); L. Boffo, 'Iscrizione del precinto del tempio di Gerusalemme', *Iscrizioni greche e latine per lo studio della Bibbia* (Brescia, 1994), pp. 283–290; L.I. Levine, 'Josephus' Description of the Jerusalem Temple: War, Antiquities and other Sources', in F. Parente and J. Sievers (eds), *Josephus and the History of the Greco-Roman Period, Essays in Memory of M. Smith* (Leiden, 1994), pp. 233 ff.; E.E. Urbach, *Studies in Judaica,* eds M.D. Herr and J. Fränkel (Jerusalem, 1998), in Hebrew, pp. 541 ff.; M.F. Fenati, *Lucio Flavio Silva Nonio Basso e la città di Urbisaglia* (Macerata, 1995).

IV The Situation of the Jews in Roman Spain

On the name *Maria* used by Jews, see N. Cohen, 'The private name *Miriam* in Greek and Latin transcription', *Leshonenu* 38 (Jerusalem, 1974), pp. 170 ff.

V The Ban on Circumcision as a Cause of Bar Kokhbah's Rebellion

V. Marotta, 'Politica imperiale e culture periferiche nel mondo romano: il problema della circoncisione', *Index* 12 (1983–84), pp. 405 ff.; A. Kasher, *Edom, Arabia and Israel (332 BCE–70 CE)* (Jerusalem, 1988), in Hebrew; E. del Covolo, *I Severi e il Cristianesimo. Richerche sull'ambiente storico – istituzionale delle origini cristiane tra il secondo e il terzo secolo* (Rome, 1989); M. Goodman, *State and Society in Roman Galilee AD 132–212* (Totowa, NJ, 1983); P. Schäfer, *Giudeofobia. L'antisemitismo nel mondo antico* (Rome, 1999), pp. 133 ff.

VI On the Relations between Diocletian and the Jews

D. Rokeah, *Jews, Pagans and Christians in Conflict* (Jerusalem–Leiden, 1982); L.I. Levine, *The Rabbinic Class in Palestine during the Talmudic Period* (Jerusalem, 1985), in Hebrew; A.M. Rabello, *Giustiniano, Ebrei e Samaritani alla luce delle fonti storico-letterarie, ecclesiastiche e giuridiche*, II (Milan, 1988), p. 795; B. Isaac, *The Limits of Empire. The Roman Army in the East* (Oxford, 1990), pp. 77 ff.; E.H. Rubin, *The Patriarch in the Roman–Byzantine Era – The Making of a Dynasty*, PhD thesis (Tel Aviv, 1991), in Hebrew; M. Goodman, 'The Roman State and the Jewish Patriarch in the Third Century', in L.I. Levine (ed.), *The Galilee in Late Antiquity* (New York–Jerusalem, 1992), pp. 127 ff.; G. Rinaldi, 'Giudei e pagani alla vigilia della persecuzione di Diocleziano: Porfirio e il popolo d'Israele', *Vetera Christianorum* 29 (1992), pp. 113 ff.; S. Safrai, *In Times of Temple and Mishnah. Studies in Jewish History*, I (Jerusalem, 1994), pp. 194 ff., in Hebrew; A. Yisraeli-Taran, *The Legends of the Destruction* (Tel-Aviv, 1997), in Hebrew; on the *Episcopalis Audientia*, see M.R. Cimma, *L'Episcopalis Audientia nelle costituzioni imperiali da Costantino a Giustiniano* (Turin, 1989); G.. Crifó, 'A proposito di episcopalis audientia', in *Institutions, societé et vie politique dans l'Empire Romain au IVe siècle après J.C.* (Rome, 1992), pp. 397 ff., p. 408; on Paneas, see Y. Tsafrir, L. Di Segni and J. Green, *Maps and Gazetteer* (Jerusalem, 1994), p. 199.

On the *Collatio legum Mosaicarum et Romanarum*, see G. Barone-Adesi, *L'età della 'Lex Dei'* (Naples, 1992); E.J.H. Schrage, 'La date de la *Collatio legum Mosaicarum et Romanarum*, étudié d'après les citations bibliques', *Mélanges Wubbe* (Fribourg, 1993), pp. 401 ff.; G. Pugliese, 'A Suggestion on the *Collatio*', *Israel Law Review* 29 (1995), pp. 161 ff.; L.V. Rutgers, *The Jews in Late Ancient Rome. Evidence of Cultural Interaction in the Roman Diaspora* (Leiden, 1995), pp. 210 ff.

VII La première loi de Théodose II et la fête de Pourim

R.Z. Wilken, *John Chrysostom and the Jews: Rhetoric and Reality in the Late 4th Century* (London, 1983); R. Larefot, *Pagans and Christians* (Bungay, 1986), p. 486 f.; B. Blanchetière, 'La législation antijuive de Théodose II. C.Th. 16.8.18 (29.5.408)', *Ktema* 5 (1980), pp. 125 ff.; A.M. Rabello, *Giustiniano, Ebrei e Samaritani alla luce delle fonti storico-letterarie, ecclesiastiche e giuridiche*, II (Milan, 1988), p. 765 f.

On the penalty of crucifixion, see P. Winter, *On the Trial of Jesus* (Berlin–New York, 1974). Winter reaches the conclusion that the crucifixion was not a Jewish mode of execution and was never carried out by an official Jewish judicial body. See also H.H. Cohn, *Reflections on the Trial and Death of Jesus*, The Israel Law Review Association (1967) (the article is reprinted from *Israel Law Review* 2 (1967) pp. 332–379). Cohn agrees with Winter that the crucifixion was never carried out by an official Jewish body and finds the source of all the confusion in the faulty use of terminology (due to the confusing translation of the word 'crucify' from Hebrew to Aramaic, and vice versa). M. Hengel, *Crucifixion in the Ancient World and the Folly of the Message of the Cross* (Philadelphia, 1977/82), contends that the crucifixion was a Jewish mode of execution as well. On the conventional Jewish death sentences, see also the unpublished doctorate of P. Segal, *Liability under Divine Jurisdiction – The Death Penalty by a Human Court and by Divine Hand* (submitted to the Senate of the Hebrew University in February 1986), in Hebrew.

VIII L'observance des fêtes juives dans l'Empire Romain

A.M. Rabello, *Giustiniano, Ebrei e Samaritani alla luce delle fonti storico-letterarie, ecclesiastiche e giuridiche*, II, (Milan, 1988), pp. 773 ff.; H.H. Scullard, *Festivals and Ceremonies of the Roman Republic* (London, 1981); L.H. Feldman, *Josephus, A Supplementary Bibliography* (New York–Leiden, 1986), p. 470; P.R. Trebilco, *Jewish Communities in Asia Minor* (Cambridge, 1991), pp. 6, 193; on the privileges, pp. 6 ff., 10 ff; F. Millar, 'I giudei della diaspora greco-romana fra paganesimo e cristianesimo, 312–438 d.C.', *Giudei fra pagani e cristiani nell'Impero romano* (Genova, 1993), pp. 133 ff.; P. Schäfer, *Giudeofobia. L'antisemitismo nel mondo antico* (Rome, 1999), pp. 117 ff.

On the privileges, T. Rajak, 'Was There a Roman Charter for the Jews?', *Journal of Roman Studies* 74 (1981), pp. 161 ff.; *eadem*, 'Jewish Rights in the Greek Cities under Roman Rule: a New Approach', in W.S. Green (ed.), *Approaches to Ancient Judaism* 5 (Atlanta, 1985), p. 33; L.H. Feldman, *Josephus, A Supplementary Bibliography* (New York–Leiden, 1986), p. 469; M. Hadas-Lebel, 'L'image de Rome auprès les Juifs, -164 +70', *Aufstieg und Niedergang der Römischen Welt*, II, 20 (1987), pp. 789 ff.; V. Scarano Ussani, *Le forme del privilegio. Beneficia e privilegia tra Cesare e gli Antonini* (Naples, 1992); M. Pucci Ben-Zeev, 'Roman Documents in Josephus' Antiquities: What Was Josephus' Source?', *Scripta Classica Israelica* 13 (1994), pp. 46 ff.; *eadem*, 'Caesar and the Jewish Law', *Revue Biblique* 102 (1995), pp. 28 ff.; *eadem*, 'Did the Jews Enjoy a Privileged Position in the Roman World?', *Revue des Etudes Juives* 154 (1995), pp. 23 ff.; *eadem*, 'Jewish Rights in the Roman World: New Perspectives', in B. Isaac and A. Oppenheimer (eds), *Te'uda, 12 Studies in the Jewish Diaspora in the Hellenistic and Roman Period* (Tel Aviv, 1996), pp. 39 ff.; *eadem*, 'Ant. 14.186-267: A problem of Authenticity', in

R. Katzof (ed.), *Classical Studies in Honor of David Sohlberg* (Ramat Gan, 1996), pp. 193 ff.; *eadem, Jewish Rights in the Roman World* (Tübingen, 1998).

On Paneas see: Y. Tsafrir, L. Di Segni and J. Green, *Maps and Gazetteer*, Jerusalem, 1994, p. 199.

IX Divorce of Jews in the Roman Empire

L.H. Feldman, *Josephus and Modern Scholarship (1937–1980)* (Berlin–New York, 1984), p. 945, and *idem, Josephus, A Supplementary Bibliography* (New York–Leiden, 1986), p. 470; R.B. Bagnall, 'Church, State and Divorce in Late Roman Egypt', *Florilegium Colombianum* (New York, 1987), pp. 41 ff.; I. Ben-Shalom, *The School of Shammai and the Zealots' Struggle against Rome* (Jerusalem, 1993), pp. 216 ff., in Hebrew; J. Mélèze-Modrzejewski, 'Diritto romano e diritti locali', *Storia di Roma*, III/2, *I luoghi e le culture* (Turin, 1993), pp. 985 ff.

X Il problema dei matrimoni fra Ebrei e Cristiani nella legislazione imperiale e in quella della Chiesa (IV–VI secolo)

G.L. Falchi, 'La legislazione imperiale circa i matrimoni misti fra cristiani ed ebrei nel IV secolo', *Atti Accademia Romanistica Costantiniana* 7 (Naples, 1988), pp. 204 ff.; G. De Bonfils, *Gli schiavi degli ebrei nella legislazione del IV secolo. Storia di un divieto* (Bari, 1992); F. Lucrezi, 'CTh.16.9.2: Diritto romano-cristiano e antisemitismo', *Labeo* 40 (1994), pp. 220 ff., and subsequently published as 'Ebrei e schiavi', in *idem, Messianesimo, regalità, impero. Idee religiose e idea imperiale nel mondo romano* (Florence, 1996), pp. 125 ff.; A. Linder, *The Jews in Roman Imperial Legislation* (Michigan–Jerusalem, 1987); S. Treggiari, *Roman Marriage.* Justi coniuges *from the Time of Cicero to the Time of Ulpian* (Oxford, 1991).

XII Jewish and Roman Jurisdiction

R. Bonfil, 'Giustizia, giudici e tribunali nelle Comunità ebraiche dell'Occidente cristiano', *La giustizia nell'alto medioevo (secoli IX–XI)* (Spoleto, 1997), pp. 931 ff.

XIV The Attitude of Rome towards Conversions to Judaism (Atheism, Circumcision, Proselytism)

S.J.D. Cohen, 'Crossing the Boundary and Becoming a Jew', *Harvard Theological Review* 82 (1989), pp. 13 ff.; *idem*, 'Rabbinic Conversion Ceremony', *Journal of Jewish Studies* 41 (1990), pp. 177 ff.; E. Klingenberg, 'The Roman Imperial Legislation prohibiting Jews from owning gentile slaves', *Jewish Law Association Studies* IV, ed. B.S. Jackson (Atlanta, 1990), pp. 89 ff.; P.R. Trebilco, *Jewish Communities in Asia Minor* (Cambridge, 1991), pp. 31 ff. n. 133; M. Goodman, *Mission and Conversion: Proselytising in the Religious History of the Roman Empire* (Oxford, 1994); P. Schäfer, *Giudeofobia. L'antisemitismo nel mondo antico* (Rome, 1999), pp. 153 ff.

See also the observation of C.R. Whittaker, *Land, City and Trade in the Roman Empire* (Aldershot, 1993), article XIII, p. 167: 'A Complete Title in the Theodosian Code *ne christianum mancipiam Judaeus habeat* (C. Th. XVI.9) is not necessarily an indication of court control . . . but the possibility seems quite high.'

XV A Tribute to Jean Juster

About Jean Juster I have received from Professor Valentin A. Georgescu of Bucharest University, the following information from the personal file of J. Juster; he was born under the name of Ianku Iuster on the 27 November 1881 and he began his studies at Bucharest University in 1900.

For a more recent version of this article see A.M.Rabello, 'The Legal Conditions of the Jews in the Roman Empire', *Aufstieg und Niedergang der Römischen Welt*, II, 13 (Berlin–New York, 1980), pp. 662–762; see also G. Stemberger, *Die Römische Herrschaft im Urteil der Juden, Wissenschaftliche Buchgesellschaft Darmstadt* (1983); J. Schwartz, *Jewish Settlement in Judaea after the Bar-Kochba War until the Arab Conquest (135 CE–640 CE)*, in Hebrew; M. Goodman, *The Ruling Class of Judea: The Origins of the Jewish Revolt Against Rome AD 66–70* (Cambridge, 1987); A.M. Rabello, *The Jews in the Roman Empire in the Light of the Legislation* (Jerusalem, 1987), in Hebrew; *idem*, *Giustiniano, Ebrei e Samaritani alla luce delle fonti storico-letterarie, ecclesiastiche e giuridiche*, I (Milan, 1987), II (Milan, 1988); M. Goodman, 'Diaspora Reactions to the Destruction of the Temple', in J. D. Dunn (ed.), *Jews and Christians* (Tübingen, 1992), pp. 127 ff.; D. Jacoby, 'Les Juifs de Byzance: une communauté marginalisé', *Practica Emeridas. Oi peritoriakoi sto Byzantio* (Athena, 1993), pp. 103 ff.; F. Millar, 'I giudei della diaspora greco-romana fra paganesimo e cristianesimo, 312–438 d.C.', *Giudei fra pagani e cristiani nell'Impero romano* (Genova, 1993), pp. 133 ff.; M. Bohrmann, *Flavius Josephus, The Zealots and Yavne: Towards a Rereading of 'The War of the Jews'* (Peter Lang, 1994); J.A.S. Evans, 'The Outsiders: Jews, Samaritans, Pagans, Heretics', *The Age of Justinian – The Circumstances of Imperial Power* (Jerusalem, 1996), pp. 240 ff.; J. Mélèze-Modrzejewski, *Les Juifs d'Egypte de Ramses II à Hadrien* (Paris, 1997), pp. 271 ff.

On the privileges, L.H. Feldman, *Josephus, A Supplementary Bibliography* (New York–Leiden, 1986), p. 469; V. Scarano Ussani, *Le forme del privilegio. Beneficia e privilegia tra Cesare e gli Antonini* (Naples, 1992); M.Pucci Ben Zeev, *Jewish Rights in the Roman World* (Tübingen, 1998), see also *supra*, no.VIII. On the problem of the distribution of rations free of charge, J. Durliat, *De la ville antique à la ville byzantine. Le problème des subsistances* (Rome, 1990); C. Virluouet, *Tessera Frumemtaria. Les procédures de distribution du blé public à Rome à la fin de la République et au début de l'Empire* (Rome, 1995). On the corporations, L. De Salvo, *Economia privata e pubblici servici nell'impero romano. I corpora naviculariorum* (Messina, 1992). On the Imperial cult, L. Cerfaux et J. Tondriau, *Le culte de souvrains dans la civilisation gréco-romaine* (Tournai, 1957); S. Weinstock, *Divus Julius* (Oxford, 1971); D. Fishwick, *The Imperial Cult in the Latin West* (Leiden, 1991); G. Bonamente, 'Il senato e l'apoteosi degli imperatori. Da Augusto a Teodosio il Grande', *Macht und Kultur im Rom der Kaiserzeit* (Bonn, 1994), pp. 137 ff.; *idem*, 'Apoteosi e Imperatori cristiani', in G. Bonamente and A.Nestori (eds), *I Cristiani e l'Impero nel IV secolo* (Macerata, 1998), pp. 107 ff. On the *defensor civitatis*, add V. Mannino, *Ricerche sul 'Defensor Civitatis'* (Milan, 1984). On Jewish law in this period, A.M.Rabello, 'L'interpretazione del Talmud babilonese e del Talmud gerosolimitano: il Midrash halakah', in S.J. Sierra (ed.), *La lettura ebraica delle Scritture* (Bologna, 1995), pp. 103 ff.; *idem*, 'Diritto Ebraico', *Enciclopedia Giuridica, Enc. Italiana Treccani*, aggiornamento IV (1995), pp. 1 ff. On Justinian and the Jews, and in particular on Novella 146 of Justinian, see P.T.R. Gray, *The Defense of Chalcedon in the East (451–553)* (Leiden, 1979); E. Klingenberg, 'Justinians Novellen sur Judengesetzgebung', *Festschrift für H. Lange* (Cologne, 1992), pp. 139 ff.; P.T.R. Gray, 'Palestine and Justinian's Legislation on non-Christian Religions', in B. Halpern and D.B. Hobson (eds), *Law, Politics and Society in the Ancient Mediterranean World* (Sheffield, 1993), pp. 241ff.; G. Veltri, 'Die Novelle 146 PERI HEBRAION. Das Verbot des Targumvortrags in Justinians Politik', in M.Hengel und A.M.Schwemer (eds), *Die Septuaginta zwischen Judentum und Christentum* (Tübingen, 1994), pp. 116 ff.

INDEX OF SOURCES

Rabbinic Sources

New Testament and Early Christian Literature

Patristic Literature and Church Councils

Greek and Latin Sources

Inscriptions and Papyri

Roman Law

Barbarian Sources

INDEX OF NAMES AND SUBJECTS